Edwin K. Gedney

PATTERNS OF EDUCATIONAL PHILOSOPHY

OTHER BOOKS BY THEODORE BRAMELD

The Climactic Decades: Mandate to Education
Cultural Foundations of Education—An Interdisciplinary Exploration
Design for America
Education as Power
Education for the Emerging Age
Ends and Means in Education
Japan: Culture, Education, and Change in Two Communities
Minority Problems in the Public Schools
Patterns of Educational Philosophy
Philosophies of Education in Cultural Perspective
Toward a Reconstructed Philosophy of Education
A Philosophic Approach to Communism
The Remaking of a Culture—Life and Education in Puerto Rico
The Use of Explosive Ideas in Education
Values in American Education (coeditor and coauthor)
Workers' Education in the United States (editor and coauthor)

PATTERNS OF EDUCATIONAL PHILOSOPHY

Divergence and convergence in culturological perspective

THEODORE BRAMELD
University of Hawaii

HOLT, RINEHART AND WINSTON, INC.
New York Chicago San Francisco Atlanta Dallas
Montreal Toronto London Sydney

Parts of this book have appeared in *Patterns of Educational Philosophy*, copyright 1950 by World Book Company; in *Philosophies of Education in Cultural Perspective*, copyright 1955 by Holt, Rinehart and Winston, Inc., and *Toward a Reconstructed Philosophy of Education*, copyright 1956 by Holt, Rinehart and Winston, Inc.

Library of Congress Catalog Card Number: 73-135130
SBN: **03-085258-7**
Printed in the United States of America
4 3 2 1 038 9 8 7 6 5 4 3 2 1

To
the Memory
of My Mother

PREFACE

The pervading theme of *Patterns of Educational Philosophy* is the critical reconsideration of two interdependent propositions. The first is that the period of civilization through which we are now speeding is one of ominous, perilous crisis. The second is that philosophies of education, when they are treated with practical seriousness and candor, also become philosophies of culture.

One term thus recurs intermittently: "crisis-culture." This is not at all a novel term, certainly not in my own previous writings. Nevertheless, the motivation that has led to the present work is central. Let me make the point as sharply as possible. If it was legitimate to regard the 1940s, 1950s, and 1960s as decades of anxiety and violence, but also of extraordinary achievement and adventure, then it becomes doubly legitimate to anticipate the 1970s and beyond in comparable ways. Furthermore, if it was legitimate to interpret, as I attempted to do, the major patterns of educational thought as symbolic barometers of the alternating storms and calms of recent history, then it becomes at least equally legitimate to interpret them in this manner as we accelerate toward the twenty-first century.

Since this theme is to be elaborated at length, let me assert at once that its framework embraces three major disciplines that are frequently and deliberately fused into one: philosophy, anthropology, and education. How this fusion came about in my personal genesis is, I trust, sufficiently relevant to permit what may be called a prefatory confession.

It was toward the conclusion of my undergraduate years that I "discovered" the field of philosophy. Like innumerable youthful learners, my major subject (English literature, as it happened) had been selected prematurely and inadvisedly. Only when it became much too late to shift to another major did I find that philosophy was trying to tell me what I, again like innumerable fellow students, had been groping for: that is, for some serious notions of what might conceivably become the meaning of my own selfhood and my own place in the world, of my family and my community, and, at moments of bewilderment or anguish, perhaps even of the "nature and destiny of man." Bolstered then by a mixture of intellectual curiosity and *Weltschmerz,* plus a superabundance of immaturity, I decided to confront philosophy head on.

After three years of considerable travail as a graduate student, followed by several further years as a college teacher of ethics, logic, and other conventional courses, I made another "discovery": philosophy was not enough. For one of my temperament at least, I came to find less intellectual and emotional congeniality with my peers in this discipline, excellent though some were, than with a number of other scholars who were closer to the firing line of the human condition. Severe economic dislocation, world wars, virulent nationalism, racial and class exploitation—such issues as these not only preoccupied their concern but on occasion resulted in their doing something about them.

From a number of such associates, moreover, I learned for the first time that education could itself prove to be a fascinating area of controversy. Like other typical products of the liberal arts, I had learned earlier to look condescendingly upon professional educators as busy, superficial bores. Not that I had been completely misled: close subsequent connections with schools of education have convinced me that some "educationists" fully deserve the stereotype. Some others, however, assuredly do not deserve it, and among them were men who had helped me to realize the potential role of education as a powerful enterprise in man's struggle for advancement. And so, when the opportunity arose to affiliate with the education faculty of a large university, I accepted enthusiastically because I was confident that new ways could be found by which to put philosophy to work on the frontiers of American life. Quite aware that my meager place in the academic pecking order would be demoted still further, I forsook "pure" philosophy for the "applied" philosophy of education. Despite abundant qualms, I have never really regretted this choice.

Still, over a period of some time, I gradually realized once again that something else was seriously lacking. All the important problems of education were, to be sure, grounded in philosophy, and I continued as well as I could to treat them so. Nevertheless, it became more and more apparent to me that philosophy and education each had to be interpreted and applied within a wider setting—the indispensable setting of the human environment out of which both disciplines, after all, emerge and which in turn they serve. When, therefore, an invitation was extended to undertake a research study of the ways that representative school systems across America were trying to develop viable policies concerning Negro, Mexican-American, and other minority groups, I welcomed this opportunity, too. It led, in turn, to active participation in the pioneering field of "intercultural education" being developed at a second large university. Here I continued to work in education and philosophy, but now with somewhat clearer awareness of the need to interweave both of these disciplines together with a third: anthropology. For this, the most encompassing of all behavioral sciences, could complete, I now believed, the "triadic model" for which up to then I had been searching.

The required next step, of course, was to learn (mostly under my own tutelage) as much as I was capable of learning about this still relatively vernal discipline. Thus I tried not only to probe into the conceptual foundations of anthropology and to become acquainted personally with several of its greatest representatives, but to build upon these foundations by venturing, well beyond my previous research study, through prolonged involvement in two foreign cultures. Both field studies dared more precociously to utilize anthropological methodologies (participant observation, for example) than my amateur qualifications doubtless deserved. But they were even less orthodox in other ways: they incorporated both philosophy and education into their research designs. The first study occurred in Puerto Rico, the second in Japan—two very different countries, yet strikingly comparable in their rapid pace of industrial modernization as well as in their concern for ways by which the philosophy and application of education may become the staunch allies of cultural patterns, cultural dynamics, and cultural directions.

My justification for sharing this record is not, of course, to impose one author's autobiography, however sketchy, upon undeserving readers. Rather, it is to explain in part why the four anthropological philosophies of education to be considered at length have undergone a certain evolution in the interpretation I have sought to provide for them. This evolution may be underscored by various alterations that appear in the chapters to follow.

One of the most rewarding of fairly recent concepts introduced to me by anthropologists is termed "value orientations." This concept at once implies a connection between philosophy and culture: it focuses upon the clusters of beliefs that all cultures cherish as integral to their ways of life. Accordingly, in both Puerto Rico and Japan, I tried to search for the value orientations of their people as both distinctive from and common with those of other cultures. But in the latter of these investigations another step was taken: aided by Japanese colleagues, I fashioned a research instrument that might help to compare both the impressionistic knowledge acquired through firsthand participation and the precisely controllable evidence of how people express their values in the context of their own ways of life.

The key to this instrument, although far from meticulously

polished, was constructed out of the formula, I-M-T, defined as the "Innovative–Moderative–Transmissive Continuum." In reverse order, the intent was to detect whether people, of at least the communities I knew most intimately, were disposed toward conventional and traditional values, toward conciliatory and temperate values, toward audacious and venturesome values, or toward so complete a mixture that no one of these alternative orientations could be considered dominant.

This aspect of the Japanese study led soon after to another in the United States where, again in cooperation with codesigners and practitioners, I developed an instrument also based on the I-M-T formula but adjusted to several thousand social studies teachers. Both before and after this study, I also engaged in a whole series of elementary anthropological field experiences with graduate students who were trying to develop the still infantile subdiscipline of "educational anthropology." These projects, incidentally, were followed through in a third university to which I had moved but within which educational philosophy still remained my prime responsibility.

That both design and interpretation of the present work are influenced by such experiences may be noted by glancing at the Table of Contents. The earlier design is retained, but its significance has, I hope, developed more meaningfully and fruitfully. The triple value orientations symbolized by I-M-T is now extended to a quadruple symbol—I-M-T-R—"R" standing for the "restorative" orientation, the other three terms remaining intact. My intent here is not, of course, merely to substitute one symbol for another. It is to convey a shift of interpretation influenced primarily by the kinds of theory and practice that have intervened between editions. The shift is revealed not only in many minor details but in major omissions and substantive additions.

Perhaps the most important of these additions may be depicted as a kind of metaphoric spiral; that is, having moved successively upward along the three levels or areas of philosophy, education, and anthropology, I have recently found myself concentrating again upon the first. This has been imperative because only too painfully have I realized, as have many others in comparable situations, that when one becomes immersed in, say, prolonged field research, one is bound to lose contact with certain associations elsewhere. Such has been the case with contemporary movements in philosophy. Though I had tried to take them into account, it was only after completion of the second field study that I was able again to devote a major proportion of my attention to such important movements. Yet even this attention has been affected, as it should, by the spiral-like (or, if one prefers, dialectical) process which I have tried to suggest. Take existentialism as one of the movements to be considered: surely it is not to be treated as just another fascinating theory; rather, as a number of influential existentialists would be the first to insist, it becomes both a condition and a consequence of the crisis-culture of our time.

A further point more directly underscores my personal, cultural, and philosophic development. In mentioning field research of the value orientations in two cultures, I may have left the impression that my concern here was almost too dispassionately objective. This would be misleading. True, I did hope that my investigation with the I-M-T instrument would further refine and clarify my interpretation. Nevertheless, its motivation was still affected primarily by my interest in how people think, feel, learn, and function on the intimate level of everyday experience. I believe it may be claimed fairly, indeed, that I came to regard some of my informants (whether farmers, peddlers, teachers, students, artists, or artisans) as very close friends whose relationships I continue to cherish.

This privilege has resulted, therefore, in another shift toward reformulation. I mean the shift from what I now consider in retrospect to have been an overstress upon the group—the collective, and the institutional—and an understress upon the individual as a person. That the former stress rightly remains heavy will be evident. But that I have also come to realize more clearly that the ultimate hope for the future of mankind is to be found, after all, in the simple dignity of everyday human beings will also, I believe, prove evident. For without the direct and precious quality of kinship that I came to identify in a sugar-cane field, or on a fisherman's boat, or in the private quarters of a Buddhist priest—without this consummatory and intrinsic quality I cannot really justify either the expectations or the aspirations which this philosophy of education and culture seeks to express.

This is not to contend that the alterations selected above as examples amount either to a repudiation of preceding formulations or to the claim that I have produced a new book. On the contrary, I wish to emphasize that the original paradigm, as well as a fair proportion of the original content, is retained simply because I have concluded (with the expert advice, I may add, of critical consultants) that it *should* be retained. Granting, in common with still other critics, that I too have on occasion questioned the continued productiveness of this paradigm, nevertheless I have reached the conclusion that if effectively updated and refined it may well prove to be far more productive because far more relevant to our surging decades than it could have been when first presented.

Even so, inadequacies remain obtusely apparent. The astonishing range of reactions that preceding editions have generated, both in the articles and books of my peers and among many students, has received respectful attention. But I am also aware of how controversial both the theme and its elaboration continue to be; I am aware, too, that interdisciplinary explorations always face hazards of superficiality and generality.

In any case, the expectation still remains that others will follow much further in the refinement and application (especially by practicing teachers) of an anthropological philosophy of education appropriate for the future. This expectation is perhaps best manifested in the concluding chapter. There I try to point toward *the hope and the goal of a transcending, converging mankind.*

So momentous a task obviously requires all that can be bolstered by the very best authorities available—especially authorities in each of the three most germane disciplines. Therefore I have appended a series of suggested, annotated readings documenting and otherwise helping to enrich the propositions and contentions that permeate the emerging theme. A selected bibliography contains specific data for both suggested readings and footnotes.

One word of acknowledgment. A roster of the many professional associates and other fellow learners from whom I have benefited beyond measure would be so extensive that I have decided to choose only those most immediately helpful to completing this task. They are David Boynton, of Holt, Rinehart and Winston, who has cordially encouraged my work over a number of years; his associate, Deborah Doty, who has patiently assisted me in many ways; Dean Philip E. Kubzansky, who facilitated much-appreciated grants from the Graduate School of Boston University; and Midori Matsuyama, who has prepared the manuscript with consistent enthusiasm and conscientiousness.

November 1970 Theodore Brameld

CONTENTS

PART 2

PROGRESSIVISM: EDUCATION AS CULTURAL MODERATION

PART 3

ESSENTIALISM: EDUCATION AS CULTURAL TRANSMISSION

PART 5

RECONSTRUCTIONISM: EDUCATION AS CULTURAL TRANSFORMATION

PATTERNS OF EDUCATIONAL PHILOSOPHY

PART 1

Philosophy, culture, and education

CHAPTER 1

A time of great debate

AT NO PERIOD in American history, not even in the early decades of the nineteenth century when public schools were first established as a permanent institution of our culture, has education stirred such heated controversy as during the one or two decades preceding our own midcentury, and even more heatedly during the decades since. Traditionally, the American people have tended to behave rather complacently about education, honoring it perhaps more widely than many other people, but also taking it for granted. They have usually left what to teach and how to teach to those professionally responsible.

But public attitudes toward education have changed drastically. Far from being taken for granted, education is more likely to be discussed in language that discloses powerful feelings at least as often as knowledge of facts. In hundreds of communities across the nation, citizens have taken sides—sometimes angrily. Such organized groups in the community as Negroes and other minorities, chambers of commerce, churches, patriotic bodies, and self-righteous guardians of tradition—all have come to consider education as their prerogative. Never before, moreover, have periodicals with vast circulations considered education to be a subject certain to arouse their readers and to attract countless new ones. In torrents of articles, these periodicals, as well as others of smaller circulation but of substantial influence, continue to feature conflicting positions on a wide variety of educational problems. Newspapers and magazines with nationwide circulation, books and pamphlets, radio and television networks, public forums, powerful national organizations, even state legislatures and the Congress of the United States—all have joined in the debate.

Even more dramatically and sometimes violently, the phenomenon of student unrest has staggered and baffled citizens everywhere—a phenomenon that emerged almost imperceptibly but gradually accelerated to a stage where increasing thousands of college students became involved and then spread downward into the high schools as well as upward to the graduate and teaching sectors. Almost simultaneously, student unrest became endemic in various countries of Europe, South America, and Asia. It was almost as if by transoceanic contagion an epidemic of resentment, skepticism, and even rejection of education as it had long been accepted was spreading across the globe.

What deeper trends and conflicts lie behind this bitter, persistent controversy? The question is far easier to ask than to answer. Many explanations might be suggested—some worthless, others convincing; some superficial, others profound; some inconsistent and confused, others logical and clear. Our first purpose should be to try to answer the question by placing education in wider perspective—in the perspective both of contemporary American culture and of cultures historically and geographically beyond our own. But it is not enough to attempt even this enormous task. It is necessary, in addition, to find a way whereby culture and the educational processes within it can be effectively examined and interpreted. This, we believe, is a chief role of philosophy.

For philosophy, as we shall try to show, may be defined as the effort of any culture to become conscious of itself—to face critically and stubbornly its weaknesses as well as strengths, failures as well as achievements, vices as well as virtues. Contradicting the common notion that philosophy at its purest is an aloof discipline unsullied by either the miseries or the joys of everyday life, we shall develop the thesis that it is the supreme instrument by which, through the ages, man comes to terms with his own beliefs as he struggles to organize his existence within culture. It follows that, because education even within the simplest cultures is indispensable to that struggle, the only way we can hope ultimately to understand education is to subject it to philosophic scrutiny.

This way of depicting philosophy requires a reformulation that as yet is seldom attempted. In order to symbolize our own approach, we have chosen to adopt from the outset a fairly novel term: "culturology." Although occasionally utilized elsewhere, we wish to make clear that *by culturology we mean here a philosophy of mankind that is primarily governed by, and exerts profound influence upon, the life of members of culture.* Education, in turn, is perceived and judged as the ubiquitous process through which this life of men not only is conveyed to each successive generation but becomes established, modified, or even drastically altered in the course of that process.

General statements such as these require, of course, substantiation and delineation. Thus, the next three chapters of Part 1 aim to develop our meanings somewhat more fully, although still in a preliminary way: Chapter 2, by regarding the context of philosophy when viewed, as it were, through the lens of culture (particularly through the science of culture—anthropology); Chapter 3, by considering philosophy as a tool of culture—with special concern for education; and Chapter 4, by sketching several contemporary developments in philosophy that also react, directly or indirectly, upon the mood and status of contemporary culture. The three chapters are complementary: each may be considered separately for purposes of conceptual distinctions and comparisons, but all three eventually become interdependent throughout. It is this central theme of interdependence that comes into focus in culturology as our prime guide of appraisal in approaching far-reaching expressions of educational thought and action.

Yet, far-reaching though such expressions are, we must not lose sight of the intricate, indeed combustible, issues that pervade them. For it is the latter issues which, after all, justify and challenge us to turn for guidance by our most insightful, most sensitive, and cosmopolitan interpreters of man and his place in the universe.

Issues of significance are, of course, numerous. Often they seem almost too overwhelming to enable us to confront them with any satisfying sense of resolution. This is so, moreover, precisely for reasons already implied: by no means are they *merely* educational issues; on the contrary, they weave in and out of the fabric of culture itself. Thus they interconnect with all of the multiple institutions constituting culture: education, certainly, but also politics, economics, religion, art, and science. Each institution, in turn, is fraught with its own conflicts, instabilities, and uncertainties. Each, therefore, permeates education in covert or overt ways, just as education permeates them.

But institutions, though providing as it were the structural framework of culture, constitute far from all of it. Because each institution is fashioned by man, each is both the product and the agent of his own wants, his own feelings, his own thoughts, as manifested in both his own personality and his relationships with other personalities. Thus we perceive at once that man everywhere is laden with perceptions and attitudes of how he sees and judges himself and his world, at the same time that such characteristics are deeply influenced and subtly shaped by the institutions that he has constructed himself.

May we exemplify a few of the issues that thus arise within this complex network? They are issues, we repeat, that prove inevitably educational, yet that flow continuously through the tidal mainstream of the culture that benefits from and sustains them. Our examples, in turn, are of two broad sorts—those, on the one hand, that may be regarded as broadly *institutional*; those, on the other hand, that are *personal or interpersonal.* But let us bear in mind, too, that both kinds—the institutional and personal—depend upon one another. So, too, do philosophy, education, and culture which together create the design of this book.

Among institutions, consider *politics* first. Here its fusion with education is immediately apparent. Education as an institution has itself become, especially in the modern world, an "arm" of politics. Whether we are speaking of American, European, or Communist countries, the construction and operation of schools and universities have become a colossal enterprise. So, too, have they become increasingly so in Asia, Africa, and in the underdeveloped areas where education often holds high priority. The task of abolishing the illiteracy that remains in over half of the world's population is itself urgent enough.

However urgent, this task is still not a very helpful example of the acute issues we have in mind. As a general objective, the goal of worldwide literacy receives widespread if still inadequate support. What does become debatable quickly enough is the complexity of meanings inherent in one concept—*control*—an issue stretching all the way from advocates of strictly local community autonomy, after the manner of town meetings in New England, to those advocates of international authority who contend that only adequate and enforceable financial responsibility operating through the United Nations (or, preferably, a much stronger international body) can possibly solve any single crucial problem of education, such as illiteracy. In between these extremes are proponents of centralized control on the national level (as in Japan or France) or on intermediate state and provincial levels (as in the United States or Canada).

Nor does the issue cease at the point of financial responsibility. Our own country, for one, is fraught with divisiveness: no consensus has emerged as to whether such responsibility should *primarily* lie with towns, with states, or with the federal government. Even more divisive is the issue of what levels of authority shall determine academic standards, and with these a whole cluster of disturbing questions about the most effective ways of learning and teaching, about criteria of evaluation, about student participation and involvement, about faculty authority, and many others.

Yet behind all issues of control lies a still more fundamental political and/or educational question: Is it the obligation of the nation-state to establish guiding principles not only of *how* but of *what* we shall or shall not choose to educate? The question is simply enough answered in some countries—in, for example, the Soviet Union or its allies: there the governing bodies, and doubtless a large proportion of citizens, too, take for granted that communism provides the "right" principles; therefore, every academic subject from history to science must be planned and taught accordingly. But in democratic countries such as England, America, or Norway, this superimposition is ostensibly repudiated. Hence general policies of control are likely to seem more negative than positive—that is, control is more or less officially exercised to prohibit any one kind of all-inclusive doctrine in favor of fair consideration of many doctrines.

We say "ostensibly repudiated," however, because whether the locus of authority is extremely centralized, extremely decentralized, or a blend of the two, the boundaries to which officially democratic countries do, in fact, tolerate such diversity are, again, far from precise. Here we are confronted with the familiar but always thorny question of academic freedom. The history of education in the United States alone chronicles innumerable cases of intimidations, restrictions, even severe retributions, for what is judged to be one or another infraction of proper limits as determined by one or another level of authority.

In important respects, to be sure, those advocates of the increase of academic freedom, broadly regarded, may feel encouraged by developments following World War II. Organizations such as the American Association of University Professors have long held firm to the right of dissent in the classroom and to the right of participation in unpopular causes. The two largest organizations of teachers—National Education Association and American Federation of Teachers—have likewise, at times, not only defended members under fire, but at other times have dared to stand up firmly against political pressure in their demands for respectable standards of salary, tenure, and other conditions they deem necessary to upgrading their profession.

Students, too, have been asserting themselves in ways that have rarely, if ever, occurred in the history of American education. They have pressed not only for more involvement in the control of all forms of educational procedure but also for basic changes in the curriculum itself. One must recognize, to be sure, that the phenomenon of student militancy which began most aggressively in the early 1960s and spread subsequently across a dozen or more countries generated a good deal of confused and negative public reaction. Yet the fact remains that the new spirit of criticism and collective action was also welcome not only to many citizens but to many educators as well. It demonstrated that participants in the educational enterprise need not necessarily be coerced into silence or passivity by those who control other enterprises, most notably the political.

Accompanying or even instigating teacher and student dissent has been the emergence, too, of movements among black and other minority groups. Here the interdependence of educational and political institutions becomes unusually complex. The famous Supreme Court decision of 1954 (a belated recognition that segregated schools are unconstitutional) especially was evidence that political control may sometimes accelerate rather than retard democratic education. True, enforcement remained extremely weak. But the struggle for civil rights, especially in the South, became stronger partly as a consequence of this decision—a struggle with which growing minorities of white citizens, especially students, also allied themselves.

In subsequent years, student and black power have scarcely resulted in unmitigated progress toward academic freedom in any inclusive sense. Nevertheless, the gradual sharing of faculties and students in educational policy-making and planning, the establishment of courses and institutes devoted to black history and black problems, the increasing employment of black teachers and administrators, and further decisions by the Supreme Court or lower courts in behalf of integration—these have become unprecedented accomplishments.

On balance, however, a key problem remains that may, in turn, be stated as two questions. The first: Does or should education, even in formally democratic countries, remain ultimately and decisively the servant of political and allied institutions? The second: Does or should education, notwithstanding continued restrictions and weaknesses, rise to new heights of responsibility, new conceptions of professional and personal freedom, and, above all, new recognition of its role as participating partner in political authority and power? The answer to either question is far from one-sided. Granting, for example, that the frightening period of McCarthyism in the early 1950s gradually receded, no astute interpreter of the American scene would be likely to assert that McCarthyism as symptom and symbol of reaction has disappeared; none, moreover, would predict that it will not recur. The term, "backlash," was introduced into popular language as a reaction to black and student aggressiveness. Along with it, severe penalties were either being threatened or imposed all the way up to the Congressional level. How far penalties against allegedly intransigent behavior will decrease or increase, or how far, as one consequence, academic freedom may be strengthened or weakened, are contingencies not likely to be fully resolved, perhaps for decades to come.

They do, nevertheless, underscore very well the urgency of a thoroughgoing culturological interpretation. For they exemplify, we think, the wider questions just asked—questions that can be effectively confronted only when such philosophic issues as the nature of academic freedom are discerned and interpreted in the setting of their pervasive cultural relationships.

That these relationships embrace other than the two institutions of politics and education should be obvious. Economics, for one, is so enmeshed with politics that frequently it becomes almost impossible to decide where one leaves off or the other begins. Certainly one of the most debated questions in the philosophy of history has been whether economic institutions and practices do not most pervasively determine *both* politics and education.

But let us turn to another example of how educational issues may be galvanized by means of culturology. This is the issue generated by *religion* when it, too, is viewed as another major institution of culture. Hardly less than the seething political events of recent decades, religious events undergo extraordinary tensions, conflicts, and reforms. No doubt the ecumenical congresses in Rome and their aftermaths have received most attention. Yet, again in the United States itself, only the most orthodox or fundamentalist among religious sects have insisted that no reconsideration of their original tenets of faith and creed is warranted.

Among the great majority of churches and synagogues, profound issues arise in religious thought to challenge the most searching, unrelenting examination possible. Traditional conceptions of divinity; the place of ritual and myth; the distinction, if any, between religion and science; theological justification of moral conduct; the role of religion in social change—these are typical issues. As they persist, education itself becomes increasingly persistent, for many learners, too, desire wide opportunities to pursue religious problems with the same privilege of unqualified criticism and disputation that they desire in confronting political or economic problems.

Here, the Supreme Court, stepping once more into a controversial arena, has proved itself again the proponent more than the opponent of academic freedom. In 1963, it forbade the practice of scripture-reading or prayers within the public schools. Its argument was simple: the Constitution guarantees separation of church and state; therefore any action that weakens this wall by indoctrinating children in behalf of sectarian creeds is unconstitutional. Although less frequently than in its decision against school segregation, the Court's interpretation has been ignored or violated frequently. But only a trivial minority of schools have heeded another feature of this second momentous decision: granting that indoctrination in the sense of imposition upon children of any religious creed cannot be legally justified, this is not to deny—rather, by implication, it is to favor critical informed attention to—the cultural role of religious experience. The typical issues just mentioned could, from this point of view, become legitimate and stimulating areas for curriculum study.

In short, when the institution of religion is approached, not as separate from but as integral with human evolution, we perceive that it becomes quite as germane to education as does politics. At once, therefore, a culturological interpretation opens whole clusters of questions concerning both the actual and desirable place that religious institutions may occupy in the global life of man.

A philosophy of education that is simultaneously a philosophy of culture must be considered, we have suggested, from multiple perspectives. The two examples thus far discussed, both of which occupy attention in subsequent chapters, have been viewed primarily as cultural institutions. We have promised, however, to consider one or two examples from another perspective—namely, that of personality. The point is that culture and personality are bipolarities of the same reality: neither, in actual experience, can exist without the other.

Here we choose as one example the kind of issue that has troubled so many young Americans during the postwar decades: *sexual morality*. This issue, obviously, is also institutional. Throughout history, acceptable conditions of courtship and marriage have been recognized by formal law, custom, or both. Religious orders, too, have invariably concerned themselves with the relationships of love in both their moral or immoral manifestations. Nevertheless, institutions are scarcely the sufficient cause of these manifestations; more correctly, they are their consequence. Sexual behavior, after all, is both deeply personal and deeply interpersonal: personal, because the libidinous desires of every normal human being are intimately and privately his own; interpersonal, because these desires project toward their object of satisfaction—ordinarily, toward persons of the opposite sex, although by no means exclusively so.

Disturbing issues of moral conduct, all of them traceable to basic philosophic questions, thus arise when we realize—for the social revolution has compelled us to realize—the wide ranges of behavior beyond heterosexuality. Both homosexuality and autosexuality, particularly, have become openly recognized to such a degree (and here institutional authority again becomes concerned) that encrusted laws of prohibition against deviancy are being modified, if not repealed, in many parts of the United States as well as in other countries. Simultaneously, the spread of birth control, the relaxation of laws against abortion, and widening permissiveness among the young in premarital experience—these are all drastic shifts both in attitudes and behavior.

Transformations that affect sexual morality have been occurring with the encouragement, meanwhile, of another multifaceted institution: that of the arts. Everyone knows that sexuality has long been a preoccupation of artists in prose and poetry, in the theater and dance, in painting and sculpture. Nevertheless, throughout much of Western civilization, it has usually been treated delicately if not surreptitiously or guiltily. Even more so, formal education has almost universally regarded sexual experience as a taboo.

But compare these conventions with recent developments. Literature and the theater are only two of the arts that treat erotic themes with an exactitude worthy of clinicians. In schools, one may find millions of adolescent students reading and discussing vivid novels with the zestful encouragement of their teachers. Moreover, within scarcely a decade, "sex education" has become so familiar that, although invariably it stirs the ire of some citizen groups, it meets the hearty approval of others.

The moral and immoral ranges of sexuality are by no means, then, simple to delineate. We suggest that they can best be considered, especially in their relevance for education, as a culturological question. That is, they require the closest partnership of two disciplines: philosophy, in its analyses and evaluations of the assumptions upon which all morality rests; and anthropology, in its descriptions and interpretations of the fantastic diversity in sexual roles that human beings perform both within and across the cultures of the earth.

One concluding example, likewise intertwined with our preceding ones: few single concepts in the psychological sphere have stirred more keen attention during the post-midcentury years than that of *alienation.* Although recognized for a long time by insightful observers of human nature, only occasionally in earlier periods did the concept inspire either penetrating theory or sustained research. Certainly scientists of human behavior did little to prepare for, much less to cope with, the spread of defiance against conventionality—a defiance so pronounced as to require newly invented labels such as "beatnik" and "hippie" to differentiate such groups from "ordinary" young people. Moreover, their often surprising behavior radiated not only across the Americas but across other continents as well.

But alienation in its broad connotations has by no means been limited to vocally rebellious youth. Resistances against war or other oppressive foreign policies, against racial discrimination, against sexual or drug proscriptions and inhibitions, against religious asceticism or authoritarianism, and, perhaps most commonly of all, against technological domination and depersonalization—these are widespread phenomena that have been examined and appraised by scores of interpreters. Once again, accordingly, we perceive how the personal and institutional become inextricable.

Certainly it does seem plausible to contend that, in the experience of alienation even more clearly than in many other experiences currently besetting the human condition, "the alienated man" is trapped by a vicious circle. As documented by a classic study in social psychology—the "frustration-aggression complex"—we learn that repressions of normal needs and aspirations generate counter reactions and sometimes violent ones: in severe personality disorders, in sometimes brutal class conflicts, and in intra- or even international racial revolutions against dominant and usually white establishments.

These comments, no less than others evoked by our preceding examples, deserve further attention as we proceed. Here, the only contention we wish to underscore is that, whether we are considering issues of politics, religion, sexuality, alienation, or any other crucial issue, all of them admonish us to consider their bearings upon education. Alienation, surely, is at least as relevant as any others that might be exemplified: students and faculties who resent what they adjudge to be irrelevant curriculum requirements, or who challenge outmoded administrative policies, or who maintain that financial resources to education are grossly disproportionate to other public budgets, or who consider their institutions to be controlled openly or covertly by the "political-industrial-military complex"—these may as surely contribute to uncomfortable but far-ranging feelings of alienation among uncounted, nonvocal multitudes as they do to those minorities who articulate overtly hostile attitudes and sometimes erupt into destructively aggressive tactics.

Our time of great debate in education becomes, then, all-encompassing. It penetrates the depths of the psyche; but also, it stretches to the edges of the globe—indeed, in our dawning age of space, vastly farther still.

At the same time, any productive culturological interpretation of educational philosophies must discover ways to focus sharply upon, and thus also to exclude from, an enormously wide and hazardous landscape—the landscape of man and culture as these exist within the still wider spheres of nature and the universe. In venturing upon this exploration, we hope to consider both practical as well as theoretical phases of the educational enterprise, some of them as immediate as methods of daily classroom teaching, others as inclusive as educational-cultural designs for world civilization. All such phases are bound to create varying, perhaps even sharply conflicting, patterns of belief and programs of implementation. Simultaneously, however, all of them invite fertile opportunities for rapprochement and synthesis.

Following the next three chapters, which together provide the groundwork for our approach, the successive four parts will select four points of view as culturologies of education.

CHAPTER 2

A culturological approach to philosophies of education

DELINEATION OF CULTUROLOGY

IN CHAPTER 1, the point was made that philosophies of education are to be regarded within a conceptual framework that shall be termed *culturology*. This term is scarcely accepted, as yet, either by philosophers or even by those few anthropologists who point most directly toward its emerging formulation. Nevertheless, we choose to adopt it as somewhat less awkward and more focal than terms closest to its intent: philosophical anthropology and/or anthropological philosophy. The former of these is somewhat familiar; it includes a number of important thinkers at least as far back as Giambattista Vico of about three hundred years ago, up to and beyond the twentieth-century Ernst Cassirer. But the latter term (rarely, if ever, found in philosophic literature) is the more accurate; it suggests that philosophy is the discipline to which anthropology, in turn, contributes most.

Either way, the distinguishing feature of culturology is this: *culture is regarded as the fulcrum of an effort to interpret the meaning of man, his existence, and his actions.* In this sense, one might even contend that culturology is virtually synonymous with "anthropocentricism": because both look upon and interpret the world from the posture of the human species, therefore either may be questioned by some philosophers for its limitations just as egocentricism may be questioned by others for connoting a pattern of beliefs allegedly emanating from and returning to the ego.

Granting, then, that culturology, no less than any other provocative concept, is open to controversy, it is adapted here as a productive way to describe and evaluate the remainder of this book. But it differs from, say, anthropocentricism in the sense that it carries less invidious implications of restriction: it depends very directly and consciously upon the scientific and philosophic study of man when he is seen as the carrier and fashioner of culture in its relations to still wider spheres of reality, such as the geological.

Now it is this inclusive relationship that utilizes culturology in order to examine and evaluate one of culture's major institutions: education. Of course, a comparable effort could be attempted for any other major institution. This is simply the case because, in one way or another, each institution proves integral with the culture that embraces all of them.

But let us further emphasize that, while culturology as an abstract term need not, as such, become associated with any *one* systematic interpretation of education, our own adaptation of culturology is further characterized by a definite orientation. *This orientation is an anthropological philosophy that is frankly naturalistic, experimental, and radically democratic.* To anticipate, we find no objection to retaining a phrase utilized elsewhere: "an anthropological philosophy of education."[1] It is this orientation that not only receives primary attention in Part 5; it also governs our preceding evaluations of three other, still more conspicuous, philosophies of education in Parts 2, 3, and 4.

Meanwhile, we may try to encapsulate our adaptation of culturology. This concept aims to interpret alternative educational theories as primary orientations of *culture*. At the same time, it rests upon *philosophy*—a term not yet well defined but that we may anticipate as both deriving from and influencing the cultural experiences of our hazardous times.

Only too obviously, this encapsulation is nothing more than the bare bones of an organic unity toward which, one step at a time, we shall try gradually and meaningfully to evolve. Our next step is to introduce a more focal concept that acquires additional significance from the culturological point of view.

A later chapter refers to the influence of Karl Mannheim and to his theory, the "sociology of knowledge." Here, with the aid of various scholars who have followed Mannheim further, let us recognize and extend his influence. We are thinking, for example, of the brilliant study by Peter L. Berger and Thomas Luckmann, *The*

[1] Brameld, *Education for the Emerging Age*, pp. 112ff.

Social Construction of Reality—A Treatise in the Sociology of Knowledge. Sociology and anthropology are, to be sure, so closely related sciences that experts are far from always agreed as to proper distinctions. Even so, we prefer the term "culturology of knowledge" for reasons that may be clearer when the culture concept is delineated more fully. At the moment, let us simply assert that "culture," as we understand it, is more inclusive than "society" and that the culturology of knowledge is therefore more relevant than Mannheim's more restrictive term.

But let us go still further: a guiding hypothesis is proposed for our entire study of viable influential educational philosophies. Very simply, teachers and students (not to overlook rank-and-file citizens equally concerned about education) can hope most successfully to understand and act upon this cultural institution if and as they very seriously consider and, in their own terms, put into operation the culturology of knowledge.

This hypothesis, if it is to be sustained, must be tested in many specific and partial ways—in learning-teaching, in curriculum experimentation, and in methods of administrative control. More broadly, what the culturology of knowledge suggests to education is that we can most effectively *know* best and also ultimately *value* best the beliefs and practices of the *real* world when, and only when, we perceive this world in terms of man as a creature and creator of culture.

Yet, to speak of "man as a creature and creator of culture" is to beg a key question. What, after all, do we mean?

THE CULTURE WE LIVE IN

That culture is among the most fruitful of all the concepts that have lately emerged in the social sciences is a proposition in which a considerable majority of scholars in these fields would concur. The phrase, "lately emerged," is precise because, while culture as a concept is very old, its clarification by the scientific discipline most directly concerned with it, anthropology, is comparatively new. Indeed, the first academically respectable definition of culture (still by far the most quoted) was offered in 1871. In this year, the English scholar, Edward B. Tylor, wrote at the very opening of his *Primitive Culture*: "Culture or Civilization . . . is that complex whole which includes knowledge, belief, art, morals, law, custom, and any other capabilities and habits acquired by man as a member of society."[2]

[2] Tylor, *Primitive Culture*, p. 1.

Components of this definition are multiple. In the phrase "complex whole," Tylor is hinting that any culture, however numerous or diverse its parts, still possesses some kind of pattern or configuration. Also, it embraces innumerable personal activities along with their nonpersonal or objective manifestations. Morals, for example, are in one sense covert, but in another sense they attain overt expression through the behavior of families as well as through courts, legislatures, churches, schools, and other institutions. Again, Tylor implies by "law," "custom," and "habits" that culture connotes regularities of human behavior rather than merely idiosyncrasies or accidental occurrences—regularities upon which, be it noted, he passes no judgment of approval or disapproval. All characteristics of culture, moreover, are acquired: they are not inherited, not carried by the genes or other biological equipment from generation to generation. Finally, the individual cannot fashion culture by himself; he does so only insofar as he lives and works with other men—that is to say, cooperatively.

A case could be made for the contention that Tylor's successors down to the present day have devoted most of their energies to refining, elaborating, and testing his famous definition. Virtually every word has been subjected to scrupulous analysis and has generated endless debate and vast research. As briefly suggested, consider the term "society": What is its precise relation to culture? Are culture and society synonymous? If not, why do even anthropologists still so frequently interchange the two terms in their own writings? Part of the answer lies in the fact that anthropology, relatively speaking as a young discipline, is even less refined in terminology than, say, economics or political science. Part of the answer also is that, by fairly wide agreement among experts, society is one very important aspect of culture; hence, when talking about that aspect they quite properly use the term "society." Anthropologists often view a human society as the situation in which people find themselves when associated together, as in a family, or club, or village. A *society* assumes the character of *culture* when it acquires habits, values, institutions, and skills that are cherished in common and transmitted to successive generations.

Other terms in Tylor's definition are equally provocative. Habit, for example, demands careful psychological interpretation. Thus, the first widely influential anthropologist in American history, Franz Boas, defines culture as follows: "Culture embraces all the manifestations of social habits of a community, the reactions of the individual as affected by the habits of the group in which he lives, and the products of human activities as determined by these habits."[3]

Or let us consider the term "civilization," which Tylor regards as equivalent to culture. Many authorities, likewise, continue to follow his lead here. They do not contrast "civilized" with "uncivilized" cultures, preferring to regard all cultures, however different from one another, as civilized within their own context of beliefs, habits, and practices. For this reason, authorities also increasingly reject as misleading the term "primitive." When they wish to distinguish between one culture (such as the American or French) and another (such as the Australian aboriginese), they more often use the terms "literate" and "nonliterate," the latter merely denoting that the culture possesses no written language. But this terminology is not universally accepted among scientists, historians, and philosophers of culture.

The meaning of culture is perhaps best interpreted in *Culture: A Critical Review of Concepts and Definitions* by two stellar American anthropologists, Alfred L. Kroeber and Clyde Kluckhohn. Their review demonstrates that, despite wide ranges of emphasis and perspective on the central idea, a high degree of consensus also prevails toward its core meaning. They recognize, of course, that older, honorific notions of culture as cultivation—"to achieve or impart refined manners, urbanization, and improvement"—is still entirely legitimate so long as we are clear that this is what we intend. As used by social scientists, however, culture is at least that "set of attributes and products of human societies, and therewith of mankind, which are extrasomatic [not bodily or organic] and transmissible by mechanisms other than biological heredity, and are as essentially lacking in sub-human species as they are characteristic of the human species as it is aggregated in societies."[4]

Culture as a concept becomes even more fructifying when applied pluralistically. Consider for a moment the *variety* of cultures existing upon the earth—all of which have something in common, each of which is also distinguishable from others by its own qualities of consistency and harmony. Some such cultures have vanished, except in historic memory or in the important respect that certain of their features have been absorbed by later cultures; thus to speak of ancient Egypt and Greece as once having had great cultures is also, in one sense, to speak of our own period of

[3] Boas, "Anthropology," *Encyclopædia of the Social Sciences*, Vol. II, p. 79.

[4] Kroeber and Kluckhohn, *Culture: A Critical Review of Concepts and Definitions*, p. 145.

history. But it is equally true that, while peoples of various races and nationalities are today in closer contact than formerly, profound dissimilarities exist between the institutions, customs, and beliefs of, let us say, the Orient and the Occident, or between those of Europe and North America, and even those of central Africa and Madagascar. Still further, we recognize the existence of *sub*cultures within a whole culture; it is not improper to regard subcultures such as those of the American Indian as manifesting distinctive patterns. In short, what we should keep in mind is that the totality of "culture" carries many smaller "cultures" within it—that is, smaller patterns or ways of life which, while capable of differentiation, are also inextricably bound to larger ones. Institutions, such as those mentioned above (politics, for one), illustrate a somewhat comparable phenomenon.

This view of culture, in terms of what may also be considered overlapping configurations, suggests a further refinement of meaning. We have been talking about what may be termed the *order* of culture, but we have not noted explicitly two other concepts that prove equally fruitful: these are cultural *process* and cultural *goals*. Let us epitomize them:

> Order refers to the patterns of relationship to be found in every culture—its layers of class and status, say, or its widening concentric rings of family, neighborhood, community, region, nation. Process refers to the dynamics of culture—to the ebb and flow of its membership, its institutions, its innumerable contacts both within its mobile parts and with outside cultures. Goals refer primarily to the values of culture, to its sense of direction and purpose as it undergoes change within its ordered patterns of relationship. Each of the three concepts can, of course, be subdivided many times; each is also intertwined with the other two. Yet we may select one or another in turn, and apply it to actual events.[5]

All three of these concepts are of equally rich significance. Thus, just as the order of culture may help to clarify the nature of reality in its manifold meanings, so process in culture may also prove clarifying. Consider only one familiar anthropological term, *enculturation*. Often this is interpreted to mean the cultural process that occurs through transmitting or "socializing" skills, habits, and attitudes by means of formal and, especially, informal teaching

[5] Brameld, *op. cit.*, p. 116.

and learning. But some authorities perceive enculturation as much more than such a transmissive process; for them, teaching-learning may provide room for modifying or even transforming skills, habits, and attitudes in the direction of goals. Interesting questions are evoked, in turn, by the culturology of knowledge: surely, to enculturate presupposes that what we are learning and teaching in the course of cultural experience must be dependable and so, in some vague sense at least, true. For why, otherwise, should we want to engage in the process at all?

Enculturation, nevertheless, is concerned at least as much with values as it is with truth. As Tylor reminds us, knowledge is important to culture, but so too are such features as morals, custom, and art. No wonder, then, that values enter into our grasp of culture; they provoke questions not only as to the course in which a particular culture may be evolving but also whether these directions, in turn, are desirable and, if so, achievable.

The crucial point is that any or all of these beliefs often acquire quite different significance when culturally perceived. No longer do they remain pure exercises of intellect immune from the patterns, the dynamics, or the purposes of everyday human life; rather, they become indigenous features of man-in-culture. Thereby they provide a further step toward the meaning of an anthropological philosophy—that is, of culturology—and this, in turn, of an anthropological philosophy of education.

Although the American culture is far from our exclusive concern, it enriches our culturological awareness to focus next upon a few of its past, present, and future characteristics. The ultimate intention is to improve our capacity to appraise philosophies of education. For these, too, are cultural experiences. They spring from the culture; they develop and mature within it; they react upon it. They cannot be understood without it.

Yet, merely to inquire into the nature of the American culture is to reveal how difficult—nay, impossible—is any single definition. Historians, sociologists, philosophers, novelists, and other artists have been seeking a definition almost since the moment America was born—and they are still seeking. This is not unfortunate. America is boundlessly rich, not only in natural resources but in spirit and stamina. It is young as cultures go and certainly complex. No wonder, if it is seen differently through different eyes, or if the scene is changed in time by viewers' different emotions and characters.

How do American anthropologists view America? They are

only beginning to apply their special competencies to their own culture, for the majority of them have concentrated on simpler, more nonliterate cultures. Still, an increasing minority is beginning to operate nearer home: not only do they study fairly distinct subcultures, such as Indian tribes, Negroes, or other minority groups, but some have examined whole American communities and still others have examined single institutions *within* communities—education being one.

An influential example of how Kluckhohn regarded his own culture some years ago still remains one of the most perceptive. He found that Americans are characterized by, among other traits, a capacity for generosity, laughter, and optimism; a faith in the rationality of the common man; a high moral sense; a glorification of action and work; a dramatization of the individual; a worship of success; a faith in "progress"; a tendency to conform to majority standards; a warm regard for recreation; a consciousness of diversity in cultural and biological origins; a "relatively strong trust in science and education and relative indifference to religion"; a love of gadgets and bigness; a high degree of restlessness and insecurity.

In common with many other social scientists, Kluckhohn observed sharp discrepancies between the beliefs and practices of American culture. Thus, we may cite his statement that "it is only the *tradition* of economic independence which truly survives. For all our talk of free enterprise we have created the most vast and crushing monopolies in the world." Further illustrations of such divergence are, first, the "intolerable contradictions" in our creed of equality and our treatment of minorities, and second, the existence of a status and class structure that tends to stratify people to a far greater extent than is so blandly assumed by our long-held belief in freedom of movement and opportunity. "Americans are at present seeing social change of a vastness difficult to comprehend . . . World War II appears to have destroyed the old equilibrium beyond repair."[6]

This quotation raises the question of whether America can be diagnosed as a "crisis-culture." Were Kluckhohn still living, he might very well have answered even insistently in the affirmative than during the 1940s when this statement was first made. A few other anthropologists would also probably answer affirmatively or at least recognize the importance of crisis as a cultural event. A number have also been enlisted in the difficult task of assisting

[6] Kluckhohn, *Mirror for Man*, pp. 228–261.

underdeveloped peoples to adjust to rapid technological advances with accompanying tensions.

One of these anthropologists, certainly, is Laura Thompson in her *Toward a Science of Mankind* and in her earlier *Culture in Crisis*, a study of the Hopi Indians of northern Arizona. Her definition of culture-crisis is "the manifestation of critical imbalance in one or more essentials of a culture structure in environmental setting."[7] Again, the culturologist, David Bidney, has defined culture-crisis as "a state of emergency brought about by the suspension of normal, or previously prevailing, technological, social, or ideological conditions."[8] And H. G. Barnett, another anthropologist, has explained that in a state of culture-crisis:

> . . . a familiar universe of associations and sanctions has been distorted or destroyed, and must be reorganized. The wrenching away of any control mechanism . . . requires a reorientation. Unsettlement for any cause creates a fluid condition in which the old values are no longer operative. With the old sanctions and compulsives gone or of doubtful validity, the way is open for the creation and the acceptance of new interpretations.[9]

Such definitions are probably acceptable to the too few historians and philosophers of culture who believe that the present age is one of profound crisis. The Englishman, Toynbee, is one. Another is the American, Mumford, who has long contended that:

> The period through which we are living presents itself as one of unmitigated confusion and disintegration: a period of paralyzing economic depressions, of unrestrained butcheries and enslavements, and one of world-ravaging wars: a period whose evil fulfillments have betrayed all its beneficent promises. But behind all these phenomena of physical destruction we can detect an earlier and perhaps more fundamental series of changes: a loss of communion between classes and peoples, a breakdown in stable behavior, a loss of form and purpose in many of the arts. . . .[10]

[7] Thompson, *Culture in Crisis*, p. 161.

[8] Bidney, *Theoretical Anthropology*, p. 349.

[9] Barnett, *Innivation: The Basis of Cultural Change*, p. 89.

[10] Mumford, *The Condition of Man*, p. 14.

We propose, then, to designate the man-made environment of the present period of American history as a culture in crisis. On the basis of the definitions given above, our own usage implies that institutions, habits, symbols, beliefs, and faiths are almost all infected by chronic instability, confusion, bifurcations, and uncertainties.

At the same time, the crisis through which much of the world is now struggling has by no means struck every facet with equal force. Various institutions and faiths, including some schools and churches, tend to build in their members habits of acquiescence in, rather than a feeling of concern about, the current of events. It is true, of course, that these events cannot disturb all of us at every moment. We tend to go about our daily routines, as far as we can, accepting those attitudes and practices to which we have grown accustomed, from which we draw security, and upon which we depend. If for no other reason than that the constant strain upon us would be unendurable, we often overlook or deliberately ignore many symptoms of abnormality in the culture.

This "normal" tendency to conceal "abnormality" is peculiarly characteristic of the American people. More than any culture of modern times, perhaps of any time, ours has seemed to be an optimistic culture. We have enjoyed an abiding faith in the inevitability of progress. We have possessed limitless confidence in our youthful virility, ingenuity, resources—our "bounce." Most important, we have thus far escaped the worse effects of the epidemics that have swept so much of the earth—the epidemic of war, especially. Although parts of our land have suffered terribly (the Civil War still leaves deep scars), our cities have hitherto escaped bombing, our fields and farm lands have not been ravaged, our civilian populations have not been scourged. Nor have we been threatened too seriously, thus far, by the totalitarian movements of Europe and Asia. We entered World War II to destroy fascism, but few of us feared it could conquer America. True, the long period of Cold War generated new fears. Many of us have continued to believe, nevertheless, that the "democratic way of life" is quite invincible—that the ideals of "liberty" and "equality," though never quite attainable, are secure forever.

Yet, granting that the United States appears to be less directly affected by our crisis-culture than are some other regions, we cannot assume that ultimately it is less involved. On the contrary, by comparison with many nations, it is *more* involved. As the leading world power it can set, not only its own course, but the course for lesser powers. Thus it may either deepen the crisis of our time, or it may greatly relieve, perhaps resolve, that crisis. It may hasten the complete collapse of civilization, or it may contribute immeasurably to cultural renewal.

OUR "SCHIZOPHRENIC" AGE

But if America is to assume the solemn responsibilities thrust upon it by its own dominance, one of the first tasks of its thinking citizens is to look critically and honestly inward to examine the condition of their culture. Can it be, for example, that the habit of many of us to gloss over our frailties and to shy away from sharp analysis of our personal and social instabilities—the easy confidence with which we like to believe that opposing forces can be persuaded to act reasonably and to cooperate amicably—is itself symptomatic of cultural disturbances? This question may be answered only as and if we are first able to demonstrate that internal conflicts, tensions, and hostilities do permeate the fiber of our culture.

In the language of psychiatry, our culture may be diagnosed as, in grave respects, a "schizophrenic" culture. Accurately stated, the personality elements of a schizophrenic individual are not only in conflict but often are out of contact with one another, so that the term is applied to culture with awareness that it has the defects of every analogy: strictly, a culture is never schizophrenic in the sense that a person is. Our own culture, moreover, lacks the extreme manifestations of this disease in that its multiple areas of conflict still maintain varying degrees of communication. These areas of conflict have, indeed, so long permeated our history that few, if any, have developed only within preceding decades. Nevertheless, having qualified the analogy, let us note several symptoms that prove especially disjointed in the present period.

Self-interest versus social interest. Traditionally, American culture, borrowing from modern Europe, has been concerned to promote the self-interest of its individual members. This is observed not only in the shibboleths of competitive enterprise, but also in the daily conduct of countless persons. Self-aggrandizement, self-display, self-promotion; an ethic that rewards and praises those who practice shrewd dealings; the elevation to civic dignity and high political office of individuals who win pecuniary success by such dealings; the feeling that family loyalty precedes if it does not deny all wider loyalties—these are common to our way of life.

Still, although common, they are not exclusive. Side by side with attitudes and habits of self-interest are others that reveal a strong social interest. Admiration for the gifts of philanthropists; the generosity with which people of small income "chip in" to support public causes; an ethic that praises service to others, the ideals of brotherhood and honesty in business; the eagerness with which groups, ranging from Rotary Clubs and Boy Scouts to huge fraternal organizations, manifest good fellowship and cooperative effort; the zeal with which some high-school and college students join in projects of urban renewal or child and health programs—these, too, are characteristic of American communities.

Inequality versus equality. What Gunnar Myrdal called, in a now classic work, *An American Dilemma*, is another example. The term refers to our failure to provide full civil rights, fair job opportunities, and respect for millions of citizens at the same moment that democratic rhetoric subscribes officially to "equality for all." Myrdal was concerned with the 10 percent of our population that is Negro, but since his work was published the dilemma has compounded—and only too frequently in violence between the white and black races. Other minorities becoming increasingly restive are Mexican-Americans of the Southwest, American Indians, and Puerto Ricans. Millions of white citizens, too, are denied economic, social, educational, or other privileges. Jews constitute one instance; women in business, professions, and politics, another; the "poor" of Appalachia and other depressed areas, still another.

Nor is the dilemma confined to our failure to practice what we preach. The truth is that, even as an ideal, American culture is by no means universally committed to equality. Recall the first conflict noted above: when success is measured by the "ability" with which a man wins over others in the struggle for financial gain, the implication is clear that individuals either should be condoned for their superiority or blamed for their inferiority. In this perspective, it is not equality that deserves praise so much as the kind of inequality that enables one to stand economically and socially well above the average.

Again, however, gross inconsistencies appear in practices and attitudes. Legislative efforts to provide equal privileges for blacks and other minorities indicate that inequality is by no means universally approved. The Supreme Court decisions declaring unconstitutional segregation of Negroes in public accommodations, including public schools, have given powerful sanction to that disapproval. Still more significant is the growing insistence that economic failure is not necessarily the mark of inferior ability. In an industrial system as huge and bloodless as ours, a person can only too easily be victimized by circumstances utterly beyond his control. Hence, equality of security, if not of opportunity, must be guaranteed by medical care, cooperative agencies, and other public services.

If it be asked whether such illustrations do not muddy the concept of equality, the reply is that, even if they do, there is no avoiding them. The culture itself has muddied it. The fact is that, if judged by its behavior, America does not agree with itself as to what equality means.

Planlessness versus planning. Does our culture agree any more harmoniously as to the need for, or meaning of, social-economic planning?

To some, the very term *planning* smacks of "communism," "socialism," or other obnoxious "un-American" proposals. To others, not only is careful planning desirable in such an intricate social order as ours, it is a dire necessity.

The advocates of planlessness are often governed by a self-interest that profits by economic inequality. They want their businesses, families, and personal lives to function as independently as possible, without interference "from the outside." If they have theorized about their beliefs at all, they doubtless contend that such independence will, in the long run, produce the greatest welfare for the most people.

Yet it is startling to observe with what circumlocutions even the most rugged of rugged individualists square their verbalizations with concrete actions. Recognizing that recurrent depressions with their heavy toll of suffering are undesirable, even the professed opponents of planning are reluctantly willing to plan within particular localities or states; yet they also continue to look with suspicion upon trends toward centralized control of federal direction. And although these proponents of planlessness opposed the economic and social planning of the New Deal, Fair Deal, or Great Society, and labeled such projects of regional development as the Tennessee Valley Authority "creeping socialism," such huge corporate enterprises as General Motors or the Du Pont "empire" are themselves magnificent demonstrations of *planned* efficiency—not only of technological integration but also of interlocking directorates, hierarchical supervision, price-setting policies, and deliberate subversion of inventions in favor of contrived technological obsolescence. Nor are they averse to regulation by government—so long as such regulation strengthens their own power, their own right to plan as *they* see fit for *their* own ends.

But the advocates of wider social-economic planning are not

agreed on how much and what kinds of political controls over economic life should be approved. Some are willing to settle for a curious conception termed the "mixed economy." The economy they tend to endorse is "mixed," not only in its wavering proposals for planning here but no planning there; too often it is a confession of mixed attitudes as well—another significant symbol of a culture that tends to conceal its bifurcations from itself by patchwork remedies.

As one instance of this confusion, we may consider the attitude of organized labor toward planning in America. Though in certain other countries—Sweden, let us say—labor has supported national planning by democratic means, our own powerful unions hesitate to propose any measures that might jeopardize ultimate domination by the captains of commerce. True, labor is not timid in pressing for higher and higher wages. True, also, it sometimes supports partial measures of planning—for example, health insurance, unemployment compensation, retirement benefits, and education. By and large, nevertheless, struggle between the forces of capital and labor is confined primarily to determining how they shall divide profits accrued from the traditional economic structure which they both endorse. The recent history of the American labor movement is itself an ironic commentary upon economic, political, and moral schizophrenia.

Nationalism versus internationalism. Hans Kohn, the historian, has written in disturbing terms:

> . . . the "one world" of the twentieth century offers the apparent paradox of an unparalleled intensity of economic and cultural intercourse between peoples . . . and at the same time a completely novel bitterness in conflicts between nations. . . . A unified humanity with a common cultural design seemed to emerge at the beginning of the twentieth century, but at the same time the divisions within mankind became more pronounced than ever before; conflicts between them spread over wider areas and stirred deeper emotions. Cultural contact had engendered and intensified conflict between nationalities.[11]

This statement is diagnostic of how the crisis from which we suffer extends beyond the boundaries of America; how, in our kind

[11] Kohn, *The Twentieth Century: A Midway Account of the Western World,* p. 19.

of world, cultural illnesses cannot possibly be confined in some "isolation ward." They are contagious illnesses.

Ours is the first century in history in which not merely one, but two,, world wars have been fought—and these less than a quarter century apart. Subsequent to these catastrophes, a whole series of lesser wars has exploded into suffering and destruction across many areas of the earth—East and West alike—each one a threat to planetary conflagration. Moreover, the brand of nationalism that has developed under such labels as fascism and Nazism has been unprecedented in its fanatical fury and hatreds, its techniques of creating mass hysteria, the shocking speed with which it replaced democratic-libertarian practices with autocratic-authoritarian practices. Soviet and Chinese communism, too, have appeared to become more nationalistic, less concerned to promote the Marxian ideal of an international socialist democracy than to strengthen their own pyramids of power.

Nor is the spirit of nationalism by any means lacking in America. Here are familiar symptoms: restrictive immigration laws; tireless agitation by isolationists against not only the United Nations but "internationalists" of all kinds; a gargantuan armaments program that deprives educational, health, recreational, and other services of desperately needed funds; a foreign policy that speaks more often for national than for world economic interests and still more often acts as though our nation alone were innocent of wrongdoing.

Though familiar, these trends, too, are offset by others. Communication within and among large-scale cultures has increased more rapidly in the past few decades than in the whole of preceding history. Air travel and electronics have brought all parts of the globe into closer proximity than was formerly dreamed possible. Rapid infiltration of Western technology is transforming great areas which, only a few years back, were primitive in economic productivity. Recognition that war has become infinitely more destructive than ever before has brought persistent demands for world government with enforceable authority over individual nations—demands that signalize the possible emergence, at last, of a unified mankind.

In terms of our crisis-culture, utmost danger lies in the grim threat that these dichotomies between nationalism and internationalism will not be resolved in time. Force, not only in atomic, chemical, and bacterial weapons but also as a rationale for collective behavior, has become stronger at the same moment that the power of communication and skills in collective arbitration have become stronger. The insistence that might makes right, the superstition in countries such as South Africa and Rhodesia that the white is inherently destined to rule over others (just as some individuals are inherently superior to other individuals)—these are not the heresies of a few "crackpots." They are widely maintained not only in foreign lands where fascism concealed often by innocent-sounding labels is still openly or subversively practiced, but in the United States where alarming proportions of citizens are zealous to respond. Yet, they are maintained side by side with equally fervent convictions of opposite tenor: reason above force, the equal worth of nationalities and races, and the goal of a powerful but democratically governed community of nations.

Absolutism versus experimentalism. Permeating all these cultural cleavages, and extending beyond them, is the more subtle struggle between absolutism and experimentalism, regarded here in a broadly cultural rather than in any strictly philosophic sense. On the whole and granting exceptions, we may say that self-interest, inequality, planlessness, and nationalism tend in our culture to be absolutist in spirit and action; whereas social interest, equality, planning and internationalism tend in our culture to be experimentalist in spirit and action.

Thus advocates of private enterprise may attempt to ground the assumption of self-interest in an absolute law of nature. The same attempt might seek to justify not only the right of the "superior" to unequal privilege but also a "free competition" which alone, friends of planlessness insist, guarantees a workable economic system. Absolutism is also a familiar feature of nationalism; common examples are the inviolable sovereignty of each nation, the supremacy of a leader of a racial elite, the prevalence of dogma, and the play upon passions.

At the same time, experimentalism, typified by the promotion of social interest in the Scandinavian countries, has been powerful in its own motivations. Even in individual-centered America, we may recall the experiments of the 1930s with federal works projects; such successful planning ventures as the Tennessee Valley Authority and social security; the later federal programs in interracial housing, employment, education for the disadvantaged; federally supported projects in the fine arts and cultural exchange; the abortive but pioneering League of Nations after World War I; and the more hopeful United Nations after World War II. It is clear, also, that the whole spirit and method of social science have gained immense prestige and influence.

Whether experimentalism makes a greater *total* impact than

absolutism, however, is far more clear. For one thing, the natural sciences have been under attack in recent years. Nuclear physicists create such fiendish devices as hydrogen bombs which have the force to destroy their creators along with everyone else. Other experts invent jet-propelled airplanes and missiles which, while knitting the world together, also preclude adequate defense against enemy invaders. Still others build computers, radios, television sets, movies, automatic printing and recording devices, which create unprecedented opportunities for world enlightenment while, at the same time, provide those who control them with a stranglehold on public opinion and mass mentality. For another thing, science is held to be weak in moral or social responsibility and purpose. The fact that its creations are so often used to destroy, maim, or poison rather than to build and improve life is evidence enough for many of its critics.

This is not to say that absolutism provides what experimentalism thus far lacks. On the contrary, absolutism is itself open to grave charges. Consider its religious forms. American culture, like virtually all cultures nonliterate or literate, is saturated with supernatural faiths. The dominant creeds—Catholic, Jewish, Protestant—are more or less alike in their acceptance of a Supreme Being, Who is the source of natural and moral law, and to Whom mortals look in facing the travails of this earthly realm. All three creeds unite, likewise, in their stand that science is inferior to religion as a final source of protection and authority.

Here religious unity ends. Not only do sects differ as to how much and what kinds of science are permissible; they dissent bitterly in their interpretations of religious doctrines themselves. Often, too, they disagree on social, political, and other policies: some disclose sympathy with nationalism, self-interest, inequality, planlessness; others tend toward internationalism, social interest, equality, planning. No wonder if, in the face of these internal disorders, experimentalists criticize religious absolutists for their escapism, anarchism, and dogmatism quite as severely as the latter criticize them. No wonder if, as against the absolutist's dependence upon some secular or divine power, the experimentalist holds that men, their skills and intelligence, are the sole reliable guide to their own destinies. No wonder, finally, if he insists that moral confusions must be solved and purposes fashioned not by less but by *more* experiment—for all absolutisms tend to build cultures that are closed and static rather than open and dynamic.

In the decades of the Cold War and beyond, the conflict between absolutism and experimentalism has centered on still another issue: the scope and limits of free speech, assembly, and other privileges guaranteed by the Bill of Rights. Those of experimental temper have generally insisted that these privileges must be scrupulously protected because essential to the rational and scientific exploration of every sort of human problem. Those of absolutist temper more often support political and other maneuvers that, in the name of "law and order," would restrict the right of dissent, the right to belong to unpopular parties, and especially the right to advocate beliefs "contrary to the public interest." On this issue, religious groups are again divided—some strongly supporting civil liberties because of their concern for religious liberty itself, others tending to confine religious liberty to their own preordained creeds. But experimentalists are themselves often unclear or inconsistent: in recent years, many have taken equivocal stands as to the kind and degree of freedom that they would grant to those political minorities who, once in power, they contend, would destroy all freedom. True, the fears and intimidations generated by the mutually hostile attitudes and policies of the Soviet and American power blocs have been mainly responsible for these vacillations and confusions. The question that has not yet been resolved, however, is whether the extreme restrictions that are proposed for combating "communism" (a term seldom well defined) will not lead to the same absolute ruthlessness of suppression and the same conformity in behavior that characterize totalitarian policy.

Man-against-himself versus man-for-himself. Our concluding illustration is recapitulation of the preceding ones, but observed more closely from the vantage point of culturology. In our time, man seems to be his own worst enemy as often as his own best friend. It is enough to remind ourselves that America's sanitariums are crowded; that the number of qualified psychiatrists falls far short of need by many thousands; and that millions of men, women, and children who should receive treatment are not receiving it. To denote the extremes of mental illness, we now use the term "schizophrenic" more strictly as the mental disturbance of split personalities. But the *tendency* to schizophrenia, which we may characterize as "schizoid," is so insidious and so widespread that no one can say how many people are in varying stages of this form of illness.

The kinds of disturbances from which individuals suffer in our culture are, of course, numerous. As we shall suggest later in discussing neo-Freudian ideas, psychiatrists and psychoanalysts today are far from agreed either in theory or practice on how far Freud was right in tracing mental illness especially to malfunctioning of the sexual drive. They do more fully agree that until inner conflicts are removed, until a equilibrium is established in the patient, he cannot hope to be "happy." Typically, they explore the patient's emotional behavior, especially his unconscious motivations, with the expectation that if he can be made aware of such motivations, he will be able to face his problems and adopt an internally harmonious pattern of behavior.

However helpful this kind of psychotherapy may be in particular cases, the difficulty is that too frequently it leaves untouched much of the patient's cultural environment. It seeks to remove conflicts within, but it does little if anything to remove conflicts without. It concerns itself insufficiently with the problem of whether many individuals can achieve *internal* harmony so long as they do not struggle with other individuals and groups to achieve *external* harmony. If man is against *himself*, the question is (as the anthropologist, Jules Henry, has asked) whether, more basically, the culture is not against *itself*. If countless individuals suffer from emotional frustration, from violation of "normal" rules of sexual conduct, or from other troubles, can it be that these are largely caused by instabilities or cleavages in the institutions, customs, and beliefs with which man has surrounded himself? Can it be contended, for example, that, while orthodox Christian absolutism often frowns upon sexual expression as a necessary evil, the naturalism of a social-experimental way of life looks upon it much more emphatically as life-affirming and a necessary good? Has man not been taught to accept an economic system that encourages him to behave acquisitively, in support of self-interest and inequality, yet at the same time is also taught to behave generously in support of social interest and equality? Can it be that the nationalism that exploits so many hatreds and fears, that now threatens to destroy mankind itself in time of war, that produces political fanaticism and violence, is in mortal combat with an internationalism that encourages man to regard all peoples with respect and that promises world peace?

To the extent that psychiatry and allied sciences do not squarely face such questions—to the extent that they are governed by a psychological approach rather than by one that is equally sociological—they themselves perpetuate those bifurcations of culture reflected in the human beings who make up culture.

Fortunately, however, the nonsubjective approach has its own quota of able advocates. These defend "man for himself"—the kind of man who says "Yes" rather than "No" to himself and to his children; who seeks to satisfy rather than deny the widest possible spectrum of his deepest wants; who appreciates that abundant self-expression requires equally abundant and hopeful social-expression; who dedicates himself accordingly to a purposeful, expanding program of life fulfillment for himself and the widest possible circle of his fellowmen.

One further interpretive view should be added to our cultural portrait. The examples selected to illustrate the thesis that ours is a crisis-culture do not adequately reveal that, in various ways, the tensions generated between polar institutions, behaviors, and attitudes are already past the breaking point. That is to say, the energies dammed within them are bursting through the floodgates into the open. The result is that ours may also properly be called a time of cultural revolution.

The concept "revolution" should be defined. It is the shifting of cultural patterns at such accelerated rates that patterns hitherto dominant begin rapidly to collapse, looking toward replacement by others that have never before been tried. According to this definition, revolutions may embrace huge areas of the earth; or they may be confined to smaller cultures, to subcultures, even to aspects of a single culture. They need not generate overt violence, although sometimes they do. Nor can we say that revolutionary events inevitably produce fresh cultural patterns. Sometimes they simply collapse; at other times they become *counter*revolutionary, in which case the direction of change is reversed toward patterns still older than those presently disintegrating.

True, change is always occurring, even in the most static of cultures. Indeed, it is often a matter of interpretation whether a particular movement is *evolutionary* (meaning "in a state of gradual transition") or *revolutionary*. That numerous evolutionary changes are taking place in present cultures, including America's, is obvious. What is not obvious is that many of these slower movements are also cumulations of cultural strain, carrying within them the potentials of revolution. They are connected beneath the surface with streams of energy flowing from and to all parts of the globe—energies in some cases of volcanic energy. Three illustrations may be cited in behalf of the contention that we live in a time of revolution.

Technology. Our first illustration has been anticipated: the swift realignments caused by the partnership of science and industry that has produced social transformations far greater than at any other time in human history.

The single most fearful invention, atomic energy, has already changed our outlook on war—its practices, its horrors, its immeasurably destructive force. Atomic energy has not succeeded in bringing about a sufficiently strong international government to control its dangers. But it has stimulated the need for such a government as never before.

Meanwhile, technology has reshaped the character of our culture in other revolutionary ways. The automobile has transformed rural life (especially in America) to such a degree that the former isolation of farm families has virtually disappeared. The same isolation has been drastically reduced by mass media of communication —magazines, newspapers, telephone, telegraph, movies, radio, and television (the last two of which have brought voices and images not only across continents but interplanetary distances within seconds).

New methods of production and distribution are equally cyclonic. The use of electric power makes it entirely practicable to decentralize industrial production and to raise its efficiency manyfold. Under the pressures of global war, quantity production via the assembly line has accelerated within the span of a few years. Certain commercial enterprises (General Electric is one) have acquired resources far greater than all those of some whole states of the union. The speed of commodity distribution, which multiplied rapidly with the coming of railroads, has now reached the stage where it is not unusual for herds of cattle to be shipped from continent to continent by air freight. Atomic energy, too, has boundless potentialities, not only for revolutionizing the manufacture of industrial power, but for medicine, transportation, and dozens of other fields as well. Already it has reached the stage of practical use; yet its potentialities in the future defy imagination.

Last but by no means least is the burgeoning revolution in automatization and computerization. Cumbersome methods of recording are being displaced almost overnight by lightning speed. Related to these phenomena is the awesome if not frightening creation of cybernetics—the science of human controls replaced by electronic mechanization.

Economics-politics. The twentieth century is signalized by economic-political revolutions interrelated with the technological revolution. The most dramatic of these is the Russian—a revolution that not only overthrew an autocratic order but also replaced it with the first system in history where the main instruments of industrial and agricultural production are owned and controlled by a nation-state. If we recall that, since 1917, a predominantly illiterate population much larger than that of the United States, and occupying far greater territory, has become literate; that the Union of Socialist Soviet Republics is already the second most powerful nation; and that communism is spreading throughout other parts of the world, most notably China but also countries as close to our own as Cuba—if we recall such events, we can scarcely deny that the Russian Revolution became one of the most earth-shaking events in the annals of man.

Authorities in politics and economics disagree about the extent to which the USSR has regressed in various respects to cultural habits reminiscent of czarism. But far less disagreement prevails about the regressive character of fascism and Nazism or their excrescences. To be sure, granting that certain of these movements overthrew earlier regimes, the truth is that they also replaced them with systems that were grossly counterrevolutionary. As against Communist beliefs in equality of race or sex, for example, they restored ancient-medieval patterns of strict inequality—a pattern still influential in parts of Europe (for example, in Spain), in South America, in South Africa, and even in the Deep South of North America. Yet, in skillful exploitation of propaganda methods, in encouragement of state programs of recreation, and in other ways, fascist-type regimes, too, have disclosed revolutionary symptoms.

Changes less violent and sweeping in character but still far-reaching have occurred, or are occurring, in countries as far apart as New Zealand and Finland, and in the African countries. In some, despite temporary attacks and compromises, the shift is often toward democratic socialization and public ownership of major industries and natural resources. Yet the patterns that will later emerge are seldom, if ever, clear.

Of all great nations, the United States, thus far, is perhaps least affected by the revolutions of other countries. Yet even here rapid changes have occurred, particularly in what is often termed as "the black revolution." Some authorities anticipate that these changes may well produce new institutions similar to those of democratic-socialist countries—if they do not produce an Americanized fascism. The cautious increase of public ownership of electric power, the growth of consumer cooperatives, the rise of federal agencies responsible for education, health, old-age security, and other public welfare—these and other developments are all under way. Yet the trend is neither consistent nor universally supported. In the years since World War II, popular choice has alternated between political leadership that favors an extension of federal responsibility and that which strongly disfavors it. And the pendulum continues to swing, depending upon political, military, or economic tensions and crises.

Abundance. By abundance, our third and last illustration, we mean the economic, social, and esthetic transformations through which the peoples of the world might be provided with resources of healthful, creative, cooperative living. This revolution is, in large part, the effect of our technological and economic-political revolutions. Not wholly an effect, however: as abundance (medical care, adequate nourishment and shelter, instruction, art) is made possible for hitherto impoverished people, these, in turn, become powerful causal agents of cultural restlessness, as in the case of black upheavals in Africa and in America itself.

Not that the third revolution has thus far embraced vast areas of the earth. In this sense, perhaps to a greater extent than the others, it is far more potential than actual. What is not potential is our increasing awareness that abundance *can* be provided only if human beings, as the makers and remakers of culture, are wise enough to do so. Medical science already knows that the sick and ill-nourished, wherever they may be, are capable of becoming healthy and well-nourished. Psychology and related sciences already know that the average illiterate, whoever he may be, can learn to read, write, cooperate, and operate machines. Applied arts and sciences (chemistry is one) already know that plastic, nylon, and countless other new synthetics can be shaped into equally countless useful articles—from household appliances to clothing.

Nor is the fact that the world's population is still rapidly increasing necessarily fatal. Actually, both the declining rate of infant mortality and the rise in life expectancy are largely consequential of more abundant health and economic opportunity. Various scientists insist, moreover, that abundant sources of food have never yet been tapped—in the oceans, for example, or the arctic regions. At the same time, the need to control population growth in many countries (India, say) is considered by many authorities to be paramount—a need, if the population explosion is not to result in famine and chaos, that will require earth-wide experimentation and powerful programs of international action.

Yet, still more deep-cutting than any of these potentials of abundance are the potentials within man himself. Frustrated as he has so often been by life-denying customs, by ignorance and superstitions, by cleavages in loyalty and other values, man has never approached anywhere near full command of his own energy, creative intelligence, and strength. He has been ruled over far more frequently than he has ruled. He has been starved, hoodwinked, exploited, cajoled, intimidated, frightened far more often than he has been decently fed, well informed, respected, encouraged, aroused. With all the weaknesses that remain for him to conquer, "the next development in man" is the mature social development of man himself. This revolution, too, is already under way. Whether man can learn to direct this development before he is inundated becomes, very climactically, the foremost question of culturology in general and of education in particular.

CHAPTER 3

Philosophies of education in a crisis-culture

BOTH PHILOSOPHY AND EDUCATION permeate the fiber and texture of culture. Philosophy does so because every culture, literate and nonliterate alike, symbolizes a pattern of basic beliefs providing those who accept that culture with greater or lesser articulation and significance. Education does so because every culture endows its members with formal or informal symbols and trainings which aim to enculturate its philosophy into attitudes, habits, and skills. If philosophy expresses the beliefs of culture, education helps to carry them out.

However they may be judged in terms of sophistication, worth, or adequacy, equally apparent is the fact that philosophy and education each varies tremendously in the quality and extent to which it functions in time and place. Nor is this true only of nonliterate cultures. Oriental philosophies and school systems are both very unlike Occidental ones. The Soviet Union and Communist China construct their school systems upon a definite philosophy (dialectical materialism) and build their institutions, from nursery schools to universities, with conscious insistence that everything they teach shall demonstrate that philosophy. Fascism and Nazism have expressed views of the world that were not only transplanted into their schools but have left heavy excrescences of influence upon millions.

But it is the democratic cultures in which we are principally interested. Both philosophy and education have been of utmost importance to modern England, France, Norway, Mexico, Japan, and other countries. The same generalization applies to the United States. Philosophers have sought to give distinctive expression to the beliefs, attitudes, and functions of the young nation all the way from pre-Revolutionary days to our own. Education, too, has been endorsed as one of our chief instruments of cultural solidarity and progress. The history of American *philosophy,* interpreted in the perspective of American *education,* is at the center of the adventure which is American *culture.* Yet, we cannot and should not isolate this triple relationship from still wider relationships. They are wider, not only in the sense that America's present and future are bound up with the present and future of the Soviet Union, of Asia, indeed, of the world; they are also shaped by cultures extending much deeper into the past than do America's few short centuries.

Let us underscore our all-pervading theme. In approaching influential philosophies of education, we do so in terms of a point of view. This point of view is governed not only by the general meaning of culturology as we choose to regard it (namely, anthropological philosophy) but by a still more selective meaning (namely, an interpretation of the culture of our time as beset by both crisis and revolution).

This more general meaning depends upon a number of basic features of the nature of culture which may now be summarized and supplemented. Any culture is:

(1) a product of physical, biological, psychological, and social levels of the environment;
(2) a distinctive level of nature, man-made, and not reducible to any of these other levels;
(3) an intricate unity of all animate and inanimate, physical and nonphysical things or events that have been created or affected by man as a member of society;
(4) a pattern of configuration of these things and events that possesses regularity in time and space, and is made possible by habit, custom, law, and other man-made processes or structures;
(5) a continuity of human experience manifested through learning and communicating that experience rather than through biological heredity;
(6) a way of life that profoundly conditions the attitudes and conduct of each individual member;
(7) a symbol encompassing all humanly built objects; all institutions—economic, religious, political, social; all arts,

languages, philosophies; all mores, routines, practices, artifacts; all attitudes, faiths, values; and

(8) an interweaving, flowing complex of order, process, and goals.

Now it is only fair to reiterate that culturological interpretations of educational philosophy are by no means commonly accepted. Even the most comprehensive histories of thought have failed, with few exceptions, to project philosophy sharply upon the screen of specific cultures. This negligence is understandable. For one thing, knowledge and expertness in the behavioral sciences, although indispensable to such an interpretation, are relatively recent and limited. For another, much theory, including the philosophic, appears so specialized and so quarantined from experience that one may be tempted to regard it as purely intellectual, completely self-contained.

As we are able, however, to expand our knowledge of economic and political forces, of anthropology and sociology, of class and racial influence upon psychological, esthetic, and religious experience, we find more careful attention being paid to the near heresy that philosophers, too, are human beings. Like other human beings, not only do they affect their cultural environment but they are profoundly affected, in turn, by that environment. Hence, while experts in culture are doubtless influenced by philosophic beliefs (what we shall now prefer to call metacultural beliefs), equally true is the fact that philosophers are influenced by cultural experience. To take one classic instance that will be noted in Part 4, Plato and Aristotle are occasionally treated less as geniuses spinning speculations out of the fecundity of their intellects than as Greek citizens—that is, as patriots brilliantly interpreting the upheavals that rocked the Athenian life of their generation and offering grand-scale solutions in accordance with their own aristocratic postures. Others may be similarly treated—the Englishman, John Locke, for one, or the American philosopher-statesman whom he influenced, Thomas Jefferson, for another.

It is unnecessary to argue that everyone who philosophizes does so solely because of his interest in the culture. Although philosophers who engage in "pure" thought are still, like speculative mathematicians or artists, inescapably members of their culture, let us grant that philosophers may engage in speculation for the sheer intellectual delight that it affords. Nevertheless, as we study the biographies of influential thinkers, let us also note how often they, too, were or are alive to the foremost issues of their own generations. Let us ask whether the moments of philosophy's highest creativity, highest originality, and most powerful effect upon cultural life have not usually been moments when issues were keenest and the need for fresh interpretations most desperate. Here may also prove to be the central challenge of culturology.

The present culture—however strained, "schizophrenic," or explosive in many ways—presents, then, a magnificent opportunity. It calls upon philosophy to exercise the highest possible integrity in order that our institutions, habits, and faiths may be scrutinized, reaffirmed, modified, or, if need be, thoroughly rebuilt.

PHILOSOPHY: SOME RELEVANT FUNCTIONS

Let us approach this opportunity more explicitly. Remembering that only secondarily are we concerned with philosophy regarded as a more or less self-contained discipline, it still becomes important, we think, to pay more than casual attention to some of its relevant, if elementary, functions as copartner of anthropology. This is so because our primary purpose, after all, is to interpret education by means of the bifocal concept now termed culturology. To punctuate the point in another way, this chapter (together with the next) hopes to prepare us to interpret educational theories primarily from the "inside out," just as the preceding chapter prepares us to view them primarily from the "outside in"—that is, from the perspective of culture. Neither approach is sufficient. But both are indispensable. Both depend upon each other.

Yet, in some respects, the meaning of philosophy is still more difficult to epitomize than is anthropology. For the latter, although but a "child" by comparison with the ancient discipline of philosophy and although still insufficiently mature, is recognized by virtually all of its own theorists and practitioners as embracing fairly common attributes. One reason for this, we suppose, is that anthropology as it becomes a science is governed by increasingly respected criteria of both subject matter and methodology. Not so philosophy. It is not a science, however profoundly concerned with science. It is not an art and certainly not a religion, although again it pays endless attention to both of these fields.

In our own time, moreover, philosophy has compounded its own uncertainties as to just how it is supposed to function and just what its responsibilities are supposed to legitimatize. Philosophers themselves disagree, often so vituperatively within the very field where they are supposed to be expert, that one wonders (as not a few of their critics have wondered) whether philosophy is becoming little more than a sterile exercise in latter-day sophistry. At the least, as Chapter 4 will demonstrate, prominent contemporary movements in philosophy frequently give the impression of sharing very meager features in common.

How then shall we confront the dilemma that besets any attempt to characterize philosophy today—the dilemma either of simply taking sides with one or another movement (with, say, the philosophic analysts and their allies who seem extraordinarily confident that only *their* interpretation is any longer intellectually respectable) or of rejecting philosophy as a discipline entirely? We suggest that the dilemma itself is faulty; rather, the state of philosophy may well be the consequence less of philosophers than of our cultural age of confusion and ambivalence which they themselves tend to reflect in their professional roles.

What we are suggesting, in short, is that until philosophers and their work are themselves reinterpreted contextually—above all, culturologically—it becomes more than likely that they will exacerbate still further rather than alleviate an already violently disturbed human situation. If, however, philosophy can once more be recognized less as an erudite specialization than as a searching interpretation of men as cultural beings, then the most persistent, indeed classical, problems of philosophy may once more rise out of their shrouds and become vitally pertinent to every significant aspect of our dawning twenty-first century civilization. Far from being treated contemptuously as obsolete, these problems come again into sharp focus because, although reformulated to suit an age radically different from that of, say, ancient Greece, they compel us to confront them just as urgently today as they did millennia ago.

From this viewpoint, philosophy proves pertinent equally to education. For education, too, shares the perplexities, obstacles, choices of men together with the foremost creation of their own genius: culture. Formally or informally, education is infused throughout all cultures, simple and complex alike. Therefore, it can no more escape philosophy than cultures can. Conversely, cultures are able to escape neither philosophy nor education.

Let us consider, therefore, some of the more elementary features of this powerful discipline. As we proceed, our philosophic definitions and classifications are to be *used*. They are to function throughout the remainder of this book as tools of analysis, criticism, synthesis, and evaluation. Meanwhile, four main topics are to be considered: (1) When do we philosophize?; (2) philosophy:

its branches; (3) the relations of philosophy; and (4) levels of belief.

WHEN DO WE PHILOSOPHIZE?

You and I (innocent though we may be) have often tried to phrase, in terms of our own experience and background, certain beliefs that concern us dearly—beliefs about religion, love, freedom of speech, politics, labor unions—each involving questions important to thinking, maturing people everywhere. Whether we call it philosophy or by some other name, *we all philosophize whenever we try to express what we believe about our lives and about our relations to the rest of life.*

Educators are certainly no different from others in holding beliefs and utilizing them. When they philosophize about the schools they simply concentrate upon one very important area, an area in which people not only have strong views but also prove exceptionally quick to talk about them. Most of the time such expressions of belief are not *called* philosophy. Often, they are made by practical-minded school executives or by professors of the "science" of education who sometimes assert that philosophy is an outworn exercise.

Philosophy, then, is inseparable from living experience. However unexpressed in technically philosophic terms, it is always in the background, helping to shape and being shaped by the tangible means through which we carry on our day-to-day responsibilities. In every phase of life—material, spiritual, lay, professional—we believe certain things about the activities we perform. And these beliefs, usually to a far greater extent than we realize, not only reflect our day-to-day activities but, in turn, mold and direct these activities.

As a matter of fact, we could not do without our beliefs. A businessman would fail if he did not assume and act upon the legitimacy of making a profit from his enterprise. A conscientious preacher would suffer severely if he felt that he ought to reexamine his faith every Sunday morning before services. A school principal might accomplish little if he thought that his duties rested upon a crumbling foundation of beliefs. There is nothing more necessary to mental health, to personal and social harmony, to consistency of action purpose than to be fairly well satisfied with the beliefs that underlie everyday conduct. They constitute a type of habit pattern that enables us to proceed with some degree of efficiency, orderliness, and confidence in what we are doing.

If, however, it is true that we take our beliefs for granted much of the time, equally true is the fact that few of us can take them for granted all of the time. Either or both of two main causes may jolt us into sudden questioning of what, up to this point, we have been inclined to accept without much question.

The first cause is the discovery that one's cherished patterns conflict with someone else's patterns. Sometimes, it is made by reading a provocative book, seeing an exciting play; occasionally, by contact with a stimulating teacher or by participating in the far from trivial pastime of college "bull sessions."

The second cause is the awakening, sometimes a wrenching one, that one's beliefs are in contradiction not so much with those of another person as with one's own. We detect an internal inconsistency that what we believe is not consistent at all points with how we behave. This is another way of saying that what we *profess* to believe and what we *really* believe simply do not harmonize. Often we make this second discovery after having made the first one. In either case, the important point is that something similar happens, at one time or another, to most of us.

But surely, it is far from enough to exhort ourselves to raise critical questions. A main reason why we often philosophize badly is that we do not know how to philosophize well. It is one forward step to recognize that, in some sense and at some time, virtually all human beings perform that function. Still, several steps remain before we are at all qualified to philosophize about education.

As we climb toward a more definitive conception, please remember that at no time is it departing from our original culturological approach. We shall simply try to understand more thoroughly what we do when we analyze and synthesize our patterns of belief about educational habits, attitudes, and practices.

PHILOSOPHY: ITS BRANCHES

One of the rewards of the study of philosophy, for those who are willing to be patient, is that as we move slowly along we find that philosophy develops ever wider ramifications of meaning. The degrees of sophistication and awareness, of agreements and disagreements in the expression of our beliefs, vary sharply among the most highly trained theologians, artists, and scientists as well as among ordinary individuals.

The same plurality of meanings applies to the nature of "belief." That we all have beliefs of some sort is undeniable. But what it is we imply when we say we believe something can hardly be taken for granted. Those of us who have ever attended a large political rally have no doubt been impressed by the earnestness of the speakers. Each seemed to be quite convinced of his own views. For him, they were apparently *real,* and not only real but *true,* and not only true but, in the most earnest sense of the word, *good.* Whether each speaker was equally sincere or equally able to defend reasons for so regarding his views may have been difficult to determine from his behavior. But that each speaker desired us to believe him must have been apparent.

Such a desire is not peculiar to philosophers. Is it not a common observation that the beliefs we ordinarily profess seem true to us who hold them—seem so true that, whether we are followers of the Republican party, of Christian Science, or of the college elective system, we are inclined to look upon disbelievers as victims of the false? Is it not apparent that the institutions of culture, the structures of nature, or the practices and faiths of men seem real to their participants? Is it not an observation, also, that we often regard certain of these institutions, structures, practices, and faiths as essentially good—so good that those who maintain very different beliefs about them seem to be believers in the bad?

Through philosophy's long history, the attack upon these plaguing questions proceeds from a number of fronts. Philosophy has been divided into specialized branches, methods, and divisions, each of which concentrates upon one major area of belief. This is an admission, perhaps, that the question is simply too complex to be treated as a whole. As to the number of such divisions, philosophers have differed among themselves—some speaking of four or five, others of as many as eight or nine. But let us confine ourselves to three, regarding others as subsidiary to them. These are: study of the principles of reality; study of the principles of knowledge; and study of the principles of value.

Historic labels for these branches of philosophic investigation are *ontology, epistemology,* and *axiology.* Their tasks are to clarify, as far as possible, our underlying criteria or principles of belief about the areas of reality, truth, and value, respectively. Each is indispensable to education not only in theory, but in practice as well.

Although we shall try to characterize all three as they have been familiarly characterized in the conventional terms of philosophy, it is worth noting that even these are not acceptable to all philosophers today. Also, we shall usually defer concrete illustrations, since they will become abundant when applied to practicing philosophies of education.

Study of beliefs about reality. Suppose that you are gazing intently at an object that you take for granted so much of the time as seldom to think of its existence at all—the floor in the room where you are reading this book. Suppose you ask yourself to describe its simple characteristics: well, it is solid, flat, and smooth, you say; its color is brown; whether concrete or wood, it surely is a substance of a thoroughly material quality. This is what almost anyone would mean, no doubt, by calling the floor *real.*

Suppose, however, that at this point a teacher of physics enters the room. You ask him the same question you asked yourself. He replies that, strictly speaking, the floor is made of molecules; that molecules consist of atoms; atoms of electrons, protons, neutrons; and these, finally, of electrical energy alone. Thus the *real* floor—the "energetic" floor—is to him not at all identical with what a layman apparently perceives.

Or let us consider the floor from another point of view. The color of the floor, he tells you, is merely light waves of a certain length striking your retina and then translated through your optical nerve into visual response. Do you not in this case, therefore, contribute something *to* its nature through a nervous system which, after all, is peculiarly yours?

Thus, it would seem that you are standing on at least three floors rather than one. The *first* is "out there" in the material world. The *second* is the construction of the scientist—certainly not the one you perceive directly with your eyes. The *third* is the product of external fact plus your own nervous response. Which, then, *is* the floor—or are all three blended into one? *This is the task of ontology: to determine what is real about any and all aspects of the world.*

It should be apparent even from this naïve illustration that schools, too, are confronted with problems of reality. For they deal at every level with countless objects of nature—inanimate and animate, subhuman and human—and the scope of their ontological concern reaches as far as the kind of universe they expect children to accept. The differing assumptions about reality that divide Roman Catholic parochial schools from public schools; the widespread influence of such superstitions as astrology and palmistry upon millions of "educated" adults; the inability of many teachers to articulate the most elementary traits of existence (for example, what it means to say that nature everywhere *evolves*)—all these are random instances of an educational system that too seldom examines its own body of ontological beliefs.

Education, it is commonly alleged, fails to prepare the young to face the "real world." In great measure, this allegation is well-founded. Curiously, however, those who shout the accusation loudest are often themselves victims of ontological myopia. They gaze upon reality with vision literally and figuratively distorted by images on the television screen, or still more pervasively by prejudice, propaganda, worship of custom, or other influences of which they may not even be aware. Education for reality rather than for illusion is, then, one major obligation. We can hope to meet it successfully not by yielding to warped conceptions of the real but by utilizing constantly the service that philosophy, particularly ontology, may best be qualified to render.

But the general study of reality can be approached by means of even more specialized terms, two of which—*metaphysics* and *cosmology*—are familiar in philosophic discourse. The former is defined in various ways, sometimes as a synonym for ontology itself. Literally, however, metaphysics means "beyond the physical"; even today, many people associate it with some sort of elusive, esoteric art—with an attempt to discover realms of being quite outside the realm of everyday experience. In this sense, metaphysics is strictly *one kind* of ontology; we may term it loosely as "other-worldly" by comparison with "this-worldly" kinds. Actually, ontology, as such, does not prejudge the question of what the principles of existence may turn out to be: it searches for them wherever they are and whatever their forms, be they physical or spiritual, one or many, fluctuating or permanent. If some philosophers believe that reality at its most real is metaphysical in that it transcends the fleeting events of everyday experience, others are just as emphatic in holding that these are the only ones that exist.

Cosmology centers primary attention upon characteristics of reality that seem to disclose a universe of system and order. No doubt, the aim of many ontological quests in intellectual history has been for a cosmology. Others, however, may conceivably be satisfied to determine the character of particular things and limited spheres; in this regard, cosmology, too, is subsidiary to ontology. For the latter is equally interested in *both* the particulars and the universals of reality. It does not assume, necessarily, an all-embracing cosmos any more than it assumes, with metaphysics, the primacy of a realm above or beyond the physical.

How, then, are these subsidiaries of ontology also important to the schools? They are important whenever children or adults are taught to believe in a realm of eternal existence beyond the here and now. Important whenever they learn that the world of which they are part is a vast, ultimately perfect harmony of order and law. Important when, on the contrary, they are told neither eternity nor cosmic harmony is demonstrable but that reality is a multiplicity of ever-changing facts and events. Important, in short, whenever or however their minds are conditioned to assure them that here, indeed, is the only *real* reality.

Study of beliefs about knowledge. So far as education is concerned, the problem of knowledge with which epistemology deals is at least as crucial as the problem of reality. Reduced to elementary terms, *epistemology enables the teacher to discover whether he may be conveying the truth to his students.* May he find principles upon which he can rely when going about the crucial business of developing that most precious of possessions—human knowledge? Or must he simply trust his "intuition," his sensations, the opinions of his superiors, faith in some "infallible" document, or still other tests that happen to be conveniently at hand?

Note these four familiar remarks:

(1) "You can't kid me, brother; I *know* a crook the moment I see one."
(2) "Of course I *know* she was cribbing; I saw her."
(3) "Certainly I *know* what I'm talking about; doesn't the Constitution say so itself?"
(4) "We *know* the bridge is safe because six of us just crossed it."

In each of these instances, the speaker "knows." In each instance, however, his reason for knowing is obviously different from the other instances. The first rests upon common sense or intuition, or some other judgment that is fairly spontaneous and personal: plainly, one does not rely solely upon observation in such a case; one does not literally *see* a crook unless in the very act of committing a crime. The second instance, on the contrary, is based upon direct observation: the speaker asserts a truth precisely because his senses have reported to him what he sees. The third rests upon prestige and authority, upon a revered document—hence, not directly upon either common sense or observation. The fourth instance suggests that knowledge is the product of tested experience in which sense perception is an ingredient but in which the effect of what happens is the basic measure. Behind each instance (and it is easy to add others) lies some kind of belief about how and when we know in contrast with how and when we do not know. In short, we believe "truths" because, consciously or not, certain epistemological criteria underlie belief.

Epistemology is closely related to the other two main branches of philosophy, ontology and axiology. At the moment we are more concerned to note how *logic* and *semantics*, although sometimes regarded as distinct branches of philosophy, may be subsidiary to epistemology, just as metaphysics and cosmology may be subsidiary to ontology.

Logic is concerned with the reasoning *process*. It demonstrates that, however accurate a person's reasoning may be, he does not thereby necessarily attain the truth. One authority may argue, for example, that since children have low intelligence quotients because of bad environments, therefore Johnny has a low IQ because of a bad environment. In this case, the observer is reasoning with complete logical accuracy, but he is not necessarily telling the truth about any of the facts. Thus, the precise relations between logic and epistemology are far from simple. But if, by careful attention to *how* we think, we are enabled better to detect strengths and weaknesses in *what* we think, logic becomes a useful technique in the determination of knowledge. It establishes rules for connecting links in a chain of thought so that they can be depended upon to hold fast. These rules also enable us to recognize flaws and weaknesses.

Two classic types of logic—deductive and inductive—both illustrate this function. *Deductive logic* is a formal process from premises to conclusions (the illustration regarding Johnny's intelligence is a common form). *Inductive logic* proceeds from particular data to only partially conclusive judgments (the instance, above, of men crossing a bridge, is typical). In either process, logic helps to make us more conscious of how we reach sound or unsound beliefs about the true or false; in this respect, it is not only a legitimate but an indispensable aid to epistemology.

Semantics has elements in common with both epistemology in general and logic in particular. It helps to clarify the connections of languages with events, the relation of concrete terms to abstractions, the devices that serve to conceal facts behind confusing and deceptive smoke screens of words, and other difficulties that block common understanding. Some semanticists, like some logicians, might object to regarding their field as a subdivision of epistemology. Surely, connections between the two are far from elementary. Nevertheless, it would not be difficult to contend that semantics is also concerned with beliefs about knowledge. How, for example, can we discover measures by which to determine: first, whether what we try to communicate coincides with what we *mean*; and, second, whether what we mean coincides with the facts or events that our words *represent*?

A word of anticipation needs to be said also about *philosophic analysis*, to which we shall refer often in Chapter 4 and beyond. That it overlaps with both semantics and logic should be apparent, but that it is to be regarded as a subdivision of epistemology might be challenged by some enthusiasts.

In any case, that logic, semantics, philosophic analysis, or all three, are necessary tools in education can easily be illustrated. To learn how to reason from step to step, to detect common fallacies in thinking, to practice the inductive method of arriving at verifiable results in laboratories and classrooms, to appreciate the necessity of cautious reliance upon past deductions—all these are logically indispensable. At least equally so are the ways in which educators may be helped to clarify their ordinary language—language frequently proving to be very murky indeed.

Study of beliefs about value. Axiology, the last major branch of philosophy, confronts problems of belief about value. It is subdivided into three fields, in each of which values are predominant: moral conduct, esthetic expression, and sociopolitical life. Each of these fields has been treated ordinarily by three respective disciplines: *ethics, esthetics*, and *sociopolitical philosophy*. We have chosen, however, to regard them as having one denominator in common—that of value itself. Thus they are subsidiary to axiology, as logic may be subsidiary to epistemology.

The problem of axiology is to clarify criteria or principles by which we determine what is good in human conduct, what is beautiful in art, what is right in social organization, and, finally, what these have in common as well as what distinguishes them from one another. The significance of axiology for us is, then, to *examine and integrate these values as they enter into the lives of people through the institution of education.*

The way in which the axiologist determines what is "good" is by no means always simple. Just as those who have not explicitly philosophized may suppose that anything we "know" is in some sense "true," so at first glance it is quite easy for us to suppose that anything we "value" is in some sense "good." Yet on second thought we discover that "good," too, has a wide range of meaning. Let us consider the implications of these remarks made casually in the course of a day by an imaginary child:

(1) "Gee, this ice cream's *good*."
(2) "All right, mama, I'll be *good* and obey you."
(3) "That was mighty *good* medicine; it cured me in no time."

(4) "Boy, wasn't that song *good*?"
(5) "What're you reading, Dad? Oh, 'The *Good* Society.' "

The implications contained within these and other apparently simple meanings of one word have led to entire philosophic doctrines. Thus, the first statement suggests a theory called *hedonism*—the theory that only what is pleasurable can really justify the label "good." No doubt the hedonist can argue a strong case, but he would be challenged by consistent believers in the value implied by the second statement. In that case, good conduct is judged by the standard of someone in authority, a standard that may extend so far beyond the home as to circumscribe the conduct of millions of political subjects. The third statement illustrates what ethicists sometimes call an *instrumental* good, a means to some desired end. The fourth implies two criteria rather than one: an *immediate* good (as an end in itself rather than as a merely useful means) and an *esthetic* good, a certain kind of "taste." The final statement signifies a *social* valuation; the author of such a book is writing not of the good of individuals alone but of the good or goods relating to organized associations of people.

This final example helps us to understand why we have need for such a comprehensive term as axiology; here *both* ethical and social values are included under one caption. How completely the values we hold interweave with values of the home, neighborhood, city, and state is a fact no teacher, for example, could possibly ignore. To consider the values of art in isolation may also prove unsound. We must ask whether they, too, do not arise in social media—whether the painter, composer, poet, or architect is not always conditioned by the interrelations of human experience at the same time that he responds to these interrelations.

Thus, like the issues arising in the first two branches of philosophy, issues of axiology may carry us far afield. Moreover, as we detect the complexity of values, we seek their overlapping as well as their distinctive qualities. In the case of education, we ask and try to answer such questions as these: What are the grounds upon which schools confidently and traditionally teach that certain rules of morality are good and others are bad? That certain kinds of literature are beautiful and others are ugly? That certain forms of government are right and others are wrong?

THE RELATIONS OF PHILOSOPHY

To continue the process of dividing and subdividing would be misrepresenting philosophy. We should be giving the impression that it is solely a series of specializations rather than equally a subject concerned with *connections among* beliefs.

If, in recent years, philosophy has seemed more and more to confine itself to the less and less, the same trend is noticeable in other fields of scholarship and research. Like many experts, philosophers have seemed often to delight in narrowness rather than breadth; in a "trade" vocabulary rather than familiar language; in the life of the "ivory tower" rather than that of the market place. In some respects this is perfectly legitimate; as our knowledge of the modern world has increased, the criteria by which we judge it have also become increasingly technical.

The history of philosophy also attests, however, to its age-old concern with the totality of life—in fact, as intimated by our brief reference to cosmology, even with the totality of the universe. In terms of our original conception of philosophy, we are concerned not merely to express many *heterogeneous* beliefs but to determine how far they may be *homogeneous*, too. This is often what is meant by "system" in philosophy: it is an effort to bring all important human thought into some kind of design, to create what is aptly called in German a *Weltanschauung*, a unified view of the world. We shall find that the philosophy of education is as much interested in this effort as in utilizing such specialized tools as axiology. Meanwhile, philosophy may be viewed, in its general sense, by considering: first, its *internal* relations (those *inside* the boundaries of philosophy as such); and second, its *external* relations (those that relate it to *outside* major fields, like science or art).

Philosophy's relations: internal. A twofold question now arises: (1) How is *each branch* of philosophy concerned with the question of its own homogeneity—that is, with whether there is *truth* or an indefinite variety of *truths*; *value* or many *values*; *reality* or many *realities*, and (2) are epistemology, axiology, and ontology separated by insurmountable walls, or do they overlap and join into some inclusive pattern?

The problem of the "oneness" or "manyness" of each major area—reality, truth, and value—is as ancient as philosophy itself. The levels of belief that are called skeptical and agnostic tend to question whether any solution of this problem can be found. Nevertheless, the farthest reaches of antiquity disclose in fragments of Greek thought how Thales, Anaxagoras, Parmenides, and others hoped to discover a principle of reality that would reduce all physical objects to such basic "substances" as water or fire. In our time, with the aid of massive cumulations of scientific knowledge, the search continues in the effort of cosmologists (Albert Einstein, most famously) to encompass the seeming disparities of the earth and the heavens under a unified equation of mathematical physics.

Traditional terms common to this problem of oneness or manyness are *monism, pluralism,* and *dualism.* Thus, a monist in the area of knowledge is one who believes he has found some all-inclusive criterion by which he can judge the truth or falsity of every idea. A pluralist insists that various criteria are essential, depending upon the nature of the ideas we are dealing with, the time and place in which they are expressed, and similar qualifications. A dualist in epistemology believes that the plurality of types of knowledge is limited to two. He might hold, for example, that science produces one type and religion a second; each is regarded as reliable in its own sphere, neither being reducible to the other.

The problem of oneness and manyness is equally important in the area of values. Many of us are troubled, to take one example, by the appearance of dual sets of values in family and business relations: the devotion and generosity that a father shows his children may seem quite opposite from the competitive acquisitiveness with which he runs his office or store. Likewise, in the past half-century we have asked, with increasing anxiety, whether the nations of the world can find a common standard of right and wrong or whether each must be left free to be its own supreme judge and sovereign authority. If the latter should continue to be the case, moral standards on the explosive plane of international affairs will continue to be pluralistic, as well as dangerously antagonistic.

The answer to the second half of our question (Are the branches of philosophy, in their concern for reality, truth, and value, related to one another?) is implied by our answer to the first. One who tends toward a monistic pattern of belief in the area, let us say, of reality, is likely to wish to extend that pattern to embrace knowledge and value also—to encompass all three by some single sweeping principle. Typically, although not invariably, the same rule holds for pluralists and dualists: a pluralist in axiology may be pluralistic in epistemology and ontology; a dualist in epistemology tends to find reasons for dualizing his beliefs in ontology and axiology.

A few additional terms help to point up these generalizations. In the long history of thought, the terms *empiricism* and *naturalism* refer, respectively, to philosophies of this-worldly experience and of nature. The terms *idealism* and *transcendentalism* refer, respectively, to philosophies of spiritual existence and sometimes of other-worldly perfection. Each pair of terms suggests a kind of partnership of beliefs: thus, the empiricist and naturalist tend to be theoretically closely allied, as do the idealist and the transcendentalist. Each pair of terms also suggests others that we shall find fruitful. To illustrate, the empiricist and the naturalist may be allied with *materialists* (who believe in the universality of "matter" as the basic reality); while the idealist and transcendentalist may find themselves allied with *absolutists* (who often believe that the key to reality is to be found in a final, immutable, eternal Being).

Such abstractions may seem irksome. Yet, they are as relevant to the great conflicting choices among beliefs about life and education in our time as they have been at any time in human history. For our present discussion, they become most important because they serve to *join together* the three chief branches of philosophy. Thus, we shall find that a belief pattern may be thoroughly naturalistic from beginning to end in its approach to ontology, epistemology, *and* axiology. Such philosophies as idealism may also cut across reality, knowledge, and value and combine all three into patterns of belief that seem to be even more unified than are naturalistic patterns.

Philosophy's relations: external. But philosophy encompasses much more than the relations that help to supply its own internal homogeneity. It probes inquisitively into the assumptions and purposes of *every* field, revealing that, for some philosophers, it apparently has no fixed boundaries at all. Hence, to speak of external relations is really only a convenient term for differentiating its outreaching characteristics from those relations that bind it within.

Ideally, the philosopher, far from regarding other fields as isolated from his, has a special responsibility to become familiar with them. Thus, to philosophize in the vast field of science, he must seek some understanding of, say, physics, biology, geology, sociology, psychology; in the field of art, some understanding of painting, music, poetry, the dance, the theater; in the field of education, some understanding of the curriculum, teaching methods, the principles of learning and administration. And to philosophize about the interrelations among all three fields, he must hope to understand science, art, and education together.

It may be argued that such an objective is no longer possible.

Perhaps it *was* possible for an exceptional man of ancient Greece or Rome to possess most available knowledge; the civilized earth was narrow, and what men knew of it was meager. Today, however, not only has most of the earth been brought under direct observation; knowledge of it and the surrounding universe is expanding at the most unprecedented rate in human history. Shall we not, then, be satisfied with less presumptuous objectives? The answer, for several reasons, is definitely *No.*

In the first place, the very scope and depth of modern knowledge constitute an urgent reason why philosophy should attempt to relate major fields both to one another and to itself. Where mutual understanding is missing, the activities of men result in confusion, cross-purpose, complacency, skepticism, and negativism. Such a phenomenon is only too commonplace among nations, in politics, religion, art, and science, among professional educators, and still more in the contempt in which academicians too often hold such educators. *In the necessary and fruitful but also dangerous growth of specific knowledge, only one discipline seems to remain that specializes in nonspecialization: philosophy itself.* Far from diminishing, the need today is increased by the very difficulty of meeting it.

In the second place, achievement although arduous is not unattainable. There is a difference between being familiar with the most important knowledge of a given period (an achievement possible for Aristotle in his period but impossible for any man in ours) and being familiar with the major summarizations, implications, and presuppositions of such knowledge. The best that a single student can accomplish is to master the outstanding premises, issues, conclusions, and laws about which experts are concerned within their own fields. This in itself is surely no meager task.

In biology, for example, the philosopher need not—indeed, cannot—retrace the steps of intricate laboratory experimentation to understand its development or to verify its findings. He need not be a priest in order to appraise the foundations of a church, nor a professional politician to examine the premises underlying principal laws enacted by a senate, nor a superintendent to evaluate the main objectives of a school. If he has had experience in these fields so much the better; if he is acquainted with their guiding beliefs and richest results so much the better still. Ralph Barton Perry, an American philosopher, makes the point effectively. The philosopher, he says, must:

> . . . enter fields in which specialists have already staked their special claims, and where the philosopher finds himself an amateur among professionals. He cannot hope to do their special work better than they do it, but only to incorporate their results and add items and relationships. The philosopher is accustomed to this somewhat shameless role. He does not, however, undertake the task arrogantly or overconfidently. For it is the philosopher who, having undertaken the task, is most acutely aware of the difficulty.[1]

In the third place, the success with which anyone can understand the position or significance of various fields is always a matter of degree, differing very widely even among highly trained philosophers. A few contemporary thinkers—such as Dewey, Russell, Maritain—have possessed such huge funds of information about the content and achievements of major fields that they become guides and interpreters for many lesser practitioners. But it is a mistake to think of the philosopher exclusively in this professional sense. Just as anyone who expresses his beliefs is thereby practicing philosophy in minor ways, so anyone who expresses beliefs concerning the ordered connections of experience is practicing philosophy in more substantial ways. He is doing so, moreover, whether he is called a philosopher or a political leader, scientist, artist, or educator functioning as a philosopher.

In the last place, if teachers, nevertheless, are intimidated by the prospect of synthesizing knowledge, or of helping young people to obtain an ordered outlook upon their culture, this hesitancy could be caused not so much by inability as by habituation. The schools themselves have often become victims of specialization. Subject-matter compartments—English, science, mathematics, foreign languages—are decidely not conducive to the development of integrated education. Teachers so frequently concentrate in single departments that, if they succeed in building any broader conception, they are likely to do so in spite of rather than because of their professional preparation. Still, we shall see that this truncated preparation is neither necessary nor desirable.

Thus, to return to our contention that, despite the undeniable difficulty of the task and the imperfection of accomplishment, philosophy today may be properly concerned with wholes as well as with parts, with connections *among* facts as well as with facts as such. Of course, it may choose to focus upon relations within

[1] Perry, *Realms of Value*, p. 14.

one rather than another major field. The "unity of science" movement, which has attracted wide attention, is an example of how the philosophy of science delineates the common principles of the physical, biological, and social sciences. The philosophy of religion is concerned not only with various Christian creeds but also with how these may or may not harmonize with Oriental creeds.

In this relational function, philosophy may utilize any of the concepts or branches introduced above. Thus, some philosophies of religion are dualistic in that they predicate a separation of body and soul. Contemporary philosophies of science are usually empirical, pluralistic, and naturalistic. In any case, we can expect axiology, epistemology, and ontology to serve as indispensable tools of analysis and synthesis precisely to the extent that value, truth, and reality are indispensable within any one great area of knowledge and culture.

But let us note, finally, that, just as these branches and concepts are not merely principles of connection *within* philosophy itself but also *between* philosophy and art, for example, or philosophy and science, or philosophy and education, so they may be useful as links among *all* such fields or institutions. Thus, axiology becomes important everywhere; it is a bridge connecting the islands of history *and* science *and* education *and* art. Moreover, if such concepts as idealism and empiricism, or monism and dualism, are fundamental to single areas, they may become even more fundamental to great systems of philosophy—to sweeping views of man and the universe.

The philosophy of education exemplifies, moreover, each of these widening relations. It is concerned with characteristics that unite the innumerable aspects of education into one great field, but also with the manner in which they reach out to encompass other fields. In either aim the philosophy of education is less comprehensive than philosophy taken as a whole. Yet the philosophy of education may on occasion—and, indeed, should more often—function as *a complete philosophy of life viewed from a particular perspective*: from a hilltop overlooking the plains of the world. As the great American philosopher, John Dewey, has said: "The most penetrating definition of philosophy which can be given is, then, that it is the theory of education in its most general phases."[2]

[2] Dewey, *Democracy and Education*, p. 386.

LEVELS OF BELIEF

The outline we have drawn of some relevant functions and relations of philosophy, granting that it may appear crude to some and arid to others, is indispensable as prerequisite of the entire task and purpose of this book. Yet at no time have we forgotten two interdependent features: one, the reliance of philosophy upon culture; two, the importance of philosophy to understanding and interpreting not only culture but education as symbols of our own culture in crisis. No such comprehensive approach can, of course, explicate every point at once: just as anthropology at a given moment may be treated quite "autonomously," so too may philosophy. This we have deliberately attempted above by encapsulating a few of its conventional features.

As our discussion has proceeded toward its "external" relationships—that is, toward intricate connections with other fields of experience—we were already reaffirming, however, our original conception of philosophy as indigenous to the culturological point of view. For, in an entirely plausible sense, philosophy becomes coalescent with, rather than isolated from, those manifestations of human life which, as typified by art or science, constitute the fabric of culture itself. Equally, education becomes thus typified. To borrow a famous phrase from Ruth Benedict, philosophies of education, too, become integral with "patterns of culture."

At the same time, as Benedict also depicts so graphically, patterns of culture are sometimes remarkably divergent. To recall our earlier question—why do we philosophize?—we do so because we human beings intermittently become so concerned, even obsessed, about incompatible beliefs that we feel compelled to reexamine and perhaps drastically to reformulate them. We are thus compelled, moreover, because we seek to satisfy a fundamental need to bring these beliefs into active, meaningful internal as well as external relationships.

Hence it is that, whether or not deliberately aided by such refined instruments as epistemology, axiology, or ontology, men sometimes realize that just as patterns of culture suffer from disequilibrium, so, likewise, do patterns of belief which are, after all, their symbolic counterparts. And when this occurs, many of us, enthusiastically or not, are compelled to decide more or less deliberately as to what we shall do about such disequilibriums. This decision is not simply an arbitrary choice between agreement and disagreement, between Yes and No. On the contrary, a number of levels of choice emerge:

(1) We may refuse, of course, to allow a disturbance of belief

to affect us after the first moment of reaction. Instead, after begrudging it a minimum of attention, we may settle back upon the old comfortable cushion and pray that nothing will happen to upset us again. Typically, we tend to resent any disturbance of our belief habit pattern; and, the more deeply entrenched it becomes, the more we are resentful. This, the least reflective level, may be called the *complacent* choice.

(2) We may feel compelled to analyze our beliefs with some care—to ask why they seem to be in conflict either with other beliefs of our own or with those of different individuals—but this examination will not necessarily lead to resolution of the conflict. It ends with the examination itself so that, in a sense, we have taken apart our beliefs but have not put them back together. This is the *negative* choice.

(3) We may decide that our entire body of major beliefs is now open to such severe question that the most honest course is to doubt them. This takes us one step beyond mere negativism in that we are now definite in our *dis*-belief. This may be termed the *skeptical* choice.

(4) We may reach the opinion, after careful examination, that it is simply impossible to accept one set of beliefs in preference to another. We cannot decide whether they are true *or* false. Neither affirming nor denying, we remain as neutral and noncommittal as humanly possible. This is the *agnostic* choice.

(5) We may fasten together many different beliefs, not fusing them into a harmonious pattern but keeping them as separate pieces, ready to shift about into different positions, checkerlike, as the need arises. This is the *eclectic* choice.

(6) We may decide, despite or perhaps because of our analysis, that our original pattern of beliefs is, on the whole, sound and worth perpetuating. As against choice (1) above, we make this judgment not before but *after* careful consideration. This may be called the *transmissive* choice.

(7) We may decide to test out degrees of rearrangements of the pattern as a whole—a process that involves some trimming of its original elements, some gradual improvement and modification. This we shall call the *moderative* choice.

(8) We may conclude that what is needed is to substitute for the pattern in which we have been placing our trust another pattern—one that was widely followed in some

earlier age. We return to this pattern, however, not because it is old but because, to us, it is more permanently satisfying than any other. This is the *restorative* choice.

(9) We may decide, finally, to substitute a fairly new pattern —new not merely in the sense that it supersedes the one we have been holding but that it is different from any that has been commonly held thus far either in our own period or in the past. This may be termed the *transformative* choice.

These main choices are not, of course, as mutually exclusive as they seem when stated as generalizations. They overlap in actual experience; at best, they are rough approximations of alternative emphases. Also, we may shift from one level to another or possibly combine two or more. Strictly speaking, the final choice above—to consider one—is possible only theoretically. Since no one is able to invent a completely original pattern of beliefs, it is possible to contend that the "transformative" overlaps with other choices—the "moderative," for example. Again, the "restorative" choice is, in one sense, "new" if the person who accepts it is not yet aware of its ancestry or if he insists that the beliefs he aims to restore demand constant restatements of the still original pattern. Equally true is the fact that even the most far-reaching change one individual makes in beliefs may be made at about the same time by other people. Most important, we hold no brief for the finality of the nine levels; other and more refined or elaborate series might well be constructed.

How often we do decide to choose depends both upon our sensitivity to the impact of conflicting beliefs and upon the frequency or force of that impact. In times of severe tension and rapid change, the compulsion to do so is greater than in times of comparative stability. The probabilities are, however, that most of us make any far-reaching choice only once or twice in our whole lives, if we do so at all. Moreover, the frequency of choice tends to diminish as we grow older. Typically, although by no means invariably, we are perhaps more and more often drawn to settle upon the *first* level of choice (the complacent), less and less often upon the *last* (the transformative).

THE CHOICES BEFORE US: PHILOSOPHIES OF EDUCATION AS PATTERNS OF CULTURE

Let us try to recapitulate this challenge in another way. A crisis-culture is not likely to be one for whose ills we find any single diagnosis or any single prognosis. The deeper and wider the turbulence, or the more complex the schemes of living that make up a given culture, the more numerous and perplexing the choices that it confronts.

Such a time is our own. Individuals, groups, and nations are by no means agreed on what is right or wrong with basic patterns and choices of belief. As a matter of evidence, violent clashes of opposition and disagreement constitute one of the clearest symptoms of crisis itself.

Nevertheless, it becomes possible to organize the great choices before us and thus to observe how those patterns of belief that were considered from the "inside" (that is, in terms of philosophy as such) grow here in significance when viewed, in turn, from the "outside" (that is, from the standpoint of culture). Were these patterns restricted to purely personal alternatives, we should be perpetuating a fallacy of some philosophy textbooks. We should be assuming that patterns of belief are largely creatures of a self-contained intellect, whereas in fact they are likewise and more fundamentally political, economic, familial, and moral.

This contention is best clarified by returning to the several levels of belief epitomized above. All of these (or perhaps still further choices) have their own coteries of contemporary spokesmen in philosophy. But our point now is that a comparable scale is applicable to beliefs about and interpretations of culture. That is, instead of referring any longer to these choices in terms of philosophic belief exclusively, let us now propose to utilize more frequently a term mentioned earlier: philosophic patterns of cultural orientation—that is, culturological patterns. Consider, then, a few relevant examples.

First, the complacent level. While scarcely philosophic in any full sense, it is not uncommon even in such a time of bewildering uncertainty as our own. Many citizens, in schools and out, do refuse to face the issues between two such powerful cultures as those of Russia and America. Others yield to whatever pressures toward conformity happen to be dominant at a given time. Still others gloss over the disturbances created by shifting moral or esthetic standards. In brief, we discourage the critical expression of beliefs by training young people to suppose that what *seems* on the surface to be real, true, or good about our culture *must be* real, true, or good.

The second and third levels—negativism and skepticism—are also widespread. When common opportunity, social harmony, or peace is rare, not only do negative reactions become exceptionally numerous but some skeptics cry that trustworthy patterns of belief are not possible at all. Doubt arises about the efficacy of most conventional activities. Indeed, as noted in Chapter 1, the widely discussed phenomenon of "alienation," or such commonly related symptoms as uprootedness and social deviation, appear to be chronic among large minorities of the young. These are said to have lost their own "identity" and to reject all affirmative proposals toward concerted action or purposeful commitment.

The next two levels of expression—agnosticism and eclecticism—are equally commonplace. In education, the latter is symbolized by a polyglot of courses that presents smatterings of many things without purpose or design; the former, by the extent to which, in the fraternity of scholars, impartiality becomes a badge of academic virtue and partiality a vice. Yet, granting the case for diversified curriculums, granting also that to see "all sides of every question" is a worthy aim when not merely a smoke screen for timidity or hidden biases, we may also question whether these choices, too, do not mirror tensions in our culture. Could it be that the perplexing diversity of economic forms, the cross-purposes of scientific research, the mutual hostility of political philosophies, the fierce oppositions between absolutism and experimentalism—could it be that such phenomena, rather than the reasons more frequently professed, are responsible for the current fashion of ethical "neutrality" and scientific "objectivity"?

The levels of expression thus far glimpsed through the lens of our crisis-culture are by no means, then, the most adequate ones. Not that these orientations are useless; from the Cynics of ancient Greece to the Skeptics of the eighteenth century, and down to the "impartial spectators" and agnostics of today, periods of eruption have induced critiques that act as healthful purgatives. But these still remain preliminary to the central task. Full expression of patterns of belief should be organic and constructive. It should aim, not merely to unearth defects, but to seek and estimate our strengths. It should aim also to weld truth, value, and reality into unified relations that overarch the various fields of nature and of man. Hence, in order to follow further as philosophers of education, four chief routes remain most compelling:

(1) *We may, on the transmissive level, consciously and clearly confirm those habits of living and expressions of belief that have hitherto prevailed in modern culture.* In education, should we settle upon this choice, we would identify ourselves with the kind of educational theory and practice that we shall call the *essentialist* orientation.

(2) *Or we may, on the moderative level, prefer to revise our beliefs and practices one step at a time.* Neither lagging too far behind nor moving too far ahead of the rate of change of the present culture, we would choose in education the program and doctrine of the *progressivist* orientation.

(3) *Or we may, on the restorative level, celebrate the spirit and principles of an earlier and, for those of such persuasion, a nobler human order.* Convinced that the present culture is failing man, we would insist, educationally, upon a resurrection of the premises and proposals of the *perennialist* orientation.

(4) *Or, finally, we may, on the transformative level, envision and share in the innovation of cultural designs.* Convinced, too, that the present culture is no longer adequate, we would subscribe to the educational beliefs and actions of the *reconstructionist* orientation.

This is not to say, of course, that these four are the *only* preferable orientations. Nor does this mean that every philosophic approach to education of any consequence *must* fit into one of these large categories. Indeed, as will be considered in the following chapter, some certainly do not; yet, these additional approaches may, in turn, throw further light upon the four orientations to which primary attention shall be paid. In any case, our contention is this: Whatever approaches are to be considered, or however carefully we may seek for common ground as well as differences among them, they must not be adjudged in purely philosophic terms. They *are* philosophic, of course. But more basically, they confront our distraught and, in some ways, revolutionary culture. The choice or choices that we make could well help to determine in momentous ways the structures and methods, not only of education, but also of virtually all major institutions, habits, faiths, and practices.

Meanwhile, a further word of precaution is in order. If we are to deal fairly with any model of large organizing categories, whether in educational theory or in any other field (history, for example), we must recognize that by no means are they so concisely and discretely organized as one is easily tempted to suppose. In our own model, for example, each orientation has something in common with the other three. Essentialism and perennialism especially, will be found to share a good deal of the same philosophic, educational, and cultural outlook, as do reconstructionism and progressivism share theirs. A diagram may help here if we bear in mind that, in no way, does it measure the precise *extent* of overlappings either among the four positions regarded as wholes, or among individual advocates of these positions.

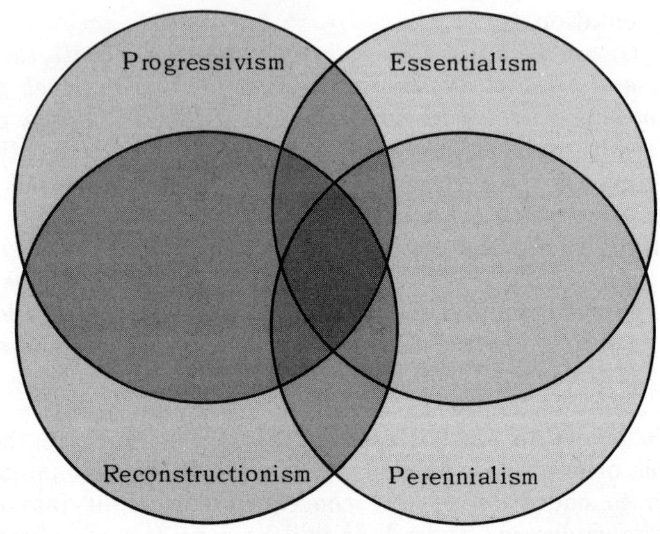

Still another caution is called for. The concepts through which we have chosen to organize and interpret major culturologies of education are *only* concepts—that is to say, they are not to be regarded as objectively "real" systems that exist, as it were, independently of man's critical operations with and upon them. Exactly as in the case of the concept "culture," they are, rather, to be utilized as *abstractions or intellectual tools* that help us more clearly to organize, analyze, and evaluate interrelated, yet often quite heterogeneous, bodies of educational and cultural experience. In brief, they are what we shall later term "operational" categories through which to interpret the orientations that they symbolize.

CHAPTER 4

Contemporary philosophic movements: culturological anticipations

BEFORE TURNING directly to the predominant orientations in educational philosophy that were delineated at the conclusion of Chapter 3, one additional step is imperative. We must try to characterize several contemporary movements of thought that have attracted the attention not only of "general" or "academic" philosophers but of many theorists in the physical and social sciences, in religion and art, and certainly in education.

Now as any one knows who claims to be even mildly familiar with twentieth-century philosophy, not a single one of our own preferred categories—essentialism, progressivism, perennialism, and reconstructionism—is standard to the typologies of conventional philosophy. In one respect, this is fortunate: we wish by means of culturology to supersede such easy and, from our vantage point, often sterile typologies. Instead, the four approaches that we have chosen, although intended to embrace a good deal more than the institution of education as such, are interpreted precisely because they are both the products of and contributors to that institution.

Since they become the chief preoccupation of all subsequent chapters, let us say no more about these approaches at the moment. Instead, we wish here to select each of the following philosophic positions for brief consideration: (1) existentialism; (2) neo-Freudianism; (3) neo-Marxism; (4) philosophic analysis; and (5) Zen Buddhism.

But why *these* positions? Only two—existentialism and

philosophic analysis—are conventionally treated by philosophers of education, while one, Zen Buddhism, is almost totally neglected. The answer must be that, granting that our own selection of philosophic movements can no more prove to be adequate or conclusive than can our several levels of belief, *these movements provide useful supplementations of or commentaries upon our preferred fourfold model of educational philosophies.* All of them, certainly, are significant for the world of thought in our time.

Speaking in other terminology, we hope to discover that our chosen cluster lends itself with greater or lesser relevance to the value orientations that have been termed transmissive, moderative, restorative, and innovative. In this lending, we cannot, of course, expect to interpret any one of our contemporary philosophic movements in meticulous detail; such an effort would be impossible without at least one companion volume of comparable magnitude. All that can be suggested is that our fourfold culturological perspectives upon educational philosophies may be, respectively, strengthened or weakened when existentialist, neo-Freudian, neo-Marxian, philosophic analyst, and/or Zen Buddhist ideas are woven into them. In turn, however, it is likely that these movements may become strengthened or weakened when they, too, are considered intermittently from the four perspectives. Please note, finally, the *alphabetical* order: no one of our selected philosophic approaches is ranked preferentially. Each, rather, may prove of fairly comparable interest and value.

EXISTENTIALISM: THE QUEST FOR AUTHENTICITY

Still, because our first selection almost immediately demonstrates that it cannot possibly be located exclusively on any one level either as philosophic belief "within" or as culturological interpretation "without," perhaps we are fortunate to begin with existentialism. Such diversity applies just as well to the "lower" levels (the skeptical, for example) as it does to the "upper" ones (the restorative, for example). Thus, many existentialists have been relegated to the lower levels of belief either because they reject familiar points of view or because they seem to lend themselves so vicariously to beliefs about, say, religion or politics that one may wonder just what it is they do believe. In any case, some existentialists, partly because they repudiate all "systems" of philosophy, seem able to relate to the transmissive orientation, for one, as spontaneously as other existentialists seem able to relate to the transformative.

Nevertheless, one need not conclude from the existentialist's pliability that he maintains no central theme at all. He does: indeed, this is epitomized so frequently by a maxim attributed to the most famous twentieth-century existentialist, Jean-Paul Sartre, that we record it here: "Existence precedes essence." Long before Sartre, however, Sören Kierkegaard, the "founder" of this movement expressed it this way: existence "constitutes the highest interest of the existing individual, and his interest in his existence constitutes his reality."[1]

What may these strange phrases mean? In brief, they are simply declaring that the fundamental nature of human life is far more central and prior than are any of the elaborate formulations of classic philosophies, ideologies, or theologies. In this respect, existentialists may even be termed "antiphilosophers": they hold that systematic, rational forms or "essences" of thought (such as those of G. W. F. Hegel, the great German philosopher against whom, particularly, Kierkegaard rebelled) lead us away from the most precious of all truths: man in his existence came first and last; all else lies in limbo between.

Kierkegaard, a Danish thinker, remained obscure well into the twentieth century. Then, philosophers such as Sartre, Gabriel Marcel, and Albert Camus in France; Karl Jaspers and Martin Heidegger in Germany; Ortega y Gasset in Spain; Martin Buber in Israel; and Paul Tillich in America began to reinterpret and extend his own brilliant but literally quite agonizing ideas. They came to recognize, too, that the German thinker, Friedrich Nietzsche, who had already attracted wide attention in rather different ways, belonged within their fold. So, too, did the Russian philosopher-novelist, Fëdor Dostoevski.

A competent culturological interpretation of existentialism is yet to be undertaken. In concert with many others, let us merely suggest here that this movement becomes a repudiation of the ruthless power of modern civilization conspiring to overwhelm individuality and personal integrity. The objectivity and icy neutrality of a cosmos reducible to scientific formulae; the burgeoning of an industrialism that cares only for more and more production and consumption of commodities (many of these useless or injurious); the succession of wars that threaten to destroy the earth along with millions of people in total indifference to human well-being—these are only some of the more glaring circumstances that generate the existentialist's critique.

But a radical shift, away from the dominant philosophy

[1] Kierkegaard, as quoted in Burtt, *In Search of Philosophic Understanding*, pp. 79f.

inherited especially from nineteenth-century Europe and toward an existentialist reinterpretation, cannot be pictured as a relaxed, easy choice. However most existentialists continue to dispute among themselves—and they do—none would deny that unequivocal confrontation of one's own integrity must be accompanied by suffering and anguish. Thus the dreadfulness of impending death is an inescapable facet of life (a theme often developed by Heidegger), but neither can it be mollified by fictions of immortality as portrayed by Christian or other doctrines. "Nothingness" is a familiar term among existentialists. So, too, is "absurdity," a term suggesting that no beautifully rational interpretation of reality can be justified; we only deceive ourselves if we suppose that any metaphysical speculation guarantees human destiny at all.

The existential philosophy, as Kierkegaard so profoundly demonstrated, is also paradoxical. The very depths of despair and loneliness are, likewise, ultimate challenges to selfhood. Thus in Marcel, for one, this affirmation centers in love; in Jaspers, it centers in the vision of world civilization; in Sartre, in abundant social order for all common men; in Tillich, in "the courage to be." All of these and other existentialists vary, perhaps, as widely as they converge, yet through all of them one belief seems paramount: human freedom as unmitigated self-affirmation, human freedom made possible again only by the paradox of its impossibility and its denial. As Sartre has put it, the existential man is condemned to be free: whether in a concentration camp, or a police state, or a monolithic religious order, man alone is compelled to maintain his own integrity without which, after all, life is meaningless.

It seems fair, indeed, to suppose that some interpreters of existentialism thus portray man not only as an autonomous entity but as completely self-sufficient and independent of other entities. After all, can it be otherwise when one's own inner freedom, however dreadful, is the capstone of one's own life? Nevertheless, this is a misleading view. Certainly no existentialist of the stature of a Sartre, Jaspers, Marcel, or even a Kierkegaard, can be satisfied with mere withdrawal into subjectivity or moral anarchy. For all such philosophers, the principle of existence is bipolar: just as *I* must be free in order to become human, so likewise must *you* be free.

But it is Buber, probably most persuasively, who has focused upon such human reciprocity. The very titles of his famous *I and Thou* and *Between Man and Man* symbolize this categorical imperative. While he, too, is deeply concerned about what he terms the "Single One," he recognizes equally that communication, silent or vocal, is crucial to human affirmation. Therefore, whether he is discussing religion or politics or education, *dialogue* becomes the pervading theme. This is typical of the Buberian "dialogic philosophy": "Being, lived in dialogue, receives even in extreme dereliction a harsh and strengthening series of reciprocity; being, lived in monologue, will not. . . . The basic movement of the life of dialogue is the turning toward the other."[2] But we are not to suppose that such a movement is ever a process of mere thinking: it is always of two or more persons who commune in many ways—nonverbal and verbal, affective and cognitive.

We are tempted to continue much further, but it becomes necessary to conclude our initial comments upon existentialism by returning to the thread that runs through abundant and sometimes conflictive interpretations. Sartre is again as incisive as any: "Man is nothing else but what he makes of himself."[3] But such a making is also, as Buber insists, the mutual making with other selves as well.

NEO-FREUDIANISM: METAPSYCHOLOGY AS INTERPERSONAL THERAPY

That our selected contemporary movements of thought frequently intermesh, just as we shall find that they do among our chief orientations in educational philosophy, is excellently illustrated by one development called existential psychology or existential psychoanalysis. Well-known advocates of this movement in America include Rollo May, Abraham Maslow, and Carl Rogers, although (as in the case of existentialism itself) one sometimes finds it difficult to draw neat distinctions between their agreements and disagreements either among themselves or with disparate schools of psychotherapy.

In any case, the influence of Kierkegaard, Sartre, and others is acknowledged for their stress upon the search for authentic personal identity—a search more or less central to all specialized forms of psychotherapy, to be sure, but especially highlighted by existential practitioners. Certainly, it is no cause for surprise that May, for one, has discovered a common motif between the Kierkegaardian concept of dread and the Freudian concept of anxiety: both are phenomena chronic to the human failure to achieve harmony either within one's self or with other selves.

[2] Buber, *Between Man and Man*, pp. 20, 22.

[3] Sartre, as quoted in Kaplan, *The New World of Philosophy*, p. 104.

Our primary purpose, however, is neither to elaborate upon existential psychology nor to assess the gigantic contribution of Sigmund Freud. It is true, we think, that Freud's genius lay at least as much in the field of modern philosophy (an apt term for Freudian theory is "metapsychological," reminding us of the parallel term, "metacultural") as in the psychological sciences. But we are interested here in how a few of these contributions have been modified and adapted by the generation after him.

Who are the neo-Freudians? Some interpreters, surely, would include the existential psychologists just mentioned. Others might properly include the influential rebels from Freudian orthodoxy: Carl Jung and Alfred Adler. In America, those perhaps most widely known as neo-Freudians have been Harry Stack Sullivan, Karen Horney, Erich Fromm, Abram Kardiner, Franz Alexander, and Harold D. Lasswell—all of whom have been considered psychotherapists with the exception of Lasswell, a political scientist and theorist. Others could, of course, be chosen for consideration.

Let us try again to ferret out merely one or two common denominators. All, of course, recognize the original influence of Freud himself—an influence to which we return briefly in later chapters. At the same time, they modify most of his own concepts: thus, unlike Freud, they refuse to consider man as so completely determined by his instincts—notably, those manifested in sexuality and aggression. Rather, they hold that environmental conditions, especially social conditions, are at least equally influential. Thus for Freud the Oedipus myth, to select one of his most famous concepts, is rooted in deep instinctive feelings between, mother, father, and child that are frequently, although unconsciously, destructive; while for Horney and others, because these feelings respond chiefly to family influences, they may prove to be either destructive *or* constructive depending upon environmental circumstances.

Another basic modification is symbolized by the term, "interpersonal relations"—a term central to Sullivan. Here one is reminded of Buber, although it is much more likely that Sullivan was influenced, directly or not, by the transactional theories of American pragmatists to whom we shall refer in Part 2. In any case, an emphasis upon the resilience amidst interacting individual and group experience suggests that neo-Freudians have been in direct line with the culturological approach to human life in general and to education in particular. That is, they have been convinced that human behavior, granting that it stems profoundly from inherited biological roots, is the product at least as much and usually far more of sociocultural conditions that vary almost infinitely not only among families but among subcultures and whole cultures.

It follows that neo-Freudians also deviate from their master in that they assume the evolutionary, virtually limitless, growth of the human species and the mental health of which it is capable. Recognizing that some interpreters of Freud maintain that he, too, reflects this optimistic assumption, it does seem reasonable to agree with other interpreters that at times he appears at least ambivalent toward this assumption, whereas neo-Freudians are much less so. On the whole, they are melioristic—that is, they believe that civilization can progress, if only we give it a fair chance—an attitude that seems to be entirely congenial with what we have called the moderative level of belief. By contrast, Freud often appears pessimistic in concord with the "reality principle" that civilization inevitably becomes warped and constricted because of the compulsion to restrain those unconscious, destructive forces that seethe within the human psyche.

Where both the classic Freudian and neo-Freudian metapsychologies tend to converge focally is in the crucial functioning of conscious awareness—that is, in the often thankless, frustrating task of attempting to assuage the relentless tensions that pervade the bipolarity of unconscious drives toward unlicensed pleasure at one extreme, and the repressions of conscience as expressed in taboos, customs, or other social mandates at the other extreme. Differences between Freud and the revisionists may lie not so much in the centrality of consciousness, however limited, as in the conviction of Sullivan and his colleagues that this mediating role is best achieved when we come to recognize, first, that human drives are shaped by a complex of outside influences, especially cultural influences, and second, that conscious mediations occur not merely *within* the psyche (as it were) but *between* psyches. The therapist, moreover, may become involved in this relational process to a much greater extent than in the strictly Freudian, more neutral treatment of the patient as a scientific object of analysis.

Almost endless ramifications of both insight and clinical evidence in neo-Freudian theory could, of course, be pursued. Thus, Kardiner's contributions, in collaboration with anthropologists, to the concept of modal personality (for example, of an Indian tribe) has contributed richly to culturology by enabling us to regard the individual less as a unique human entity than as a kind of abstracted cultural type, even to the extent of "national character." Others (among them the psychiatrist, Henry Murray, whether properly regarded as a neo-Freudian or not) have helped us to appreciate that the domineering authority of objective cultural restrictions should be reinterpreted less in terms of transmissive beliefs than in terms of "ideal" patterns of the future—that is, of transformable, directive human goals.

In this overview we have tried, as far as possible, to avoid technical psychoanalytic terminology. Our primary purpose, rather, has been to spotlight a metapsychological mood that, though it by no means supersedes Freud, does attempt to amend him through the channel of twentieth-century developments in the human sciences. This attempt centers in the hopeful conviction, perhaps more vehemently and influentially expressed by Fromm than by any other neo-Freudian, of "man for himself"—a conviction realizable only as, or if, man discovers how to escape from the false freedoms of distorted personality and debilitating sociocultural habits foisted upon him by outmoded and enslaving institutions. In this conviction (not all neo-Freudians, of course, share equally his own radical enthusiasm), Fromm points directly toward the next among our cluster of philosophic movements.

NEO-MARXISM: THE STRUGGLE FOR CULTURAL HUMANISM

Just as existentialism provides, for some exponents, a link with the neo-Freudian movement, so the latter leads, for others, toward neo-Marxian thought. In Fromm, this transition is unusually apt: his interpreters continue to debate whether it is really Freud or Marx from whom he has learned most. What is less debatable is that few if any influential American writers have found richer value in rapprochement between both great pioneers. As Fromm himself puts it succinctly, "I believe that Marxism needs such a psychological theory" (that is, a neo-Freudian "humanistically oriented" one) "and that psychoanalysis needs to incorporate genuine Marxist theory. Such a synthesis will fertilize both fields. . . ."[4]

It is this kind of fertilization that suggests what we mean by neo-Marxism, although the synthesis is not necessarily limited exclusively to any two philosophic movements. Existentialism, for one, permeates some recent work of philosophers who still regard

[4] Fromm, in Fromm (ed.), *Socialist Humanism*, p. 244.

themselves primarily as Marxists—particularly those in the smaller Socialist countries which have been trying, despite severe Soviet pressures at times, to loosen the official Communist ideology while yet maintaining what they consider to be the vital core of Marxism.

No less than in neo-Freudianism, the question of what this core may mean is anything but simple to answer. One fertile approach to the question may be to contend that just as Freud's stern, instinct-anchored metapsychology needs to be corrected by a still-emerging culturological interpretation, so also does the rather old-fashioned Marxian world-system traditionally known as dialectical materialism require its own far-reaching supplementations.

The meaning of this world system is in itself a subject of ceaseless controversy—some of it bitterly hostile (especially in capitalist countries such as the United States), some abjectly worshipful (especially in the Soviet Union and Communist China). Orthodox interpretations of dialectical materialism are being increasingly modified, however—one of the most potent influences resulting from the discovery, publication, and translation of early writings by Marx himself. Known as the *Economic and Philosophical Manuscripts of 1844*, Marx outlined, at the age of twenty-six, his entire theoretical viewpoint. It is these writings that have appeared especially to affect Fromm and his disciples, as well as a number of influential philosophers not only in Socialist countries but in England, Japan, France, Italy, and now even in America. For they reveal Marx to be extraordinarily predictive of the global problems, tasks, and goals that now beset civilization.

This reinterpretation is more totally culturological, we think, than are any of the other selected contemporary movements now under review. That is, neo-Marxism is a thorough-going anthropological philosophy—a view of man engaged in an immensely dynamic, sometimes violent, sometimes peaceful life of history and culture. At the poignant center, man is thus depicted as a self-searching and evolving being who, in conjoint struggle with others, desires fulfillment of a great cluster of human needs—economic ones most persistently, but all other needs, too, such as love, adventure, and satisfying creative work.

Tragically, however, such fulfillment is only too often denied man. The early writings of Marx emphasize especially the theory of alienation to which we alluded in Chapter 1—a phenomenon familiar enough to contemporary social philosophers and scientists but which Marx foresaw almost clairvoyantly as a chronic disease of the technological-industrial order of power and production. "Estrangement"—another familiar term today—is repeated again and again in his early manuscripts. Thus, speaking of the extraneous impersonal tasks that millions of workers must perform in mechanized factories, Marx writes: "An immediate consequence of man's estrangement from the product of his labor is man's estrangement from man."[5] But this condition extends not only to himself and to others; it extends to nature: one's work very often becomes so vacuous and splintered that one fails to discover any significant relationship between discrete parts either within society or within the world of inanimate and animate beings.

This is not to suggest that neo-Marxism amounts merely to a revivification and updating of the original Marx. Sweeping changes that have taken place since his death in 1883 (Freud, for example, was then only twenty-seven years of age) require innumerable complementary influences. Consider but one instance: the central Marxian concept of "class consciousness." Anthropologists such as Kluckhohn and psychotherapists such as Kardiner have helped us to perceive, whether intentionally or not, how such a phenomenon as class consciousness may also occur as a kind of "class *un*consciousness"—for example, how frequently we may blithely pronounce some value judgment about an implicitly endorsed and reinforced cultural practice (and not only about class patterns, of course, but also about those of race, religion, and family, among others), yet toward which, on closer examination, we prove to be entirely insensitive and uncritical. Here we are reminded of our preferred term, the "culturology of knowledge," as a theory of epistemology that not only amends classic theories of realism and others, but also challenges such relatively new theories as analytic philosophy.

Meanwhile, let us mention only one or two additional aspects of the neo-Marxian approach. (Further brief attention will be paid in Part 5 to Marx's own contributions.) That both the Freudian and Marxian positions have much in common despite profound divergences is alone indicated by their heavy stress upon the irrational (or what we shall later prefer to call the "unrational") dimensions of man. In Marx's case, to be sure, these are far more the consequence of environmental, especially socioeconomic forces, than of inherited, biological factors. Yet both positions frequently leave the impression that man is so powerfully determined by one or another of these primary forces that the opportunity for

[5] Marx, in Josephson (ed.), *Man Alone*, p. 101.

human freedom through deliberate human action is, if not virtually paralyzed, constrictive indeed.

Perhaps the single most challenging revision of such versions of nineteenth-century theories of determinism is a common thesis of both neo-Freudians and neo-Marxists. This is the thesis that man, enriched by new knowledge and world-expanding experience, can at last begin to come into his own and to discover how he and his fellowmen may galvanize and release the powers he latently possesses—powers that have hitherto remained only, at best, obscure or distorted. As already intimated, neither Freud nor Marx wished to repudiate a philosophy of personal and/or cultural rejuvenation. Certainly, in any case, many of their followers, seeking to recrystallize both Freud and Marx, often seem less concerned with original meanings than with flexible, operational interpretations that apply directly to our own period of revolutionary transformation.

This concern is well typified by the Yugoslav neo-Marxian philosopher, Gajo Petrović. In contradicting, for example, any simplistic explanations of economics as the cause of history, he carefully distinguishes between sufficient and necessary conditions of human belief or behavior. While economic factors are, he agrees, of vast necessary influence in shaping attitudes, habits, and conduct, this fact does not at all compel acquiescence in the dogma that such factors are alone decisive.

The contentions of Petrović are scarcely original; many beside him have been making them for a long time. Nevertheless, they do invite the conclusion (surprising as it may seem to average Americans and, surely, to many teachers) that the Marxian fountainhead, far from having gone dry, bursts with fresh exuberance and fresh aspirations of an "ideal superego"—that is, as a design for man-in-culture no longer fettered by such life-denying malignancies as alienation but portrayed as the prospects of "liberation" when these are delineated by another neo-Marxist of unique perspicuity: Herbert Marcuse.

PHILOSOPHIC ANALYSIS: CATALYST OF OBFUSCATION

Although at first glance one might suppose that little if any connecting implications can be detected between neo-Marxism and philosophic analysis (intermittently, we shall prefer to say "analytic philosophy"), at second glance even these two very disparate movements, when compared culturologically, suggest at least tenuous common features.

For one thing, the philosophic analyst is sometimes depicted as a therapeutic methodologist. Indeed, the ". . . philosopher's treatment of a question is like the treatment of illness."[6] Thus far, he shares congeniality not only with neo-Marxian therapeutic analysts of the social unconscious but, likewise, with neo-Freudian therapeutic analysts (existential or otherwise) in their preoccupation with the individual unconscious. The acute distinction, of course, is that the analytic philosopher is allegedly and exclusively concerned with conscious, logical mind. In this concern, he aims to rid not only philosophic language but *all* language of a monstrous depository of scientific, ethical, religious, in fact, every sort of verbal debris by which men have been entangled and deluded throughout intellectual history.

Philosophic analysis reveals at least one other quality in common with our selected cluster of contemporary positions. That is to say, it too appears as one type of reaction to the cultural convulsions that have extended across the earth and all the way from the two world wars well into our own period. To be sure, the average philosophic analyst (if there is an average one) seems indifferent to these convulsions as germane in any way to his own specialization. Nevertheless, he, too, is expressing at least a sense of indignation toward ways of interpreting philosophy and culture through, for example, such "outmoded" doctrines as objective idealism.

But whatever his motivations this much, we think, may be said. The analytic movement—usually omitting now the adjective, "philosophic"—has become the most widely attended contemporary development among professional philosophies of the non-Socialist and non-Communist world. Some of our most distinguished twentieth-century philosophers, unfamiliar though most of them are to the public, are analysts of one or another school: Ludwig Wittgenstein, Bertrand Russell (although he embraced much more), G. E. Moore, Rudolf Carnap, Herbert Feigl, Moritz Schlick, Gilbert Ryle, C. E. Ayer, Hans Reichenbach, and J. L. Austin. This roster, too, could well be extended.

We say "one or another school" because as is true of, say, existentialism, styles of interpretation vary greatly. Logical positivists, logical empiricists, linguistic analysts, scientific empiricists, and ordinary-language theorists—all these have occupied high seats of academic prestige. Moreover, debates among analysts, no

[6] Wittgenstein, as quoted in Cornforth, *Marxism and the Linguistic Philosophy*, p. 135.

less than debates with their nonanalyst opponents, continue furiously if heatlessly—a situation that we cannot resist wondering about in turn: Is this state of ironic disputation due *merely* to quests for clarity of meaning, or is it due, in addition, to the astonishing opaqueness of so many analysts toward the overwhelming complexities that permeate an age of psychic frustration, socioeconomic alienation, cultural schizophrenia, or all three?

We hope to entertain such questions as our culturological perspectives upon educational philosophies proceed into subsequent chapters. Here, our obligation is again merely to pinpoint any perceptible threads that run up and down the analytic movement as a whole. Let us then borrow at the outset from the cosmopolitan-minded American philosopher, E. A. Burtt, whose appraisal of analysis is both sympathetic and cautious:

> Analytic philosophy is a way of thinking that emphasizes the logical dissection of concepts and statements to reveal their precise meaning, and tries to draw all the distinctions required if this process is to be carried out with scrupulous thoroughness. Why is such meticulous discrimination important? Because no thinker has ever been able to deal with any serious issue without careful analysis; to be concerned with a problem is by that token to wish one's understanding of it to be clear, accurate, and systematic. In the absence of such discrimination one inevitably falls into obscurity, confusion, and loose-jointedness.[7]

Surely we must applaud this mandate. Even so, different analysts travel widely varied routes. Doubtless one of the earliest of these routes was pursued by the famous Vienna Circle (which flourished, interestingly and perhaps not altogether coincidentally, only a few years after the period when Freud and his disciples, also in Vienna, were forging a very different sort of analysis). The logical positivists, as they were often then known and whose followers entrenched themselves in major English, American, as well as other universities, performed at least two powerful roles: first, they repudiated as empirically "meaningless" all metaphysical and, frequently, even ethical questions that had long been sacred to traditional philosophy (at best, these were termed merely "pseudoquestions"); and second, repudiation was accompanied by alternative approaches, among them, and perhaps centrally, the "verifiability principle" of Schlick and others.

[7] Burtt, *op. cit.*, p. 43.

Burtt's epitomization of this principle is again worth quoting:

> Unless one can specify a procedure by which a given assertion is testable, so that either it or the contradictory assertion can be confirmed by adequate evidence, the assertion not only has no right to claim truth—it has no sense.[8]

This principle, of course, overlaps, with other epistemological theories (especially pragmatism and some versions of realism) but it has often led to a sharp dichotomy between, on the one hand, the alleged verifiability of evidence as accurately describable by scientific investigation and, on the other hand, the alleged *un*verifiability of moral, esthetic, or other spheres of human conduct—spheres which have been termed merely "emotive" or otherwise subjective and arbitrary reactions.

Although logical positivism has been refined and qualified through the years by such sophisticated philosophers as Ayer in England and Feigl in America, we fail to discover that subsequent formulations depart drastically from their earlier ones. We do find, however, other startling departures among analysts that doubtless stem more directly from the original insights of Wittgenstein than from the Vienna Circle (although, to be sure, he in turn profoundly influenced Carnap and other Viennese pioneers).

Wittgenstein, who in stature has been compared by his disciples with Darwin and Einstein, differs from both of these geniuses in fascinating respects—one, he never formulated a unified theory (such as evolution or relativity) that evolved consistently through the main trajectory of his thought; another, some of his disjointed writings are anything but analytic in the sense of Burtt's depiction. Rather, they have been described by some as so "cryptic" and even "mystical" that one may wonder whether Wittgenstein is as much a herald of our disorganized, however creative and innovative, period of history as he is the archadvocate of impeccable rational clarity.

Analysts themselves rarely, if ever, raise this kind of question, but they do pay close attention to Wittgenstein's pioneering logical and linguistic contributions. His strongest concerns were focused originally upon the necessity for ideal forms of language, especially those in science. But later he became the prophet of the ordinary-language theory which has troubled Feigl, among others, and which maintains that the reliability of thought is to be anchored less in the artificiality of philosophic and scientific constructions than in familiar, habitual usages of everyday discourse.

[8] *Ibid.*, p. 45.

Although we doubt whether either Wittgenstein or his analytic disciples were, or are, intellectually intimate with his contemporary, the culturologist, Cassirer, nevertheless one is struck by suggestive comparisons between the latter's interpretation of man as "animal symbolicum" and Wittgensteinian notions of "ordinary language." Both philosophers challenged merely formal, austere, tightly logical structures in favor of multiple styles and levels of communication (there are "countless" kinds of symbols, said Wittgenstein). At the same time, while both philosophers respected the imperatives of linguistic precision, they also pointed in their distinctive styles toward the need for philosophic reconversion through the common symbols of human intercourse.

Here it could even be contended that the earlier concern of analysts for epistemological criteria—most notably the verifiability principle—is transcended by the ideal of maximum, though never perfect and always developing, "probabilistic" linguistic forms that lie, as it were, beneath or beyond the observable data of man and nature. Moreover, because these forms are not at all dependent upon empirical evidence, they are (in familiar, logical terminology) purely "analytic" rather than "synthetic" propositions which do depend strictly upon such observable data. Analytic language, then, is located by some on the level of "metalanguage," the import of which stems directly from Wittgenstein's oft-repeated dictum: "Whatever can be said at all can be said clearly."[9] This dictum also delegates to philosophy its only legitimate prerogative. All other activities are abortive and futile.

ZEN BUDDHISM AS ESTHETIC COMMUNION IN MAN AND NATURE

If analytic philosophers are right, Zen Buddhism is not a "philosophy" at all. Here, indeed, some of its own proponents agree, although for very different reasons from those of analysts. Yet one has only to glance backward toward our preceding philosophic sketches in order to appreciate that Zen (here we omit the second term) comes full circle by at once inviting affinities with at least the first of our positions: existentialism. Despite wide variations again, both Zennists and existentialists join forces in challenging the objective, neutral, and unemotional posture of scientific philosophers (and thus, of course, of those analysts who have often been intimately allied) that so often apparently mirrors our

[9] Wittgenstein, as quoted in Kaplan, *op. cit.*, p. 57.

age of impersonal and industrial giantism. Equally, both positions probe the deeper recesses of man as human being and repudiate man as mechanized equation. Nor is it accidental that, among neo-Freudians, Fromm, particularly, has traced subtle but fruitful interconnections.

In any case, the proliferation of Western interest in Zen during approximately the same time span that embraces our other selected movements surely suggests at least partially comparable culturological influences. Perhaps the most distinctive of these influences is the relatively recent proliferation of cross-cultural exposure—one that enables a growing number, if still a paucity, of citizens in various countries to awaken to radically diverse cultural interpretations of man and nature than were hitherto assumed. After all, if the "mysterious East" still remains mysterious to most of us in the West, this is less so, at least, than it was a century ago. Especially in the case of Japan and the United States, the acculturative process has compounded so radically that few are astonished if the impact of the former nation proves as forceful in some respects as the impact of the latter does in others. Zen and pragmatism, respectively, are both fascinating instances of this process.

But Zen departs strikingly from our preceding philosophic positions still further. Thus, although its central character has changed but meagerly, it is by far the oldest historically among our selections. Its own origins are traceable to China from about 500 A.D., and its career of subsequently continuous influence in Japan dates from the twelfth century. Yet, not until about World War II did Zen begin to attract serious, not merely dilettante, attention in America and Europe. Since then, the influence of one remarkable Japanese Zennist, D. T. Suzuki, has doubtless overshadowed all others. Writing and speaking in eloquent English as well as in other languages, he was able, through many decades of a productive life and several volumes of his own interpretation of the great Zen sages, to reach expanding audiences. Meanwhile, Western scholars, too, were becoming fascinated by Oriental philosophies, one of whom, Alan W. Watts, has paid unusually persuasive attention to Zen. Among still others, we note only such eminent twentieth-century Europeans as Carl Jung and Martin Heidegger, or such Americans as Huston Smith and F. S. C. Northrop—the latter a culturologist whose *The Meeting of East and West* was one of the first impressive pleas for solid bridges of understanding across the vast distances of space and time that separate some of the greatest of all civilizations in history.

But how, in this concluding sketch, shall we try to capture the intrinsic quality of Zen? Suzuki surely speaks as authoritatively as any. It is, he says:

> . . . an altogether unique product of the Oriental mind, refusing to be classified under any known heading, as either a philosophy, or a religion. . . . Zen must be studied and analyzed from a point of view which is still unknown among Westen philosophers. . . . There is . . . no escapism, no mysticism, no denial of existence, no conquering of Nature, no frustrations, no mere utopianism, no naturalism. Here is a world of the given.[10]

Suzuki's statement, however provocative, seems more negative than positive. Let us then venture a statement or two from Watts:

> For living Zen . . . is above all a process of unlearning, of the abandonment of ideology, of all fixed forms of thought and feeling whereby the mind tries to grasp its own life. . . . Zen is closer to . . . the "unspeakable" level of reality—the non-verbal, non-symbolic, and totally undefinable world of the concrete as distinct from the abstract . . . for Zen is to move with life without trying to arrest and interrupt its flow; it is an immediate awareness of things as they live and move, as distinct from the mere grasp of ideas and feelings *about* things which are the dead symbols of a living reality.[11]

Both Suzuki and Watts are trying to tell us that before we of the West can even begin to grasp Zen, we shall have to undergo an intellectual and emotional metamorphosis which very few of us are willing to take at all seriously. The most that we can fairly expect, actually, is superficial exposure to several of Zen's guiding concepts. Nevertheless, it is also true that no inviolable obstacle prevents the arduous few from grasping them any less fundamentally than does the master of Zen himself. Here are several of the more familiar of these concepts:

Enlightenment. This is the core principle of Buddhism as immortalized by its founder in India, Gautama, a thousand years before

[10] Suzuki, *Studies in Zen*, pp. 84, 201.

[11] Watts, *The Spirit of Zen*, pp. 13, 52.

the emergence of Zen. The latter movement perpetuates this master principle, however multiple Buddhism's sectarian creeds. In essence, it is the search for release from frustrating, unsatisfying, boundless desires, yet a release attainable not by ascetic denial (as in Hinduism, say) but by universal identification with the totality and reverence of nature.

Satori. One cannot help but be reminded here of Maslow's pseudo-existentialist theory of "peak experience"—a psychotherapeutic insight pointing to individual awareness at moments of unsullied, exceptional clarity and understanding of oneself. In Suzuki's terms, satori is a state of liberating tranquillity; in Freud's or Marcuse's, it could be interpreted as the joyous celebration of Eros. But it is also the climax of Buddhist enlightenment and therefore of maximal, nonverbalized well-being or attunement to oneself and nature.

Mundo. This is a rigorous question-answer technique through which Zen disciples are pressed by Zen masters to confront and resolve merely rational dilemmas that often appear to be, on the surface, absurdly inconsistent. Mundo is aided by koan, a baffling but crucial process because it requires the would-be Zennist to work his way toward solution to the most penetrating of human problems. Yet they are never reachable by orthodox logic if only because such problems are themselves rarely, if ever, logical. Satori is the highest and rarest achievement of mundo and koan, but Suzuki also has a great deal to say about intuition defined as *prajna*—a Chinese term connoting pure, undifferentiated unity as contrasted with *vijnana,* itself reminiscent of a kind of Western pluralism and discordance.

Esthetics. Among authorities, the question of the scope and specific ways through which Zen is expressed esthetically appears controversial. Nevertheless, many close observers of Japanese arts have insisted that their most indigenous features are directly traceable more to Zen than to any other influence. Even a novice may appreciate, for example, the delicacy of the tea ceremony when performed by a specialist of long training in one or another school devoted exclusively to this ritual. And one may respond, sometimes very deeply and immediately, to the centuries-old stone gardens of Ryōan-ji and other Zen temples in Kyoto—a response which may well convey something of what Suzuki must mean by prajna. But whatever the medium—whether poetry or painting, architecture or gardening—authentic Japanese arts are unique both in their exquisite symplicity and in their nonesoteric, nonsymbolic delight in things and events as plain as a cricket or a cup of tea.

But every interpreter of Zen is equally emphatic in stressing its toughness and masculinity. Wrestling, archery, and fencing are all arts claiming Zennist influences. Also, as pictured so graphically in *Three Pillars of Zen* by Philip Kapleau (an American who became a full-fledged monk after arduous years of apprenticeship), monastery life can be as earthy, practical, and humorous as it can be intensively contemplative and solemn. In this, as in many other respects, Zen thus proves to be a paradoxical way of life or, in Western terminology, dialectical. In the Zennist's continuous search for rhythmic wholeness despite the antipodes of man and his world, one thus expects Suzuki to speak quite as readily of "unknowable knowledge" without necessary contradiction as one might suppose the Freudian or neo-Freudian to speak of the "conscious unconscious."

This series of philosophic portraits may legitimately reiterate our primary intention. We have tried neither the impossible task of embracing all influential movements of thought in our time nor of depicting any one of them with pretensions of adequacy. What we have tried to suggest is simply this: however dissimilar their motivations or formulations, these selected movements may prove, in culturological perspective, to be influential ways of responding to and offering directions for an age of revolution. In this sense, each of them likewise offers contributions to our understanding of education when this institution, too, is viewed in culturological rather than in conventionally academic or professional terms.

None of these movements, furthermore, can be identified exclusively, or even primarily, with *any one* of the four culturological approaches to education which, based upon correlative levels of belief, constitute remaining parts of the present work. Rather, we hope to find that *all* of them—though in diverse manners, to be sure—contribute provocatively to each of these four orientations. With this hope in mind, we propose to take note of them at varying and intermittent points, but particularly in our successive evaluations of their relevance to philosophies of education—relevance, that is to say, when such philosophies are regarded not only from "within" but from "without," and therefore as philosophies of culture.

CULTUROLOGICAL APPROACHES TO EDUCATION: A DESIGN

The central challenge of Part 1 and of this entire book is, in essence, that education in our times is faced with the stern obligation to assess its failures and successes honestly, relentlessly, and fearlessly. Reasons for such an obligation do not, however, become evident merely by the study of education as such. Rather, our first need is to analyze both divergent and convergent views that beset theory and practice by placing education in clear relationships with two other spheres of human endeavor and creation: the first, culture; the second, philosophy. Only as this is accomplished shall we be able to examine and select wisely among the major alternatives confronting America and the world. We have tried to exemplify some of the salient and controversial features of our approach to education as these may be considered subsequently by way of what is termed a triadic interpretation:

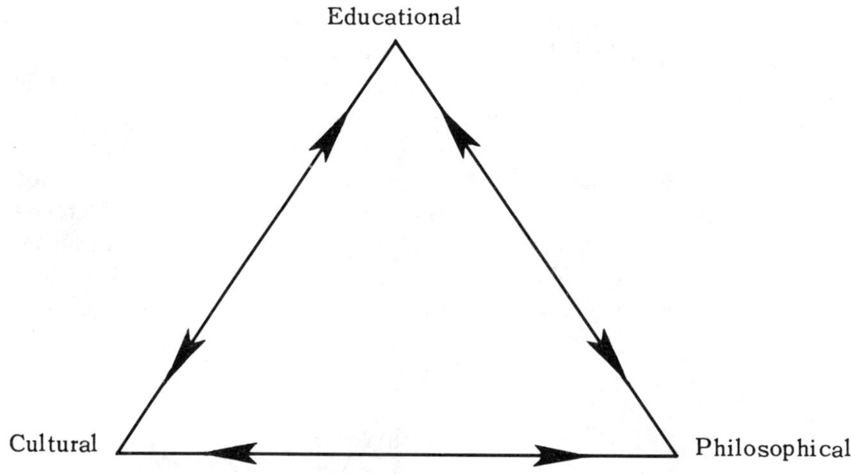

Now, by way of design, let us observe that this interpretation does not proceed in chronological order but rather, in one sense, as a time sequence that begins with the *present*, moves next to the recent *past*, then still further into the past, and finally, toward the *future*. Yet, in another sense, all four are also "present": each exerts gargantuan influence upon the culture and education of our own period.

In any case, progressivism is considered first because, among all four selected culturologies of education, this is most "present-centered" both in its own dominant beliefs and in the respect that it is the most articulate and influential school of social, philosophical, educational thought and action in twentieth-century American culture. But even when unsuccessful in bringing institutions and methods into harmony with its own central beliefs (of course, it frequently has not), it receives widespread and sincere homage. Moreover, until recently at least, it has commanded more attention in American education than has any subsequent movement among the contemporary philosophies named above.

But success never goes unchallenged. While we shall recognize that both perennialism and essentialism are much older philosophies in the history of education, these levels of education and culture have acquired fresh and militant vigor. Their recent formulations are conditioned, moreover, not merely by explosive events and ideas of the present period of history, but by progressivism itself. Indeed, both of these formulations (expressive also of the restorative and transmissive levels, respectively) may now be interpreted as counteroffensives against progressivism. Still more broadly, they can thus be judged as influential alternatives to the moderative orientation toward educational and cultural experience.

Reconstructionism is, in certain respects, also a counteroffensive. Yet, more frequently than in the case of either essentialism or perennialism, this culturology of education often finds itself in rapport with progressivism at the same time that it seeks to supplement and strengthen the latter in ways considered to be far-reaching and transformative.

Although attention must be focused upon the *educational* expression of these four constructive levels, our philosophies are thus to be viewed in wide perspective. The unities or disunities among them (sometimes subtle, sometimes crass, sometimes friendly, sometimes hostile) are, at bottom, *cultural.* Their manifestations through curriculum structures, psychologies of learning, and school administrations are all symptoms of beliefs, attitudes, habits, and institutions that permeate many strands of experience, whether economic, political, religious, scientific, esthetic, social, or personal. Teachers or others who accept one or another of these basic choices may not always be consistent about them; they may not always admit, either to themselves or to others, that the beliefs they hold about education are tied by a thousand knots to their beliefs about culture. Nevertheless, it is our business to show that the knots are there, even if hidden, and that we need to examine them in order to see whether they are sufficiently secure.

But it is our business for deeper reasons than simply because teachers, students, and citizens are expected to have some knowledge of educational theories as part of their intellectual equipment. Much more seriously, we are concerned to test major educational patterns because America and the world are at a decisive juncture in history—a juncture upon which we hope to throw more light as we proceed.

In America, to be sure, the compelling choices before us are usually couched in less extreme forms than those that convince so many millions elsewhere in the world—the Communist forms, perhaps, most powerfully. Indeed, all of the major philosophies of education that we are to examine profess devotion to the ideal of democracy. Each sincerely holds that *it* is the most real, the truest, and the best exponent of that ideal. Yet, whether such claims can be sustained at all under inspection remains to be seen. With the analytic philosopher, for one, one needs to become ultrasensitive to the *meaning* of such words as democracy—to determine in what ways the perennialist's conception, say, differs from, or agrees with, the progressivist's, to decide which of the two is the more defensible, and to ask whether either one is any longer acceptable. Finally, one needs to inquire whether, in view of America's strategic position as the leading world power, its chief philosophies of education and culture are not bound to affect deeply, and to be affected by, those of other world powers.

In order to come to terms with this kind of inquiry, we propose to design the remainder of this book in parallel stages. Thus, in each Part that follows, we shall usually consider, *first*: (1) an epitomization and preliminary evaluation of its underlying philosophy; (2) historic roots of that philosophy; (3) its beliefs about reality; (4) its beliefs about knowledge; and (5) its beliefs about value. Then, *second*, we shall consider the educational theory that rests upon its philosophic base: (1) its historic backgrounds; (2) its beliefs about learning; (3) its beliefs about the curriculum; and (4) its beliefs about the control of education. And, *third*, we shall consider how each of our predominant philosophies may be appraised in culturological perspective. As we proceed, the several movements of contemporary thought outlined earlier in this chapter are interwoven at whatever points that seem apropos; in this third stage, however, we shall usually pay more critical attention to their actual or potential significance for education than in the first and second stages.

One last word by way of design. The concluding educational theory, reconstructionism, is the youngest of our chosen orientations. Doubtless partially for this reason, it is also the least systematic or most vulnerable. But because reconstructionism nevertheless is adjudged, *from our own viewpoint*, the most impelling of the four positions, more extended attention is provided to both its philosophic and educational beliefs than to its fellows. Part 5, accordingly, is arranged into sequential sections or clusters of chapters. But an exactly parallel structure prevailing in our interpretations of progressivism, essentialism, and perennialism prevails here as well.

PART 2

Progressivism: education as cultural moderation

CHAPTER 5

Philosophic beliefs of progressivism

PREVIEW OF PROGRESSIVISM

AS A TWENTIETH-CENTURY philosophy of education, progressivism has won the support of more outstanding American theorists than any competing philosophy. It has influenced foreign educators both of East and West. And it has affected practice on every level, from nursery school to adult forum. Yet it has also generated violent criticism as well as downright hostility among philosophers and scholars of differing orientations. Although less directly influential as a theory than it was earlier in the century, and although modified if not at times overshadowed by partially congenial theories, progressivism has been and still remains a vastly important point of view. No teacher and no citizen earnestly concerned with the schools of America or of the world can ignore or pass lightly over this philosophy and what it means for culture and education.

Such immense influence derives not so much from its theoretical formulation as from the modern milieu of which it is a sweeping, and sensitive interpretation. This milieu has been of such a character as to encourage widespread acceptance and implementation of the beliefs peculiar to progressivism. In Chapter 7 we shall pay further attention to the social, economic, and political conditions that have not only made progressivism a powerful movement but are largely responsible for negative attacks upon it and for the present formulation of positive counterphilosophies. At this point, please recall only one salient emphasis from the picture sketched in Part 1: *the technological, experimental, this-worldly habits and accomplishments that potently shape our modern culture.* Such habits and accomplishments, above all others, dominate the progressivist outlook.

This outlook may be called "the liberal road to culture." It is the road considered by far the safest and most promising of all those open to us and along which we are, therefore, urged to continue traveling. We do not refer here merely, or even primarily, to political attitudes. By "liberal" used as an adjective, we mean rather the flexible, curious, tolerant, and open-minded attitude. By liberal used as a noun, we mean the kind of person who not only holds such an attitude but carries it over into adventurous, exploratory, continuously developing experience. He reminds one of the scientist who is curiously engaged, day in and day out, in the controlled remaking of some part of his environment.

It follows that effective education is, above all else, the scientific method at work in every area of experience. Far from being limited to academic laboratories, this method is equally applicable to personal and social life. But it is more than a precise method—more than the exactitude with which personal and social problems are solved. It is the very quality with which humanity should approach *all* pressing problems. It is the spirit of open inquiry, of tireless investigation, of willingness to listen to opposing ideas and to give them opportunity to prove their worth. Above all, it is the belief in man's ability to face the world with his own skills and to solve his problems through his own alert intelligence.

Good schools built upon such a theory are held to be potentially, though not always actually, culture's greatest single agency for genuine progress. Through them, the people can learn slowly how to act experimentally and so how to overcome the obstacles that always arise in the path of their onward march. Through them, the liberal way of life becomes synonymous with the democratic way. For democracy, to the progressivist, is the inclusive way of thinking and behaving.

Nevertheless, with all its strengths, with all its contributions both to education and to society at large, progressivism is open to certain stubborn doubts. These, too, spring from the soil of our culture, which now suffers from chronic instability. In such a period, confidence in the methods of experimental change is sure to be less widespread than in a period of relative stability. Disturbing questions arise, in turn, as to the adequacy of liberalism when it is understood to be the cultural-philosophic expression of that kind of confidence. As critical voices challenge the sufficiency of the liberal outlook, they challenge also its educational counterpart.

This does not mean that all critics are agreed either on what is wrong with liberalism (and therefore progressivism) or what should be proposed in its place. As a matter of fact, their proposals appear often as much in opposition to one another as to the theory that, in various respects, serves as their common foil. In Parts 3 and 4—where the essentialist and perennialist philosophies of education are considered—we shall find that both raise grave doubts about the adequacy of the liberal-progressivist outlook.

In contradistinction to either of these, our own culturological critique centers on one thesis. *Progressivism is a philosophy of transition between two great cultural configurations.* It is the major rationale of a culture that is (1) shifting rapidly *away from* those ways of living that Western culture has achieved in the past and (2) shifting rapidly *toward* new ways of living that are still to be achieved in the future. In brief, progressivism is a *transitional* philosophy, standing between cultural patterns that are increasingly obsolescent and cultural patterns that still await an opportunity to prove their desirability and practicality.

In this perspective, progressivism is to be judged not as a philosophy deserving wholesale repudiation but as one to be refurbished and strengthened. Its priceless contributions to modern civilization and education should be incorporated within a larger framework. This framework should utilize progressivism's experimental approach to nature and man, should accept the evolutionary and technological beliefs as well as the achievements of recent decades, but also should translate these into audacious conceptions of thought and programs of action commensurate with our revolutionary age.

ANCESTRY AND BACKGROUND OF PROGRESSIVISM

THE GENERAL CHARACTER OF PROGRESSIVIST THOUGHT

Progressivist beliefs, formulated in philosophic terms, embrace two classes: in some matters they are negative and diagnostic; in others they are positive and remedial. The former are expressive of opposition to authoritarianism and absolutism in all its forms, modern as well as ancient: religious, political, ethical, epistemological. The latter are expressive of man's confidence in his own natural powers, particularly his self-regenerative power to face continuously and to overcome satisfactorily the fears, superstitions, and bewilderments of an ever-threatening environment.

The philosophic term popularly used to characterize this outlook is *pragmatism*—a term made famous by a book of this title by William James. Today, although labeled by other terms, such as "instrumentalism" or "experimentalism", pragmatism is still widely held to be the single most original, most typically American of all the philosophies that have been formulated in our history.

Strictly speaking, pragmatism is a theory of logic. As Dewey says, the term "means only the rule of referring all thinking . . . to *consequences* for final meaning and test."[1] For our purposes, we shall use the term to connote an organized expression of beliefs about nature and man, with logic and epistemology its philosophic fulcrum.

Of all the sciences that employ this cultural matrix and have thus contributed to pragmatism—as it has contributed to them—we mention particularly biology, anthropology, psychology, and physics. Biology—because man is seen as an evolving, struggling organism interacting with his animate and inanimate environment. Anthropology—because man is also an organism with a very long history of interactions with his fellows living together in cultures. Psychology—because man is a behaving-thinking animal, subject, no less than other animals, to experimental understanding. And physics—because by means of this and allied sciences, man has proved his astonishing capacity to come to grips with nature.

And yet this very capacity raises a problem of modern culture to which pragmatists never tire of returning. Can human beings, living together in societies, learn in time to transfer their genius in the natural sciences to the human and social sciences? Can they do for themselves what they have done for the soil, for the fluids and energies of matter and space? That they have the competence, pragmatism does not doubt. But that they will learn to use that competence is of considerable doubt. Yet, even on this question, pragmatism is optimistic. Has not the culture of which it is the great liberal herald already shown that striking progress can be made in conquering man's *whole* environment, even including man himself?

The task before us, then, is to specify this competence as

[1] Dewey, *Essays in Experimental Logic*, p. 330.

exactly as possible and at the same time to test it in actual practice. In the language common to pragmatism, what we must do if we are to move ahead is to put ideas to work. We must think not primarily for the sake of thinking but for the sake of doing. We must reject the spurious inheritance of pure intellectualism. First of all, we must apply our minds to the huge job of living. We must reject all doctrines of human helplessness which submit to mysterious, overpowering forces. In this spirit of confidence, education, far from being regarded as a passive conditioner of our existence, must be accepted as the greatest of all cultural instruments.

PHILOSOPHIC THREADS

No philosophy springs full-blown from the soil of a single moment or locality. Although pragmatism is native to our recent American environment, it is also the descendant of a long line of ancestors—a line quite as long as written history.

Some of the philosophic threads woven into the developed pattern of pragmatism-progressivism can be traced as far back as ancient Greece. Heraclitus, for example, expresses the belief that all reality is characterized by constant change, that nothing is permanent except the principle of change itself. In Socrates, we find a noble attempt to fuse epistemology and axiology in the principle that knowledge is the master key to virtue. The Sophist, Protagoras, sketches the theory that both truth and value are relative to time and place.

Even Plato and Aristotle, whose doctrines we shall find to be often in conflict with progressivism, provide it with elements that are by no means trivial. To consider but one example, the temperate spirit of the progressivist outlook is foreshadowed in Aristotle's frequent preference for moderation and compromise.

One cannot always trace the ways such remote influences have entered into this philosophy. Certainly, they are more indirect than those of the earlier "modern" centuries beginning, perhaps, with the seventeenth. No doubt, such philosophers as the Englishmen, Francis Bacon and John Locke, or the Frenchman, Jean Jacques Rousseau, helped to generate the liberalism that is associated with pragmatic and hence progressivist attitudes. Bacon helped by his effort to refine the experimental method; Locke by his doctrine of political freedom; Rousseau by such beliefs as the goodness to be gained simply from being one's natural self. We must also mention the influence of such German thinkers as Immanuel Kant and G. W. F. Hegel. The former attempted to ground a liberal glorification of the individual in the unassailable dignity of human personality; the latter insisted upon the dynamic, ever-readjusting processes of nature and society.

The American philosophic influences flowing into progressivism are easier, though not too easy, to trace. Benjamin Franklin, Thomas Paine, and Thomas Jefferson—the last strongly influenced by Locke—made important contributions. We may note their sophisticated attitude toward religious dogma, their belief in individuals, their vigorous democratic spirit. Such eloquent idealists as William T. Harris and Ralph Waldo Emerson, although closer to essentialism, must not be forgotten. Harris directly influenced Dewey, the most powerful of all progressivists, as did Emerson, whose transcendentalism is flavored with American practicality and common sense.

Not until almost the beginning of the twentieth century, however, did a genuinely "native" outlook and interpretation of American culture begin to emerge. Through many media—through the arts, especially literature (Mark Twain is one example), through the psychological and social sciences, through education and even religion—the young nation began to break its European fetters and to reveal in philosophy an independence of imagination and creative power that it had revealed earlier in political revolution.

Two contributors to this declaration of cultural independence stand high above all others, prior to Dewey himself: Charles S. Peirce and William James. The stature of Peirce has grown steadily through the years although he was little known in his own lifetime.

It was from him that James gained and developed his central philosophic principle: ideas are meaningless unless they make a difference in experience, unless they "work." Peirce is thoroughly scientific, naturalistic, and empirical in his thinking. The entire function of thinking, he says, is to habituate us to action. Feeling, muscular effort—these are such typical manifestations of human activity that it is not only improper but impossible to separate them from the merely intellectual.

The influence of James has, of course, been very great throughout the twentieth century. His famous *Principles of Psychology* is still, in various respects, the foremost single achievement in this field by any American scholar-scientist. His works in philosophy have seemed as a fresh intellectual breeze blowing over the land. As in Peirce, the dominant point of view is one of living organisms that function through experience, action, flowing feelings, habit patterns. Concern is nearly always with the total self viewed in a range of overlapping perspectives—spiritual, emotional, physical.

Although Dewey alone has matched the genius of Peirce and James as a philosophic emancipator, many philosophers, sociologists, and psychologists have absorbed and reworked their beliefs in various ways. One of the most brilliant, George Herbert Mead, strongly stimulated Dewey as well as a number of able American philosophers of pragmatic orientation, such as Charles Morris. Mead's theory of the self, developing out of its active social relations with other selves in a process of continuous communication and role-playing, has grown in influence at a rate comparable, perhaps, only to that of Peirce's ideas. Another distinguished American philosopher, C. I. Lewis, regarded his own distinctive formulation as "conceptual pragmatism," while in Europe the best known spokesman was F. S. C. Schiller, an Englishman.

Only two other pragmatic philosophers may be mentioned: Max Carl Otto and Ernest Nagel. A great university teacher, Otto devastatingly exposed the paraphernalia of traditional philosophy and culture, including the shortcomings of supernatural religion. Nagel, as John Dewey Professor of Philosophy at Columbia University, has achieved preeminence as a philosopher of science.

FOUR CULTURAL INFLUENCES

Other thinkers and movements might readily be added to this list, but here we prefer to emphasize important cultural influences upon progressivism. As its defenders would readily agree, at least four such influences, each closely interrelated with the others and with philosophy as such, are especially significant: the Industrial Revolution, modern science, the rise of democracy, and the American environment. Each is here depicted as concisely as possible.

The Industrial Revolution. This familiar term is used broadly here to mean the era of modern economic change extending from the decline of feudalism to the rise and maturation of capitalism. Rumblings of this change were heard as far back as the fourteenth century, although it was not until the end of the nineteenth and the beginning of the twentieth that the Revolution began to attain its greatest force. During these five or six centuries, the transformations that have taken place throughout the Western and, more recently, the Eastern hemispheres are so breathtaking that even in our own generation we are still seeking to comprehend and adjust ourselves to them. To recall our characterization of philosophy as the expression of beliefs, we are still suffering from the shattering effects of the Industrial Revolution upon the beliefs and conduct of man.

The full impact of the Industrial (more recently characterized as the technological) Revolution upon men's attitudes and habits has been sensed with particular keenness by pragmatist-progressivists. Certainly they have emphasized the gigantic power over natural forces that accompanied the exploration of the earth and the development of machines. At the same time, they have been among the foremost critics of that power.

Modern science. As both cause and effect, modern science has developed in close relation to the Industrial (and technological) Revolution—cause, since science was a chief instrument in the building of machines and the conquest of natural resources; effect, since science was supported and encouraged by the new economy. Science has generously repaid the support and encouragement it received through invention, efficiency, and expansion of the whole productive process.

The chief significance of science to such philosophies as progressivism lies in its powerful new method. It is a method that seeks to meet difficulties continually arising in the course of human adjustments to nature, not by placating fearful and awesome powers or by appeal to authority or dogma, but by scrupulous examination, explanation, and control of the factors in each situation. Mathematics, measurement, laboratory precision come into prominence. Induction (the forming of generalizations from the comparison of particular data) becomes integral with deduction (the logical process of explaining particulars from prior generalizations) in the sense that the scientific method is "hypothetico-deductive."

True, this method began to develop long before the modern era, but its achievements in the last two centuries have been far greater than in all preceding history—achievements still accelerating at breakneck speed. Before the Renaissance, scientists were only vaguely aware of the powerful impact of their own method upon the perplexities of nature and man. But, by the nineteenth century, perhaps no better example of that impact could be selected than the epoch-making *Origin of Species* by Charles Darwin. This is not to say that scientists still accept the evolutionary theory exactly as Darwin developed it. But its major axioms—namely, that plants and animals, including man himself, have a purely natural history, that all living forms are the products of natural selection, and that change implies emergence of new forms from the old—are vastly important for modern philosophy in general and for pragmatism in particular.

The rise of democracy. As are both industry and science, modern democratic society is woven into the design of modern culture—of which all three are parts. Unquestionably, the first two developments speeded the advancing ascendancy of democracy. In order for them to succeed, they had to be unbound from the chains of medieval church and state; above all, they needed political arrangements guaranteeing maximum freedom to the rising bourgeoisie (the young middle class), which carried the torch of their new power. The product of these joint influences was an explosive upsurge of confidence in the capacity and right of men to rule themselves and to direct their own lives.

To be sure, the roots of democracy extend deeper still—into the Judaic-Christian heritage of respect for personality and a faith in human brotherhood, and into the Greek heritage of devotion to rational capacities. But until men had learned how to implement these values through concrete economic, scientific, and social practices they could only dream—they could not actually test out democracy in the laboratories of wide social practice.

A favorable cultural environment. None of these pervasive influences could fructify without a favorable environment. They required an environment that, on the one hand, could provide abundant natural resources, and, on the other hand, would not be too cluttered with the bric-a-brac of earlier beliefs, institutions, customs, habits, faiths.

Such an opportunity loomed from the moment of America's discovery. In its unbelievable fertility, its boundless territory, its rivers, minerals, forests—all of them opening before the awed gaze of its pioneers—the American continent provided ideal conditions for the firm establishment of an industrial order, for unhampered scientific work, and for the practice of democracy.

Naturally, the impress of even earlier periods could not be dismissed. European culture, particularly in some halls of learning (so well exemplified by modern philosophy itself), has continued to our own day to be influential in America. Even able thinkers like Emerson, responding as they did to the thrilling promise of the virgin continent, still seemed oftener to be under the influence of inherited cultural patterns than emancipated by the new.

Nevertheless, a set of beliefs that was characteristically

American began to emerge slowly and to find philosophic expression suitable to our culture. These beliefs, too, are partly the effect of European thought and practice, partly of still wider cultural influences. Yet, when Dewey, particularly, has been called the foremost American philosopher, this is a tribute not only to his technical brilliance but also to the fact that he has so sensitively, and profoundly, expressed a way of life that has come to be regarded as distinctively American.

Accordingly, we shall confine our exposition of pragmatism-progressivism largely to Dewey's own interpretation, but the views of fellow thinkers are included, too, when these seem to contribute. The aim is to understand this American philosophy because it constitutes the theoretical substructure of virtually every principle that has emerged as progressive education.

PROGRESSIVIST BELIEFS ABOUT REALITY

By ontological beliefs, please recall, we mean those expressing attitudes, convictions, and assumptions about what one believes to be fundamentally real as opposed to the unreal, the illusory.

The question is sometimes raised as to whether the progressivist position is grounded in a genuine ontology at all. It repudiates any attempt to discover and describe what James called a "block universe"—a fixed, forever-the-same, predesigned reality. It warns us that whenever we make such an attempt we invariably get lost in a hopeless tangle of arbitrary, meaningless speculations.

In fact, pragmatists doubt whether even the term "*uni*verse" —a term implying that existence is one vast, completed cosmos— is anything more than verbalism. Many of their writings are severe critiques of all doctrines of absolute reality. Throughout the centuries, they contend, these doctrines have allowed their advocates to play the pleasurable but futile game of escaping from practical life into a realm created by and existing largely within otherworldly imaginations. In their opposition to traditional cosmology and metaphysics, pragmatists are philosophic heretics. Here, especially, the theories embraced variously by such terms as philosophic analysis and logical empiricism share a common attitude with pragmatism at the same time that they are often at odds among themselves and critical of pragmatists as well.

If, however, we search for an ontology that faces directly *toward* the here and now—that describes surroundings more modestly, less comprehensively, perhaps, but in the long run, more fruitfully than absolutist doctrines—the key may be found in the titles of three of Dewey's famous works: *Experience and Nature*, *Art as Experience*, and *Experience and Education*. Why is experience the key concept?

Ordinary usage offers the cue. When we assert that a person is "experienced" in business, we mean that he has learned how to perform his job by direct frequent contact with the methods, materials, and people involved. We contrast him with another who has been isolated from such contact—who may be excellently trained but who has not yet put his training to practical tests. We get closest to reality, in short, when we are in the thick of things—when we are tilling the earth or running machines, when we are participating wholeheartedly in the events of our communities, when we are challenged by the never-ending curiosities, hazards, excitements of ordinary personal life.

To immerse ourselves thus in the empirical stream is not at all to conceal either the weaknesses in nature and society or their perfections and strengths. Immediate human experience, with its terrible sufferings, its delights, sorrows, joys, beauties, uglinesses, hatreds, and loves—this is the reality into which, for better or for worse, all men are born and in which they perform their roles until they die. As Peirce expresses it, "Where hope is unchecked by any experience, it is likely that our optimism is extravagant."[2]

Ontological beliefs founded on experience may be said to possess also a strong *evolutionary* quality. Experience is struggle. Life is action and change. Chance, the unexpected, the novel, and unforeseen always play a major role. Men, like other animals, survive and advance as they, too, change and struggle, explore and dare, probe and act.

But, just as certain animals survive more successfully than others because they possess some such capacity as strength of jaw or speed of foot, so man survives because he, too, possesses a function that is more highly developed in him than in any other animal. This, says the pragmatist, is the power of intelligence—the power to remember, to imagine, to relate, to symbolize, to solve problems, and to communicate his thoughts to others of his kind.

Man's mind, accordingly, exists *within* the flow of experience—not at all *outside* of it. Mind is not some mysterious entity that defies scientific explanation. As a matter of fact, it is not an entity, a distinct organ or object, at all. On the contrary, mind behaves in organic relation with the body, the feelings, the habits, and the other responses of the total organism. It exists only in

[2] Peirce, in Fisch (ed.), *Classic American Philosophers*, p. 57.

terms of its activities, of its ways of behaving, of what it does to give definite advantages to the organism of which it is part. It *is*, indeed, what it *does*. But what it does is part and parcel of the tissue of that reality that is man living as a part of nature. Mind is, in essence, an especially important way of experiencing. It is mind*ing*.

Since further attention is given below to the way in which experience as "mind" operates, we shall merely note four additional attributes of the progressivist ontology.

(1) *Experience is dynamic.* It moves at varying rates, pauses at temporary resting places, then once more is on its way. This characteristic suggests that its dynamic action is also rhythmic—a kind of alternating, but never merely repetitive, process of adjustment and readjustment, which ever continues because such is the way of nature. Life is never static. Though rates of change vary immensely, change is everywhere.

(2) *Experience is temporal.* As planets, forests, animals, cultures emerge and develop, they are never quite the same today as they were yesterday. Certainly, they will be different in the days, and years, and centuries to come.

(3) *Experience is spatial.* While experience pushes forward, it pushes also outward, spreading fanwise ever more widely, yet, never reaching the outermost limits of the universe because there are no recognizable outermost limits.

(4) *Experience is pluralistic.* It is composed of a vast network of multiple relations, which are just as real as the things related are real. At once spiritual and material, complex and simple, intellectual and emotional, experience enfolds all of the natural world within itself—the pebbles of the beach, the beasts of the forest, the simplest peasants and wisest statesmen of the human realm.

PROGRESSIVIST BELIEFS ABOUT KNOWLEDGE

IMMEDIATE AND MEDIATE EXPERIENCE

An empirical ontology is indispensable to the pragmatic outlook only as it falls within the range of man's observation, judgment, and control. This does not mean that man, by his power to perceive, literally *creates* objects in his surrounding world. Nature was *there* in that world eons of time before the species *Homo sapiens* emerged upon the evolutionary scale. In remote areas of the heavens and even on our own earth, elements of nature exist that have never once come within the scope of human observation.

But, says the progressivist, having made clear this qualification, all of us distinguish between the *foreground* and the *background* of reality. The distinction is between experience that is in the focus of awareness and that which hovers on the dim periphery. Backgrounds shift to foregrounds as they become resources of reflective processes; foregrounds become backgrounds as they recede for the time being from sharp attention and concern.

A different way of describing our most distinctive human role—the operation of "knowing"—is to consider the relative distinction between two orders of experience: *immediate* and *mediate*. Let us suppose, for example, that at this moment I am relaxing in my armchair so that, without at all expressing what I feel, I achieve a pattern of adjustment, unity, and balance with both my surroundings and myself—with my study, books, pictures, the log fire, the landscape I glimpse outside; with my feelings of the moment, my fleeting thoughts, my quite unconscious breathing and posture.

Experience here is *immediate*. It seems so completely fused, so internally direct and harmonious that, as I experience them, I and my environment are completely unified. This is what Dewey often calls the "undergoing" of an experience; in any case, it certainly is *not* knowledge.

But, let us suppose now that the telephone rings. I lift the receiver to hear a voice cry that an accident has occurred two miles from where I live. A friend is badly hurt. I am wanted there at once. I grab my hat, dash down the stairs and, reaching the corner, peer anxiously along the avenue. What shall I do next? Start walking rapidly? Call a taxicab? Try thumbing a ride? Or, though none is in sight, wait for a streetcar? Which has the best chance of getting me to the accident in the shortest time? Taxi service, I recall, is unreliable and slow. Streetcar service is just as bad. Automobiles move with greater speed, and I've seen students getting rides from friendly passersby. I'll try that, and then, if no one stops, I can count eventually on a streetcar anyway.

Now, this fairly common situation may be regarded as *mediate* experience for the simple reason that, to turn the adjective into a verb, "I mediate." I build a bridge between the starting point, where my sense of equilibrium was disturbed, and the ending point, where once again I shall hope to enjoy equilibrium. The entire episode exemplifies that rhythm of experience epitomized as undergoing-doing-undergoing, where "doing" suggests a span of mediation. Still more centrally, however, it enables us to observe thinking or intelligent behavior in its precise sense of reflection.

The span of mediation is crossed by five familiar but fundamental steps; taken together they constitute an "act of thought." The *first* is little more than a tendency to keep moving on the same even keel in the face of the blunt impact of some obstacle in the flow of immediate experience. In many instances, we do exactly that; an obstacle may be so slight that we glide over it hardly aware that it is there.

Often, however, it stubbornly remains; in such instances, we take a *second* step. We stop, and we observe just what it is that interferes. We recall similar, though not identical, experiences. We weigh, measure, take apart. In short, we estimate the obstacle with whatever care its persistence and its size demand.

The more thorough our task, the more ready we are for another step, the *third*. Here one or two or perhaps dozens of suggestions (taxis, streetcars, walking, automobiles) for conquering the measured obstacle flash across our minds. Such suggestions, when they have reached a point of quite definite specificity and clarity, eventually develop into what Dewey himself sometimes liked to call "ideas."

As we narrow down the possibilities, we take still another step, the *fourth*. Here we imaginatively follow through, or anticipate, the consequences most likely to ensue were we to act upon one or another of the likeliest proposals that have just occurred to us. We *infer* what would happen, without actually overtly testing our inference. This is a privilege that not only saves time but also avoids many of the bumps and bruises that other animals and some human beings suffer by more clumsy, less intelligent, trial and error.

When, however, we are tentatively satisfied that one proposal is promising enough to risk the trial, that it offers most assurance of leading to a resolution of the difficulty that first induced our thought, we take the *fifth* and final step. In other words, we carry through. We test our inference overtly. We *do* in fact what hitherto we only imagined ourselves doing. We discover by experiencing actual effects whether our choice of one rather than another idea was the judicious one.

The plausibility of this theory invites easy misconceptions. Thus, it must not be supposed that people think only when coerced by fears, discomforts, or other maladjustments. To be sure, need is the prime impulse of reflection. Yet it would be foolish to deny that some experts in, let us say, mathematics, manipulate ideas mainly for the joy of symmetry or the stimulation afforded by puzzling ideas.

Equally necessary to avoid is the simplicity that whenever people think they inevitably proceed in the exact sequence of the five steps outlined above. Actually, a person may stop at any point. It may be argued, for example, that thinking ceases with step four whenever, as in the case of more or less exclusively intellectual pursuits, a problem can be solved without strictly overt action.

Reflection, moreover, zigzags back and forth. Consider the frequent need to regress from step three—where suggestions most often occur—to step two, in order to examine and recall other factors that were missing at first. The less sure we are of this or that suggestion, the more we need to be sure that our analysis has been as thorough as possible.

Again, some situations require greater attention to one phase of thinking than to others (such as reasoning out, in step four, the consequences of an intriguing possibility). Yet, in most problematic situations, each phase of thinking functions in relationship to other phases; each step is taken successfully only as one is sure of all the other steps.

Finally, this whole dissection is far more artificial than is the actual process of thinking. For one thing, it is not only at the fifth step that, in a strict sense, action first occurs. Thus, in step two, analysis may require extensive physical manipulation. For another thing, the time taken to complete an act of thought varies tremendously; in many instances, the minor complications arising in daily experiences are met with greater speed than the time required to recount them. Yet, in other instances, hours, days, months, years, or decades are required to break through crucial obstacles. Thus, in the case of a baffling disease (whether of the human body or of the body politic), whole generations may be required to meet the task successfully.

Whether simple or complex, the puzzles that all men face, that all men must attempt to solve, are common grist for the common mill of thought. No chasm divides primitive from highly educated persons. No wall separates a child from a completely mature adult. The degree of care with which they think differs a great deal. The central process does not.

One can understand, then, why mind may be viewed as an ubiquitous instrument with which to operate upon nature and society. Such an operation is frequently crude, but it is also capable of remarkable refinement and dexterity. When of this character, mind is truly *scientific* because of the method it employs—scientific whether utilized by a highly trained physician or by a skillful mechanic with no formal training. The point is that the possession of this precious instrument is by no means the franchise of an intellectual minority. Mind functions at some level whenever man, struggling to survive, tries to solve his daily problems by thinking and acting. Yet, today, it functions far less fruitfully and widely than it must if our culture is to achieve the status of which it is capable—a status governed by intelligence and thus by scientific method everywhere at work.

KNOWLEDGE AND TRUTH

We now come to the progressivist's conception of the character of knowledge and truth. The fruitfulness of ideas is, of course, a common way of stating this conception. For Peirce, an idea acquired true meaning by giving significant relationship to things that previously lacked meaning. For James, the test of truth (or at least *a* test of truth, for he offered several) was the satisfaction a person derives from having worked an idea through to harmonious conclusion and reward in terms of adjustment.

Although James greatly refined this simple pragmatic notion, and although the profundity and complexity of Peirce's philosophy are still being appreciated, it is Dewey who has given instrumentalist logic its most influential treatment. Such ancient terms as inquiry, meaning, judgment, inference, and verification take on rich and sophisticated significance in his creative thinking. Influenced by Mead, he constructed a theory of language that regards communication as the most important of all media of social evolution. With a fellow philosopher, Arthur F. Bentley, he has refined the logical process with extraordinary sophistication and given wide acclaim to the term "transaction" as a key to reflective inquiry. Although we cannot venture here into these technical phases, one point should be emphasized: *the crucial test of whether an idea becomes true is its long-range effectiveness in the conquest of difficulties demanding that reflection shall mediate, thereby permitting us to resume our union with immediate experience.*

To say that an idea turns out to be true when it succeeds in reintegrating experience is to say that one may have innumerable ideas that turn out to be false because they fail to effect such reintegration. If, strictly speaking, ideas become for laymen what hypotheses are for scientists, then all ideas, like all hypotheses, must be weighed with caution. They should rest upon rigorous analysis of the problematic situation out of which they emerge and which they are designed to correct. They should be "thought through" in terms of what would happen if we were to apply them. Finally, they should be tried out in action and rejected or revised whenever found to be inadequate.

But even ideas that produce the consequences desired never remain permanently true. Although some consequences are much more durable than others, each successive problematic situation in which ideas are employed will be different in some slight way from preceding ones. Thus each new problematic situation calls for reinterpretation of ideas that hitherto seemed fairly satisfactory.

Knowledge as "passive." It is, therefore, plausible to contend (at the risk of a more artificial distinction than actual experience in thinking warrants) that we can differentiate between what is strictly "true" and what we merely "know." Although Dewey would perhaps not have approved of this differentiation wholly, there seems to us a sense in which knowledge can be viewed as a kind of reservoir of information, facts, laws, habits, principles, and processes, which each person accumulates as he lives through the interworkings of experience. Further, knowledge is that vastly greater fund that other people have accumulated and from which an individual learns either by direct association with others or by indirect acquaintance through the records they have left. No problem a person confronts is ever so unique that he cannot draw upon his personal memory or the communal store. But some problems remain unsolved precisely because an individual's knowledge remains too limited to provide the cues needed for successful reflection.

Knowledge, we also see, is social as well as individual. An individual's chances of resolving life's recurring difficulties are greatly improved as he becomes acquainted—firsthand and secondhand—with other individuals, groups, nations, races, mores, common practices.

Knowledge, still further, is a product of definite activity. The more often we cope directly with demands of our environment or the richer our experience in practice, the greater our preparation is for inevitable demands of the future.

Knowledge, therefore, grows. New experiences constantly enrich and change the import of whatever we already know. By these same terms, however, knowledge always falls short of perfection. We cannot guarantee that what, by the test of its success yesterday, turned out to be true will necessarily be true tomorrow by mere repetition of that test.

Truth as "active." At this point the relation of truth and knowledge begins to crystallize. Knowledge, we might say for purposes of classification, is comparatively *passive*; it is cumulation of experiences and information waiting to be used again. Every truth, on the other hand, is comparatively *active*—the particular *result* of knowing, of choosing and directing some segment of knowledge through the hazards of a rough terrain. It is the effect of a mediating process, which invariably reshapes that segment so as to qualify, rearrange, and supplement the content of the knowledge reservoir itself. To search for any particular truth would be impossible without a general fund of knowledge. But a general fund of knowledge is itself an accumulation of those products of active mediation that are designated as truths—a fund that would remain forever sterile and inert except for new truths.

To assure that this relationship is clear, let us consider the example above: my imperative need to reach an accident. As I rehearsed various means in my imagination, I was recalling whatever "knowledge" I might already possess. In this case, knowledge had been obtained mainly from actual experience in getting from one place to another rather than from reports of how others had done so. Yet the idea that seemed most likely to succeed in this emergency—thumbing an automobile ride—was one that I had never tried. I had only seen students utilize the idea, with enviable results. Here, therefore, was a simple case of what might be termed *indirect* knowledge; I could not really claim this particular experience as my own without having applied it to the fresh problem that I was now trying to meet.

Having once resolved to test out my preferred idea (or hypothesis, the more formal term), it was essential that my store of *general* knowledge of travel in cities be applied to this *specific* case. I had to decide whether my best chance of stopping a car would be at one point on the avenue, or at the stop-and-go light a half block ahead. I had also to decide whether, imitating successful connoisseurs of this art of the machine age, I should jerk my thumb in rhythmic intervals or whether I should step into the middle of the street and frantically wave my arms. When, within a moment, I had decided upon the stop-and-go light for my point of trial; when, within a minute, I had flagged a car and caught my ride; when, within ten minutes, I had reached the accident; when, accordingly, my idea was carried out and unified with action—then my previous knowledge of transportation as a means of connecting two geographically separated points had become definitely modified as "truth."

I would probably remember this experience, then, and at the next relevant experience would dip into a richer reservoir of knowledge than I had possessed before. I would be more confident. Yet, I would also find that my greater knowledge had undergone still further revision through the need to apply it to a situation not wholly like the previous one. It would be a situation, therefore, in which once more my knowledge would be submitted to the means of thinking and testing—to the criterion of whether such means could produce an anticipated end and, thus, still another truth.

Intelligence and operationalism. Dewey often emphasized his preference for the term "intelligence" to such terms as knowledge," "truth," or "mind," freighted as they are with historic connotations that pragmatism rejects. Intelligence is, in essence, the experimental way of living, the central method of human interaction with environment. In Dewey's richly meaningful language it is ". . . the product and expression of cumulative funding of the meanings reached . . ." in ". . . special inquiries (undertaken because of the presence of problems). . . ."[3] Here "product" implies the dependence of intelligence upon past experience, past knowledge; "expression" implies the active functioning of intelligence in the ongoing present; and "special inquiries" implies the particular difficulties of experience by which intelligent behavior is always motivated.

In still other words, intelligence is the habit of dealing with nature not by blind obedience or routine but by the relationship of what we have previously known to what we do not yet know for certain. It is a habit that enables us to maintain continuity between the two by means of richer, more productive relationships, interpreted and reinterpreted according to the consequences that they produce. Whether these consequences are more properly called "knowledge" or "truth" is of less importance than that they are dependable only to the degree that they meet the canons of experimental inquiry.

Pragmatic epistemology may also be regarded, accordingly, as an anticipation and expression of the theory termed "operationalism." First stated by Peirce and developed by such philosopher-scientists as P. W. Bridgman, operationalism regards even the most universal laws of nature as tools of scientific interpretation and control rather than as objective, fixed, eternal ordinances. Actually, science as a whole is treated as such a tool. By means of it, man engages in the manipulation of the raw materials of the physical,

[3] Dewey in Schilpp (ed.), *The Philosophy of John Dewey*, p. 521.

biological, and other spheres, brings them within the compass of conceptual relations, formulates hypotheses, and tests them under laboratory conditions. As the surgeon *operates* upon a sick body after diagnosis and consideration of various possible cures and relevant laws of medicine, so the chemist or sociologist operates in comparable fashion upon bodies made up, respectively, of material compounds or human groups.

The operational method of utilizing ideas has already been implied, both by the concept of culturology and by the concepts of progressivism, essentialism, perennialism, and reconstructionism. It will be recalled that all of these are to be regarded as *symbols* by which to organize and explain patterns of culture and education. *They are not objective systems or existences but fruitful ways of approaching and interpreting human problems.* And they are continually subject to modification, further clarification, and fresh application to the evolving character of education as a personal and social experience.

PROGRESSIVIST BELIEFS ABOUT VALUE

AN EMPIRICAL APPROACH

Turn now to axiology, the third philosophic area underlying progressivism. A first relevant point is that values are profoundly related both to beliefs about reality and about knowledge.

On the one hand, values arise out of the desires, urges, feelings, and habits of human beings—values that we possess both as biological and social animals. In this sense they are quite as real as any other facts, events, experiences. On the other hand, values are closely related to knowledge. If the test of ideas is the effectiveness with which they bring readjustments to immediate experience, then one may, indeed, contend that an idea is true when it is ultimately good and good when ultimately true. For values are, after all, "identical with goods that are the fruit of intelligently directed activity. . . ."[4] What, then, is the place of values in this potent philosophy?

The answer to this question requires a further refining of terms. An operational distinction somewhat parallel to mediate and immediate experience is to classify values as *instrumental* and *intrinsic*. Strictly speaking, instrumental values are those we attach to experiences that serve as a means to some desired end other than themselves. An operation for appendicitis has an instru-

[4] Dewey, *The Quest for Certainty*, p. 286.

mental value: an individual hardly cherishes the experience for its own sake; he endures the pain, the inconvenience, and the expense because of the restoration of health that it offers as a reward. Health may be taken to exemplify an intrinsic value. A normal person cherishes good health because it is immediately satisfying. In this sense, we may speak of health as a kind of good in itself.

Progressivism is careful to warn, however, against any sharp distinction between these two classes of value. In some contexts, instrumental values themselves become intrinsic; in others, intrinsic values seem largely instrumental. Thus an operation often gives to the surgeon who performs it a certain intrinsic satisfaction that he has done his work with precision and fine skill; at the moment, he may not think much beyond the operation to the beneficial effects that will follow for the patient. But health is, in some ways, as much an instrument as an intrinsic value. Even though most individuals regard this value as immediately good, it is also regarded as a necessary means to economic opportunity, leadership, successful education—indeed, to a variety of ends extending far beyond itself.

Strictly speaking, all values—instrumental and intrinsic alike—are properly so labeled only as they emerge from the process of reflective deliberation. To feel a pleasurable sensation, let us say, is not even intrinsically good until it has become meaningful through experiences involving the activities of mind. In this sense intrinsic values bear some analogy to knowledge. They are cumulations of human experience that we continue to cherish as moral habits, traditions, symbols, immediacies. Instrumental values, by this analogy, are closer to truths, in the sense that they are freshly created effects of intelligence in controlling the moral aspects of life. Like most analogies, however, this one is far from exact. The two kinds of value depend on each other, even as knowledge and truth do.

Another helpful, if equally artificial, distinction appears between *social* and *personal* values. In the first place, all values inevitably reveal a social quality. Individuals learn better to appreciate good health, let us say, as they associate with other healthy individuals. (Health is here taken to mean freedom from the many varieties of political and psychological disease as well as from contagious and organic physical diseases.) Certainly both the social and medical sciences become instruments of good health today because of the wide *sharing* of discoveries, diagnoses, and cures by countless experimenters across both centuries and national boundaries.

The social character of values appears to be still more fundamental when we analyze the self. In order that the individual may become a self at all he must actively participate in a community of selves. The infant is not born a personality; he becomes one as he is gradually made conscious of his self by becoming conscious of other personalities. This occurs as the young child learns to communicate—a process that involves the anticipation of responses that others make to his own vocal, written, overt gestures. Through these responses, he discovers that other selves exist and that he, too, is a self with similar desires and capacities.

In the second place, values are personal. Pragmatic axiology disagrees emphatically with theories sometimes advanced that all doctrines of good and evil are little more than traditions, folkways, mores molded into individual life by streams of tribal evolution. Not that we can ignore the heavy residue that these streams deposit upon all human experience. But pragmatism does refute the simple equating of custom, let us say, with moral standards. Just as inherited bodies of knowledge are essential to but not identical with the truth-seeking process in its concern with current problems, so rules of right and wrong that each present generation inherits from *past* generations are essential to, but not identical with, what may be most distinctly valuable for individuals *now*. After all, societies exist only insofar as individual human beings exist. There can be no such thing as a society without individuals, or vice versa. Even though it be equally true that individuals apart from society have no meaning, either to themselves or to others, we must never forget that individuals do have the intelligence and the potential power to criticize, reject, or qualify whatever social standards of good and evil they find prevailing at a given time.

We conclude that for the pragmatic philosophy values constantly develop in the interplay between fresh personal experiences and cultural deposits—experiences that only real individuals, after all, can have, examine, direct. We conclude, also, that values not tested and retested by intelligence are scarcely worthy of being labeled values at all. They become little more than clichés or pious slogans on a very low plateau of social routine.

Such an axiology as pragmatism's avoids dogmatic commandments or rigid moral axioms. Values, as an integral part of experience, are relative, temporal, dynamic. Just as in physics or biology, laws should be defined as instruments of operation and control that often require revision in achieving scientific truths, so laws that express convictions about values likewise need constant redefinition and reapplication in our striving world of morals.

Values such as *growth* thus come to be strongly emphasized. When an organism grows, it adds steadily to its life by broadening its connections with cross sections of the present cultural and natural environment. Simultaneously, it explores endless opportunities for adventurous experience that time so abundantly provides. Growth affords, in a sense, its own sufficient criterion of value: it is relative to itself and therefore intrinsically good. But it is also relative to further growth and, therefore, also good instrumentally.

Dewey found in this value the nucleus of all pragmatic values:

> . . . the process of growth, of improvement and progress, rather than the static outcome and result, becomes the significant thing. Not health as an end fixed once and for all, but the needed improvement in health—a continual process—is the end and good. The end is no longer a terminus or limit to be reached. It is the active process of transforming the existing situation. Not perfection as a final goal, but the ever-enduring process of perfecting, maturing, refining is the aim of living. Honesty, industry, temperance, justice, like health, wealth and learning, are not goods to be possessed as they would be if they expressed fixed ends to be attained. They are directions of change in the quality of experience. Growth itself is the only moral "end."[5]

THE PRAGMATIC APPROACH TO ART

Various students of Dewey have remarked that his great study of esthetics may eventually come to be regarded as his most enduring contribution to philosophy. In any case, no achievement of any pragmatist more completely challenges traditional philosophies of life as well as of art or more richly expresses the healthful energy, the this-worldliness, the breadth and depth of human experience.

Values properly designated "esthetic" emphasize the *undergoing* phase of man's development—the having and enjoying of an experience. This is what Dewey often called the "consummatory" moment in the rhythm of continuous interplay between individuals and their surroundings. Such values are, of course, related

[5] Dewey, *Reconstruction in Philosophy*, p. 177.

not only to values of other kinds but also to reality and knowledge. They are not to be pigeonholed according to some static formula of classification; rather they are regarded as events within the time flow of nature.

One who loses oneself in the mood of fulfillment expressed in a symphony, a painting, or in a humbler object such as a flower garden is thereby attaining esthetic value. This is true whether the individual has himself given shape to the particular work of art or has simply shared it sympathetically with its creator. The important point is the wholeness, completeness, harmony that a composer or painter, listener or spectator achieves by identifying himself with whatever experience is designed—that is, carried through to a new balance of the forces and materials indigenous to it.

Thus it is that art emerges from "the live creature" of nature. Although it occurs only at the cost of tension, imbalance, and disequilibrium, its culmination is its own reward. In Dewey's characteristic terms: ". . . only when an organism shares in the ordered relations of its environment does it secure the stability essential to living. And when the participation comes after a phase of disruption and conflict, it bears within itself the germs of a consummation akin to the esthetic."[6] As art this consummation takes a multitude of forms: a pair of well-made shoes, a graceful dish, a bridge, a carefully planned street, a play, a dance. Great art, then, does not isolate itself from life. On the contrary, it strives through countless media to enrich the meaning of whatever in experience is most vital and significant.

It follows that the pragmatic philosophy regards science and art not as separate but as complementary achievements. Notwithstanding the strong emphasis placed upon the consummatory or intrinsic phase of creative experience, art also demands full utilization of the reflective, or, more precisely, the instrumental phase. Such utilization is perhaps more apparent in some arts than in others; the so-called applied arts (for example, weaving, metalwork, ceramics) obviously require a wide range of practical and technological skills, processes, and knowledge. But even the so-called fine arts (Dewey was skeptical of any rigid distinction between the fine arts and the applied arts) have similar requirements: music depends upon mathematically stated tempos; painting, upon spatial principles.

Indeed, any idea that art requires less exacting or active in-

[6] Dewey, *Art as Experience*, p. 15.

telligence, strictly defined, than does science is completely spurious. The difference, again, is one of emphasis, not of kind. Both utilize essentially the same experiences of nature; both try to bring these experiences and man into a more meaningful relation. The artist, like the scientist, faces problems and tries to think them through and to *do* something about them. The need of readjustment because of maladjustment is just as real to him as it is to the scientist—often, perhaps, more real in the sense of being more directly and passionately felt.

The artist, however, tends to identify himself more immediately with the qualitative material of his particular medium of expression, and he is always intensely concerned to attain the fulfillment of form that that material (social events, stone, paint, steel, words, bodily rhythms, musical notes) challenges him to fulfill. The scientist, in contrast, is often less intimately identified with the material (the mathematical physicist works almost entirely with abstract symbols). Typically, he regards the "doing" events of his experience as of more strategic importance than the "undergoing" events, which, we noted, highlight the esthetic mood.

DEMOCRACY AS VALUE

The rise of modern democratic states, as indicated above, has been one of the major sources of this American philosophy. Distinguished pragmatists do not, however, confine democracy to a political definition. It is political, to be sure. But it is much more—a pattern and program for the whole range of life. Democracy is a challenging expression of values, attitudes, and practices. It is an ideal that we win in the very process of fulfilling it, an object worthy of religious faith, and, in a certain sense, a work of art.

Democracy has already been encountered in this sketch of progressivist beliefs. Ontologically, the democratic way is that dynamic and interdependent *experience* that is living at its best. It is an outlet for some of the deepest drives of the individual—that is, for his need of dignity, respect, association, and responsibility.

Epistemologically, democracy is both seed and fruit of the widest practice of *intelligence*. It is a questing for truths that, in its most carefully delineated sense, is nothing less than science operating in and through the intermingling of men with their environments. In different words, it is the life of reflection applied to social intercourse. Inevitable issues of concrete group relationships are faced not merely by selfish interest and blind appeal to precedent or violence but, by the same type of diagnosis, they are a searching for hypotheses and experimental programs that the individual relies upon when he applies his intelligence to difficulties more narrowly his own. If thinking, like communication, is a phenomenon of the *social* self, then democracy is the institutionalization of that social self. In a broad sense, it is the five steps of the act of thought, writ large, in the efforts of people to meet the recurring issues of their communal life.

Axiologically, the meaning of democracy has already been inferred. Its values are both instrumental and intrinsic. As a plausible ideal, it is "the *pursuit* of happiness," the steady effort to find mediating ways to the attainment of adequate ends, but it is also the immediate satisfactions enjoyed by such attainment. Democracy is both individual and social. *Each personality* requires the greatest opportunity and freedom to solve the problems that are distinctively his; but at the same time he so much needs the strength and experience of *other personalities* that, without them, his own freedom or equality is largely an illusion. Finally, democracy is symbolic of the supreme value of growth. It is not a fixed objective toward which we strive but that we can never hope to reach; it develops wherever and whenever men, within the flow of history, associate in mutual respect. If democracy has a moral meaning, as Dewey said, it is this: ". . . the supreme test of all political institutions and industrial arrangements shall be the contribution they make to the all-round growth of every member of society."[7] We win democracy, in short, only as we *practice* it at every stage along the way—within our homes, clubs, trade unions, businesses, schools, states, and perhaps, eventually, within a family of nations.

The winning of democracy by practicing it implies that democracy conceived as value should be regarded as both critique and norm of human experiences. Far from being merely a phenomenon to be described objectively and neutrally, it becomes, on the one hand, an instrument for criticizing individual and social weaknesses and, on the other hand, a norm or standard toward which men should strive in order that the life of democracy can prevail. Let us briefly consider this key value from both points of view.

As *critique*, democracy calls sharp attention to social obsolescences and failures of both the past and the present. Governments enforcing obedience to monarchic, autocratic, or theocratic power; economic systems exploiting many individuals by compelling them to toil for the benefit of a few other individuals; cultures

[7] Dewey, *Reconstruction in Philosophy*, p. 186.

stratifying and segregating races, classes, and creeds—all these, and many other failures, are condemned. Contemporary society is judged guilty on a long list of counts: blind acceptance of dogma or outworn custom; meek subjection of uncounted millions to religious, political, or economic hierarchies, widespread discrimination against minorities; lack of economic and other forms of opportunity, a lack that frustrates or destroys ambitions and abilities; absence of scientific planning by social institutions. Little wonder that the pragmatist is hostile to all doctrines that are openly or surreptitiously totalitarian. He opposes fascism, religious authoritarianism, and Soviet Communism alike in that they are inimical to the value of democracy.

As *norm,* the democratic value is the closest approximation to any ultimate ideal that the pragmatist-progressivist is willing to accept. We say closest *approximation* because his experimental temperament compels the pragmatist to admit that such a norm might conceivably be reshaped by the long course of events ahead of us, until even it no longer could be regarded as truly democratic. To consider such a contingency at the present stage of history is, however, to quibble over the improbable, to raise a merely academic question. To our own culture, and to all cultures as far as we can see, *democracy symbolizes that kind of growing life in which, first, each person consciously seeks and finds the fullest and the most varied satisfactions of his own capacities and in which, second, each group of persons seeks and finds comparable satisfactions through interplay with other groups.* Thus, the degree to which democracy ever manifests itself is the degree to which such a measure can be adequately met. In this framework, men may rally 'round it as a religious symbol of "a common faith" in their capacity to rule over all nature, over all groups, and over themselves—and to do so in an ever more rational, more generous, more humane and cooperative way.

Finally, democracy for the pragmatic philosophy may be regarded, profoundly, as a cultural work of art. If, as we have observed, art is at its core the free expression and consummation of creative human energies, then the democratic process becomes art at its very best. It is the privilege of each man to control, reshape earth and culture so that both he and his fellows are invigorated and enriched.

Like all values that we think of as esthetic, democracy is by no means, then, solely intellectual. The joy a person feels in freedom, in achievement and growth, in comradeship with others working with a sense of common aim, even in appreciation of the harmony and order of a culture that the majority of men themselves design and regulate for their own purposes—the joy inherent in these experiences points to the fact that democracy is warmed and colored by creativity in its varied hues of feeling, change, rhythm, tension, struggle, balance, movement. The greatest art, the richest consummatory experience that human beings in modern life are capable of undergoing, is democracy itself.

These, then, are among the more basic beliefs undergirding progressive education. Our treatment has surely not been comprehensive, and our interpretation, conditioned by a point of view, has doubtless affected what strives to be a friendly overview. Our main purpose has been to highlight general features of particular importance to the progressivist theory and program of schooling. To these, we now turn.

CHAPTER 6

The progressivist pattern of educational beliefs

PROGRESSIVISM THEORY IN FOCUS

PROGRESSIVISM, the term, is here used more strictly to denote a cluster of systematic beliefs about education, which rests upon another cluster of harmonious and systematic beliefs about philosophy—the American philosophy denoted by such terms as pragmatism, instrumentalism, and experimentalism. To change the metaphor, the beliefs outlined in the preceding chapter can be regarded as substructure and the beliefs outlined in this chapter as superstructure. If we were to carry this metaphor still further, we imagine that the superstructure, in turn, consists of two stories: the first, educational theory; the second, concrete practice in school and community.

Actually, these ascending levels only roughly approximate the relationship between theory and practice. For one thing, progressivism as education and pragmatism as philosophy have been fused to an extraordinary extent through the work of Dewey. Far more insistently than any influential American philosopher, he maintained that the philosophy of education, properly understood, is also a philosophy of life. His first great decade of influence (1894 to 1904 at the University of Chicago), during which many of his most fundamental views were formulated, was a period of fruitful educational as well as technical philosophizing. After that time, he devoted more of his attention to exploring the areas of ontology, epistemology, and axiology. But his interest in education never waned in the least, and the channel between education and wider philosophic areas was likewise kept open by able disciples.

But the free flow of ideas was not limited even to philosophy combined with educational theory. Experimental application of pragmatism-progressivism to practice, which began toward the close of the nineteenth century, and in which Dewey pioneered through his own laboratory school, accelerated in the twentieth century. Pragmatism as formulated by Peirce, enriched by James, and matured by Dewey, has now permeated directly or indirectly a fair proportion of all public schools in America. It has affected the characters of generations of young people. And it has influenced uncounted teachers and pupils in other countries.

We cannot be specifically concerned here with the "second story" of day-by-day experimentation. But it is important at least to note that any effort to distinguish philosophy, educational theory, and educational practice by rigidly delimited categories does violence to the facts. As much as any influential philosophy of our time, pragmatism-progressivism has insisted upon the interdependence, the continuity, and interaction of all kinds of experience, however theoretical at one extreme, however practical at the other. More than this, it has viewed all kinds of human experience, of thinking and of acting alike, as dynamic manifestations of culture.

This is not, of course, to maintain that all educational progressivists are equally conscious of, or consistent in, their reliance upon underlying philosophic principles. The fact is that influential spokesmen sometimes go so far as to deny any logical relation between, let us say, pragmatic epistemology and progressivist methods of learning. Such attitudes are a reflection, however, not so much on the basic nature of pragmatist-progressivist thought as upon the eclecticism or superficiality of some of their spokesmen. Certainly, as this position is symbolized by Dewey—and who, after all, is a better symbol?—progressivism should be viewed as the conspicuous inlay of a huge cultural mosaic. It is a mosaic in which general philosophy, school practice, and wider institutional patterns are all significant parts. To an important degree, this same complex fusion will become apparent when we study in later pages the three remaining interpretations of education—essentialism, perennialism, and reconstructionism—as well as interweaving influences such as neo-Marxism, existentialism, neo-Freudianism, and others.

BACKGROUNDS OF PROGRESSIVE EDUCATION

EUROPEAN INFLUENCES

Just as strands of direct or indirect influence on philosophic thought can be traced through intellectual history from ancient Greek speculation to American pragmatism, so strands of influence can be traced through the history of educational thought. To mention one, note Plato's insistence that his leaders experience, as part of their long educational training, years of "learning by doing" in the rough-and-tumble environment of politics and war.

But it is from the Renaissance world with its revolts against medieval authoritarianism that "the new education" (as it is sometimes called) obtains more of its germinal ideas. Johann Comenius, for example, discovered a whole array of visionary proposals. Although his views influenced other theoretical positions besides progressivism, nevertheless his beliefs in "work experience" and in fitting instruction to the child, rather than the converse, are astonishingly modern in early childhood education.

A philosopher-educator still more clairvoyant was Jean Jacques Rousseau. One of the great prophets of the French Revolution, he was concerned, above all, to establish a profound faith in the natural power of man. Rousseau prepared the ground, as no one before him had, for what came to be known in our century as "the child-centered school"—one of progressivism's most fertile conceptions. He was concerned, above all, to encourage children to express their natural impulses; accordingly, he opposed the stern discipline and forced "learning" that characterized the schools of his day. This is not to say that Rousseau's beliefs have been embodied in progressivism in the way he expressed them. Dewey himself was critical of such inadequacies as his romantic and sentimental faith in the innate goodness of man. Nevertheless, Rousseau's has been one of the most powerful influences in behalf of an education that would free children from fear and superstition, or adults from domination by political and religious potentates—an education centering on man as a natural and social creature capable of mature, cooperative self-direction.

As with Comenius, it would be difficult to say whether the great educational triumvirate of the Enlightenment—Johann Pestalozzi, Johann Herbart, and Friedrich Froebel—have had a greater influence on progressivism or on essentialism. As writers of their age, all three (but particularly Herbart) remained apologists for the dominant culture while, at the same time, offering innovations in education that were genuine and modern.

Pestalozzi, for example, often seems as strong a proponent of "self-activity" as Comenius or Rousseau. Direct observation rather than mere verbal learning, creative work, family life as educational experience—these are typically progressivist heresies. Herbart anticipated the concept of the "whole child" by insisting upon harmonious and justly proportioned development of all the learner's capacities, a development made possible educationally by building upon cumulative interests. Froebel, known as the founder of the kindergarten, insisted, with Comenius and Rousseau, upon the right of the child to be free in expressing his nature. Thus he conceived the role of the teacher as guide, not as commander. He was one of the first to regard play and games as rich learning experience. As in Pestalozzi, too, discipline becomes more a matter of cooperation based upon love for children than a military regulation enforced by threats of reprisal.

AMERICAN INFLUENCES

Granting that the strongest influences upon progressivism in America were not primarily theoretical but rather cultural in the sense discussed in Chapter 5, nevertheless, certain directly educational influences did lend added strength to progressivism's mature interpretation. James, for example, influenced the profession through his *Talks to Teachers on Psychology* which expounded his characteristic belief that the strengthening of acquired habits in behalf of individual well-being is the essence of good education.

More directly influential was the monumental leadership of Horace Mann, Henry Barnard, and Francis Parker. Although none of these three educators was a first-rate theorist, each was a forerunner of progressivism. In Mann, one senses the deep faith of a pioneering democrat—an educator who actually believed, a century ago, that schools can become agents of social reform! Barnard, although more conservative, became one of the first influential opponents of private schools as class-divisive and one of the first proponents of public schools as class-unifying.

Among these great frontiersmen of the American public school system, it was Francis Parker who manifested most strikingly the early spirit of progressivism. Much of the revolutionary romanticism of Rousseau and Froebel was regenerated in Parker's brimming optimism, his faith in children, his love of nature. Probably more than any professional leader before our own day, he insisted upon a central place in education for the creative arts and for creative work—an insistence that bore abundant fruit in his own experimental schools at Quincy, Massachusetts, and

Chicago. Like James, he was strongly individualistic (he always made the self supremely important) ; but, more than most progressivists before or since, Parker did not hesitate to criticize frankly our socioeconomic system for its failure to provide sufficient security and opportunity for enough ordinary people.

Many other American educators might be mentioned as early contributors. Felix Adler, founder of the Ethical Culture Society, is one. Others, less theoretical, but nonetheless important because of their pioneering in laboratory schools, include Junius L. Meriam and Marietta Johnson.

While Dewey, of course, remains the dominant intellectual force behind progressivism, two American philosophers of education stand above all others as devoted and able interpreters and original supplementers of his work: William H. Kilpatrick and Boyd Bode. Both scholars successfully restated the original beliefs of pragmatism for teachers, students, administrators, and parents. Both have been so articulately concerned with the psychology of learning that our section below on this subject draws often upon their formulations. Both have positive convictions about the power of education to determine the course of history in an increasingly democratic direction.

Others of varying influence and originality have been identified intermittently with the John Dewey Society, both in the United States and in other countries—most notably, perhaps, in Japan. Some of these thinkers, too, have strongly influenced progressivist beliefs about learning, curriculum, and control—the three large areas of educational theory to which we now turn.

PROGRESSIVIST BELIEFS ABOUT LEARNING

THE CHILD IN HIS ENVIRONMENT

The child is an experiencing organism, an integral part of the flow of events, relations, feelings, thoughts, things. Thus we need to approach him as a natural being, associated with other natural beings and, like any other object of nature, subject to scientific analysis and individual development.

It follows that the child's behavior is wholly within the realm of his experience. In some respects, he is an animal more like than different from other animals. For he, too, is engaged in the recurrent conflicts, the defeats and victories, of nature. He, too, is immersed within the endless stream of emergent change.

Nevertheless, the child's powers are very different in their potential refinement and complexity from those of even the highest nonhuman animals. This is especially true of his intelligence, his ability to face and resolve problems. It is this ability that has enabled his species to achieve its mastery over all lower species as well as over inanimate nature. Accordingly, it is the practice and improvement of intelligence that is central to education.

The school is "good" when it enables him to grow through such experience, when it provides ways of expression for his total behavior pattern, when it permits him to act in relationship to the actions of others. It is "bad" when it blocks expression of his feelings, when it denies satisfaction to his curiosity, when it turns him away from his own problems and interests, when it fails to provide opportunity for him to cope with them directly, overtly, experimentally.

The progressivist general psychological viewpoint may now be epitomized in six important generalizations.

(1) *This psychology definitely, consistently applies the underlying pragmatic philosophy.* It is a way of looking through the triple lenses of reality, knowledge, and value as defined by such philosophers as Peirce, James, and, above all, Dewey. The more polished these lenses and the more expertly we learn how to adjust them so that the image of the child in his environment is seen as an integrated whole, the more clearly we shall have perceived the vibrant core of progressive education. Thus, for example, the ontological influence of organic evolution is strong in a psychology asserting that all animal and, therefore, all human life is characterized by natural processes requiring careful scientific explanations. Thus, too, the dynamic, re-creative qualities of reality are epitomized in the nature of the child: in his zestful enthusiasms, his eagerness, his amazing sensitivity and responsiveness, his endless questionings and discoveries—most important of all, perhaps, in the fact that the child repeatedly modifies and is modified by the experiences through which his behavior develops.

(2) *As a direct inference from our first generalization, learn-itself becomes a natural experience.* In a comprehensive sense, it is simply the recurring effort of every organism to remove obstacles and reduce disturbances by building new responses into its own patterns of development. The smallest child learns, as his tendencies and responses are more and more organized, to select some stimuli from among the welter that impinge upon him and to assimilate

and react to these more than to others. From this viewpoint, learning is as functional to organic life as, say, nourishment. And, like the latter, it is most fully operative only when accompanied by appetite—appetite for the experiences that endlessly confront human beings as they explore their bewildering but intriguing world.

(3) *Such a view of learning means that "the whole child" is necessarily involved in learning, not only his "mind."* Mind is, in any case, simply a term for relatively specialized behavior: it is the function that seeks to exercise deliberate control over one's relations by foreseeing consequences and meanings in events. Hence, even the most intellectual processes are not cut off from feeling in some form, from habit, and from bodily response. On the less refined levels of experience, learning is certain to embrace —at least as intimately as on more refined levels of experience—the muscular, glandular, emotional, and other constituents of any total structure of behavior.

(4) *The child's surroundings are as fundamental to his nature as is his own body, which, in a way, is also part of his surroundings.* The self is always social and, as the child learns with his whole nature not with something separate called a "mind," his learning requires the steady aid of his environment. Each cooperates in changing the other.

(5) *Learning functions on rising levels of complexity, the highest of which is intelligence.* We should hardly say that the rabbit is able to reflect intelligently; we do say that he learns. Apes not only learn but apparently show considerable intelligence. But men often learn also as lower animals do; they build responses into their behavior by sheer trial and error, impulsive acts, hasty choices, which involve, at most, one or two steps in the act of thought. The point is that reflection differs from other kinds of learning more in degree than in kind. Reflection is more cautious, thorough, analytical, constructive, imaginative, and certainly more dependable than learning that is more overt, fumbling, and direct.

(6) *Several concepts concerning the nature of the child, although still held by influential traditional psychologies, are rejected.* The child is not endowed with innate mental attributes; he conceals no chrysalises of intellect that unfold their wings at the proper time. Nor is the child a mechanism that responds to stimuli in the environment as

> a motor responds to drops of gasoline. In short, he is neither a "soul stuff" to which bodily activities have little immediate relationship nor mere atomic particles in which mental processes are altogether physical. In the older language of psychology, the child is not all mind or all matter for the excellent reason that he is both at once.

By "both," however, the progressivist again must explain what he does *not* mean. He denies that the physical and the mental are parallel planes of human existence or that they are ultimately always separate, dualized, static, and discrete substances or elements. The older psychology's concept of "instincts," to consider one example, is replaced by a concept of plastic, overlapping tendencies which are capable of being modified and directed in manifold ways. Likewise, progressivism discards the widely held theory that response follows stimulus in a one-two order of cause and effect, that behavior is merely the product of exercising and strengthening sequences or bonds of stimulus-response. Agreeing that a given stimulus helps to determine the nature of the particular response, progressivism holds that the responses of which the child is capable (according to his capacities, interests, habits, environment) are themselves selectors and conditioners of particular stimuli. The child *invites* a certain stimulus because he has been conditioned to invite it. Response and stimulus are thus *interactive* because each is a function of the other.

LIVING AS LEARNING: AN ILLUSTRATION

In order to apply these generalizations more concretely to the progressivist theory of learning, we select for illustration a timely controversial problem—juvenile delinquency. That this problem is becoming dangerously chronic in many American communities, that, perhaps, its most dangerous aspect has been the increase of drugs among youth in their teens, few observers could deny.

American educational leaders also recognize the existence of this problem. They may even admit, on occasion, that maladjustments in family life induced by such factors as family migration and employment of both parents, by strains of insecurity and false allurements of success create new tasks for public education. Yet even when these leaders have not been wholly preoccupied with teacher competencies, budgets, and curriculum routines, they often hesitate to examine forthrightly the nature of the community, or their students' own family and social values. Some hesitate because they regard the curriculum as already overfilled with more important subject matter—some because they fear reprisals from religious, patriotic, or other groups who consider such values to lie beyond the proper boundaries of education.

Does this mean, then, that most young people are learning nothing about the habits and morals of youth as these are exemplified by such fads as drug-taking? The question is rhetorical. Of course, they are learning. They are learning when conflicts or tensions occur at home. They are learning from their classmates, in neighborhood gangs, in dance halls, from movies, down the alley, behind the barn, at the neighborhood "joint." They are learning afternoons and weekends, when school is out. They are often learning when they least recognize that they are learning at all.

The progressivist does not ask us to choose, then, between learning in school and nonlearning out of school. Rather, the issue is between *two kinds of learning*. One is expertly directed toward constructive consequences; the other is nondirected and determined by unexamined, conflicting behavior. The difference, in other words, is between what Dewey calls genuinely *educative* as against *miseducative* learning. One stimulates growth and enriches personal and social relations; the other weakens or destroys the individual's capacity to grow.

In short, if education is to deal with juvenile delinquency, it must shift radically away from traditional structures of fixed courses, fixed hours, fixed rules, fixed objectives and toward widening patterns of subject matter that encompass nothing less than the entire, complex environment. If drugs are tempting to many young people, then the serious problems they generate are important to the school. If family stability is important to them, then that is important to the school. If sexual experience is important to them, then the school program should reach out into the late afternoons and evenings, into weekends and summers, and should extend throughout the whole community in which the child carries on his daily activities.

A public education that walls itself off, then, from the most deeply felt aspects of living and instead concerns itself chiefly with courses and academic requirements that are the least deeply felt aspects of the child's experience is an irresponsible education. At its door must be laid no small part of the blame for juvenile delinquency.

We are now better prepared to rephrase and supplement, in terms of progressivist learning, some of the general statements made above about the child and his environment. Implicit or explicit in the illustration are the following concepts especially relevant to the progressivist theory of learning: (1) interest, (2) effort, (3) purpose, (4) intelligence, (5) habit, (6) growth, (7) organism, and (8) culture. We shall try to dissect the core of each concept as interpreted by this theory.

Interest. To say that a child is "interested" in a particular experience is to say he is responding to it because it "clicks." It arouses a feeling or a whole cluster of feelings, emotions, impulses. It has meaning for him to the degree that it can be associated with meanings already derived from previous experiences. But its meaning is not identical with such experiences. Rather, each new one provides an element of the novel and the uncertain, which invites him in turn, to discover how this element may be brought into harmony with older experiences and hence to become more meaningful.

What is often termed "the teen-age revolution" is surely an urgent case of which the drug problem is only symptomatic of more complex causes and effects. How shall it be met? By soft-pedaling and circumventing or by involving the younger generation in confronting and coping with it?

Effort. Dewey's *Interest and Effort in Education*, an early and little-known book, is actually one of his richest contributions to education. In it, he argues that a correctly organized effort in learning—prolonged, intellectual concentration or hard practice in developing a manual skill—will not be separate from but must be fused throughout with interest.

This is merely to say that all of us work most intensively at tasks in which we are motivated by our own impulses, desires, talents. To force effort upon children when they are not in the least interested, when they fail to see any significance in what they are compelled to do, can mean only that they will probably learn far better to dislike that kind of effort than they will learn the content or skill that is the ostensible educational objective.

The total effort required in learning to understand the confusions and disturbances of teen-agers in a given community may be far greater than that involved in grammar-drilling or fact-memorizing. It may, for example, require firsthand investigations of social agencies or ghetto districts as well as prolonged sociological involvement. Yet, it becomes problematic, meaningful, and vital to many young people.

Purpose. Interest and effort combine with a third important factor, purpose. Although progressivist theory seems to certain of its critics to have inadequately analyzed this concept, nevertheless, progressivists insist that purpose, in some sense, is essential to all effective learning.

By purpose, in the present context, Dewey and his disciples mean the foreseen consequences of a particular interest and its related effort, both being biologically derived. Educationally speaking, learners need to see where a given experience may lead and why it is important for them to clarify it and so to satisfy the impulse that motivated them in the beginning. Kilpatrick, in an excellent discussion entitled, "Purpose: Its Place in the Life of Learning," epitomizes the progressivist view: ". . . purpose . . . permits a higher degree of efficiency of action than otherwise would be possible; but it also means that desirable results will be affected in the degree that purposes are critically chosen and intelligently directed."[1]

Intelligence. Between motivating interest and achieved purpose is the all-important phase of learning earlier called intelligence. This is the careful, sustained effort to think through and reorganize a disorganized situation. When we act immediately, spontaneously, on impulse, the end result is likely to be far less satisfactory than when we stop to consider what will happen *if* we act. By *observing* carefully as many relevant elements in the situation as possible, by *recalling* past observations and past experiences somewhat similar to the present one, and by *judging* the significance of the latter in terms of the former, we are able to reformulate and carry out our purpose, confident that its attainment is most likely to be the best possible under the circumstances.

This crucial phase of learning is, of course, what is termed above "mediate experience." In this relation we may say that "knowledge" stands to "recollection" as "truth" stands to tried-out "purpose."

Again, the illustration of juvenile delinquency is apt. One of the major reasons why experimentation with drugs often becomes destructive is that it may be merely impulsive. Its consequences are not sufficiently thought through. To bring intelligence to bear upon it, therefore, is to delay response in order to consider as many facets of the experience as possible. Such an examination requires all the care of observation, recollection, and judgment

[1] Kilpatrick, *Philosophy of Education,* p. 254.

that can be mustered. Educationally, this involves the difficult responsibility of studying the history and record of drug addiction, of noting its changing patterns in perspective, and of weighing its effects upon mental illness, illegitimacy, and family disintegration.

Habit. "The basic characteristic of habit," said Dewey, "is that every experience enacted and undergone modifies the one who acts and undergoes, while this modification affects, whether we wish it or not, the quality of subsequent experiences."[2] The importance of this progressivist conception of learning is threefold.

First, habit is often an obstacle. To the degree that the learner is tempted to fall back upon routine reactions, he too often fails to bring intelligence to bear upon new situations, following instead habitual behavior patterns regardless of whether they are appropriate. Nevertheless, he thereby modifies both himself and his ongoing experience.

Second, habits prove to be indispensable aids to learning because they help the learner to perform a great many actions automatically or reflexively, thus enabling him to give primary attention to consciously reflective action.

Third, he can, if he is encouraged to do so, acquire the habit of reflective behavior, just as he can acquire habits on routine or motor levels of action. He can become *habitually* intelligent. He can "learn to learn."[3]

Progressivist learning of habits is properly concerned with decreasing negative and with increasing positive effects. Habits are "bad" when they become flabby excuses for avoiding reflection, "good" when they become its ally.

Today our most imperative intellectual need in education is to devote attention and practice especially to the third kind of habit—that is, to controlled, experimental reactions to the problems we meet in our environment. Just as the scientist learns to analyze, infer, and test his hypotheses with habitual expertness, so the average citizen can learn to meet his everyday problems far more reflectively than he now does. If juvenile delinquency is to be coped with successfully, both young people and adults will have to face it much more often with habits that stimulate reflection, much less often with habits that do not.

[2] Dewey, *Experience and Education*, pp. 26–27.

[3] See Arnstine, *Philosophy of Education: Learning and Schooling*, pp. 41–44.

They will, to be sure, resort to habits of the second kind as well. For example, they will employ the skills of written and spoken communication as they investigate scientifically the causes of drug usage in a particular community. But habitual skills such as these are not at all antithetical to the habit of intelligence. Contrary to distorted views of progressive education (for example, that it fails to teach the three R's), progressivism insists upon habits of skills as well as habits of reflection. Correctly understood, they are entirely complementary.

Growth. Learning is also an axiological experience. That is, it tends either to improve or to damage the child's physiological, psychological, and social values. Only when it strengthens the whole learner by enabling him, bodily and spiritually, to pursue his deepest interest with sustained and efficient effort, only when it efficiently and continuously strengthens his habits of motor skill and his habits of reflection, does it help the child to grow.

Juvenile delinquency signifies, by the same measures, just the opposite of the value of growth. If our public schools are to be appraised by this value, they will become good insofar as they help to create a constructive and wholesome social environment. They will provide an abundance of learning experiences in which the same intelligent process of reflective thinking and action is applied to drug and other human-relations problems that is frequently applied to far less germane problems. Frustration, conflict, superstition, orthodoxy, silence, taboos, rote learning of moral rules—these are widespread evils that must be uprooted from education. Only as young people gain in critical self-awareness, self-confidence, positiveness, and articulateness about the learnings that are at the very core of their experience will they really grow.

Organism. The child's responses are a function of the unity of the organism. He learns, therefore, with his body as well as with his mind. More strictly, he never learns with merely the one *or* the other because neither exists without the other; neither functions except in some degree *for* the other. The familiar term "organismic" denotes the complete interrelatedness that characterizes progressivist psychology, as do also two other popular terms—"gestalt" and "field." Both of these connote the flexible unities and patterned configurations indigenous to the fusion of all individual and social life, to the dynamic wholeness of man's inner and outer experience.

One helpful way to bring out the significance of organism

for learning is to note once more the import of immediate and mediate experience. We recall that by the former, as distinguished from the problem-solving quality of the latter, is meant the undergoing or consummatory phase of behavior. We enjoy a sense of full communion with ourselves and our surroundings as an artist enjoys identification with the designs and symmetries of a concerto or a mural. Here, particularly, one is struck by resemblances between the esthetics of progressivism and of Zen Buddhism. Both are philosophies of human holism.

Learning is most completely organic, in short, when it is both immediate, in the way of esthetic appreciation, and mediate, in the way of scientific analysis. Each phase of learning is polaristic, not antagonistic, to the other. Just as the student of painting may become quite scientific, so the student of chemistry may sometimes become quite artistic. The important point in this regard is that the continuum of *immediacy-mediacy-immediacy*, which we noted in discussing pragmatic beliefs about reality and knowledge, is not only, in another context, the continuum of *intrinsic-instrumental-intrinsic* values but is also the continuum of *undergoing-doing-undergoing*. All three hyphenated phrases simply suggest, in different perspectives, the rhythmic fusion of learning. They suggest also that feelings of the body and ideas of the mind function as partners in a unified, organic enterprise.

Culture. Although the concepts we have thus far defined imply the sociality of learning, this final aspect should become explicit. That the child never learns in isolation from others is a truism progressivists never tire of affirming. The "self" that the child acquires is, in great measure, the product of communication with other "selves." It is the blending of responses that develop into personality "roles" as he slowly learns to anticipate how others expect him to respond.

Our conception of culture, as stated in Chapter 2, includes, then, much more than a sociopsychological recognition of human interdependence. Kilpatrick partially expresses this conception when he says that culture means: ". . . all those transmitted results of prior human experience and contrivance through which the group now carries on its life. This includes, especially, language, customs, tools, institutions, knowledge, distinctions, ideals, and standards."[4]

[4] Kilpatrick, in National Society for the Study of Education, *Forty-first Yearbook*, Part I, "Philosophies of Education," p. 61.

In this context we may say that schools are set up by a culture primarily to *guarantee its continuity*. The institutions and practices erected by the long, arduous trials and struggles of earlier generations must be maintained by later generations. This is not merely because men cherish them for their own sakes, but because without them each successive generation would have the impossible task of starting from scratch to develop controls over its hazardous surroundings.

Such a view of the cultural necessity of moderative learning is pregnant with implications for the developing culture. On the debit side, it tempts us to consider learning as a mere device to reinforce tradition—a mirror of historical events. On the credit side, the progressivist is careful to point out that, although certain societies have cultivated an education chiefly to preserve the past, every culture, no matter how static it appears, is continuously evolving. Education does not operate in its full sense, accordingly, unless it recognizes and relates to this evolution—accepting the *bequests* of the culture, certainly, but also recognizing their *pertinence and usefulness* to contemporary practices and problems in ongoing communal experience.

The progressivist concept of learning, now in terms of culture, again dramatizes the obligation of public schools to confront the problem of juvenile delinquency. When schools explore honestly and thoroughly the problems, customs, and ideals of family life, they must conclude that the achievements slowly maturing through the ages are worthy of profound respect. Without them, we would be thrown into a state of moral chaos. But this conservative conclusion is not inconsistent with the recognition that the *meaning* of such problems, customs, and ideals must be reinterpreted to meet the changed conditions of each successive generation.

THE EXPERIMENTAL CURRICULUM: CONTENT AND METHOD

THE SUBJECT MATTER OF PROGRESSIVE EDUCATION

The proper subject matter of a curriculum is any experience that is educative. This means that the good school is concerned with every kind of learning that helps students, young and old, to grow. No single body of content, no system of courses, no universal method of teaching is inappropriate. For, like experience itself, the needs and interests of individuals and groups vary from place to place, from time to time, from culture to culture.

The well-constructed curriculum is not unlike a laboratory. It is unceasingly experimental, and all its participants—teachers and students alike—are, in some fashion, staff scientists. Thus, it becomes necessary to avoid rigidity in school requirements, absolute boundaries, mechanical standards, preconceived solutions. Just as the experimental method is flexible, exploratory, tolerant of the novel, curious to try the hitherto untried, so too is its educational symbol.

At the same time, advocates of progressive education are quite willing to recognize that certain learning areas, to which traditional subject-matter labels may be attached, are proper organizational devices. They are equally willing to try various forms of curriculum structure. Belying the caricatures of progressive education, which depict it as disorganized, atomistic, and planless, Dewey and his followers have never denied the need of careful structuring and planning. What they do insist upon is a curriculum that grows through cooperative interests, thinking, and action. It is in this sense that Kilpatrick calls the term "emerging curriculum" his ideal.

In assessing its accomplishments during the last half-century, Harold Rugg, one of the great pioneers of progressivism, found five major types of effort to rebuild the curriculum—of which the first four are greater or lesser compromises with the traditional curriculum pattern:

(1) reorganization within a particular subject: juggling items about with little actual redesigning;
(2) correlation of two or more bodies of subject matter: for example, between English and the social studies;
(3) grouping together and integrating related subjects within broad fields of knowledge: for example, "general education" in the natural sciences or arts;
(4) "core curriculum": a loosely used term to suggest blocks of learning experiences around common needs;
(5) "experience-centered curriculum": dissolving subject-matter lines and emphasizing "units."

The units of the experience-centered curriculum, which cut across fields and clusters of needs, are generated and shaped by the experiences of learners themselves. They are directed toward the total personality development of each learner by exposing him to a wide range of emotional, motor, intellectual, and social experiences. In the order of these five, we can observe increasing degrees of emancipation from traditional curriculums with the core curriculum by far the most progressivist of the subject-matter types and therefore closest to the full-fledged experience-centered pattern.

The way in which a particular subject matter becomes a creative learning experience offers many examples. History, however, is particularly apt because of the familiar criticism that progressive schools too often neglect intensive study of the past.

It is true that progressivists rebel against the conventional teaching of history. They deny that study of the social heritage, divorced from present impulses, problems, and purposes, can be fully educative learning. They are devastating, therefore, in their critique of segregated courses in ancient, medieval, or modern history as these have usually been taught in public schools and colleges.

At the same time, progressivists insist that history is an indispensable educative tool if properly utilized. Indispensable because the scientific method requires knowledge of what has already happened in order to anticipate what may happen. Indispensable because the continuity of culture, which education helps so powerfully to reinforce, requires the deepest possible understanding of habits and institutions evolving from the past into the present and toward the future. Indispensable, finally, because the flow of temporal events is always from immediacies that have already been, through mediacies that are now, into new immediacies that become fresh consummations and syntheses of those events.

For history to be learned on these premises, two guiding rules must be implemented. One is that the ongoing *present* is always the fulcrum of interest; hence if history is to be significant, it must necessarily be drawn upon whenever learners see its significance *for* the present. Once they do see it, then a motivation for historical study is provided. As Dewey pointed out:

> Just as the individual has to draw in memory upon his own past to understand the conditions in which he individually finds himself, so the issues and problems of present *social* life are in such intimate and direct connection with the past that students cannot be prepared to understand either these problems or the best way of dealing with them without delving into their roots in the past.[5]

[5] Dewey, *Experience and Education*, p. 93.

The second rule, which applies especially to the primary and secondary school, is that history should often be taught, not as a separate subject, but as a phase of every larger unit of learning. This rule is implemented by the most advanced curriculum structures listed above. In the experience-centered curriculum, especially, history proves so natural to each designed unit that its subject matter becomes one basic experience within the total process of living as learning.

PROGRESSIVIST METHOD: SOME CENTRAL ISSUES

A number of selected issues elucidate the curriculum principles of progressivist theory.

The nature of real problems. Teachers and administrators in charge of conventional curriculums often remark that they are already practicing "sane" progressive education. Look at the "problem approach," they say. Such skills as mathematics deal with problems, do they not? And do not science courses, too? And is it not a common approach in the social studies, arts, and other areas as well?

As with other issues, the best way of appraising such a contention is to square it against relevant philosophic beliefs. When we do, we find that what is *called* progressivist is too often not at all in accord with progressivist beliefs. The problem approach is not in accord when problems are artificially contrived without careful consideration of whether they bear upon meaningful situations. A large proportion of ordinary exercises in, let us say, arithmetic, have no such bearing. They are, in fact, counterfeit problems—textbook stereotypes divorced from economic occupations or any other cultural interests.

The problem approach fails again when problems become merely recipes which, when ingredients are mixed and stirred according to direction, are guaranteed to turn out dishes quite identical with those of previous cooks. To change the metaphor, we are reminded of puzzles in a magazine with solutions hidden on a back page: the student's job now is to ferret out answers which the teacher carefully conceals. This type of learning by recipe or predetermined answer exemplifies one method of deduction—the application of a given formula to prove or illustrate some specific case.

Progressivism does not deny the need for practice in the form of exercises or deductions at the proper time and place. It does deny that they should occupy a central position in the curriculum. The experimental method can never function *merely* by drawing upon a reservoir of knowledge—upon rules, laws, given facts—or upon repetitive skills. The evolutionary quality of all experience imparts to every genuinely problematic situation a similar quality—a quality of the temporal, unique, and particular. Speaking again in terms of logic, such situations are, in essence, inductive: they examine all factors relevant to the search for relationships, and they are guided throughout by tentatively maintained ends-in-view which, when tried out, aim to eliminate the initiating quandary.

The use of drill. How, then, can progressivists justify a place for drill? If they do, are they not inconsistent? If they do not, are they not guilty of failure to produce well-trained citizens?

Their reply rests upon the now familiar psychological position that memorizing and rote practice as such rarely succeed in stimulating interest, much less any strong impulse to carry on intelligent activity. But interest geared to this kind of activity very often leads to recognition of the necessity for dexterities that demand concentrated practice, for memorizing of appropriate material, and for the logical and manual abilities that help to carry out the deductions required by more inductive tasks.

The best way to perfect a given skill is by its constant use in whatever vital projects students pursue. The effective use of either foreign or native language, for example, is not taught as well by formal grammar and vocabulary lessons as it is by permeating the curriculum at every point with language opportunities—above all, by providing communication among students, teachers, and resource people of the community. Words, say instrumentalists, are man's chief tool of meaning and control—a view generally in accord with Cassirer's theory of man as the animal symbolicum. But as with any tool, one becomes expert in their use only by applying them as a means to obtain worthwhile ends. Repetitious exercise is justified, therefore, only if it is commonly perceived by all participants as such a means.

Work versus play or work and play? A partly related issue is raised by the contention of critics that progressivist methods often confuse work and play. Education, if it is sound, is hard work, they say, and "sugar-coating" of courses or skills by reducing them to "easy fun" merely encourages laxity.

The progressivist replies that to identify schooling with work and outside activity with play means again that the former is divorced from ongoing experience while the latter remains an intimate part of such experience. Only when work is cut off from the drives, enthusiasms, and talents of growing individuals does it become a necessary evil—an onerous task to be completed as quickly as possible. Labor, under these conditions, is considered antithetical to leisure-time activity.

But work that is meaningful and creative, is not a burden to be avoided. In the joy and satisfaction it affords, one might properly contend that it is similar to play. The latter, on the other hand, has many of the qualities of work; children's games and adult diversions often require reflection, imaginative planning, and exhausting energy. Recreation as learning provides a good illustration of Kilpatrick's concept of "concomitant learning"—learning that occurs not so much by deliberate or formal instruction as by the fact that the human organism functions as a unified whole, and hence, that every experience affects the learner's personality.

Still, progressivists also recognize distinctions between the two activities. They call attention to the fact that work of any kind, in school or not, requires alternating relaxation. They perceive dangers in types of work that cause people to react to monotony or drudgery by resorting to unhealthful, falsely stimulating pleasures—drug indulgence for one. But hard work that permits individual capacities to function on a high plane of intelligent activity, this calls, too, for respite and recreation. We may even say that play is one form of what has been termed "immediate experience." In esthetic terms, it sometimes appears as a more consummatory, undergoing phase of human life.

Immediate experience, however, is by no means disjoined from preceding and succeeding activities that require conscious effort and control. If activities of mediate experience arise out of immediate experience, they also continuously regenerate and recondition it. Play, then, must be removed from the fringes of school programs, where it is inaccurately termed *extra*curricular. Children learn equally from work *and* play when both are functional to their personal and social growth.

The issue of indoctrination. If, to the progressivist, the experimental method is at heart inductive in the way that science is inductive, if it is thus tolerant of various kinds of evidence and alternative points of view, will he not necessarily oppose all programs of education that seek to impose some single doctrine—

religious, political, moral, or of any other category? The answer is unequivocal: he will, of course, oppose them.

But this answer is too negative and too simple. No education, say progressivists, is strictly impartial or objective. All teachers are influenced by values, attitudes, customs—the entire philosophic equipment of culture—and these saturate content as well as practice throughout. Hence, educators should not be deluded by the superficial rationalization that they can immunize themselves from these influences. Their task is rather to bring them all as closely as possible within the range of critical scrutiny, and to ensure that teachers and students alike be frank and clear about their beliefs.

Several inferences follow. One is the necessity of academic freedom as the right of children or adults to confront any controversial issue of any importance. It implies unrestricted opportunity to examine facts and test hypotheses. But the choices that result from intelligent activity are still not to be indoctrinated—that is, they must not be taught so as to preclude questioning or possible alternatives. A second inference is that choices are true for a limited time, always subject to the probability that they will need to be revised. Finally, an underlying conviction prevails that the method of intelligence is by far the best method men have found by which they are able to advance. This conviction is as close to indoctrination as progressivism ever approaches in theory. Nevertheless, we shall find that even this conviction, which it would like all of us to share, is open to rigorous inspection and debate.

Child-centered or community-centered schools? A further issue, particularly significant to our culturological evaluation in the next chapter, is whether the center of a good school is the individual child, his interests and growth, or the problems and development of the community of which the school is part.

Stated so baldly, the distinction between child-centered and community-centered schools is, of course, sharper than either the theory or practice of progressivism warrants. All advocates would insist that no school can or should be exclusively either. Nevertheless, strong differences of emphasis are discernible.

The child-centered emphasis is revealed in characteristic concern of the progressivist curriculum for rounded, organismic learning—a curriculum that encourages individual initiative, release of feelings, spontaneity of ideas, creative expression. Such a curriculum requires that the teacher know every student as thoroughly as possible—not by class grades alone (in fact, these are usually of minor consequence) but by his family relationships, his emotional and physical health, his special abilities and limitations. Thus, the abundant use of tests and records is intended to produce a comprehensive profile of the student—his knowledge, social sensitivity, appreciations, interests, progress, skill in problem-solving. But he is allowed wide deviations in terms of his individuality and in the pace and ingredients of class study. Lock-step courses are taboo.

The community-centered school, as a model, is equally sound progressivism. If learning permeates the lives of individuals, then it follows that the school should constantly utilize and mold into its curriculum the widest possible resources of living. Such a curriculum includes nothing less than the resources of the entire human community—from the school block to the farthest reaches of our planet. Children should spend a large part of time in direct contact with every feature of their natural and cultural surroundings that thus become material to be analyzed, reworked, assimilated into personal behavior.

Application of this principle may be illustrated almost boundlessly. Students discover the *arts* everywhere around them: in trips to museums, of course, or in plays, movies, and symphonies, but even more so in everyday materials and incidents (landscapes, clays, metals, folklore, the daily tragedies and comedies of their neighborhoods). In *social studies*, they may have direct acquaintance with ghetto conditions, factories, markets, farms, courts, mines. The *natural sciences*, too, may be related to their immediate environment. Chemistry analyzes drinking water as a project in consumer education; physics studies the efficiency of the local power station; botany investigates a plant disease that has been plaguing nearby farms.

Why adult education? Ideally, the community school becomes a vibrant center of neighborhood life—a center from which activities of students and teachers radiate in all possible directions and also toward which other members of the community gravitate. No wonder that adult education becomes a corollary of this wider approach to education of children.

Progressivists view the learning of mature men and women with special urgency. For, while it is true that men *may* continue to grow throughout their lives, no certainty whatever proves that they *will* do so. Stated otherwise, if children learn beyond as well as within the rigid boundaries of the public school (much too often to their detriment), then parents may learn also. Yet, again like their children, they may be victimized by crosscurrents of belief, propaganda, superstition, and outright falsehood. As a matter of fact, the average adult is perhaps even more susceptible than children to learning that inhibits or distorts rather than stimulates growth. Children, at least, have the benefit of some organized educational direction, whereas adults, bound by the prejudice that education ceases at the age of leaving school, frequently lack even that much direction.

Education through the years after formal graduation is not to be regarded, then, as a comfortable leisure-time activity. It is just as mandatory for healthy community living among adults as for their children. Moreover, it enables citizens to face the issues of our unstable time not with prejudice, ignorance, or whim, nor with mere classroom knowledge soon made obsolete by changing community circumstances, but with self-confident capacity to analyze and act upon these issues.

PROGRESSIVE EDUCATION AND SCHOOL CONTROL

THE DEMOCRATIC SCHOOL

Progressivist theorists find themselves returning again and again to the problem of freedom. Characteristically, Dewey regarded it as soluble *educationally* only as it is examined and interpreted *culturally*. Thus, if the classroom teacher is perplexed over how much and what kinds of freedom to encourage among his students, or how much discipline and initiative to exercise, he must first ask himself: "What does freedom mean in society at large? What does order mean? How can freedom be related to order so as to become its ally rather than its enemy?"

The most generalized answer progressivists offer to such questions is that freedom means positive opportunity for men to release their powers in behalf of individual and community growth. Politically, freedom is not a negative absence of restraint —the doctrine of *laissez faire* and minimum government. Freedom is a potential realized only through social arrangements that at once protect and encourage every person to deal forthrightly and cooperatively with all his problems. Peirce's anticipation is succinctly stated: ". . . the problem becomes how to fix belief, not in the individual merely, but in the community."[6]

This doctrine of *shared* experience must be underscored as central to progressivist theory. It is the normative principle that

[6] Peirce, in Fisch (ed.), *Classic American Philosophers*, p. 63.

freedom is genuine only when individuals, working and living in groups, are able to discuss and express their interests fully, continuously, together. Any social institution that blocks such interplay, that prohibits members of a race or religion from joining at *every* point in the activities of the community, that subordinates women, that denies working people complete participation in economic affairs, is so far *un*democratic and, therefore, *un*free.

The order resulting from maximum sharing is, in the most unqualified sense, *man-made* order. It is not order superimposed by some supreme ruler, individual or collective, divine or mundane. Therefore it is less final, more modifiable and pluralistic than the metaphysical, religious, or political order resting upon a foundation of unchallengeable authority. But just because it has been fashioned from the needs and impulses, the actions and purposes, of real human beings, it also proves more substantial and satisfying in the long run. It grows as democracy grows; its means ever reshape its ends; its ends change into new means. The key to order, finally, must be intelligence; for it is chiefly the freedom of intelligence that enables individuals, and therefore the democracy created by individuals, to deal with their natural and social environment constructively, unifiedly, developmentally.

This encapsulation of major pragmatic beliefs about freedom and order applies at every point to the truly democratic school. Freedom in education means freedom to achieve—an encompassing synonym for all constituent and integrated aspects of learning: interest, effort, purpose, intelligence, habit, growth, organism, culture. It is opportunity for pursuit of interests by every child. But, it is also opportunity for pursuit of interests by the group to which the child belongs. It thrives in the kind of school where experiences are shared fully by *all* children.

Discipline assumes quite different meanings, accordingly, for the tradition-harnessed teacher and for the progressivist. Recognizing that order in education is desirable and necessary, the latter holds that the surest and best order develops out of the joint experience of those involved. When students help to make their own rules because they come to see that regularity of procedure is necessary to attain their own purposes, problems of discipline are rare. Controls are established by their beneficiaries, and although less refined or exacting than if determined "from above" they may, for that very reason, achieve all the more stability.

It follows that the progressivist teacher is more a guide and fellow explorer in the educative adventure than a taskmaster. This by no means implies that his function thereby becomes less crucial; on the contrary, his role becomes more important and difficult, more painstaking and energy-consuming, than in the formal school where his own and his students' duties are carefully routinized and preplanned. If effective, he must know each child as intimately as possible. He must encourage maximum give-and-take in and out of the classroom, accepting criticism of himself. He must, with the cooperation of students and colleagues, constantly modify each plan of study; therefore, he must always resist the temptation to fall back upon a repetitious, mechanized program. He must, in short, practice as well as preach democracy. This is hard work.

As progressivists in the field of school administration have often argued, the kind of freedom and order that applies to democratic society at large should apply to classrooms and to school systems as well. Perhaps the severest indictment made against typical administrative practices is that they tend to exaggerate such values as efficiency in business at the expense of values (growth and cooperative planning, for example) that prove more educationally rewarding. So, too, are colleges and universities. The progressivist principle of continuous interplay among all individuals and groups, the highest test of any democratic community, is violated by this kind of system. Students take orders from teachers, teachers from principals or deans, principals or deans from the superintendent or president. He, in turn, is responsible to governing boards which, although at times nominally democratic, frequently represent only that small segment of the population that is willing to endorse efficient educational administration.

The progressivist administrator, on the contrary, encourages faculty participation in all important matters affecting the school. Curriculum plans, budgets, and tenure rules are all subjects of thorough discussion, and often faculty decision. Students have their own councils in which problems relevant to discipline, recreation, and courses of study are examined and approved cooperatively. Parents, too, are urged to involve themselves with school programs; parent-teacher associations, advisory committees of citizens, and adult forums are all influential in the best types of progressivist schools or colleges.

THE SCHOOL AS AGENT OF DEMOCRATIC PLANNING

The progressivist belief that schools are established by a culture to guarantee its continuity—a belief to which we have already alluded and shall allude still further below—offers a clue to this philosophy on the issue of education and social change. No progressivist would defend the familiar view that education is inevitably and chiefly, not the moderator, but the transmitter of cultural tradition and habit. Particularly, those who urge community-centered schools agree that, while education must always recognize and respect the milieu within which it operates, it can and should criticize social weaknesses, make clear-cut proposals, and act strategically to bring about improvements.

The familiar concept of interaction clarifies this position. The effective school works *with*, not *against*, its environment. It assesses obstacles and resistances that stand in the way of evolution and then utilizes these experimentally. It neither sits back and rationalizes its feebleness, nor does it overestimate its own strength and impatiently try to effect immediate and radical change. Again, the central belief is in the scientific method, now crystallized in terms of *social* intelligence. Education *could* become a gigantic force for democratic evolution if it would only free itself from false psychologies of learning, from false philosophies of historic change—if it would only face and solve problems of culture with the same productive brilliance that physics and other laboratory sciences demonstrate.

To spell out the progressivist approach to social problems by applying abstract formulas to concrete problems is not, however, so simple. Even within the ranks of leading theorists, astonishing differences are to be found on such practical questions as how teachers should act together to exert influence not only within the public school but also upon the wider environment. Despite broad agreement that teachers should function in community life, no general agreement has prevailed as to the extent to which this implies aggressive participation in and loyal identification with economic or political movements. Kilpatrick, for example, strongly opposed affiliation with organized labor: such affiliation too often results in teachers' losing their freedom to think independently, because they become propagandists for and servants of special interest groups. On the other hand, outstanding progressivist theorists such as John L. Childs have taken a different view. Dewey himself contended in a famous statement:

> If teachers are workers who are bound in common ties with other workers, what action do they need to take? The answer is short and conclusive. Ally themselves with their friends against their common foe, the privileged class, and in the alliance develop the character, skill, and intelligence that are necessary to make a democratic social order a fact.[7]

[7] Dewey, *Education Today*, p. 307.

The assumption here is that social intelligence means social action and that social action does not occur in a vacuum. Teachers must themselves choose whether to associate with those organized forces in our democracy that strive to improve opportunities for men and women to live more fully. In this conviction, as much perhaps as in any other in all his educational writings, Dewey repudiates the more innocuous and "safe" interpretation of which some of his followers have been accused.

Nevertheless, it is possible to find even in Dewey's writings a strong note of warning against what he would regard as too extreme or militant an approach to social action and social control. On several occasions, he abruptly questioned Marxism, the official philosophy of the Communist movement, and rejected it on several grounds: that it substitutes violence for intelligence; that it sets up a philosophy of history which, despite its materialistic basis, is seldom less absolutistic than old-fashioned theology; and that it predetermines its own development by predicting a planned society.

But it is against the doctrine of a planned society that he and virtually all leading progressivists have warned teachers and citizens to be on their guard. For, in a planned society, we may detect a counterpart of ancient and medieval faiths in fixed and final ends. Worst of all, we find lurking here an insidious ethic of the ends *justifying* means—of the belief that because the end of a planned society is presumably moral, therefore any means, however cruel or violent, that may be necessary to attain it are also moral.

How then *should* education approach these problems? First of all, honest analysis reveals certain facts about the dangers and failures of what is called "free enterprise." Dewey, far more forcefully than most other progressivists, severely criticized capitalist economic practices. He showed how miseducative are the effects of a system that exaggerates pecuniary gain to the extent that it becomes the supreme aim of life, the final criterion of success. He indicted this system for failing to assure security against the ravages of unemployment, old age, war. He pointed to the fact that millions perform jobs so routine and atomized as to arouse in the worker no feeling of significance, no sense of social aim.

Education, meanwhile, too often compounds our confusion. Where it has concerned itself with the economy at all, it has often taught young people to be acquiescent and uncritical. To the extent that it has ignored explosive economic problems, wishing to be left in peace, it has allowed cultural confusion to be reinforced by learning-living situations outside of school—situations that prove frequently purposeless, chaotic, and destructive.

The alternative is testable programs of action. On the one hand, schools need to become much more democratic within their own walls. On the other hand, as social institutions, they need to teach average citizens why and how to improve democratic structures outside their walls. Such a tremendous task points, above all, to *a fresh patterning of order.* It should become an order in which cultural affinity with the heritage of freedom is firmly maintained but which recognizes equally that ruthless, competitive individualism can no longer be tolerated in our closely knit world. Hence it must be an order which would substitute, for planless economic practices, varying degrees of planning—an order correctly termed a "planning society."

This task is not in the least inconsistent with the theory of progressivism. By means of it, rather, schools become channels through which flow the most exciting, pressing issues, practices, events, proposals of the local, national, and international community. The planning society is, in fact, a graphic demonstration of widescale democratic learning. It is a hypothesis which, like every hypothesis, must be shaped and reshaped as it evolves from specific stage to specific stage, from present plan to present plan, from means to ends, from further means to still further ends.

Since, finally, the most crucial of such means, in school and out, is the universal practice of free intelligence, here is the most compelling of all reasons why art, broadly understood, becomes central to progressive learning-teaching. Art, after all, is the artists' freedom to express by identifying themselves with and transforming the materials of nature and culture. Hence it becomes, in turn, the very essence of democratic and educational endeavor blended into one. And scientific method, which too often we identify only with cold and impersonal specialization, becomes a full working partner of esthetic creativity—the master instrument by which men everywhere share in planning and cultivating their lives in the ever-growing garden of experience.

CHAPTER 7

A culturological evaluation of progressivism

THE BELIEF OF DEWEY that the history of philosophy is a critical portrait of the history of culture applies not only to patterns of belief with which he was unsympathetic but equally to his own pattern. If, then, we are successfully to evaluate his position and that of his associates, we shall have to observe pragmatic-progressivist behavior in its natural setting of economic, social, political, and similar trends. We shall have to study its character not as an erudite system of thought immunized *against* experience but, taking it at its own word, as a product *of* experience. Thus far, pragmatism-progressivism is in accord with the culturological approach through which each major position is viewed within this book—namely, that American philosophies of education are varying expressions of the patterns of American culture. This approach has been formulated in Part 1.

Indeed, the constant cross-fertilization of cultural events with beliefs about those events is so central to progressivism that, in both preceding chapters of this part, we have found it necessary to record many instances of such cross-fertilization. Particularly, we underscored four influences without which Dewey, or Peirce and James before him, could scarcely have been able to formulate their mature doctrines—without which, therefore, neither Bode or Kilpatrick could have formulated theirs. These influences are the Industrial Revolution, modern science, the rise of democracy, and a generous environment.

The chief value judgment we shall place upon pragmatism-progressivism has also been stated in a preliminary way. Pragmatism-progressivism is the highest philosophical and educational embodiment of what may be termed the *liberal way of life.* Therefore, like liberalism itself, it is in some ways a powerful and adequate interpretation of contemporary culture; in other ways, it is a feeble and inadequate interpretation. Its success in exposing and criticizing the beliefs of earlier cultures has been striking; its success in articulating and justifying the motives, habits, and aims of our younger American culture—especially of the past century—is, likewise, of the highest order. Its success, however, in providing a sufficient rationale and program for a mature, designed culture is far less substantial. Rather, progressivism, like liberalism, is *transitional* to that kind of culture. Both are ways of moderation.

EDUCATION IN A LIBERAL CULTURE

THE IMPACT OF INDUSTRIALISM

The emphasis that progressivism gives to culture is revealed by its characteristic assumption that education is an institution established by organized groups of people to guarantee the continuity from generation to generation of their habits, structures, customs, attitudes. To quote Dewey: "It is the function of education to see to it that individuals are so trained as to be capable of entering into the heritage of these values which already exist, trained also in sensitiveness to the defects of what already exists and in ability to recreate and improve."[1]

If, in good pragmatic fashion, we apply Dewey's statement to the development of American culture and education, we note a trend of far-reaching consequence. This is the trend from agrarianism to industrialism. The Industrial Revolution, which began to transform Europe even before the thirteen colonies had joined to form a federal union, soon transformed America as well. The cherished dream of Jefferson—that the population of the new country should be composed chiefly of small, self-sufficient, but independent farmers—was fading rapidly by the time the nineteenth century had reached its midway mark. Before the century's end, many American cities had become huge, machines had become more intricate and efficient than had ever been imagined, and businessmen had obtained ever larger shares of political as well as economic power.

[1] Dewey, in Kilpatrick (ed.), *The Educational Frontier*, p. 292.

What has been the effect of this trend on the nation's schools? The story of how they were established by the young nation as public, tax-supported institutions for all the children of all the people is one of the most glorious stories in educational history. From the progressivist viewpoint, however, the way in which schools have carried out this purpose is considerably less glorious. Some, perpetuating the customs of the European heritage, have from earliest times reflected the belief that the main purpose of education is to prepare young people to become "ladies and gentlemen" by veneering them with the classical tradition—a belief for which we find imposing support even today. Many other schools, from the beginning of American history until the Civil War, reflected the impact of the agrarian period. Although industrialism was already on the march, this was a period when most young people took part in cultivating fields, caring for livestock, making their own clothes, and helping with the many tasks connected with a hardy, pioneer environment. Thus they acquired skills and facts important to their culture by sharing immediately and directly in it. Their other educational needs—reading, 'riting, 'rithmetic, and a smattering of "wisdom"—were provided by the school.

If, during this agrarian period, the educational division between what children learned informally through intimate acquaintance with their surroundings and what they learned formally within their classrooms was not wholly justifiable in terms of all we now know about good education, it was at least plausible. It made sense in the period of direct and significant participation by children in the simple, isolated, self-sufficient community of the typical rural family. From the two spheres of home and school, children learned much of what was most essential to their experience.

Yet, for the same reason that the division made considerable sense for our earlier agricultural society, it makes very little sense for our later industrial society. As industrialism has grown toward its present giant stature children have shared less and less directly in their parents' occupations. Division of labor has extended so far that now these occupations rarely have any direct connection with family experience. American farmers today almost never make their own clothes or produce all their own food, and many consume only minor parts of what their lands ordinarily produce. The home, moreover, is far less typically the center of family activity and interest not only for the father, who is probably the wage earner, but often also for the children and the mother. Outside amusements, rapid transportation, stuffy apartments, commercialized excitements, and group affiliations—all produce a serious challenge to education itself.

This challenge, insists the progressivist, is that an industrial order and an agrarian order demand different kinds of schools. If we apply the psychological principle of "living as learning" to such a historic setting and if we recall that the primary purpose of education, according to this principle, is to provide learning that meets the needs and interests of living, we may say that a three-R's curriculum merely combined with family experience cannot possibly meet contemporary needs and interests. For this reason, the school's obligation becomes much greater—to ensure that the concerns of culture created by an industrialized age will be met educatively. This is the first responsibility of good public education.

Thus, we see why, for Dewey and others of his persuasion, this responsibility has at least three aspects: (1) to ensure that the school helps individuals to enter fully into the existing industrial-technological order; (2) to teach them to be critical of such cultural weaknesses and failures as family instability and unemployment; and (3) to help them correct these wherever and whenever possible. Any less comprehensive a program can only assure that a great gap will continue to separate curriculums and methods of learning from our turbulent economic, political, and moral culture. Rote learning, sterile subject matters, and authoritarian discipline are all instances of cultural lag. Functional learning, relevant subject matters, and self-discipline are instances of efforts to catch up with the culture.

INDUSTRIALISM AND LIBERALISM

Thus far our sketch of progressivism in its cultural context has been derived largely from its own theorists; it demonstrates our contention that they are themselves culturally oriented. From this point on, our interpretation, at times, derives less from progressivists themselves than from a more critical culturological perspective.

We need, therefore, to consider further the value judgment that progressivism is an educational expression of liberalism—a term embracing clusters of political, ethical, and social attitudes as well as correlative practices, all peculiarly suited to the civilization that emerged with the Renaissance and reached the peak of its vitality early in the present century. While the Industrial Revolution generated many of these attitudes and practices, liberalism, in turn, often provided intellectual and moral sanction to industrialism.

To etch the present picture as sharply as possible, let us imagine modern culture on three mutually supporting levels of experience: first, the "bottom," or foundation, level of industrial life with its network of socioeconomic relations typified by the factory system, division of labor, technology, and business control; second, the "middle" level of liberal attitudes and practices that articulate, reflect, and reinforce the industrial level; and third, the "top" level of organized education resting upon both liberalism and industrialism while helping to give meaning and strength to both. Imagined in this way, each level supports the other two; with modern industrialism still the most basic and with liberalism operating somewhere in between it and organized education.

But the picture is distorted in at least one respect. Like many oversimplifications, it does not take account of the factor of time. Actually, all three levels—liberalism as a diffused way of life at the center level, the educational level of belief and practice above, and the industrial level of technology and power relations below—have undergone historic evolution. All three have, together, experienced at least two major, although *overlapping*, periods. The first, which we call "early liberalism," extended from the seventeenth to perhaps the first third of the nineteenth century; the second, which we call "later liberalism," has extended from the latter time to our own generation, reaching its widest range of influence in about the middle third of the twentieth century.

Early liberalism. This was a pattern of attitudes and practices designed to bolster a "new" culture that was partly agrarian, partly industrial, and decreasingly feudal. Therefore it was, above all, a symbol of the kind of liberty required by men in revolt against a decadent and outmoded medieval order. As an ideal, it epitomized what men increasingly sought in practice, namely, the right to inquire about and engage in commercial, industrial, and agricultural activity unrestricted by inherited privilege or by monarchical or theocratic power. In essence, this was *laissez faire* liberty—freedom from restraint. It was exactly what was needed by the new, high-spirited, competitive economy manned by groups of individuals struggling ruthlessly against other individuals for markets and profits. Similarly, as viewed by various interpreters, it was an age of wide protest resulting in religious as well as political reformation.

Moreover, while early liberalism was providing theoretical justification for habits and values of the emerging industrial era, it was also supporting the kind of education that would enhance these habits and values. This was the education, proposed by such early liberals as Locke, that was designed especially for those who were taking over political as well as economic control of the new system.

Later liberalism. This period was not so much a rejection as a modification and widening of earlier liberalism. While it continued to oppose the medieval order and to stress with unremitting vigor such values as independence and freedom of inquiry, it challenged the narrowness, negativeness, and remnants of absolutism that still lurked in classic liberal doctrine. Early liberals really cared little about liberty for everyone. They were much more interested in guaranteeing that the virile, young middle classes have the right to oppose restrictions upon their power than in guaranteeing that the lower working classes—who depended on the upper classes for employment—should also enjoy certain rights, especially the right to a job. Educationally, too, early liberalism was concerned with teaching young people that their first duty and their best chance of success lay in adjusting both to marketable skills and to major tenets of the industrial system. Thus, education provided justification for subservience to an order that, although different from the ancient and medieval orders, could be no less domineering over the lives of ordinary men.

Later liberalism not only called attention to these limitations of its precursor but also sought to correct them. Early in the nineteenth century, a number of critics had begun to speak out. Some, such as Robert Owen, were already advocates of a more radical philosophy; others, such as John Stuart Mill, were eloquent advocates of a liberalism that guaranteed liberty not merely to the middle-class citizen but to *all* citizens. By the time of the American Civil War, the beliefs, for which Mill was probably the most brilliant European spokesman, began to find ready response in "the land of opportunity."

Such a widened liberalism was especially plausible in the generous, natural environment of America (to which we refer above), and it was strengthened and widened by the unique spirit of the American frontier. True, as Frederick Jackson Turner and other historians have shown, such a spirit could not be captured by any simple formula (Turner's own theses have often been criticized), nor could it be said to have influenced only those who experienced the life of the frontier directly. Its qualities included assertiveness, shrewdness, optimism, toughmindedness, restlessness, ingenuity, adventuresomeness, self-respect. Such qualities, as developed in generations of pioneers who pushed back the boundaries of a vast and rich territory, seemed to be reflected in habits and attitudes of the more settled populations in the East. George S. Counts, a leading educational interpreter, sums up both the liabilities and assets of the pioneer influence:

> If there was much in this early society that we would be happy to leave to history—the bitter toil, the lack of refinement, and the crudeness of manners—there was also much that we would like to preserve as the essence of American character. The life on the frontier and on the farm bred in our people a sturdy and self-reliant quality, an inventive and resourceful mind, a sense of individual worth and integrity, an abhorrence of show and pretense, a fierce assertion of human equality, a deep love of personal freedom.[2]

We can understand, then, why some interpreters of liberalism wished to imply far more than unhampered freedom of a minority to engage in exploitation of the majority. It still meant this to some, of course. But it meant to others the freedom of every individual to pursue his own ends by exercising his fullest nature, powers, and capacities. It meant, finally, *public* education—an education not limited to those who could afford to pay, not open merely to the few who expected to domineer over the many, but an education for rich and poor, black and white, high and low alike.

The development of later liberalism and of related theories in education was not completed, however, in the nineteenth century. The environment's capacity to provide such magnificent opportunity for enterprising individuals could not remain indefinitely the same. As we have seen, the agrarian culture was increasingly supplanted by an industrial culture. Successful conquest of geographical frontiers—lands, forests, river power, minerals—meant that eventually no such frontiers would remain to be conquered. As we approached and entered the twentieth century, the rise of economic empires within the nation, the spread of rapid communication, transportation, and interstate commerce persistently called attention to the fact that *the individualistic*

[2] Counts, *Education and American Civilization*, p. 103.

period of our history was waning. Even the pioneer faith that the majority of our problems could be solved locally or, at most, at the state level came to be questioned as evidence accumulated that they were not being solved on these levels. In short, technology and industrialism were liquidating our provincialism. Spurred by transportation, communication, and cooperation, they were compelling Americans to unify and direct ever larger segments of their economic and political experience and even to consider joining cooperatively with other nations.

Such leaders as Dewey responded to these changes. They urged schools to join hands with the culture, to take industrial life into account, to emphasize social and interdependent as well as individual and independent aspects of experience.

The swinging pendulum. Let us summarize our discussion of liberalism to this point. Early liberalism—with its counterparts, on the cultural level below, of individualistic capitalism, small-scale enterprise and agriculture, and, on the level above, of an education reflecting that order—has been waning for at least a century. Later liberalism, meanwhile, has gradually come into prominence. It is a liberalism still characterized by regard for such frontier and agrarian virtues as self-reliance and self-assertiveness; therefore, in important respects, it is *continuous with* earlier liberalism. In fact, many values of our early American heritage remain vital. But later liberalism is also characterized much more strongly and self-consciously by such virtues as cooperation, community participation, and collective responsibility.

Now, the important point for our understanding of progressivism is that the education and, indeed, the culture for which it stands are profoundly saturated with *both kinds of virtue*—individual *and* social, personal *and* communal. Although, as we have seen, progressivism rejects the three-R's school of the agrarian period, it does not reject the individualistic values that were hidden corollaries of that kind of school. Although it rejects quite as strongly any kind of totalitarian education that threatens to submerge the individual, nevertheless it insists that modern education must give much stronger attention to the problems and needs created by the larger whole of an interlocking political, economic, and social order.

Swinging pendulum-fashion between these two poles of value—individuality and sociality—progressivism as educational theory and practice reflects the two great levels of culture below it. It reflects the industrial level because, in America certainly, economic life remains individualistic at some points (witness the small farmer and shopkeeper), collective and centralized at other points (industrial monopoly and growing federal authority). It reflects and reinforces the liberal level because, as the later period clearly reveals, that level is also concerned to preserve and respect the same two poles of values.

Here is a conception of liberalism which, constructed out of the history of modern culture, prepares us to understand more clearly why progressivism plays the role that it does in our own day. Opposed to all "either-or" philosophies, it tries to become, and largely succeeds as, a mediating philosophy of "both-and." Although sensitively opposed to any "extreme view," any "absolute choice," any "blueprinted future," it accepts from its heritage the positive worth of liberty as the right to speak, think, worship, act, live as far as possible according to one's deepest personal needs. At the same time, it stresses, especially in recent decades, the importance of the community and the purpose of increasing unity and cohesiveness among groups. It strives, therefore, to give a fair hearing to economic, political, ethical proposals that might further liberate men and help them to find better ways of growing together with their fellows.

But let us also bear in mind that the liberal temper is essentially cautious. It is resilient, tolerant, sympathetic, open-minded, curious about novel suggestions and new ways of planning. Equally, however, it is suspicious of dogmatic proposals, rigid tradition, arrogant authority, stubborn prejudice. The liberal is on his guard against any kind of "extremism." Granting that ours is a period of inevitable change, of unique social demands, he never strays too far from the path along which our culture has been patiently moving for so long. Progress must occur in many areas, step by step, gradually. To edge forward a little at a time, from where we were, to where we are, toward where we might later be —testing, trying, planning, replanning, modifying—this is as essential to the liberal's mood and strategy of moderation as it is to the scientist whom, above all others, he seeks to emulate.

That later liberalism has succeeded in profoundly influencing and in giving voice to a large proportion of American institutions, practices, habits, and attitudes is a matter of record. In politics, it grew in power and prestige through such presidents as Theodore Roosevelt, Woodrow Wilson, and, above all, Franklin Roosevelt. In the world of economics, supported by the world of politics, the working people were increasingly protected in their right to organize; political experiments in a "mixed economy" and in new federal responsibilities were encouraged. In law, both political and economic experimentation was supported by the constitutional interpretations of such liberal Justices of the Supreme Court as Oliver Wendell Holmes and William O. Douglas. In education, progressivist schools were established in many parts of the country as well as abroad; they not only attracted wide attention but also influenced countless others on every level and in many localities.

To contend that the liberal road has been the only road along which our culture has traveled in recent decades would be, of course, a gross distortion. We Americans have been much too diversified, too fluid, too busy "succeeding" to know or care very much whether we have always been unified in our efforts, consistent in our direction, or harmonious in the beliefs that serve as our guides. Nonetheless, after all reversals, contradictions, and vacillations have been taken into account (one may cite the conservatism of the Coolidge-Hoover period of the twenties, the Eisenhower period of the fifties, erratic decisions of the Supreme Court, resistance to welfare legislation such as public health, the reactionary period of McCarthyism, and widespread resistance to progressive education), it is still impossible to deny that liberalism-progressivism has been, and remains, an attractive, impelling choice. In its value orientation it has seemed to suit, as no other choice has suited, a culture at once individual and social, independent and interdependent, private and public. Above all, it has seemed to fit a culture much more preoccupied with the process of expansion and growth than with viable boundaries and determinable goals. Even when it has not succeeded in capturing the whole of a particular institution—as experimental education has never captured the public schools of America—the confidence and optimism of advocates, such as Kilpatrick and other progressivist theorists succeeding him, still remain influential.

PROGRESSIVISM ON THE DEFENSIVE

But such confidence and optimism remain open to serious doubts. Like the liberal culture it espouses, the fact is that progressivism has been on the defensive in many places. Spokesmen for educational tradition and for classical learning (against whom Dewey and his lieutenants took the offensive in earlier years of our century) have themselves mounted a powerful counteroffensive while critical voices of more radical inflection are also increasingly heard. Meanwhile, many educational spokesmen scrupulously avoid the term "progressive education." Or, if they use it at all, they refer to the past, as though it were an outmoded educational fad to be viewed condescendingly but no longer as a force in the schools. No wonder that the acclaimed historian of progressivism, Lawrence A. Cremin, should have declared that the movement has suffered a "dismal end." Indeed, it has "collapsed."[3]

Nevertheless, one detects in some of Cremin's interpretations an overtone of half-wishfulness. Actually, as he also notes, perceptive interpreters have long subjected progressivism to sharp criticism for some of its own frailties, both in theory and action. For example, Bode, as far back as 1938, indicted it for what he regarded as real or apparent inconsistencies: method versus content, individualism versus cooperation, intellectualism versus overt experience, and others. In the same year, Dewey, too, recognized how easily progressivist schools might pervert his philosophy. Therefore, he warned against anarchy as a spurious substitute for genuine freedom in education, against lack of careful curriculum planning, and against the tendency to other faulty educational practices of which overzealous, but inadequately trained, teachers and administrators have sometimes been guilty.

As their most relevant defense, meanwhile, progressivists have continued to call attention to concrete educational achievements. Granting mistakes and conceding weaknesses, the record is impressive not only in that the average child learns as well by progressivist as by more traditional methods, but that he frequently learns much better. Some competent psychologists, to be sure, have been convinced of a greater need for structure or for formal exercise in certain skills. But, in acquiring and utilizing the knowledge of society, art, and, to a large degree, natural science; in developing critical attitudes, initiative, and individuality; and in participating cooperatively and happily both in school and community affairs—in ways such as these progressivist learning has frequently proved to be more effective than that based on more customary or routinized procedures.

The progressivist also reminds us that many of his basic ideas, which only he and his associates advocated a few decades ago, are now accepted by many who do not associate themselves with these ideas at all. Rather, they are accepted by some of the very leaders who like to ridicule the label. Accordingly, he seeks further opportunity to test his hypotheses. Is it not absurd, he asks, to condemn wholesale the weaknesses of public education

[3] Cremin, *The Transformation of the School*, pp. 348, 350.

and even of democracy by calling these institutions overprogressivized when, as a matter of fact, the majority of public schools are only now beginning to catch up with the philosophy of progressivism—when, indeed, they are only now becoming full-fledged partners of our technological and democratic age?

THE MODERATIVE CHARACTER OF PROGRESSIVISM

Thus far, we have taken two steps toward a culturological evaluation of progressivism. The first step carried us to the judgment that progressivism, along with its philosophic core of pragmatism, is the educational corollary of later liberalism. Therefore, it seeks to encourage schools that are, both in theory and practice, genuinely liberal. Like the scientific method, which is their most frequently applied guiding belief, they are mobile and inductive. Also, at their best, they are strongly individualized in their approach to learning at the same time that they aim to become strongly socialized.

The second brief step in our evaluation led to the generalization that progressivism's earlier aggressive, often victorious, attacks upon traditional types of education have shifted to a defensive position in the face of strong counteroffensives. This is not to say that all progressivists have remained silent; they have sometimes replied convincingly to their critics both inside and outside the profession. Some have maintained their influence in practice as well as theory.

Nevertheless, the counteroffensive continues, waxing and waning, according to the shifting public mood created by particular educational and cultural issues. Our third and final step thus remains to be taken. We shall inquire into some of the reasons for this stormy climate of opinion, especially reasons discernible in the cultural milieu with which progressivism is allied.

LIBERALISM IN A CRISIS-CULTURE

To inquire into the causes of this controversy, it may be helpful to recall a few of the characteristics of our crisis-culture. In Chapter 2 we discussed some of the shocks to which contemporary institutions, habits, and beliefs are being subjected. Alternating periods of precarious peace and ruinous war, of revolution and counterrevolution, have made the twentieth century one of the most fearful and destructive in recorded history. In sum, ours has been a century of pervasive and deep-cutting conflicts within and among nations.

It is in this climate of fluctuations, confusions, and cross-purposes that the deepest causes of much of the present skepticism and hostility toward liberalism in general, and toward progressivism in particular, may be detected. For if it is true, as we have asserted, that liberalism more than any other outlook has implemented and verbalized the meanings and intentions of recent American culture, then it is liberalism that is certain to be severely attacked when that culture suffers from such painful and chronic tensions and disturbances as we have described.

Look once more at the record of events. The outstanding liberal apostle of internationalism in our time, Woodrow Wilson, not only failed to prevent World War I but failed also to establish a workable League of Nations. And not only did his great liberal heir, Franklin Roosevelt, fail to prevent World War II, but the social measures taken under his leadership as "cures" for the worst depression in American history were often discarded the moment postwar prosperity had lulled the people into a sense of dubious security. Even such eminently liberal interpretations of the Constitution as those of Justice Holmes have not been firmly established as legal precedents; on the contrary, decisions of the Supreme Court fluctuate so curiously that we can only predict that the philosophy of law most likely to govern any particular case is seldom, if ever, predictable.

Let us grant that Presidents Wilson and Roosevelt, or the presidents who have followed them, could no more be held wholly responsible for the tragedies in which they played such prominent roles than could the jurist, Holmes, or the philosopher, Dewey, be held responsible for failures of their culture. Nevertheless, in the spirit of fairness for which liberals are themselves notable, we must insist that if these men deserve a share of credit for the assets of our period, then they also deserve a share of responsibility for its debits. The plain truth is that, when inventories are taken, the proud achievements of our liberal culture are marred by grim liabilities of fear, deprivation, and violence both within and among nations.

Persistent and plaguing questions are, then, to be expected. Can America any longer rely so buoyantly upon its zestful ingenuity, its energetic capacity to extricate itself from difficult situations, its haughty self-sufficiency, its rich natural resources, its eagerness to try proposed schemes, and to venture along whatever path the moment offers? Can we expect to solve the problems that now beset us by continuing to resort to pseudo-optimistic beliefs in compromise, in growth for the sake of further growth, in cautious progress? Can we rely so confidently and so exclusively upon the reasonableness of the scientific method and the experimental mode of thinking to direct our cultural development? Can we afford to gaze so intently upon the flow of *present* experience that we must regard the future as intangible? Is the liberal's typically moderative approach to problems of exploitation, segregation, and global war adequate to cope with pressures and faiths that are daring and uncompromising?

That the liberal's answer to such questions is earnest and often persuasive has been made evident in his educational theories and cultural accomplishments. The progressivist, too, may contend (and we should agree with his contention) that the counteroffensive against experimental schools by forces outside, as well as inside, the profession may arise largely not so much from asserted *educational* objections as from unasserted *cultural* premises. Thus, he may argue that such opposition is often traceable to a fear that progressivisim, were it to become widely influential in public education, would encourage widespread criticism of the system of private enterprise, or that it might educate the peoples of the earth (not of one nation) to believe that *they* are the sole determiners of their ultimate fate. Still more crassly, hostility stems, so progressivists might also assert, from a fear that they promote classroom practices of excessive cost to the taxpayer.

Moreover, on a still broader plane, we should remember that, because liberalism is opposed to any kind of absolutist outlook, it *tends* often to lend its influence toward the more or less experimental side of the chief conflicts of our crisis-culture: toward social-interest rather than self-interest, toward equality rather than inequality, toward planning rather than planlessness, toward internationalism rather than nationalism, toward man-for-himself rather than man-against-himself. Similarly, it often supports extensive changes in behalf of greater technological achievement, greater economic-political freedom for average citizens, greater abundance. Finally, the liberal could well point out that social, religious, or other organized forms of opposition to him derive, in large part, from lack of confidence in, or fear of, his own genuinely amenable, democratic spirit.

On the whole, however, liberalism as a pervasive rationale of institutional and behavioral experience has perhaps as often demonstrated remarkable skill in reconciling or accommodating itself to economic, political, or other cultural conflicts as in committing itself firmly to one as against another side of many such conflicts. And, after all, is not a conciliatory mood entirely in harmony with its frequent actions? Despite all the failures of recent history, the liberal insists that, by his mediating strategies, cultural gains have clearly outrun cultural losses. By free speech and fair play, by cautious evolutionary change, he has helped to ventilate the minds of men. He has encouraged them to make decisions on basic issues only after they have considered all relevant aspects and to question whether any one answer is necessarily the only right answer. Moreover, his conviction that advances can best be effected moderately discourages hasty actions. True, his approach to problems demands consummate patience. Yet this very patience ensures greater improvement in the long run of personal and social progress than impetuosity or carelessness. So many thousands of reforms have been effected in economics, politics, education—indeed, in every phase of cultural experience—that we may expect still more reforms if we will but pursue the liberal road along which we can claim to have traveled successfully thus far.

What, then, is our overall appraisal of both the critique and the defense of liberalism as these are variously expressed? That it has often proved to be a capable, devoted servant of American civilization is clear. But the primary issue before us is not whether it *has been* but whether, during the period of acute stress that we have already entered, *it can continue to be* equally capable and devoted.

A disturbing question thus persists. *Is later liberalism, like early liberalism a century ago, becoming defective in its capacity to interpret and direct the course of dominant events?* Just as later liberalism, however, did not so much reject as supplement and strengthen early liberalism, so the paramount need today may equally be to supplement and strengthen later liberalism as well.

Let us turn our attention, accordingly, to two related and comprehensive areas in which it becomes pertinent to inquire whether later liberalism and, so, both pragmatism and progressivism respond adequately to the crisis of our time. Each area may be conceptualized as an area of *tension* between broad pairs of theoretical but also practical terms: the first, tension between means and ends; the second, tension between individuality and sociality. Our considered judgment is that, with all its energy and competence, this philosophy of education-and-culture in its characteristic formulations is incapable of satisfactorily releasing either state of tension. On the contrary, it often adds to their severity.

THE TENSION BETWEEN MEANS AND ENDS

Hypothesis and commitment. As our first illustration, recall the key concept defined above as an "act of thought." This is the problem-solving methodology also stressed in progressivist learning.

Although the logical clarity as well as usefulness of this methodology must not be minimized, the practical question here is whether the centrality of problem-solving as a process does not invite philosophic justification for lack of strong commitment to anything so much as the process itself. Emphasis, in other words, is more often upon "how we think"—upon analyzing, setting up, and testing hypotheses—than upon the clear-cut conclusions, objectives, or commitments that may be attained as results of such thinking.

Mead himself, moreover, reinforces this judgment in finding that Dewey's philosophy insists ". . . upon the statement of the end in terms of the means. . . ." As such, it is an expression of the American belief that ". . . the ideal phase of politics and business has been found in the process rather than in their objectives. . . ."[4]

True, many passages in the writings of progressivists, especially of Dewey, recognize the need for positive, far-sighted conclusions. Not only does his fruitful concept of immediate experience as capable of becoming an intrinsically valued end provide an ontological basis for the view that intelligence mediates in behalf of such experience but, we recall, the test of truth lies in the *consequences* of thinking. Thus, to argue that ends are not important along with means would be an absurd distortion.

Nevertheless, when ends are attained, they become subject to such further modification that often they seem to slip from our grasp. When, accordingly, the progressivist is asked to specify to *what* ends we should be committed, one of his favorite replies is against inflexibility and dogmatic authority. And, after all, is it not true that no single feature of pragmatism-progressivism is as prominent or distinctive as its brilliant delineation of the *process* of inquiry?

Now, the point to be noted is that such an *emphasis* upon process is strikingly congenial to twentieth-century American culture. If any aggregate of characteristics has dominated this culture, it is precisely those of movement, development, action, change. Just as liberalism—notably, in its later forms—has aimed to liberate men from the constrictions of exploitation and limited

[4] Mead, "The Philosophies of Royce, James, and Dewey in their American Setting," *International Journal of Ethics*, Jan., 1930.

privileges and rights, so pragmatism-progressivism has aimed to liberate men from fixed categories, static routines, and strict dominations. In their place, it provides a common faith in the growing, ongoing, continuous, and evolutionary.

Progressive education, plausibly and typically, has accented much the same kind of methodological concern. In rebelling against the rigidities of authoritarian schooling, it upholds the *solving* of problems as supremely important. But it has not as persistently upheld the need for commitment to solutions that should result *from* problem-solving—especially not if such solutions take the form of encompassing cultural goals. Just as capitalism and technology opened up vast resources of nature to investigation and exploited these resources with minor concern for eventualities, so schools geared to our burgeoning era may encourage the investigation of novel, ever-expanding frontiers of experience and yet subordinate whatever inclusive achievements might be desired as the results of such investigation.

We reiterate that the choice—strictly speaking—is never between mutually exclusive alternatives, and defenders of the progressivist position correctly claim that artificial issues are raised by critics who attempt to dichotomize ends and means. What is not artificial is the point of stress. The *stress* of the progressivist is upon "how" rather than "what," upon process rather than product, upon hypotheses rather than commitments. Or, to state the difficulty less severely, let us say that the "what" is always somehow *contained in* the "how," the product *in* the process, commitments *in* hypotheses. As one relevant example, we may note that such an astute disciple as Bode concluded an impassioned plea for fresh cultural direction and purpose with little more than a restatement of experimental method as the ideal democratic end.

Tolerance and conviction. A state of tension may also be observed in the use of pragmatism by some progressivists in ways to discourage strong, manifest convictions. The teacher, especially, is tempted to suppose that such convictions may be incompatible with democratic education. Hence, correct opposition to indoctrination becomes, on occasion, much more doubtful opposition to programs of learning that seek expression of systematic and positive beliefs.

Granting that progressivists, again, are not always unified or explicit in this matter, even Dewey sometimes, in effect, discouraged clear-cut convictions among teachers and students. Thus he and his disciples have disapproved (as we shall note in Chapter 20) the careful study of religious doctrines by public education, for example, apparently because they question whether the curriculum could deal critically enough with doctrines antithetical to those with which they are themselves in sympathy. For partially similar reasons, some progressivists have, at times, bitterly opposed the right of a Communist to teach even if professionally qualified in his own field. In short, many have seemed curiously reluctant to risk giving to a teacher, whose own beliefs may be attained by methods or principles contrary to theirs, the privilege of holding and defending them in the open forum of democratic classrooms.

Moreover, the argument is not persuasive that the teacher of strong convictions contrary to those of progressivism would refuse to submit his own beliefs to thorough scrutiny. Before proposing to exclude his views from democratic schools, one would suppose that progressivists, to be consistent with their inductive and cooperative methods, would first experiment with policies and programs offering the dissident teacher opportunities to *demonstrate* his capacity or incapacity for objective analysis—the opportunity, also, to share his convictions with others, and to subject them to the comparison and criticism of differing students and fellow teachers.

In the light of such quandaries, one wonders, indeed, whether progressivists are always as tolerant as they earnestly profess. No doubt they are tolerant enough of tolerance in the abstract—that is to say, of scientific inquiry and of openmindedness. Sometimes individual progressivists go further (again, Dewey is usually the best proof) by taking fairly radical stands on political and economic issues. While it is therefore difficult to generalize on the issue of tolerance and conviction, perhaps a fair statement is that the extent to which convictions are encouraged by the progressivist depends upon the extent to which they are congenial to the liberal climate of habit and opinion. For this reason, the most congenial—and surely, the safest—conviction is sometimes lack of conviction except in behalf of the careful and moderate means by which ends may be attained.

Present and future. A final example of the tension between means and ends is the liberal-progressivist view of time. Past, present, and future are all conceded to be objective events. Not only is the study of history, for example, indispensable to progressive education but also, as in his concern with ends, the progressivist teacher by no means altogether disregards the importance of the future. After all, since experience is temporal, it must inevitably encompass all three common dimensions.

Again, however, the question to be answered is not whether the pragmatic philosophy of time includes the future in its ontology but where it focuses its attention. Here the answer is clear. Seldom, if ever, have Dewey and other liberals tried to shape any definite designs of a future order toward which, precisely because of such formulation, we might be better prepared to take confident steps. More strongly, they ordinarily dismiss all such formulations as utopian—a term that, to them, is, more often than not, repugnant.

The rapidity of present social change and the conviction that conflict and uncertainty are ultimate traits of existence even provide a rationalization for minimizing attention to the future. As Kilpatrick expresses it:

> The world of affairs is clearly changing more rapidly in our day than ever before, and the stream of events always develops in novel fashion. The future becomes thus even more uncertain than hitherto. Some things we can, to be sure, in reason foretell: Seasons will recur; children will be born, grow up, live out their time, and die. . . . But who can foretell what specific significant events will happen, what new problems will arise? . . . Who can now foretell what Europe, or the world, will be like in another twenty years?[5]

But Dewey had anticipated Kilpatrick's remark some half a century earlier: "With the advent of democracy and modern industrial conditions, it is impossible to foretell definitely just what civilization will be twenty years from now."[6]

These quotations help us to understand how progressivism, again like liberalism, derives its beliefs not primarily from philosophy but from its cultural environment. Especially the American environment has been one of process and movement and, correspondingly, one of short-range vision and strong preoccupation with the present. Such preoccupation is not surprising. A youthful country brimming with opportunity and enticement, with untapped wealth, with unbounded optimism, with problems

[5] Kilpatrick, in National Society for the Study of Education, *Forty-first Yearbook*, Part I, "Philosophies of Education," p. 65.

[6] Dewey, in Archambault (ed.), *John Dewey on Education*, p. 429.

needing to be settled quickly should not be too worried about what lies far ahead—or, accordingly, with mature cultural designs.

We can well understand that this kind of interest is reflected in progressive education. Of course, time is never conceived as a momentary "specious present," for learning always involves some stretching back into the past and forward into the future. But when we ask, "*How far?*" the answer usually given is that we cannot reach too far ahead without jeopardizing our dependence upon passing experience. In a culture hitherto fairly content with its immediate resources and exuberant abilities, the correct statement that we cannot clairvoyantly "foretell" what the future *will* be comes to imply easily that we must not try to foresee too concretely what the future *could* or *should* be. Thus, Dewey's sound insight that good schools cannot merely prepare for later adult life is subtly, perhaps unconsciously, transformed into the far less defensible belief that education should be so centrally concerned with current events of living as to neglect sustained attention to aggressive programs and comprehensive purposes for the potential period of cultural transformation looming before us.

THE TENSION BETWEEN INDIVIDUALITY AND SOCIALITY

Our characterization of later liberalism has suggested that it is a philosophy expressed through both individuality and sociality, through both the personal and the communal. Perhaps its greatest appeal lies in this interactive principle—a principle that Dewey stated with great cogency as far back as 1897 in *My Pedagogic Creed*. We quote in part here:

> . . . this educational process has two sides—one psychological and one sociological—and . . . neither can be subordinated to the other, or neglected, without evil results following. Of these two sides, the psychological is the basis. The child's own instincts and powers furnish the material and give the starting-point for all education. . . . Knowledge of social conditions . . . is necessary in order properly to interpret the child's powers. The child has his own instincts and tendencies, but we do not know what these mean until we can translate them into their social equivalents. . . . In sum, I believe that the individual who is to be educated is a social individual, and that society is an organic union of individuals.[7]

[7] *Ibid.*, p. 428.

Now the problem posed by this relation lies not so much in its plausibility as in its meaning for a period of history increasingly and pervasively different from that in which it was first expressed. We have already met this problem in various forms. Its most disturbing features may, however, be restated in two questions: (1) How can the individual hope to develop his "powers" and "tendencies" in the midst of and in active relation to cultural patterns and institutions that are constantly becoming more gigantic, more powerful, more impersonal, and more collective? (2) If hope prevails that the individual can achieve this development, what kinds of cultural institutions and practices should he help to build and apply so that they, in turn, will lend support to his development?

The individual emphasis. Despite many qualifications, liberal-progressivists lead us to believe that the best way for an individual to develop himself, and thereby society, is to utilize fully his capacities, especially his intelligence. This belief is supported by the potent individualistic influence of James. It is supported still more strongly by the insistence of Dewey that the powers of the child are the "starting-point" of all education, by his delineation of the reflective capacities of the individual, by the psychology and logic of an "act of thought," and by the progressivist view of the behavioral patterns of human nature. Further, we should not forget that the individualistic stress in progressivism, even today unacceptable to many conventional schools, has been a legitimate protest against the stern formalism of traditional education.

Whatever the causes of their concern with the individual, it is interesting to observe how many of Dewey's disciples persist in emphasizing the biopsychological aspects of experience. To be sure, they consider at times the sociological aspect as carefully as did Dewey himself. Yet, it would be difficult to deny that Bode's most characteristic contribution is his brilliant psychological study, *How We Learn,* or that the same type of psychological concern likewise overshadows others in the creative writings of Kilpatrick and of such latter-day progressivists as Ernest Bayles and Donald Arnstine.

No wonder, then, that the child-centered school, referred to above, has played so prominent a role in the history of progressive education. Despite the tireless insistence of all able exponents that the good school is *both* individual and social, despite progressivist enthusiasm for shared interests and community life, the child-centered emphasis remains conspicuous for its frequency and popularity in the professional education, especially of elementary teachers. Here the major premise of the individualist emphasis, which may at times reflect the spirit of Rousseau more genuinely than that of Dewey, is this: the most fruitful way to deal with acute problems of our culture is, above all, for each individual to be conditioned and encouraged to study the culture primarily from the point of view of an *individual* living with *other individuals*. Help the child to live richly and intelligently, release him from the bondage of traditional authority and passive learning, and the good society will most surely emerge.

The social emphasis. Although it may be shown, then, that the child-centered approach continues to be more influential in practice than the community-centered school, nevertheless the community-centered approach to education has not been neglected. Dewey himself, let us not forget, always manifested a marked social concern both for educational experiments and for political and social as well as educational theory. Nor should the sociocultural aspects of Kilpatrick's summation of a lifetime be overlooked in his *Philosophy of Education*. Finally, progressivists must applaud reinvigorated interest in community schools that are increasingly advocated for large cities as ways to involve citizens in their own educational and neighborhood problems.

By their social emphasis, progressivists may thus recognize the weakness of their individualistic emphasis. Some may even agree that overconcern for the individual in education is a more or less subtle reflection of the competitive economic order, and of the faith in pecuniary success attained by self-interest at the expense of social-interest. They would, perhaps, even agree that the cult of child development could be symptomatic of cultural lag—an aftermath of the earlier liberalism that later liberalism inherited but failed to integrate fully into its own cultural beliefs.

Remaining doubts. The two emphases just epitomized create a state of tension which now come into focus in the first of our two earlier questions: How can individuals develop their capacities in the face of such impersonal social configurations and power structures as now prevail in the culture? Our doubts about progressivist responses to this question are expressed as briefly as possible.

(1) *The continued influence of the psychological, individual-centered phase of the liberal-progressivist movement is too dominant to permit it to unite solidly around a straight-*

forward social orientation. This results partly from Dewey's keen interest in the process of intelligence, probably still more directly from the views of his psychology-minded followers, but most of all from the culture that supports their movement. The American culture, in various ways, is still individual-centered, still vacillating and uncertain as to the extent to which it should relinquish, for example, private enterprise for social enterprise, local authority for federal authority, national rights for international rights.

Moreover, the communities which have been most resilient to progressivism are largely suburban middle class, well-to-do, well educated, and they pride themselves on their hospitality to liberal trends. But their school systems are very unlikely to challenge seriously the heritage of individualism so long as this heritage remains a half-expressed rationale for the status of their controlling citizen groups.

(2) *The social emphasis is further obfuscated by the reluctance of liberal-progressivists to assess sufficiently the stubborn, illogically maintained obstacles that impede their own pleas for intelligent action.* True, these obstacles are not ignored. Such pragmatists as Otto devoted many years to exposing absolutism—especially the authoritarian, antidemocratic qualities inherent in traditional religion. Others have vigorously protested comparable qualities in political totalitarianism.

But does it remain at all certain that liberalism-progressivists appear, as a whole, persistently or aggressively realistic in providing the kind of diagnoses and prognoses requisite to coping with obstacles such as these? Is it not the case, for example, that the emphatic *psychological* concern of a Bode or a Kilpatrick largely bypassed *psychoanalytic* aspects of human behavior, and hence the hidden, unrational springs of learning experience? Still more seriously, have most pragmatic philosophers paid probing, realistic understanding to the military-industrial complex, to the political power structure that sustains it, or to the potent machines of mass communication untilized in behalf of both that complex and that structure? And thus to the degree that intellectual leaders of progressivism temper *their* concern for sharp negative analyses of such obstacles in the path of democratic progress, may we really expect the administrator or teacher who looks to these leaders for guidance not to temper *his* ostensible concern?

(3) *The uncertainty or direct avoidance of sharp negative analyses of psychocultural obstacles invites a judgment of insufficiency as to positive social strategies for coping with these obstacles.* The general character of the progressivist method—centered in scientific problem-solving—is of inestimable importance; it needs to be applied far more universally than hitherto. Moreover, the pragmatist's contention that social science lags behind natural science, and that we have not as yet approached most economic, national, and similar issues in an experimental manner, is equally urgent. But the question stubbornly persists whether thus far we are even offered a workable model through which to approach these issues. The liberal-progressivist's moderative value orientation, his caution against undue haste, his warning that we must never resort to impatience—all surely aggravate the question whether "the failure of reasonable man" is not his reluctance to assess the unreasonableness of his enemies, especially of his enemies' ruthless political and national power.

Dewey's somewhat belated concern with the problem of social struggle against such enemies highlights the grounds for our critical judgment. His legitimate opposition to the Marxian theory of dialectical materialism, because it is absolutist and even metaphysical, seems to have deterred him from asking squarely whether other aspects of this theory might not have strengthened his own methodology in dealing with, let us say, economic conflict. In one or two books, he cautiously raised this question. But he did not answer it; he did not admit that the concept of "class struggle," operationally interpreted and adjusted to a culture differing acutely from that of Marx himself, might be utilized for both fruitful diagnosis and vigorous democratic action. Meanwhile, the great majority of progressivists have flatly rejected this neo-Marxian concept, if they have considered it at all. Instead they have resorted to the more comfortable, more congenial way of multiple means and social compromises because, for one thing, these are far more congenial to the central mood that pervades their beliefs.

This is not to overlook contributions that some theorists of progressivist strain, such as Kenneth D. Benne, have made to the philosophy and psychology of *group* behavior. The collective world that has risen like a giant undoubtedly affects such fruitful developments as human relations and group dynamics. With the exception, however, of Dewey and Mead in developing their concepts of the social self, perhaps the two sociological theorists who have most directly impressed American educational thought in shifting toward social-centered and away from individual-centered action have been European-trained: Karl Mannheim and Kurt Lewin. Among more formal philosophers, one of the most influential has also been European educated: Martin Buber. Yet it remains doubtful whether any one of these three seminal scholars has exerted substantial impact upon everyday education. Certainly only meager empirical evidence of such an impact upon progressivist practice, much less theory, is thus far discernible.

What, then, is the common denominator of the several points we have tried to sharpen in centering upon progressivism's social emphasis? In brief, it is that liberal-progressivism has not convincingly answered our first question above: How can the individual hope to develop his "powers" and "tendencies" in active relationship to cultural patterns, institutions, and groupings that yet are constantly becoming more powerful, more impersonal, and more collective? The personal-psychological emphasis that continues to deemphasize sociological and anthropological areas of interpretation, plus faltering analyses of inimical social forces and corrective strategies, combine to produce a state of tension in which average individuals cannot find aggressive, systematic, or dedicated ways of acting in concert with their fellows.

The need for a cultural norm. Turn at last to our companion question: If hope still remains that the individual can achieve rich personal development, what cultural institutions and practices should he help to build so that they, in turn, will lend support to this development? The implication of our question is that individual and social processes need to be guided by explicit norms if they are to have clear intent and expectation. Does the philosophy with which we are here concerned provide any such norms?

In a degree, of course, it does. Our exposition of its axiology has disclosed the devotion of progressivism to the ideal of democracy—an ideal defined sometimes in terms of maximum interaction among growing individuals and groups; sometimes, as the experimental method in personal and social operation. Nevertheless, as is true in the other areas of tension, a certain quality of ambiguous hesitation haunts the quest for certainty. We have felt this quality throughout our examination of the means-ends relationship. In the appreciation of commitment, there is a stress on hypothesis; in the recognition of the future, a stress on the present; in the admiration of conviction, a stress on tolerance. The same hesitation, in another context, has appeared in the tension of individuality and sociality. The liberal's commendable concern, on the one hand, to maintain both aspects in dynamic balance prevents him from providing, on the other hand, culturally designed objectives that are sufficiently concrete or unequivocal to include both individuality and sociality.

This generalization might be illustrated in many concrete ways, but let us consider a more basic contention. Dewey and his colleagues insist that individuals should enjoy the right to growth, to equal opportunity and participation—in short, to all values of democracy. But they do not outline graphically the normative contours of a culture by which we could measure our failures and successes in attaining individual satisfaction of these democratic values. Indeed, one may ask whether we are even afforded an adequate conception of the good individual. For so long as we are deflected from any substantive description of the good society, how can we conceive of the good individual when, on the progressivist's own premises, he becomes meaningful only in the full context of that society?

A still more dramatic example of hesitation in answering our second question follows from progressivism's opposition to a "planned" society and its equally strong support of a "planning" society. Reasons for this position have been sufficiently provided so that it becomes necessary only to ask whether they are convincing.

Does the liberal-progressivist philosophy, which offers such persuasive objections to religious and political absolutism, offer comparably positive anticipations of democratic fulfillment? In its legitimate opposition to totalitarianism, does it not fail to envisage alternative arrangements for an increasingly cooperative but also libertarian order? In its rejection of cultural uniformity, does it not often shy away from the objective of cultural plurality synthesized with the magnificent ideal of humanity? In its key belief that education is an agent of cultural progress, does it not hesitate to agree upon clear directions for such progress? In its resentment against traditional individualism and motives of self-interest, does it not also discourage us from fashioning viable institutional arrangements based much more strongly upon cooperation and motives of social-interest—arrangements by which to channel the revolutions in technology, politics-economics, and abundance toward worldwide democratic goals? In objecting to "blueprints" on the ground that we cannot know in advance what should be *planned,* does it not divert us from deciding for what people should be *planning*? In correctly warning us against the fanaticism and bigotry that sometimes accompany strong commitment to social purposes, does not liberalism-progressivism disavow also that esthetic fervor or religious dynamic without which men never create greatly or hope boldly?

Satisfying answers to such entangling questions are never purely negative or positive. Indeed, as we have suggested, progressivism itself frequently provides abundant materials *for* just these answers. Nonetheless, when the balance is struck, the fashioning is far from accomplished. Like the rapidly shifting cultural patterns embracing it, here is a philosophy midway between the fixed universe against which it rebels and the designed culture which still awaits creation. Liberalism is the rationale of this unrelieved tension between means and ends, between individuality and sociality.

And so progressivism, in the revealing terms of Harold Taylor, ". . . will accept as true the fact that *education is an instrument of social transition.* It will thus be a liberal philosophy, taking as its goal the development of free men in a changing social order."[8] In still franker terms, progressivism is the educational effort of an adolescent culture, suffering from the pleasant agonies of growing up, from preoccupation with the excitement of present events, from the cultural period of trying and erring when the protections of infancy have been left behind but the planned autonomies of maturity await future delineation and fulfillment.

CRITIQUE OF PROGRESSIVISM: CURRENT PHILOSOPHIC VIEWS

Our preceding judgment of progressivism, viewed as personal-cultural moderation, deserves one additional consideration. Recalling the several movements of contemporary thought sketched in Part 1, our intention here must again be even more selective: to prevail upon one or another of these movements to assist us in striving toward further culturological evaluation of the liberal-progressivist orientation—an orientation which, although one

[8] Taylor, "Education as Experiment," *Antioch Review*, Summer, 1949 (italics supplied).

powerful symbol of the crisis-culture that pervades it throughout, requires the kind of reinforcing supplementations that we shall now consider.

Neo-Marxism. The most immediate example of this kind of assistance recalls the tension noted above between individuality and sociality, particularly the observation that contemporary progressivists almost invariably tend to denigrate several relevant features. Certainly, it seems evident that neo-Marxism, one of the most impelling philosophic movements of our age, receives even less attention from younger progressivists than it did in the depression years of the thirties—a fact easily demonstrated by subsequent progressivist-oriented textbooks in educational theory where Marxism may be entirely omitted from the index. Also noteworthy is the discovery that one collection of essays by a dozen commentators upon Dewey's educational philosophy includes none at all that could be considered even vaguely neo-Marxian, much less Marxian, in critical "appraisal."

This is not at all to suggest that neo-Marxism is ignored elsewhere. In the United States, the work of Fromm, Marcuse, and others abundantly testifies (however much they also differ among themselves) to its resounding influence. Still more impressively, a profusion of scholars, especially in European countries, demonstrate the vitality of neo-Marxian thought outside the Soviet Union. In many such writings, one may note devastating objections to Marxian forms of orthodoxy, on the one hand, and tough-minded confrontations of radical sociopolitical change in democratic directions, on the other. To cite only a single source, the international symposium, *Socialist Humanism*, edited by Fromm, embraces a prolific range of critical themes and projective interpretations that compare, inferentially at least, the main expressions of neo-Marxian thought with what we have called both early and later liberalism.

The implication here should be evident enough. Neo-Marxism, because its main social thrust is by no means wholly at odds with that of progressivism, might contribute abundantly indeed were it to be taken seriously once more—but this time, we trust, by more than a mere smattering of educational philosophers.

Neo-Freudianism. Because, however, the progressivist tension between individuality and sociality avoids sufficient attention to *both* polarities, it therefore underemphasizes individuality in some important senses just as it does sociality in others. In either case, as we have also noted, progressivism tends to pay much less searching attention to irrational or unrational factors than it does to rational ones.

The argument may be reemphasized by Dewey's cursory references to Freudian theory. *In Human Nature and Conduct* (1922), it is not hard to understand that "psycho-analysis" is mentioned but five times, and then, as a rule, mainly to protest characteristically against the fallacy of reductionism—in this case, reduction to the sexual drive as sufficient cause of human behavior. Dewey was too astute to ignore the unconscious altogether. But neither he nor Mead, and certainly not their later disciples, have demonstrated anything like intense interest in Freudian, or even emerging neo-Freudian, theory.

As in the case of neo-Marxism, therefore, contemporary neo-Freudian metapsychology invites us to consider a far more adequate interpretation of progressivism. As Chapter 4 intimated, Freud and Marx are complementary and paradoxical: both exposed the subterranean forces of man (the one psychically, the other socially); both perceived the interdependence of these forces; but both were therapeutic in their eagerness to correct the distortions and dangers generated by them.

Neo-Freudianism, again like neo-Marxism, embraces, we recall, a vast range of both theory and practice, and some of its spokesmen afford fruitful opportunities for rapprochement with progressivists. Nevertheless, our "remaining doubts" about the psychological, individualized side of progressivism are, if anything, intensified. Guidance and counseling, especially, become vulnerable on related scores; not only do progressivist practitioners and their influential leaders (Carl Rogers, for example) play down the power of social and other cultural patterns by playing up the role and primacy of personality, but they even usually tend to minimize the explosive significance of such Freudian concepts as the unconscious itself.

Thus, the practical consequence of neo-Freudian theory as exemplified by some of its proponents could become, for progressivists, both a weakness and a strength—weakness to the degree that it reinforces the imbalance toward individuality; strength to the degree that it encourages, with Fromm and others, to press for incorporation of updated Freudian concepts in direct conjunction with Marxian ones.

Zen Buddhism and existentialism. The more adequate culturological evaluation of progressivism, toward which we are now fumbling, extends our search for more rounded and mature conceptions of individuality than progressivist theorists, thus far, seem able to provide. We have just suggested that one step toward this conception could be fuller incorporation of neo-Freudian theory. What has not been suggested is that both Zen Buddhism and existentialism might contribute still further steps. Neither, so far as we know, has been considered very seriously by most progressivists—whether by Dewey in his influential works or by his loyal disciples.

We fail to discover these movements taken seriously in most post-Deweyan writings, either. One timely example of disregard may be mentioned—*Students Without Teachers,* by the zealous, progressivist philosopher-administrator: Taylor. In two chapters, titled "The Radical Element in American Thought" and "The Return to Progressive Thought," one searches in vain for any reference, much less positive or even negative discussion, to any one of the potent contemporary philosophic developments thus far mentioned. It is not surprising that the "radical element" embraces little more than recapitulation of James and Dewey. One is surprised even less at the ironic term, "return."

The potential contributions of both Zen Buddhism and existentialism to a more modernized appreciation of individuality are partially anticipated by our comments upon neo-Freudianism. Each offers significant insights—Zen in its search for intensity of awareness, especially through esthetic experience; existentialism in concentrating upon the meaning of selfhood as incorporated by, say, the school of existential psychoanalysis.

Neither of these movements, obviously, is new. But their American influence has expanded only with and after the mid-twentieth century—something like half a century after the core of Dewey's own philosophy crystallized. Thus, among pragmatists-progressivists, only one or two works began to take Zen at all seriously (together with Taoism and other Oriental philosophies): *Zen and American Thought,* by the philosopher, Van Meter Ames; and *Imagination,* by the educator, Harold Rugg. Both works, although still neglected, are remarkable demonstrations of how individuality may be broadened and deepened both be removing it from the provincial settings so typical of American culture and by fusing it with a more intercultural, more universal, image of man.

As for existentialism, virtually the only perceptible influence upon a few progressivists or neo-progressivists (Benne, perhaps, most sensitively) has been Buber. His "dialogic philosophy" with its concern for communication in education resembles in various ways the more prosaic renderings of Dewey and Mead of the transactional self-other process. We have no doubt that the insights of Buber could enrich the moderative orientation much more than they ever have thus far.

Philosophic analysis. In fairness to Taylor, it should be noted that he does, incidentally, note some connection between the philosophy of pragmatism and logical or philosophic analysis. This is not unexpected. For many years, pragmatists have been recognized by analysts for their concern with precisions of language as essential to the methodology of experimental science.

But in the context of our present evaluation, two further points deserve attention. The first is that philosophic analysis can be of genuine assistance in reducing the tension between ends and means by attacking the ambiguities that lurk in the relationships of, say, hypothesis and commitment or, in more neutral terms, of process and product.

These ambiguities could be reduced through more exactitude in refining all the terms relevant to the central methodology of problem-solving. Thus, as Israel Scheffler, an analytic philosopher in education, has noted, Dewey's continuous opposition to dichotomies in logic as well as in nature or culture has blurred rather than sharpened the precise terms necessary to reflective thinking. The need for clarification of language applies to any kind of philosophy of education, but its special relevance to progressivism is that the latter otherwise weakens its role as liberalism's ally by virtue of its propensity to discourage definite distinctions in favor of the spirit of flexible accommodation.

The second point is also suggested by Scheffler, although not quite as he intended. Dewey's concern for practical relevance underestimates ". . . the value of detachment from environing social conditions . . ." and thus ". . . fails to do justice to abstract, theoretical considerations in the scientific assessment of evidence."[9] Here, the analytic philosopher is pleading for greater intellectual objectivity in place of too-frequent, indiscriminate encouragement of problem-solving as the key to good education. Still, although this point, too, may be well taken, it at least equally invites the kind of antiprogressivist, transmissive orientation toward which we shall find later that we are sometimes lured, unwittingly or not, in the name of objectivity.

[9] Scheffler, in Archambault, *op. cit.*, pp. 103f.

Recalling, in brief, all five recent philosophic positions together, our principal conclusion is that progressivism, with perhaps somewhat more exception in the case of analysis than in the others, has largely circumvented these movements because they are considered ostensibly irrelevant. A consequence is that, if its formulations remain as unmodified significantly as most of them have since the height of Dewey's influence, we can scarcely afford to be astonished if its direct impact upon education has comparably diminished. One crucial problem that remains then is whether, strengthened by critiques and amendment from contemporary philosophic developments, progressivism may now begin to evolve toward newly potent and relevant levels of theory and practice not only in America but in world culture.

PART 3

Essentialism: education as cultural transmission

CHAPTER 8

The essentialist pattern of philosophic beliefs

PREVIEW OF ESSENTIALISM

FOR VARIOUS REASONS—perhaps the habit of ultra-caution or a stake in established institutional arrangements—some philosophers of education, no less than some citizens, find themselves encouraging the preservation and transmission of practices and beliefs that have characterized the cultural patterns of the period leading up to our uncertain and unstable present. The error of the present culture, according to them, is that it has strayed altogether too far from the road laid out for it by the past. The surest solution for its difficulties is to return directly to that road. Then, and only then, can it hope to regain confidence in itself; then, and only then, can it move forward with certainty and stability.

In this metaphor is to be found the culturological key to essentialism, whether as *critic* of an educational philosophy such as progressivism, or as *advocate* in its own right of an alternative philosophy. As critic, it finds in progressivism, which it regards as perhaps its chief opponent, an embodiment of all the precarious fluctuations of our time—a way of life and education that reflects only too accurately the desperate gropings of rootless and restless persons and, therefore, glorifies the very cultural characteristics most congenial to its own spirit: activity, tentativeness, flexibility, self-direction, trial and error. As advocate, essentialism recognizes certain values in these cultural characteristics, but other values stand higher. These are much more needed as stabilizers: structure and content, orderly sequence, inherited principles, guided discipline, and other patterns derived from the highly complex culture and correlative philosophies of at least four centuries. Their origins are often dated from the Renaissance; their endings, at their highest maturation, were clearly discernible by the latter half of the nineteenth century.

The aim of Part 3, to sketch essentialism in broad strokes and to evaluate it in terms of conspicuous beliefs of the long era of postmedieval civilization (hereafter referred to as the "modern era"), is faced by even greater difficulties of interpretation than that of other major points of view considered in this volume. Progressivism, for example, and notwithstanding its own inadequacies, is more systematic and coherent than a philosophy of education that weaves into its own pattern so great a variety of diverse strands. Indeed, one basic characteristic of essentialism is its *eclecticism*, typified especially by the presence within its own camp of both professed idealists and realists. Even so, we shall see that this curious and sometimes uncomfortable fellowship is quite understandable when judged, not primarily in technical philosophic terms, but rather by the culture that they both help to justify and in behalf of which they both would muster education's arsenal of resources. For allied reasons, we shall see too that philosophic movements other than either realism or idealism—indeed, movements often opposed or indifferent to them on philosophic grounds—become to a remarkable extent compatible agents of cultural transmission through education. We refer particularly, though not exclusively, to philosophic analysis and existentialism, while reiterating that these and other movements are as capable of modifying essentialism *in diverse ways* as they are of alternative philosophies of education.

Allowing for many differences of emphasis and sometimes outright contradictions, what then is the central contribution of essentialism? In briefest compass, it views the established beliefs and institutions of our modern heritage as not only real but true, and not only true but good. It recognizes, of course, that this heritage is marred by flaws—war, disease, and poverty—but it insists that these are usually if not always the results of mistakes in human judgment, not evils inherent in the universe or in man. "Ignorance," in other words, is a term for misjudging the underlying rightness and order of the universe; "understanding," a term for accurately judging its rightness and order.

Thus, the essentialist orientation, however erudite its varying formulations or labels or however earnestly some of its representatives may protest their liberal spirit, has often been utilized skillfully and overtly, as well as subtly, to maintain inherited cultural patterns. Its import becomes clearer, moreover, as the internal conflicts of our age become sharper. No previous era has undergone radical transformation without eloquent and loyal resistance from those who believed they had little to gain by change and, perhaps, much to lose. Our own is no exception. It may be asserted without exaggeration that the transmissive mood, as reflected by popular books and scholarly works of historians, literary critics, and economists, is today as fashionable (certainly in some intellectual circles) as in any other mood. The essentialist in education also reflects this mood. The very character of his doctrine (although sometimes denied by his *professed* intent) would utilize schools to strengthen and refine rather than to alter the complex structure of attitudes, beliefs, and institutions so patiently and expensively erected by the predecessors of our own period of culture.

Having provided this general setting, essentialism will be interpreted under three large headings paralleling those of the preceding three chapters. Chapter 8 considers beliefs of a general philosophic quality; Chapter 9 considers beliefs about education specifically; and Chapter 10 provides a culturological evaluation of essentialism. As in the treatment of progressivism, all three topics are interwoven. Hence, even our more descriptive approach to the first and second is by no means unaffected by our opinion that, despite great lasting contributions, essentialism is no longer satisfactory as a philosophy of education either in its wider connotations or in its direct, practical applications.

It is no longer satisfactory for one overwhelming reason. However complex or attractive the transmissive mood and attitude may be, an age of sweeping change such as our own cannot establish a stable yet dynamic culture by perpetuating either beliefs or habits that were much more suitable for an age now well beyond its crest of maximum achievement. In the respect that the preponderant influence of essentialism under whatever rubric is directed toward such an objective, it may be regarded as the supreme example for our day of a cultural lag in educational philosophy. Yet it is important that we also conscientiously try to respect and benefit by essentialism.

ESSENTIALISM IN THE HISTORY OF THOUGHT

PATTERNS AND OBJECTIVES

Like other important philosophies of our time, essentialism claims a long and honorable ancestry. We should therefore expect its most typical contemporary feature—an articulate, sophisticated concern with the transmission of inherited culture patterns—to derive in certain respects from the very earliest Western philosophers. Plato, particularly, should be mentioned, for he is often regarded as the founder of *objective idealism*—one of two dominant forms of contemporary essentialist theory. Equally important from the point of view of what we shall call *objective realism* is Democritus, who developed the first systematic theory that the whole world, including man, is composed of atoms—particles of matter differing from one another only by such quantitative relations as size and shape. Aristotle, too, was fascinated by the structures of objective reality; although a disciple of Plato, he tried to provide a philosophy as realistic, in some ways, as the Democritean.

But such thinkers, including those of medieval civilization, are chiefly precursors to essentialism. We shall observe in Part 4 that the thought of Plato and Aristotle provides the pattern not so much for essentialism as for perennialism. Essentialism is, above all, a *modern* theory—a product of the Renaissance centuries and beyond. *In place of an ancient and medieval absolutism symbolized by unchallengeable, dogmatic authority of ancient-feudal political and religious institutions, modern essentialist philosophy aims to provide a systematized, unified conception of man and the universe that will be as appropriate as possible to modern needs and institutions.*

Sometimes this conception is developed in almost if not entirely natural and material terms. In this case, we tend to view it as does the modern *realist.* To be sure, it is not easy to define realism concisely, for different exponents of the position tend to stress different facets of the overall position, and we emphasize that classical realists, particularly, are more likely to be associated with some expressions of perennialism than with essentialism. Nevertheless, it may help to quote an epitomization of recent realism by one educational essentialist:

> Realists insist that the qualities of our experience are real independent facts of the external world. They are unchanged by entering the ken of the knower, and do not depend on any mind, finite or infinite, for their existence. The qualities of experience stand on their own feet. The world about us is a real world, not a world of phantasy. . . . However, realists do not agree when they go on from this point to build a metaphysical system. Some of them believe in God even

> though they do not reason their way to that belief via the route of idealism. The existence of God is not made necessary for them by the nature of human knowledge. Other realists do not believe in God. They think of reality in a purely naturalistic sense. Still others suspend judgment as to the existence of God, while accepting the world described by science as the real world.[1]

At other times, essentialism is developed from more spiritual or mentalist premises, in which case we tend to view it as does the modern *idealist.* One may be helped to obtain a preliminary notion of idealism, too, by considering some of its meanings:

> Ultimate reality is of the same substance as ideas. . . . Behind the phenomenal world is an infinite Spirit that is both substructure and creator of the cosmos. . . . The existence of God is made necessary by certain factors in selfhood. . . . Since nothing can be conceived to exist without being in relation to other things, many idealists believe Reality to be a logically unified total system, a Universal Mind.[2]

It will be noted that in both the realist and idealist positions the stress may be either on the universe as a whole or on the self and its ideas or perceptions. Both positions, in other words, attempt to take into consideration the world *and* the individual, with a concern for their interrelations.

Finally, essentialism may be depicted as an adroit *combination* of realism and idealism in one system of philosophic thought. Indeed, we shall find that in educational theory this combination tends to become more significant and useful than the attempt to divide realism and idealism into two completely antithetical positions.

Regardless of such differences, which may become extremely involved, the leading thinkers of the era beginning in about the fifteenth century are, with some exceptions, concerned with two wide objectives. The first is to build a set of beliefs by which men can live in a culture increasingly secular, increasingly scientific, increasingly industrial. The second is to ensure that this set of beliefs continues, in some way, to provide a foundation of cer-

[1] Butler, *Four Philosophies and Their Practice in Education and Religion,* p. 248.

[2] Butler, *Idealism in Education,* pp. 37, 67.

tainty to which men can subscribe and in which they can trust. Essentialism's task is to translate these objectives into workable educational practice—a task in which it succeeded so well that it captured virtually all secular schools from the time of the Renaissance until the rise of progressivism.

MODERN THINKERS CONTRIBUTING TO ESSENTIALIST BELIEFS

Since essentialism has matured during several centuries of our modern era, perhaps the best way to understand it is to make the acquaintance of some of its historic contributors. The aim here is again to provide only a sampling of modern thinkers, preparatory to considering their influence upon contemporary essentialism.

Undoubtedly the greatest period in modern idealism occurred in the Germany of the seventeenth and eighteenth centuries—in such intellectual giants as G. W. Leibnitz, Immanuel Kant, G. W. F. Hegel, and Arthur Schopenhauer. All four are excellent representatives of the paramount objectives mentioned above. Leibnitz, a brilliant mathematician and man of affairs, constructed a theory of the universe in which all events and facts are related in a system of perfect "pre-established harmony." Kant endeavored to preserve the venerable beliefs in "God, freedom, and immortality" by arguing that, though they cannot be established by the canons of "pure reason," they remain necessary assumptions of the moral life, of "practical reason." Hegel attempted to reconcile the scientific and spiritual approaches to life in one breathtaking speculation: all nature and all society are arranged with such exact logical order that they express necessarily the perfect "reason" of a Supreme Being. The sensitivity shown by Hegel to dynamic qualities in the emerging civilization also appears in Schopenhauer's sorrowful speculation that human life, in essence, is an insatiable longing for satisfactions that are never fully achieved through experience. Such longing can be overcome only by being obliterated in that eternal and absolute nothingness to which age-old Oriental philosophies have beckoned us.

These idealists differ from the medieval philosopher and theologian in their tireless efforts to build a philosophy that might withstand the scrutiny of rational analysis and allow room for new developments in science and culture. Hegel's solution is typical of this objective. It embraces every fact and every event in a sweeping conception of spiritual reality. The meaning of the term *objective* is thus especially unequivocal in the Hegelian system:

the spiritual or ideal (here synonymous terms) is by no means an inner, private phenomenon; it is not equivalent to one's own soul or subjective mind; rather, it is the universe itself in which all individuals and all physical things perceived by our senses are members.

Somewhat prior to but overlapping the German idealist movement is British empiricism—the forerunner of contemporary realism. The greatest thinkers in this movement include Thomas Hobbes, John Locke, George Berkeley, and David Hume. Hobbes's greatest fame rests, perhaps, on his contributions to political philosophy. He endeavored to justify absolute monarchy by proving that men are materialistic, egotistic beings who need to set up an all-powerful authority to protect themselves against their own predatory impulses.

Locke's empiricism had a different political purpose. As the most influential philosophy of early liberalism (discussed in Chapter 7) and as support for the Revolution of 1688, it seeks to prove that, since ideas are derived solely from man's own perceptions and reflections, he may be properly subjected to no other political or ecclesiastical authority than himself. There are, for example, no "innate ideas" to which tyrants can resort as authority for their acts. Yet Locke succeeded not so much in rejecting all forms of absolutism as in substituting a more modern, middle-class variety for the monarchical absolutism to which Hobbes remained loyal. Moreover, as Berkeley contended, Locke's kind of empiricism logically requires a spiritual base—a Supreme Being who is himself the ultimate cause of the very sense perceptions that Locke emphasized.

It was left, then, for Hume to follow the argument to its logical outcome by demonstrating the superfluity of the cumbersome apparatus of metaphysical absolutism that his British colleagues tried to construct on either a material or a spiritual substructure. But this was an outcome so distasteful to the culture that even Hume qualified it. Modern philosophy has devoted itself, in considerable measure, to "refuting" his heresy.

That such idealists and realists (with the partial exception of Hume) could still, despite all their differences, aim toward ultimate objectives that are more common than not is revealed by Baruch Spinoza. A philosopher of Jewish background who spent many years in Holland, Spinoza brilliantly conceived of the geometrically exact and uniform world of nature as, at the same time, a world of the spirit. For him "the intellectual love of God" is identical with scientific understanding of the universe. Even human action and appetite are treated as if they were "lines, planes or bodies"; and freedom may be attained only by understanding the complete, predetermined regularity of a world operating according to God's decrees. Thus, Spinoza sought, without making compromises between them, to *identify* what we call the idealist with the realist patterns of belief.

Until the recent development of pragmatism and instrumentalism, the course of philosophy in America followed closely the European pattern. Such an emulation may be explained by the fact that the new land was settled almost exclusively by people educated in the literature, art, and politics of the Old World. Thus, one might expect that both idealism and realism should have been imported to our shores, to be developed further in the young nation.

Idealism in America is frequently dated from Jonathan Edwards. Strongly influenced by Berkeley, among others, this outstanding thinker of the Puritan period tried to prove the unqualified supremacy of God but to leave a place for the exercise of free will—a reconciliation congenial to an infant culture already given to encouraging individualism and self-reliance. Although idealism has continued to be extremely influential since Edwards's time, we shall mention here but four other figures: Ralph Waldo Emerson, the great transcendentalist; Josiah Royce, often regarded as the most original American idealist down to the present day; and the later, twentieth-century idealists, W. E. Hocking and E. S. Brightman. Still, the cultural significance of these and other idealists is perhaps as well revealed by Emerson as by any other. Influenced by German thought, he was fascinated by the vision of "the One," which embraces animals, trees, moons, and men. But he was already sufficiently a man of his time and country to emphasize the need for individual assertion and control over environment.

The attempt of American realism to break away from idealist-religious philosophies began early in our history. Yet it was not until James, whom we recall primarily as a pragmatist, that the outlines of a realist position with native coloration could begin to emerge. Since James, two Englishmen who resided in America for various periods have been among those who have especially deepened the realist philosophy: Alfred North Whitehead and Bertrand Russell. George Santayana, part European and part American, is a third important contributor. In America, John Wild has been recognized as an outstanding realist philosopher, but it should be noted that he identifies himself with classical rather than contemporary realism in the mechanist, materialist emphases that we have placed upon it.

The range of thinking among recent realist writers is, accordingly, so wide that it would be difficult to determine whether some realists belong more to progressivism or to essentialism insofar as some of their educational and social ideas are concerned. Whitehead, for example, is often admired for his "liberal" ideas, while the eclecticism that we have already noted in essentialism was frankly admitted by Russell who often denied any logical or otherwise necessary connection between, say, his scientific and moral or social beliefs. Yet one may note that much realist interest in the structures of external nature and in the relationships of individual minds with those structures is often traceable to its forerunners—Aristotle, Hobbes, Locke, and others. Certainly, insofar as earlier American realists of the twentieth century are concerned, it has been a consuming preoccupation of many to prove that *objects exist prior to and are independent of the operations of the mind.* More recently, however, under the influence of Russell and other major European philosophers, this interest shifted to scientific logic—above all, to the analysis of language—and away from ontological or epistemological problems which, in any case, are considered largely outmoded. Although at first glance such concerns seem remote from the practical affairs of education, we shall find that they and their implementers may have considerable significance for the schools of our time.

Meanwhile, the influence of both modern idealism and realism upon American political beliefs is easier to establish—even in this prefatory sketch. The American Revolution revealed many evidences of the stubborn effort to reconcile the demands of freedom with age-old habits of compliance with preestablished cosmic order. One may note, for example, how directly the Declaration of Independence relied philosophically upon the realist Locke—especially upon the doctrine of natural rights. This doctrine holds that laws of nature give men certain divinely inspired, inalienable rights, which, by the very fact that they are so given and hence are prior to any fluctuations of experience, cannot rightfully be abrogated. Thus, just as the hand of Puritanism, exemplified by Jonathan Edwards, still weighs heavily upon our religious and moral habits, so the historic beliefs associated with thinkers such as Locke still weigh perhaps as heavily.

The most influential of all political essentialists in modern history, however, may well be Edmund Burke, the archexponent of the contention that perpetuation of a given value over a long period of time is the strongest possible argument in favor of its permanent worth. His reverence for established institutions led him to the judgment that "The place of every man determines his duty. . . ."[3]—a place presumably fixed by historically prescribed patterns of order. That the Burkian view, directly or indirectly, continues to affect transmissive attitudes in politics, economics, religion, and certainly in education is apparent in a wide range of cultural experiences down through all the decades of our own century.

In turning now to ontological, epistemological, and axiological highlights of essentialism, one is surely justified in focusing largely upon the mighty forces symbolized by the historic concepts of idealism and realism—concepts which continue to influence numerous scientists, religionists, and educationists as well. At the same time, it is necessary to be reminded that essentialism as represented by these two movements has been presently overshadowed (as, indeed, has progressivism in some respects) by other culturological expressions of the essentialist mood, often in quite other terms—for example, philosophic analysis. In the concluding section, we shall make brief note of these expressions while paying somewhat closer attention to them in the next two chapters.

ESSENTIALIST BELIEFS ABOUT REALITY

A common denominator of the essentialist ontology—its beliefs about reality—is the conception of a world governed by unimpeachable order, a world conceived both by classical idealists and realists as ruling over or through man according to its inviolable dictates. It is a conception in which, therefore, whatever meaning man possesses must be reconciled as far as possible with that kind of world.

OBJECTIVE REALISM AS WORLD SYSTEM

If by this term is meant a systematic view of the physical, natural order and of man's place within it, one may then assert that two major scientific fields have dominated all others in shaping objective realism. The first is the field of physics, including such sciences as astronomy and chemistry, which entered its great modern period of influence with Sir Isaac Newton. The second is biology, especially as interpreted through the theory of evolution

[3] Burke, as quoted in Randall, *The Making of the Modern Mind*, p. 435.

with which we first associate the name of Charles Darwin. Both these fields have, of course, influenced philosophies other than essentialism, but in diverse ways.

To consider the physical sciences, let us recall that it was Newton's supreme achievement to carry the researches of his predecessors, notably Copernicus and Galileo, to a logical and apparently ultimate conclusion by proving that every aspect of the physical world can be brought within the compass of all-inclusive order. With nothing in nature determined by chance, the simplest incident can be explained by physical laws, such as the law of gravitation. All nature operates with the efficiency and regularity of a clock. From the time of Newton until our own day, this theory, which we may call *mechanism*, has continued to exert immense influence—the theory, in brief, that the world itself operates by the causes and effects, the pushes and pulls, of a monstrous machine.

Mathematics is central to the theory of mechanism. All motions and relationships in physical nature are reducible to quantitative terms which, expressed in abstract equations, aim to encompass and explain every event in nature. It is as if the whole universe had become a magnificent system of geometry. So it was with essentialist philosophers as far back as Spinoza; so it remains for many scientists, philosophers, and laymen today.

Now the point to which we must pay strict attention is that the world as a machine is moving perpetually under its own power. The method of science consists primarily in reducing all observed processes to a mathematical account, to an expression of law and of universal order, which exist in nature itself. It is true that to build this awe-inspiring structure, Newton and his scientific descendants carried on many important experiments and thus foreshadowed the meaning of the experimental method as it is understood, for example, by instrumentalists. It is also true, however, that the emphasis in traditional mechanism has been strongly *deductive*. That is, it has been in large measure concerned with postulating, extending, and applying general mathematical laws of nature to an ever-widening range of particular phenomena. The *inductive* method, the building up of generalizations from particular observations and experiments, is by no means ignored; indeed, it is regarded as indispensable. Nevertheless, the essentially deductive character of much mechanistic science was well expressed, a century after Newton, by the Frenchman, P. H. D. Holbach:

> Man . . . is the work of Nature. He exists in Nature. He is submitted to her laws. He cannot deliver himself from them. . . . The universe, that vast assemblage of everything that exists, presents only matter and motion . . . an immense, an uninterrupted succession of causes and effects.[4]

This simple and comprehensive picture of the world has now been amended, for nature is found to be far more complicated than Newtonian physics assumed. First molecular physics and then atomic physics, which led to the most devastating scientific discovery in history (atomic fission), accelerated a shift in thought that had already begun a hundred years before. To the new physicists, the universe appears to be an expanding field of explosive *energies* rather than a body of mobile *matter*. But such changes in recent science have not fundamentally modified beliefs about the universe that we associate with the realist and, especially, the mechanist position. These beliefs, we reiterate, are still geared to the acceptance of a physical world governed chiefly, if not wholly, by mechanical processes and physical elements. The order of nature, even if far more intricate and manifold than previously supposed, is *still there waiting to be revealed to man* in all its awesome regularity.

The second great scientific contribution to modern realism —evolution—holds that every organism, from the simplest plant to the most complex animal, may be brought within the compass of natural explanation. Although the particular laws that Darwin formulated are no longer universally accepted by the scientific world, realism's approach to evolution and biology is often considered analogous to its approach to physics. Our task, the biological realist maintains, is likewise to observe causes, effects, and other temporal events in the organic sphere and to explain them in terms of uniformities in nature.

Darwin himself was not a mechanist in certain respects. But it is interesting to note how, long before his time, scientists were reducing organic structures and processes to biochemical compounds and reactions. In terms of such analyses, living things became as mechanical as, let us say, chunks of earth or burning gasoline. Life itself, many biologists now believe, will be produced in the laboratory as soon as we learn more of its chemical relations. Moreover, the science of genetics is now able to effect such radical changes in plants and animals that it can literally produce

[4] Holbach, *ibid.*, p. 274.

new species and thus demonstrate laws of heredity within the laboratory.

The evolutionary theory has also been applied to astronomy, geology, and sociology. Not only was our earth, for example, "born" from the sun in some remote era, but it has slowly developed through different stages to its present stage. Cultures, too, have evolved systematically: The founder of modern sociology, Auguste Comte, and the philosopher of evolution, Herbert Spencer, both tried to show how group life is subject to forces that carry men along in a current of inevitable change.

OBJECTIVE IDEALISM AS WORLD SYSTEM

The central point to be made is that, although objective idealism is distinguished from realism by greater "cosmic optimism" and in other ways, its formulations in modern philosophy are governed by a preoccupation to encompass both modern religion and modern science.

Perhaps the most influential application of this synthesis is Hegel's spiritual theory of history, which attempts to establish the laws of every stage of civilization, to demonstrate why each stage followed its predecessor as it did, and to account for the powerful forces of social change that seem to deny fixity to any one period of history. The Hegelian answer to these difficult questions is still accepted in essence by some thinkers of our generation: briefly, it is that *history is God thinking*—thinking His way through, and thus expressing, the eternal dynamic shiftings of the world, which is itself spiritually real. Clearly, this interpretation of history, far from denying the facts of movement and conflict, regards them as fundamental; indeed, it has been well said that Hegel's God is a "man of war." Although Hegel lived before Darwin, it is significant that he anticipated the struggling, restless qualities of reality upon which evolution, as a scientific theory, rests. Yet, counterbalancing his stress upon *becoming*, upon endless movement, he emphasized equally the *being*, the necessity, of each event in history. No war, no government, no social achievement is accidental; each step in the march of civilization is spiritually ordained.

Hegel leads us also to a pair of philosophic terms not previously mentioned—*macrocosm* and *microcosm*. The former refers to the entire universe and usually connotes cosmic design and unity, that is, a cosmology. The latter refers to the single part, the separate fact, or, on the human level, the individual man or institution, each of which in design and unity minutely reproduces the universe. For example, analogies are drawn between the vast solar system and the tiny atom: the nucleus of the atom resembles the sun, and the electrons resemble the planets. Hence the macrocosm-microcosm polarity may be fruitfully utilized even by objective realism.

It is, however, more often utilized by idealism to clarify the spiritual affinity between God and man. Thus, according to the Hegelian theory of history, God, instead of being apart from the human world or directing it from "on high," is *immanent*. He is a manifestation of and exists within history itself. The macrocosmic God, in short, is a universal Mind, which includes within itself all things, all energies, all time and space, all individual minds. Every law of science—physical and physiological alike—is an equally marvelous expression of the harmony and reliability of God's own handiwork. It is unnecessary, then, to deny the multiplicity of events that lead many contemporary thinkers to regard the world as pluralistic; numerous though these events may be, they are ultimately joined in one unified and spiritual whole, of which God is the supreme source. He is the Thinker thinking his thoughts and thereby creating everything real.

In fact, the literature of objective idealism is rich with ingenious logical devices, often borrowed from science, to prove God's existence. The famous "argument from design," for example, attempts to demonstrate that the mechanistic perfection of nature requires a Maker, a Supervisor, just as any clock requires someone to construct and wind it. Closely related to this argument is the equally familiar "cosmological argument," an adaptation of the law of causality: if, as science itself holds, every natural effect without exception is caused, then so, too, must the whole world have a Cause. (We shall later note comparable arguments by perennialism.) Although many philosophers have raised doubts about the validity of such arguments (analytic philosophers reject them completely), they continue to be expressed and widely accepted by many holding idealistic beliefs.

The traditionally religious tone of objective idealism might lead to the suspicion that the theory of organic evolution has a disturbing effect upon it. It is true that if one identifies religion with Christian fundamentalism, with a literal acceptance of the Biblical story of creation, one cannot, of course, believe that man emerged from lower species of animals. The sophisticated philosophy we are now considering, however, finds little trouble in accepting evolution. As might be expected, we need only include the objective uniformities observed in the development of species along with any other given uniformity of nature and to assert that they too are ordinances of a macrocosmic God. Just as civilizations pass through logically ordered stages, so do plants, lower animals, and human beings.

Meanwhile, if man still finds difficulty in comprehending the spiritual macrocosm in any complete sense, he is able at least to comprehend in some measure the most perfect earthly microcosm of that reality—himself. Even the human body is an amazing demonstration of symmetry and order (consider, for example, such a complicated but efficient organ as the eye). Still more revealing is the human mind. Its capacity for logical reasoning, for proceeding logically from step to step to a finally valid conclusion, is a microcosmic demonstration of the systematic process that we discern in the macrocosmic steps of historic development.

Recent idealism develops this microcosmic concern with the individual by its concentrated attention on the self and the person. (One of the more influential contemporary religious philosophies is called *personalism*, made famous by E. S. Brightman, Peter Bertocci, and others.) The aim of this attention is to reveal the spiritual uniqueness of the self, which is, indeed, a phenomenon of nature but also more than natural—more than a fact capable of scientific analysis. It is aware both of itself directly and of other selves in a community of selves attuned with one another. Here one detects a fraternal spirit with some expressions of existentialism—Buber's, perhaps most notably.

At any rate, in the individual's awareness of other individuals we find an anticipation of the idealist's social philosophy (developed so beautifully by Royce in his *Philosophy of Loyalty* and other works). For, since a community of selves is already a more inclusive spiritual reality than any single self, it partakes more fully of the universal Self. It is, we might say, intermediate between God Himself and the human person, who is, as the idealist, Hocking, expresses it, ". . . an imperfect image of the whole cosmos. . . ."[5]

This is not to say, of course, that (as *subjective idealism* might hold) man himself is the *source* of reality. Rather, although he may first come in contact with God through intimate awareness of his own spiritual self, the fact is that God's Self, as universal, is prior to and the Cause of man's self. You and I, in short, are basically real because we are the personal representatives of an ideal cosmic being. We approach Him only as we reflect Him in our own spiritual life, or, more exactly, as we develop our own divine quality by closer approximation of God.

[5] Hocking, *Types of Philosophy*, p. 409.

ESSENTIALIST BELIEFS ABOUT KNOWLEDGE

The theory of man as a reflection of God provides a direct bridge to an understanding of essentialist beliefs about knowledge. For if man, at his most real, is a microcosm of the universe, then *he knows* in the degree to which his mind is able to *reflect* that universe—to reproduce accurately and adjust to the historical and contemporary contents of the physical, biological, social, esthetic, religious spheres. This generalization again applies, on the whole, both to the idealist *and* the realist.

THE BODY-MIND CONTROVERSY

One must not argue, of course, that differences between realist and idealist types of essentialist thought are not far-reaching. Indeed, much modern philosophic writing has been devoted either to a continuous battle between these two schools within the very area we are now entering—namely, epistemology, the theory of knowledge—or to deviations from both.

Very simply, idealists take the position that, since the spiritual is the key to reality, we know within and through the mind; the body, like all physical objects, is ultimately subject to and embraced by the mind. Realists take just the opposite position: since the material is the core of reality, we know within and through the body. For many realists, the mind is itself ultimately physical and obedient to the same rules that govern all other physical objects. Highly technical discussion has thus been devoted to the effort of recent realists to disprove the case for idealism, especially in its epistemological emphases.

The realist, Ralph Barton Perry, has been among the more eminent of these thinkers. He has demonstrated with great cogency that idealists commit a fallacy when they premise that, because human beings know objects only through their ideas, therefore ideas and mind are *responsible for* objects. The fallacy derives from attributing causal efficacy to the "egocentric predicament" that we perceive things only if we are present to perceive them.

A third position, also militantly defended by epistemologists from the Frenchman, René Descartes, to the American, Arthur O. Lovejoy, is that mind and body cannot actually be united and, hence, *dualism* is inescapable. The old religious belief of the separateness of the soul is often, although not necessarily, implied in this third position.

The mind-body controversy likewise permeates modern psychology—so deeply, indeed, that it illustrates perfectly how philosophic assumptions must underlie all scientific work, the protests of some scientists notwithstanding. As a matter of fact, the psychological dispute over the *primacy* of mind or body or the *parallelism* of mind and body has often been scientifically fruitful. It has influenced excellent techniques of experimentation, the results of which, in turn, have enriched our understanding of human behavior. The main point here, however, is that either the body approach or the mind approach, if followed far enough, supports modern essentialism in its doctrine of knowledge. We shall find that both approaches develop attitudes and habits of practical consequence for education and for the culture it serves.

THE IDEALIST APPROACH TO KNOWLEDGE

We know most truly, say the idealists, as we understand our own spiritual selves, but such understanding is enhanced as we come to recognize that the marvelous rationality of which our minds are capable is but a small part of the perfect rationality of Infinite Mind. But the various ways in which this general position is elaborated by idealism are astute and comprehensive. For example, it is possible to speak of at least four main types of idealism in the history of American philosophy—personal, speculative, dynamic, and absolute—all of which try, in one way or another, to take into account scientific knowledge and thus to reflect the experimental mood of the young culture. As Royce expresses it, "The very existence of natural science, then, is an illustration of our thesis that the universe is endlessly engaged in the spiritual task of interpreting its own life."[6]

It would be difficult, however, to find an American who is as convincing in his analysis of the psychology of idealism and thus of the process by which knowledge is obtained as the British idealist, T. H. Green. Men approach their own spiritual selves most closely, says Green by *introspection*. Thus, we discover that the unique feature of mind is a consciousness that cannot possibly be identified with sensation, for every mental experience involves *relations among* sensations. The element of redness, for example, would be meaningless *as* redness; it becomes meaningful only when the power of consciousness organizes it into a related whole, as in a red sunset. And since this power is not itself reducible to a sensation, it must be, strictly speaking, an "extranatural" principle. Mind itself becomes a *substance*—not a material substance, to be sure, but one possessing its own spiritual autonomy and uniqueness.

For many idealists, and especially for those of Hegelian tra-

[6] Royce, in Fisch (ed.), *Classic American Philosophers*, p. 240.

dition, this mentalistic substance expresses its own laws of logic, which, in turn, offer the main cue to laws of the universe. The *dialectical* process of thinking from step to step in an irreversible sequence is found to be strictly comparable to the process, for example, by which cultures evolve from stage to stage according to God's laws of history. In the language of modern religious philosophy, the inspiration which enables me, as a *finite* being, to know that I have found a universal truth is the realization that my mind is attuned to God's *infinite* mind—that I am in complete, rational harmony with Him. By the same criterion, I err, I am victimized by falsehood, when this harmony is incomplete, when communication between me and the cosmic Self is clouded by the welter of my feelings or distorted by my sense perceptions.

THE REALIST APPROACH TO KNOWLEDGE

Realists in psychology and epistemology are largely within the great tradition heralded by Newton in the physical sciences. One of the main aims of realism has been to observe human beings as it does any other material objects and to explain mind and its operations in terms applicable to the explanation of a machine. Although this aim has been beset by great obstacles, realism for nearly a century has prevailed over idealism in psychology precisely because it has utilized much more fully the methods and canons of the physical sciences. We sketch briefly three historic movements in realist psychology—*associationism, behaviorism,* and *connectionism*—all of which have greater culturological implications than their scientific proponents usually appreciate.

The first realist movement in psychology, associationism, stems from British philosophy, especially from Locke. The ideas or contents of the mind are an association of elements—"atoms" of sensation and perception. The associationist studies them chiefly by introspection (a method often employed also by the idealist) but he does so without preconceptions about the "soul" or other spiritual substances which presumably glue them together.

Despite the exclusion of such preconceptions, associationism faces many theoretical difficulties. As in the case of the idealist, Green, the associationist is constantly forced to resort to some extranatural principle to perform the *associating* of mental atoms. And he is never sure that the ideas each of us holds is a reliable, a "true," mental image of the object we perceive outside ourselves. We are, as it were, prisoners of our own subjectivity.

The second realist movement in psychology, behaviorism, arose largely as a protest against just such difficulties. The term "behavior" is preferred to "mental life" because the total organism, in its neurological, physiological, and biological experience, is the psychologist's concern. In behaviorism's most orthodox formulation, such terms as "mind" and "consciousness" are only confusing relics of a prescientific approach. Purely objective methods of observation and measurement replace such methods as introspection, the chief psychological process being that of *conditioning* the organism to respond to stimuli and thereby to form habits. The body is the fundamental fact. Even thinking may be regarded as a complex of neuromuscular habits centered in the larynx, by which we respond with and to silent or spoken language. Personality is the name we give to the individual's pattern of conditioned reactions.

Although behaviorism as it was originally conceived has been modified, its guiding assumption is still that the individual is essentially explainable in mechanical terms. It substitutes the postulate of materialism (human beings are subject entirely to physical laws) for that of idealism (human beings are subject entirely to spiritual laws).

Behaviorism has influenced a number of psychologies of our day (the progressivist, for one), but probably its greatest impact has been upon the third conspicuous realist approach to knowing and knowledge, namely, connectionism. Although difficult to characterize in few words (its leading exponents are also, at times, rather eclectic), the term "connectionism" itself is simple enough. It implies that all animals, including human beings, build patterns of response by "stamping in" and "stamping out" *connections between* stimulus (S) and response (R). In this way bonds of connection are built up or broken down. The chief "laws" governing this process include "the law of exercise" and "the law of effect." The former suggests that frequency and recency of stamping will strengthen connections; the latter that the individual tends to retain responses that are satisfying (that is, pleasurable) and to eliminate those that are annoying (painful). Since the S-R-bond process can be measured with a high degree of precision, psychological experiences can be subjected to exacting quantitative experimentation.

THE CORRESPONDENCE AND COHERENCE THEORY OF KNOWLEDGE

In discussing the idealist or realist *approach* to knowledge, we have not yet indicated how genuine knowledge, as contrasted with error or falsehood, is allegedly *attained*. We should note that the correspondence and coherence theory of knowledge (as the characteristic statement of this process is known) holds that, in general, what we know to be true is the product of an agreement obtaining *between* the facts, relations, processes, or laws of the objective world *and* our individual judgments about these phenomena.

This is not to say that "correspondence" and "coherence" are merely synonymous theories. Like every other epistemological position, complex difference of degree or even of kind have prevailed here, too. But, since we are required to restrict our treatment, let us choose the late American idealist, Theodore M. Greene, to speak for us. By correspondence, in brief, is meant (borrowing from Kant and paraphrased by Greene) ". . . conformity to all available and relevant data . . .," whereas by coherence is meant ". . . the internal consistency of our individual judgments or of our closely related clusters of judgments and, even more importantly, the mutual consistency of judgments issuing from different experiences or types of experience." In brief, the terms "conformity" and "consistency" together are based on "trustworthy evidence or data."[7] Correspondence and coherence are complementary. But realists and idealists are rarely satisfied with any single generalization; rather, one finds varying expressions of the common epistemological point of view. In America, two main types, neorealists and critical realists, were influential in earlier decades, and both types have been philosophic allies of related psychological movements.

Neo-realists are psychologically close to behaviorism. Knowledge is presented to the mind directly from the world. It is therefore interpreted as a body of specific responses to external stimuli with little or no reference to intervening intellectual processes.

Critical realists are more in the tradition of Locke and the associationists, who, we recall, premise intellectual mediators or substances which fuse clusters of sensations. Knowledge is *re*-presented through these mediators. Perhaps the most famous critical realist has been Santayana, whose theory of the "realm of essence" holds that a kind of bridge connects the outside object and the inside idea of the object, partaking of the essence of both object and idea without being either one. Hence, he speaks of a realm not of existence but of "subsistence." In Santayana's theory,

[7] Greene, in National Society for the Study of Education, *Fifty-Fourth Yearbook*, Part I, p. 101.

the strange alliance of realists and idealists again begins to appear, for the realm of subsistence is characterized by numbers and shapes that are real yet cannot be perceived in the material world. Recent realism revivifies in this theory some of the characteristics of classic realism.

The arguments of these schools of thought and the various terms they attach to their respective theories of truth often become so complicated that it is fortunate if, for our purposes, we need not analyze them in depth. Three main inferences to be drawn from them are, nonetheless, relevant to our interest.

The first inference is that realist psychologies and philosophies are inclined to accept a more or less completely mechanistic world, within which human beings exist and function. It is a world governed primarily by the cause-and-effect determinations of physical-chemical processes most accurately conveyed to the mind through mathematically formulated laws.

The second inference is the realist assumption underlying correspondence and coherence theories—namely, that the "stamping in" of responses to stimuli (as stressed particularly by connectionism) provides *reliable* knowledge. Without such an assumption, there could not be any need to encourage techniques of stamping. Hence, stimuli that emanate from the given environment—both of nature and society—are the source of the truth process; human responses are the product. The "mind," or whatever the organ of response formation may be called, is exposed to this environment in much the same way as camera plates are exposed to light. While the apparatus of exposure, timing, and position is often complex (especially in critical realism), the net effect is similar.

The third and, for our purpose, most significant inference is that the correspondence and coherence theory of knowledge, allowing for some substitution of terms, is often *equally appropriate to the theories of idealists and realists*. For both, the universe of order is the source and criterion of everything we know. True, idealism insists upon a correspondence and coherence between the finite self and infinite Self, while realists speak of the mind's dependence upon "nature" or "matter." Realists are also more neutral and objective about what they perceive as cold facts and uniformities than their more optimistic idealist allies, who, in contrast, find the universe to be radiating with rosy hues of hope and purpose. But both realists and idealists assume a cosmic source of truth with which it is the business of mind to correspond and/or cohere.

ESSENTIALIST BELIEFS ABOUT VALUE

That the essentialist's beliefs about reality and knowledge strongly condition his beliefs about value is revealed by the common denominator of his axiology: values, like truths, are rooted in and derived from an objective source. The character of this source and of values deriving from it often depends upon whether the view is that of the idealist or the realist.

Nevertheless, one may discover emphatic similarities between the realist and idealist wings of this momentous educational philosophy, especially when they are appraised from a point of reference beyond themselves—namely, the culture. From this point of reference, we find that both wings of essentialism strongly tend to substantiate and transmit inherited principles and practices of morality, art, and social conduct.

THE IDEALIST THEORY OF VALUE

Idealists have usually assumed that ethical laws are themselves cosmic laws. Hence, you and I, as selves, succeed in becoming good only as we share actively in them. The practical effect is obvious. In less philosophic language organized religion, for example, teaches the same doctrine: God's Ten Commandments can solve all problems of moral conduct for those who are ready to accept and practice them. While upholding this authoritarian doctrine of values, idealists are, nevertheless, eager to convey the impression that the individual person is himself an active determinant of values. They do so by interpreting the self as becoming more and more fully a self in its unity with other selves and so, finally, with the Supreme Self. Nevertheless, it is this Supreme Self who is always the source as well as the goal of the values for which you and I strive.

The way in which idealists develop this position is a striking illustration of how modern philosophy differs from its medieval forebears. Wishing to adapt themselves to the "this-worldliness" of modern civilization—a wish shared by idealists as well as by realists—objective idealists, especially those of the Hegelian strain, do not deny the existence of evil. On the contrary, they regard evil as a real human experience. But since their universe is warmly toned with the qualities of inherent goodness, some of them (Royce is one) try to prove that evil is always subordinate or, at least, that it is meaningful only when contrasted with its exact opposite.

Emphasis on logical argument rather than on mere dogma is

another example of the spirit of modern idealism. Thus one may consider the brilliant ethics of Kant, who still commands many distinguished followers. Deeply disturbed by the threat to traditional faiths—a threat to which he himself lends support in his philosophy of science—Kant seeks to ground standards of conduct in unimpeachable moral law. Therefore, he sets up a "categorical imperative" of obligation to duty, which, he insists, is completely consistent and unconditional whether it is ever obeyed or not. Paraphrased, the law states that each of us should always act as we would want such acts to be performed by all of us everywhere and at all times. For example, it is our duty to be strictly honest because honesty is a good we universally approve; hence, even if we violate our duty in respect to honesty, we could not possibly wish to see acts of stealing become the general rule.

A further example of the influence of modern attitudes upon idealist ethics is its tendency to stress the freedom of the individual. Kant is again a dominant figure, for he argues in behalf of moral freedom and other axiological principles threatened by the strict cause-and-effect determinations of modern science. The moral self is free precisely because it has emancipated itself from these determinations and has joined hands with other selves in a spiritual union that is ultimately supernatural. The law of duty, in other words, requires the assumption of sufficient freedom to carry out its commands. This assumption requires, in turn, that we hold membership in an order of reality where freedom is possible —a reality above and beyond our world of necessity and ruled by a Being able to grant immortal membership to mortal beings and to reward them for their acceptance of the categorical imperative.

Since the time of Kant, many thinkers have tried to strengthen or modify his original formulation to accord with contemporary conditions. Shorn of its complications, it reveals how men may seek personal goodness regardless of how overpowering the pressures of heredity and environment or how strong the temptations of a lustful and competing world.

Idealism's approach to ethical values is paralleled by similar approaches to social and political thought. Hegel, for example, found increasing spiritual quality in every social institution from the family to the nation—a spirituality that, in turn, justifies an ardent nationalism and patriotism. Under the terms of this spirituality, the state becomes sacred—becomes, indeed, the expression of God Himself—a point of view adapted with telling success over a century later by the idealist philosophers of totalitarian Italy and Germany.

The spiritual totalitarianism of Hegel and his disciples is by no means the only social consequence of objective idealism. The strong individualistic spirit of postmedieval culture is reflected frequently in thinkers such as Kant, and even to some extent in Hegel. Green and Royce are among recent idealists who have insisted upon the profound value of liberty for the self and in relationships among selves. Nevertheless, whether the emphasis is microcosmic or macrocosmic, modern idealists tend to agree that the social and political life of man manifests his membership in a community of spiritual persons, the Supreme Ruler of whom is God.

The erudite and frequently transmissive implications of this social philosophy are epitomized by the American idealist, Hocking, who states:

> . . . the authority of Society is derived. . . . Society can expect every man to do his duty, on one condition: that it speaks for a divine Will, which expects every man to do his duty. It is this being beyond Society which provides the staying power for a flagging conscience and a flagging love. . . . God is the law of a normal social life.[8]

Finally, let us try to sample the esthetic flavor of idealism. Virtually all of its great representatives have been fascinated by the philosophy of art, but again none more profoundly than Kant. Men enjoy "disinterested pleasure" in objects of beauty, says Kant, which enables them to forget their limited and warped perceptions; thus they glimpse together, momentarily, their common and eternal unity. Hegel's esthetic theory echoes the same tone: a work of art, whether in architecture, poetry, music, or any other medium, is an expression of the spirituality of life. Men grasp the universals of reality through the feelings and sensations induced by a natural object such as a piece of wood or the sound of a bell. Other idealists have stressed this feeling tone in their theories of art, and so have tended to ally themselves with an esthetics reminiscent of modern naturalism.

On the whole, however, idealists judge the beauty of an object by the extent to which it penetrates through the crudity and ugliness of everyday experience to those symmetrical, harmonious patterns of nature that resemble the workings of the logical mind.

[8] Hocking, *Science and the Idea of God*, p. 83.

The idealist sculptor, Saint-Gaudens, removes the blemishes and uncouthness of the individual, physical Abraham Lincoln in order to "idealize" him—to reveal his spiritual universality and perfection as we have come to conceive them in our spiritual imaginations. Here, he says, is the "true" Lincoln. Here, also, is the meaning of the immortal dictum of the poet, John Keats, that "beauty is truth, truth beauty."

THE REALIST THEORY OF VALUE

The simplest introduction to realist ethics is through its ontological belief that the source of human experience lies in regularities of the material environment. Therefore we must try to approach values as we approach knowledge, namely, by objective understanding of facts and events to which people happen to attach judgments of worth and for which they express desire, admiration, dislike, disapproval. Sometimes, the consequence of this objective approach is to discount values as purely arbitrary concepts beneath the dignity of "scientific" investigation—an attitude prevalent today in many university departments of social science. It is also reflected among logical positivists and their offshoots when some contend that values are merely "emotive" or, at any rate, scientifically unverifiable and arbitrary.

Yet, traditionally, realists have sometimes expressed genuine concern about axiological problems. One of their most influential theories, for example, may be called *ethical determinism.* Since all elements of nature, including man, are linked together in an endless chain of causes and effects, therefore it follows that whether the individual is good or bad depends entirely upon the past causes that have shaped his present conduct. Similarly, what he will be in the future is largely determined by the causal chain now being forged.

The difficult implications of such determinism, as it is often termed, has led some philosophers of realist preference to discuss ethical principles in different ways. Thus, the utilitarians of the nineteenth century, anticipating progressivism later, preferred to approach human conduct by analyzing psychological motivations and consequences in purely natural terms. Usually, however, they reflected the individualism and mechanism of their own age, attempting to measure values by a kind of calculus of pleasures from which they may determine "the greatest happiness of the greatest number."

But it is impossible to embrace realism's beliefs about values in a single harmonious interpretation. Perry, for example, regarded value as any object of *interest*—a theory suggestive of progressivism. More influential was the famous realist, Russell, who, although not always harmonious even with himself, revealed in his famous essay, "A Free Man's Worship," a favorite mood of many realists. Man, he says, must be understood in the world which Science presents for our belief . . . a world of cold causality in which one's hopes and fears are the product of the accidental collocations of atoms"; a world in which facts, not goods, are supreme; a world where "omnipotent matter rolls on its relentless way"; yet a world in which men do somehow manage to fashion ideals and a "passion for eternal things. . . ."[9]

Thus the transition from the realist view of individual ethics to social philosophy is a plausible one, for political and economic values are toned with much the same scientific neutrality that Russell discovered in the "free man." Most social science of our day is realistic in this sense: economics seeks to discover and objectify the inviolable laws of the market or the business cycle; sociology, the structures of social organizations; political science, the behavior of pressure groups or political parties. Vilfredo Pareto may be mentioned here as one of the most influential social realists of earlier decades; Emile Durkheim as another. Long before them, however, Adam Smith was attempting to universalize the laws of capitalism; still earlier, Niccolò Machiavelli was establishing objective principles of politics by showing how "the Prince" behaves in "real life." Both Smith's and Machiavelli's influence have remained prodigious down to our own time.

The theory of evolution, a more recent basis of the realist's social beliefs, illustrates especially well how the cultural milieu may color ostensibly impartial findings. Thus Spencer argued from biological doctrine of the struggle for existence, being a fundamental law of all animate beings, to a defense of self-interest and self-aggrandizement—a convenient doctrine, still widely approved, for justifying the profit incentive. William Graham Sumner, another "social Darwinist," contended in the name of science that attempts to ameliorate the inhumane social effects of economic competition are contrary to natural law. In the struggle for existence, "Nothing but might has ever made right . . ." and ". . . nothing but might makes right now."[10] Folkways are the cultural habits of peoples, the effects of natural forces that men set in operation and allow little or no exception because they are devoid

[9] *Selected Papers of Bertrand Russell*, pp. 2ff.

[10] Sumner, *Folkways*, p. 62.

of intellectual reflection and intent. For Sumner, the study of folkways has much the same importance to sociology as the study of cells has to physiology—a good example of the way in which social realists may emulate natural scientists.

We do not mean to imply that Spencer and Sumner are typical of all social realists; moreover, even their own extreme determinism and conformism become, on occasion, qualified by more liberal tendencies. Yet, their attempts to ground moral conduct upon presumably objective descriptions of group behavior illustrate one of the most common logical devices of the realist: to hold that what has been and is characteristic of man and society (*descriptively*) is by this very fact what ought to be (*normatively*), because such conduct is natural, orderly, and inevitable. This inference, however cautiously or unconsciously made, allies the social values of some realists with those of some idealists. For, like the idealist, the realist may contend—and now with the prestige of science to support him—that "whatever is, is right."

Realist theories of art also deserve brief note. Although even more difficult to categorize than beliefs about conduct and society, realist esthetic beliefs concentrate largely on expressing life "as it is" and therefore on its complex pleasures and pains, its alternating harmonies and disharmonies. In their crudest forms, these theories symbolize the timeworn belief that art is *imitation* of nature. Few realists, however, would interpret imitation as mere reproduction in mirrorlike fashion, but rather as honest *expression* that conveys some aspect of the world clearly and significantly through the chosen medium of the artist. The emphasis of realist art is not upon beauty in the idealist's sense of patterns of spiritual perfection behind the facade of appearances, but rather upon *both* beauty and ugliness—in fact, upon all elements of reality.

As in other philosophic areas, realists and pragmatists have some affinities with regard to art: both are down-to-earth; both reflect the influence of science. But the tone of the realist esthetics of Santayana, for example, is again different from that of the pragmatist esthetics of Dewey. Santayana stresses more strongly the hedonic—that is, pleasurable—factor in art, just as other realists stress still more strongly the factors of emotion and will.

The quality of realist esthetics may be illustrated, finally, in its more determinist mood through the works of the American novelist, Theodore Dreiser, or the American painter, John Steuart Curry. Running through Dreiser's novels is always the relentless power of cause-and-effect upon the fate of individual human beings—a power analogous to the pull of the sun upon the planets.

The viewer of Curry's paintings feels the virile honesty of his effort to portray the regions of America as a great pageant of tragedies and joys. But one may also sense in these paintings an effort to disclose more than the eye perceives: one fixes upon detailed facts that somehow have the capacity to expand into universal experiences. Curiously, it is just this universality that is present, too, in the artist-scientist-philosopher Spinoza. Both are trying to paint, as it were, a picture of the *real* world. Both aim to depict it as exactly as possible. But both aim also to reveal a profound and determined order running through the storms and stresses, the fluctuations and discords, of nature and life.

RECENT STRAINS IN ESSENTIALIST THOUGHT

As we have pointed out, the two great traditional movements of modern thought—idealism and realism—have generated considerably less philosophic excitement in the postwar years of 1950s and beyond than they did in earlier decades. For this reason, it could be contended that essentialism is now of greater historic curiosity than of crucial relevance for the present and future. But the contention is a dubious one: it is not so much that essentialism has diminished but rather that its advocates acquire somewhat different formulations of their beliefs than they did before.

Since a number of these formulations reflect the influence of one or another of the five contemporary developments (neo-Freudianism, for example) that we have chosen for comment in preceding chapters, we must return to them especially in our culturological evaluation. But, as also noted, these developments remain too pliable, too unsystematized, and sometimes even too ambiguous to lend themselves exclusively to any one philosophy of education, essentialist or otherwise. On the contrary, they are amenable in specific ways to each of the major patterns encompassed by this book.

Some recent philosophers of stature do, however, belong quite predominantly within the essentialist framework as we regard it, yet may still not properly deserve categorization according to any one of the more influential essentialist orientations previously mentioned—traditional *or* contemporary. That is, they are neither clearly representative of idealism or realism nor are they easily distinguishable according to other conventional criteria.

Here one may recall twentieth-century thinkers as influential and diverse as Oswald Spengler (philosopher of history), Pitirim Sorokin (philosopher of society), José Ortega y Gasset (philosopher of society), Reinhold Niebuhr (philosopher of religion), Michael Polanyi (philosopher of science and ethics), and Leslie White (philosopher of the science of culture). True, some of these men, whether or not they deserve it, are bound to be classified under one or another of the philosophic rubrics (idealism, say) thus far utilized. At the same time, no one who knows their work will insist that they represent pure models of the transmissive cultural-educational mood. Such a contention has validity if only because seminal thinkers can never be reduced merely to formulas—a generalization equally applicable, of course, to pragmatists, say, as well as to realists and idealists. Nevertheless, we think that each of these men well exemplifies our contention that essentialism in its current expression deserves far more appreciation than that of a merely dated assessment. Indeed, depending largely upon the directions of cultural evolution, its influence upon education (as well as upon other institutions) may substantially expand in the decades ahead.

Let us illustrate by mentioning two quite different but relevant spokesmen: White and Polanyi. A research anthropologist as well as theorist, White maintains that culture is a "superorganic" reality different from all levels of nature. As such, man is just as subject to his own laws of order, process, and goals as he is to laws of genetics or electricity. The primary task of anthropology is to discover and formulate these laws. Education, it follows, is not to be regarded as an instrument of cultural moderation or transformation; rather, its primary role is to engage in the restoration and transmission of culture.

The flavor of Polanyi's sophisticated essentialism may be savored by a single quotation:

> I have tried to affiliate our creative endeavors to the organic evolution from which we have arisen. This cosmic emergence of meaning is inspiring. But its products were mainly plants and animals that could be satisfied with a brief existence. Men need a purpose which bears on eternity. Truth does that; our ideals do it; and this might be enough, if we could ever be satisfied with our manifest moral shortcomings and with a society which has such shortcomings fatally involved in its workings. . . . Perhaps this problem cannot be resolved on secular grounds alone. But its religious solu-

tion should become more feasible once religious faith is released from pressure by an absurd vision of the universe, and so there will open up instead a meaningful world which could resound to religion.[11]

[11] Polanyi, in Buford, *Toward a Philosophy of Education*, p. 493.

CHAPTER 9

The essentialist pattern of educational beliefs

IN ASCENDING from the philosophic foundations of essentialism to its theory of education, the reader should guard against several misconceptions. First, it is not our purpose to demonstrate that essentialist educational theory invariably proceeds directly and logically from essentialist philosophic beliefs. Although, in general, the fundamental philosophy and the educational theory are interrelated, essentialist beliefs about education sometimes modify, supplement, or even deviate from the beliefs of such eminent philosophers as Berkeley, Kant, or Santayana. Even so, while neither all idealists nor realists are necessarily systematic educational essentialists, it is probably reasonable to say that a fair proportion of educational essentialists have been either realists or idealists, or, in at least important ways, congenial to one of these two great modern philosophic orientations.

Second, the reader should observe that our presentation of essentialist education will be no more detailed than was our presentation of its philosophy. Both are so selective that, as in Chapter 8, the reader should be prepared for certain simplifications that can be elaborated only by additional acquaintance with the literature.

Third, this chapter is concerned primarily with basic educational theory. Hence, the day-to-day practices of essentialist schools can be considered only incidentally.

Fourth, it is extremely important to recognize, again, that certain educators who, although included within the general operational schema of essentialism, would not accept either an idealist or realist characterization. Our previous insistence that essentialism is especially susceptible to eclectic tendencies is underscored. Still more relevantly, essentialism is not to be interpreted, in any case, as a technical philosophic outlook merely or even primarily, but rather as a pervasive symbol of our age.

This culturological approach tends to express, sometimes explicitly, sometimes implicitly, the transmissive conception of educational theory and practice. In earlier stated anthropological terms, essentialism therefore underlies a range of theory and practice of what could be regarded by some interpreters as the process of enculturation—defined conventionally as the universal human facility to teach and learn when that facility performs the predominant role of maintaining cultural stability and order.

THE RISE OF ESSENTIALIST EDUCATION

HISTORIC BACKGROUNDS

The educational theory of essentialism reveals both a negative and a positive purpose. Negatively, its representatives struggle to emancipate themselves as do modern philosophers in general from the world view of the Middle Ages. Positively, they aim to substitute for it another world view appropriate to a more secular, scientific, industrial civilization. We find, therefore, that the great educational thinkers of essentialism extend over a long period of history. Although ancient-medieval beliefs contribute to the total pattern, its more distinctive features emerge with Renaissance educators, such as Erasmus, and reach fruition in twentieth-century Americans.

The spirit of the early revolt against medieval otherworldliness and dogma is nowhere more courageously exemplified than in Erasmus, who lived in the late fifteenth and early sixteenth centuries. In urging curriculums devoted to a "humanism" of classical learning and an international outlook, he was bitterly opposed in his own time. But it was a time of increasing susceptibility to new ideas. Hence, his influence in behalf of well-trained teachers and schools for the middle class as well as for the aristocracy could not be totally suppressed.

Comenius is one of the first Renaissance educators who sought to systematize the teaching process. He foreshadowed modern realism in his insistence that "everything be taught through the senses"—a belief he carried into practice by including pictures in his famous textbook on foreign languages. But, like so many leaders of his era, he was also deeply absolutist: he believed that the world is at once dynamic and purposeful and that education's chief task is to shape the human creature into an image of the Divine.

Among academic philosophers mentioned in the preceding chapter, none is more representative or educationally influential than the realist, Locke. As the archadvocate of the seventeenth-century, middle-class revolution, we recall that he substituted a new social theory of adjustment to external nature and social order in place of the medieval theory of adjustment to supernatural and monarchical authority. This substitution had immense, if not always obvious, significance for the kind of school he advocated. A "this-worldly" thinker (though making some provision for deity), he wished to gear education more closely to practical situations. But he was also interested in the education of "gentlemen" who are "set right"—that is, are taught the proper rules and habits of the economic and political order that they are assigned to govern—and who "once set right . . . will quickly bring all the rest to order."[1] Needless to say, "the rest" could only mean the lower classes of working people who, for another three centuries at least, were to remain subservient to these same gentlemen. It is no wonder that, along with more humane proposals, Locke also favored "working schools" for pauper children, who would be trained for industry in order to repay what the community had spent to keep them alive.

Of the many other historic figures who might be chosen to illustrate the development of essentialist ideas, some also influenced other educational movements. Chapter 6, for example, noted that Pestalozzi, Froebel, and Herbart might be claimed by progressivism as well as by essentialism, depending upon which aspects of their thought are emphasized. Perhaps the most accurate generalization that can be made about all three is that, although they sought valiantly to break through the historic philosophies and cultural habits that tied them so securely to their age, they could not fully succeed. Thus, Pestalozzi believed deeply in "Nature" (indeed, he is often close to Rousseau), and in this mood, he anticipated the naturalism of such thinkers as Dewey. Yet he is, at the same time, essentialist in that he is unwilling to deny the transcendental. "God," he says, "is the nearest relationship of man."[2]

Froebel sought the same difficult synthesis. Deeply devoted

[1] Locke, as quoted in Ulich, *History of Educational Thought*, p. 204.

[2] Pestalozzi, *ibid.*, p. 261.

to the education of little children and eager for them to express themselves creatively, he nevertheless perceived an ontological quality in such expression. Indeed, no statement by an essentialist educator of the idealist wing is more clearly ontological than this: "Education consists in leading man, as a thinking, intelligent being, growing into self-consciousness, to a pure and unsullied, conscious and free representation of the inner law of Divine Unity, and in teaching him means thereto. . . . This Unity is God."[3]

Of the three, however, Herbart is most clearly essentialist. A critical disciple of Kant, he insisted that the goal of education is to attune one's soul to a "vision of the Absolute," from which one may derive one's faith "in the ultimate victory of the good."[4] Also deeply influenced by the theory of associationism, which he derived especially from Locke, he is sometimes regarded as the first systematic educational psychologist. His famous laws of instruction were reframed so convincingly by his followers that even today some "lesson plans" follow the five mechanical steps of "preparation, presentation, association, systematization, application." Herbart was a believer in "mental states," which are linked together somewhat as chemical elements are linked to form a compound.

The influence of these and other theories upon American essentialism is so powerful that whatever educational philosophy developed in the first two centuries of American history was strongly imitative of them. True, a Benjamin Franklin or a Ralph Waldo Emerson might flavor his beliefs with ingredients of the new culture. Our first professional philosopher-educator, William T. Harris, who became a United States Commissioner of Education, is much more typically European, however, than native American in outlook.

Harris, a devout follower of Hegel, applied objective idealism with relentless consistency to the emerging public-school system. Believing that reality unfolds according to an inevitable design of spiritual unity, he insisted that education's chief task is to acquiesce in this process. He even defended the rise of industrial capitalism as both necessary and desirable and thus implied that opposition or criticism by the worker is nothing short of traitorous. Like Spencer and Sumner, who argued from the premises of scientific realism, Harris, the idealist, concluded, too, that on the whole "whatever is, is right." The school, in short, is dedi-

[3] Froebel, *ibid.*, pp. 286f.

[4] Herbart, *ibid.*, pp. 281, 283.

cated to preserving inherited values and adjusting man to society. For this obligation accords with absolute ontological law.

TWENTIETH-CENTURY ESSENTIALISTS

Until the 1930s, essentialism continued to be overshadowed by progressivism in explicit philosophic formulation. Then, in the Depression years, a well-organized counterattack upon progressivism was launched, spearheaded by the Essentialist Committee for the Advancement of Education. The commander of the counterattack, William C. Bagley, although not regarded as a professional philosopher, considered himself a realist and appreciated the importance of a philosophic grounding for education. It is significant to note that he found himself identified with other thinkers who were educational idealists; prominent among them was Michael Demiashkevich, who is said to have coined the term "essentialist," and who cooperated closely with Bagley in the Committee. H. H. Horne was widely known as a self-styled "idealistic theist" and (as J. J. Chambliss has noted) the "best known advocate" of this position for several decades of American education. Among the realist members were Ross L. Finney, Isaac L. Kandel (the first American leader in comparative education), and Frederick S. Breed. These educators and their peers are, however, regarded more as contributors to a previous period than to subsequent ones.

And yet, although the *term*, essentialism, has likewise lost much of its popularity, we would not be at all correct to say that the cultural *mood* it reflects and the educational posture it represents have themselves become outmoded. Despite shifting terminology, despite, also, a reluctance of some to be classified by any label—essentialist perhaps most of all—the fact remains that the culturological posture we have termed "transmissive" is an extremely influential one when tested both by its recognition in educational theory and, in a more inclusive sense, by what kinds of educational behavior are favored and practiced. Recalling the pragmatic test of "consequences," essentialism perhaps remains not only as pervasive a position as ever but, in important respects, still more pervasive.

ESSENTIALIST CONCEPTS OF LEARNING

THE CORRESPONDENCE AND COHERENCE THEORY AS PRESUPPOSITION

Although learning is studied as a psychological process, it also presupposes, more or less explicitly, an ontology, an epistemology, and an axiology. That is to say, it presupposes a body of beliefs about the nature of the reality we study, the reliability of the knowledge we presumably derive from study, and the values related both to reality and knowledge. The essentialist may not always acknowledge such presuppositions, but their presence is nicely illustrated in the fact that all historic varieties of essentialist learning rest more or less directly upon the correspondence and coherence theory of knowledge. This theory, we recall, seeks to establish the truth of an idea by the accuracy and consistency with which it presents or, more popularly, *re*-presents an object to the mind.

As earlier indicated, correspondence and coherence are not to be regarded as synonymous concepts; some philosophers, indeed, would insist on important distinctions. Certainly, in either case, the theory can become extremely complex. Hence it is necessary to reiterate that whatever we try to say here requires much more elaboration than we are able to provide.

These distinctions apply at least as importantly to the idealist and the realist, who differ in their interpretations of the nature of the object. The idealist will usually characterize the object as spiritual, immaterial, or ideal; the realist, as physical, material, or mechanical. Yet in either case, and despite a variety of refinements, the central device for testing ideas is the same—namely, by correspondence, representation, coherence, or preferably a combination of all three. Learning is then measured by the degree of skill, exactitude, and permanence with which this testing is effected.

At any rate, in educational theory if not always in "pure" philosophy, explicit support for the compatibility of realism and idealism may be found in the essentialist camp itself. Consider this statement of Horne, one of our most ardent earlier representatives:

> . . . true ideas *represent* the situation correctly. The proposition, the sun shines, is true because the sun does shine. A true proposition states what is so. It is only a question of fact. There is no question of making the sun shine, or controlling the shining of the sun, but only of the fact whether the sun shines. Truth is the agreement of statement with fact. . . . *This view is held by realists and idealists alike.* Realists and idealists differ, not in their theory of truth, but in their theory of reality.[5]

[5] Horne, *The Democratic Philosophy of Education*, pp. 500f. (italics supplied).

Educationally, the significance of this approach to knowledge is to place students in a position of being receptive to and spectators of the contents of the universe. Whether the universe be conceived as primarily physical or spiritual and whether the particular course of study be concerned with history, art, geography, economics, biology, or any other segment of the whole body of knowledge—the aim of learning is receptive. Teachers are agents of that whole, selecting relevant elements from the welter of historical and contemporary facts, laws, practices, customs, achievements that compose its contents. They then organize learning situations that seem to them most conducive to transmitting the elements selected.

In accordance with these theoretical premises, it is practicable to determine by objective measures whether a particular student is entitled to promotion, graduation, or other honors. Insofar as he is able to *re*-present coherently the world to which he has been exposed, he is educated; insofar as he is incapable of doing so, he is uneducated. In this sense, the correspondence and coherence theory of knowledge governs the construction and application of essentialist types of examinations. Strictly speaking, to examine means to determine the fullness and accuracy of the mind's agreement with reality.

In this preliminary statement, we have sought to epitomize only the common core of essentialist learning in its more traditional formulations. Even within these limits, we are painfully aware that almost every theorist within the essentialist movement would insist upon further qualifications—qualifications governed, to some extent, by divergent emphases of idealists and realists within the common orientation. Let us keep these divergencies in mind.

THE IDEALIST THEORY OF LEARNING

Idealism as a philosophy of life tends, oftener than realism, to begin with the individual person, the much-emphasized self, and then to move outward toward understanding of the objective world. To recall previous ontological terminology, microcosm supplies the cue to macrocosm. As the self learns about its own thought processes and gradually formulates laws of the mind, it simultaneously acquires insight into processes and laws of other selves and eventually of the universe. Thus, as conceived by Kant, time and space are really creations of the mind, even though they must be projected in external events before men can grasp their meaning.

It follows that idealism often tends to respect and to stress subjective psychological ideas and processes. Introspection and intuition, for example, are more congenial to it than to realism. Moreover, the capacity of the mind to combine related parts into qualitative wholes of meaning suggests that idealism, thus far, anticipates the Gestalt approach to learning.

On this subjective and personal premise, learning may be defined as the self-development of mind as spiritual substance. In this sense *mind creates itself*. And the kind of education that emphasizes the training of faculties includes the ability to remember, to reason logically, to comprehend the unity among things, to know the "permanent" values and truths of our heritage.

But we have also found in our brief review of idealism that, when viewed in the great perspective of modern culture, it cannot be interpreted merely in subjective, or individualist, terms. Although such an emphasis is inevitably strong, especially in democratic countries like England (recall the idealist, Green) and America (Royce), the need to ground the individual in cosmic order is almost invariably stronger and cannot be suppressed. The idealist movement is ultimately an *objective* movement. As the potent tradition of Hegelianism reveals, it is a theory of the macrocosm, of the world, which the individual mirrors in himself.

Thus we turn to the central feature of idealist learning. The individual learns as he gradually acquiesces in the spirituality of total Being—that is, of God. He may, to be sure, *begin* with himself in this process, for we must not disregard the idealist's stress upon *self-creation*; indeed, we feel a strong esthetic quality, reminiscent of Plato, in this spiritual outreaching. Nevertheless, except in the case of a reversion to subjective idealism, idealists hold that the individual always comes to know himself better by having grasped his relationship to the cosmic ground. Learning does not usually *end* with the self.

The phraseologies with which this position is developed by earlier essentialists vary greatly, of course. Horne speaks of the learner ". . . as a finite personality growing into the likeness of an infinite ideal." Repeatedly, he calls attention to the purposeful nature of the cosmos, which one increasingly appreciates as one develops ". . . reverence for the spiritual realities of existence."[6] Demiashkevich stresses divine laws and eternal truths, which all individuals should learn, and derives from the concept the need

[6] Horne, in National Society for the Study of Education, *Forty-first Yearbook*, Part I, "Philosophies of Education," pp. 154–156.

". . . to educate children for the respect and preservation of fundamental social values. . . ."—for the "ultimate certainty" of "metaphysical faith."[7]

The most distinguished idealist among American educators since the period of Horne and his essentialist compatriots has been Robert Ulich. Still, it would be misleading to regard him as typical of the essentialist orientation, for he has always been reluctant to identify himself with any one "ism." Moreover, he is invariably ready to include scientific and naturalistic ideas within his theory of learning even though, as a disciple of Kant, he builds his outlook upon a firm belief in "transpersonal" spheres of reality, a "deeper dimension of Being," and "the immanent laws of the universe." While often radiant with liberal and radical ideas applauded by educational philosophers of other persuasion, he also states that ". . . the mind of man . . . participates in a higher rational order which represents the unity of principles and laws. . . ." Hence, after all possible concessions, Ulich's overall educational position rests upon belief in a spiritual universe that governs all learning and serves as a final judge of what is and is not good education. In a book called (by the idealist, Hocking) his "magnum opus," Ulich pleads for ". . . common participation in the world of the mind . . .," for the hope ". . . that we may arrange our lives according to universal laws . . .," for a "feeling of unity with the All-Embracing . . ." and for ". . . the divine ground. . . ."[8]

Yet, the philosophic cosmopolitanism of Ulich is so admirable that, in his case even more than in many others included in this work, we run the constant risk of simplistic judgments. For example, one may find implications of the coherence theory of knowledge in a statement such as this: "From the idea of *thinking as an ordering process* it follows that good thinking has the tendency toward the creation of coherent structure."[9] Yet it is also significant that he has been the first distinguished educational philosopher in America (although a German expatriate) to weave colorful existentialist strains through the fabric of his neo-

[7] Demiashkevich, *Introduction to the Philosophy of Education*, pp. 348, 143, 358.

[8] See Ulich, *Crisis and Hope in American Education*, p. 168; *Fundamentals of Democratic Education*, pp. 97, 151, 143; and especially, the book he considers most fully expressive of his philosophy: *The Human Career—A Philosophy of Self-Transcendence*, pp. 232, 235, 245.

[9] Ulich, *The Human Career*, p. 114.

Kantian idealism. Ulich's influence upon a number of devoted students, who have since become influential scholars in their own right, remains substantial, of whom we mention only three: Solomon Lipp, Van Cleve Morris, and Paul Nash.

Existentialist strains in learning are directly indicated also in another educational theorist who, so far as we know, developed his position quite independently and subsequently of Ulich. We refer to Philip H. Phenix. Like Ulich, Phenix is far too sophisticated to allow easy characterization. Although he classifies himself as a realist, he is as appreciative as is Ulich of numerous elements in progressivism and other positions. Yet, in the context of his strongly transcendental religious concern, it is difficult to avoid an overall impression of an essentialist orientation. For example:

> The principle of devotion to truth, whether or not anyone's interests are served by it, is the cardinal presupposition of intellectual activity. Truth is not something that is fashioned in response to human wants. It is not created, but discovered. . . . Truth is not what anyone subjectively wishes or determines, but what objectively is."[10]

No wonder, then, that an ". . . enduring and progressive democracy rests on common loyalty to a law of truth and right which is found and given, not constructed by human decision. . . ." Or that ". . . the affairs of politics within the nation and between the nations are seen as occasions for discovering and obeying the universal law of right to which all are subject and in which the ends of life are fulfilled."[11]

THE REALIST THEORY OF LEARNING

Despite the continued influence of idealist theories of learning on school theory and practice, realist views have undoubtedly received far greater attention from recent educational psychology. Moreover, the outstanding American realist in educational psychology for many years was Edward L. Thorndike, whose theory of connectionism we have referred to above and to which we shall refer below. Here one may merely recall that, despite significant contributions to the science of learning, Thorndike was not as immune to philosophic assumptions as he and his followers some-

[10] Phenix, *Education and the Common Good*, p. 35.

[11] *Ibid.*, pp. 248, 251f.

times wish us to believe. Not only does connectionism seek to reduce the study of the human being largely to mechanistic, quantitative explanations analogous to, if not identical with, those of the physical world ("whatever exists, exists in some amount," Thorndike insists[12]), but it also tends strongly to encourage learning through adjustment to "the given." By "stamping in" and "stamping out" responses to stimuli, the teacher acts as agent of reinforcement for habits and beliefs congenial to dominant institutions of the inherited culture. The S-R-bond psychology, as a derivation of this theory, has probably been the single most influential one in teacher-training programs.

In the interim, to be sure, we must record the impact upon education exerted by a number of other realists of earlier relevance: Breed, Bagley, and Finney, especially. Yet, none of these educators exerts anything like the post-half-century influence exerted by Thorndike's creative and persuasive successor, B. F. Skinner.

With facility in translating his version of behaviorism into a whole range of testable, provocative experimental models, Skinner has persuaded not only innumerable psychologists but social philosophers and practical educators as well that the human being can be conditioned and determined to build the kind of world he wants and deserves. In this respect, to be sure, Skinner can not be regarded as stereotypic of essentialist patterns. Indeed, his novel, *Walden Two*, attests to qualities that express not only some progressivist but even reconstructionist values. The central point for our purpose, however, is not so much what Skinner himself may have intended; rather, it is how hosts of his followers have chosen to apply his own principles to the learning-teaching process.

Culturologically speaking, in short, "operant conditioning" (a term popularized by Skinner) thus invites almost limitless, testable "technologies" of teaching in harmony with essentialism. "Programed instruction" is, of course, the most comprehensive of these technologies, since it can embrace cybernetics, "computerology," and a whole range of remarkable inventions called "teaching machines."

Let us consider this contention with the help of Mary Jane Aschner's able encapsulation of Skinner's psychological approach: ". . . all behavior is externally caused and externally controlled. . . .

[12] Thorndike, as quoted in Rugg, *Foundations for American Education*, pp. 125f.

By manipulation of the initial situation, behaviors could be created, designed, shaped, and changed almost at will." For operant conditioning ". . . consists in the systematic manipulation of situational variables so that the *consequences* of a given instance of behavior become the *locus of control* over that kind of behavior. . . ."[13]

Now the term "consequences," as we recall, is of special concern to the progressivist philosophy. In axiological context, it leads to the question of "ends in view" and hence, to the whole theory of values which, for the progressivist, endorses the dynamics of growing individuals and growing societies. That Skinner himself inclines toward this kind of human direction is clear (survival, in a broad sense, is sometimes depicted as his highest value) and that he certainly does not hold merely a transmissive value orientation is also clear: "An effective educational policy cannot be satisfied with the replication of great historical achievements."[14] As he also recognizes, however, not only is it entirely possible but often the case that education can be extremely replicative. And this is where operant conditioning readily lends a hand: although itself axiologically neutral, it leads particularly well to consequences that are far from neutral. In this respect, realist-behaviorist learning and teaching become especially welcome to perpetuators of the inherited cultural order—a fact supported by multimillion investments in the construction and adoption of new technologies that stem so largely, in turn, from the work of Thorndike and Skinner.

Even so, in trying to typify the nature of essentialist learning from a realist viewpoint, one must keep in mind the distinction already drawn between such contemporary scientific protagonists as noted above and those classic realists who, in some ways, anticipate perennialism at least as legitimately as they do essentialism. Perhaps the best American spokesman who might be claimed for either orientation is Harry Broudy. In perspective, however, he belongs much more definitively among essentialists than among their perennialist brethren. For example, he has almost nothing to say about Thomism in his most comprehensive interpretation of educational theory (*Building a Philosophy of Education*)—an omission which no good perennialist, as we shall see, could tolerate.

[13] Aschner, in Nash, Kazamias, and Perkinson (eds.), *The Educated Man*, pp. 395f., 399.

[14] Skinner, *The Technology of Teaching*, p. 237.

Broudy is unusually well informed of viewpoints other than his own—so much so that in discussing the teaching-learning process, for example, he recognizes the progressivist focus on problem-solving, and he also admits that ". . . pedagogy has something to learn from the various theories of mind and knowledge offered by philosophy."[15] Even so, his version of realism leads him to conclude that, since mind is the "form of forms," therefore, the great task of knowing is ". . . the attainment of accurate concepts and precise relationships among them."[16]

THE ESSENTIALIST CURRICULUM

The essentialist curriculum, by and large, is a miniature of the world that teachers, administrators, and their supporters wish young people to regard as the real, true, and valuable world. But this certainly does not mean that essentialists advocate only one curriculum pattern for all types of schools; many different patterns have been proposed at different times and places.

Despite this variety, a casual search for common denominators already reveals them in the original Essentialist Platform which (although no longer endorsed by any active group) nevertheless remains as a kind of guideline. The platform advocates, for example, ". . . a rich, sequential, and systematic curriculum based on an irreducible body of knowledge, skills, and attitudes common to a democratic culture." It is a curriculum, moreover, in which there is ". . . stress upon adequate mastery of the content . . ." and ". . . presentation of this material as economically as possible . . ." according to ". . . rigorous standards of scholastic attainment as a condition of promotion." Indeed, the child has the right "to be guided, disciplined, and instructed."[17]

Phrases such as these invite profitable exercise not only in linguistic but in culturological analysis. Thus, the phrase "irreducible body of knowledge, skills, and attitudes" evokes the question of how we can determine what is irreducible, a question that cannot be answered without searching into essentialism's foundational beliefs. There we discover the presumed existence of absolute laws and inviolable processes and facts. Every individual must know these in order to adjust to the universe and, hence, to the culture of which they are the fiber. Again, the implications of such

[15] Broudy, *Building a Philosophy of Education*, p. 353.

[16] *Ibid.*, p. 339.

[17] Essentialist Committee, "Summary of Theses" (mimeographed).

phrases as "mastery of the content" or "rigorous standards" require us to attune our minds to these laws, processes, facts—and to do so with utmost thoroughness, persistence, and exactitude.

It is interesting to compare such language with that of the Council for Basic Education—an organization that inherited much of the original spirit of the Essentialist platform. To be sure, in its "program of aims for the public schools," the Council has never provided any systematic theoretical framework despite its recognition that the ". . . present educational situation, like all crucial controversies, has its roots in philosophy." One does, nonetheless, note such phrases as "the transmission of tradition," "basic or generative subjects," "unchanging philosophic faith or view of human nature," and "ends which are sufficiently realistic to be within the grasp of the majority of existing school systems in the United States."[18]

Moreover, what the Council has advocated programatically is clear enough. It amounts primarily to a series of subject-matter fields long familiar to the schools and colleges not only of America but of Europe. Spokesmen are very much concerned with upgrading standards but they are not in any noticeable way concerned, except skeptically, with methodologies urged by progressivists. Substantial increase in the study not only of Greek and Latin but of languages such as German, French, Spanish, and Russian is typical of the Council's curriculum recommendations. Thus, as one writer on modern languages puts it:

> Consistent and intelligent effort over a long period will be called for to overcome neglect and indifference, to find and train qualified teachers, to reorganize and revitalize classroom instruction. . . . If these things are done, however, we can at least look forward to a generation of linguistically competent young Americans who can support the nation in its role as the world power and whose minds have been deepened and broadened by some knowledge of a culture and language other than their own.[19]

Whether or not directly influenced by the Council, the fact remains that in the decades of postprogressivism, a substantial shift has occurred in curriculum organization that is frequently harmonious with the Council's own posture. This shift could

[18] See Koerner (ed.), *The Case for Basic Education*, pp. 3ff.

[19] *Ibid.*, p. 151.

hardly be described as essentialist in any systematically theoretical sense, but certainly it has exerted prodigious influence upon essentialist-tempered mood and practice. One need only review, for example, such reports as *Current Curriculum Studies in Academic Subjects* to observe the extent to which the sciences, especially physics and biology, have been restructured as disciplines, and how even the social studies and language arts (although more feebly) have been promoted according to "high" standards of scholarship. As one report notes, many millions of dollars have been spent by the federal government for summer institutes in the teaching of modern science alone.

That some of this effort has resulted in modernizing and upgrading sections of the curriculum is to be commended. Yet a close look, for example, at the ironically titled *Revolution in Teaching* or comparable documents is surely cause to wonder just what the "revolution" is supposed to produce. Certainly, with minor exceptions, no forthright attention whatever is paid to the kinds of revolutions that have been epitomized in Chapter 2—that is, in politics, society, or morality—as these directly and acutely affect man's own dilemmas or man's own future.

Yet, it would be unfair to assert that most of the active promoters of the Physical Science Study Committee, the Commission on Mathematics, the National Task Force on Economic Education, or comparable bodies, have deliberately and consciously expressed the transmissive mood in cultural attitudes or behavior. More often than not they have, if anything, supported such a mood rather by default than by intent. Characteristically, therefore, they have rarely if ever clarified their own metacultural meanings even when (as in the case of the analytically inclined philosopher, Michael Scriven, or the philosopher of science education, Joseph Schwab) they write so learnedly of *The Structure of Knowledge and the Curriculum*, or elsewhere, that the reader may feel humbled by their remarkable self-assurance when perhaps he ought to feel dubious indeed.

Earlier idealist or realist theorists on the curriculum such as Demiashkevich or Breed also leave so much uncertainty among critics as to their exact intent that it is scarcely difficult to understand why, so often, they have been circumvented or superseded in later years. Accordingly we shall avoid these pioneers here except to comment upon the idealist, Horne, as an example. In some respects, Horne, too, is amenable to progressivist ideas: he urges us to consider the needs and abilities of children; moreover, his "essential" studies include the scientific method, the inorganic and organic physical world, the human environment, and appreciation of as well as skill in the arts. But Horne's language affords equally good exercise in linguist or metacultural practice; indeed, how meaningful, really, is a sentence such as the following unless it is judged in culturological context?

> The chosen subject-matter should teach pupils to know the facts and opinions they need to know in order to feel and act as they need to feel and act; to feel as they should feel about the values of living in order to think and act as they should; and to do the useful, proper, and right things in order that they may think and feel as they should.[20]

What does Horne mean by "need to know," by "should feel," by the "useful, proper, and right things"? Is not the answer that these concepts and commandments are derived from "a sense of cosmic adjustment"—from the "mutual fitness of man and his environment"[21]—a position wholly congenial to those habits of reinforcement to which even the liberal-tempered Horne thus lends his support?

We are not trying to suggest that approaches to the transmissive-oriented curriculum, whether idealist or realist, are invariably typical of Horne's. Thus, in the closing section, we shall turn to several writers who are not so readily classifiable at all. Moreover, some more recent philosophers of education such as Broudy have tried to take into account a substantial range of knowledge and research that produce, in turn, quite elaborate designs—for example, in general education. Still others have viewed the curriculum in different light, although none perhaps more influentially than the general philosopher, Whitehead, in his famous and stimulating series of essays, *The Aims of Education.*

Yet, on the whole, it seems fair to conclude that the curriculum of essentialist or pseudoessentialist theorists must fulfill one obligation before all others: to assure that a series of fundamental, durable bodies of knowledge are conveyed to the learner as expertly and excellently as possible. This is not always to say (although the Council on Basic Education might lead us to think so) that great issues of human life such as race, sex, and class are to be ignored. Phenix, for example, confronts these and other

[20] Horne, in National Society for the Study of Education, *Forty-first Yearbook,* Part I, "Philosophies of Education," p. 160.

[21] *Ibid.,* pp. 162ff.

issues with sensitive concern, as does Ulich. Yet, among those of the generation that have followed the pioneer group of American essentialists, Phenix speaks as eloquently as any in regarding "intellectual excellence" as the keystone of both learning and the curriculum.

ESSENTIALIST VIEWS OF THE SCHOOL'S ROLE IN SOCIETY

THE GENERAL POSITION

American essentialists, without exception, believe in democracy. Some of them have been ardent defenders of the Bill of Rights, and it is possible to find among them educators all the way from Bagley onward who, on specific political issues, have assumed liberal or even radical postures.

At the same time, they often tend *as a group* to interpret democracy in terms more closely related to the early liberalism of Locke than to the later liberalism of Dewey. Democracy is likely to be conceived less as an experimental process of interaction between individual and society, between means and ends, than as a corpus of inherited principles which education has the duty to convey and citizens the duty to revere and respect. The student may detect, therefore, a strong note of transmissiveness in many essentialists even when they qualify their views with a more moderative stance and thus reflect something of a progressivist-tempered view. Idealists, influenced perhaps by Rousseau, may conceive of democracy as a spiritual fusion of selves—a kind of superperson. Realists may also regard the trend away from laissez faire individualism as a progressive symbol of organic evolution. Still others, as we have also noted, may not consider themselves either as realists or idealists; yet they reveal sympathy for the essentialist orientation.

On the whole, perhaps because so many essentialists tend to assume metaculturally that schools fulfill their primary obligation when transmitting habits and practices from generation to generation, they disclose less penetrating and persistent interest in the school's role in society than in learning and the curriculum. Some essentialists almost never express any precise views on the subject of school and society; in those writings that discuss the subject at all, the essentialist position occasionally lacks consistency. In still others, as in the case of Broudy's systematic book (already mentioned), neither "administration" nor "control" seems sufficiently germane to warrant indexing. Yet we find it difficult to avoid the impression that, on balance, Broudy reflects a good deal of the values of early liberalism in such statements as this: ". . . education for democracy is a call to abolish the mediocre in favor of high grade individuals."[22]

As expressed in the heyday of essentialism, the essays of the realist, Kandel, are probably still more representative of the predominant tone. He has frequently repeated that the primary and proper responsibility of education is to "reproduce the type, to transmit the social heritage, and to adjust the individual to the society" by inculcating facts, skills, knowledge.[23] Yet on occasion he, too, has endorsed a less acquiescent and more creative cultural role for the school.

A similar observation might be made of the position of more contemporaneously influential philosophers such as Ulich and Phenix, whose discussions of school and society also swing back and forth from the pole of education as cultural reinforcement to that of guide to social change. They could well assert, for example, that the aim of education is both to reinforce established principles and practices drawn from the cultural heritage and to change the culture progressively toward the perfection of an all-inclusive reality.

This does not mean that essentialism would limit education's services to the select few; all children and youth are to be educated. To be sure, the high-school curriculum ought to provide adequate subject matter for those who are preparing for college and, thereby, for an eventual place in the upper stratum of community life. (Here, indeed, is one of the central, if not always explicit, cultural causes of the curriculum we have noted above; for the good college is itself assumed to be essentialist in structure and aim.) But the school must also provide industrial or other kinds of training for millions of future workers—workers who must be sufficiently skilled to serve the economic order and hence the dominant group that shapes and administers school policies; workers who, accordingly, learn that it is to their own advantage to be loyal to those upon whom they are financially dependent. Essentialism's entire position on school administration is at least implicitly premised on the fact that the capitalist-industrialist economic society is itself "line-staff"—with lines of authority running from top echelons of managers to lowest ranks of workers.

Acquiescence in dominant culture patterns may help us

[22] Broudy, *op. cit.*, p. 199.

[23] Kandel, *Conflicting Theories of Education*, p. 32.

further to understand why the essentialist conception of discipline extends far beyond the school and well into the culture. Thinkers such as Schwab and Ulich are, to be sure, often interested in the *intellectual* discipline they consider necessary to learning. But the cultivation of such learning habits as memorization and acquisition of facts in sequential order is also educationally suited to building the cultural habits needed by efficient workers. In accordance with the "Puritan ethic," even distasteful and uninviting work sometimes appears in this setting to be a desirable educational objective. Still, it is only fair to point out that now and then an essentialist-oriented thinker, such as Phenix, becomes extremely critical of this inherited value; instead, he prefers to look upon work as indigenous to a "democracy of worth."[24]

A common character of the essentialist position may, then, be adduced from the literature. Since society is integral with reality as a whole, it is also integral with, and subject to, the same spiritual or physical universalities as are other aspects of reality—universalities of law, order, custom—which it is the primary duty of education to disclose and perpetuate. Although variously formulated and amended, this is the explicit or implicit major premise of all leading essentialists.

DIVERSE INFLUENCES IN THE ESSENTIALIST MOOD

At this point, brief attention must be paid to several additional educators of influence who, as already anticipated, cannot be clearly associated with either realism or idealism, yet who tend to exemplify the general cultural-educational character just epitomized. Most of these educators, to be sure, are not philosophers, nor is it at all unusual for some of them to ridicule or at least to avoid philosophic expertise because they consider it too vague or impractical to deserve patient attention. A few others, however, are very much concerned with philosophy according to their own notions of that discipline. We shall select instances of both kinds as they relate particularly to our concluding theme in this chapter.

The former have become more or less familiar public names at different moments in the postwar years—among them, Hyman G. Rickover, Arthur Bestor, Mortimer Smith, James D. Koerner, Jacques Barzun, Max Rafferty, and James B. Conant. It would be absurd, of course, to place this diverse group on a single plane of intellectual stature. Yet, with all the qualifications and differences required in any detailed review, it is still probably fair to

[24] Phenix, *op. cit.*, p. 103.

assert (as does Gurney Chambers, writing of "Educational Essentialism Thirty Years After") that men such as these have exerted, and continue to exert, a great deal of common influence in terms of essentialism as ". . . the prevailing educational philosophy in the U.S." For, after all, let us not forget that ". . . transmission of the cultural heritage should continue to be one of the major aims of education."[25]

Conant may be chosen as a representative of this "prevailing educational philosophy." Although his books, too, are dated oftener than not, no one could fairly challenge the assertion that *The American High School Today* and several lesser known ones exerted a great deal of influence over some period. Nor is this fact hardly surprising in its reassurance: multitudes of conventionally-minded teachers, parents, and, above all, administrators, must have welcomed statements such as this: "I believe no radical alteration in the basic pattern of education is necessary in order to improve our public high schools."[26] Equally, most of Conant's proposals for "strengthening" the curriculum have surely been applauded as a model by the Council for Basic Education.

At no time, moreover, does he take clear issue with line-staff structures of administrative authority. But he does pay a good deal of attention to the "academically talented," who are first of all measured by their ability in mathematics and foreign language.

At least as fully as any of the other nonphilosophic writers mentioned, Conant has been earnestly devoted to education as he conceives it, and at times (his proposal for the "comprehensive high school," is perhaps most famous), he appears to be more far-sighted than they. Even so, when his implicit assumptions are exposed critically, he emerges as a congenial but persistent ally of the transmissive approach to American education and culture.

Let us turn, finally, to spokesmen of the second kind—interpreters of education who are far less superficial and, therefore, more philosophic in their approach than are Conant and others of the first kind. In mentioning the writings of three, please bear in mind that we are not interested here in philosophic categorization so much as we are in their overall effect upon cultural structures, practices, and purposes. They are James E. McClellan, R. S. Peters, and Jerome S. Bruner.

Although McClellan has been especially intrigued by ana-

[25] Chambers, "Educational Essentialism Thirty Years After," *School and Society*, Jan., 1969.

[26] Conant, as quoted in Brameld, *Education for the Emerging Age*, p. 51.

lytic philosophy, the title of his book, *Education and the New America,* written with Solon T. Kimball (an educational anthropologist), suggests wider questions. Our interest in its predominantly essentialist orientation, however, is limited in that McClellan appears to deserve this judgment almost despite his total disregard of major American advocates during earlier periods of the same movement which he echoes—for example, Bagley, Horne, Kandel, or even Ulich. Nor do peers such as Broudy and Phenix receive more than incidental notice, if any. Indeed, the central problem could well seem existentialist (How is personal commitment possible amidst the corporate society of "new America"?) although the term itself is not indexed.

In any case, McClellan's solution is anything but existentialist. It is reduced to a plea for intellectual excellence in the "fundamental disciplines." Thus, while avoiding any specific educational methodologies that might enable us to grasp his contention that the "new society" (which deserves our "assent") is concerned "only" with "powerful, dynamic means," the book concludes that these disciplines provide ". . . the primordial rules of thought that guide our most fundamental interpretations of the world." They are, indeed, the "institutionally legitimate modes of social control" and consist disparately of four: logic and mathematics, experimentation, natural history, and esthetic form—none of which is "discussed in behavioral, operational terms," and all of which are left dangling. Only after several dizzying detours are we finally led to commitment itself, now defined as "a firm intellectual grasp" of the "nature of this system"—that is, of the "public, corporate world" which "despite everything, is *real.*" For ". . . knowing ourself as a part of a social system *is* accepting the moral demands inherent in that system. . . ."—a statement surely celebrative of transmissive attitudes radiant all the way from Burke to Sumner and even well beyond.[27]

R. S. Peters, our second example, is an English philosopher of education often admired by Americans of similar affinity. But, again, our interest is not so much at the moment with his own speciality (also, analysis) but rather in what he implies about the wider cultural role of education. On this score, Peters looms even more forthrightly than McClellan as an essentialist-tempered philosopher. For while the latter still leaves the reader puzzled over many uncertainties as to his intent, and while much of what

[27] Kimball and McClellan, *Education and the New America,* pp. 17, 303, 313, 321.

Peters, too, has to say is neither especially enlightening nor provocative in terms of our culturological concern, one discovers nothing at all ambiguous about the principal thesis of his Inaugural Lecture at the University of London or in his *Ethics and Education.* Perhaps as precise an encapsulation as any is this statement:

> The underlying idea of all such education must surely be that children should recapitulate in a brief span the more gradual development of their ancestors. They should be initiated into traditions in which the fundamental principles of reason are implicit. At first they will learn to act from others who know how to act, without understanding the reasons. Gradually they will come to grasp the principles underlying their actions, which make reasons relevant, and will be able to act with understanding and to adapt their practice to novel situations. They may also come to challenge some practices as being no longer rationally defensible.[28]

Now, on first glance, as any analytic philosopher should be the first to agree, this statement is vulnerable to as many linguistic questions (consider only the phrase "fundamental principles of reason") as it would be to scientific questions raised by any anthropologist sensitive to such familiar cultural terms as "recapitulate" or "initiate." Although one fails to discover any meticulous consideration (at least in the works cited) of either anthropology or even of the scientific concept of culture, what does nevertheless emerge emphatically is that "initiation" is the master key to education. And initiation, it turns out, "is always into some body of knowledge and mode of conduct which it takes time to master" —a phrase entirely in accord with enculturation defined as White, for example, would define it. No wonder that education ". . . involves essentially processes which intentionally transmit what is valuable in an intelligible and voluntary manner and which create in the learner a desire to achieve it. . . ."[29]

But Peters' comments about these processes suggest further evidence of his transmissive-culturological propensities. Almost *ad infinitum,* for example, he presupposes values such as "worthwhile content," or the need for "impersonal standards" and "rigor-

[28] Peters, *Ethics and Education,* p. 213.

[29] Peters, in Archambault (ed.), *Philosophical Analysis and Education,* pp. 103, 102.

ous canons." Also, in common with many others chary of progressivism, he insists that critical thinking is futile "without handing on anything to be critical about." Indeed, some statements match the best of Horne or other idealist philosophers of tradition: "In science it is truth that matters, not what any individual believes to be true; in morals it is justice, not the pronouncements of any individual."[30] Thus, one can hardly be expected to profess astonishment when, as Arnstine has noted, Peters falls back upon "formal ethical principles based on Kantian models"—models that provide "only minimal help in adjudicating practical disputes."[31] Even so, they may be extremely "practical" in other ways, as the potent cultural contributions of essentialism attest.

Our third example derives not primarily from a philosopher but from a psychologist, Bruner, who nevertheless demonstrates as does his colleague, Skinner, a lively interest in philosophic dimensions of his field. Nor need Bruner, again like Skinner, be depicted as a consistent advocate of essentialist belief. Even so, and partly perhaps because some of his own assumptions have remained fluid if not opaque, important features of his work have also lent conspicuous comfort, intentionally so or not, to the transmissive orientation.

Bruner's essay, "After John Dewey, What?" may be cited to sharpen the point. After conceding that education is ". . . not only a transmission of culture but also a provider of alternative views of the world . . .," and after echoing ideas of what Dewey had said earlier, he still so clearly sounds the clarion call of "excellence" in education that one can well appreciate the wide applause he has received for assertions such as this: "The goal of education is disciplined understanding. That is the process as well." Conceivably, his attention to the "structure" of knowledge, to "discovery," and to other psychological concepts could contribute, if elaborated further, to progressivist or even reconstructionist as well as to essentialist educational practices. Yet, it is scarcely difficult, meanwhile, to detect clear and oft-repeated essentialist overtones:

> . . . the subject matter of education is knowledge about the world and its connectedness, knowledge that has a structure and a history that permits us to find order and predictabil-

[30] *Ibid.*, p. 104f.

[31] Arnstine, "Review Article—The Cartography of Education: R. S. Peters' Ethics and Education," *Educational Theory*, Spring 1968.

> ity in experience and delight in surprise. . . . All of these things depend in the end upon cultivating and giving expression to the forms of excellence that emerge in our varied society."[32]

These essentialist-attuned phrases are due, we suggest, not merely to Bruner's psychological interpretation but to his relative neglect of the bipolarity that this interpretation demands—that is, of the sociological and anthropological dimensions of human experience. Yet, it is precisely this polarity which Dewey recognized but Bruner has failed to consider in his essay. However insightfully he may at times supplement progressivist concepts such as reflective thinking, one may wonder, in fact, whether he does not actually invite regression rather than progression in his interpretation of knowledge and knowing. Certainly, if June T. Fox is correct in her comparison of Dewey and Bruner, the latter's shift in emphasis is rather "away from the social and back to the individual." Granting hopefully that other shifts may yet occur, it is still within the psychological framework where she belives Bruner has exerted his primary influence. Thus: ". . . the environment, when development proceeds according to an intrinsic and self-contained logic of its own, serves only as a kind of preservative force which can encourage or inhibit development but which cannot determine its course."[33] In terminology closer to our own, the human environment, which is primarily culture, has remained in Bruner's thought largely outside or beyond the power of humanly organized direction and renewal. His more recent projects in the social studies may lead, however, to a less transmissive orientation than has appeared evident thus far.

[32] Bruner, in Archambault (ed.), *Dewey on Education--Appraisals*, pp. 222, 226.

[33] Fox, "Epistemology, Psychology and Their Relevance for Education in Bruner and Dewey," *Educational Theory*, Winter, 1969.

CHAPTER 10

A culturological evaluation of essentialism

AS A PHILOSOPHIC and educational movement, essentialism seems less willing to investigate its own cultural motivations than, for example, progressivism does. This unwillingness may derive partly from the fact that essentialism has been so much identified with the inherited characteristics of modern culture that it has failed to achieve the perspective on itself that more dissident movements are able to achieve. An individual whose strongest motive may be to comply with the demands of his environment is unlikely to probe deeply into the cultural forces that affect him. Similarly, a philosophy of education and culture primarily dedicated to transmitting or reinforcing hitherto dominant patterns of belief and conduct is unlikely to examine too critically the complex milieu surrounding it.

This certainly does not mean that philosophically minded essentialists are oblivious of the critical age in which we live or of rapid social change. All of them offer many comments upon the instabilities, the failures, and successes of our culture. Let us assume, indeed, that all essentialists, because they operate on a constructive and not a complacent level of belief, are more or less willing to recognize strains and conflicts in our culture. Let us grant that, however eclectic at moments, they are all earnestly concerned to defend their own concepts of the democratic way of life. And let us even grant that the term, essentialism, is itself now so fraught with obsolescence that it would be better to substitute another—"disciplinism" perhaps. Even so, our major evaluative judgment is that the general position represented—whatever the symbols that may be preferred—is not, for this age, an adequate position. The essentialist critique of our inherited culture, when offered, is unable sufficiently to release its ties to that culture. Constructed primarily to sanction the hopes and ambitions of modern industrial civilization, essentialism can no more severely challenge the major assumptions of its own intellectual and educational system than it can repudiate the culture that has sired those assumptions. Essentialism, a child of the postmedieval world, is its devoted heir.

Thus, in the history of cultures, the services performed by the transmission of beliefs are not always equally defensible. It becomes less and less defensible in our own culture. An age sickened by crisis—racked by revolutions in technology, politics, economics, even human nature—is not to be cured by sophisticated apologias for time-honored structures and habits. Primarily for this reason, essentialism, despite its rich contributions to our modern past, remains an unsatisfactory philosophy. Whether, however, it may be supplemented and strengthened in order to function more effectively than hitherto is a final question to be raised toward the conclusion of this culturological evaluation.

MODERN IDEALISM AND REALISM: UNDERPINNINGS OF MODERN CULTURE

PHILOSOPHY OUTSIDE THE CONTEXT OF CULTURE

Philosophy, as we have observed, is an indispensable tool for any mature person—certainly for any professional worker in education—who seeks to be clear about his basic beliefs, about their relationships to the culture which affects them, and hence about the personal and social actions that should follow from them.

That too much of the so-called philosophy taught in our teacher-training institutions does not meet this conception of its practical roles may be illustrated by several widely adopted textbooks. Although sometimes carefully prepared, they classify educational theories into such conventional types as idealism, realism, pragmatism, scholasticism, existentialism, and philosophic analysis. But none of these expositions ever clearly poses the question of how far conventional philosophies are the product and rationale of the institutions, habits, attitudes, and customs that compose the man-made environment called modern culture. Instead, the reader is often asked to assume that every philosophy is primarily an intellectual creation that somehow generates itself by its own logic, that each incubates its own self-contained system of beliefs, as though the culture scarcely existed. In effect, the student is left to choose arbitrarily among these philosophies. Lacking any other legitimate criterion of choice, he may reach the dangerous conclusion that one philosophy can hardly be determined, except by personal preference, to be more valid or defensible than any of the others.

Our position, in contradistinction to this overintellectualized and compartmentalized approach, is that thinkers who build profound conceptions of the world are also real human beings living in real cultures. However sophisticated their interpretations may be, they cannot escape the cultural impact. This is no less true, moreover, of philosophies that choose to exclude explicit awareness of the social or psychological roots of their central beliefs than it is of other philosophies that deliberately and consciously include such awareness. That pragmatism is one of the latter philosophies is so apparent that even the sorts of textbooks mentioned above can hardly ignore altogether its cultural motivations. But that such philosophies as idealism and realism also reflect, as well as support, an important era in cultural evolution evidently seldom occurs to the textbook authors.

Not that idealism and realism are by any means the only philosophies subject to this criticism. As our two preceding chapters have reiterated, these positions have receded from their earlier prominence. Yet, the same kind of question may arise about other positions that have tried so zealously to supersede them. Again, we are thinking in particular of philosophic analysis and existentialism, neither of which rarely pays serious attention, if any, to contextual interpretations developed by, say, the philosopher of language, Ernst Cassirer, or the anthropologist of language, Edward Sapir.

But let us stress again that our intention is not to appraise either of these relatively contemporary movements (any more than others we have chosen for occasional comment) as *necessarily* allies of essentialism. That either can prove to be such an ally in some important instances has already been suggested, especially toward the close of our previous chapter; it will be suggested further toward the close of this. But that it need not prove to be so will also be further emphasized.

Meanwhile, our obligation here is to pay primary attention to the two great philosophies that have functioned hitherto most powerfully in modern history. It is these, we must contend, that have thus far contributed much to the transmissive value orientation and thus to its educational embodiment.

PHILOSOPHY WITHIN THE CONTEXT OF CULTURE

Idealism and realism, despite their complex conflicts and multiple deviations, have aimed at one supreme objective: to supplant the static, closed worldview of feudal culture with one that would be more congenial to the economic, scientific, and political events that, beginning with the Renaissance, transformed the character of Europe and America.

The cultural relations of modern philosophy may be clarified by another reference to the rise of modern physical science and the industrial order. Increasingly since Copernicus, we recall, science has sought to explain the phenomena of physical nature by objective, often quantifiable and otherwise exact canons—canons that exclude caprice, revelation, magic, or mere dogmatic authority. During the modern period, too, philosophers have sought to produce an organized and consistent system of beliefs in harmony with the parallel scientific study of the universe, society, and man. Descartes, Hobbes, Spinoza, Locke, Kant—all of these and many others dedicated themselves to this tremendous task.

What we have not sufficiently emphasized in our discussions above is that modern science itself arose because of the occurrence of cultural events that encouraged and supported the revolutionary departures that it symbolizes. These events include the exploration of uncharted seas and continents, the construction of great cities, and the rapid growth of a new type of industrial system called capitalism.

Capitalism, as a profit-making economy, utilizes very different productive techniques from those utilized by the feudal economy—techniques that require the continuous collaboration of science. For, whereas feudalism was based largely on handcraftsmanship (on the production of single commodities by single individuals), the new economy is based upon mass methods of production that are made possible only by the vastly greater speed and efficiency of technology (by which we have meant the alliance of science and industry). Indeed, despite the magnificent contributions of pure science divorced from practical interests, and despite the influence of other factors such as climate or nationalism, cultural historians build a very strong case for the thesis that the insatiable appetite of the industrial system for increasingly efficient, expanding instruments of production has probably given greater impetus to the development of science than has any other single factor.

At the same time that the processes of nature were being subjected to scientific explanation, thinkers were hard at work exploring social and individual processes and attempting to explain them by comparable principles. Thus, Adam Smith and his associates sought to formulate economic and political laws with the same finality and regularity that philosophers of science ascribed to the natural world. Locke, Hume, and others prepared the ground for an equally inclusive science of mental processes—a psychology that would explain phenomena of the mind in terms as objective as those of modern chemistry or physics. Pervading many such efforts (for example, Berkeley's) was a deep religious concern to show that the elements and events of both inanimate and animate nature are the ordinances of a spiritual Being Who is Himself the Supreme Maker of law, the Author of nature, and the Cause of all we perceive. In short, it was possible to discover and formulate natural, political, economic, psychological, *and* religious laws that could stand, each in its respective area, as coordinate manifestations of the same orderly universe. Each law would thereby have the direct and indirect effect of supporting all others.

Thus, in the perspective of over four hundred years of cultural evolution, one can well understand why the modern world view came to serve as solid foundation for the industrializing countries which, by the eighteenth and nineteenth centuries, already dominated most of the European and American continents. It offered a rationale for the burgeoning technological age by demonstrating how its enterprises are governed by undeviating economic law. It accounted for religious belief, when that was desired, by demonstrating that spiritual law is harmonious with scientific and social law. It even justified political revolts by demonstrating that men must sometimes fight to protect the inalienable rights established by laws of nature.

In many ways, this great world view succeeded magnificently. The industrial-scientific culture was a releasing force of vast power, proving its superiority over earlier cultural orders by establishing, among other advances, a higher standard of living and greater opportunities for millions of people. The philosophies that it produced not only probed more deeply into man's inner being, giving him a renewed sense of his significance, but projected their findings upon nature, history, art, religion—upon every important segment of reality. The idealist, for example, found cosmic support for his strong belief in individual, spiritual freedom. Furthermore, the beliefs propounded by modern thinkers were, in *their own time*, often radical—at once thoroughgoing and future-looking. They helped, on the one hand, to speed revolt against monarchical, papal, manorial authority by puncturing and collapsing the flimsy pretensions upon which so much of that authority depended. They anticipated and sanctioned, on the other hand, such institutions as political democracy and modernized economy—institutions that in an earlier age were heretical or immoral but for men of the new age were both daring and desirable.

As is true of all efforts at generalized interpretation, qualifications and limitations could now be compounded. But we must confine ourselves to three that prove unusually pertinent to our culturological approach to essentialist thought.

(1) *Despite their multiple contributions to a common cultural thrust, philosophic patterns, certainly insofar as they offer support to essentialist beliefs, have been and continue in many ways to be dissimilar.* We have recorded above a few such differences. The idealist, to choose one, tends to look upon man and the world more optimistically and warmly than does the colder, material-minded realist and, hence, to view progress as inherent in a purposeful reality. It can also be argued cogently that idealism tends to emphasize the selfhood and subjectivity of the individual much more strongly than realism, thus allowing wider room for personal freedom and autonomous action. The soul seems to be striving, even emotionally, toward spiritual perfection. Again, idealism often favors a monistic conception of the world which, at times, contrasts with the pluralistic propensities of realism. More basic than all of these, at least to their traditional exponents, is the "stuff" with which each builds its system of reality: idealism, a spiritual substance identified with mind; realism, a material substance identified with body.

Nevertheless, such demarcations between idealists and realists are not necessarily as abrupt as some conventional historians of thought or education still like to contend. One may observe, for example, an undercurrent of cosmic optimism expressed by modern philosophers of realist sympathies, such as Spencer, or an emphasis on individual freedom expressed by other realists, especially by friends of lassez faire, such as Locke. In regard to the old philosophic argument of monism versus pluralism, some mechanistic materialists (Holbach is one) seem quite as monistic as are most objective idealists, while some idealists (Green is one) seem as pluralistic as are most realists.

Although these similarities and overlappings could be extended almost indefinitely, we wish to emphasize once more that *we are not predicating any logical or otherwise formally philosophic identification of realism and idealism.* Despite the unifying philosophy of a Spinoza aiming to transcend them, such an identification would be absurd in view of the fact that the history of modern thought is so largely devoted to disputes between them. For several reasons (temperamental or cultural as well as more precisely philosophic), the two schools are in genuine opposition at many more points than we are able to suggest.

But the question that should disturb the ease with which idealists and realists have regarded themselves as implacable foes is why, if this is so, they can so often join hands congenially in a *practical, socially consequential* movement such as essentialist-directed education. (The same question may be asked, as was anticipated near the close of Chapter 9, of some recent educational theorists who seek to repudiate both idealists and realists.) Is their congeniality *merely* a coincidence? The answer is strongly negative. The distinctions among particular thinkers and schools, although interesting, legitimate, and subject to endless ramifications, are not at all subject to the easy compartmentalizing that one finds in the culturally rootless, artificial classifications of so many textbooks. *For, despite all their differences, modern realism and modern idealism, as well as their less classifiable heirs, belong to a united front; they are engaged in a task so momentous as to require the talents and interests of both: the task of constructing the intellectual and moral foundations for a modern industrial culture urgently congenial to both.*

The realist's great contribution is a world view that is largely physical, orderly, natural, and subject to examination and understanding by men who are themselves subject to exactly the same precisions because they are part of this same universe. The idealist's great contribution is a world view that is largely spiritual, orderly, and subject to understanding by persons who are themselves spiritual and thereby possessed of some of the qualities of *this* same universe. Our two remaining qualifications and limitations are devoted mainly to further support for this pivotal contention.

(2) *Renaissance and post-Renaissance thought do not at all relinquish the full spirit or substance of the absolutism that was central to ancient and medieval thought.* Absolutism has been retained because, for one thing, the modern era has demanded its own types of sanction for its own types of domination over the lives of ordinary men. But modern thought does not, therefore, simply retain inherited patterns of such sanction; rather, it usually succeeds in substituting scientifically and rationally sophisticated formulations for the outmoded ones of an earlier era. Whether in the form of Hegelian-influenced "dialectic idealism" or of Newtonian-influenced "mechanistic materialism," these philosophies hold that the order and design of the universe are completely established and increasingly known. Thus, to take the example of "freedom" as reinterpreted in the light of these philosophies, the idealist tends to regard the individual self as ultimately "free" insofar as it abides by the laws of freedom established by the cosmic Self. The realist tends to interpret the individual as "free" insofar as he understands and accepts the laws of nature as determined by science. In all varieties of influential expression, however, both realism and idealism provide sanction for the kinds of microcosmic freedom congenial to a modern macrocosmic order—an order often accompanied, no less than the one it supplanted, by overarching authority and ruthless power.

(3) *The institutions and practices of the modern world, far from being hostile to such a sanction for freedom, welcome and encourage it in every possible way.* What we must not forget is that this era has been structured so as to place great responsibilities upon certain groups—notably, the rising middle classes which, from their beginnings, have been eager to promote economic enterprise, trade, experimentation, and exploration. Sometimes very profoundly (as in Spinoza), sometimes more obtusely (as in Spencer), philosophy comes again and again to the service of these middle classes. With differing arguments—cosmological, ethical, religious, logical—philosophy provides an intellectual bulwark that, on the one hand, supports the right of emerging groups to criticize and act against the hitherto dominant groups of a feudal and theocratic culture and, on the other

hand, defends their equal right to establish new patterns of authority for an industrial, secular culture in which they themselves would rule.

In this double task we have found both modern idealism and modern realism to be generous allies. The former pictures a spiritual universe in which man is good when he expresses his own spiritual self and thereby strives to embrace God by revering. His benevolent mandates. The latter pictures a material universe in which man is good so long as he understands and abides by its orderly natural and social processes. To be sure, no two philosophic systems highlight the same vistas or color their canvases with the same pigments. Since each possesses its own esthetic uniqueness, the picture created by idealists tends to be warmer, more emotionally toned than that created by realists. The particular focus, moreover, may be upon the individual in his search for independence of expression and movement, or upon the state, or upon religion, or upon a science such as physics, biology, or sociology. Seldom, however, does any philosophy of the modern era become influential if it fails to provide support in some form for the industrial, increasingly technological, pattern of civilization which, by the eighteenth century, had already pervaded most of the Western world.

It is in this qualification that we detect the main import of essentialist education as a potent agent of modern culture.

TRANSMISSIVE ROLES OF ESSENTIALIST EDUCATION

THE REAL, THE TRUE, AND THE GOOD

Essentialism, as a theory of education and culture, is much too sophisticated to deny that contemporary institutions and practices have failed in many ways to meet contemporary needs. Nevertheless, it steadfastly maintains that the supreme educational task is to develop in men sufficient acuteness and skill to enable them to penetrate the dark clouds of ignorance that conceal from them the underlying reality, truth, and goodness of the natural and/or spiritual world. Such an educational task is, of course, vast. Not only do men differ widely in capacity but even the exceptionally able may all too easily misinterpret that world. Hence men often mistake some part for the whole; or the processes of nature and society may themselves be undergoing such swift changes that, although still expressions of basic unity and order, they are thus far too elusive to grasp.

How, then, shall we confront the predominant, if not always equally explicit, aim of essentialist education: to maintain and strengthen inherited patterns of modern culture as wisely as possible? Let us face this question more fundamentally than heretofore by considering two important, related means to achieving that aim. One means is to rely on the *practices, habits, and institutions* that have been discovered, established, and tested. The other is to become increasingly aware of the *axioms, rights, laws, and principles* that, existing beneath practices, habits, and institutions, may or may not have been discovered and revealed. To illustrate: the Constitution of the United States may be revered by the essentialist for its authorship and accepted as a symbolic actuality (his encouragement of learning via the printed page or teaching machine can reinforce such acceptance) ; or the essentialist may stress "natural rights" and other moral mandates whose significance lies in universal principles more real, more true, and more valuable than the Constitution itself.

Although the essentialist might stress both *institutions* and *principles*, a difference in emphasis is important enough to reveal some disagreement among essentialists over the chief service to be rendered by their doctrine. Educators who stress the heritage of institutional arrangements such as private enterprise may seem more conservative in practical attitudes than those who devote primary attention to rights and axioms; thus the latter may argue persuasively that certain institutional changes are needed in order to fulfill such rights and axioms. This second type of emphasis, nevertheless, may produce an even more profound and more long-term transmissive effect than the former. Here, then, we are required to analyze two further points of interesting distinction.

In the first place, the frame of mind cultivated by the emphasis upon rights and axioms leads us to recognize their existence within an already designed cosmos, whether or not such rights and axioms have been previously discovered or are still to be discovered. The student exposed to this frame of mind thus learns to recognize or accept what the world presents to him—whether as institutions and practices, or as laws and principles not yet perhaps fully understood but capable of recognition and acceptance.

In the second place, emphasis upon rights and axioms performs a transmissive function because abstract laws, axioms, and principles are, after all, derived from institutions and practices—

that is, from social, political, economic, religious, and other cultural arrangements. They are *abstract* only in the sense of being *abstracted from* such arrangements. Upon close inspection, the essentialist's universal axioms prove to have a cultural history of their own: they were created to support definite institutions and practices of very definite periods.

Although substantial historical evidence could be offered, we choose only one familiar example of the abstraction of universal laws: the famous doctrine of "natural rights." It was developed by such thinkers as Hobbes, Locke, and Rousseau for political purposes at a time of great social and economic upheaval. Devised, first of all, to give moral support to the struggles of the rising middle classes in behalf of new economic patterns, it provided justification for their right both to rebel against feudal types of authority and to establish revolutionary authorities of their own choosing.

Thus the question of how essentialism operates as an agent of cultural transmission invites at least one plausible answer. In urging the primacy of rights and axioms, it thereby exerts its influence in behalf of historically established institutions or practices for which such principles were originally devised and which, in turn, they loyally support. In this way, essentialists have helped to strengthen and encourage whatever continued vitality and relevant meaning these institutions or practices may still possess.

RECEPTIVE LEARNING

The reinforcing propensity of essentialist education is revealed also by approaches to the learning process. For, granting once more that important psychological distinctions prevail between realists and idealists (not to mention others who are neither), it must be remembered that both of these philosophies agree on one presupposition of learning: they both tend to interpret the mind as receptor of the world of natural or spiritual realities, truths, and values. Such a theory of receptivity is, of course, congenial also to the theory of existent principles and/or institutions. Thus in this respect learning, too, serves to cultivate acceptance of these principles and/or institutions.

But receptivity affords another related way to encourage cultural transmission. Through the process that the essentialist realist, Finney, once aptly termed "passive mentation," the "immature" learner not only acquires the facts, practices, beliefs, rules, and responses selected by those who, being "mature," believe it is their duty to select them; of even greater consequence, he acquires the *habits* of absorption. With continuous practice as he grows into adulthood, the average individual thereby so firmly develops more and more of the attitudes and responses of "passive mentation" that he is less and less likely to change them. Whether the essentialist derives his theory from hereditarian or from environmentalist preferences, or whether learning consists largely of stocking the mind substance, of enriching mental states, of discovering (with Bruner) the structure of knowledge, or of raising (with Skinner) the standards of "excellence" by programed instruction, the practical effect may be the same. In relegating critical thinking, the questioning attitude, cooperative planning, and other characteristics of progressivist learning to secondary roles (if he seriously includes them at all), the essentialist-oriented educator helps to form the habits of citizens who most readily learn to receive whatever contents and skills may already be selected by those in authority.

Of course, the pupil will develop beliefs about "individual initiative" and "freedom of speech" as well as about other traditions that presumably encourage an active, critical response to his environment. Indeed, his teacher often believes sincerely in such traditions, and may very well provide some place for problem-solving or even, in elementary ways, for philosophic analysis. But, because he is afforded little experimental opportunity to translate generalities into classroom or community experience, his belief in them often becomes verbal substitutes for personal or social practice and involvement.

THE OBSOLESCENCE OF ESSENTIALISM

"TRANSMISSION," PAST AND PRESENT

Essentialist perpetuation of the traditions of postmedieval culture is directly relevant to another important question: How far is essentialism an adequate and defensible theory of education for our present culture-in-flux? Certainly, it should not be denied that this theory performed a valuable service (for example, by providing training in industrial skills and in cultivating virtues, such as thrift) throughout the long era during which the middle classes grew to positions of dominance. The momentous influence of Locke, Harris, Thorndike, and numerous other thinkers of earlier periods testifies to this service. It tried to recognize the place of religion in modern education, especially if congenial to Protestant and nonperennialist belief. And it performed the service of placing education on more scientific grounds by insisting upon precision of data and measurement.

But culture changes—sometimes at cyclonic speed. Beliefs once forward-looking or strongly supportive of relatively productive institutions may gradually come to retard them. When this occurs, as it often has in history, older patterns of belief—whether or not philosophically formulated—may become *opponents* of novel, emerging cultural arrangements, and *proponents* of patterns with which men have long been comfortably familiar and to which they render habitual allegiance.

With this historical perspective, we may appreciate more and more clearly the stellar transmissive role of essentialism, particularly in the twentieth century. As political, ecclesiastic, military, and other lieutenants of the industrial structure solidified their control over institutions; as recurring periods of war and unceasing exploitation of millions proved the inability of these upper strata to guarantee a stable, satisfying life for the multitudes; as criticisms of early liberalism by Mill, Marx, Dewey, and others became more devastating and bitter; as the later measurement movement initiated by realists in education and the social sciences often proved to be even more apologetic for the rightness of "whatever is" than had objective idealism—as such trends and realizations crystallized simultaneously throughout the nineteenth and twentieth centuries, the essential value of inherited arrangements no longer seemed so easy to condone.

Thus traditional objectives of education took on a different, far more defensive connotation in the dominant role of essentialism. Despite apologias, qualifications, and even intents that ally essentialism with later liberalism, its principal task, whether always overtly or not, is pronounced. This is to maintain, by both justification and revivification, the cultural habits and correlative beliefs that have captured much of the cultural orientation that still pervades substantial proportions of Western civilization. Little wonder—when we consider how deep the impress of the long era preceding our own time—that its protagonists continue to be vociferous, numerous, and, on occasion, shrewd.

ESSENTIALISM AS CULTURAL LAG

Yet, with all due appreciation, the earnestness of those protagonists of essentialism who work in the social sciences, religion, education, and other fields also reveals the presence of cultural lag. It is a lag, moreover, of gravest consequence for the future life of man.

The period through which he is now passing is often and properly characterized, we recall, as a period of revolution. It is revolutionary in the sense that abnormally rapid, fundamental innovations are occurring in every area of human experience—in morals, science, art, and certainly in economics and politics. These innovations call for a twofold reaction: on the one hand, maximum awareness of their causes and characteristics; on the other hand, fullest consideration of every important proposal to reshape modern culture toward ends that seem desirable as alternatives to, or supplements of, earlier patterns of belief and practice.

Those of the essentialist mood have themselves sometimes sensed certain revolutionary symptoms in the present period. Indeed, it is because of profound feelings of disturbance that they have objected to what they regard as one serious contributor to the current confusion of cultural aims—namely, progressive education. They fail to meet the demands of our time, however, in respect to the twofold reaction noted above. They do not analyze adequately the significance of such movements as progressivism in its cultural matrix of later liberalism; hence, they cannot successfully judge its significance for our revolutionary period. And they do not consider objectively to what extent their own proposals would resolve the present confusions and conflicts of our culture, or to what extent these proposals would perpetuate the very patterns of belief, habits, and associated institutions that may seriously exacerbate such confusions and conflicts.

Let us consider, again, what is perhaps the single most pervasive example of essentialist support of traditional patterns of belief—namely, belief in freedom of enterprise founded upon the post-Renaissance system of economic relations. Notwithstanding doubts raised by deviants among essentialists, especially among those no longer identified with realism and idealism, the greater part of their philosophic apparatus has operated uncritically in behalf of the system's perpetuation. Indeed, it becomes possible to detect three interconnected cogs in that apparatus: (1) the glorification of our social heritage; (2) the correspondence and coherence theory of knowledge, with its corollary of receptive learning; (3) the central belief in an ordered world of institutions that applies as well to laws and principles.

Social heritage as concealment. The central difficulty caused by essentialism's reinforcement of cultural tradition is not that it glorifies the social heritage but that it does so uncritically. That is to say, it helps students insufficiently to distinguish between past achievements that are decidedly worth understanding, even worth preserving, and those that, having served their original purpose, are no longer worth preserving. Many essentialist thinkers thus tend to commit the familiar logical fallacy of identifying parts with the whole—of implying that because modern culture records great accomplishments in *some* areas, therefore it does so in *most* or *all* other areas.

Some interpreters of essentialism, it is true, attempt to distinguish between the essentials of the social heritage and the mere traditions of custom and habit. The essentials, they say, are the permanent and indispensable features of that heritage; it is these they wish to preserve. So long as no judgments of culturological appraisal are provided, however, the distinction is difficult to maintain: essentials and traditions are easily confused with each other by anyone who wishes to find in the latter convenient examples of the former.

The confusion of essentials with traditions may be illustrated by reference to the essential virtues—honesty, respect, duty, devotion, and many others—which this type of education selects for inculcation in the young. Seldom does it question whether they are meaningful in the abstract; almost never does it seem aware that *these virtues are meaningful only when delineated within the experience of living cultures.* Seldom, accordingly, does it either ask or answer the question: How shall we decide *which* elements of the heritage are to be retained and perpetuated? Yet, again and again, essentialists tempt us to suppose that the heritage is itself a *sufficient* criterion—that in and of itself it provides a primary source of goodness and truth.

Returning specifically to the dominant political-economic system, the point is that *generalities* about the past tend to conceal *specificities* that apply neither to all of the past nor certainly to the present and future. Consider, further, the value of freedom. Undoubtedly it is true that, with the rise of a new industrial order, freedom was achieved in newly significant ways by *some* individuals—especially by individuals of the middle classes. But it is grossly inaccurate to conclude therefrom that freedom was achieved by *all* or *most* of the people—especially by the working classes, including disadvantaged minorities. Groups of people are not free in any sense that is empirically meaningful so long as they are subjected to domination by others—so long as they are denied the opportunity to satisfy a large part of their wants or to participate, by means of political and economic authority, to a degree commensurate with their numbers in determining policies under which these wants are to be satisfied.

Such subjection and such denial have proved very widespread throughout modern culture. In some respects, indeed, they have become even more widespread than in the earlier period of modern history, with its relatively open, competitive system of small-business capitalism. For this system has been increasingly superseded by the relatively closed, noncompetitive monopolistic, corporate technology of the present period where fewer and fewer individuals are free to work, earn, or plan as they please. In a century of worldwide wars, fewer are free even to *exist*. Nevertheless, whenever citizens are taught to accept freedom in some absolute or undifferentiated sense—whenever they are taught that freedom is somehow grounded in a universal, orderly system of nature and/or in a universal God—they thereupon fasten still further strands to their heavy bonds of acquiescent, uncritical response.

The correspondence and coherence theory of knowledge as concealment. Granting the network of refinements noted in Chapter 9, traditional forms of the essentialist theory of knowledge provide a second main device of concealment geared closely to the first. Thus the idealist's epistemology, for one, may suggest an active meeting of mind with Mind; yet the practical effect of his way of learning is often not too different from the realist's. So long as the learner is placed in the role of understanding the given culture by coherently presenting or *re*-presenting whatever content is chosen for him to assimilate, he is ill equipped to analyze the reliability of that content. He is ill equipped to determine in what ways it is incomplete, distorted, or unobjectively selected by his teachers, many of whom have identified what should be learned with what most controlling groups in the culture (school boards, for example) want him to learn. His primary duty is to incorporate that content into his mind substance (or whatever the preferred term) and then to reflect it as faithfully as possible in his own knowledge, habits, and behavior.

We may appreciate, then, why it is that essentialist education so often receives wholehearted support from those in established positions of social power who benefit by retention of inherited institutions. Whether via operant conditioning through teaching machines, or via microcosmic-macrocosmic harmonies of religious idealism (as in Christian Science education, for one), any shrewd advocate of the inherited structure fully recognizes its usefulness in developing citizens amenable to his own metacultural beliefs. For, *even if we assume that some essentialists do not consciously intend that their doctrine shall be utilized to serve controlling cultural interests, the program they endorse has the effect of making them, more often than not, useful partners of these interests.*

Our analysis of how essentialist learning serves as an invisible barrier against transformative or even moderative change may now be epitomized. In a culture suffering as ours presently suffers, one of the ways by which men seek to maintain stability is by teaching people to accept and revere the given order. Whether the given order is in reality what it is pictured to be (men are "free," for example) is of less importance than that, in the interests of those who sanction it, the accepted picture must be firmly impressed upon receptive minds and emotions of the largest possible number of citizens, young and old.

"Antecedently uniform reality" as concealment. The final important cog in essentialism's apparatus of concealment has been a crucial belief that the reality to be assimilated is one of established if not always articulated uniformity—a reality governed by physical and/or spiritual regularities which are themselves cosmically and permanently established. This belief, a carry-over from medieval culture and philosophy, expresses itself in one of two major practical directions. Either it is a way of inviting conformity with already existing institutions, or it is a way of inviting conformity with the axioms and principles that underlie institutions whether or not the latter currently exist. How can this kind of ontology operate as still another device to conceal the actual character of contemporary economic, social, political and moral experience?

It can do so because, for one thing, it reinforces the premise of classical economic theory that laws governing our traditional economic system (the law of supply and demand, for example) are so inviolable, so universal, that we must respond to them with the same obeisance that we respond to the law of gravity. Habituation to this kind of response serves both forms of concealment noted above: the first (the social heritage), by identifying a *particular* economic order with the *general* order which, embodied in that heritage, is assumed to be the fountainhead of all important knowledge and value; the second (the theory of knowledge), by disclosing to us the laws of social life through receptive, if not replicative, learning.

The theory of an antecedently uniform reality, insofar as it is taught as the exclusive theory, serves as concealment in other ways. It fails, for example, to consider the challenge of a radically different approach to reality, namely, the operational theory of scientific discovery. By interpreting laws of, say, economics as instruments constructed for the purpose of controlling the human environment, operationalism challenges the whole acquired structure of social and natural order assumed by essentialism and, along with it, the whole habit of acquiescing in that structure. It demonstrates further that, however complex the problems involved, men can approach economic experience, including our particular form of economic order, as an area of life on which to operate for the purpose of frequent modification and innovation.

Essentialists also fail to appreciate clearly enough that their theory, no less than any other, is the product and expression of a historic and cultural age. Hence, as emphasized above, the laws, axioms, rules, and principles held to be universal prove, upon more scrupulous inspection, to be articulations and rationalizations of that very definite age. In short, they establish a foundation for economic, scientific, political, and other practices required to bolster and assure the alignment of cultural forces.

But historic ways in which philosophy has been and continues to be utilized in order to provide this foundation have not, to this point, been sufficiently emphasized. Subtly overlapping tendencies may be reconsidered: for one thing, philosophy has assumed a realist-scientific form *or* an idealist-religious form; for another, it has assumed an objective and worldly form *or* a subjective and personal form. Expressed in other terms, the search for a given and uniform reality is the search for a harbor of security—in some cases, the objective reality of nature or God; in others, the being of the natural or spiritual person. The attraction of the latter harbor (the subjective and personal) has been the support it provides, above all, for the individual who is struggling to attain new rights and power. The attraction of the former (an objective world of physical and/or spiritual law and order) is that it provides a harbor large and deep enough to include and protect all such rights and power. Therefore, it also includes multitudes of ordinary people allegedly dependent upon both kinds of harbors.

A history of modern philosophy might still be written around disputes over these two great sanctions of security—the objective and subjective. Such a history would need to point out that both these worldly and individualistic forms have each assumed the same premise of a uniform, objective set of principles, laws, and axioms, which presumably establish the supremacy and indisputability of their own point of departure. *Both are finally absolut-*

istic. And each, because it *is* absolutistic, has often embraced and justified the other by its own favorite system of laws and axioms. The "subjectivist" (Berkeley, for example) builds an objective Supreme Being out of the substance of self; the "objectivist" (Hobbes, for example) builds a law-abiding, if still material, self from the stuff of physical nature. Each one often becomes a smooth *reflex*, reflecting the other as in a mirror: *the self and the world of modern philosophy are both the intellectual symbols of a culture unwilling, or unable, to disavow the medieval belief in and reliance upon an unchallengeable and objectively established universe.*

But the subjectivist-objectivist orientations are also symbols of the grave instabilities chronic to modern culture. Having established little more, finally, than their own ultimate sanction—the microcosmic and/or the macrocosmic—nevertheless, having suffered acutely from the failure of political, economic, religious, and other orders to provide a stable and peaceful way of life with full participation by the common man, these philosophies have continued to swing from the subjective to the objective pole and back again. One can well understand that, in their restless search for rest, men of historic cultures have tended to seek justification for their erratic behavior in some unimpeachable, institutional authority transcending themselves. But in modern Western culture, especially, this authority may also conveniently justify such behavior by equating it with "freedom" or other "inalienable rights" endowed in the individual.

The issue is admittedly complex, for the reciprocities of modern culture and philosophy are themselves complex. Nevertheless, the essence of the third major concealment may be simply stated: *the whole doctrine of an already existing, indubitable reality becomes a powerful cultural device to reinforce attitudes of compliance either with objective institutional arrangements, or subjective wishes and habits, or both.* To teach, for example, that economic practices are governed by laws as impersonal and inviolable as the laws governing the stars is only to nourish a convenient belief in the righteous inevitability of those institutions and individual wishes.

To teach, however, that no such laws exist—that laws are intellectual tools constructed by men, that by means of these tools men gradually learn to shape and reshape a stubborn cultural environment by operating upon it as engineers operate upon the equally stubborn surface of the earth—to teach this is to threaten the "established" order. To the cultural and educational essentialist, this is also sufficient grounds for questioning or even ridiculing (in the name of scholarship, of course) any philosophy that dares to propose such a heresy.

CRITIQUE OF ESSENTIALISM IN THE LIGHT OF CONTEMPORARY PHILOSOPHIC MOVEMENTS

REINFORCING INFLUENCES

Toward the conclusion of both preceding chapters, we tried to suggest through more or less random examples that essentialism in its contemporary character can no longer be confined so predominantly to the historic doctrines of idealism and realism. Although these doctrines have been stressed most, by no means are they exclusive. Such diversity helps to account, we have also said, for an unusual degree of eclecticism in the essentialist outlook; or perhaps more correctly, this outlook is both the condition and consequence of a range of philosophic ideas far from always harmonious with one another.

Nor is it too hazardous to conjecture one explanation. Under whatever label, the essentialist mood of our time is one of the most potent systems of symbols that have evolved through modern culture—a culture not only undergoing extraordinary confusions in our own period but, consciously or not, compelled meanwhile to maintain characteristics of political, economic, religious, *and* educational authority beneficial to established forces very much concerned with precisely that kind of maintenance.

Thus, as one might also expect in the face of its primarily transmissive role, the strength of essentialism may be drawn from abundant philosophic and educational resources. Although we have been suggesting and will suggest in subsequent chapters that other influential philosophies of education may likewise find ways to strengthen their formulations by drawing upon some of these same resources, essentialism as we regard it has already begun to do so more persistently thus far than has, say, progressivism. This is so, we think, because essentialism has needed to supplement if not to replace much of the two historical doctrines, realism and idealism, upon which it has so heavily depended thus far—doctrines which are so abrasively challenged by opposing viewpoints, including progressivism itself.

Contributions to the essentialist mood by the several contemporary philosophic movements already touched upon are, to be sure, very diversified. Certainly, we do not pretend, without much greater knowledge than research studies thus far afford, to weigh these contributions with anything like precision. As will also be noted further, it is entirely possible that they may help to modify essentialism in promising, even innovative directions. Meanwhile, let us note a few of their more predominantly reinforcing roles.

The most inclusive contribution may prove more negative than positive—that is, a frequent disinclination on their part to deal directly, much less exhaustively, with the very issues that we consider of supreme urgency—issues of social, moral, or other forms of struggle and uncertainty typified by our discussion in Chapter 2. To be sure, not all such issues are ignored by contemporary philosophic movements; yet, if one surveys the representative educational writings of analytic philosophers, for example, one cannot help but be struck by what Abraham Kaplan, a sympathizer of this position, calls their "remoteness" and "antiseptic air." Certainly, the representative books of analysts widely required in graduate education classrooms (*Philosophy and Education*, edited by Scheffler, is a fair example) appear, to say the least, cold-blooded. And, when their advocates do venture into germane questions of cultural or even educational "purpose" or "aim," they appear again only rarely to find such questions directly related to the goals of young citizens—except perhaps to conclude that "normative" goals such as, say, student democracy are arbitrary anyway and hence beyond any kind of verification or other justification according to "descriptive" rules of analytic logic.

Our point, then, is that many analysts, when they follow their own ground rules, either remain aloof entirely or offer a case for objectivity which encourages, in turn, moral and social neutrality. That the practical consequence is supportive of whatever cultural patterns prevail at a given period is a persuasive objection to the analytic movement still not advanced anywhere emphatically enough.

Not that all exponents do remain neutral, of course. As we have noted briefly, several analysts in the name of their prestigious academic specialty prove remarkably facile in defending educational policies sympathetic with much the same kind of transmissive cultural orientation endorsed by the very idealists or realists whom they like to deplore. Others seem even concerned to make an elaborate case for their own normative values which, although still admittedly arbitrary according to their analytic criteria, somehow manage to emerge as naïve and cloudy preferences for what William K. Frankena, for one, terms "the good life"—whatever that may mean.

In varying ways of more or less subtlety, it might be equally possible to demonstrate that one or another of each remaining selected movements can be, indeed have been, utilized in behalf of the essentialist approach to culture and education. Two of these, however, could thus be adjudged only were we to distinguish them from their more orthodox expressions: neo-Marxism and neo-Freudianism. Let us only assert here then that Marxism, when utilized as the official ideology of the Soviet Union, has frequently been interpreted not only as a materialistic form of realism, but has provided justification for extreme techniques of receptive learning under the aegis of communist-indoctrinated education. Also, orthodox Freudian psychoanalysis, although rejected by Soviet ideologists and not often directly utilized by educators elsewhere, nevertheless serves to reinforce assumptions entirely congenial with other facets of conventional realist belief: its cluster of assumptions about the determined, instinctual drives of human nature can and does, at times, provide a therapy of "adjustment" to the imperious demands of the superego—that is, to traditional standards of conscience culturally assumed to be "right."

As for Zen Buddhism and existentialism, we find no clear evidence in educational literature of essentialist inclination that the former has thus far been considered even tangentially. But such is not the case, of course, for the latter: we have found that several theorists (most notably, perhaps, Ulich and Phenix) have received a good deal of existentialist inspiration for their underlying idealist and/or realist beliefs. Yet it becomes no more plausible to assert that existentialism is the inevitable ally of essentialism than to insist that philosophic analysis is—especially so, since as noted in Part 1, existentialist beliefs range far and wide in culturological perspective.

Virtually all, then, that can properly be claimed for the influence of existentialism in the period of post-idealist and post-realist essentialism is, rather curiously, comparable to analytic philosophy. On the one hand, existentialists may render support to transmissive patterns not so much by what they do assert as by what they do not: in dismissing many major cultural problems of our time as irrelevant at least to them (take the collective technology as one), some may rather cavalierly invite the student to shift attention away from these problems to his personal and subjective existence. Such problems remain as urgent as ever, to be sure, but either their diagnoses or their prognoses are, if offered at all, confined chiefly to the possible meaning of this existence.

On the other hand, other existentialists (again by no means all) provide quite explicit support for orientations that reverberate with attitudes reminiscent of early liberalism. Van Cleve Morris, to cite one articulate proponent, has frequently interpreted education existentially in terms of "complete, undiluted, and absolute freedom"—terms which, however qualified, not only take severe issue with progressivism's individual-social transactional process, but insist that education rightly understood is predominantly "individual-centered." Whether Morris is expounding his personal views may not always be clear; what does come clear is that, for existentialists as he views them, ". . . the way to the good life . . . is not through social reform." Indeed, if ". . . democracy means group decision, let us have none of it." For the ". . . only adequate socio-order is one which recognizes and values the absolute freedom of the human person." Hence each man must be "his own supreme court of value."[1]

SOME POSSIBLE AMELIORATING INFLUENCES

That our chosen movements of modern thought may be considered in diverse perspectives has been emphasized sufficiently so that we propose to close this culturological evaluation by turning now to a few suggestive ways that might contribute to the essentialist orientation in other than the predominantly *reinforcing* influences considered above. Let us take these more *ameliorating* influences at random.

Neo-Marxism. Surprising though it may seem at first glance, this influence may be included, for one, because of its contributions to what we wish to call "sociological realism"—that is, its attempt to expose and assess socioeconomic structures which are bolstered, in turn, by military-industrial-political superstructures. Such an attempt differs in an important way, of course, from the classic Marxian philosophy of dialectical materialism that so often has undergirded receptive educational patterns in Communist countries; yet it stems partially from a comparable philosophy of objectivity and universal law of the sort detected among essentialists themselves of both traditional and more recent strains. White is again an example: though no professed Marxist, his insistence upon the *sui generis* (that is, self-generating) level of human existence known as culture may serve to toughen our awareness of its recalcitrance in the face of organized efforts to bring about directed change, educationally or otherwise.

White's formulation may be questioned, of course, for its

[1] Morris, in Van Cleve Morris (ed.), *Modern Movements in Educational Philosophy*, pp. 363, 369ff.

subordination of a scientifically operational interpretation of culture by a reified (that is, an objectively concretized) one. Nevertheless, we think that, granting qualifications, the heavy stress of sociological realism upon the conserving power of transmission rather than upon liberal moderation or radical transformation deserves salutary respect.

Neo-Freudianism. Essentialist educators have rarely paid direct attention to orthodox Freudian theory, much less to this one. Yet we suggest that such relative neglect is itself easy to explain. Although Freud was one of the supreme realists of the age (Who, indeed, can point to any other pioneer of psychical exploration more ruthlessly insistent upon analyzing human nature for traits largely avoided elsewhere?), yet the interpretation of man that he presented to the nineteenth and twentieth centuries remains so distasteful to defenders of Western custom that, even today, it remains ignored or misunderstood by many of these defenders.

It is regrettable, therefore, that educational psychologists, exemplified by realist essentialists such as Thorndike, have made almost no effort to supplement or synchronize their own assumptions with either Freudian or neo-Freudian ones. This is not equally true of all educational psychologists—certainly not of Bruner who, as we have noted, cannot in any case be corralled within the essentialist fold without debatable limitations. Nevertheless, when he speaks of Freud as the "child of his century's materialism" who perceives man in "the continuity of organic lawfulness," Bruner invites educational psychology to incorporate Freudian thought into a more adequate, perhaps neoessentialist, conception. For example:

> It remained for Freud to present the image of man as the unfinished product of nature: struggling against unreason, impelled by driving inner vicissitudes and urges that had to be contained if man were to live in society, host alike to seeds of madness and majesty, never fully free from an infancy anything but innocent. What Freud was proposing was that man at his best and man at his worst is subject to a common set of explanations: that good and evil grow from a common process.[2]

Zen Buddhism. Bruner may also possibly come to recognize that, just as neo-Freudianism is capable of enriching educational

[2] Bruner, in Benjamin Nelson (ed.), *Freud and the 20th Century*, pp. 279ff.

theory, so too is this theory. His interest in "art as a mode of knowing" anticipates this possibility, as does his provision for intuition in knowing. But these are intimations at best.

It is perhaps unfortunate that a philosopher of education such as Ulich, despite his interest in Oriental thought, avoids discussion of Zen Buddhism in his best-known writings. Or that in a series of fine-etched portraits of *The Educated Man* by several writers (dedicated to Ulich), no space is available for a single Oriental portrait, Zen or otherwise.

Such inadvertence among American scholars is, of course, more common than not. Essentialist-inclined theorists, no less than those who are progressivist-inclined, still tend to view education myopically within the frameworks of Western culture. We suggest, nevertheless, that Zen Buddhism, reinterpreted for our age, may offer at least as much to the revitalization of essentialist patterns as do our other contemporary movements. Like neo-Freudianism and now existentialism, to which we turn, Zen Buddhism centers upon the intrinsic qualities of man's nature. In this respect, it too nourishes the roots of individualism and personality in ways not altogether uncongenial to the values of early liberalism in their more American stylizations.

Existentialism. Perhaps more generously than others, this modern movement, we have found, can be interpreted in virtually innumerable ways not only by essentialism but by other philosophies. That existentialists may render support to the transmissive orientation has already been noted. What has not been noted is that they can have a great deal to say that amends, if not radically alters, this orientation.

The point is exemplified by the American existentialist, Ralph Harper, in his interpretation of education. Although his primary interest appears to be religious, Harper discusses educational aspects that are as practical as the curriculum, the learning process, and society in relation to the school. Therefore, he demonstrates (largely with Ulich's approval, incidentally) that the essentialist way of interpreting man is multilateral. Yet its root ideas still remain grounded in assumptions entirely congenial to his own attitudes as well. Thus: ". . . existentialism is concerned about the unfolding of the individual as a whole in the situation in which he finds himself. . . . The unfolding, the development of the subject, is the end which the existentialist works toward."[3]

[3] Harper, in National Society for the Study of Education, *Fifty-fourth Yearbook*, Part I, p. 223.

Analytic philosophy. Although instances of the congeniality of some analysts with traditional essentialism have already been noted, other ways may also be considered. For example, all contemporary analysts pay tribute to the pioneering thought of the realist and naturalist, Russell, and thus reflect some of his own mood of skepticism, if not repudiation, of historic absolutism—religious or not. Similarly, their contributions to educational theory have been substantial in exposing the dubiety of "pseudo-questions"—questions largely of metaphysical vintage that, in fact, have no meaning because devoid of empirical observation and verification. Yet it is also interesting to find that some types of analysts (Herbert Feigl, as a logical empiricist, is one) reveal considerable affinity for moderative and even transformative orientations which, they contend, rest upon scientific and logically supportable foundations.

In general, however, the richest contribution that analysts can make toward what might again be termed neoessentialism is similar to its role as critic of progressivism or of any other major theory. This, of course, is its relentless exposé of loose, unrefined language. Here Scheffler's *The Conditions of Knowledge* and *The Language of Education* are acute; so, too, are some of the essays by Robert Ennis, B. O. Smith, and others in *Language and Concepts in Education.*

But with the same spirit of vigorous criticism in which analysts take pride, we must equally insist that many of them beg more profusions of questions about educational theory than they claim to answer. This is at least as much the case of Jonas F. Soltis, as it is of D. F. O'Connor whose *An Introduction to the Philosophy of Education* was one of the first analytic ventures into this discipline. Both writers seem almost totally oblivious, for example, of the culturology of knowledge which would surely insist, with them, upon clear educational "meanings"; yet it would extend far beyond the levels of their own constricted realms of discourse in order to incorporate such fundamental dimensions of cultural and educational experience as economic or social conflict. Without these "meanings," indeed, we are compelled to conclude that the contributions of analysts to any philosophy of education, essentialist or not, still remain more barren, trivial, and vapid than their pretensions to relevance could conceivably justify.

PART 4

Perennialism: education as cultural restoration

CHAPTER 11

Philosophic foundations of perennialism

PREVIEW OF PERENNIALISM

RECALLING the culturological premises from which philosophies of education are being appraised in this volume, this central question must be raised as we embark upon an interpretation of perennialism: How does our third major theory propose to deal with the world crisis confronting the life of man?

At heart, the reply is that no other sure way is open through the impasse of our time than through the common principles that are restorative of the attitudes and habits of ancient and medieval culture. Let it be noted that the term, "restorative," has no invidious connotation whatsoever; it merely suggests that *the perennialist reacts against the failures and tragedies of our age by rejuvenating those axiomatic beliefs about reality, knowledge, and value that transcend every age.*

Perennialist theory thus offers a distinctive and influential contribution to both the theory and practice of contemporary education. When a civilization is disturbed by turmoil, bewilderment, and cross-purposes, when the need for moral and intellectual as well as economic security becomes both severe and chronic, many citizens are sure to seek anchorage in the safe harbor of long-enduring order. Such a civilization is our own.

The chief motivational force of perennialism is not to be regarded, then, as nostalgia for values long-remembered and revered. Rather it is a conviction, bolstered by extraordinary philosophic acumen, that the core beliefs of ancient-medieval culture apply as vitally to the twentieth century as they did to the thirteenth century after Christ or the fifth century before Christ. Hence, we must appreciate that the perennialist would seem to oppose the very frame of reference so important to our own interpretation of his philosophy. He insists that the proper principles of concern to philosophy have no relationship, per se, to cultural origins or effects; on the contrary, since they are axiomatic, timeless, and spaceless, such principles rise above all history and, therefore, all cultures within history. Precisely because they have these qualities, they can serve as reliable guides to any period, including our own. They are, indeed, the *only* reliable guides.

Our study also requires understanding of why perennialism appears even more in contrast to progressivism as moderation than it is to essentialism, the philosophy of cultural transmission considered in Part 3. For, although essentialism is allied to perennialism and both join in counterattacking the progressivist-liberal outlook, such characteristics as an eclecticism and an eagerness to accommodate itself to the industrial-scientific era force essentialism to admit virtues in that outlook that perennialism is more reluctant to admit. Perennialism is less eclectic and less transmissive than essentialism; with some exceptions, it is also more internally unified as a philosophy. Hence, any concessions that it makes to other philosophies of education are likely to be offered more frequently on its own premises than on theirs. To be sure, we shall find that perennialism supports many essentialist and even progressivist or reconstructionist beliefs as far as they go. But it insists that they fail to go far enough. Still more important, they are frequently considered poorly grounded philosophically.

But this preliminary profile fails to emphasize the resilient qualities manifested in perennialism. Granting that it is viewed as encompassing and unifying, let us grant also that historically it is sometimes remarkably sensitive to cultural as well as to several philosophic movements other than its own—and perhaps never more dramatically than in the post-midcentury years to which we have been paying intermittent attention. We do not doubt that the foremost demonstrations of this sensitivity, moreover, were the ecumenical congresses of Vatican II in the 1960s (initiated by Pope John XXIII), the consequences of which continue to have repercussions far beyond their occasion.

This does not suggest that still other influences have not been disturbing to the perennialist outlook. In accordance with our culturological framework, it would be more correct, indeed, to contend that the ecumenical spirit has itself functioned much less as cause than as effect of such deeper, more elusive influences as we have earlier touched upon—among them, surely, science and technology. In any case, because perennialism as educational theory and practice also proves itself to be in greater flux than earlier in the century, it becomes even more hazardous than in preceding decades to characterize its principal features without the constant risk of oversimplification and gross generalization.

Yet, granting this risk, and viewing perennialism once more as an expression of cultural dynamism, we shall be compelled to form a sharply critical evaluation of it. Granting, too, its very rich contributions to the history of philosophy and to the experience of Western civilization, we are compelled to adjudge perennialism in its still dominant forms to be a precarious road for our culture to follow.

It remains precarious because, among other reasons, it would still tempt us to turn the course of history backward. Its admiration for broad aspects of the medieval culture suggests that it is a reflection, after all, of historic habits and institutions, of time and place. In denigrating the potent environmental influences that continue to shape its character, perennialism asks us to accept it as a cultural guide without having carefully considered either its own cultural derivations or its cultural consequences.

Perennialism jeopardizes the contention, too, that institutionalization of democracy on a planetary scale is the most pressing of all obligations facing mankind. Despite his sometimes arduous defense of liberal or even radical ideals, despite his occasional forthright defense of academic freedom and other human rights, despite his sympathy for the common man, the perennialist, when we regard him as representatively as we can, cannot be sufficiently democratic. Whether in the place of democracy there would arise an aristocracy of high-minded directors of the masses of plain people, or whether the very nature of his doctrine would open wide the door to corruption of authority, is an option we might not enjoy facing. It is, however, an option we would have to face because it would be inescapable.

But this anticipates our evaluation of the restorative alternative that will be developed in Chapter 13. There we shall also hope to consider some features that could serve effectively to correct some of the more vulnerable characteristics of perennialism in favor of a more innovatively cultural and educational orientation. Meanwhile, Chapters 11 and 12 present an exposition and interpretation of perennialism paralleling those of the two preceding parts.

HISTORIC BACKGROUNDS

THE GENERAL CHARACTER OF PERENNIALIST THOUGHT

If the term, "perennial," is defined to mean "everlasting," analogous to a species of flower that blooms continually season after season, then we begin at once to understand the general character of perennialist thought. Here, we are told, is the historic meaning first termed by the seventeenth century genius, G. W. Leibniz, as *philosophia perennis* and adapted by many philosophers since. As suggested in our brief preview above, its core belief is precisely a kind of "everlastingness." It recognizes that individual persons, like individual experiences and individual flowers, come and go, bloom and wither with the passage of seasons and years. But the patterns or forms common to all things recur as patterns or forms century after century, era after era—indeed, forever.

To discover and characterize these common recurrences becomes the most important undertaking of which any civilization is capable. Without them, human beings are rootless, hapless victims of circumstance. With them, they are not only able to withstand the buffetings of chance and change but are also able to look upon their own lives and the lives of others with serene awareness of inner significance and outer stability.

Fortunately, a philosophy of everlastingness is already available to us. To find it, however, we need to restore and apply to twentieth-century culture the metaphysics, logic, esthetics—in fact, virtually all the basic beliefs—of three great thinkers who stand above all others: Plato, Aristotle, and Aquinas. Reliance upon these thinkers does not imply that perennialists bow to every word of their theories or that other thinkers are unimportant. As in the case of the individual flower, some of the "petals" and "leaves" of, let us say, Aristotelianism are unique to its own author and to the period of history that gave it birth; yet, its central principles, as a species of thought, may be applied to any era.

We must also reiterate, as we did of progressivism and essentialism, that the leading contemporary spokesmen for this third philosophic outlook are by no means completely in accord. For example, some are not identified with any ecclesiastic movement or organization at all, preferring to remain secular. Equally important to emphasize is the fact that contemporary perennialism has by no means remained immune to any one of the five philosophic movements to which we are giving intermittent attention: this is probably truer of existentialism than of the others; yet we shall find that even neo-Marxism, much less neo-Freudianism, Zen Buddhism, and analytic philosophy all receive a quantum of respectful attention.

The one central belief, however, upon which agreement among perennialists is most universal is that, if our sick culture and our still sicker education are to be restored to health, we shall need first to restore to their positions of prestige and guidance the greatest "doctors" of all time. With their help, far more than with that of any others, we can hope accurately to dissect our deep troubles and to construct a curative program that will prevent the chaos and death threatening to devastate the earth.

THE GREEK HERITAGE: PLATO AND ARISTOTLE

The few pages allotted here to historic backgrounds cannot even begin to reproduce the vast landscape of ideas swept by the searchlight minds of the Greek philosophers and by their successors. Therefore let us merely sketch in some of the most relevant beliefs of Plato and Aristotle, returning to them frequently throughout this Part.

Plato. Like Socrates, his immortal, half-mythical teacher, this philosopher was concerned above all else to strip the superfluous, the secondary, the transitory from the inner core of reality, truth, and value. It seems plausible that he was impelled to this search because everywhere about him he perceived cultural decay induced by doubt, immorality, sophistry, and wars—evils that threatened the very survival of his beloved Athens.

It had been Socrates' chief contribution to insist upon scrupulous, relentless examination of beliefs by exposing their inconsistencies and fallacies and by developing more defensible formulations which men could respect because they had thought them through. Plato built his own system by this "Socratic method," by ascertaining how, in the midst of conflicting standards, men may follow the path of virtue.

Of all the dialogues of which the Platonic philosophy is pieced together, none compares either in length or depth with the *Republic*. Here the author reached his highest peak of speculative vision and offered his most mature formulations. He believed that the only certain way of building a society at once stable and just is to determine the precise status of each person and each class according to his or its proper capacity. Those with most wisdom and virtue will occupy leading positions at the top; those with least, at the bottom; and the mediocre, in between. At the bottom are placed slaves and artisans; in the middle, soldiers; at the top, the small class of "philosopher-kings," who, through many years of arduous education and training, have proved their superiority in resisting temptations of evil and in living according to the highest good.

The exploration of this highest good, without which men are unsure of their standards, becomes the central problem of the *Republic.* It is solved by the famous doctrine of "Ideas," anticipated by Plato in earlier dialogues. Platonic "Ideas" are not to be confused with the "ideas" that men develop and discard as they engage in everyday affairs: the latter are fleeting, temporal, particular; the former are permanent, eternal, universal. Once grasped, they become the only sure way by which daily events, passing impressions, fickle opinions can be measured, classified, and evaluated. What is most important, Ideas provide leaders with moral and political criteria, the most inclusive of which, justice, becomes also the highest good of men living in an association organized according to their worth.

Plato was at heart a practical man committed to his principal beliefs. But he couched much of his thought in such poetic, even mystical, language that it is not always easy to distinguish between literal and metaphorical aspects.

Aristotle. It was against these poetic and perfectionist qualities that Aristotle often rebelled. More prosaic and precise, more objective and strategic than Plato, he devoted much of his mature life of thought to tempering the extremes of his teacher. Especially did he rebel against Plato's frequent efforts to lure mere mortals away from this world of travail to the "heaven above the heavens," where all fleshly ills and guilts, all confusions and temptations are resolved in the transcendent calm of spiritual contemplation. Although he did not at all succeed in freeing his thought of the Platonic doctrine, Aristotle wished to provide, in such works as *Ethics* and *Politics*, sound rules of conduct which men might learn to trust. Thus, *Politics* proposes a limited constitutional rule over willing subjects, suggesting the "polity" as a compromise between Plato's concept of a stern aristocracy of philosopher-kings and such "inferior" political forms as democracy. For Aristotle, in short, Platonic Ideas tend to be much too ideal, much too perfect, to be very useful. The task is to bring them back into direct, organic relation with ideas and experiences of daily life, with feelings, pleasures, pains, individual things and events.

The ingenious device he created for this purpose is frequently called *hylomorphism* (*hylo* derived from the Greek word meaning "matter," and *morphism* from the Greek word meaning "form"), a theory of form *within* matter, ideas *within* things, souls *within* bodies. By the use of this device, Aristotle attempted to resolve the Platonic dualism of form *and* matter, ideas *and* things, soul *and* body, to which he so strongly objected. In contrast to the concept of two worlds of spiritual perfection and material imperfection, the Aristotelian world is a single cosmic order of *increasing* perfection—a hierarchy of lower and higher forms, patterns, and ideas. Near the base of his ontological pyramid, one finds the greatest proportion of mere matter and, hence, the smallest proportion of form. Near the apex, one finds the greatest refinement of spiritual form and, hence, the least matter. At the very peak of the pyramid, form is so completely free from the contaminations of mortal experience that it defies full human comprehension. Called the Unmoved Mover, it becomes a kind of deity which, although it does not itself change, eternally draws all lower forms toward it, somewhat as a magnet attracts iron filings in their own patterned field. The inner tendency of reality is thus toward greater and greater *actuality* (that is, purity of form) and away from mere *potentiality* (that is, impurity of matter). Most levels of experience with which we are familiar are a fusion of actuality and potentiality, which Aristotle called *substance*.

Human beings themselves afford the best example of substance, for seldom are they actually what they seem capable of becoming potentially. Their ideas are often dormant and cloudy rather than vital and clear; their development toward actuality is more or less retarded by the relatively formless, stubborn "mud" of their earthly existence. Nevertheless, some men do succeed in rising far above the level of their physical natures. As they do so, their spiritual selves become increasingly dominant; their thoughts abstract more and more from the particularities of everyday life; and they approach, although they never completely attain, that state of rarified actuality of which the Unmoved Mover is the final end and final form.

We may conclude from this sketch that despite Aristotle's propensity for prosaic, realistic, practical attitudes, his philosophy emerges less as a departure from Plato's than as a fascinating elaboration of it. The this-worldly emphasis, although much stronger than in Plato, nevertheless is counterbalanced by a kind of spiritual-intellectual beatitude or other-worldly perfection attainable only by entering the realm of the *super*human and *extra*natural. Even Aristotle's famous ethical doctrine of moderation—the Golden Mean—is supplemented by his conviction that the highest good is contemplation for its own sake. Likewise, his theory of political compromise concedes that the middle-class polity is less ideal, therefore less real and less good, than the pure aristocracy or even than the monarchy ruled by the leader-thinker.

THE MEDIEVAL HERITAGE: FROM THE STOICS TO AQUINAS

During the long era bounded by the decline of Greek civilization and the rise of modern civilization, philosophy, in the sense of critical examination and reformulation of basic beliefs, was overshadowed by faith. The prevailing tone was one of devotion to whatever beliefs might be assumed and inculcated as important, finished, indubitable.

Yet, at no time was philosophy dormant; at no time after the creative Greek period, even during the Dark and the Middle Ages, were thoughtful men content with a life of blind obedience to dogma and absolute authority. The Roman period, for example, had produced such able thinkers as Epictetus and Marcus Aurelius, both of whom lived during the first two centuries after Christ. They expressed, in a more highly developed form, the theory of Stoicism that had germinated in Greece, a theory holding the universe to be a predetermined whole within which man functions successfully only as he acquiesces in that whole. In the third century, Plotinus revised Platonism in such a way as to give it a more explicitly religious character. With such concepts as "God" and "soul" becoming more predominant concerns, it is not surprising that the fine mind of Augustine should, in the early fifth century, have interpreted reality in strongly dualistic terms—spiritual and material, soul and body, good and evil, heaven and earth, salvation and damnation. The longing for the life hereafter, for the "City of God," which Plato had already predicated in nontheological terms and which Paul had infused with theological ardor, now captivated the Western world. For about ten centuries, *a thousand years and more,* philosophy concerned itself chiefly with elaborating and justifying Christian tenets within the medieval culture.

From the ninth to fourteenth centuries, this concern crystallized in the important intellectual movement called *scholasticism.*

Its central aim was to demonstrate, among kindred beliefs, the existence of God and the assurance of immortality. Anselm, in the late eleventh century, was especially skillful in such argumentation by proving, for example, that we cannot conceivably doubt God if we are willing to reason the matter out, because God is, by definition, a perfect Being from Whom no attribute can be excluded and Who, therefore, includes *existence* as necessary to that very perfection. But scholasticism, too, was far from a completely systematic philosophy, having evolved through several stages reflecting, successively, the influence of Plato and neo-Platonism, of Aristotle, and, in the period of its slow decline, of such thinkers as William of Occam, who challenged its central postulates. Judged by its permanent influence, however, the Aristotelian period of scholasticism was, by far, the most important.

The chief protagonist of this period was Thomas Aquinas, "the angelic doctor" of the thirteenth century. His philosophy encompasses in one syncretic outlook, without emasculating the essential qualities of either Aristotelian or Christian principles. Although he largely accepted the teachings of the immortal Greek, he insisted that beyond the substances of soul-body or spirit-matter lies a realm of faith which rational judgment cannot sufficiently explore. Both realms—the "rational" and the "revealed" —are indispensable to any whole individual or any whole civilization. Thus, although the existence of God or the soul may be demonstrated by scholastic arguments, such arguments might weaken the more important immediate, self-sufficient faith in God. So, too, with ethics: we can and should build moral rules out of the stuff of dynamic experience, but surmounting these rules are the supernatural virtues—faith, hope, charity—derived not from experience but from the spiritual fountainhead.

Aquinas remained true to the ancient-medieval tradition. Although perhaps clairvoyant of a restless culture approaching the threshhold of modern revolutions, and although eager to confront perplexing issues of human life and destiny, nevertheless he was able to preserve an authoritarian creed while at the same time encouraging critical reflection. Following Aristotle, Aquinas postulated pure form, intellectual and spiritual, as the compelling power, the final end, beyond all matter. Following Plato and Augustine, he interpreted man-on-earth as preparation for man-in-heaven.

But partly, also, because he never disparaged or ignored man-on-earth and because he recognized the importance of daily work, pleasure, creation, and association, he has commanded a host of followers in the modern era—a host quite possibly larger than the following of any other one philosopher in Western history. Even in our own time, Thomism (as we may term it) continues to have many adherents. For it can comfort and persuade men who may desire to justify *both* the reflective and the dogmatic, *both* the earthly and the divine.

PERENNIALISM IN MODERN THOUGHT

From Aquinas to our own generation—a span of about seven centuries—the essence of his great system has often been accepted as the pseudo-official philosophic doctrine of one of the most venerable and powerful institutions of all history, the Roman Catholic Church (referred to below as the Church). Both Plato and Aristotle have also commanded their quota of secular followers among modern thinkers. We may recall that Platonism permeates, indirectly or directly, all systems of objective idealism. Likewise, Aristotelian beliefs in a universe organized in ascending levels of eternal forms within matter and nature was assumed by most biological scientists until after Darwin's experimental disproof of the fixity of plant and animal species. And it is virtually the keystone of classic realism.

But from the fourteenth century onward, the ancient-medieval world view was steadily superseded by philosophies that sought to adjust their conceptions to the jolting events that heralded new industrial and political arrangements. Although essentialism, the offspring of perennialism, did not so much repudiate the old absolutism of its parent philosophy as substitute new absolutisms (idealistic or realistic), the substitutions have been sufficiently original and refreshing to justify the claim that modern thought is far from being a mere reworking of Greek or scholastic thought. Science, art, economics, religion, and education all found it more and more discomforting to fit their expanding knowledge and experience into the framework of a closed universe and a revealed faith. Even within institutions of learning controlled by organized religion, perennialism in its original formulation continued to wane.

In the course of the past half-century or so, however, the perennialist philosophy has been marked by a revival under such labels as neoscholasticism and neo-Thomism. Indeed, in some quarters, it has recently become so vigorous as to support its own contention that, however dormant they may appear during some historical periods, its principles are truly perennial. Today, it commands the allegiance of a roster of intellectual leaders who, whether or not identified with the Church, regard their beliefs as sufficiently congenial to justify our classifying them as perennialists.

Thus, three eminent French perennialist thinkers—Etienne Gilson, Gabriel Marcel (often called a "Christian existentialist"), and Jacques Maritain—have achieved international distinction for their modern elaborations of this ancient philosophy. In addition to years of teaching in America, Maritain served as ambassador to the Holy See and was a prominent figure in UNESCO. This is not to imply that he is either *the* official or philosophical spokesman; on the contrary, lively dispute continues to wage over his ideas, some of which have been repudiated by other perennialists especially in the period after Vatican II. Even so, it seems likely that authorities, whether Church-affiliated or not, would consider him at least as representative of, if not more influential than, any other twentieth-century philosopher of this outlook. We shall therefore rely most heavily upon him in the sections that follow.

The fact already noted, however, that perennialist thought continues to be reformulated from decade to decade must not be overlooked, even more so at a time when cultural change is abnormally rapid. Particularly, we must not overlook the influential Jesuit philosopher-paleontologist, Teilhard de Chardin, whose book, *The Phenomenon of Man*, has been widely read by many nonperennialists. Also, the involvement of the clergy in political, racial, and even moral controversy (birth control, most conspicuously) has generated worldwide theoretical as well as practical concern toward the complex issues of perennialism as a viable philosophy of man and the universe. Nor is it at all surprising that recent philosophic movements such as existentialism and neo-Freudianism may likewise affect these issues.

Yet, notwithstanding all such qualifications, let us bear in mind, above all, the pervasiveness and constancy of perennialist thought. As Mortimer J. Adler, a non-Catholic philosopher, once put it, "Aristotle and St. Thomas have answered more philosophical questions than any other thinkers in the European tradition."[1] Whether Adler still insists on this assertion, it is certain that his French colleague, Gilson, more than concurs: "The three greatest metaphysicians who ever existed [are] Plato, Aristotle, and St. Thomas Aquinas."[2]

[1] Adler, *Problems for Thomists*, p. 3.

[2] Gilson, *The Unity of Philosophical Experience*, p. 317.

How shall we understand their importance for reality, truth, and value through the minds of their contemporary heirs—Maritain especially?

PERENNIALIST BELIEFS ABOUT REALITY

What men need above all is the guarantee that *reality is universal*—that *it is everywhere and at every moment the same.* This is a guarantee that can be fulfilled only by laying bare the harmonious forms that always lie, even though they may be concealed, beneath the material crust of changing events and fleeting ideas.

Individual thing, essence, accident, substance. In typical Aristotelian fashion, we begin not with arid abstractions remote from the concrete and the visible but with simple *individual things* perceived everywhere about us: stones, grass, dogs, people in their endless array of shapes, sizes, colors, activities.

Although in our daily lives we never escape from such physical embodiments, these are but paths to the inner sanctuary of existence—to what the philosopher calls their *essence.* For what is important about individual things is not their multiplicity and variety; it is their essential nature. If we are thoughtful, we do not say, for example, that a friend is characterized above all by a special talent, such as skating, or by a common attribute, such as eating; rather, we search for the quality that makes him most intrinsically human. We find that he alone, among all objects of reality including the brute animal, is able to engage in the kinds of practice we call deliberation, demonstration, and speculation. This discovery enables us to state that, in essence, man is a reasoning animal. We do, of course, view our friend in a wide variety of particular ways: we like to watch him skate and we like the neckties he wears. But he is still to be characterized in the same way—by his rationality—if he never skated in his life or if he never wore neckties. These are his *accidents* and not his *essence.*

Nevertheless, really to understand the ontology of our friend, we must return to the study of him as an individual and therefore as a whole human being. Regarded in this way, his essence is still the most important discovery we can make about him—so important as to constitute the deepest reality of his nature. But when we behold him with our senses, we still see him, accidents and all, *as* an individual. So, likewise, do we see all other things, from mountain peaks to mice. To recall the Aristotelian roots of this fascinating theory, we may see things simultaneously *both* in their particular, accidental, and material characteristics *and* in their universal, truly essential, formal, and spiritual characteristics. This union of the two aspects of an individual is the meaning of *substance*—a fusion of matter *and* form.

Teleology. One of the most important properties of substance, we found from Aristotle, is its tendency to move upward out of its own potentiality toward its maximum actuality. The perennial example is the oak from the acorn. The actual form of the species, oak, remains potential in the acorn until the proper conditions for unfolding occur. The individual thing, the particular oak, then takes the shape that has been latent within the seed.

This example introduces us to the principle of *teleology*, which we have not treated explicitly above, despite its use in varied forms especially by objective idealism. To say that reality is teleological is to say that it is inherently purposeful: not only is it governed by an end which determines its predominant means but it is destined eventually to attain that end by its own inevitable course. Not, of course, that all individual things do actually attain their own ends. An oak tree does not grow from every acorn. Individual men as human beings, a church or a nation as a historic institution, seldom approach the actuality of which they are fully capable.

Even so, if we look at reality in broad enough perspective, its direction clearly appears: the City of God, in Augustine's terms, will inevitably arrive. In terms of this doctrine, then, we may explain why, of the four main "causes" operating in reality—matter as *material cause*, motion as *efficient cause*, form as *formal cause*, and end as *final cause*—the last is the most fundamental. Moreover, the final cause fuses with the other three causes in the sense that matter, motion, and form are present together in the purposeful substances of individual things. This is to say that the changes (motions) occurring in any given material object (for example, that budding rose on yonder bush) are induced by its hylomorphic character—that is, by its form which is also its own end.

The fourfold classification of causes under imperial authority of the final cause is pure Aristotelianism, but neo-Thomists prefer to state such principles in language familiar to moderns. Thus, in once discussing war and peace, Adler has held "an optimistic view of history" which predicts that eventually we shall achieve a peaceful world. He confesses the "probability" that it will not occur for about five hundred years but that it *will* occur is not at all improbable. World peace is a higher, a more real, end than national sovereignty and conflict; we may therefore assume that it is a certainty in the same sense that final cause is a certainty. How could it be otherwise so long as ". . . ultimate ends are always potentially present in the means, for the means are the ends in the process of being realized. . . ."?[3]

The supernatural. Whereas some neo-Thomists often like to focus upon the mundane, other neo-Thomists are more concerned with what they regard as the ultimate and supreme end of reality. This end lies beyond even a peaceful world, in the *super*mundane, *super*natural—in other words, in God Himself. But God, as pure Spirit, pure Actuality, pure Form, is so utterly devoid of substance that, although reason is in some ways helpful, we cannot conceive of Him in any adequate way except by a faith above reason and filled with mystery.

Indeed, we cannot grasp the import of teleology itself except by faith and by dogmas such as the Trinity. Despite all the philosophic equipment of modern perennialism, the supernatural reality is always present. It is repeatedly called upon as the final determinant upon which all else depends.

Here, of course, ecclesiastic or clerical perennialism deviates from lay or secular perennialism. Indeed, the creed and dogmas of the Church, which radiate to and from this supernatural reality, are considered so crucial to its members that Churchmen may insist upon their sharp separation from other philosophers whom we include here as perennialists.

Realism versus nominalism. The teleological approach to reality may be epitomized in the distinction between two terms familiar to every student of historic philosophy: *realism* and *nominalism.*

Realism as a perennialist doctrine requires careful attention to avoid confusion. In its *modern* sense, as applied to essentialism, realism often refers to the priority and externality of the world's contents—an interpretation also acceptable, up to a point, to *medieval* realism. Essentialist and perennialist realists both believe that there is a genuine objectivity about whatever exists; both therefore repudiate such doctrines as subjective idealism, which insist upon the prior reality of inner thought.

Except for these common premises, however, the two theo-

[3] Adler, in National Society for the Study of Education, *Forty-first Yearbook,* Part I, "Philosophies of Education," p. 226. See also Adler, *How To Think about War and Peace,* Chap. 14.

ries are more often in disagreement than in agreement. Whereas essentialist realists in the tradition of Locke consider most real the physical world of multiple elements (objects, events, data), those in the Aristotle-Aquinas tradition consider the universality, the form, *among* elements to be most real—a reality recognized through the individual's reason but never identified with such reason. This position, as already noted, is often termed classic realism. Ontologically, therefore, it is closer to perennialism than to essentialism, although it also overlaps a good deal with objective idealism and thus bridges both culturological orientations—the restorative and transmissive.

In any case, it was the attacks of Occam and others upon Thomist or classic types of realism that weakened scholasticism and prepared the way for modern philosophies of science. Under the banner of *nominalism*, the view gradually took root that the ideas people hold are nothing more than the *names* with which we label things in nature. Thus, the species rose has no reality of its own, for there is no objective pattern that embraces individual, living roses. At most, there is only the word "rose" with which we label them. The nominalist theory was, in a sense, the precursor of a pluralistic materialism brought to prominence by such thinkers as Hobbes and reflected in one of its most extreme formulations: orthodox behaviorism. In this respect, therefore, nominalism resembles recent realism more than it does the medieval or classic realism against which it is aligned.

But we must not suppose that the issue between Occamist nominalism and Thomist realism is of interest merely to antiquarians of philosophic lore. On the contrary, it reappears in many guises, occasionally expressed even in its classic terminology. As one writer observed, the defeat of Thomist or classic realism ". . . in the great medieval debate was the crucial event in the history of Western culture; from this flowed those acts which issue now in modern decadence." For when Occam ". . . propounded the fateful doctrine of nominalism, which denies that universals have a real existence . . .," he raised the issue of ". . . whether there is a source of truth higher than, and independent of, man; and the answer to the question is decisive for one's view of the nature and destiny of humankind."[4]

But if the "source of truth" is so important, then epistemology as well as ontology must find a place in the perennialist mosaic of beliefs.

[4] Weaver, *Ideas Have Consequences*, p. 3.

PERENNIALIST BELIEFS ABOUT KNOWLEDGE

TRUTH, SELF-EVIDENCE, AND REASONING

Actually, epistemology has already hovered nearby. For, says the perennialist, only as we *know* can we apprehend the basic meaning of reality at all—unless, of course, we resort to faith and revelation. To be sure, the "unless" is finally paramount. Yet, as rational animals, we are still able to achieve understanding of ourselves and our world.

Begin again with our perceptions of individual things. Truth, indeed, may be defined as the conformity of thought to things—not, however, to temporal things as they appear to the naked eye, as some essentialists believe, but rather to things as they eternally *are*, to their very being—their essence. Since awareness of truth is ultimately awareness of essence, philosophy should first elucidate the principles by which this task can be achieved.

Perhaps the most important of such principles is *self-evidence.* If we are willing to look diligently enough, the perennialist believes we shall discover propositions which convince us as "indubitable and incorrigible" by their precision. They spring, as it were, from their own common sense, and cannot possibly be denied by anyone honestly willing to consider them. One example is the self-evidence of sheer existence. You and I must accept this proposition, for *to reject it would be to reject the existence even of our rejection*; this is an impossibility if we think about existence at all. Another example, on a somewhat different plane, is the self-evidence of mathematical axioms: such simple rules as those of multiplication disclose to us that three times three always results in the same product.

No one, of course, knows *all* the self-evident propositions that are possible to know, any more than one ever completes the search for essences. One can only infer that, inasmuch as some are discovered, more will be. But they are the groundwork of philosophy—the concern of what Adler calls "first-order questions" upon which such "second-order questions" as those of philosophic analysis rest.

The term *first principles* is applied to those propositions that are at once so abstract and self-evident that, temporarily at least, they can be recognized apart from all material content. The principle of being or existence, noted above, is one. But probably the most important first principle of all is that of causality. From this principle—namely, that everything has a cause—philosophers may proceed to "prove" the existence of God as the First Cause of all being.

The study and establishment of first principles is the great task of *metaphysics*—the "science" of speculation or intuitive reason. But we must not infer from its abstract character that this most profound of disciplines is remote from the world of reality; on the contrary, it is concerned precisely with what is *most* real—pure form, pure essence, pure Idea. The meaning of the Greek term *meta*, "after," helps to elucidate the task of *meta*physics: it is the search for that which comes after we have perceived things in the variety of their immediate appearance—the search for their ultimate reality.

The discovery of truth is aided, too, by laws of reasoning, for logical definition and demonstration proceed according to them. First stated by Aristotle, they are employed not only by perennialists but by students taught through typical logic textbooks down to our own day.

Perhaps the most familiar laws of reasoning are those of the *syllogism*, which formalize the logical relationships among major premise, minor premise, and conclusion. To cite a perennial example: if we accept the premise that all men are rational animals (and we cannot possibly deny this as a first principle), and if we recognize that Mr. Smith is a man, we must conclude that Mr. Smith is a rational animal. This is a classic example of deduction and serves as the model for innumerable scholastic thinkers. For them, the major premise is invariably, although sometimes only implicitly, traceable to some first principle which either is held by metaphysics to be true or is asserted as a revealed dogma. The minor premise and the conclusion are then related to the major premise by a chain of rigid links that constitute allegedly inviolable syllogistic laws.

We have just implied that the logic of perennialism, like every other important division of this philosophy, is dependent upon its beliefs about reality—not only upon its beliefs about thought. Thus, despite the emphasis upon deduction, an important role in logic is also played by *induction*—that is, building general judgments by noting resemblances among particular data. This role is important because, as already observed, perennialism by no means denies the particulars of reality; rather, it strongly insists that these particulars, as we sense them in individual things, are the starting point of all human efforts to understand the world.

The role played by induction is better appreciated if we distinguish Francis Bacon's conception of it from that of Aristotle. For Bacon (and for many others—Dewey, for example), the general judgments we attain by examining and correlating specific data are, literally, outcomes; they are not inherent in the data as such, hence are at all conclusive (and even then approximately so) only when we reach them inductively. For Aristotle and his followers, on the contrary, induction is primarily a device necessitated by our mortal limitations. We move clumsily toward general judgments only because, in our potential state, we are unable to recognize the universality that in essence is inherently present. Because, in short, we are human and cannot move at once to the actuality, to the form, of things, induction facilitates our approach to the truth: it helps to achieve clearer understanding of the major premises, the universals, which are always the source and goal of formally logical constructions. Only when finally in a position to move confidently forward from these premises deductively, however, are we able to understand any concrete thing or event by virtue of its membership in the prior, encompassing whole.

The issue is resolved by Aquinas in a few words when he insists that ". . . though the act of sense-perception is of the particular, its content is universal. . . ."[5] This is so even though we do not recognize the content explicitly until we have engaged in the inductive process by beginning with particulars.

THE SCIENCES AND PHILOSOPHY

The sciences (biology, physics, sociology, and others) are concerned with what Maritain ingeniously calls "empiriological analysis"—that is, examination of individual things and events at the level of experience and nature. The perennialist should become as familiar as possible with this level and with the facts it determines. Here we may be sure that philosophic analysis, in its current mode, is entirely acceptable, too, provided that its strict limitations are clearly kept in mind. Similarly, the inductive method of science is indispensable.

But just as induction is subordinate to deduction, so the sciences are subordinate to philosophy—above all, to philosophy's own highest "science" of metaphysics. Here the term "ontological analysis" is useful since it indicates the kind of analysis that produces knowledge of first principles and that proceeds by its own laws of reasoning.

The relationships between the several sciences and philosophy, although often complex when delineated by scholastic methods, are not difficult to explain. For, although empiriological and ontological analysis are helpful to each other, and although

[5] Aquinas, as quoted in Brother Benignus, *Nature, Knowledge and God*, p. 392.

both ascend in a kind of continuous and orderly hierarchy of knowledge, philosophy ultimately, solely depends upon its own canons. It does not depend at all upon the sciences for its most conclusive demonstrations or discoveries.

To be sure, so long as the sciences remain in their allotted territory, independence may also be granted to them. They operate according to their own canons, of induction, especially. But as soon as they venture into areas beyond these canons they, too, require formal guideposts for such first principles as causality. Thus, ". . . the premises of scientific syllogisms are either self-evident truths or rest thereon . . ." says Adler.[6] In this respect, the sciences are vastly more dependent upon philosophy than it is upon them.

Maritain sums up his views here in essays *On the Use of Philosophy*:

> As a result, we have to realize that . . . philosophy . . . deals with aspects and explanations in which science is not interested. Thus matter . . . is composed, in the eyes of old but still valid Aristotelian hylomorphism, of two elements: pure and indetermined potentiality. . . . and determinative form . . . (which, in man, is spiritual soul). . . . It is up to philosophy to try to bring into some sort of unity our knowledge of nature, not by making science's explanations part of its own explanations, but by interpreting them in its own light.[7]

PERENNIALIST BELIEFS ABOUT VALUE

THE SPHERE OF ETHICS

How characteristic of perennialism to recognize the importance, within limits, of common human experience! Neo-Thomists are fond of speaking of ethics, esthetics, and politics as branches of "practical philosophy," which is, to be sure, on a lower stratum than "speculative philosophy" but is, nonetheless, philosophy. In short, these branches are also concerned with universal principles, albeit principles of everyday practice in ethical conduct, esthetic creation, and political organization.

One must not forget that the highest good for neo-Thomists is union with God. Just below this highest level is the life of rea-

[6] Adler, *Art and Prudence*, pp. 238, 242.

[7] Maritain, *On the Use of Philosophy*, p. 57.

son, for in speculation we come as close as thinkers can to such a union. But on the practical level, perennialists would doubtless continue with Aristotle to regard happiness as the most important value—happiness defined as maximum fulfillment of personal capacities.

Practical philosophy is further illustrated by perennialist recognition that pleasures are also a legitimate part of earthly happiness. Here the ascetic propensity of Platonism is countered again in Aristotelianism by deeper appreciation of emotions and appetites which, however, should never be indulged excessively; when they are, man's material nature is bound to dominate over his spiritual nature. Passion must always be kept under the strict rule of reason. Indeed, the life of reason is itself considered the most rewarding of all pleasures—nay, the greatest happiness. Here is a worldly ideal which, though very difficult to achieve, is sufficiently attainable so that, for a few men at least, it may be experienced in fairly high degree.

Let us merely touch upon Aristotle's brilliant design for ethics. For him, as for many of his present-day disciples, there are two main classes of virtues: the "intellectual" and the "moral." These virtues are arranged in a kind of hierarchy, in which moral virtues, built by habit formation, are at the "bottom," while intellectual virtues, built by teaching, are at the "top."

The lower type belongs, as it were, to the "irrational" part of man, although it also partakes of the rational. Moreover, standing midway between extremes are the virtues of moderation: Courage, for example, is the mean of foolhardiness and cowardice; modesty, the mean of bashfulness and shamelessness.

The higher, or intellectual, virtues belong to the "rational" part of man. Among these, intuitive or speculative reason is first in the hierarchy. But both prudence and art are also included among the intellectual virtues because, although they stand at the level of human action and production, they are likewise subject to rational controls. Prudence, for example, is most concerned with individual conduct. It therefore commands the special attention of men as they go about their daily lives, for it establishes the rules by which they act morally while also acting vigorously and practically. The prudent man is properly self-interested and, therefore, clever; he is the "individual thing" of reality acting out his ethical role. Nevertheless, because he also deliberates about the universal forms that hide behind his particular actions—because he is "substance"—his aspiration is to be truly philosophic and hence purely rational about those actions.

THE SPHERE OF ESTHETICS

Art is another important "intellectual virtue" of concern to practical philosophy. "The Man of Learning," says Maritain, "is an Intellectual demonstrating, the Artist is an Intellectual operating, the Prudent Man is an intelligent Man of Will acting well."[8] By the "Intellectual operating," he suggests that the artist impresses his forms upon matter in order to give them, in actuality, the meaning that is in them potentially. The matter upon which the artist operates may be stone, paint, or such symbols as musical notes or words.

At any rate, beauty is the supreme value of esthetics in the same way that speculative reason is the supreme value of ethics. Also like speculative reason it is, in a sense, self-evident, for it is intuited directly rather than demonstrated logically. Beauty differs, however, from other forms in the respect that we behold it with an immediate *delight.* There is something ecstatic about pure beauty—so much so that, in its presence, philosophy finally fails us. Only a state of grace can fully appreciate, Maritain insists, that:

> God . . is the most beautiful of beings, because . . . His beauty is without alteration or vicissitude, without increase or diminution: and because it is not like the beauty of things, which have all a particularized beauty . . . He is beautiful by Himself and in Himself, absolutely beautiful.[9]

Such language is reminiscent of the famous doctrine of "Platonic love"—the love of the spiritual—which Plato's *Symposium* identifies with love of pure beauty unsullied by passion.

But the art of everyday life is very much concerned with things—it is the one intellectual virtue that is chiefly so concerned. Moreover, it involves pleasure, for we experience a pleasurable emotion when we hear fine music or witness fine drama. As Aristotle insisted, however, another and even more important value in such enjoyment is that of *catharsis.* By participating vicariously in the passions of actors on the stage, the spectator in the audience releases his own tensions and so, when he leaves the theater, finds himself better able to regulate his personal life. Such purgation, says Adler, ". . . temporarily relieves the burden of

[8] Maritain, *Art and Scholasticism,* p. 20. See Adler, *Art and Prudence,* pp. 432–436.

[9] Maritain, *Art and Scholasticism,* p. 31.

every-present passion, and thus aids reason in its office of discipline and control."[10] Man may thus also derive a rich value from listening to music or watching a motion picture.

THE SPHERE OF POLITICS

Introductions to perennialist philosophy are still being written with virtually no reference to politics—an omission which tempts the conjecture that its disciples sometimes become so engrossed with eternal things that such a worldly activity scarcely concerns them. Actually, however, the current crisis-culture has deeply troubled some perennialists: the single most vocal symbol of perennialism (the Church) has become increasingly articulate about flamboyant issues that accompany war, economics, politics, and race.

At the same time, it becomes almost impossible currently to epitomize perennialist political thought. Differences sometimes become so acute that even such terms as "left wing" or "right wing" are not uncommon. One reason for these differences, moreover, is explicitly philosophic within the hierarchy of beliefs: situated, that is, on a relatively "low" axiological level, politics is regarded as rather distant from, although still related to, the ruling axioms of metaphysics. In this respect, politics is roughly analogous to the sciences; epistemologically, it also lies somewhere between opinion and pure truth, just as in ethics it partakes of both the moral and intellectual virtues. Yet it is still capable of intellectual analysis and hence of the development of sound, because philosophic, principles.

Another reason for differences is that those perennialists who are friendly to the forces of democratic expansion may feel discomfort in reconciling such friendliness with Aristotle's or Thomas's preference for aristocratic political values. Nevertheless, we find Maritain, Teilhard, and others, vigorously and openly endorsing "democracy" as the best of all social orders. Since, in this conception, they reach a good deal further than their venerated masters, we are especially concerned with the legitimacy of such an endorsement. Let us turn once more, then, to Maritain.

The term "political personalism" is focal to his outlook. The developed person as a whole, rather than the individual who is but partially developed, is considered to be the finest model of political life. This model is developed in terms of "true humanism"

[10] Adler, *Art and Prudence*, p. 204. See also Maritain, *op. cit.*, p. 65.

—a humanism which ". . . tends to render man more truly human and to make his original greatness manifest. . . ."[11]

By the whole person, Maritain assumes a core perennialist belief. Man is integrally both material and spiritual, but he becomes fully himself in the degree that he rises to the heights always latent within him. Such an effort is really successful only under divine guidance—under the magnetic pull, we may say, of deified Form. In this sense, political personalism also rests upon theological, supernatural grounds and supports Maritain's firm contention (developed also by the right-wing Anglican, T. S. Eliot, in his widely read works) that the ideal society must be Christian at heart or fail.

A Christian society, we are told, cannot be maintained either by fascism or communism. It cannot be maintained by the former because the state swallows up the person or because it discriminates among persons on such false grounds as race. Nor can it be maintained by the latter because it, too, is totalitarian and, even more, because it rests upon the philosophy of materialism. Yet fascism and communism are not alone in this failure: the same judgment may be applied to that truncated kind of humanism which, in the name of democracy, limits itself to a merely "anthropocentric" conception of man by insisting that you and I are socially self-sufficient, earthly individuals. Rousseau, Comte, and Dewey are all repudiated because they commit this grievous fallacy.

Nevertheless, it is not to be denied that Maritain, in contrast to some perennialists, has earnestly sought to reconcile his philosophy with the revolutionary events of our century and to apply it in behalf of humane values accepted by the most ardent advocates of a radically socialized order. Occasionally he goes so far "leftward" as to insist that capitalism as an economic system has largely outlived its usefulness; that the working class has become the most important single force in shaping the destiny of humanity; that considerable collectivization of industrial processes is now needed; that the people should properly be the determiners of public policies and their chosen leaders the "vicars" of their interests. All such proposals are considered under the general category of the secular or "temporal city," and Maritain carefully points out that, within this kind of regime, it is necessary to tolerate many differences in religious allegiance, including even the difference of those individuals who swear to none.

[11] Maritain, *True Humanism*, p. xii.

But the temporal city, finally subordinate and secondary to spiritual order, exists "on a lower plane." In his attempt to bring the two "cities" into juxtaposition, Maritain utilizes his superb scholastic training to draw innumerable fine distinctions. They are distinctions which, in all likelihood, are symptomatic of considerable personal as well as intellectual suffering induced by the struggle between his devotion to complete Thomism, on the one hand, and his sensitivity to contemporary issues and dangers, on the other. He speaks of the secular state ". . . as an end and principal agent—but not . . . the final end or . . . the highest principal agent." He insists that the "spiritual and temporal planes" are "clearly distinct"—yet "they are not separate." He regards Church and state as independent of each other but willingly admits that the Church not only should discern its own political interests but, as the "deposit" of revealed truths, is entitled to direct temporal affairs "from above." Conversely, the state even has the "duty" to "assist the Church in the free accomplishment" of its mission (which is, of course, to promulgate its absolute and unchallengeable doctrine). Thus, despite his own preference for "democracy," he is able to say that the Church, as a church, ". . . is compatible with all forms of government worthy of man." And we can understand from this relative valuation of Church and state why Maritain seems to accept without reservation the authority of papal pronouncements, even referring to them repeatedly in firm support of his own arguments.[12]

Maritan touches upon so many other provocative questions in the political sphere and shows such comprehension of philosophies such as Marxism (toward which he is, nonetheless, hostile) that our presentation barely samples his thought. In closing this chapter we should, however, note two other qualifications. The first is that, through the years, Maritain himself has somewhat modified his political views, so that one can never be quite sure in a given criticism that one is expressing his *current* view. The second is that he remains much further "left" than many others who proclaim their devotion to perennialist precepts.

If, indeed, there is any validity in the progressivist view that the ultimate and most reliable test of beliefs is their active consequences, we may conclude that Maritain is politically a rather atypical perennialist. In its recent history, the hierarchy of the Church has, in practice, much more often aided political regres-

[12] See Maritain, *True Humanism*, pp. 100, 158, 180ff., 230, 170f., 288f., 293, 172; *Christianity and Democracy*, p. 37; *Ransoming the Time*, p. 206.

sion (its role in the Spanish Civil War is a tragic example) than it has supported Maritain's objectives. Actually by the test of consequences, one might contend that the conservative assayist, Hilaire Belloc, has been more representative of predominant perennialist attitudes when he expresses grave doubts about majority rule as the basic criterion of democracy, or when he places the Church above the popular majority even to the point of insisting that, in moral choices, the faithful should, if necessary, resist civil law in order to obey the law of the Church.

But this generalization is also open to scrutiny. Belloc, after all, was writing during the first half of the twentieth century, while Maritain's most creative period continued scarcely a little longer. More recently than either, the perennialist viewpoint, as we have reiterated, has undergone extraordinary self-criticism and cultural involvement. This mood reacts severely upon Maritain himself who, in the ninth decade of his life, became once more a storm center of *philosophia perennis*: his book, *The Peasant of the Garonne*, warns ominously against the heretical deviations that he detects alarmingly in Vatican II. For is it not, after all, the self-evident, everlasting realities, truths, and values that provide perennialist doctrine with all its historic viability, all its eternal nobility?

Nor should we be surprised in the least that even this almost angry book was quickly succeeded by still another of gentle adoration. Its title is the epitome of Maritain's undeviating beliefs in the duality of both the eternal and the temporal: *On the Grace and Humanity of Jesus.*

CHAPTER 12

The perennialist pattern of educational beliefs

THE QUALIFICATIONS with which essentialist beliefs about education were treated in Chapter 9 apply in considerable measure to perennialism. It is not contended that perennialism's educational beliefs invariably depend upon its philosophic substructure. Nor is every Platonist, Aristotelian, or Thomist necessarily a consistent, self-avowed, educational perennialist. Finally, the educational beliefs of perennialism, far from being treated in exhaustive fashion, are limited to their more general features.

THE SWEEP OF PERENNIALIST EDUCATION

ANCIENT-MEDIEVAL BACKGROUNDS

Considering the overwhelming contributions of Plato, Aristotle, and Aquinas to the perennialist world view, we may assume that their attitudes toward education are also influential. That this is so is demonstrated by the fact that many of the outstanding proposals by perennialists of our own day are derived from these three masters.

Plato. The educational beliefs of Plato are adjuncts of his aristocratic position in politics and are even more immediate adjuncts of his pivotal doctrine of Ideas. This is the doctrine, we recall, that finds the essence of reality, knowledge, and value to consist of eternally existing patterns—the archetypes of all particular things, truths, and goods. Since a just social order is really possible only as these Ideas become the standards by which we are governed, the single most important objective of education is to train leaders to recognize and to apply them in every possible way.

The *Republic*, particularly, outlines its program of education. Since this program continues almost from birth to the age of fifty, we might suppose that it is an ancient recognition of the popular current view that people can learn continuously throughout life. But Plato showed little interest in training the majority of the people. His program so rapidly weeds out the "unfit" that only a few continue into the later years. Until the age of twenty, the student concentrates on music, gymnastics, the three R's, and military training; from twenty to thirty on mathematics and science; from thirty to thirty-five on philosophy; and from thirty-five to fifty on practical experience in society where moral and intellectual stamina is rigorously tested. The artisan class receives least education because it is least competent. (The huge class of slaves beneath the artisans is simply ignored.) Those who qualify as soldiers are almost all selected by the time they are twenty; those best suited for secondary offices in the state, by the time they are about thirty. Study of philosophy—the all-important subject—is therefore confined to an elite who, over a five-year period, acquire knowledge of first principles and who, after prolonged periods of practice, are then, and only then, ready to rule as philosopher-kings.

The Platonic psychology pervades this entire program. Man is endowed with three capacities: appetite, will, and reason. Education should consider all three—hence the emphasis on gymnastics and music, especially in the earlier years, as aids respectively to the physical and energetic, or "spirited," qualities of human nature. But reason requires the most exact training if it is to rule effectively over both qualities, and if each is to exercise its proper function in relation to the other two.

This "tripartite soul" likewise corresponds to a "tripartite society." Artisans are those in whom appetite is strongest; soldiers, those in whom will is strongest; leaders, those in whom reason is strongest. The just society is measured by the hierarchical order of these classes, in the same way that the just man is measured by an analogous order of his psychological traits. In this sense education is "good" insofar as it establishes justice both in political institutions and in human beings.

Aristotle. Our earlier contention that Aristotle was fundamentally a Platonist is supported by the extent to which his writings reinforce Plato's major educational principles. He did not, of course, merely repeat them. Yet, in his insistence that the cultivation of reason by means of the sciences—and especially by philosophy—is the single most important task of education and, in his conception of such training as having the political purpose of wise leadership, he was in complete agreement with his teacher.

Aristotle was more original in his emphasis upon habit formation as the primary purpose of elementary schooling. In this respect, he foreshadowed the view of various essentialists, for he held that obedience to moral rules, to tradition and law, is properly and most easily inculcated during the earliest years. Ontologically, he implies that children require firm guidance because of the dominance in their natures of matter and motion over form and purpose—a dominance that may recede as their actuality comes to prevail more fully over their potentiality.

Also distinctive in Aristotle was the emphasis upon happiness as a goal of good education. Yet, even in this emphasis, the Platonic influence is noticeable. Not only did he stress the concomitant cultivation of the several components of human nature—the physical and emotional as well as the intellectual—but he finally agreed that the highest happiness is a life of speculation. In his delineation of man as a hylomorphic being, however, Aristotle sometimes conceived of happiness in a more rounded or balanced fashion. Indeed, it is in terms of this conception that some perennialist educators try to adapt the progressivist conception of the "whole child" to their learning and curriculum programs without doing violence to their own principles.

Aquinas. The skill with which Aquinas incorporated Aristotelianism within his own medieval-Christian system of beliefs is nowhere more aptly illustrated than in his views on education. The purpose of education is to draw dormant capacities of the learner from their hiding places within him so that they will become active and real by his consciousness of them. Thus the teacher's role is primarily to instruct, in the sense of giving aid to the susceptible human substance, but, above all, to help the learner to reason clearly and to intuit first principles. In this task, learning through words becomes more fruitful than learning through the senses, for words are symbols of essences.

An interesting analogy may be drawn between teacher and physician. Just as the latter assists sick or wounded organisms in their inherent tendency to heal themselves, so the former assists ignorant men in their inherent tendency to become wise. Were the tendency not already present, neither physician nor teacher could possibly succeed, for neither can create what is not potentially existent. Both, in this sense, are agents of reality, the teacher acting as direct channel to the mind of the student from the final source of reality—the divine headwaters of Truth.

Such Thomist views found solid support in the historic structure of medieval education. Although secular control continued to operate to some extent, the Church was certainly the most important agency of learning over an era of several centuries. Under it, elementary and secondary schools emphasized the rote study of Latin, taught some music and arithmetic, and enforced discipline by frequent corporal punishment. The first universities emerged in the twelfth and thirteenth centuries and, with them, teaching slowly gained the status of a prestigious profession. (Aquinas himself was a professor at the University of Paris.) The typical university curriculum consisted of the seven liberal arts—subsumed under the *trivium* (grammar, rhetoric, and logic) and the *quadrivium* (arithmetic, geometry, astronomy, and music). To these, other studies were gradually added, especially Aristotelian "science," ethics, politics, and metaphysics, all of which were strictly prescribed under faculties licensed by the Church. The import of this curriculum for contemporary perennialist education will be made clear.

PERENNIALIST EDUCATION IN MODERN TIMES

The medieval theory and practice of education have remained influential down through the centuries. Even today, the organization of our most modern universities reflects their medieval predecessors. Learning through words, advocated so strongly by Aquinas, is still the predominant practice, and surely the study of Latin still required in many secondary schools is a medieval inheritance.

To be sure, classic ideas about education have carried over into modern culture in many ways, just as into education and the whole of modern philosophy. But, except within parochial circles, the historian is hard pressed to find educators in the original medieval tradition who exerted much influence during the centuries following its height of influence and power. An exception was the Church leader, Cardinal John Henry Newman, whose *The Idea of a University*, published in 1852, continues to be quoted frequently for its eloquent defense of perennialist higher education. In America, probably the most eminent Catholic educator during the nineteenth and early twentieth centuries was

Bishop John L. Spalding. His beliefs about education, always in the framework of his faith, are still a good index of beliefs among far-sighted Church leaders.

The American revival of interest in perennialism derives less from Church than from lay educators. In the twenties and early thirties, a new movement in behalf of classical education, expressed under the old name of humanism, attracted wide attention. Although not directly grounded in any one philosophic tradition, its exponents included the Thomist, Louis J. Mercier, and the intellectualist, Norman Foerster, both of whose views on university education reveal the influence of Newman and anticipate those of the influential lay perennialist, Robert M. Hutchins.

Indeed, future historians who write about our amazing century may give more credit to Hutchins than to anyone else for the movement sometimes termed neo-Scholasticism or neo-Thomism. Although he does not formally attach either label to himself, and although admittedly less well equipped philosophically than his former associate, Adler (to whom he has given major credit for his own "education"), he has been able, as former Chancellor of one of the world's great universities, the University of Chicago, and subsequently as founder and inspiration of the Center for the Study of Democratic Institutions, to extend himself widely.

As the Jesuit philosopher of education, John W. Donohue, has indicated, this is not to convey the impression that the Hutchins-Adler partnership or, for that matter, the whole neo-Thomist movement has remained as popular in the post-midcentury period of strife and confusion as it did earlier. What does remain true is that both Hutchins and Adler have continued to rephrase and supplement their ideas in terms that they consider more appropriate to later decades. Nor should it be forgotten that most Church leaders enthusiastically welcomed the rise of perennialism within secular circles. (Maritain, for one, has written admiringly of Hutchins and others.) Church specialists in the philosophy of education would, to be sure, insist upon their differences as well as their agreements with secular perennialists. Also, in the ecumenical spirit of Vatican II, they recognize the need for educational reform. Nevertheless, when viewed in broad educational perspective, both Church and secular perennialist educators share so many underlying principles that our approach to their beliefs about learning, curriculum, and educational control must be derived from the writings of both groups.

Perhaps Donahue epitomizes a fair contemporary attitude toward the role of this philosophy as it springs from the Thomist fountainhead:

> . . . the investigator might find it more rewarding to follow the lead of those thinkers who have been, to some extent, inspired by Thomas without ever taking over his total construction. In this case, one would look for certain master-ideas in Aquinas that would have a continuing significance and can be synthesized with contemporary thought.[1]

PERENNIALIST BELIEFS ABOUT LEARNING

But let us recall that perennialist views, despite the demand for unity, are by no means wholly unified. The Platonist, for example, would not be expected to agree on every point with the Aristotelian nor with the Thomist. Nevertheless, just as the core beliefs of Plato, Aristotle, and Aquinas are much more similar than dissimilar, so the range of agreement among their disciples is, likewise, strikingly wide. It is upon this broad area of agreement that we now turn our spotlight.

MENTAL DISCIPLINE: THE FOCUS OF LEARNING

Perennialists concur in the proposition that exercising and disciplining the mind is one of the first obligations of learning—or, more strictly, is paramount in the *higher* learning. Accordingly, they insist that any theory and program of education that in general ranks vocational skill, overt action, interest, or similar concepts over mental discipline for its own sake has clearly put last things first and first things last. Behind this standard—central and explicit in the writings of some advocates, more implicit in the writings of others—lies the elaborate psychological apparatus with which we have become briefly acquainted in our survey of perennialist beliefs about knowledge and related beliefs about reality and value. Learning theory is a restatement in different context of more basic philosophic theory.

Consider the perennialist contention that man is distinct in kind as well as in degree from all other animals. The scientific evidence provided by Darwin and by subsequent evolutionists—that man has descended from lower species—is completely irrelevant because, in last analysis, man's distinctiveness is "proved" not by science but by speculative reason. The rationality common to all men is self-evident; one cannot even reason against the existence of such rationality without using reason. This is a first principle that would be true at any conceivable time or place in which man attempts to consider rationality at all. Thus, by deduction,

[1] Donahue, *St. Thomas Aquinas and Education,* p. 19.

we proceed from the major premise that man is universally rational to the conclusion that any particular man whom we may meet is likewise rational.

But the principle of rationality generates, out of its own self-evident clarity, a second highly important principle, namely, that of freedom. To be sure, the skills of metaphysics and logic utilized by perennialists in order to convince us that they believe in freedom are far more elaborate than this brief statement can suggest. Consideration of freedom leads, for example, to the age-old problem of free will and, eventually, to the solution offered by theology: man has the will, if he will but exercise it, to save himself from the damnation that his fallen state of sinfulness continually threatens.

But the quality of freedom in which we are most interested can best be cultivated by education. It is the power to act voluntarily, which depends in turn upon the power of reason itself. Since, according to perennialism, the authority of reason is the source of freedom, it follows that the supreme purpose of education is to perfect that authority as far as possible. In this doctrine lies an important meaning of liberal education: to "liberate" man by helping him to become his essential self—a self which, distinct from the brute, is a *rational* animal and, therefore, free. All learning must be dedicated to this end of man's maximum actualization.

How is man to undertake so difficult a task as learning to reason? To anticipate our discussion of the perennialist curriculum, we may say that he must begin with correct habit formation during his first years of schooling. The skills of reading, writing, and computation are so necessary that they easily take precedence over all else. But these are chiefly preparatory. Learning to reason, in the strict sense, becomes a major objective of secondary and college education—an objective attainable only by continuous exercise in the related disciplines of grammar, logic, and rhetoric. We begin to achieve the greatest power, to reason, as we learn how to relate words to one another so that they acquire clarity and order—as, further, we learn how to communicate inwardly, with ourselves, and outwardly, with others. In this effort, recent developments such as philosophic analysis are helpful, but many of the required rules about the "meaning of meaning" are to be found in such thinkers as Plato, Aristotle, and Aquinas.

Still, we cannot assume, say perennialists, that all logicians teach us to reason. The logical theory of Dewey, for one, has done inestimable harm to education by identifying the reasoning process almost exclusively with experimental problem-solving. Actually, not only is problem-solving limited to the area of discovery and research but the knowledge it produces, being largely inductive and therefore only probable, is of a distinctly lower order than that obtainable by employing the critical faculty of reason proper.

Thus, learning how to reason, in the highest sense, consists in learning how to philosophize as we develop the intellectual virtues. By means of metaphysics, reason, as man's highest natural attainment, ascends even above logic and becomes purely intuitive, completely disengaged from experience. Reason, says Maritain, is ". . . visible only by means of abstraction and universal concepts. . . ."[2] In this rarefied atmosphere, and only in it, man becomes for the moment utterly free. But it is a freedom earned only at the cost, paradoxically, of prolonged mental discipline.

LEARNING TO LIVE: THE PERENNIALIST RECIPE

But mental discipline, although at the apex of the pyramid of learning, does not constitute the whole. Aristotelian perennialists, especially, are quick to insist that they are equally concerned with the substance of the student and therefore with the material, or bodily, as well as with the spiritual, or rational, part of his nature.

Because of this concern, Aristotelian perennialists incorporate to their own satisfaction many doctrines of modern psychology. Despite his charge of the "inductive sterility" of much psychological research, Adler, for example, accords a limited recognition to the importance of recent experiments in reading and in psychoanalysis. The late educational philosopher, William F. Cunningham, went so far as to accept certain findings of the realist, Thorndike, and such important psychological concepts of progressivism as interest and motivated learning. Maritain, with characteristic breadth, has suggested work experience as desirable learning experience, and he is insistent that, up to a point, elementary education should encourage the free play of imagination, the "kind of bounding, temperamental, and lucid freedom" that is natural to the child.[3] Hutchins has also been known occasionally to approve the methods of progressive education. So, too, has Adler.

But the significance of a remark in the chapter above should be recalled: *whatever concessions perennialism makes to psychol-*

[2] Maritain, *Education at the Crossroads*, p. 46.

[3] *Ibid.*, pp. 45f., 60f.

ogy or to other fields are always made on its own premises, never on theirs. Since this is so, the reader of treatises by lay perennialists should not be seduced by sophisticated persuasiveness until one is certain of their major premises. One should be careful, also, not to isolate specific passages for approval until he has determined that they are valid indices to those premises—an admonition with which perennialists, concerned as they are with syllogistic reasoning, would surely condone.

Returning to the perennialist recipe for learning to live, it should not then be overlooked that human nature is flavored far more abundantly with one ingredient than with any other—namely, learning to reason. That is to say, learning to live, in any morally defensible fashion, becomes impossible except under the authority of the thoroughly educated—meaning the metaphysically equipped—mind. The Thomist goes beyond this doctrine by insisting that both learning to live and learning to reason are but two steps on the path to eternity. Hence, in addition to such universal human needs as health, family, economic security, leisure, and knowledge, there is the superlative need of that "divine security" that absolute faith alone can satisfy. Thus, another ecclesiastic educational philosopher, William J. McGucken, has stated forthrightly that ". . . the thing of ultimate importance is not here but hereafter. This world has genuine value only insofar as it leads to the next."[4] Psychologically, this last and crucial step is well accounted for by the same principle that accounts for others—by man's hylomorphic, teleological being which ever drives him, however faltering his progress, toward expression of the essence abiding within him. Learning, to be precise, is the development of substance: it is the purification of man's actuality.

Perennialists still seem also to find quite beyond compare the analogy between the art of teaching and the art of medicine, as immortalized by Aquinas. Thus, Maritain insists that each art stimulates the spontaneous inclination of the human organism both to be healthy and to learn—an analogy that reminds us of the role of Socrates. Just as the "gadfly of Athens" sought to disturb the tranquillity of his listeners by challenging their vague, half-formed beliefs and by pointing out contradictions and comparisons, so the teacher today is effective when he performs a similar role. Surely, then, it is a role deserving the admiration of

[4] McGucken, in National Society for the Study of Education, *Forty-first Yearbook*, Part I, "Philosophies of Education," p. 273.

analytic philosophers, as Adler has implied in his mature reformulation, *The Condition of Philosophy.* Lectures, too, can be helpful but never for the sake merely of conveying information; they must also provide enlightenment by interpreting and pointing up implications in the subject matter being taught. When the teacher thus functions as physician of the soul, we have here "learning by instruction." It is distinguished from "learning by discovery" because, in the latter, no teacher is needed at all—the student learns by himself if he knows how to read actively and creatively. Each type of learning can, of course, reinforce the other: learning by instruction should stimulate the self-education of learning by discovery.

The teacher, according to perennialists, is, then, not at all a mere conveyor belt of information between world and mind—a recognition which distinguishes perennialist theories of learning from some popular essentialist theories. Indeed, the teacher becomes himself a learner to the degree that his own capacity for self-discovery is increased as he instructs others. Nevertheless, the teacher ought to exert "moral authority" over his pupils because, if he is professionally qualified, he is properly superior to them.

The perennialist approach to learning and teaching is distilled by a quotation from Maritain. It should enable us to test our skill in detecting subtle overtones of Aristotelian-Thomist symbols which, taken out of context, might apply to philosophies completely in conflict with his:

> What is learned should never be passively or mechanically received, as dead information which weighs down and dulls the mind. It must rather be actively transformed by understanding into the very life of the mind, and thus strengthen the latter, as wood thrown into fire and transformed into flame makes the fire stronger.[5]

PERENNIALIST VIEWS OF THE CURRICULUM

Because perennialism, like other philosophies of education, has practical effects on the schools today, its views of the curriculum are affected by current practices while at the same time steadily influencing those practices. Two main levels are surveyed: (1) elementary and secondary education; (2) the higher learning and adult education.

[5] Maritain, *Education at the Crossroads,* p. 50.

THE ELEMENTARY AND SECONDARY LEVELS

One of the most revealing differences between progressivism and perennialism is in their respective attitudes toward "education as preparation." Whereas the Dewey school rejects the doctrine that schooling is preparation for some later period of life, many perennialists insist that schooling in the early years is precisely that. Their belief is that the child is still primarily potential rather than actual; hence the first task of education is to prepare him for his maturity, his life of reason, by guiding him toward that maturity.

Here we have a philosophic justification for the attack upon those elementary schools that fail—as perennialists often say they do—to teach the three R's adequately and thus fail to provide the child those rudimentary skills without which he cannot, in later years, act rationally. On this issue, although proceeding from somewhat different premises, certain perennialists argue in the manner of certain essentialists.

It is true that one can find other perennialists (curiously, perhaps more often among parochial educators than among some secular ones) who have tried to reconcile the progressivist type of "activity curriculum" with their own principles. A few have gone so far as to insist that their schools are the most "progressive" of all—especially if, as some are, modeled after the theory of the Italian educator, Maria Montessori. Maritain also occasionally invites such an interpretation. More conspicuous, however, is their Aristotelian stress upon habits that can be toughened into permanent human possessions only by continuous exercise and familiarity with right content.

And what is "right" content? Most important on the elementary level is "reading, writing, and figuring" with some consideration for history, geography, literature, science, and a foreign language. As Hutchins put it in his first book, the educator must, above all, avoid the concept of the elementary school as in any sense "an agency of social reform." In a book published seventeen years later, he even proposes that elementary education ". . . not bother inexperienced children with what are called the social studies."[6]

Equally important for some perennialists is character training in the early years. This may be discovered, upon careful inspection, to be another term for training in the moral rather than the intellectual virtues—the latter, as with Aristotle, being more

[6] Hutchins, *No Friendly Voice*, pp. 66, 114; *The Conflict in Education*, Chap. 3; and *The University of Utopia*, pp. 56f.

properly the subject of later education. Reading is heavily stressed throughout.

Although the dividing line between the elementary and secondary levels varies for different perennialists, one finds extraordinary unanimity in their proposal that almost all adolescents engage in a program of general education or in trade and skill training, with one type or the other open to every normal young person between the ages of twelve and twenty.

The students who receive most attention (the percentage ranges from less than forty for Mercier to approximately one hundred for Maritain and Hutchins) are those eligible for general education. For students under the age of about sixteen, the stress by several perennialists is upon foreign languages—Greek and Latin as well as modern tongues. For those between the ages of sixteen or seventeen and twenty, the stress is, first, upon the related disciplines of logic, rhetoric, grammar, and mathematics—the master keys of reasoning—and, second, upon the "great books" of all time.

This unanimity of general purpose should not be taken to imply that all perennialists are agreed upon the best plan for general education. Just as we have found differences among progressivists and among essentialists, so, too, perennialists sometimes differ vigorously. Cunningham offers a plan for general education which is characteristic of his breadth of mind and his eagerness to consider criticisms and proposals from educators of other orientations. It is significant of the differences among perennialists that he finds much that is unsatisfactory in the adult-education program associated especially with Hutchins and Adler.

Nevertheless, it is this program that, more than any other, has brought perennialist education to public attention. For nearly all leaders of this allegiance, the most certain means to sound general education for every educable citizen is careful reading of the most important, most perennially influential, works of the leading minds of history. Thus the intellectual center of secondary education should extend to adult education as well—a conviction that has been carried out in large numbers of communities. Since it is obvious, however, that beliefs of the authors of the great books are by no means always in harmony with perennialist beliefs (they are sometimes at opposite poles), the question arises as to whether the great books program either on the secondary or adult levels is a good example of the perennialist philosophy of education. Certainly such men as Maritain have lauded the program. More impressive is the fact that Hutchins' own prescription for general education, although on occasion tempered by alternative possibilities, is typically Aristotelian: "In general education we are interested in drawing out the elements of our common nature; we are interested in the attributes of the race, not the accidents of individuals. . . ." —attributes which are "the same in any time or place." Moreover, since the "truth is everywhere the same" (Aquinas is cited as authority for this self-evident principle), therefore "education should be everywhere the same."[7] This prescription is harmonious with Adler's position (in discussing his own experience, the latter has often mentioned, "Mr. Hutchins and I"). Indeed, Hutchins reaffirmed this prescription well after he had left the University of Chicago: "The aim of an educational system is the same in every age and in every society . . .: it is to improve man as man . . . [who also is] the same in every age and in every society. . . ."[8]

Nevertheless, in the case of Hutchins, particularly, let us appreciate his exceptional resilience to the cyclonic events of his time. Thus, in *The Learning Society* published over three decades after *The Higher Learning in America*, he has nothing to say about the great books but much to say about the need for continuing education of adults for an automatized age of increasing leisure. Also encouraging is his admiration for the Danish Folk Schools which, seen in a different framework than his, lend themselves to decidedly nonperennialist interpretations. Whether this means that Hutchins may have swerved from his earlier philosophic course is not always clear.

What does seem clear is that, unless they have repudiated this earlier course, Hutchins and his associates still expect the great books to be read not merely for the mental discipline provided—although this is important—but also for the distillations of transcendental truth that they allegedly contain. The fact that scientific treatises appear quite frequently in the list of great books may be justified on one or both of two grounds: first, that these, too, contain first principles which may be explicated through learning by instruction and by discovery, and, second, that they offer contributions to those subphilosophic levels of knowledge obtainable by "empiriological analysis." Similarly, works on ethics or politics by a Mill or dramas by an Ibsen are included because they help the reader to understand the two great intellectual virtues of practice: prudence and art.

[7] Hutchins, *The Higher Learning in America*, pp. 61–87. See also Hutchins, *The Atom Bomb and Education* and *The Learning Society*.

[8] Hutchins, *The Conflict in Education*, p. 68.

Church educators would, of course, deny that any program that fails to give priority to study of theology could possibly be perennialist in their sense. We reemphasize and respect this distinction, again calling attention, however, to the many common beliefs of Church and secular perennialists. Once more, Maritain may be the strongest spokesman of the former, for he is convinced that teachers who encourage study of the ". . . heritage of philosophical wisdom . . . may always hope, indeed, that by virtue of its very truth, the philosophy which they think to be true, as I do Aristotelian and Thomistic philosophy, will gain momentum among their fellow men, at least in the generation to come."[9]

THE HIGHER LEARNING

In some respects, our outline of perennialist general education has anticipated the treatment of higher learning. For Hutchins and his sympathizers, however, its organization is a compromise forced upon it by the prevailing American pattern. Actually, general or liberal education should, according to Hutchins, be relegated to the junior college, which is usually classified as in the field of secondary education and should be freely available to all normal young citizens everywhere. The higher learning proper should begin after general education has been completed—and then only for those students who, at the age of about twenty-one, have clearly demonstrated their superior ability.

Perennialists are often scathing in their denunciation of the present university for its eclecticism—its disorganized accumulation of courses and requirements, its duplications, its emphasis on education for money-making and other kinds of merely utilitarian training. They would correct these evils by an "ordering principle," the model for which they often candidly derive from the medieval university. Granting that the latter found its own ordering principle in theology, today's leading perennialists (excepting Churchmen) find theirs in metaphysics or speculative philosophy —in what Hutchins has called "the intellectual love of God."[10] Indeed, Hutchins' own writings belie his claim: "I am not here arguing for any specific theological or metaphysical system. . . .";[11] for it is clear in the context of his ideas that he argues very often for at least one specific metaphysical system—the Aris-

[9] Maritain, *op. cit.*, p. 73.

[10] Hutchins, *No Friendly Voice*, p. 67.

[11] Hutchins, *The Higher Learning in America*, p. 105.

totelian. Indeed, when he speaks of the necessity of "divine aid" and of faith in "the fatherhood of God,"[12] one wonders if there are very consequential distinctions between his views and those even of the clerical Thomist.

Fact-finding research, to be sure, is included in the higher learning. Such experience is as indigenous to such research as matter is to the Aristotelian pyramid of reality, which is its ontological archetype. But just as the level of facts and sense data in the latter is inferior to the level of reason and form, so the collector of information is inferior to the seeker of self-evident first principles. Accordingly, "research institutes" (a term he retains in his later writings) should be established on the fringe of the university; its members, who would hold nonfaculty status, would be helpful in providing material to illuminate such principles.

Hutchins would also permit the establishment of "technical institutes" for training in the "routines" connected with such learned professions as law, teaching, and medicine. But, since these professions would emphasize the intellectual and moral virtues, the most important part of the higher education necessary for them would be offered, not in the institutes, but to pre-institute students by faculties of the university proper. All university students would likewise have had a general education of the type advocated for the junior college. This would make it possible for them to concentrate upon those principles of philosophy (ethics for the prospective lawyer is an illustration) held to be most important to their intended specializations. Throughout the entire educational plan, only slightly qualified in later writings, experimental science is accorded a subordinate position, because "all the most important questions of human existence" cannot and "do not yield to scientific inquiry."

The Hutchins plan for higher education is modified in certain respects by other perennialists, just as is the plan for general education. Thus Maritain and Cunningham, understandably, stress theology more heavily than does Hutchins. Still, in many perennialist discussions, the medieval university is frankly admired as a model. The terms "quadrivium" and "trivium" are revived as appropriate captions under which their proposals are classified, and Hutchins has written: ". . . no universities since the Middle Ages have been able to duplicate the accomplishments of those that existed then."[13]

[12] Hutchins, *The Atom Bomb and Education*, pp. 13–14.

[13] Hutchins, *The Conflict in Education*, p. 100.

PROBLEMS OF SOCIAL AND EDUCATIONAL CONTROL: THE PERENNIALIST SOLUTION

"THE TWILIGHT OF CIVILIZATION"

One of the deep interests of perennialists is with the difficult question of how educational institutions can be organized and controlled so as to exert the strongest possible influence upon the world of concrete events. That theorists of neo-Thomist persuasion are concerned about such events is philosophically implied by the life-centered aspects of Aristotelianism.

Few educators have been more outspoken in their conviction that (to employ the title of a Maritain tract) we are already deep in "the twilight of civilization." Few American philosophers indeed, can't be fairly compared with Maritain in respect to the acumen with which he has analyzed faults in the political, economic, and cultural scene. To be sure, Hutchins has on occasion warned of the dire threat to human survival which his own university helped to generate by its experiments with atomic energy. He has expressed clearly his strong distaste for "witch hunts" and extreme "anticommunism" and has, for these expressions, received wide acclaim from educators who may otherwise reject his ideas. He has even offered public condemnations of contemporary social practices ranging from the ruthless wastage of soil to compulsory military training and inadequate housing.

Moreover, Hutchins' defense of academic freedom, as he defines it, has been more forthright than that of many educators. Certainly his Center has encouraged free flow of dialogue about many pressing, concrete issues. For these admirable reasons, Hutchins has been defended against our demonstration that, considered in the perspective of his range of thinking, he remains a perennialist. We can only reply, therefore, by reassessing this perspective. For example, how are we to appraise critically his plea for world government if we are also to ignore his Aquinas lecture, *St. Thomas and the World State* (delivered before the Aristotelian Society of Marquette University)? In this lecture, he refers to St. Thomas' *Treatise on Law* as "the greatest of all books on the philosophy of law" and the supreme guide to world peace.[14]

To what extent he or other perennialists would unite in specific solutions to the major problems confronting our midcentury is less relevant to our present interest, however, than their

[14] Hutchins, *St. Thomas and the World State*, p. 38.

very considerable agreement on the most common cause of these problems. Maritain on the social "left," Adler and Hutchins somewhere "left of center," the Englishmen, Belloc and Eliot, on the "right"—all agree that *the cause is the spiritual-intellectual bankruptcy of modern man.* This bankruptcy already began to appear with such early heralds of modern science as Occam and Bacon. It was aggravated by such individualists as Rousseau and culminated in the pragmatists, James and Dewey. While agreeing that the "material," particularly the economic, levels of life are not at all satisfactory, perennialists repeatedly contend that the problems they generate are more effect than cause of our troubles.

THE CENTRALITY OF LEADERSHIP

Surely it does seem clear, in perennialist terms, that attainment of the required "moral, intellectual, and spiritual revolution" is shared by two institutions, the Church and the university. Whether the Hutchins group would, if pressed, admit with the theologians that the Church is ultimately the more important of the two, we cannot say. They are, however, unequivocal in their insistence that the university must provide strong leadership for the "revolution."

We return, then, to the issue of social and educational control. Granting that men must bring rational and ethical order to the world, let us ask: Who is to determine its principles? Who is best qualified to decide finally who shall control? Who shall direct whom? As perennialists themselves insist, we cannot restore order in the culture if each man is left to be his own arbiter, for we have been told that only immoral anarchy results in the long run from individualistic, "anthropocentric" interpretations of freedom. What, then, is the source of those principles that alone can guarantee that the required controls will be grounded in "justice" and "righteousness"?

This question leads us, once more, to the heart of perennialist education. The required principles, say perennialists, can be found only in philosophy—not in any philosophy, of course, but in one that has been found to consist of a systematic, positive structure of beliefs about reality, knowledge, and value. More specifically, since we are here concerned with the practical spheres of society, economics, and politics, reliable criteria in these areas of life are ascertainable ultimately through the moral and intellectual virtues. These virtues, in turn, are derived from metaphysics—hence, from an intuitive awareness of eternally real and true first principles.

The supreme purpose of the university becomes, therefore, the education of those who engage in such high philosophic pursuit. The objective is not merely philosophizing for its own sake but philosophizing in order to create leaders who *know* with certainty what justice and righteousness *really* are. A paradox can even be detected in this argument: the best way to solve the greatest problems of man is to turn our backs upon them—to develop leadership by immunizing our minds from the confusions and accidents of experience and thus by purifying them in the distilled essence of Ideas.

But perennialists are not always in agreement in their conception of leadership as it relates specifically to the problem of control. Maritain, especially, has professed faith in the capacity of ordinary people to solve their problems according to their own best judgment—a faith that leads him to find in working and farming people the single greatest reservoir of future social hope. In holding that ". . . the man of common humanity is not possessed of a less sound judgment and less equitable instincts than those social categories which believe themselves to be superior . . . not because he is more intelligent but because he is less tempted . . .",[15] Maritain meets directly the underlying issue of control. His position is that, in the long run, "common humanity" is more likely to recognize its own interests than is any single person or any minority. This is a position, however, that even he cannot reconcile, except by scholastic logistics, with such beliefs as the infallibility of the Church, its final superiority to the state, and the unimpeachable authority of the hierarchy which issues the Church's mandates. Since ". . . all authority derives from God as from its primordial source . . .", it follows that a leader "can establish a genuine *right* to be obeyed" only as his "supreme ordinating Law" is derived from "the Cause of being. . . ."[16]

In considering the issue of leadership and control, we recall how most American perennialists have agreed that general education should be open without restriction to every average young man or woman. In this respect, they seem to concur thus far with Maritain's confidence in "common humanity." Actually, however, when the perennialist plan is traced back to *the Aristotelian belief in hylomorphism as it bears upon the school*, one begins to detect limitations. For, while every human being tends to develop from

[15] Maritain, *Christianity and Democracy*, p. 78.

[16] Maritain, *Scholasticism and Politics*, pp. 103ff.

matter to form, from potentiality to actuality, from appetite to reason, most of us succeed in doing so very imperfectly.

The perennialist conception of the inequitable distribution of power in society is thus well stated by Eliot. While denying that he is defending aristocracy, nevertheless he insists upon the principle of hierarchy:

> What is important is a structure of society in which there will be, from "top" to "bottom," a continuous gradation of cultural levels: it is important to remember that we should not consider the upper levels as possessing *more* culture than the lower, but as representing a more conscious culture and a greater specialisation of culture. . . . The levels of culture may also be seen as levels of power, to the extent that a smaller group at a higher level will have equal power with a larger group at a lower level . . . and in such a society as I envisage, each individual would inherit greater or lesser responsibility towards the commonwealth, according to the position in society which he inherited—each class would have different responsibilities.[17]

In this statement, we perceive a strong reason for the kind of program of general education that perennialists have developed. The potentially highest men, few in number, are most likely to be discovered in the process of providing for all the opportunity to blossom intellectually. General education will thereby select and prepare those few who are fit for the higher learning and so for the fundamental and necessary leadership of superior minds.

Let us grant that perennialists, however divergent in their proposals for general education, are all concerned with the good life, as they conceive it, for the masses of men. Even so, two crucial aspects of this conception must be recognized. The first is that, for secular perennialists at least, only the university is capable of creating the intellectual, moral, and spiritual elite necessary for the survival of civilization. The second is the affinity between such a conception of an elite and the ancient-medieval philosophy of leadership from which it directly derives.

Hutchins himself has avowed this affinity. As a young university president, he believed not only that the higher learning should be a "privilege," not a "right," limited strictly to those with demonstrated "ability" and "interest," but also that there

[17] Eliot, *Notes towards the Definition of Culture*, p. 47.

should be *"far fewer"* students over the age of twenty (that is, beyond the level of general education) than are now enrolled in universities. (He reconfirmed this belief at the age of nearly seventy.) Further, Plato's philosopher-king has been his own model for the university administrator and the symbol of his ideal leader. This rare person is a true aristocrat of the mind and spirit, to be selected by no less an ordeal than the *Republic*'s long program of education and training for potential possessors of Ideas—the philosopher-kings. Hutchins carefully summarizes the stages of his ordeal. For it is ". . . the kind of scheme which is called for if the administrator is to have the moral and intellectual qualities which the times demand."[18]

Thus, the most conclusive and consistent answer to the question "Who is to control whom?" might be epitomized as "He who is best qualified to do so." We may grant as generously as possible a great range of ramifications and concessions to current conditions and experiences. Nevertheless, the ultimate answer of perennialists is crystal clear. It is, in essence, the answer of Plato.

CONTROL WITHIN THE SCHOOLS

Perhaps the closest perennialist approximation to a democratic view of school or college administration is Hutchins' remark that the administrator should ". . . get others to join him in the search for the end and try to lead all his constituency to see and accept it when it has been found."[19] Although this view might invite widespread discussion by the constituency of the university, it in no way violates the conviction elsewhere implied that, since administrators governed by Platonic-Aristotelian beliefs are most likely to know what the end of education should be, it becomes their obligation to instruct others in their own superior knowledge. The fact, moreover, that Hutchins and his colleagues have advocated, at times, a completely nonelective and carefully systematized curriculum suggests that they regard the kind of cooperative teacher-pupil planning proposed by progressivists as superfluous —superfluous because philosophically unsound.

The theories of certain Church educators, indeed, are more akin to this kind of planning than those of some secular colleagues, just as they are more akin to the activity curriculum. Thus, a document of the Commission on American Citizenship, sanctioned by

[18] Hutchins, "The Administrator," *Journal of Higher Education*, November 1946.

[19] *Ibid.*

the Church, contains a number of suggestions for widening social and educational controls which seem quite compatible with advanced democratic principles. Cunningham, in his far-sighted proposals for general education, also reveals a cautious concern for democracy—especially for student participation in the formulation of educational policy. He writes:

> We maintain that the student should be given the widest latitude in rights and responsibilities consistent with his potentiality. We know that he is not equipped to dictate policies of the curriculum, but he should be able to conduct, under guidance, most of the extracurricular activities.[20]

Notable also is the fact that some American pioneers of teachers' unions, such as Margaret Haley, were Roman Catholics and that Bishop Spalding expressed far more sympathy with organized labor as a force for democratizing economic power than Hutchins and most other educational administrators ever expressed. Most auspicious of all are post-Vatican-II steps taken by various clerically governed schools and colleges to include laymen in boards of trustees or other policy-making bodies, as well as to provide wider academic freedom to raise heretical questions such as marriage of clergy, birth control, and even the infallibility of the Pope. But it still remains doubtful whether the dominant hierarchical structure of the Church has been breached in any far-reaching way either within the United States or elsewhere.

Moreover, we must confront the question of whether differences between religious and secular leaders are as acute as they appear at first glance. Regardless of how liberal a theoretical position in behalf of the "self-discipline" and "self-activity" that ecclesiastic educators profess, we must also remember that *the source of authority and discipline lies elsewhere—that is, "over ourselves."*[21]

What also seems very clear is that if clerical perennialists at times manifest hostility to the secularism of public education, they are not at all averse to using the resources *of* public education. A strong campaign has long been conducted to guarantee full share of federal funds for parochial schools. Church writers have persistently sought to prove that the founders of the United

[20] Cunningham, *General Education and the Liberal College*, p. 233.

[21] Cunningham, *Pivotal Problems of Education*, p. 221 (italics supplied).

States—James Madison, particularly—never intended that religious schools should be denied public support. Actually, although the Supreme Court has tended to resist religious efforts to break down traditional walls dividing church and state, many individual states of the Union do provide tax-paid services to parochial schools, ranging from bus transportation to the purchase of textbooks. Moreover, both before and after the Supreme Court's rejection of sectarian Bible readings or prayers in public schools, some infringements have continued in various states by both Catholics and Protestants. Meanwhile, the main argument in favor of federal aid is persistent: church parents are taxed twice (once for public and once for parochial education) despite the fact that, in most localities, their children are free to attend public schools. At least they are free except for the fear that, if they do attend, they and their parents will not receive the full blessings of their faith.

Behind all such militant efforts, although not always articulated, is the impregnable dictum of this philosophy that man should subordinate himself to a power superior to himself—namely, a supernatural God recognized and accepted through divine grace. Since its institutional voice is the Church itself, control is properly vested in those most certain of the principles that determine both the method and content of good education. From a perennialist point of view, this is how and why the Church, as well as the university, should lead the way to the necessary "revolution."

CHAPTER 13

A culturological evaluation of perennialism

THE MILIEU OF PERENNIALISM

THAT THE HARDY PERENNIALS—Platonism and Aristotelianism—took root in the cultural soil of Greece was no mere accident of time or circumstance. The political and economic soil of Athens provided the needed seedbed, and the social climate of the fifth and fourth centuries B.C. was favorable to its tender philosophic plants.

Added to these assets of soil and climate were others that favored the prospect that Platonic-Aristotelian beliefs would sprout, blossom, and produce generations of their species. First, there was the rich fertilizer of waste, blood, and bone that war supplies in abundance. Ancient Greece was torn by violent conflicts, both in foreign wars—notably with Persia—and in civil strife between city-states. Second, the way had been well prepared for the cultural soil. War again had helped, turning over the earth almost too continuously, but thus preparing it for fresh plantings and new germinations of belief. Still more important were the fruits provided by a long preceding period of creativity in such arts as drama, literature, and architecture, and in such intellectual disciplines as logic and mathematics. For example, the worship of magical power in numbers by Pythagoras and his disciples was exploited by Greek philosophers in their creation of a more sophisticated interpretation of nature and man. All these and still other achievements cultivated a cultural climate favorable to perennialist beliefs.

PLATO AND ARISTOTLE: CITIZEN-ARISTOCRATS

Both as human beings and as citizens, Plato and Aristotle were deeply affected by this environment. Far from being isolated within ivory towers of rarefied wisdom, both were men of action, both were embroiled in the turmoil of corruption and violence. Plato himself, according to one account, was sold into temporary slavery; even if this fact cannot be verified, he did travel widely and associated with the rulers of Syracuse as well as of Athens. Aristotle also traveled throughout much of the civilized Western world of his time: he tutored Alexander the Great and, like Plato, was directly involved with the most powerful political leadership of his age. So involved was he that, after Alexander's death, he was forced to flee or suffer the fate of Socrates, who had been martyred for his beliefs.

Of even greater culturological significance to perennialism is the fact that both Plato and Aristotle looked upon the conflicts about them from the point of view of a powerful aristocratic class. We cannot, of course, measure precisely the extent to which their own class status was responsible for their consistent support of the aristocratic outlook or for their equally consistent rejection of all other outlooks. We must recognize, too, that scholars continue to debate the cultural roles they played as well as the wider meanings of their profound doctrines. From all that we have since learned about cultural motivations of belief, however, there is little reason to suppose that Plato and Aristotle, alone among thinkers, were immune to such motivations. On the contrary, if judged by such fruits as the *Republic* and the *Politics*, it may be inferred that the closed aristocratic circle, in which they were charter members and from which their families and friends benefited, strongly influenced both their criticisms and their proposals.

Thus, Plato and Aristotle regarded unsatisfactory all three types of rule found in the countries and cities about them. They disliked the tyrants (who for a time controlled Athens) as much as they disliked those of Syracuse. They disliked the oligarchy, which placed control in "uncouth" commercial classes. And they disliked the democratic order which had reached its widest circumference under Pericles, just before Plato was born.

If tyranny was denounced as the worst of the three, it is also possible to understand why democracy might have been considered even more responsible, in the long run, for the troubles of Athens. The democratic structure of government had been expanding continuously throughout the fifth century. The aristocracy exercised progressively less power and the popular assembly, consisting of artisans, merchants, small farmers, and sailors, progressively more. During this period, although the Athenians had been engaged in imperialist struggles and were temporarily victorious, they had passed their peak of success more than a generation before Plato's lifetime. Thus he came to manhood during a period when past glories overshadowed present attainments. Even more significant for his developing thought, Plato's whole impressionable youth was spent in an atmosphere of bloody struggle within Greece. The long Peloponnesian War against Sparta ended, with the humiliation and defeat of Athens, when he was twenty-five. For him and for the younger Aristotle to have inferred a cause-and-effect relationship between violent strife and democratic control is, then, quite understandable—and especially so when we recall that the class within which they moved was forced by this control into subordinate positions.

That democratic forces were actually responsible for the decline of the Athenian Empire is, nevertheless, a dubious contention. Granting that historians differ on this question of responsibility, still one may cogently maintain that *it was not the too-rapid increase in power of the common people that produced the difficulties of Athenian democracy; on the contrary, it was the much-too-slow increase.* We must recall that, despite remarkable economic, artistic, and scientific achievements, the fruits of these achievements were denied to the greater part of the population. We must recall, too, that the Athenian economy could expand only to the limits set by the slave labor force upon which it finally depended. This limitation not only stunted its democratic growth but also blocked commercial expansion and military power.

The relevant point, in any case, is not what we are now able to understand about ancient Greece; rather, it is what Plato and Aristotle themselves must have understood. If one recalls that they believed in the inevitable course of history, but nevertheless disapproved the course Greece had been following, one can appreciate the significance of Plato's master design for a class-structured society. Whether this society, like the real Athens, depends upon a great pool of slave labor is another point on which interpreters differ; certainly, the *Republic* does not explicitly disavow slavery. What Plato did construct is a three-level order of artisans, soldiers, and philosopher-kings. With philosopher-kings in supreme authority and with the army and navy to enforce its decisions, the Platonic pattern thus becomes entirely consistent with the desired status of the author and his class. Not only does it propose to place an aristocracy in power—to be sure, an aristocracy of talent rather than blood—but also it aims to restore peace and unity by means of the ingenious formula that "justice" emerges when each member of his respective class functions according to his nature. Thus it leads to the harmonious acceptance by all classes of a hierarchical political order.

Plato's republic was not at all, therefore, the mere speculative dream of a poet-perfectionist. Although he recognized immense difficulties in establishing such a state, we must not overlook its resemblance in certain political and educational features to the real Sparta. This city-state, demonstrating its superiority of power over Plato's Athens by the dreadful test of war and by an entrenched class of hereditary landowners, was ruled with the collaboration of a strong military clique. Moreover, the ruling class not only disciplined itself sternly and rigidly (whence the term "Spartan," that we still use), but it disciplined those beneath it even more relentlessly. Its educational program, too, was mainly a device to inculcate habits of strict obedience and sacrificial service.

To be sure, Plato sought to improve upon the Spartan system. We may recall that in the *Republic* the soldiery is relegated to a level below that of the supreme rulers (philosopher-kings), for he recognized and feared the narrow callousness of the typical military character. Also, he hoped, by his psychological-political theory of tripartite harmony, to create a spirit of willing rather than coerced obedience to the corporate whole; he was too keen not to perceive that continued, stable, absolute rule is possible only if the lower, as well as the upper, classes support such rule. Moreover, it is probable that he founded his famous Academy for the training of scholars in the hope that it would produce leaders purified of the military-economic ruthlessness that contaminated the leadership both of Sparta and Athens. And it seems to have been historically established that he sought to apply parts of his program in Syracuse (his influence with Dionysius II was at one time strong), thus demonstrating his own belief in its practicability.

To what extent Plato and Aristotle were patriotic, to what extent subversive, citizens of Athens remains a controversial question. For those who have allowed Plato's intriguing dialogues to shape many of their judgments of Greek culture, such a question is perhaps shocking. But one fact we must never forget: both Plato and Aristotle apparently opposed both the progressive forces in Athens personified by the popular assembly and such pro-democratic philosophers as Protagoras and Democritus. This is so despite the fact that both men loved many aspects of their culture (they could scarcely have failed to recognize that the democratic reign of Pericles was the Golden Age of creative achievement in Greece) ; it is so despite evidence in such later dialogues as the *Statesman* and the *Laws* that Plato modified his extreme aristocratic views; and it is so despite Aristotle's greater willingness to accept some of the strengths of Greek democracy. But the fact still remains that their political philosophies are marked throughout by intensive aristocratic bias. Indeed, Aristotle perhaps revealed his ultimate discipleship to Plato more strongly in politics than in any other field.

Just how far the two philosophers influenced the ultimate collapse of Athenian democracy, and finally of Greek civilization, obviously cannot be measured. Certainly their charge against the "democracy" of their day—that it produced a society governed by excesses of "freedom" and "variety" and of equality "to equals and unequals alike"—was devastating. Through many subsequent centuries, and finally expressing itself in perennialist movements of our own day, it has continued to be one of the most persuasive and, to democratic ideas and practices, one of the most destructive influences in history. This judgment has been confirmed no more eloquently than by the historian, Arnold Toynbee:

> . . . the Hellenic Utopias [notably, Plato's and Aristotle's] . . . were conceived at Athens in the schools of philosophy that arose in the age immediately following the Peloponnesian War. The negative aspiration of these works is a profound hostility to Athenian democracy. . . . The first concern of the Athenian post-war philosophers was to repudiate everything that for two centuries past had made Athens politically great. Hellas, they held, could only be saved by an alliance between Athenian philosophy and the Spartan social system. In adapting the Spartan system to their own ideas they sought to improve upon it in two ways: first by working it out to its logical extremes and secondly by the imposition of a sovereign intellectual caste (Plato's Guardians), in the likeness of the Athenian philosophers themselves. . . . In their condonation of caste, in their *penchant* towards specialization and in their passion for establishing an equilibrium at any price, the Athenian philosophers of the fourth century B.C. show themselves docile pupils of the Spartan statesmen of the sixth. In the matter of caste the thought of Plato and Aristotle is tainted with that racialism which has

been one of the besetting sins of our own Western Society in recent times.[1]

AQUINAS AND THE MEDIEVAL PYRAMID

Not for well over a thousand years did democracy again loom, even dimly, as a natural and cultural ideal to attract the masses of mankind. The Platonic ideal of two worlds—the inferior, corrupt world of earthly experience and the superior, perfect world of spirituality—slowly enveloped Europe in the strange, occasionally grotesque disguises of theology, dogma, and superstition. Whatever philosophy remained (partially excepting the work of Plotinus, Augustine, and a few lesser men) was wrapped in the heavy trappings of sect, creed, and ritual.

But developments in the thirteenth century after Christ prove that the light of reason had never been extinguished. This fact supports the hypothesis (considered more fully below) that so long as men can breathe they will, sooner or later, struggle to combat the forces in their culture that frustrate their most basic urges, including the urge to confront and then act upon their problems.

The thinkers of this period were concerned with a twofold task. On the one hand, their time demanded that they interpret medieval civilization to itself and provide a rationale which would give meaning and justification to its most powerful political, economic, and religious institutions. On the other hand, they were motivated in this effort by the restlessness of men too long confined by the strait jackets of dogmatism, absolutism, and a static economy. In meeting these two demands, their rationale was both defensive and clairvoyant: defensive in the face of forces symptomatic of social change; clairvoyant in recognizing that, notwithstanding the philosophers' valiant efforts, these forces would continue to grow until they finally replaced the medieval order by some other way of life, perhaps a very different one.

Any brief characterization of the thirteenth century and of the centuries called the Middle Ages unavoidably distorts. Nevertheless, granting complex refinements of the medieval order, we may assert that one of its most inclusive features was the pyramidal arrangement of religious and secular levels. The Church itself was structured in ascending levels of authority—faithful masses at the base; simple clergy and monastic servants closest to the masses; above them, various orders of officials, such as bishops

[1] Toynbee, *A Study of History*, p. 183.

and archbishops; and finally, at the apex, the supreme pontiff. The economic order of feudalism may also be pictured in ascending levels—serfs at the base; professional soldiery above them; lords of the manor still higher; and, at the apex, kings. As still a third way, medieval culture might be conceived as roughly analogous to the class structure in the *Republic*: the class of commoners lowest; next, the baronage or landholding class with its coterie of knights and soldiers; highest, the priesthood with its presumed superior wisdom and spiritual authority.

Such pyramidal classifications should be regarded here as operational, designed to help clarify for us the meaning of the Middle Ages. That no such neat patterning actually existed throughout Europe is proved by the fact that individual communities were usually very small, widely scattered, sometimes quite autonomous, and frequently in conflict. Moreover, religious, political, and economic authority was sometimes vested in one person or one group. Thus, in many places, the local Church by controlling the land served literally as landlord over a multitude of serfs. In others, the lord might function as king.

Regardless of discrepancies between the unity of its theoretical design and the plurality of historic facts, this much seems to be characteristic of medievalism: so far as cultural order existed, it was to be found in *a crude, organic spirit of reciprocity* which pervaded those who belonged within it. The lord, for example, considered himself obligated to his serfs for military protection; his serfs, in turn, were obligated to provide him with a generous share of their produce. To be sure, this reciprocity was not one of equality: all positions in the hierarchy of the culture were strictly class stratified. Nevertheless, one can find some sense of corporate wholeness in the manner of interdependence, however hierarchical.

Now it was precisely this half-expressed sense of corporate wholeness upon which Aquinas fastened his philosophic attention. By articulating its principles into brilliant philosophic synthesis, he rendered the great practical service of strengthening both idea and fact. We thus observe a perfect *ontological* justification for *axiological,* and therefore political, harmony. It is a corporate harmony of unequal but interrelated members not fundamentally different, after all, from Plato's "just" harmony of classes. But Thomism crucially amends Platonism by incorporating Aristotle's teleological principle of the Unmoved Mover, which becomes suggestive of the Christian God of divine wisdom, goodness, and omnipotence.

This political theory is broad and flexible enough to allow its adherents, down to our own day, to accommodate various practices. Thus the principle that God is the final judge can be used, as it has often been used, to justify the exercise of absolute authority by rulers who insist that they alone are attuned to God's will. Aquinas himself, however, insisted that political authority should be limited by law and that even revolution against a tyrant might conceivably be justified. Following Aristotle's political beliefs, Aquinas here revealed a willingness to adopt a moderate position between the extremes of tyranny and democracy.

Nevertheless, Aquinas, like Aristotle long before him, became dissatisfied with such moderation. Law, for example, proves to be much less simple than our common understanding of the word itself. Instead of one kind of law, he considered four—eternal, natural, divine, and human. All are properly authoritative on their own levels of hylomorphic reality, but all are traceable to a single fount which is the law of God. Likewise, although he provided a place for legitimate secular power, he admitted that the authority of the Church and its rulers was, in crucial circumstances, supreme.

Thus, it seems altogether legitimate to compare Aquinas with Plato and Aristotle, not only for their many similarities in philosophic thought but also for similarities in their roles as men of practice, as leading citizens of their respective eras. It is true that Plato and Aristotle were critics and foes of the democratic tendencies that had *already* developed in their culture, whereas Aquinas, more strictly, was a critic and foe of democratic tendencies that were to emerge only *after* his time. Nevertheless, it is not unlikely that he, too, detected in his day certain current dangers to long-cherished beliefs and institutions. Plato and Aristotle were alarmed by instabilities in their culture, especially by the decline of aristocracy. Aquinas saw all about him the increasingly rapid development of cities and towns, of commerce and guilds, of the mobility of population—all tokens of expanding, although still nascent, gropings toward power and freedom by growing numbers of people. It is no more possible, of course, to determine exactly how far these events shaped the philosophic formulations of Aquinas than it is possible to measure the correlations between culture and thought in Aristotle. Certainly one discovers in both (and even to some extent in the more reluctant Plato) a readiness to accommodate themselves to impending forces of change while trying to hold their allegiance to the old.

In his theory of a corporate culture united by divine and

absolute law, Aquinas becomes the supreme apologist of his age. His *Summa Theologica* is not only the greatest philosophic portrait of the greatest medieval century; it is the summation of a millennium.

PERENNIALISM IN ITS CONTEMPORARY MILIEU

Our demonstration of the compatibility (although far from precise cause-and-effect relationships) of perennialist beliefs with the two cultural eras that witnessed their conception, birth, and maturation should prepare us to consider whether perennialist beliefs are compatible with our own crisis-culture.

A superficial view might suggest a negative answer. As noted above, the centuries following the thirteenth were marked by revolution against corporate authoritarianism in both religious and secular spheres. The rise of industrialism with its middle-class power structures, the establishment of modern science with its experimental methods of regulating both nature and man, the spread of democratic movements and the concomitant restatement of principles governing democracy and education—all of these are evidences of a great postmedieval revolution. As a consequence, the perennialist approach to culture had come, by the nineteenth and twentieth centuries, to be widely regarded as obsolete—as the fascinating interpretation of an era which had long since been consigned to the limbo of historic memory.

On sharper scrutiny, however, this conclusion is unfounded. Note, for example, how the impact of Thomism on modern culture has been perpetuated by the long-established institution that so deeply reveres it. Even though the influence of the Church has seemed to wane through much of the modern era, its dominance over vast multitudes has certainly not. It is so solidly entrenched in some European countries, such as Spain and Ireland, not to mention a large proportion of Latin American countries, that its political and economic power seems at times to be more decisive than that of national governments. Even in predominantly Protestant countries, such as the United States, the Church exerts gigantic influence in politics, in education, and in popular arts, including the motion picture.

Nor has the apparatus of medieval authority, with its many nuances of belief and conduct, been completely discarded in the modern era. As observed in our cultural evaluation of essentialism, the history of Western man since the fourteenth century has been marked by prodigious efforts to recast institutional forms so that the new requirements of secular authority for the industrial age would still justify strict controls over most people and most practices. But we observed also that, in performing this task, both the spiritual and material types of essentialism borrow freely from Greek and medieval thought: Platonism, for example, has richly contributed to all of the influential expressions of objective idealism, including contemporary expressions; Aristotelianism has affected classical and various forms of modern realism.

Thus, although perennialists frequently criticize essentialists, advocates of these two groups usually find it much less difficult to establish friendly rapprochement with each other than with such nonabsolutist, nonauthoritarian philosophers as the progressivists. (The point is underscored in *The Revolution in Education*, by Mortimer Adler and Martin Mayer, where, by inference, they seem to combine perennialists and essentialists as "traditionalists" in opposition to "modernists.") At the same time, the very weaknesses of essentialism—weaknesses symptomatic of a culture that has failed to solve its own problems of war, demoralization, frustration—offer perennialists their renewed opportunity for influence. Although it might be argued that these same weaknesses are also characteristic of perennialism, its advocates think otherwise. Drawing upon the achievements of modern thought, science, and education, perennialism restores into one complete system a theory of absolute reality, knowledge, and value and a consoling, invincible faith. Never before in our era has this momentous philosophy been so strategically equipped to exploit both the successes and failures of its closest ally, essentialism.

But even disregarding the support that this alliance affords, perennialism is one important expression of contemporary culture because it still offers one of the most revered paths to the amelioration of a pervasive cultural crisis. As in all periods of crisis, many men among us today seek a haven where their bewilderments or uncertainties, their lack of conviction or direction, can be resolved and corrected. One of the most alluring ways to security, moreover, is to rise above individual and social problems—to find succor in a realm of perfection, which presumably transcends the struggle and crassness that reflective, forthright actions always demand. If such a haven also provides a secondary place for rich experience and participation with our fellow men, so much more is our sense of obligation satisfied and our conscience assuaged. Just as Plato looked to the approximation of perfection which idealized the aristocracy of predemocratic Athens, just as he carefully incorporated in his *Republic* such features of his own culture as Spartan discipline and Socratic dialectic, so perennialists twenty-five centuries later appear also to look to the ancient-medieval archetype of philosophy and order while accommodating their principles to contemporary achievements and goals.

One of Adler's latter-day statements epitomizes the main point:

> . . . my position with respect to the ancient and medieval view of philosophy is that it is correct if it is interpreted as presenting us with an ideal to be realized—a sense of the public esteem it should deserve, a vision of the position it should occupy in the family of disciplines, and of the status it should have in our culture; but that it is wrong if it is interpreted as claiming that the philosophical enterprise as conducted in ancient and medieval time, lived up to this ideal.[2]

This restorative synthesis has a double appeal. While it offers intellectual and emotional anchorage in the remote and ostensibly more ideal past, it also insists upon its modernity. Hutchins' support of international government, to cite a relevant example, accords with the advanced thinking of our time. But even this support is strikingly consistent not only with that of Aquinas but also with that of the medieval Dante who, in accord with the Thomist archbelief in corporate unity, advocated a "spiritual empire" for the world of his time. Where, indeed, could Hutchins and his colleagues find a more noble formulation of their international principles than in this excerpt from Dante himself?

> The human race, therefore, is ordered well, nay, is ordered for the best, when according to the utmost of its power it becomes like unto God. But the human race is most like unto God when it is most one, for the principle of unity dwells in him alone. . . . But the human race is most one when all are united together.[3]

We conclude that the significance of perennialism for our times is to be evaluated in relationship to its cultural milieu, just as its significance for earlier eras must be evaluated in relation to their milieu. In all three major eras—ancient, medieval, and

[2] Adler, *The Conditions of Philosophy*, p. 235.

[3] Dante, as quoted in Randall, *The Making of the Modern Mind*, p. 106. See also Sabine, *A History of Political Theory*, p. 257.

modern—it is both a philosophic interpretation of and program for the culture as an organic whole. Yet, just as the perennialist interpretation of the medieval period (that of Aquinas) incorporates the achievements of the ancient period (that of Plato and Aristotle), so today perennialism incorporates important developments of the seven centuries since Aquinas. Its leading exponents are much too sophisticated to ignore, for example, the colossal thrusts of technology. But they also seek to respect philosophies as diverse as existentialism, philosophic analysis, and every other movement of contemporary thought. For they recognize that their perennial hope of becoming dominant is to be flexible and sensitive to contemporary public opinion and to intellectual advance.

Nonetheless, despite its many concessions to recent history, the contemporary expression of perennialism still strikingly resembles both of its earlier expressions. In all three, it reacts subtly (at times, almost despite some of its advocates) against the transformative forces of the respective eras. In all three, its basic orientation and major premises compel it to stand *against* the drive of the common people to make all final policy decisions and *for* the alternative power of a higher authority to whom the people should properly and finally bow.

Let us consider, successively, the historic roles of the common people in the ancient, medieval, and modern cultures. In Greece, we observed that artisans, sailors, and similar groups had gained rapidly in power during the period preceding Plato and Aristotle but that such instruments as the popular assembly were beginning to weaken by the time the *Republic* was composed. In the thirteenth century after Christ, a new and disturbing restlessness among the people was doubtless perceptible to Aquinas, although their characteristic attitude remained submissive. Now, in the late stages of the twentieth century, the people are in a position somewhat similar to that of both earlier cultures. Especially during the past two centuries, they have increasingly demanded and won their rights; but they chafe from frustrations and oppressions which deny them fulfillment of those rights. Like the followers of Pericles, they have tasted democratic privilege and found the flavor good; but, like the new city dwellers of late medieval Europe, they envisage far greater privileges than they have ever yet enjoyed.

In this kind of setting, the contemporary perennialist is faced with an even more acute dilemma than those of his predecessors. While professing devotion to "democracy" he is compelled by his own doctrine not only to doubt the success with which ordinary citizens have controlled their lives and institutions in the immediate past but also, as we shall observe below, to question their ultimate capacity for successful self-government in the period that lies ahead.

THE MIND AS ESCAPE

The demonstration attempted above—that contemporary perennialism is a *necessary* bulwark against thoroughgoing cultural change in ways partially analogous to the perennialist orientation of previous ages—is by no means *sufficient* to prove that it is an undesirable philosophy. The most extreme judgment that might thus far be adduced is that its claim to be finally and purely immune to political, economic, and related forces is untenable. Accordingly, we must return to the issue previously raised in discussing the role of the world's common people: Is the insistence of perennialism that the people should conform to a higher authority than themselves a desirable choice for our own culture?

This issue may be considered afresh in terms of the perennialist conception of mind. Within the context of a theory of reality, mind becomes a kind of ideal norm by which to justify the corporate unity of all classes. In other words, the system of human relations between lower and higher levels of status again resembles a pyramid—a hierarchy of ascending orders of knowledge and goodness. Near the apex of the pyramid is mind itself—the beacon by which alone, except by the help of sheer faith, we can hope to find our way through the jungles of lust, hatred, and selfishness which everywhere beset mortal beings.

We have observed how this whole system of belief is carried over into educational principles. Mental discipline, "freedom" as pure rationality, teaching as "instruction" and "discovery," schooling as "preparation," the centrality of "metaphysics" in the university—all such proposals are harmonious with the philosophic formulation of perennialism. How, then, shall we appraise them?

AFFINITIES OF PERENNIALIST AND ESSENTIALIST EDUCATION

Several aspects of our appraisal have been anticipated in our evaluation of essentialism. Notwithstanding significant deviations ranging from subtle overtones to first principles, contemporary perennialists are often as congenial to essentialist practitioners as the latter are to the former. Faculty psychology, the effort to store minds with the wisdom of the classics, an insistence upon memorizing and intense study of grammar—these are important examples of such congeniality.

We can understand, also, why those large clusters of citizens who approve the essentialist type of school for its transmissive cultural role may tend also to approve perennialist restorative beliefs. A college education devoted mainly to mastering the ideas of other ages may reasonably be assumed to be "safe" education. Thus it may discourage prolonged study or involvement in controversial problems on the ground either that these are trivial or that they can be solved only by following long, circuitous routes through great minds of the past. Further, despite its concern for logic and other mental skills, we have seen that perennialism is not always averse to those mental and moral habits conditioned by "passive mentation." On the contrary, insofar as these habits discourage the young from active participation or responsibility in educational policy-making and curriculum planning, they encourage deference to those of superior status (teachers, clergymen, or civil officers) and thus help to perpetuate patterns of the accepted social and political order.

The leader's mind: its import. Although some perennialists, like some essentialists, may be sufficiently friendly to traditional formulas for elementary and secondary schooling, nevertheless cultural transmission is by no means their *ultimate* aim. In addition, they insist upon certain basic *changes*—changes required by the failures of both the moderative progressivists and the transmissive essentialists, changes which can and should be implemented *primarily* by the training of wise leaders. Such training cannot be achieved by essentialist methods. Hutchins, for example, insists upon the primacy of the Socratic (preferably later termed *maieutic*) method of learning, in which the teacher functions as midwife of the soul. Thus, the precise character of "minds" possessed by these leaders becomes of immediate, practical importance, for they are to guide the people toward wise decisions and wise actions.

Although experimentalist methods are by no means disregarded by all perennialist educational programs, any more than they are rejected by all essentialist ones, it is significant that clues to the real "mind" lies elsewhere. Such methods are distinctly secondary and subordinate. The primary and dominant mind, as conceived by perennialists, is capable of engaging in metaphysics and of attaining intellectual virtue. It alone can grasp those first principles which become the master keys to every human experience, every institution of culture, every subject of the curriculum.

Retreat within. Are we now prepared to contend that the perennialist concept of mind in its most "real" form is also a form of retreat? A partial answer is that it withdraws *into itself*. In terms of his deepest premises, the perennialist completely denies the necessity—on the level of ontological analysis and the purest intellectual virtue (by far the most important level)—of employing experimental, cooperative testing or of checking its pure knowledge against the knowledge of other people.

To be sure, on the level of empiriological analysis and the moral virtues, such comparative testing can take place. Dewey's reflective thinking, for example, has its useful role. Nevertheless, discoveries of the highest speculative mind are discoveries *of* itself, *by* itself, *within* itself. Since it provides its own sanction *for* itself, it has no need, on this metaphysical level, to reach into the realm of social or natural experience—that is, to bring its principles into the laboratory for public inspection and approval. It provides its own authority by the unsullied purity of its own intuition.

Retreat without. But a still more important mechanism operates in this profound theory of mind. We may epitomize this as a kind of *outward* retreat. All perennialists since Plato tend to turn not only subjectively to inner speculation for guidance but also objectively to an outer ideal and permanent conception of the universe and hence of the culture. Such a conception retreats in two ways: first, away from the present into the restorative past where it finds much of its ideal theory; and second, away from the responsibility of openly, publicly examining or achieving cultural aims by experimental methods of verification, and toward a realm of timeless perfection.

The first aspect of outward retreat has been illustrated by perennialist beliefs in corporate unity and hierarchical authority (rephrased, of course, to suit modern situations) as major premises of social order. Such beliefs were central to medieval culture.

The second aspect has been variously illustrated. One illustration is the belief that the basic purposes of culture are implicit within the teleological, hylomorphic character of reality itself; they cannot, therefore, *really* be denied or doubted however much we may try to do so. Another illustration is the belief that men must rely upon an elite that is subject, ultimately and exclusively, to its own unimpeachable authority. Still another illustration is the belief that such authority springs from the same fount of eternal being and wisdom as do the subjective self-certainties of each superior mind. All such illustrations point to a similar conclusion: a transcendental, perfect universe ruled by divine law. To this, men may turn from their own troubles with the assurance that they can rely upon it to guide and comfort them.

Both kinds of retreat, the inward and the outward, are reciprocal parts of one encompassing philosophic system. No disciple of Aristotle, as Adler has reiterated, would accept the contention that the self-evidence of first principles attained by speculation has the form only of subjective thought within the field of *epistemology* alone. It is a form, likewise, of *ontology*; hence, in contrast with the earlier-mentioned nominalist doctrine that thoughts are merely words, the self-evidence of thought is the very fiber of objective reality itself. If superior minds are especially high forms of this reality, then they can reveal it to themselves in their own intellectual purity. The purposes of mind thus become those of the universe, including culture; *the one kind supports the other, according to convenience.* These purposes are also alike in their assumption that no infallible test can be found for either, except the certainty of their own highest principles. Upon them men must finally depend. And upon them all education must finally build.

THE PERENNIALIST CHALLENGE TO DEMOCRACY

THE SANCTION OF AUTHORITY

A double judgment of paramount importance now follows. On the one hand, perennialism, considered as one important cultural bulwark rather than merely as pure erudition, strikingly supports those political-economic arrangements where the common people find guidance in an aristocracy of presumably wise, virtuous leaders. On the other hand, the supreme authority of these leaders centers in the finality of *their own* wisdom and virtue. It is a finality which relies, above all, upon *inner* speculative principles and *outer* universal-cultural purposes, both encompassed by the triad of universal knowledge-reality-value.

This double judgment now compels us to confront, in turn, the preliminary evaluation with which we introduced our study of perennialism. Granted the beauty and fertility of its contributions to Western civilization, this philosophy of life and education is, in last analysis, a disturbing challenge to the democratic conception of culture.

One pivotal belief distinguishes democratic purposes from the perennialist purposes we have been studying: the belief that the majority of people in any organized society should be the sole sovereign authority over the whole of society; conversely, no single individual or minority group should hold sovereign authority in any organized society. Closely related is the important belief in the fallibility, temporality, and finiteness of judgments made by the majority in its own behalf. Such decisions of the majority are always liable to error, as well as to changed circumstances which compel a new judgment. Hence they require continuous criticism, continuous checking of evidence and introduction of new evidence, continuous experimental testing of all important facts and proposals, and continuous public testimony among as many dissenting and consenting groups as possible.

Such a conception of democracy attained one of its earliest, although limited, expressions in Periclean Athens. It was revived in the Renaissance culture by such men as Locke and was adapted to the needs of the new middle classes as they successfully rose to power. It was made more dynamic and flexible between the eighteenth and early twentieth centuries by liberal thinkers and leaders ranging from Rousseau and Mill to Dewey and Holmes. It has been widened and deepened still further by more radical thinkers and leaders such as Paine, Marx, Veblen, and others, and by the increasing strength of mass movements throughout the world. Today it threatens both the civil and ecclesiastic domination of economic and political authority, and it attacks, on a scale unprecedented in history, the frustrating network of special interests and privileges.

Throughout the two thousand years during which democracy has struggled for supremacy over alternative conceptions of economy and culture, it has met bitter opposition from minority power groups and from the intelligentsia who are their spokesmen. During that time the opposition has often successfully submerged democratic beliefs and habits which, even when they have had some practical effects, have been variously restricted or denied.

In such a setting, perennialism is then to be regarded as one important ally of such opposition. Although some exponents may earnestly insist they are not opposed to democracy (just as most essentialists insist they are not), nevertheless perennialists are often impelled to support undemocratic theory and practice even when, as is often true, they do so in spite of their own earnest protestations to the contrary. They are impelled by their own beliefs, by the cultural behavior that these beliefs reflect and bolster, and thus by a complex compound of both belief and behavior.

SELF-EVIDENCE: A CULTUROLOGICAL CRITIQUE

This interpretation is supported by further scrutiny of the insistence upon self-evidence and first principles of knowledge. Although these are to be utilized for the "good" of all people, the perennialist fails to provide any guarantee by which we can safely trust them thus to be utilized—any guarantee, that is to say, except by the presumed intellectual integrity and purity of those who maintain that they, above all, possess such self-evidence.

The point may be restated. Perennialism identifies something called "freedom" with something called "rationality," thereby insisting again upon its devotion to "democracy." But since "rationality" proves, at its highest and most real, to be another name for metaphysical speculation, "freedom" emerges as the freedom of those intellectual leaders who are best able to pronounce final judgments of truth or value. In this way the rest of the people become "free" insofar as they, too, acquiesce in these judgments.

If, however, first principles are indisputably self-evident, should they not be similarly self-evident to all those who are likewise competent to judge them philosophically? If a proposition is self-evident, should it be subject to logical disputation at all? If it can be challenged, even denied by such argument, how can it also claim to be self-evident—that is, indubitable? Such questions are persistently raised among many philosophers recognized by their colleagues for their logical acumen. These philosophers disagree so completely with such philosophers as Adler, and insist so vehemently that principles self-evident to him are not at all self-evident to them, that we are forced to question the presumed universality or dependability of those very principles.

Consider, as one illustration of their disagreement, Adler's categorical assertion, in 1942, that the two following "propositions" are completely self-evident: ". . . corporeal substances differ essentially or accidentally, according as they are individuals of different species (having diverse natures) or as they are numerically distinct individuals having the same specific nature . . ."; and ". . . the good is convertible with being. . . ."[4] Although it is

[4] Adler, in National Society for the Study of Education, *Forty-first Yearbook*, Part I, "Philosophies of Education," pp. 244f.

possible that Adler would no longer defend this statement (he has subsequently confessed that some of his earlier views are "no longer tenable"), we are unfamiliar with any repudiation. What does remain certain is that any non-Aristotelian philosopher of our acquaintance would still insist that nothing at all self-evident pertains to either of these propositions—unless it be that neither one *is* self-evident! The first involves an array of assumptions about the structure and process of reality which every philosophic analyst or every evolutionary, experimental philosopher of science could question. The second involves equally dubious assumptions about ontology in its relationships with axiology—assumptions tending to confuse two types of belief which, while perhaps related, are far from necessarily identical.

Moreover, even such highly abstract first principles as were noted in our brief exposition of perennialist beliefs about knowledge are challenged by logicians holding alternative views. Thus, the principle of causality has been examined by many philosophers with quite different conclusions regarding its meaning—some doubting that it has *any* meaning. Others have cogently argued that the use of the principle of causality to "prove" the existence of God exposes the perennialist himself to inconsistency: if everything has a cause, do we actually add anything to our knowledge by assuming a First Cause, which is an exception to the principle of causality, and calling this exception "God"?

The self-evidence of some mathematical principles is also frequently challenged. One of the most familiar disagreements derives from the alternative point of view that every mathematical system is a series of logical relations, starting from premises themselves arbitrarily assumed. Hence, it is possible to predicate varying or even opposed starting points, as do Euclidean and non-Euclidean geometry, and to proceed from these through different chains of logical relations to different mathematical results. Such a point of view clearly does not deny that starting points are needed in mathematics or in any other discipline; it does deny the perennialist contention that these starting points may be either eternal or real in any meaningful sense. In the language of deductive logic, it further denies that ontological or other major premises are ever final or universal.

Our position in regard to this issue of self-evident principles is well epitomized in the following statement by two American philosophers:

> . . . the history of human thought has shown how unreliable it [self-evidence] is as a criterion of truth. Many propositions

> formerly regarded as self-evident . . . are now known to be false. Indeed, contradictory propositions about every variety of subject-matter . . . have each, at different times, been declared to be fundamental intuitions and therefore self-evidently true. But whether a proposition is obvious or not depends on cultural conditions and individual training, so that a proposition which is "self-evidently true" to one person or group is not so to another.[5]

The consequences of the principle of self-evidence, as applied to democracy, are disastrous. Perennialism would vest ultimate control over culture in those who, by definition, cannot be contradicted because they are their own supreme authority. And it would do so without having convinced anyone except its own apologists that its highest principles, upon which that authority finally depends, are beyond error. As Gilson states it, "Reason has not to prove any of these [first] principles, otherwise they would not be principles but conclusions. . . ."[6]

Indeed, perennialism requires only one more device to ensure that the "wise" judgments of its leaders will be respected and obeyed—the device of *power*. Supported by a power sanctioning the leaders' judgments (as was Plato's military class or the armies of medieval, theocratic states), it would prove exceedingly difficult for their critics, political or philosophical, to challenge that power successfully. In fact, dissent is often and conveniently silenced under the name of falsehood, immorality, heresy, treason —as the pages of history, with their profusion of torn and bloody epitaphs, only too abundantly record.

In short, a self-evident "wisdom" that is *enforceable*—however benevolent it may be and however virtuous Plato's philosopher-kings aimed to be—is a hazardous privilege. It is especially hazardous when threatened by the taint of corruption by which great power is always threatened. Frequent though the mistakes of democratic judgment may be they are open to the therapy of public analysis, testing, consent, and correction. To be sure, democratic judgments are never infallible. But neither are they irremediable. The import of the choice between them and perennialist judgments is unmistakable.

The critique we have offered of self-evidence on the level of reason applies still more forcibly, however, on the level of revela-

[5] Cohen and Nagel, *An Introduction to Logic and Scientific Method*, p. 131.

[6] Gilson, *The Unity of Philosophical Experience*, p. 314.

tion. Here, the tenuous efforts of the "intuitive" mind to make itself plausible to other minds are no longer considered indispensable: religious communion with God replaces philosophic communion among men. Nevertheless, for this very reason, the revelatory and mystical are held to be still more real, still more true and good than the speculative and metaphysical. This is so because the rare mortal who wins such divine companionship is himself closest to divinity. Therefore, he is very properly the authority over ordinary men who, contaminated as they are by matter and passion, can at least enjoy vicariously through him the aura of spiritual blessedness.

Thus the essence of democracy is denied again by the highest of all perennialist principles. But even when this principle is not directly incorporated into the educational theory and practice of lay advocates, it is frequently, if only tacitly, sanctioned by them. Certainly, parochial education becomes in this context the very antithesis of democratic education; it indoctrinates students in the belief that the ultimate guidance of their lives is to be sought, not in their own natural capacities or in their own shared judgments, but in a supernatural Being Whose orders are most safely entrusted to His hierarchy of earthly representatives.

Maritain reflects the authentic tradition with typical forthrightness. He discusses "mixed questions," *including education*, which should be considered "primarily and above all, not in reference to the temporal order and the good of the earthly city" but in reference to the spiritual order and "the good of souls. . . ." Actually democracy, "more than any other regime," requires the absolute authority of God; and no leader deserves to be obeyed unless he derives his own authority from "the sovereignty of the Cause of being. . . ."[7]

How, then, shall we meet the contention that perennialism can still claim to be democratic in the sense that it finds all men to be "equal before God"? Everyone recognizes, of course, the ideal of brotherhood in the simple beliefs of Jesus and the Judaic tradition. Similarly, no one denies that some members of the Church and some philosophers of Thomist preference are concerned with enhancing this ideal. Indeed, let us recognize that, despite or perhaps sometimes because of the hierarchical structure, a remarkably impressive minority of clerical personnel have been demonstrating far greater courage in the face of racial or other inequities than have many professed democratic liberals or even democratic radicals.

[7] Maritain, *True Humanism*, p. 293; *Scholasticism and Politics*, pp. 103ff.

Nevertheless, one fails to detect clear evidence that such courage follows consistently *from* their own philosophic beliefs. History demonstrates that perennialism has supported and still supports various political systems, some of them rigidly antidemocratic. Even Maritain has affirmed that the Church is no more obligated to support democracy than it does other "worthy" systems of rule.

What, moreover, is the precise meaning of the doctrine that men are equal before God? The question is: *In what sense are they equal?* In the sense that all human beings are equally human? Perhaps, but this circular statement tells us nothing at all; so, too, are all animals equally animals. Are men equal in the sense, then, that they should share equally in determining all policies by which their lives will be governed justly? Clearly *no*, if we judge either by the record of two millenniums of Church control or by the theory of self-evident and revelatory justice.

Are men equal, then, in the sense that all men should seek and pray equally for eternal salvation? Clearly *yes* if the highest aim and measure of this life is the hope of afterlife. But, because the hope of afterlife is precisely such an aim and measure (certainly for all Church educators), equality on earth becomes, at best, a question of secondary interest; the Church readily supports national regimes officially opposed to equality as a political and economic end; and Maritain himself characterizes the Church as the "perfect society organized in accordance with its own appropriate . . . hierarchy, in which authority comes from above to teach souls and lead them to salvation."[8]

ROLE OF THE MAJORITY: THE PERENNIALIST VIEW RECONSIDERED

Perennialist attitudes toward the majority. The last stronghold of defense against the contention that perennialist doctrine is ultimately a negation of democracy is the insistence that it does recognize the role of the majority as legitimate and important. On this issue more than on any other, differences between the "left wing" and "right wing" are most pronounced—the right wing revealing skepticism of and sometimes contempt for common citizens; the left wing revealing greater confidence in them and, hence, in the hope of increased privileges and powers for them. We have noted that such differences are defended on the ground that perennialists may differ about social philosophy, which stands

[8] Maritain, *Ransoming the Time*, p. 199. See pp. 41, 206, 214f.

on the comparatively low plateau of the moral virtues. These will thus necessarily produce differences of opinion that are not admissible on the high level of the intellectual virtues.

Regardless of varying positions on the social, economic, or political scale, perennialists should not be satisfied with so facile an answer. To insist upon it puts them in the position of doubting their own ability to reach clear, governing principles on the cultural level of experience. This is a doubt that is inconsistent with their argument that it is exactly on that level that such principles are now so urgent. A far stronger answer—one which left-wing perennialists, at least, would emphasize—is that ordinary men, who constitute the majority, deserve the right to join in determining social policies for the simple but fundamental reason that even they are potentially capable of rational judgments. Restated still more precisely, all men, being hylomorphic, *could* ideally become rational enough to govern themselves, even if actually they have not thus far learned how to do so. But if they could, then may not democracy, as rule by the majority, also succeed? And does not admission of this possibility demonstrate that perennialists are not, after all, opponents of democracy? Does it not also follow that, theoretically, perennialists do not necessarily advocate stratified cultural structures? Even though the two greatest cultures of which this philosophy was the rationale were heavily stratified, no man is condemned by his nature to occupy one level of culture throughout his life. Therefore any man may, if he sufficiently exercises the faculties of will and intellect, rise to the heights of reason and wisdom—nay, even of revelation.

Here we have the major premise, more or less frankly admitted, that underlies perennialist programs of general education. Only when this kind of education becomes the universal pattern will the latent powers of mortal men be aroused sufficiently so that the majority may be equipped in the only way that has real significance—in behalf of *actual* rather than *potential* rationality. A solemn obligation of all civilized societies is to ensure that it does become the pattern.

This is the perennialists' last stronghold of defense. Unfortunately it, too, totters under examination.

Perennialist education is philosophically vulnerable. To begin with, the kind of general or liberal education still eloquently defended by Hutchins, even when embellished by current events or favorable quotations from Dewey and other nonperennialists, may be questioned on philosophic grounds. Since, for example, the scientific method is an inferior way to gain knowledge, perennialists would hold that any educational program, including their own, cannot be sufficiently evaluated by experimental canons. While these canons cannot prove conclusively that the perennialist model of general education is unsound, neither, by the same token, can they prove that it is sound.

Again, just as one may cast serious doubts upon the legitimacy of self-evidence as a criterion of any kind of ontological, axiological, or epistemological judgment, so one may cast equally serious doubts about any kind of education based upon this criterion. As in other cases, such as politics, argument reaches a stalemate which can be removed only if one is willing to concede its vulnerability by resorting to alternative criteria provided by, say, empirical comparison of evidence into the work of different kinds of educational programs.

Insufficient concern for democratic processes. Whether perennialist education best prepares average citizens for democratic rule may also be questioned by its relative disregard of the basic *processes* by which such rule must always operate. That Hutchins and other perennialists, even when they approach acceptance of democratic *ends*, are usually either vague or inadequate in discussing democratic *means* (indeed, the whole complex problem of social control) has been an important contention of the preceding chapter.

The perennialist model of general education is illustrative. To be sure, students occasionally *read about* majority control in Mill's essay, *On Liberty*, or other classics. Some perennialists also admit, however, charily, a limited value in the activity curriculum, inductive learning, and other aspects of progressivist theory. But we search almost in vain for democratic learnings that are advocated as active sharing in the problems and policies of education itself. Granting, moreover, that symptoms of unrest and dissent have begun to permeate some institutions of learning governed by ecclesiastic policies as well as by secular ones, indifference to the political and economic struggles of surrounding communities or to student-faculty participation in such struggles has been, traditionally, much more the rule than the exception. Nor is work experience seriously considered as promising educational experience. We find, indeed, no proof even in Hutchins' latter-day *The Learning Society* of a single major shift from his consistently maintained orientation.

With meager regard for or practice in the means by which

individuals can organize and act concertedly, the belief of perennialists in the right of every man to rise above his stratum becomes little more than a pious wish. By skirting forthright analysis of, and militant action against, economic or other cultural conditions and forces that block the freedom of people to rise by their own efforts, the perennialist program of education largely by-passes those processes and strategies that might sustain, by *overt demonstration,* its verbal disavowals of a stratified culture.

Moreover, the method of maieutic conversation, although by far the most attractive characterization of general education in Hutchins' methodology, does not establish that the program meets the criteria of democratic learning implied by full presentation of evidence, full communication of that evidence, and maximum agreement, as well as action, upon such evidence and communication. Implicit in it, rather, has been a kind of pseudo-Platonic hope that eternal Ideas of truth, value, and reality lurk somewhere in the background of each seminar discussion—patiently awaiting that enunciation by which, alone, rational answers shall at last be deduced.

Subordination of science. Our next justification for questioning perennialism's professed concern for majority rule has already been implied: its subordination of science. If perennialists begrudgingly accord recognition to experimental methods, they also frequently treat science, along with its educational allies, as a scapegoat. For it is partially, perhaps even largely, responsible for mankind's contemporary troubles.

We need not consider further the weakness of perennialist arguments against scientific method and its social effects. Although one may rightly question the sufficiency of that method as thus far exercised, doubts call not for its weakening but rather for its strengthening. One can hardly accuse science of causing the present crisis in world affairs, for example, so long as it has not been systematically applied to the intra- or international conflicts and tensions chronic to that crisis. Indeed, if we are to fix the blame at all, supernatural religion and secular absolutisms—with their concomitants of superstition, escapism, dogmatism, and mysticism—are much more vulnerable. For it is these attitudes, not the scientific method, that have more often than science long influenced and determined the course and outcome of both cultural and personal affairs.

We do need to consider further the role of science in the operation of democracy—or, more precisely, the role of science in building majority consent with respect to all fundamental policies of public welfare. Such a role is exactly the antithesis of what we have called mind as "retreat without." In a democracy, cultural problems are not faced, purposes and programs are not fashioned by restoration of a venerable conception of life dependent upon self-evident first principles. On the contrary, they are derived cooperatively from common interests, they are subjected to factual scrutiny and open testimony, and they are finally tested in cultural laboratories under publicly controllable experimental conditions. Throughout this process, democracy operates to the degree that the largest possible majority of citizens not only express their common judgments on every public policy but also are informed of the techniques required to make those judgments operative. Ordinary citizens themselves are not, to be sure, experts in these techniques; this would be impossible. But they must strive to understand and approve the character and conditions of experimental procedure. And they must express their willingness to be guided by it in deciding finally whether the product it creates satisfies their widest interests.

In these terms, democracy still remains a hypothesis far from adequately tested. But certainly it cannot be tested by any system of beliefs that subordinates the adequacy or dependability of scientific method and knowledge. Nor can it be tested by any educational theory or program which disparages that adequacy.

The elite and the majority. Finally, any viable philosophy of democracy may be justifiably suspicious of the importance and the prestige that perennialism attributes to an intellectual elite. We cannot recall, too often, the ancient and medieval structures of autocratic-aristocratic relationships from which perennialists borrow so many of their own dominant beliefs. We cannot easily overlook the fact that their program for the higher learning is designed primarily for the benefit of an exceptional few who survive the rigors of general education and for whom even that education is largely intended as a proving ground. Nor can we afford to forget that Hutchins' pattern for university administration was borrowed directly from Plato himself. We stress again that, in their frequent sympathy for, if not theological identification with, a supernatural outlook consistent with a restorative view, lay perennialists also lend support to the belief of members of the Church that "*Man craves for a power superior to himself to whom he can pay homage and under the shelter of whose authority he* *finds security.*"[9] We must recognize the historic fact that this power, although allegedly emanating from God, has been exercised for many centuries by an authoritarian and enormously powerful elite—by a hierarchy whose own mandates are frequently regarded as the highest court of appeal, standing even above civil government.

The conclusion is inescapable. Although some perennialist educators have demonstrated their indignation toward racial and other forms of antidemocratic oppression, and although they may even affirm that the majority is rational *potentially,* the whole practical weight of the perennialist program has, thus far, largely doubted the expectation that the majority can become rational *actually.* If this were not the case, one would expect such an educator as Hutchins to imply at least the necessity for universities for the majority of people. Or Maritain might intimate that perhaps, sometime, ecclesiastic absolutism will be superseded by completely democratic controls within the Church itself. Neither suggestion has been made. On the contrary, both suggestions seem absurd in the sense of being incongruous with the whole "spirit and substance," the whole elaborate apparatus of premises and deductions which constitute the Platonic-Aristotelian-Thomist *Weltanschauung.* Thus our response to such democratic suggestions and behavior as are sometimes advanced with sincerity, even with courage, is to regard them in the perspective of their total outlook as inconsistent, eclectic, or simply as subordinate to their more definitive and finally undemocratic framework of beliefs. As Hutchins stated in 1968 with disarming ambiguity, ". . . the elite school should not be obliterated, but . . . its aims should be the aims of education for all."[10]

What is not ambiguous is this: the kind of education that perennialists propose *for* the majority is not necessarily education for responsible, vigorous, participative rule *by* or *of* the majority. It is, rather, a plan by which the average citizen, relegated properly if not inevitably to lower rungs of the ladder of culture, can be sufficiently sensitized to the wisdom of great minds and, through them, to the authority of self-evident truth and revelation so that he will respect and revere that authority. Certainly, most men cannot become philosopher-kings, but, through universal education of the kind proposed, they can join willingly in

[9] Cunningham, *The Pivotal Problems of Education,* p. 221 (italics supplied). See also Maritain, *Scholasticism and Politics,* pp. 103ff.

[10] Hutchins, *The Learning Society,* p. 51.

the harmonious membership of a corporate whole. They can be comforted by their sense of unity in a cultural pyramid whose apex points toward God Himself. They can, thereby, "really" share in the maintenance of that kind of "justice" whose core is always finally self-evident to their nearly divine leaders.

CRITIQUE OF PERENNIALISM IN PHILOSOPHIC PERSPECTIVES OF OUR TIME

Although our culturological evaluation of perennialism has reflected the main thrust of its role and influence, also repeatedly emphasized is the contention that this philosophy of education, no less than any others considered in this work, reflects the uncertainties and controversies endemic to the present period of human history. We have thus repeatedly stressed the remarkable capacity of perennialism to accommodate its major beliefs to these cultural phenomena while yet retaining its own permanent—that is, everlasting—character.

Amidst such lively controversy, one would also expect some advocates to take positions that on, the surface, seem too heretical or deviant to warrant their inclusion. This has been particularly evident in the kind of clerical, left-wing political and moral activism that has attracted much interest among lay citizens as well as among professional perennialists. One notes, to cite just two examples, titles of such books as *The Underground Church*, to which one Catholic bishop and a number of other affiliated perennialists have contributed, and *The New Left Church*, by a less affiliated author, Terence Eagleton. One notes, also, a good deal of debate and dispute within such widely read Church-oriented journals as *Commonweal* and *America*.

The point of these occurrences, if our guiding theme is defensible, is that they are bound also to exercise repercussions in the sphere of philosophic movements which, although nonperennialist themselves, are symbolic of much more than philosophy per se. A statement issued under the auspices of Vatican II, concerning seminarian studies, is timely:

> Basing themselves on a philosophic heritage which is perennially valid, students should also be conversant with contemporary philosophical investigations, especially those exercising special influence in their own country, and with recent scientific progress.[11]

[11] As quoted in Donohue, *St. Thomas Aquinas and Education*, p. 18.

Existentialism. Of the five such investigations hitherto epitomized, existentialism is most easily perceived as amenable. After all, let us not forget that one of Europe's most distinguished existentialist philosophers, Marcel, became converted to Catholicism while a young man (as, incidentally, did Maritain), much of his work being devoted to demonstrating how his position is the key to such themes as *Creative Fidelity* and *The Existentialist Background of Human Dignity.*

Still more interesting to us is an attempt of such religious philosophers as Will Herberg to place Maritain in the same philosophic camp. Despite the fact that the latter's basic doctrine of Thomism is decidedly contrary to existentialism in major respects, nonetheless it is true that Maritain has contributed the paradoxical term, "existentialist intellectualism," in his book, *Existence and the Existent.* By comparison, Adler, in his own reconsideration, by no means wishes to embrace existentialism by his versions of neo-Aristotelianism or neo-Thomism. But he does recognize that it, too, is an extremely fertile movement concerned at times with such "first-order questions" as being and nonbeing, freedom and indeterminacy, life and death.

In short, let us remember that the transcendent meaning of man is regarded as of paramount importance to perennialists. Insofar as the contemporary existentialist is equally concerned with that kind of meaning, it becomes quite understandable why they should welcome his concern as well.

Zen Buddhism. For similar reasons, although by no means with conspicuous zeal, a few perennialists are beginning to turn to Zen Buddhism for whatever insights it, too, might provide. In the ecumenical spirit of Pope John XXIII (he once received twenty-eight Japanese Buddhist priests in a special audience), the more traditional attitude of religious exclusiveness is challenged by works such as *Conversations: Christian and Buddhist* and *Zen Catholicism,* both by the Thomist-oriented prior, Dom Aelred Graham.

Graham's works, to be sure, not only carry the imprimatur of his archbishop; equally significant is his frank confession that the "Catholic hierarchy, discharging its rightful function, is taken for granted."[12] But is it not also significant that the titles themselves should now be officially permitted? Indeed, the whole spirit of Graham's books express sophisticated appreciation of the cen-

[12] Graham, *Zen Catholicism,* p. xiii.

tral core of Zen as the search for more profound insight and inner wholeness. The spiritual toughness of a dedicated Zen priest practicing his monastic life reminds one, too, of Catholic monasteries in the West, such as the Benedictine.

Neo-Freudianism. What we have tried to intimate about both existentialism and Zen Buddhism applies almost equally well to neo-Freudian theory. While ecclesiastic perennialists or even most secular ones might appear to shy away from so materialistic a theory of severe erotic stresses, this is much too easy a way out. To be sure, Adler in his summation seems to find little reason to include more than a mention of Freudian concepts: after all, Freud (no less than Marx) falls outside the strict discipline of philosophy because he, too, is concerned with "second-order" activities of human experience, not with its "being."

Such downgrading is not characteristic of Maritain. He places a good deal of importance upon Freudian ideas, dividing them into three planes—the psychoanalytic, psychologic, and philosophic. Toward the first of the three, Maritain evinces strong admiration, for he recognizes the power of the unconscious and of the necessity to develop new techniques, such as transference, for coping with nervous disorders. Toward the second plane, he considers Freud's psychology to be "of a purely empiriological type," which contributes much to our understanding of neuroses, dreams, and other psychic phenomena. But when we reach the third or purely philosophic plane, both of the other two are seriously weakened in turn. Despite Freud's own repudiation of metaphysics, what emerges is a ". . . pseudometaphysics of the most vulgar type, because it combines all the prejudices of deterministic, mechanistic scientism with all the prejudices of irrationalism."[13] But Maritain tempers this sort of criticism also with admiration. And he notes the emergence of the neo-Freudian movement which includes, among other features, frontiers of explorations between religion and psychoanalysis.

Maritain, Adler, and other perennialists might benefit here from a collection of letters between Freud and a Protestant religionist, Oscar Pfister, who once studied with and greatly admired Freud: it is titled *Psychoanalysis and Faith.* Freud notes for example, how both he and his friend were searching for the same goals of deep human satisfaction—the one through supreme faith,

[13] Maritain, in Benjamin Nelson (ed.), *Freud and the 20th Century*, p. 248.

the other through psychoanalysis as ". . . an impartial tool which both priest and layman can use in the service of the sufferer."[14]

Analytic philosophy. To comment further on its possible contributions is unnecessary other than to be reminded with Maritain that perennialists have little objection to analytic philosophy so long as it functions on the level where it belongs—that is, the "empiriological." Where they differ (and here Adler, again, is helpful in distinguishing between "second-order level" of problems belonging to philosophic analysis, and "first-order level" of pure philosophy) is in the insistence of analysts that "first-order" problems (Maritain's "ontological") are largely, if not wholly, meaningless.

In our own view, these analysts are likely to prove both correct and incorrect. *Correct,* because they do succeed in exposing the vacuity of perennialist "pseudoquestions," such as the nature of self-evident propositions and first principles. But *incorrect* because, devoid of any culturologically oriented framework, analysts never confront the psychocultural motivations and consequences of perennialism discussed in previous sections of this chapter. Were, however, such motivations and consequences to enlist even simple techniques of philosophic analysis, they could perhaps contribute well beyond evaluations of perennialism to which this book has been able to carry it.

Neo-Marxism. A first glance might suppose that, just as neo-Marxism offers the most immediate affinity thus far with progressivism, so it offers perhaps the least affinity with perennialism. Historically, at any rate, this supposition seems well justified.

But in accordance with much the same texture of perennialist amenability already noted toward other philosophic movements, it is not at all surprising that postwar concerns are discernible here as well. That mutual respect can be cultivated between Church and Communist intellectuals, for example, is brilliantly exemplified in the international symposium, *The Christian–Marxist Dialogue*—a series of dialogically attuned essays, in addition to a manifesto issued by seventeen Roman Catholic bishops from several countries who plead for radical social and political action. But neo-Marxists, too (such as the Czech philosopher, Milan Prucha), seem eager to search for common ground between perennialist and Marxian beliefs, contend-

[14] Freud and Pfister, *Psychoanalysis and Faith,* p. 17.

ing that the ideological hostilities between them are increasingly threadbare. Relevantly, he likewise calls attention to the need of both movements to consider the common ground of still other modern positions, such as existentialism and analytic philosophy.

In referring again to these several positions, we have, it is hoped, demonstrated at least this: despite the severe strictures that our evaluation has been compelled to place upon perennialism, viewed as a restorative expression of cultural-educational beliefs, the abnormal time in which we live is such as to compel its more sensitive, concerned spokesmen to open their minds and feelings in ways that earlier times could not.

In this respect, no less than in the case of our companion philosophies of education, perennialism must be judged culturologically. That it remains predominantly loyal to its own restorative patterns of belief is, we think, true; otherwise there could scarcely be occasion for appraising it as the paramount, distinctive force in modern civilization that it is. Even so, our intention has been also appreciative of those nuances of thought and variations of conduct that prove its capacity to confront and to adjust. Only in such an anthropological-philosophical perspective can perennialism be judged comparatively and fairly.

SECTION 1

Philosophic beliefs of reconstructionism

PART 5

Reconstructionism: education as cultural transformation

CHAPTER 14

Fountainheads of reconstructionism

SOME YEARS BEFORE the term, reconstructionism, had been invented, the American philosopher, William P. Montague, delivered a striking lecture, "Philosophy as Vision." His theme was that the primary contribution of philosophy to civilization has been its speculations upon the possibilities inherent in man as scientist, man as artist, man as politician, man as man. Choosing Democritus and Plato to illustrate his theme, Montague showed how the first of these giants of antiquity had anticipated by more than twenty centuries the atomic theory of modern physical science, and how the second explored some of the most profound issues of ethics and politics with which we are concerned today.

Philosophy, in this view, is most vital when it ventures beyond the tested boundaries of everyday experience. Its function is to point the way for explorers who painstakingly hack out new roads, build new machinery, and erect new institutions in order to disprove or substantiate the speculative visions of the philosopher.

Whether or not Montague's generalization is fully justified, he has indicated at least one of the great historic functions of philosophy. It is this function—the envisaging of radical, innovative projections—that suggests the spirit of the theory we have chosen to call reconstructionism. More explicitly than any other contemporary philosophy of education, it directs its attention to the goals needed equally by a period of fearful danger and breathtaking promise. In the sense that its thinking extends well beyond the ways of living to which we are accustomed, it strives for the imaginative audacity that Montague lauds. The vision differs, however, from the almost purely speculative vision of a Plato or a Democritus: this philosophy seeks to design cultural patterns for the future upon the solid foundation of burgeoning knowledge about nature and man, and to develop viable means of establishing them.

The goal of our fourth and concluding orientation is, then, demanded by the revolutionary age in which we live—goals that are concretely grounded in experience and that invite practicable measures for human renewal.

HISTORIC CONTRIBUTIONS OF UTOPIANISM

ANCIENT AND MODERN UTOPIAN THOUGHT

Although the heart of reconstructionism is its orientation toward the future, it is not without historic foundations. Because the common denominator of its beliefs is a passionate concern for the prospects of civilization, it centers attention upon concretely defined cultural goals which, as they involve idealizations of human potentialities, are in the historic stream of utopian philosophy. "Utopianism" as used in this book, then, means any construction of the imagination that extends beyond the here-and-now toward realizable human, especially cultural, goals.

Because of its special importance to this philosophy, the reader should not confuse this definition of utopianism with other, invidious meanings that are perhaps more common. Utopian does not here connote a flight from reality into realms of totally unrealizable, fantastic perfection. The utopian attitude is not that of the impractical daydreamer who cannot bear to face the hard problems of his own day or his immediate environment. The vision of utopianism, is rather, an expectable one—a vision of what can be and should be attained in order that man may be happier, more rational, more humane than he has ever been.

Lewis Mumford, to whom we shall refer later, clarifies the distinction in his first book, *The Story of Utopias*, when he refers to "the utopias of escape" and "the utopias of reconstruction":

> The first leaves the external world the way it is; the second seeks to change it so that one may have intercourse with it on one's own terms. In one we build impossible castles in the air; in the other we consult a surveyor and an architect and

a mason and proceed to build a house which meets our essential needs.[1]

The utopian vision in the second sense has been shared by many thinkers of past ages, especially in periods of great crisis when old patterns of culture were crumbling and new patterns were needed.

Plato, for example, was one of the great visionaries of all time, as Montague observes. The *Republic*, his greatest work, embodies Plato's solution for the problems of his own culture. Although his scheme is one which wc are compelled to reject, it is, nevertheless, a magnificent one, extremely detailed and designed to remedy the weaknesses and corruptions of ancient Athens through an aristocracy ruled benevolently by philosopher-kings.

Another contribution from the ancient world—Augustine's *City of God*—is, like Plato's work, of much more significance for perennialism than for reconstructionism. Yet, because it interprets history as a struggle between good and evil forces in which the forces of good are ultimately triumphant, its vision falls within our definition of utopianism. In addition, Augustine raises several of the most difficult problems that later utopian philosophies have endeavored to solve. To cite one: Does the course of history encourage us to believe that our ideal goals may finally be reached?

The utopians of early and later modern history may be divided into two groups. First came those who, living in the sixteenth and seventeenth centuries, were severe critics of the institutions of the waning feudalism and enthusiasts of the emerging order. If their principal figure was Thomas More, others of great stature were Francis Bacon, Thomas Campanella, and James Harrington. The latter half of the eighteenth century and the early part of the nineteenth produced such utopian thinkers and doers as Francois Babeuf, Henri de Saint-Simon, Charles Fourier, and Robert Owen. Although they, like their predecessors, were critics of the existing order and, to varying degrees, proponents of the new one then developing, they saw ahead toward a civilization that would correct the evils already being generated in the new age. Their writings reflect the impact of science, a new concern for individual rights, the restlessness of an expanding and exploring age.

The herald of modern utopianism was More. Indeed, the title of his work is *Utopia*. It depicts communal rather than

[1] Mumford, *The Story of Utopias*, p. 15.

private ownership of property. Labor is reduced to six hours per day. Meals are taken in common. And religion is dedicated to brotherhood.

Bacon placed the scientist at the center of his ideal society: the *New Atlantis*. By abolishing ignorance and superstition, by developing education and knowledge, the problems of mankind could be solved. Although he lived more than three hundred years ago, some of his proposals, such as endowed centers for experimentation, are at least as workable today as when they were made. Bacon seems to have been prophetic of the industrial, liberal, and scientific age just dawning in his own time.

A contemporary of Bacon—the Italian, Campanella—advocated, like More, a system of communal ownership of property. Like Plato, he thought that too much devotion to one's own family tends to weaken loyalty to the state; hence he, too, favored a community of wives and children. He set up scrupulous rules of hygiene for the ideal community described in his *City of the Sun* (for example, he provided for cremation of the dead as a public health measure), and insisted that all citizens share in common toil.

The last utopian work of the early modern period to be mentioned—*Oceana*, by Harrington—is significant for primary concern with the best possible political system. It proposes such far-sighted reforms as the secret ballot, rotation of incumbency in public offices, and a two-chamber legislature, all of which have now been partially realized.

Utopian theories of the eighteenth and early nineteenth centuries reflect, in part, the incompleteness of the economic and social revolutions of preceding centuries. But they also reflect the restlessness of peoples suffering from shortcomings of the economic and political institutions of early and later modern civilization; these institutions, although an advance over those of feudalism, brought with them their own cruelties and failures.

Babeuf, for example, was influential even during his short lifetime (he was guillotined at thirty-three). His *Society of Equals* expounds the belief that only when people receive literally equal shares in the resources of society can problems of political and economic life be solved. In holding that all citizens have equal rights to food, clothing, shelter, medical care, and opportunities, he anticipated widely held (and still utopian) beliefs of our own day.

Saint-Simon followed Bacon's design for a society governed by experts. He departed from Babeuf in assuming a natural inequality of talent. The chief need envisaged by Saint-Simon was to guarantee to all humans the fullest development of their faculties; this was to be achieved by making rewards proportional to merit. Because the ideal state can be created and maintained through the practice of brotherly love and the other simple virtues of Jesus, Saint-Simon may be called the father of a later movement, Christian Socialism.

Perhaps the most relevant contribution made by Fourier was his analysis of the "passions" of man to which a soundly organized society must be adapted. So challenging were his proposals that several Fourierist colonies were established. Like other utopian designs already mentioned, Fourier's is rich in ideas that are still provocative today. An example is his belief in the complete emancipation of women from any kind of subservience.

Owen, like Fourier, exerted great influence in America as well as in Europe. A thoroughgoing environmentalist, he advocated an economic system in which almost everyone would belong to trade unions devoted to the primary task of producing cooperatively for public benefit. He also saw our great cities supplanted by a worldwide system of decentralized villages, so that town and country would no longer be separated and everyone might have the benefits of fresh air, gardens, and space in which to work and play.

THE ROLE OF MEANS

The great utopians whose thought has been barely sampled above are vulnerable to criticisms. Some of their specific suggestions are simply unworkable. The colonies actually established by followers of Fourier and Owen were little self-centered "islands" that failed, in part, because they were too oblivious to the interdependent structures of modern industrial civilization. Also, they too frequently disregarded the practical considerations involved in gaining their objectives.

The reconstructionist corrects this tendency to disregard means in favor of ends; at the same time, he insists upon the importance of cultural foresight. Therefore, it is important to ask whether there are precedents for the development of a philosophy of vigorous action in behalf of utopian objectives.

To ask the question is to point toward the answer. Many a thinker of the past has not only built philosophies *of* action but has demonstrated them *in* action. To be sure, these "action thinkers" have varied widely in their objectives; yet, by their concern for strategies and programs, they have enriched reconstructionist theory also. Among the ancients, Aristotle could be mentioned for his practical suggestions in the field of ethics. Bacon and Locke in England, Machiavelli in Italy, and Hegel in Germany are only a few later contributors to modern political philosophy.

The twentieth century has produced a number of distinguished thinkers who have also been men of action: Thomas Masaryk, the first president of Czechoslovakia; Senator Benedetto Croce in Italy; General Jan Smuts in South Africa; Albert Schweitzer in Europe and Africa; Bertrand Russell in England; Karl Jaspers in Germany and Switzerland. Within our own country, one of the greatest action thinkers, the late Justice Oliver Wendell Holmes, has even been referred to as America's philosopher-king.

The stress on social as well as individual action is also derived, of course, from the experimentalism of Peirce, James, Dewey, and their disciples.

RECENT HERALDS OF THE FUTURE

About a century or more ago, a number of voices could be heard which are still more germane to our interest. No one of these thinkers, of course, can be regarded as a master spokesman for reconstructionism; each contributes at important points, but each is thoroughly inharmonious at other points. Indeed, it cannot be stressed too strongly that the differences between them often prove greater than their similarities. None, moreover, provides a unified formulation comparable to that of Dewey, for example, for the progressivist philosophy. The thinkers to be discussed below provide, at most, certain threads to be woven into the transformative orientation.

In the opinion of many students, the most stimulating nineteenth-century contributions to social philosophy were those of Karl Marx and Friedrich Engels. Both were German by birth but spent productive years of their lives in England. Although Marx was the dominant figure, Engels collaborated with him through many years of close association. But the outlines of their utopia were never carefully worked out. They seem to have been satisfied that it would operate successfully by the criterion of their favorite formula—". . . from each according to his abilities, to each according to his needs." Had they devoted more attention to long-range goals, some of the problems and failures that have dogged socialist ventures might have been avoided.

Instead, much of the intellectual energy of Marx and Engels

was exerted in analyzing the weaknesses and evils of the political and economic system that they wished to replace and against which they developed a program of militant tactics. The principle course of such action has become famous as "class struggle." Every historic society, we are told, has centered upon the struggle between those who control the sources of economic and political power (and who naturally wish to retain control) and those who wish to secure such power for themselves. At certain periods in history, the struggle has resulted in the defeat of the hitherto dominant class, as in the change from feudalism to capitalism. At other times, class oppositions have been submerged, so that the struggle between classes is then carried on more quietly than in times of open conflict. Present-day manifestations of class struggle are the efforts of organized labor to gain a larger share of the profits of private enterprise; the confusions that beset the middle classes; and the efforts of powerful interests to silence or intimidate critical voices.

Like other utopianism in modern history, the philosophy of Marx and Engels is vulnerable. For one thing, it often oversimplifies the analysis of culture by reducing it to economic class alignments without sufficient regard for other relationships and structures. Again, its ontology of natural historic laws is partially absolutist. Most seriously, Marxism advocates a dictatorship of the proletariat as an interim political-economic order under which democratic rights and processes are to be abridged indefinitely. Nevertheless, the influence of this philosophy remains powerful in many parts of the world. In the modified and updated form of what we have termed neo-Marxism, it has relevance of one or another sort for each of our four approaches to educational philosophy, but particularly for reconstructionism.

In England, George Bernard Shaw, H. G. Wells, Beatrice and Sidney Webb, G. D. H. and Margaret Cole, Karl Mannheim, and Harold J. Laski are among those intellectual leaders who have borrowed from and modified Marxian theory in expressing their own views of twentieth-century problems and institutions. Here we shall comment upon only one—Wells—since very probably he has been the most extensively read recent English utopian. His visions are tempered by a strong note of pessimism and, at times, by considerable conservatism. He believed, for example, that a population of inferior individuals will continue to exist in society side by side with average and superior persons, and he advocated the accumulation, within limits, of private property. Like Plato and Saint-Simon, he would vest a good deal of political power in an intellectual elite of experts. Unlike most earlier utopians, he thought of his society on a world scale. The influence of modern science upon his utopia is illustrated by the importance he assigned to machinery for performing back-breaking drudgery and by his insistence upon universal racial equality.

America has produced fewer influential utopians than England and France. Reasons for this are doubtless cultural: the temper of the young nation has not hitherto responded so readily to visionary ideas as to those of the European heritage or those of its own pragmatic, present-centered philosophers. But even here one notes important exceptions. By far the most influential American utopians, both of whom flourished in the late nineteenth century, were Edward Bellamy, the author of *Looking Backward*, and Henry George, the author of *Progress and Poverty*. With amazing foresight and imagination, Bellamy discussed economic organization, political structures, the family, marriage, and dozens of other topics that he considered indispensable to a rationally planned democracy. George proposed a radical cure for the evils generated by capitalism—a single tax on land and the abolition of rents. The theories of Bellamy and George, like those of other Americans to be drawn upon, will not be discussed in detail although their proposals, directly or indirectly, strongly influence reconstructionist ideas throughout.

Of twentieth-century thinkers, two from whom our emerging theory borrows forward-looking elements are Thorstein Veblen and Randolph Bourne. Although several of Veblen's works have become classics, his basic ideas still remain far ahead of most economic theorists who praise him. He is usually regarded as the chief intellectual influence behind a short-lived but important utopian movement of the 1930s called Technocracy. Its leaders had been associated with Veblen at the close of World War I and had absorbed his theory that, in our technological age, only the social engineer is sufficiently skilled to operate the industrial-political machine.

The essays of Bourne, written during much too brief a life (he died at thirty-two), have never received the attention they deserve. He was one of the first penetrating critics of pragmatism to call attention to its liberal propensity to glorify means at the expense of ends. This criticism of pragmatism had been made by essentialists and perennialists, but has seldom emanated from theorists whose ends are future-oriented.

In any case, the outstanding American utopian thinker of our own time has been, without question, Mumford. Viewed as a whole, his philosophy is straightforward in directing attention toward the radical remaking of contemporary culture. His *The*

Culture of Cities, for example, is not only a dramatic history of the rise of cities but also a severe critique of the ugly modern "Megalopolis" and a vision for its renewal to satisfy new technological and other demands.

Mumford redefines utopianism, perhaps a little too narrowly, as ". . . the belief in the possibility of renovating society, through the application of reason and social invention to political and economic institutions." But the tone of his thinking is crystal clear. Consider only his principle of "universalism":

> To supplement a universalism based on mere mechanical uniformity and on a breaking down of physical barriers in time and space, we must create a universalism based on the spiritual wealth and variety of men: their unity in diversity achieved by working together for common ends. . . . Through this worldwide unity, the human personality, now suppressed and deformed by the very agents and organizations it has created, will begin to unfold in all its dimensions: mankind will enter upon a higher stage of development. . . . But only whole men, liberated from the automatism of both instinctual and rational organizations, integrated in all their functions, will have the vital energy to take part in this drama. By building the foundations for such a structure, our generation will invest the work of the next era with purpose and significance.[2]

Further influential interpreters, whose views are at once devastating in their attack upon our inherited culture and utopian in their diverse approaches to the future, must be largely deferred. Some of these are not, of course, strictly philosophers: we are thinking not only of such a genius of architecture and urban *re*-creation as Frank Lloyd Wright or Buckminster Fuller, but of artists who range all the way from Thomas Mann in literature to Jose Orozco in painting, Gustav Vigeland in sculpture, and Edward Steichen in photography.

Only one further lively spokesman of the utopian mood, Herbert Marcuse, may be sampled for the impact he has made especially upon young radicals of several countries:

> Up to now, it has been one of the principal tenets of the critical theory of society . . . to refrain from what might be reasonably called utopian speculation. . . . I believe that this

[2] Mumford, *The Conduct of Life*, p. 240.

restrictive conception must be revised. . . . Utopian possibilities are inherent in the technical and technological forces of advanced capitalism and socialism: the rational utilization of these forces on a global scale would terminate poverty and scarcity within a very foreseeable future. But we know now that neither their rational use nor—and this is decisive—their collective control . . . would by itself eliminate domination and exploitation. . . . Freedom would become the environment of an organism which is no longer capable of adapting to the competitive performances required for well-being under domination. . . . Is such change in the "nature" of man conceivable? I believe so. . . . For the world of human freedom cannot be built by the established societies, no matter how much they may streamline and rationalize their dominion. . . . This "voluntary" servitude . . . can be broken only through . . . a radical transvaluation of values.[3]

THE CULTUROLOGICAL CONTEXT OF RECONSTRUCTIONISM: A PREINTERPRETATION

To view now the reconstructionist orientation of cultural transformation in context, we have seen how it relates to the historic course of utopian thinking, and how it differs also from utopianism of the past in that its emphasis upon cultural goals is accompanied by equal emphasis upon the means to be employed in achieving its designs.

Although concern with far-reaching purposes and aggressive strategies is grounded in the long history of influential philosophic movements, no single school of thought can be called the chief source of that influence. There are many such sources. Like other philosophies, moreover, reconstructionism must be evaluated finally by the extent to which its motivations and intentions are rooted in the culture. These motivations and intentions are at once strongly negative and strongly positive: negative, because they are generated by acute dissatisfaction with several prime facets of our age; positive, because they give rise to constructive, organized, and future-oriented plans for a culture the outlines of which are already beginning to crystallize.

The central critique of modern culture contends that, magnificent as their services have been in the past, the major institutions and corresponding social, economic, and other prac-

[3] Marcuse, *An Essay on Liberation*, pp. 3–6.

tices that developed during preceding centuries of the modern era are now incapable of confronting the terrifying, bewildering crisis of our age. Simultaneously, the transmissive, moderative, and restorative choices of belief represented in varying styles and degrees of expression by three alternative philosophies of education have likewise been found wanting. Meanwhile, the selected modern philosophic movements discussed briefly in previous parts (existentialism, analytic philosophy, neo-Freudianism, Zen Buddhism, and neo-Marxism) have responded to this crisis in multiple ways—some very deliberately and forthrightly, some obliquely or perhaps even unintentionally, but all contributing in various respects to the revolutionary compulsions that motivate the quest for an educational philosophy of cultural transformation. The need for a compass by which we can discover our lost bearings thus challenges the philosopher as he has been challenged only in previous periods of supreme crisis. He is under obligation, together with the physicist, economist, and all other scientists—bar none—to help build a rationally designed culture and to assume full responsibility for his discoveries.

Herein is the positive obligation of those in our culture. Not only are they philosophers and scientists but also artists, teachers, and just everyday citizens who find themselves responding to the beliefs most significant for reconstructionists. A large body of knowledge-achievement is already available and waiting to be used. Belief in the practicability of a planned, democratic world civilization is bolstered by rich experience in recent years. The untouched resources available for providing economic abundance, better health, better education, richer esthetic enjoyment, and for satisfying still other ubiquitous wants (such as respect for all races) are vastly greater than those drawn upon thus far. To estimate these resources accurately, as well as to plan for their release and equitable use through organized democratic machinery, becomes our chief opportunity.

Reconstructionists, in brief, seek both to determine what obstacles lie in the way of achievement of our objectives and to determine how *the largest possible majority of people* can find strength and intelligence to remove these obstacles. Above all, reconstructionists try to make certain that any design to be transformed, and any practices that may be implemented in building it, are rooted in defensible beliefs about reality, knowledge, and value. However gigantic this undertaking, they are convinced that Western civilization is at an end if man fails in them.

Accordingly, this philosophy of education, although like

various others an interpretation of and response to contemporary problems, differs in significant ways. While these alternative philosophies, too, are stirred by the deep troubles besetting our age, they analyze them differently and their prognoses are usually less fundamental or less far-reaching. Instead of remaining satisfied with gradual moderation and transition, or with fairly constant perpetuation and transmission, or with intellectualized and/or theologized restoration, the reconstructionist throws in his lot unequivocally with those who believe (as some have always come to believe in critical times) that only thoroughgoing transformation of principles and institutions is any longer possible or suitable. The philosopher of culture, Cassirer, epitomizes this attitude when he asserts that the:

> . . . great mission of the Utopia is to make room for the possible as opposed to a passive acquiescence in the present actual state of affairs. It is symbolic thought which overcomes the natural inertia of man and endows him with a new ability, the ability constantly to reshape his human universe.[4]

To conclude, reconstructionism takes its position with the historic philosophies of vision. But its vision emerges out of the tangible, tested experiences of both the past and the present. It rests squarely upon the contributions of the physical and behavioral sciences, the pure and applied arts, and education. For this reason and without any rationalizing equivocations, its adherents would defend themselves as ultimately more practical than those who, in the name of common sense or caution, delimit their theories to the point of sterility and similar ineffectiveness.

Let us then turn to our fourth and concluding interpretation of philosophies of education by considering reconstructionism in a sequence partially paralleling our first three interpretations. *Section 1* has begun to deal with philosophic beliefs in terms, respectively, of reality, knowledge, and value. *Section 2* deals with educational beliefs in terms, again respectively, of learning, the curriculum, and control. And *Section 3*, while conceding very severe divergences among patterns of educational philosophy, searches finally for culturological convergences.

[4] Cassirer, *An Essay on Man*, p. 62.

CHAPTER 15

Beliefs about reality

LIKE THE INCONSTANT CULTURE that nourishes it, reconstructionism seems at times unfinished, at other times uncertain of its own beliefs, and at still other times responsive to innovative forces—including the forces of ideas. In this respect it, too, may reveal eclectic tendencies even if the influences to which it responds are often quite deviant from those of, say, essentialism. In any case, turning to beliefs about reality, reconstructionism is by no means oblivious to elements in ontologies other than its own, including both essentialist and perennialist. Some of these common elements, though transfused by another orientation, may become evident as we proceed.

Meanwhile, one ontological source of influence appears so conspicuous that we must highlight it at once. This is, of course, the progressivist. Like the latter, from which it borrows much, reconstructionism agrees that "experience and nature" (recall the title of one of Dewey's greatest books) constitute both form and content of the universe. By "experience" is meant the vibrant stuff of life—"things and ideals," feeling and thought, the whole ebb and flow of personality, society, earth, sky. By "nature" is meant the world within reach of scientific experimentation and understanding, a world of disorder and order, of flux and stability, of strife and harmony.

It follows that the reconstructionist, too, is hostile toward other-worldly philosophies, certainly any metaphysics that tries to establish the primacy of any supposed realm of *super*nature over that of nature. Equally, he is hostile to objective systems of presumed universal order, whether realist, idealist, Thomist, or any other. From his point of view, nature (always an elusive concept) suggests an evolving reality in which humanity, although the most important manifestation of nature, is but one element in a dynamic infinitude—soil, water, mountains, stars, plants, animals.

Sharper concentration begins with the interpretation of cultural reality. Here, the typical views of progressivism are not entirely satisfactory because, as the most convincing exponent of our later liberal culture, it has devoted at least equal if not greater attention to the individual than to society. This is not to say that it ignores social factors of the human equation; its interest in the culture and in social dynamics is too great for that. Pragmatic philosophers such as Mead and Dewey have pioneered in interpreting selfhood and language as socially derived and socially directed. Indeed, whatever meaning the self possesses as reality is dependent upon the kind of environment—especially the group environment—within which it develops.

Thus the progressivist point of view is acknowledged for immense originality and relevance to the culture, especially of twentieth-century America. Yet is not the question plausible whether current progressivists have paid anything like sufficient attention to the reality of either self or society in the light of contemporary theory or practice? Too often, for example, they soft-pedal, even circumvent, the impact of cultural forces upon the individual; only rarely do we find them providing incisive analyses of class structures and cleavages or of the phenomena of mass behavior. Neither have they very often concerned themselves with determining what institutions of an economic or political nature should be built to meet the requirements of a cooperatively organized culture. At best, their characteristic treatments leave a cluster of unresolved tensions of the kind we have perceived between individuality and sociality.

The crucial questions to be raised about reality, then, are embraced by two large themes: (1) the cultural determinants of human experience; and (2) history as reality. It should be underscored that reconstructionists, too, approach cultural reality operationally. That is, the concepts utilized are organizing instruments to provide greater meaning to cultural experience—an approach thoroughly acceptable to progressivists. And let us reiterate that, in any case, our concern is not at all with being original, even if we could. Rather, our obligation is to highlight what progressivism has sometimes left shadowy because its attention has perhaps unduly concentrated upon the moderative value orientation with which, affectively as well as cognitively, they sympathize.

CULTURAL DETERMINANTS OF HUMAN EXPERIENCE

Concern for the cultural determinants of human experience proceeds from one of our most crucial assumptions about the nature of philosophy: it is the creation of man's effort to express his beliefs with utmost clarity about the environment of which he himself is part and which he himself fashions. The innumerable occasions when traditional philosophies have sought to deal with ontology, especially in the abstract fashion of metaphysics without reference to this man-made environment, have yielded misleading and often meaningless conclusions.

This is not to deny the importance of delineating the universal characteristics of reality. Without such delineation, not only would historic ontology become as totally obsolete as many philosophic analysts consider it to be; so, too, would epistemology and axiology. What we do deny is the adequacy of any branch of philosophy without consideration of the reality of culture that sustains them.

Anthropology has begun to offer strong support for cultural interpretations of philosophic belief. Such experts as Ruth Benedict, Edward Sapir, Paul Radin, Bronislaw Malinowski, Clyde Kluckhohn, and Alfred L. Kroeber have demonstrated how patterns of belief about the reality of the universe and of man are always present and always deeply ingrained in every culture, including nonliterate ones. These patterns exert subtle but persistent influence upon even the most casual events and attitudes. Recalling Benedict's seminal work, *Patterns of Culture,* certain American Indian cultures are characterized as "Dionysian" because their pattern is one of self-assertion and outreaching in a manner named for the god of wine; others are called "Apollonian" because the prevailing mood is one of calm and restraint after the manner of the god of healing; still others show "paranoid" tendencies—suspicion, treachery, tension, the will to power, obsessive rivalry, and so on. Radin has written brilliantly of the "primitive man as a philosopher." Sapir, Kluckhohn, and Kroeber have increased our knowledge of the "way of life" which they believe to be indigenous to every culture.

Thus, Sapir speaks of "deep-seated culture patterns" that ". . . are not so much known as felt, not so much capable of conscious description as of naïve practice. . . ." Moreover, ". . . the relations between the elements of experience which serve to give them their form and significance are more powerfully 'felt' or 'intuited' than consciously perceived."[1] Kluckhohn refines this conception by distinguishing between what he calls Pattern_1 and Pattern_2—the first referring to the conscious level of cultural structure, the second to the more abstract, often covert, level of belief. The term Kluckhohn prefers for characterizing Pattern_2 is "configuration." Speaking of the Navaho Indians, he points out that ". . . many distinctively Navaho doings and sayings make sense only if they are related to certain implicit convictions about the nature of human life and experience."[2] That these convictions are axiological and epistemological as well as ontological is to be expected; they support our view that no adequate formulation of the philosophic beliefs of any culture, including our own, is possible without considering all three aspects.

In this chapter, accordingly, we are concerned not so much with nonhuman aspects of nature and the universe as with ontological beliefs that focus upon the political, economic, social, moral, and other human experiences. All beliefs about reality ultimately reveal a cultural context (although a context much less apparent at some times than at others), but we confine our discussion to *those beliefs most germane to our interest.* Moreover, the ontological beliefs to be considered have been selected for special consideration because they have been insufficiently considered by other philosophies of education. Indeed, they are often so covert and implicit that they suggest again Kluckhohn's meaning of configuration.

GROUP CONFLICTS

The history of man is a history of conflict. Indeed, periods of peace have been much briefer and more exceptional than periods of bloody strife. Few have been the moments in history of which it has been possible to say that war on either a small or a large scale was not being fought somewhere on the globe. Nor can we say that civilization has improved in its capacity to solve its problems peacefully. On the contrary, the twentieth century has

[1] Sapir, in Mandelbaum (ed.), in *Selected Writings in Language, Culture, and Personality,* pp. 548f.

[2] Kluckhohn, in Spier, Hallowell, and Newman (eds.), *Language, Culture, and Personality,* pp. 114, 126; Northrop (ed.), *Ideological Differences and World Order,* p. 359.

experienced a second "Thirty Years' War"—a series of conflicts with intermissions of uneasy "peace" which, from the beginning of World War I to the end of World War II and well beyond, spread fury and destruction across much of the earth.

The causes of war have been scrutinized by political scientists and historians for hundreds of years; yet they have reached no explanation upon which all experts agree. The immediate negative cause is clear, however: the unwillingness of nations to resolve their conflicting interests through calm, intelligent discussion and conference.

What are these conflicting interests? Here we find ourselves caught in a tangle of factors: national pride and patriotism, religious friction, political and military ambition—all have played some part in fomenting wars. Certainly, clashes of economic interest are also a major causative factor. Many wars have resulted from the grim determination of some nation to acquire more material resources as prerequisites of power—more land, more harbors, more oil, more coal, more laborers—and from the equal determination of other nations to prevent such conquests from happening. Let us grant the importance of other factors. Yet, when economic interests become more powerful than the interests of peace, and when they overwhelm the deliberations of the council table, sooner or later right is strangled by might.

But violent conflicts also explode within the boundaries of nations. Civil war, a violent means of resolving group differences, may occur when all mediation fails. The American Civil War is one of history's most tragic examples; the wars in Spain, China, Korea, and Vietnam are among the most recent. In all these conflicts, causal factors were complex. American slavery was both a moral and an economic issue. In Spain, political and economic issues were complicated by the antidemocratic power of clerical authority. In Asia, South America, and Africa an oppressive neofeudalism had offered fertile ground for communism with conflict the inevitable outcome.

Other types of group conflict vary in intensity, from very sharp and violent processes to extremely diffuse and covert ones. An example is racial hostility—sometimes it virtually coincides with conflict between nations, but more often it operates within a single country. Every American knows something of the antagonism between Negroes and whites in America, with its notorious history of hatred, prejudice, lynching, "Jim Crowism," segregation, and exploitation. Indeed "white racism" and "black power" have become symbols of the "Negro revolution." Less familiar to Americans is the virulence of inter- and intraracial tension elsewhere in the world: the caste system of India with its millions of "untouchables"; the use of Shintoism in prewar Japan to support military aggression; the spurious but nonetheless devastating belief in "Aryanism" promulgated by Nazi Germany.

Antagonism may also arise between ethnic or religious groups. This is manifested not only on an international scale, but also in the tensions between foreign-born communities of a single city, or between Catholics and Protestants as in Northern Ireland. Still another type of conflict that can be described as neither racial nor nationalistic, but which is widespread and virulent in many countries, is that between Jewish and gentile groups.

Since the economic factor in conflict and in other cultural experience has already been touched upon and will be mentioned frequently in subsequent pages, it is important to clarify the reconstructionist position. Economic rivalry, for example, is not regarded as *the* cause of group conflict, but often it is a powerful condition. The distinction is clarified by a simple analogy: water is *necessary* to sustain human life but it is not *sufficient* to sustain it.

One of the commonest types of socioeconomic conflict, at any rate, is manifested intranationally. Just as with economic aspects of international wars, so economic conditions frequently play a more or less hidden role in racial or religious differences. For example, much of the antagonism of whites toward the Negro has its roots in the agrarian pattern of the South—a pattern that still survives among ill-paid, ignorant, and easily exploitable labor. Comparably, the phenomenon of black nationalism can be attributed, at least in substantial part, to counterhostility and solidarity on the part of Negroes who bitterly resent discriminations from which they have suffered so long. Nor should we overlook the antagonism expressed toward the Jew (that is, in the form of anti-Semitism) which so often is traceable to the frustrations of groups seeking scapegoats on whom to place the blame for their own economic troubles and failures.

The socioeconomic factor, at times, may operate still more subtly. Veblen was one of the first perceptive diagnosticians of the curious behavior frequently exhibited by upper classes in order to reassure their superior status. His famous ironic phrase, "conspicuous consumption," refers to the means taken by persons of these classes to convince themselves and others of their enviable success and dignity: the kinds of houses they build, the clubs they belong to, the clothes and ornaments with which they adorn themselves—all are symbols of position.

At other times and in other places, the operation of economic factors has been perfectly apparent. Conflict between laboring and owning groups has resulted in strikes, lockouts, formation of pressure groups, and legislative contests. There can be little doubt that important improvements in working conditions could not have occurred without strong, persistent effort by organized labor against other groups that have tried just as strongly, unitedly, and persistently to prevent such improvement.

Overlapping these and other examples, yet not identical with them, are numerous other symptoms of conflict in contemporary culture that invite rough analogy with common types of mental illness in the individual. A number of such symptoms have previously been noted in Chapter 2, so that it should be enough only to recall the hypothesis that our culture is suffering from "schizoid" tendencies. They are tendencies toward divisions so acute as to prevent mutual understanding or reconciliation between those of rigidly opposing attitudes or opposing courses of action.

Let us confine ourselves to two generalizations about group conflict. First, this conflict occurs on the level of experience and nature in which we are especially interested—namely, cultural reality. Second, "conflict" is an operational term connoting cultural oppositions ranging from overt violence and war, at one extreme, to religious, economic-political, and covert struggles (including inter- and intrapersonal conflicts) at the other extreme.

GROUP ALLEGIANCES

The problem of group allegiances is so closely related to that of group conflicts that it would be difficult to say whether, in a given situation, it is the conflict that produces the allegiance, or vice versa.

Certainly, evidence is only too abundant to prove that the outbreak of war can galvanize the spirit of patriotism and nationalism more quickly than can any other occurrence. The history of both world wars illustrates the capacity of the American people, for example, to rally to a common task in the face of a common enemy.

The power of war to produce group allegiance also carries over into times of peace. Oppositions between ethnic and nationality groups within the United States is often traceable to earlier hostilities between their native lands, the memories of which serve to array them against one another even after they become American citizens. The intensity of this type of loyalty may, however, diminish after a generation or two.

More persistent manifestations of the relationship of group conflict and group allegiance occur in the sphere of racial interaction. Indeed, some social scientists employ the term "caste" to interpret further the sharp division of, especially, the black and white races. But caste subdivisions may likewise occur *within* either race in turn, according to differing statuses between higher and lower levels of economic or other cultural disparities.

The Jewish minority provides a graphic illustration of strong allegiance, both as a whole ethnic minority and as a group containing its own subdivided levels. Of primary interest, however, are the cohesive intragroup loyalties that have developed in great measure from the centuries of persecution suffered at the hands of others. Jews have often been forced to live in ghettos, have frequently been denied equal voice in economic, social, and educational matters, and have suffered torture or even mass murder. No wonder that they have tended to band together for self-protection and allegiance, or that Israel has become for many Jews the haven of communal devotion and pride.

But oppression alone cannot account for Jewish solidarity; religious and cultural factors have also contributed. Therefore, no one can say how much of the group allegiance present among Jews is due to attachment to ancient customs and values, how much to external hostility and persecution. That the latter are basic factors, however—producing on occasion a reflex of aggressiveness—is indisputable.

At any rate, we may assume that if, at the root of group conflicts, economic motivations frequently operate either directly or indirectly, we should expect them to be at work in group allegiances as well. If Negroes sometimes try to build their own nativist or tribal circles of group life, or if they have sometimes reacted to white racism with counterexpressions of black racism, this is surely understandable in view of the grim record of low wages and shameful living conditions to which they have been subjected. If Jews, too, sometimes build their own circles, this is partially due to the fact that this group has been made a scapegoat for the economic failures and fears of other groups.

The role of economic factors in crystallizing and bolstering group allegiances in an industrial nation has been most constant, however, in relations between the upper, owning, managerial stratum and the lower, working stratum. The graphic extent to which the former often establishes and subscribes to patterns of leisure-class conduct is revealed by the shock and distaste with which they may view a "traitor" to their class who dares to repudiate their cherished values. The latter stratum, too—especially trade unionists—sometimes develops its own loyalties, as is indicated by the term "brother" in unions and the term "comrade" in some of the more radical labor parties. Indeed, although the labor movement has lost a good deal of its older militancy not only in America but even in European countries where its radical roots are deeper, union members still often deeply resent any one who becomes a "renegade" or "fink" by openly siding against them in a strike or other labor-management dispute.

The allegiance of groups is, in short, so powerful a factor in cultural reality that, like patterns of group conflict, it often seems to hamper efforts at conciliation. Many groups insist that they alone should be the arbiters of standards for all others. For them, the solution of group conflict is the dubious one of compelling others, by force if necessary, to embrace their own standards. "Ethnocentrism" is a familiar term to describe the phenomenon of self-centered allegiance within a culture or a subculture.

Yet, in our view, no single explanation of allegiances, such as the economic one, is sufficient. Thus the term, ethnocentrism, must be understood also to express the sheer *stubbornness* of group behavior—what the following chapter terms its "unrational" quality. A group's attachment to certain customs and modes may endure so long after the need that called them into being has passed that it is no longer able to offer rational justification or historic explanation for them.

The psychological and cultural bases of allegiance should also be stressed. Anthropologists as well as biologists have produced abundant evidence to question the common belief that man and other animals are chiefly predatory and competitive. On the contrary, cooperation and mutuality are found to be at least as common as competition and, in the judgment of some scientists, even more common. The issue remains controversial, however. For the "naked ape" is himself a controversial creature of nature and culture.

GROUP CONDITIONERS

Implicit thus far are two important theories that have influenced, in rather different ways, essentialism and other philosophies of education. One is behaviorism; the other, evolutionism.

The reconstructionist may be called a cultural behaviorist (we have earlier employed the term, sociological realist, also) because he believes that groups are conditioned to behave as they do by the cultural influences at work upon them. The social characteristics that we attribute to Jews or to Negroes, for example, are in no sense inherent; they are the product of actions by the cultures or subcultures within which groups develop. Accordingly, much of the behavior of individuals within the group is also best explained in terms of culture—a fact which more orthodox behaviorists, because their psychology has often stressed the conditioning process of the individual, have tended far too much to neglect.

The reconstructionist may also be called a cultural evolutionist. Since he is peculiarly interested in the struggle between groups, he asks in what sense it is possible to say that the fittest groups survive that struggle. But he makes the same observation of the traditional evolutionist (in this case, the "social Darwinist") that he makes of the traditional behaviorist: both have concentrated too much upon the figure of the individual in his alleged struggle for survival of the fittest, neglecting corresponding struggles of groups. The reconstructionist, rather, accepts the familiar view of social scientists that individuals who do not succeed in our culture are not necessarily weaklings; many a brilliant or strong member of the black race, for one, has failed through no fault of his own but rather because of the weakness of the group to which he is restricted. To argue otherwise is to agree with laissez-faire doctrine, which regards evolution as a struggle between individuals in which the most enterprising ones survive.

The conditioners of group behavior have not, however, been sufficiently considered until one other question is faced: What are the conditions that operate most influentially upon groups in our own culture? It is not enough, in other words, to speak in general terms of the reality of group conflict or group allegiance; nor is it enough even to indicate that economic factors are frequently more powerful as conditioners than other factors. If reconstructionism is to hold to its temporal purposes, if its deepest concern is with plans for the future that aim to correct failures and eliminate dangers of the past and present, then it must first confront the realities shaping and directing group experience during the hazardous period of history through which we are racing.

The key to these realities is a belief to which we have given preliminary attention but to which further attention is demanded: that mankind stands at a perilous juncture—that is, between two vast constellations of forces: those dedicated to worldwide tyranny and those dedicated to worldwide liberation. A corollary is the belief that the direction civilization chooses to take will depend upon whether the power structure of private and minority control is retained or is superseded by reorganized socioeconomic patterns of democratic control.

The complexity of the domestic and world situations can scarcely be overestimated. By no means have we arrived at a completely satisfactory interpretation of the causes of World War II or its turbulent aftermaths. German, Italian, and Japanese fascism was a many-headed monster in which economic motivations were mixed with psychopathic elements, racial superstitions, and a host of other factors. Indeed, World War II has been called a war whose causes are so confused as to suggest that it was itself a terrible demonstration of the "schizophrenia" of our age. Nevertheless, one hypothesis deserving careful examination is that the genesis of World War II can be found in the efforts of several highly industrialized but unstable fascist nations to bolster their tottering systems by gaining control of strategic world markets and territories by the most desperate and dictatorial means. Other, stronger nations were not prepared to let them do so. The result was war between two powerful sets of national forces, both controlled by dominant minorities.

Should a third conflagration be fired, its pervasive causes and objectives, however complex, could prove to be far more similar to than different from those of World War II. As the earth spins toward the twenty-first century, the opposing camps of communism on the one side, and Western capitalist nations under American leadership on the other side, could only too easily burst into flame. Such a war might have the character of another violent struggle between two sets of forces which, however unlike otherwise, could both prove to be less concerned with increasing authority and fulfillment by the vast majority than with maintaining their own entrenched power.

No wonder, in the face of such explosive possibilities, that the conditioners of racial, ethnic, religious, and other cultural groups serve both to settle and to unsettle their traditional positions. As oppositions are generated by competition, by insecurity, by war itself, we can observe the sharpening of hostilities and loyalties. Yet these very instabilities may invite entire groups to relinquish their former allegiances for new allegiances more harmonious with new hopes and new allies. American black citizens are, once more, illustrative of this process. Often they are divided in their political affiliations, some still supporting the conservative Republican party out of traditional loyalty to its original antislavery stand; others, supporting liberal or radical parties and movements. The point of view of a Booker T. Washington, who held, in general, that the best way for the people of his race to get along was to adjust themselves amiably to the white man's economic and social pattern, is still held by many Negroes. But other great black leaders such as W. E. B. Dubois, Malcolm X, Martin Luther King, and their successors have convinced increasing numbers of their fellows that the only hope of achieving full citizenship is through their own militant struggles.

The unsettling effect of contemporary conditions upon group status is likewise conspicuous in the huge, shifting, diffused mass loosely called "the middle class." Here are to be found large numbers of students, farmers, small businessmen, and professionals who hold a stake in the inherited order, yet who are victimized by instabilities, frustrations, and by what Marcuse calls " 'voluntary' servitude." Some sections of this class gain enough to move toward affiliation with dominant power groups. Many more, mainly proprietors of small businesses, gravitate toward the status of wage earner (the owner of a small independent shop may become a clerk behind the counter of a great chain store). But millions of members of the middle class, the white-collar groups who are neither strictly workers nor owners but an unstable hybrid, live in a state of precarious tension and confusion.

The emergence of a cross-national "student power" movement is one graphic demonstration of how large minorities of middle-class, fairly affluent, young adults of different races can function as deviant and at times even as revolutionary opponents of the political, economic, and educational establishment. This situation contains both promise and danger. It is promising if their energies can be directed in time—directed toward new democratic, genuinely international purposes. It is dangerous if youthful, middle-class alienations are capitalized upon by the demagogue, the "image maker," and other shrewd manipulators of public opinion in order to produce false enthusiasms and spurious loyalties that may quite conceivably lead to chaos both within and between nations.

A great deal of substance could, of course, bolster our sketchy comments about the reality of group conditioners. For example, many research studies try to elaborate upon the generalization that these conditioners are a plurality, among which economic conditions are an essential though far from exclusive influence. Other studies demonstrate that groups may be defined in several ways—as classes (in which economic power or its lack is primary); as social status groups (in which prestige or its absence is primary); as more or less homogeneous groups sharing certain behavior traits (in which character or personality type is the determining factor). But behavioral scientists have not, as yet, adequately considered the relationships among these ways of viewing group experience. For example, the class to which one belongs may or may not correspond with one's status group (the teacher's economic class position is usually lower than his prestige level; that of the real estate broker may be considerably higher). Still, consideration of all these and other organizing influences on group life is helpful to our core contention: a complex of forces conditions the perception of cultural reality by groups, and these forces have produced a state of acute disequilibrium.

"MORAL MAN AND IMMORAL SOCIETY"

The realities of modern group experience are not always pleasant to contemplate; perhaps it is partly for this reason that, despite his obligation to examine every sort of belief, the philosopher of education often avoids them. That group behavior may become immoral in the sense that the group often acts solely in its own interest, regardless of how cruel the effect on other groups may be, is proved by the facts of war. Moreover, the evidence of tragic happenings such as mob violence proves that groups may become impossible to control when intoxicated by passions and hatreds.

Such phenomena indicate the need to distinguish between the behavior of individuals and that of groups. Although some individuals, too, act immorally and violently, others are able to exercise moral judgment and to restrain their impulses. At least they have learned the rules of morality and conciliation, even if they do not always follow them. And so they have developed ways of intelligent control by which they are able to master problems involving their individual thinking and conduct.

Groups, however, are less likely to exercise such restraint. Not only may they act immorally and violently; they demonstrate by their habits, conflicts, and stubborn allegiances that dispassionate methods of dealing with acute junctures of national interest and class status are often forgotten or rejected.

At times, a curious contradiction may thus arise between the behavior of a group and its individual members. Individuals wish to behave, and perhaps do behave, rationally and morally in specific situations. However, because they are members of a group that may behave differently, they find themselves swept along by forces greater than themselves. To cite an example, the individual businessman may sincerely want his employees to enjoy the highest standard of living. Yet, as the head of a firm, he may be forced to dismiss workers and bring about suffering because a decline of the market has led to a situation in which curtailment of production seems inevitable.

The individual may react to such situations of contradiction in one of several ways. He may attempt to develop a rationale of self-sufficiency in the absence of any group pattern within which he securely belongs. (Here, indeed, is probably one reason for the recent rise of existentialism, either as a more or less distinct philosophic movement or as an elusive mood that yet may influence other orientations such as the perennialist or essentialist.) Or he may revolt against the group pattern to which he has been accustomed and, for his peace of mind, devote his energies to changing social conditions that produced the contradiction. (Engels and Owen provide famous historic models.) Or the individual may seek to justify the role that his group plays—a process that often explains why the most revealing approach to an individual is by way of the group with which he is aligned. Or, finally, he may simply continue to suffer, consciously or not, from the contradictions between group compulsions and his own beliefs. This reaction, far more common than most of us have wished to admit, is an important clue to the overabundance of neurotic personalities in our time. (Apt indeed is the title of L. K. Frank's *Society as the Patient.*)

Such effects upon the individual, however, anticipate later discussions of knowledge and value, so let us return to the central point. Because the behavior of groups by no means always corresponds to that which might be expected of its individual members, any philosophy that hopes to cope with the acute problems of our culture will fail unless it first diagnoses group behavior as objectively as possible and considers its diagnosis in a total view of reality. Here is a main thesis of Reinhold Niebuhr's *Moral Man and Immoral Society*, from which much of his subsequent work has proliferated. But the extreme theory that groups are merely herdlike and that group behavior is necessarily similar to that of mobs and crowds is open to sharp question. The reconstructionist position is, rather, that groups must be confronted for what they are: that they are beset by conflicts, solidified by allegiances, and conditioned by powerful forces is a pervasive reality of culture; but that they should either be condemned cynically or accepted for their behavior patterns is by no means a foregone conclusion. Rather, through patient diagnosis, the aim is to build a strategy and program that will help to correct the weaknesses of groups, heighten their morality, and release their creative potentialities in behalf of themselves and their individual members.

HISTORY AS REALITY

A principal feature of ontological theory here being considered very selectively is the premise that all philosophies, including reconstructionism itself, are expressions of historic and therefore temporal periods. This is true even when, as in perennialism, the significance of such periods is reduced to principles held to be nontemporal. History, in short, is basic to anthropological philosophy.

Other theories have, of course, emphasized the reality of history. In the spiritual interpretation of history (for example, that of Hegel and other thinkers of essentialist preference), it is held that stages in man's progress have been manifestations of divine will and divine purpose. Again, as mentioned in Chapter 8, the famous theory of Oswald Spengler, although radically different from the spiritual one, tries to show that the pattern of all history is one of cyclical epochs of rise and decline repeating themselves eternally.

Of the most influential contemporary philosophies of education, progressivism might be expected to be most congenial to reconstructionism. With Dewey and others, agreement would converge toward belief that: (1) men become what they are largely because of characteristics of the historic period in which they live; (2) every such period emerges from preceding periods and leads into later ones in such a way as to be influenced by the former and to influence the latter; (3) no metaphysical design determines the stages of history; rather, man hammers out his own history, however awkwardly and blindly; and (4) history has no ingrained purpose, no preordained goal, for the course it takes and the goals it attains depend upon human choices, failures, and successes.

Nevertheless, just as the reconstructionist's accent in areas of group experience is somewhat different from the typical progressivist's, so his foci of interest in the area of history may be different also. We turn to them now.

SOCIAL STRUGGLE IN HISTORY

Group conflicts, it was noted earlier, pervade relations between nations as well as relations between racial, religious, and socioeconomic groups within nations. We only add that such conflicts, of varying degrees of intensity, have been common throughout recorded history. Religious struggle, for example, marked many centuries of European history. The accounts of civil struggles, large and small—between slaves and freemen, vassals and lords, aristocrats and bourgeoisie, workers and owners—appear on almost every page of history.

Innumerable historians have, of course, dealt with the fact of struggle, but they have done so in terms of varying hypotheses. Here, we offer only one example, although one of the most controversial and encyclopedic—that of Toynbee. His hypothesis, influenced directly or indirectly by Hegel and Marx, among others, is that all great cultures undergo "times of trouble" when old cultural patterns are threatened by new ones. Breakdowns, followed by periods of dissolution and disintegration, are the result. The key to such crises is the failure of an originally creative minority to remain creative; instead it becomes a merely dominant minority, sterile and imitative. This situation generates dissension and eventual repudiation by the majority, who earlier had been followers and admirers. In turn, rebels produce a new creative minority, which in time degenerates; thus the whole course of cultural history is a series of challenges and responses to challenge. Toynbee believes that our own civilization is now in the throes of a crisis such as those that have already destroyed more than twenty other civilizations, and that a resurgent religious spirit is our only remaining hope of avoiding the same fate. It is unnecessary to accept his diagnosis and prognosis, however, in order to be immensely impressed by the tough-mindedness of much of his interpretation and especially by his insistence that the history of cultures is one of recurrent conflict.

Toynbee would also hold that, just as historic struggles may generate new cultural arrangements, so short periods of relative quiescence often emerge—only to be followed by other struggles for power between new alignments of forces. Thus the age-long turmoil preceding the Renaissance and the emergence of modern European civilization resulted in victory for the mercantile and early capitalist groups over feudal lords and theocratic rulers. A period of geographical discovery and technological progress then occurred that was marked by unprecedented intellectual, esthetic, and economic vitality. But this new alignment of forces was temporary; fresh conflicts arose between the elements that had risen to power and those that were still submerged. For well over three centuries, that struggle has continued at enormous cost in suffering and waste, yet not without great achievements in the way of material invention and convenience, improved working conditions, widespread education, and great expectations.

If, then, we hope to understand our own culture we must view it in the perspective of history. Still more graphically, it is our thesis (by no means unique, of course) that we stand at a juncture in the struggle for dominance that has waxed and waned before and since the Renaissance. We stand, as was suggested earlier, between two tremendous, world-wide constellations of opposing forces.

Included in *the first constellation of forces* are those groups that strive to maintain and strengthen the inherited structure. They are, first, those whose business it is to invest money for profit; second, the increasingly important managerial class that directs the technological apparatus; third, military castes (such as that of fascist Spain) which, leagued with semifeudal lords, theocrats, capitalists, and managers, have protected their joint interest in maintaining hierarchical control of commerce and agriculture; fourth, the agencies molding public opinion—newspapers, radio and television, motion pictures, advertising, and schools, all of which are often (though by no means always) allied with the established order; and fifth, a number of miscellaneous groupings such as small businessmen whose interests are not always in harmony with those of the others, and who thus sometimes belong to the second constellation to be considered.

The modern economic system, to the preservation and reinforcement of which such groups are frequently dedicated, has undergone numerous modifications both in magnitude and complexity. Whereas in its early stages it was characterized by competition between genuinely separate businesses, it has within a century developed more and more into a gigantic system of business combinations—corporations, monopolies, and cartels—that control the production and large shares of all commodities. Competition has been sharply reduced, especially because holding companies and trade agreements prevent many nominally independent corporations from being truly autonomous. Such corporations may be enmeshed in systems of interlocking directorates which frequently fix prices, curtail production, and otherwise set the tempo of the economy.

Corporate and monopoly capitalism does not represent the final evaluation of the system, however. In recent years, state capitalism has been emerging in a form revealing the governmental machine as full-fledged partner. Economists may differ as to the extent to which the system of the Soviet Union is a form of state capitalism. Few, however, would have trouble in disagreeing that the economy of the United States is both at a stage much closer to corporate than to competitive capitalism and is also manifesting increasingly strong symptoms of state capitalism. Recall, as one example, the granting of fabulously large, government-approved loans to underdeveloped countries in order to permit not only expansion of their technologies but the substantial profit of corporate American investors. Official explanations, to be sure, are rarely as blunt as this; often the rhetoric is in behalf of the "free world" and American magnanimity. Actually, the growth of state capitalism with political and military support in many parts of the world is vast.

This sketch of the constellation of forces dedicated to preserving and strengthening the established power structure is not intended to convey more than one principal contention—that it is a primary demonstration of social struggle in modern history. If, as we have said, the violent destruction of two world wars has been the most awful consequence of the existence of this constellation of forces, we should not overlook war's aftermath of uprooted and starving millions and a succession of civil disorders. Nor should we forget the fact that neither world war has solved any fundamental problems. The struggle among nations proceeds apace. Despite marked improvement, colonial territories are still subjected to foreign domination. The United States has lost much of its earlier charisma with oppressed peoples of other parts of the world who once regarded it as the great protagonist of democratic advancement. Moreover, its own minority groups continue to suffer under the disabilities imposed by discrimination and prejudice, while dissenting groups are intermittently threatened with varying degrees of intimidation and restriction.

The second constellation of forces can no more be characterized fully in any one statement than can the first. It consists of the great factory and agricultural working groups of the industrial nations, whether or not they are organized politically and economically for self-protection and advancement. It includes some rank-and-file members of the military forces. It includes equally unmeasured numbers of professional workers (doctors, lawyers, engineers, teachers, preachers, journalists, novelists and other artists) together with middle-class clusters of small business people and students. Most importantly, it includes countless human beings in such underdeveloped countries as India, Africa, and dozens of small "backward" countries (sometimes known as the "third force") where they are only beginning to measure the strength of their voice and their will.

These groups, obviously, are far from united. Many of them are disturbed internally by jurisdictional disputes and sectarian wrangling. The consequence is that those of the second constellation are more divided than are their opponents of the first constellation, who, while they, too, sometimes fail to present a solid front, are more adept at joining hands in the face of common threats. Nevertheless, these still disunified forces of expansion also seek a common basis on which to struggle for the realization of their hopes. They fear that control of the new atomic weapons by political and military forces of the first constellation may lead to a third war which will destroy most of civilization. Above all, some are beginning to perceive the emerging outlines of a new world culture which, they believe, can eliminate such dangers and bring abundance and peace to the peoples of the earth. It is the promise of such a future that provides much of the incentive behind the struggles in which they are now engaged.

CONTRACTION AND EXPANSION OF FREEDOM IN HISTORY

Struggle as a factor in the interpretation of history should be supplemented by another principle—that of the contraction and expansion of freedom.

The inadequacy of any interpretation based solely on the principle of struggle is twofold. For one thing, it may overformalize history by explaining every event in terms of an unceasing contest between two sets of opposing forces. However prevalent struggle may be, there are times of equilibrium and harmony, and there are other times when multiple sets of forces seem to impinge upon one another. The principle must then be employed cautiously, operationally, in clarifying otherwise inexplicable events—not as an explanation that can be neatly superimposed upon history. For another thing, the principle of struggle is insufficient in that it does not supply an answer to the question: Why do groups struggle? One answer—that they struggle primarily because of economic motivations—is clarifying as far as it goes. But it should be supplemented further even though we cannot hope to exhaust so perturbing a question.

It is at this point that the conception of history as freedom is fruitful. The struggles of man may be viewed as the relentless effort to win a greater expansion of that priceless value than he has hitherto enjoyed. This effort, directed against inanimate nature, has resulted in the development of controls over floods and scourges, in scientific discoveries, inventions, and even higher living standards for some people. But it has also been directed against groups that have exercised their power to delimit the freedom of others in order to possess presumably richer freedom for themselves. Sometimes those who are thus delimited succeed in improving their status; sometimes they fail so miserably that even the margin of freedom they temporarily enjoyed has been forfeited.

The history of freedom is not, then, a one-way development, a record of slow and steady gains. Freedom is constantly changing in texture and form as it evolves through time. If, in the long pull of history, the scope of freedom has slowly expanded, these expansions have frequently intervened with periods of contraction.

This general principle is well supported by evidence. The Revolution of 1688 in England widened the scope of freedom for the rising middle classes who were grappling for the power that would assure control over the infant industrialism. The American Revolution established a new system and new privileges for those who had found aristocratic and theocratic authority too stifling in the brisk climate of the New World. The American Civil War increased freedom for some American Negroes. The Spanish Civil War decreased freedom for the great majority of citizens. Latin American revolutions, too, have been followed by a whole series of militaristic regimes. By far the biggest revolutions of our century, the Russian and Chinese, followed centuries of contraction of freedom; yet their ideals and those of smaller allied countries have been distorted by conspicuous contractions often amounting to dictatorial ruthlessness. The question of whether human freedom in these great nations will yet expand widely as the century draws closer to its end remains fearfully uncertain.

The principle of changing dimensions of freedom may be helpful, not only in observing the march of civilization as a whole, but also in developing insight toward historical events in such diverse fields as literature and anthropology. The work of great American writers, from statesmen such as Thomas Jefferson to humorists such as Mark Twain, have sought to interpret the expansion of contraction of popular freedom in their own styles. The research studies of some anthropologists, such as Malinowski, reveal comparable processes at work in both nonliterate and literate cultures. Marcuse, whose guiding theme may be termed "liberation," speaks of the "biological" foundations of human nature in terms of "a new sensibility" to the "good conscience of being human, tender, sensuous," which, in Nietzsche's words, is ". . . no longer being ashamed of ourselves."[3]

The expansion and contraction of freedom in history becomes still more pertinent when we resurvey the present century. On the one side, world forces of contraction are clustered in centers of power. These are forces which not only strive to curtail the growth of democratic institutions but, when driven desperately, resort to dictatorship, anti-Semitic persecution, military aggression, and destruction of civil liberties. Not, of course, that beneficiaries of the inherited order have always stood merely for contraction of freedom. Despite the severe limitations often imposed on rights of the ordinary man, they have, at other times, released reservoirs of fresh industrial energy, especially in the youthful period of modern industrialism. Many have sincerely believed that expansion of freedom is best achieved through the free enterprise system. The Republican party in America has symbolized this kind of sincerity, although within it powerful groups have also been callously concerned to strengthen their own corporate power with, at most, token respect for any kind of freedom except that which benefits their own interests in the long run.

On the other side, expansion of freedom is helped by growing power of the second constellation of forces. These groups, which would widen freedom to embrace all the peoples of the earth, work for programs guaranteeing equality to Negroes and other minority races everywhere, equal participation of all groups (including women) in determining political and economic policies, equal access to the resources of earth and industry, recreation facilities, art, and education. These are typical objectives in the quest for freedom in our time to which the second constellation of forces is now all too slowly learning to commit its energies.

THE CONCEPT OF "ORGANISM"

Still another principle of history as reality helps us to understand that desirable cultural objectives, such as those we have just stated, suggest social arrangements that constitute an organic whole. To state the point differently, it is not enough to commit ourselves to a series of goals that may be separately listed—1, 2, 3—and then left standing in isolation from each other; they need to become interrelated and mutually supportive. Hence it is appropriate at this stage to ask whether history affords any basis for the

[3] Marcuse, *An Essay on Liberation*, p. 21.

expectation of a future possessing organic unity or, if we wish, *a holistic pattern of culture.*

If by "organism" is meant literally what the biologist means —a unity of interdependent, harmoniously functioning cells in which the life of each is integral with the life of all—then the analogy between living things and society is false. Many philosophers and sociologists of evolutionist learnings have argued for such an analogy, to be sure, but today it is seldom defended except with severe qualifications. Society is not actually an organism, as can be seen merely by the fact that often its components do not cohere or cooperate at all.

Nevertheless, history does reveal certain examples of cultural unity in which the organic principle is involved. Some interpreters —perennialists, especially—may consider European culture in the Middle Ages to have been such a unity. Smaller wholes within a culture, such as the Roman Catholic Church or an army, have also been likened to organisms.

In the history of political thought, the organic principle has been used as a conceptual device. It was employed in Germany by such philosophers as Hegel, and in France by perhaps the greatest of all social organicists, Rousseau. His *The Social Contract* is an attempt to show how, in the good society, each person may lose his status as an individual only to regain it by becoming identified with the whole sovereign people. The organic concept in ontology is most brilliantly developed in twentieth-century philosophy by Whitehead, although the extent to which he applies it to history is not altogether apparent.

If the usefulness of the organic is strictly limited, it is also helpful in the interpretation of modern events. We have observed how the struggles of nations, classes, races, and even religions can split modern cultures asunder. We have observed, too, how these struggles may encourage ethnocentric allegiances to groups as well as hostility between subcultures, classes, races, and nations. Yet it is a fact of equally profound concern that, in our own time, organic forms of culture are beginning to supplant earlier, more fragmented cultures. Whole nations have constructed new political and economic designs in which every unit is joined with all others and guided by interlocking purposes.

These partially, or primarily, totalitarian designs are not, to be sure, of a sort that reconstructionists wish for America or for the world. But the fact of their existence and their importance cannot be denied.

Nor can promising foretokens of more democratic, organic

forms be overlooked. The Scandinavian region (perhaps most conspicuously, Denmark) has moved farther in developing these forms than any other among non-Communist regions. But even in such traditionally pluralistic nations as Great Britain, the Labor party has encouraged nationalization of natural resources, basic industries, public utilities, transportation, social services—has, in short, endorsed a program in which the disparateness of traditional English capitalism is not only increasingly superseded but is supported at various points by conservative parties. In the United States, the New Deal introduced unprecedented federal controls in the belief that political units such as countries, cities, or even states could no longer cope with nationwide problems. Some innovations of the New Deal (social security, perhaps most notably) have become widely accepted as responsibilities to the welfare of the individual and society, although such issues as federal versus state authority continue to trouble successive administrations.

These trends may still be denounced as dangerously totalitarian. And some of them are. Reconstructionist-minded theorists take the position, nevertheless, that understanding and support of the organic principle has become both necessary and desirable. It is *necessary* because the integrative effect of technological revolutions in industry, communications, and transportation cannot be disregarded; thus, to return to the more cumbersome, wasteful, piecemeal methods of an individualized, agrarian society is impossible. It is also *desirable*: for the first time, mankind may learn to produce abundance, leisure, and meaningful human freedom on a worldwide scale. Moreover, the organic principle, if interpreted in relationship to the forces of expansion, helps to satisfy the individual's need to belong to a *whole* in which he can find a rewarding role. Thus he can attain, *as an individual*, something of the profound sense of worth and satisfaction that Rousseau long ago saw to be salutary for the members of any social organism grown to maturity. To reinterpret and concretize the paradox of organism-individualism becomes, for many thinkers of our time (Marcuse, for one), the central challenge to our age.

HISTORY AS FUTURE

If time is indubitably real, it may be defined as a *continuum*—a duration of endless movement—from the past, into the present, and toward the future. The present is, in a sense, the most difficult dimension of time to embrace. Even as we focus upon the present moment, it slips into the past and is replaced by another moment which, an instant earlier, belonged to the future. We can, of course, expand our conception of the present to include a long succession of moments, and this is what we usually do in everyday life. Thereby we reach into both the past *and* the future—that is, we include a flow or continuum of moments extending in opposite directions from the present instant. This flow or continuum is sometimes termed the *specious present,* for it embraces far more than the instant which, strictly, is the only present.

Here is an excellent reason for holding that not only the past but the future, too, is real. We constantly embrace the future, even when we believe that we are concerned chiefly with the present. Thus, in turn, the reality of the future suggests another dimension of meaning: the future is necessary to understanding both the past and present. Any coherent plan (to compose a symphony, say) is one in which each step is so arranged that those at the conclusion are supported by, but also contributive to, the steps taken toward the beginning. The same continuum operates in practical affairs: a man building the foundation of a house must add the upper stories at a later time; yet the size and strength of the foundation are usually determined by blueprints of what the upper stories are to be. Past and present meanings contribute to future meaning, but the latter may equally contribute to them.

These characteristics of time operate in history. If the present moment always embraces some of the past and some of the future, then those economic, political, educational, and other affairs in which we are now engaged also become affairs in which what we *have* done, and what we *will* do, affect at every moment what we *do* do. Seen thus, history itself is always a duration of past, present, and future. Moreover, as Benedetto Croce, R. G. Collingwood, Herbert Muller, and other recent philosophers of history have observed, the present historian, because he too is subject to duration, is ever refashioning the past through his role in a temporal process which, paradoxically, is affected by the future as well.

To accept such a reality of duration suggests, in short, that if the future too is real, then it is our business to make sure that the future is considered at least as attentively as the other two primary dimensions of time. This is by no means to reject the importance of these other dimensions; for example, the conventional meaning of history as interpretation of the past remains legitimate enough. But this is also to reiterate that whereas the past and present condition the future, the future also conditions the past and present. The view of the future held by the present observer thus helps to determine what is to be interpreted and reinterpreted according to the purposes he embraces. Cassirer anticipates the reconstructionist attitude:

> In our consciousness of time the future is an indispensable element. . . . To think of the future and to live in the future is a necessary part of man's nature . . . the *theoretical* idea of the future—that idea which is prerequisite of all man's higher cultural activities—. . . is more than mere expectation; it becomes an imperative of human life. And this imperative reaches far beyond man's immediate practical needs—in its highest form it reaches beyond the limits of his empirical life. This is man's *symbolic* future, which corresponds to and in strict analogy with his symbolic past. . . .[4]

But there is special need in our period of history for devoting meticulous attention to the reality of the future. It is a need engendered by the confrontation of forces which we have discussed earlier. But beyond this lies the choice between contraction or expansion of freedom, between wholesale destruction or planetary peace. One need not hold that analyzing future trends makes it possible to know whether mankind is inevitably bound; one need not believe that the groove of the future is already mysteriously cut. But, if one is reconstructionist-oriented, one does hold that to know what the future *should* be like is essential to knowing what it *could* be like, and that, if we implement our choices with sufficient determination, we can determine what it *will* be like. As we shall stress in Chapter 21, man *is* capable of "self-fulfilling prophecies."

Nietzsche, a great future-looking philosopher of the nineteenth century, has said: "That which is ahead is just as much a condition of what is present as that which is past."[5] He thus anticipates the belief that history as future is the history of men making real their hopes and purposes.

[4] Cassirer, *An Essay on Man*, pp. 53–55.

[5] Nietzsche, as quoted in Slochower, *No Voice Is Wholly Lost*, p. 378.

CHAPTER 16

Beliefs about knowledge

THE ORGANISMIC APPROACH

BECAUSE THE RECONSTRUCTIONIST is especially influenced by important aspects of the progressivist ontology of experience and nature, it is logical that he should also respond positively to various beliefs about knowledge and truth that emerge from and depend upon these aspects. Thus he would agree that the process of seeking knowledge is entirely natural; the seeker employs no esoteric, mystical, or supernatural devices, and he rejects all claims to proprietorship over final truth. Moreover, the methods and objectives of epistemology are determined by the earthly, experiential, practical interests of men. Traditional notions of truth for truth's sake are looked upon with skepticism by the reconstructionist and progressivist alike, for they usually conceal some cultural factor or unconscious bias.

In psychological terms, the individual's thinking (hence, too, the product of his thinking) is grounded in a living, growing, striving organism. Thoughts are not independent of muscular and emotional functions; they are integrated with them. Mind is not a thing; it is a name for special ways of dealing with human situations and problems. Of these, the intelligent or reflective way, identified with scientific method, is of crucial importance. Accompanying the processes of intelligent (that is, reflective) mediation between obstacles are reverie, habitual behavior, and the esthetic undergoing of experience.

At the same time, the reconstructionist does not ignore strains of influence from epistemologies other than the progressivist (such as realism either in its classical or contemporary forms). He is also ready to accommodate certain ideas from modern philosophic movements, including neo-Freudianism or neo-Marxism.

It follows that dimensions of the knowledge phenomenon may be treated in several themes: (1) goal-seeking, (2) prehension, (3) the "unrational," (4) ideology, (5) utopia, (6) consensual validation, and (7) the "group mind." Meanwhile, the following qualifications should be kept in mind. All of these themes are still being formulated by a number of theorists; none is finished. None is autonomous. All are dealt with here largely as generalizations. (Illustrations will be considered more frequently in Section 2.) All are strictly operational concepts. All build upon the preceding chapter concerned with reality and anticipate the next chapter on values. None can be considered strictly separable from beliefs about reality or beliefs about values. All seven topics, finally, are both products and conditions of cultural experience as exemplified in Chapter 2 and beyond.

THE ROLE OF GOAL-SEEKING

That man is a goal-seeking animal has long been held by the philosopher and the psychologist alike. Indeed, no single example could better illustrate how philosophic beliefs may find the atmosphere of the study and the laboratory equally congenial.

CRITIQUE OF OTHER VIEWS

Many psychologists, nevertheless, have neglected to define their terms or to test their assertions about goal-seeking precisely enough. Some, like various analytic philosophers, have dismissed all speculations about "purpose" or "goal" as nonsensical. Others, notably perennialists, have insisted that these concepts are the prime objectives of their philosophies. Still others, especially some psychologists of realist-essentialist orientation, have begged the question by identifying goal-seeking with the "pleasure principle." Or they have given a great deal of attention to "drives," which they interpret in the framework of a neoconnectionist theory of "operant conditioning."

Functional, organismic, Gestalt, and/or other psychologies have tended to pay more careful attention to goal-seeking because of their concern for the total human organism. A central thesis in progressivism, particularly, is the interactive relationship of end (preferably defined as aims) and means. Although the end-in-view selects and conditions the functions needed to arrive at its achievement, these functions constantly reshape the end-in-view and, hence, determine their outcome. More technically, the response is constituted by the stimulus and the stimulus by the response. Organically, these are inseparable relationships even though conceptually they are not.

In practice, those who subscribe to progressivist theory are concerned, we have found, with the dynamics of growing, with the continuity of adjustments and readjustments. This theory recognizes ends ("consummatory" experiences) as well as means ("instrumental" experiences). But at no time does it allow either —especially ends—to crystallize or absolutize so as to become criterion of the other. Passages in the writings of Dewey and his associates that seem to place more stress upon the end, goal, or outcome than upon seeking must be judged in larger context. There we are invariably brought back to the key interest—not to the product, but to the process or method which we call intelligence. For the human being, too, is above all concerned with the specious present of transitional means–ends–means–ends–means. . . .

Two questions may be raised concerning the adequacy of such a progressivist psychology—one practical, the other more theoretical.

Our first question arises from Chapter 15: its interpretation of cultural reality, and our belief that mankind now faces a crisis in civilization that forces us to consider alternatives before us with a thoroughness that earlier periods considered quite unnecessary. As Marcuse, for one, has suggested, the experimental method of problem-solving, granting its utility, may become actually dangerous in such a period as this. Despite its activism, the method has the paradoxical effect of inducing complacency—of encouraging man to rest content with short-range, vaguely defined goals within the establishment of "containment and contentment" rather than to seek specifiable goals of the sort required by a revolutionary culture. In short, the imperative question is: *Where do we want to go?*—not only because seeking such knowledge will help us to know where we do and do not want to go, but because, so long as we do not know, we shall be unprepared to go there.

To relate this issue to our previous discussion of history as future, the time continuum needs to be lengthened to reach much farther. A stable culture may be satisfied with a fairly short range; a culture such as ours cannot be satisfied. Granting for the moment that the continuous means–ends process as developed by progressivism has been verified in psychological experience, the range, then, can and should be greatly expanded both in space and time.

Our second question provokes the more difficult issue of whether the nature of goal-seeking can be further clarified. What do we mean by "goals" and what do we mean by "seeking" them? A preliminary statement is called for at this point.

To begin with, goal-seeking as a personal-cultural characteristic is by no means sufficiently understood. While the scientists of man have made significant progress in recent years, many puzzles remain unsolved. Nevertheless, as the philosopher of culture, Abraham Edel, has shown, we do know enough to assert with considerable confidence that mere skepticism about the possibilities of a scientifically grounded theory of goal-seeking is no longer justified. The reconstructionist is influenced, for example, by the behaviorist theory that men are complex bundles of behavioral tendencies rather than walking department stores of instincts of faculties. Like the progressivist, he looks dubiously upon any theory that considers the goals toward which man moves to be fixed in his being as though they were his very destiny.

Again, hard-and-fast distinctions between "primary" and "secondary" drives and needs become wholly artificial. To say, for example, that man inherits the primary drive to nourish himself or to reproduce but acquires the secondary need for music or companionship is to make a convenient distinction which, in the course of time, has become less and less empirically meaningful. The fact is that so-called secondary needs can sometimes prove far more potent than those called primary. Many a nonliterate culture offers evidence of the power of taboos that, though clearly creations of culture, take precedence even when they conflict with urgent needs of life. In short, as Dorothy Lee, the anthropologist, has shown, culture may be the determinant of needs at least as commonly as needs shape culture.

Still, to say that human nature embraces an almost limitless array of diverse wants is not to say that we should neglect to determine the most important wants in a given period of culture. One consequence of recognizing this diversity and complexity is, of course, the temptation to circumvent any classification at all; the excuse is that every classification is bound to be artificial or oversimplified. But this argument is reminiscent of the equally dubious argument that, since means continually modify ends, it becomes both impractical and illogical to specify the content and form of any ends at all.

"GOALS"—"SEEKING"—"KNOWLEDGE"

It thus becomes imperative to try to specify the ends of human nature (in this context, man's individual goals) precisely because it also becomes imperative to specify the goals of culture. Terms adopted by various experts to characterize these ends are, to be sure, various. Sometimes "interests," if sufficiently defined, seem adequate; sometimes "needs" apparently serve. The terminology used by those who might accept the label, reconstructionist, is also varied. But in this discussion of man as goal-seeker, we intend to view him as he seeks to satisfy the definable wants that we are beginning to learn he possesses. Through research in anthropology and other behavioral sciences, as well as through the thinking of philosophers, operational definitions of these wants are gradually crystallizing.

The nineteenth-century utopian, Fourier, was on the right track, we contend, when he sought to classify men's basic appetites according to whether of the "senses" or of the "soul," and when he attempted to harmonize these appetites under the control of impulses both egoistic and social. The political-economic philosophers, Marx and Engels, are being increasingly supported in their lifelong contention that the sheer necessities of life—food, shelter, clothing, health—are such potent goals that, if they are denied long enough, this denial can generate violent social upheavals. The psychiatrist, Freud, was right in his emphasis upon the powerful need for love—erotic love, yes, but also interpersonal or familial love, and even the love of larger groups. The sociologist, W. I. Thomas, is known for his designation of man's four deepest "wishes": (1) for new experiences, (2) for security, (3) for response (most reminiscent of Freud), and (4) for recognition. The anthropologist, Malinowski, has made a convincing case in which the desire for freedom is shown to be man's desire for increased control, efficiency, and ability to dominate his own organism and his environment. The sociologist, Robert S. Lynd, may also very likely be proved right in his analysis of human "cravings" as including not only the foregoing ones but still others such as a desire to follow a "natural tempo and rhythm" and for "a sense of fairly immediate meaning." The social psychologist, Lewin, has made experimental advance for his theory of "need-like tensions" which are under the propulsion of a "field" of forces having both direction and magnitude—a theory supported from various points of view by neo-Freudians, by such social psychologists as Allport and Maslow, and by some existentialists.

But what, more exactly, is meant by "seeking" goals such as these? Let us put it this way: most people in most contemporary cultures so passionately seek to achieve their own goals as expressed in their own ways that their lives are devoted to this effort whether or not clearly and consciously they recognize what they are doing—whether or not, moreover, their effort is expended scientifically and systematically rather than affectively and clumsily, or vice versa. Frustration, for our present purposes, is defined as the result of being denied the attainment of such goals. Sometimes denial is self-imposed by ascetics or others who think they can destroy desires by suppressing them; more often it is imposed by cultural patterns that thwart or warp man's natural propensities. But the seeking still goes on; and whether by magic, supplication, force, conscious and systematic effort, or simply by activities prompted by the sheer immediacy of organic hunger, men everywhere exert themselves toward reaching their goals.

From this point of view the usually characterized means–ends process becomes more than a process. In our modern era, vast numbers of men struggle to realize *certain* purposes—purposes that need not remain forever undefined but that can and must be spelled out if they are to be the magnetic targets of cooperative human effort. Taken together and fused together, these purposes are capable of generating both the intense light of rationality needed for guidance and the heat of emotion needed for concerted action toward an audaciously innovated culture. Seeking can become seeking *for*. Growing can become growing *toward*. It is here that the utopian thinkers grasped a fact of profound significance: human beings must have goals in which to believe, for which to struggle, if they are to be fully human beings.

But one may still ask: What does this discussion of goals and seeking have to do with knowledge? In anticipation, let us confine ourselves here to preliminary comments.

First, if it is agreed that man is a goal-seeker, we have even in this crude agreement a powerful instrument by which to determine how much and why men wish to know and what most, if not all, knowledge is ultimately for. In short, both the ways and the fruits of knowing—both how men think and the knowledge gained by that thinking—are definitely if sometimes indirectly governed by the search for fundamental goals.

Second, it is possible to move toward delineating not only the cluster of goals shared by most peoples of the earth but also how they may go about seeking them. This is not to say that these goals, much less the means of such seeking, have been specified to the satisfaction of the scientists of human nature and culture or that they will ever be specified to everyone's satisfaction. Nor is this to say that the same goals will be sought by all men, or in all cultures, or at all times. What is contended is that *it becomes possible to determine the goals and the seeking that are important to most people in the world of our time.*

Third, understanding of goal-seeking is indispensable to understanding of knowledge and its process because the construction of future political, economic, educational, and other institutions and practices itself depends on knowledge. Such institutions no longer need be considered ephemeral creations of the speculative mind. Although they may still be utopian in the strict use of that term, they are also thoroughly practical; that is, they can be built upon all available knowledge of man's resources, capacities, and limitations. In building them, the ends or goals that are most central *personally* can be synthesized with those institutional patterns that prove most tangible and systematic *culturally*. Both can be finally accepted or rejected according to whether they are able to meet the tests of public examination and social acceptability.

THE ROLE OF PREHENSION

A second principle relevant to the needed theory of knowledge may be clarified by the term "prehension"—a term adapted from, but not necessarily faithful to, the intentions of Whitehead. In our own context, prehension suggests an experience that pragmatists and others have given less attention than it deserves. Stated as succinctly as possible, it means the unity, the organic wholeness, of natural events that constitute experience. It is a unified kind of awareness that precedes and succeeds "apprehension"—that is, the analyzed awareness of an event by which we recognize its component parts.

Time, for example, is prehended before and after it is being apprehended. It is a duration or specious present. Only secondarily do we become aware that it can be divided into distinct units or instants that succeed one another like ticks of a clock. Its prehended meaning is just as real to us, if not more so, than its apprehended meaning; indeed, the former is indispensable to the latter. Most of us have experienced time in both ways. When we lose ourselves in a symphony or a drama, for example, we remain aware of the passage of time, not as *a* series of discrete moments, but as a continuity. But, if we must sit in a railway station for two hours waiting for a train, we become agonizingly conscious of the passage of time; the hands of the clock move only too perceptibly from minute to minute.

Many students of the creative process have noted and studied prehension, although terminology for the phenomenon has varied. Dewey himself approaches it in his concepts of "immediate experience" and the "consummatory." Interesting comparisons with Gestalt psychology are also possible in view of that psychology's emphasis upon the patterned unity rather than the atomization of knowing. The great French philosopher, Henri Bergson, came still closer to the meaning of prehension in his famous doctrine of the *élan vital*, in which direct awareness of the whole of an event is regarded as a distinct kind of event. As a matter of fact, throughout the whole history of thought, men have been concerned about those elusive phenomena that somehow differ from the process ordinarily called rational or intellectual and which yet seem genuine to us who experience them. "Intuition" has been another favorite term of characterization (there is an important psychological literature on the intuitive process), but we shall avoid it here because it has been used too often in behalf of supernatural and mystical doctrines.

Perhaps an analogy will help if we remember that it is merely an analogy. A poet or painter may sit by a river and attempt to convey in a poem or painting its rippling, flowing movement. The river is prehended by the artist, and this is its essential meaning. A scientist, however, may approach the river in an entirely different way: he times the exact speed of the flow; he analyzes a sample of the water; when it freezes, he may chop out pieces that can be weighed and measured. In short, he apprehends the river.

The analogy is also helpful in reminding us of Zen Buddhism —indeed, the esthetic, intrinsic experience that is its core strikes us as very close to prehensive experience. A phrase or two from Suzuki may help:

> Let the intellect alone, it has its usefulness in its proper sphere, but let it not interfere with the flowing of the life-stream. . . . Zen [is] not subject to logical analysis or to intellectual treatment. It must be directly and personally experienced by each of us in his inner spirit . . . when this

is done we are able to seize upon the living, pulsing fact itself.[1]

To carry our discussion of the nature of goal-seeking farther, let us observe how the important goals of man are themselves prehended. Is it not evident that even the presumed simplest needs of man—for food, let us say—arise from basic hungers which have their persistent patterns of rhythm, their organic unity, their continuum flowing toward consummation? When normally expressed and fulfilled, is not sexual desire similarly rhythmic and unified? If we prehend such basic needs, which exist in our natures as unified events long before and long after we have examined and explained them, would we not also prehend less definite (though not necessarily less basic) needs, such as the need for "recognition"?

The role of prehension in goal-seeking does not mean that the method of reflective, scientific analysis is not also, perhaps even more, important. The needed purposes of our age must be achieved through the maximum use of knowledge, of which apprehended knowledge is a major type. Here respect for the experimental method of employing intelligence is reiterated. Still, if our main purpose is not to repeat but to supplement and highlight, then we must assert that knowledge has not one aspect, but two interdependent ones: first, there are the prehended unities everywhere around us—in time, in unities of the physical world, and in the existential "being" of men; second, there are the apprehensions achieved by intelligence—apprehensions which may perceive and analyze prehensions themselves.

The first of these aspects of knowledge can be broadened by noting how prehension serves not only in grasping single durations such as time or hunger, but also in binding each one to other unities. Hunger is not hunger for food alone. As we prehend it, and then apprehend it, we find hunger for food to be part of a continuum of hungers, and thus of the totality of goals for which man is striving.

But prehension also acts as an integrating force in areas other than subjective behavior—areas still more crucial to our interest in goal-seeking. For, if prehensive experience pervades our relations with nature, it also pervades that level of individual-and-social nature which is culture. This supports an expectation that the goal-seeking of the typical individual—itself a field or

[1] Suzuki, *Zen Buddhism*, pp. 9, 13.

pattern of goals—is an expression of the goal-seeking of a culture. Here, of course, the concept of organism discussed in the preceding chapter fuses with prehension itself. Here, too, the concept of empathy becomes relevant: the nonverbal, nonintellectual projection of one or more persons into the feelings and attitudes of one or more other persons.

Something of the intended point of view also permeates the culturology of Northrop. For him, as earlier implied, Eastern cultures are grounded in a prehensive configuration epitomized by his significant phrase "undifferentiated esthetic continuum." Western cultures are grounded in a scientific and rational configuration in which, accordingly, apprehension is the key to knowledge. He believes that the meeting of East and West will be possible only when these two configurations have been fused into one, each absorbing some of the qualities of the other. Should this occur, the variety of goals discernible in contemporary cultures may gradually become fused in turn—not, to be sure, to become a Purpose ordained by some spiritual Being, but to become a goal that is clear to men as their partial cultural unities coalesce into a worldwide whole. That Zen Buddhism, with its growing influence in the West, affords one such opportunity is surely in rapport with Northrop's interpretation.

THE ROLE OF THE UNRATIONAL

The unrational, to which we now turn, is one concept implicit in preceding concepts. The term "unrational" is preferred to "irrational" in order to avoid pejorative connotations of irresponsible passion, blind impulsiveness, even violence. By the unrational is meant, negatively, beliefs and acts of individuals and groups governed by other than rational powers; and, positively, the primordial forces that lie below the threshold of conscious awareness. Although the unrational may sometimes possess invidious characteristics of irrationality, this is by no means always the case. The unrational plays an important role in life—a role that cannot be condemned or ignored simply because it is not rational.

Although two chief types of related unrational experience—individual and group—have long been recognized by other philosophies of education, the subject of such experience has been given more painstaking attention in recent decades than in the whole of preceding history, thanks more to Freud than to any other scientific explorer. It has also been investigated by a long list of others, many of whom, in modifying his original hypotheses, cluster around terms already utilized such as "neo-Freudianism" and "existential psychology."

This is not to suggest that reconstructionists claim anything like an exclusive franchise. Indeed, our culturological evaluations of progressivism, essentialism, and perennialism have already noted (even if much too briefly) how neo-Freudian ideas have certain potential, if not actual, values for all three. Nevertheless, since these ideas are of special relevance to our fourth position, let us try to recall in very elementary fashion one or two of the seminal concepts which Freud himself first developed.

Beneath the surface of our minds, there burns, usually unknown to us, the seering flame of the unconscious—a turbulent energy that continually twists, and often blocks, conduct on the level of conscious behavior. Recall here the famous Freudian triad: "id," "ego," and "superego." The first refers to the wholly unconscious sphere of passions. The second derives from the id and, as ego, serves to mediate between it and the external world of cultural rules and taboos as internalized by the individual. The third, superego, acts as censor upon the ego's continuous efforts to placate the id without wholly denying its tempestuous demands.

One familiar practice growing out of this type of unrational process is rationalization—the well-nigh universal practice of finding "good reasons" for the "real reasons," or "logical" justifications for what we want to do anyway. In Freud's terms, our real desires arise from the id. What we actually do to satisfy these desires may also arise from it but may be disguised by reasons so framed by the ego that no longer do we recognize the source. Equally possible, the ego may yield to demands of the superego—usually demands to suppress an action or desire—and find supporting reasons for conduct which, again, conceals the source of these demands. Rationalization, in a word, may operate to support compulsions of either passion or conscience, or both. In any case, it is a means of justification rather than a dispassionate function of intelligence.

But the reconstructionist emphasis upon cultural reality leads to further consideration. Before one can adequately consider the potent forces inherent within the individual, one must diagnose them in relation to group experience as well. Freud's preoccupation with mental illness appears marred by failure to probe deeply enough into the unrational behavior of social and cultural experience. Had he done so, he might have perceived more clearly that, while this experience is itself integral with the individual's unrational experience (the culture of groups does not, after all, exist except as also present in individuals), it is at least equally true that your behavior or mine is affected by our relations to group behavior. The neurotic behavior of individuals may well be traced more often to the frustrations, maladjustments, and conflicts within and between groups than to any other source.

Of course, Freud by no means ignored the cultural context of individual experience, and some of his writings (perhaps, most famously, his *Civilization and Its Discontents*) are brilliantly insightful. The superego, for example, is shaped primarily by one social institution, the family. Actually, the social is fundamental in Freudian theory in the sense that neurotic or psychotic disturbances are held to result from conflict between individual desires and social demands. Moreover, some neo-Freudians have shown how conflicts between the individual and society are responsible for such phenomena as anxiety. And all would agree that ". . . the explanation of the irrational is a special task of the twentieth century."[2]

Nevertheless, both Freudians and neo-Freudians often give the impression that the unrational forces of the psyche are both chiefly responsible for the failures of contemporary culture. Only exceptional ones have paid meticulous attention to "immoral society." But these exceptions are provocative indeed in their interpretations of social unrationality; we are thinking especially of Fromm and Lasswell (both of whom are considered to be neo-Freudians) and of Marcuse (who, however, disparages neo-Freudianism as "revisionist").

Like other thinkers contained by a rubric, these men are thus difficult to compare. Lasswell, moreover, has shifted away from his earlier, severely Freudian analysis of political behavior to a more ameliorative approach. Yet they have not only often agreed that modern society is itself so shockingly unrational—so obscene and destructive—of humane values that its very survival remains precarious; they have also detected potentialities for cultural rejuvenation. Fromm speaks here for several others:

> We are in the midst of the crisis of modern man. We do not have too much time left. If we do not begin now, it will probably be too late. But there is hope—because there is a real possibility that man can reassert himself, and that he can make the technological society human.[3]

[2] Brown, *Freud and the Post Freudians*, p. 220.

[3] Fromm, *The Revolution of Hope*, pp. 168f.

But to return closer to Freud's own language, what is paramount here is that the process by which the ego consciously mediates between id and superego requires a widening of the radius of consciousness itself—that is, in terms of group and not so predominantly in individual terms. It is essential to proceed further, therefore, and to inquire how unrationality operates on the group level.

THE ROLE OF IDEOLOGY

The term, "ideology," here means the complex of attitudes, beliefs, ideas, purposes, and customs that expresses, more or less systematically and more or less accurately, the programs and practices of a culture. Fashioned on their own level of sophistication and enlightenment, the people of any tribe or any country in any period shape ostensibly reliable descriptions of their dominant patterns of practice and belief. Clearly, then, ideology should not be thought of invidiously, for it is the effort in everyday symbols of every age to depict itself to itself.

Two aspects of ideology are especially pertinent. One is that, because it serves to rationalize cultural practices and habits, it may be regarded as the social corollary of the phenomenon of individual rationalization discussed above. Thus, it is a kind of verbal and sometimes pictorial or auditory superstructure that sanctions the supporting substructure of real institutions and practices.

The other aspect is that all ideologies are historical. Like the cultures they symbolize, they emerge, mature, and wane. Hence they do not always mirror the structures and practices of their cultures with equal accuracy. An ideology may reflect a culture more vividly at the height of maturity than at any other stage. In the youthful period, it may also serve to accelerate development by pointing ahead to new meanings and new needs. In the aging period, it may perpetuate an image which less and less resembles the "real" culture. This later stage supports the theory of cultural lag; ideologies tend to move more slowly than the cultures they purport to symbolize.

In language appropriate to the contemporary philosophic position which we have called neo-Marxism, the ideology of any culture thus becomes a device by which its institutions are preserved even when their effectiveness has declined. The chief service of the agencies that shape public opinion, for example, may prove ideological when manipulated by those who benefit most by the status quo. Thus, in our own culture, the prevailing ideology sometimes portrays the economic order as sacrosanct and glorifies it by the shibboleths of "free enterprise," "individual initiative," and a host of others—all of which manage to conceal changes actually taking place. Again, the current ideology builds attitudes of self-righteousness in those who benefit most from the preservation of inherited patterns, just as it may encourage complacency in those they dominate.

But we are chiefly interested in the significance of ideology for the theory of knowledge. Ideology may reflect unrational factors, for example, as indicated by its abundant rationalizations of cultural practices that are sometimes very different from the accepted depiction. The institutions that assist in that rationalization—newspapers, churches, schools—may be totally unaware of the disparity between their ideological descriptions and cultural actualities. Because ideology is one kind of group expression—a potent one at that—we require (as anticipated in Chapter 2) a culturology of knowledge that is contributive to maximum understanding of any given cultural order, or its process, or its goals.

THE ROLE OF UTOPIA

The term, utopia, now assumes a richer meaning than in earlier discussion, although it is well to be reminded that our definition excludes invidious connotations of this term ("daydreaming," for example). Simply, utopia means any world picture of attitudes, practices, ideas, and institutions that supports a conception of culture admittedly different from the prevailing one.

Thus, a utopian may conceivably look backward as well as forward in constructing his design. He may deplore the prevailing ideology and, instead, advocate a cultural pattern which existed, or is thought to have existed, at some distant time in the past. (Perennialism and essentialism both manifest utopian tendencies in this sense.) More often, he looks toward the future, as, for example, did More or Bellamy or as Mumford does in our period.

Because utopia must also be understood in terms of historic situations, one may sharply distinguish ideology from utopia only for purposes of classification. On the one hand, ideologies seldom, if ever, lack all elements of vision: such an ideology as laissez-faire liberalism acquires utopian coloration in that it embraces the possibility of a largely individualistic, competitive economy that would actually work as Adam Smith once said it should. On the other hand, utopias seldom, if ever, lack ideological elements: no speculative social imagination is capable—indeed, would be useless if it were capable—of creating a cultural design for the future so utterly unique as to show meager influence of past or present experience.

It is helpful, then, to think of ideology and utopia as a kind of spectrum rather than as two opposing concepts. Toward one end of the spectrum are ranged those ideas that depart most drastically from given or presumed cultural structures, and are therefore most utopian; at the other end are the expressions of maximum acceptance of these structures. Somewhere between these extremes, the two often meet in a blend of ideological-utopian hues that only a prism of logic could separate.

Furthermore, the utopias of one period of history may become the ideologies of the next. Locke, in one sense, was the archutopian of the period in which industrial culture was emerging, even though ideological factors were already pronounced. In America, Jefferson and Franklin glorified virtues such as self-reliance that heralded and sanctioned the characteristic beliefs of an economic and political order suitable to eighteenth-century individualism. Seen in the perspective of our day, however, their original utopianism has changed character; the incipient ideology of their age is the full-blown ideology of our own. The early liberalism which such men helped to sanction and symbolize has concealed or retarded the emergence of interdependent and cooperative methods and institutions. The utopian proposals of our time, if ever carried out, would also very likely become ideological in the course of further evolution.

But if it is true that many cultural patterns can be most accurately likened to historic spectrums in which both ideology and utopia appear, it is also true that periods of extraordinary strain and conflict sharpen the distinctions between them. Thus, during the age of European history in which feudalism was giving way to industrialism (roughly, the fourteenth to seventeenth centuries), theocrats and other defenders of the old order sought to strengthen their own ideology to the utmost—often ruthlessly, sometimes deviously. Yet, the age was also one of such tradition-shattering utopian thought that the lines of the spectrum became sharper at its extremes. Both the established ideology and the envisaged utopia were strengthened by opposition to each other.

Examining the present turbulent period of history, we see more clearly, then, why current utopian thought is to be judged, not at all as a dilettante exercise in future-speculating or crystal-gazing, but as response to imperative need. The demand is for new goals and for new institutional arrangements under which we can resolve problems that old arrangements have generated and failed to resolve.

By comparison with the utopian end of the spectrum that tended to crystallize during the transformation from feudal to modern culture, the utopian end of our spectrum is, to be sure, as yet ineptly defined. Skills and resources at the disposal of those who oppose change enable them to utilize such new ideological weapons as cybernetics, television, radio, and movies with a success totally unknown to earlier cultures. Yet, despite such success and the scarcity of clearly defined utopian goals, contemporary utopian movements have been gaining more and more adherents —so many, indeed, that apologists for the status quo, already thoroughly alarmed, utilize every means at their command to strengthen their skills of reinforcement, acquiescence, and transmission.

In this situation, the obligation before us is twofold. On the one hand, we need to analyze and interpret the use of ideology as a device for retarding democratic change and blocking utopian propensities. On the other hand, we need to intensify such propensities by fostering future-looking attitudes and defining cultural objectives while developing effective strategies for reaching them.

Just what these attitudes and objectives may mean in terms of definite cultural designs will be considered subsequently. Enough has already been said, however, to point toward some of their features. The utopian order that now increasingly demands our commitment is one built by, and for, the forces dedicated to expansion of freedom. It should be organic, earth-wide, and geared to the satisfaction of the maximum number of wants of the maximum number of people.

The direct import of utopia for a culturological theory of knowledge is aided by Mannheim, whose important theories have greatly influenced this discussion. He himself would have insisted that logic and science should be as fully utilized in constructing a utopia as in developing an ideology; both are tools for testing its pertinence to a specific culture at a specific time. Yet, in his view as in ours, they are not adequate criteria. The ideology of, say, later liberalism is to be judged by the extent to which it describes the culture of our time; and in reaching such a judgment criteria of evidence and communication, as well as those of, say, analytic philosophy, must be applied. But it is also to be judged by how well it expresses the interests of all those in the culture which it intends to depict; and interests are determined, at least in part, by economic, political, and other forces operating on groups and individuals that are not merely described as true or false but also (as we shall see in the next chapter) good or bad. Until these forces are taken into account, we can no more pass judgment upon any utopia than we can upon any ideology. We can, however, recognize that the knowledge relevant to it becomes cultural and axiological as well as "purely" epistemological.

In important respects, therefore, the principles of knowledge discussed in this chapter bear upon utopia. Like ideologies, utopias are tinged with the unrational in the sense that they are, in part, shaped by factors such as group conflicts and allegiances that cannot be sufficiently explained by rational principles or exclusively controlled by rational methods. Moreover, utopias spring from man's goal-seeking proclivities—proclivities that we have seen to be closely related to both prehensive and unrational processes.

Finally, the utopian attitude is permeated with emotional experience—the kind of experience for which some existentialists, for example, seem to be searching. As the vision of human possibilities crystallizes into clear-cut goals, those who share it may develop a fervor once akin to that of Fourier and his American disciples or, in our own day, to a visionary existentialist philosopher such as Jaspers. Nor should we deplore the affective dimension; on the contrary, we should welcome it. To regard enthusiasm and dedication as barbarous, as beneath contempt, or to ridicule the warm glow of loyalty to such a great purpose as world civilization, is to deny a demonstrable want-satisfaction of man and to confess one's own moral bankruptcy.

At the same time, we may properly warn of several dangers associated with this value. There is the danger that emotional fervor may cause the more dispassionate, objective qualities of utopian thought to be suppressed. Or utopianism could take the form of an escape mechanism, a compensation for overburdening problems of the present. Again, such thinking may itself turn into a kind of inverted rationalization—that is, a way of disguising one's failure to cope with problems of today by wishfully fancying hopes of tomorrow.

Such dangers, however serious, are avoidable. At a minimum, the great utopian purposes required for our age can, and must, be achieved through the interfusion of reflective thinking, emotion, and consensual validation. Let us turn to the third of these necessities.

CONSENSUAL VALIDATION IN TRUTH-SEEKING

The principle of utilizing consensual validation in truth-seeking may be defined, in preliminary fashion, as follows: the truths of vital experiences in group life within any culture are determined, not merely by the needful satisfactions they produce, but also by the extent to which their import is agreed upon and then acted upon by the largest possible number of the group concerned. Without this agreement, followed by actions that test the agreement, the experience simply is not validated as "true."

Consensual validation is not presented as *the* criterion of truth. Certainly, the progressivist method of seeking truth through employment of experimental intelligence is indispensable. Moreover, proponents of that method may or may not wish to insist that their own formulation encompasses consensual validation. In any case, it is not contended that the principle is itself adequate for dealing with scientific problems involving the determination of facts about nonhuman phenomena, although it may be helpful even to these problems. What is contended is that consensual validation should be given much more emphasis and that it should be much more clearly explicated than it has thus far. For the crucial functions of goal-seeking and future-making, it could well be the most important single process within the subdiscipline of epistemology.

To put this process in operation, it becomes imperative to submit the evidence about fundamental goals (delineated with the aid of other principles already outlined) to an open court of recognition, appraisal, and active testing. For example, although such wants as food, sexual expression, or personal recognition are directly evident to those who immediately experience them, they can also be drawn into the sphere of communication, where individuals and groups testify that they actually have experienced and do now experience them.

The importance of testimony about evidence as to man's wants and needs is that it takes the prehensions, the desires arising in the id, and the goals of men and groups out of the private sanctuary of individual experience. The purpose of testimony is to make subjective goals public and expressible (and, in this sense, objective) insofar as possible.

Here the disciplines of conceptualization and abstraction are indispensable. The task of achieving consensual validation involves the development and clarification of symbols (including esthetic and religious as well as scientific symbols) through the use of which people can convey their personal experiences so that these can be examined and agreed upon as being common to the group. Semantics and philosophic analysis are, of course, essential here. But so, too, are every skill and art related to communication —including the Zennist. Moreover, all the knowledge that can be mustered concerning the arts of persuasion, of influencing people's opinions and feelings, is equally required. Such knowledge is both safeguard against false consensuses and guide to truer ones.

To the degree that this sharing and agreement are accomplished, consensual validation becomes the expressed consent of one man (or many) that the testimony another has offered makes sense in that it articulates an experience that both recognize.

This method, on second glance, is neither strange nor novel. The sciences, too, presuppose agreement about and, hence, the ability to communicate evidence germane to a given field of research. "Intersubjective judgments" are, indeed, recognized by Feigl or by other philosophic analysts of variant persuasion as necessary to all scientific investigation leading to validation.

Reconstructionists, however, are especially interested in the kind of agreement and the consequent action obtained by those who constitute a group or by the many groups that constitute a culture. The process for all groups is, or should become, similar, and the result—agreement upon a truth which can now be utilized for social purposes—is likewise similar.

SOME MAJOR IMPLICATIONS OF CONSENSUAL VALIDATION

This outline of the principle under examination has several fundamental implications. To begin with, however scientific our methods of gathering evidence may be, however cautious in self-examination and communication, a point arrives at which (unless we simply abdicate) we must either agree or disagree upon the testimony that has been offered as to the nature of our goals.

This moment of validation or invalidation may follow a period of prolonged consideration. As we testify, we may experiment with various ways of describing our experience. With the aid of the insights given by, say, neo-Freudian theory, we may become sensitive to the ease with which we deceive ourselves about the desires we are trying to express. With the help of philosophic analysts, we may become aware of how often we becloud our testimony even when we have no wish to do so. Guided by clinical psychologists, we may utilize reports of experimentation with humans or animals in order to increase our grasp of what to report as our experience.

At last, however, we must reach a point where insights into our goal-seeking interests can be sharpened no further. Like awareness of time or of hunger for food, they are ultimately to be grasped as direct awarenesses. Prolonged analysis and apprehension may deepen or sharpen them, to be sure, but prehensive, unrational or existential awareness of them both precedes and succeeds analysis and apprehension.

Another implication of the process is that no individual or group should agree with the testimony of another individual or group until convinced as far as possible in a given situation that such testimony is in accord with awareness of the experience being communicated. Theoretically, it would be possible for the process of consensus-seeking to stop long before consent is ever gained. Thus, the extreme theory called *solipsism,* holding that the only reality is that of oneself, insists that there is no way to guarantee that my experience is identical with yours; so it denies that any similarity between our respective experiences can be proved. In the same way, pure *anarchism* in political philosophy denies the existence of any sound criterion of social order other than the judgment of the individual.

We have just noted, moreover, how difficult it is to establish similarity between two experiences—how, after all possible examination of such experience has been undertaken, you and I must fall back upon sheer awareness of our experiences. Precisely because of the ever-present danger of incorrect testimony or self-deception, for example, no individual and no group should overlook any possible instrument of clarification, such as logic, or any encouragement of such noncognitive and interpersonal experiences as empathy. Certainly no one should agree with another individual or group quickly or impulsively. Rather, it should always become part of the responsibility of all of us to serve as critics and correctors of those who *have* agreed. Section 2 will discuss more fully how communication and evidence-giving operate in the educational process of achieving such consensual validation. Here we wish only to stress the necessity for both.

But such achievement is by no means merely academic. It is, in addition, to facilitate action—that is, to make a difference, especially in group behavior. Obviously, depending upon the issues and problems involved in a specific effort, testing through actions themselves can vary endlessly in quality and quantity. In many cases, an action may be delayed for a long time. In others, action may be negative in the sense that a group decides against delay or termination. Again, the action may be more in the nature of a tacit change of empathic feeling rather than in overt, verifiable behavior. Basically, however, consensual validation (always depending upon the most reliable evidence and best means of communication available) is a way to seek and attain the goals of groups and, therefore, of their members. "Seek" and "attain" are verbs of action, not of contemplation.

In one sense, insistence upon the consequences resulting from the operation of this criterion is not essentially different, epistemologically, from that of the progressivist. The workability of an agreement still remains the final test of its truth. The difference of degree lies in the issues and techniques that the two philosophies tend to underscore in their respective formulations. The reconstructionist stresses those that are more often related to interactions of groups. The progressivist's concern for intelligent, critical judgments as the conclusive test of truth is thus incorporated to embrace still greater stress upon the need for concerted thinking, sharing, empathizing, agreeing, acting, and finally validating. Moreover, the process we are outlining incorporates a number of fruitful concepts such as "group dynamics," "sensitivity training," and "anthropotherapy," to which we expect to pay further attention.

Fresh distinctions between ideology and utopia here become striking. An ideology may be reconsidered as consensual validation about a culture more or less established; a utopia, as one not yet established. As we have seen how utopias may be created as counterproposals to ideologies, the problem at any particular time is that of determining which of the two more accurately expresses the goal-seeking interests of the culture to which they belong. Utopians are those who, as critics and aggressors, insist upon the need to revamp an existing culture pattern; ideologists are those who, as apologists and defenders of an existing pattern (or one allegedly existing), deny that need. Both offer testimony in support of their claims with a view to winning consent. The utopian aims to expand his influence to the point where he is stronger than the ideologist; the ideologist aims to protect his entrenched position against encroachments by the utopian.

It follows that truth-seeking through consensual validation becomes an important effect of interrelations between the cultural factors we have termed conflicts, allegiances, and conditioners. In seeking truth, evidence is essential (for example, evidence as to the causes and effects of aggression or ethnocentrism, which function as conditioners affecting racial or class status). So, too, is communication within any group or between it and other groups. Thus, in many specific ways and on its own level of enlightenment, the group tries to decide one of the most difficult questions about truth that it could attack: What do we, at this time and in this place, seek as our fundamental goals?

IS CONSENSUAL VALIDATION WORKABLE?

In confronting the question just raised, let us inquire further into the extent that consensual validation may prove to be a practical device. What defense is there against the common objection that it is too theoretical, too ideal, or perhaps not enough of either to serve successfully in actively resolving the issues of our time?

Any cursory review of history testifies that this process, under whatever name, has seldom, if ever, functioned perfectly. Neither individuals nor groups have often united to engage in the process of communication, testimony, agreement, and action. Economic classes, racial groups, religious sects, and nations are united largely because people have been born, or coerced, into these groups. Also, the goals governing activities of groups are seldom enunciated clearly; in literate as well as in nonliterate cultures, motivating purposes are likely to be mingled with powerful customs. Nor can we overlook the abundant record of mistakes in popular judgment about nature, economic policies, moral sanctions, or almost every other aspect of human experience.

Occasionally a purpose, even if it is fairly clear to members of a group, may seem, in a narrow sense, to be as much negative as positive. Thus certain groups (for example, organizations dedicated to improving the lot of Negroes, or associations concerned with establishing world order) work to supplant the isolation of race or the sovereignty of a nation by some more inclusive unity; success in such purposes could eliminate their reason for existing. Again, the *professed* ends of an individual or group may, upon careful scrutiny (as our discussion of both the unrational and ideological shows), turn out to be shockingly unlike the *actual* ends toward which the individual or group is working. The term, ideology, suggests still another fact: agreement about the goals of one group often conflicts in some way with that of another group—a fact abundantly verified by the historic record of suspicion, hostilities, and actual warfare among classes, races, and nations.

It must also be remembered that consensual validation too often turns out to be only one part of some group—a part that is able to dominate the remainder because it controls the instruments of power and propaganda or, perhaps, because others are too indifferent or ignorant to care. Then, too, groups often are not able to function well as groups even when they agree on the desirability of doing so. Like individual personalities, they are seldom completely harmonious within themselves; sometimes, they are severely disunified. Some of the conditions under which disunification occurs have been considered in the preceding chapter; in addition, personality differences among individual members and variations in capacity for leadership or followership mitigate against effectiveness. For reasons such as these, a partial or majority agreement and action may be the best that can be obtained. And even this much may appear quite impossible.

The reconstructionist would be likely, however, to defend the usefulness of consensual validation with the same vehemence that he admits and emphasizes difficulties such as those just outlined. The following arguments are sketched in that defense.

(1) *History and culture provide support.* Despite its clumsy and incomplete operation, despite the profusion of errors that result from its operation, the principle is both workable and valuable. Even nonliterate people do, after all, reach group decisions in the more or less explicitly expressed belief that they understand one another's interests. In some respects, the process has been used more commonly than we have implied—in fact, too commonly, because too often arrived at hastily or uncritically.

Perhaps the most familiar and clearest example in our own culture is the jury system. This system rests upon the major assumption that a group of individuals, because of their varied perspectives and backgrounds, are more likely to find the truth and mete out justice in situations involving the activities of human beings than would be one individual judge: someone guided by legal precedent alone or by arbitrary authority. That juries err frequently enough is obvious; yet many of us prefer to trust them because, as substantial studies have shown, consensual validation demonstrates that the system produces, on the whole, more dependable decisions than those reached by any alternative way thus far known.

Moreover, as was stressed in discussing history as reality, a consensus which begins originally as that of a small group may widen to embrace much larger spheres of individuals and even other groups. In this process, the first consensus may be superseded by a later one which is more expressive of, and therefore closer to truth about, the goals being sought. Indeed, though it is a fact that contractions of freedom may follow expansions, it is also a fact that the forces of expansion have often been aided in the modern era by the increasing literacy, cohesiveness, and cooperativeness of groups—and this despite opposition which, in some areas and at some times, has also increased. In politics, the process of consensual validation, though seldom as precisely as one could wish, is employed in popular government; in the economic sphere, it functions through relatively useful techniques such as collective bargaining; in science, the mass of accepted evidence about nature and man, together with experimental controls over them, is cumulative; in technology, there is widening recognition of both the fact and desirability of communication and transportation, so that even the most remote groups of the earth now approach closer and closer proximity with all other groups.

(2) *The sociality of goal-seeking enhances its practicality.* The practicality of consensual validation is enhanced further by increasing knowledge, supplied by social sciences such as anthropology, that goals are not merely individual, but are shared. In actual practice, we do not first testify about our wants and then seek to convince others; we first learn about such wants through the testimony and behavior of others and then gradually recognize them in ourselves. Others, of course, learn in the same ways from us.

Moreover, the goals in which we typically become interested, far from being unique or private, are frequently mutual ones. Clear illustrations of such needs are love, security, appreciation, and a dozen more—all of which depend upon the participation of others.

(3) *Recent experience has borne fruit.* Historic and scientific evidence is supplemented still further by recent experience. In the economic sphere, opposing groups (however acute their deeper conflicts may be) do learn, at times, to resolve their immediate differences. In religion, unprecedented steps have been taken in the dramatic ecumenical movement. Even nations, more conscious of the dangers of total destruction than they have ever been, are trying persistently to devise effective machinery of testimony and agreement which may develop to the point where disputes can be settled through international concord.

These efforts, though some are crude and ineffective, point to the fact that, to a greater degree than ever before, worldwide concern prevails for the need to deliberate over human problems and to attain viable solutions. This is a concern that has even led to attempts to bridge the differences separating ideologists and utopians.

(4) *Ideology-utopia refines consensual validation.* But the very existence of differences and conflicts may also serve to refine the process as a working principle. Although an ideology is often employed to divide groups or to confuse people about their interests so that they can neither honestly testify nor clearly agree (the propaganda of patriotic and economic groups is one endemic example), it may perform alternative functions. Thus, during a culture's youth and virile maturity, its ideology may, we recall, reflect its own purposes with considerable accuracy; later in the development of the culture, as it is forced upon the defensive by utopian-oriented interpreters, the ideology may counter with renewed adroitness.

Even more significant is the practical effect of utopias. For they may disclose facts and meanings that have been overlooked, if not deliberately distorted or hidden, by particular ideologies. Thus, utopian thinkers of the Renaissance, such as Bacon, contributed truths both about inadequacies of the culture they attacked and about the culture they envisaged. More recent utopian thinkers, such as Marx and Mumford, have played the same dual role of critic and visionary. Today, as ideologists find themselves performing as defenders and rationalizers of traditional cultural structures and practices, utopians are more likely than ideologists to confront facts, to expose false beliefs, to seek clarity of communication, and to rationalize less often.

(5) *The principle is self-correcting.* Consensual validation can be defended further (against charges of failure or impracticality) on the ground that it is a self-correcting and, in some ways, experimental principle. In all fairness, then, it should not be judged merely by its failures; it must also be judged by how well it operates as it is more widely used and as it profits by its own mistakes.

Such a cautionary statement has been implied in our earlier discussion of the principles of knowledge. Goals, for example, depend upon our delineation of human nature in its social and individual aspects in a given period of history; the means used in seeking their attainment vary in turn, of course, according to the nature of those goals. Again, the facility with which an individual or group has learned to testify is always subject to improvement. Both because of the explosive increase of scientific knowledge and because of the immediacy or directness of goal-seeking, never-ending criticism and clarification of testimony or agreements are indispensable. It follows that ideologies and utopias, as cultural formulations of past, present, or future cultural objectives, are also subject to continuous modification and supplementation. Every utopia must meet the final test—the degree to which, in practice, it attains those goals to which it is dedicated and which then prove (or disprove) effective.

The most important feature of the dynamic character of consensual validation, in short, is that the principle is improvable —a principle which, in democratic political parlance, goes by the term: *due process.* By constantly providing for maximum communication, evidence, and testing among participants, the principle assures that the dissenter and the deviant, as well as any individual member, will have a full voice.

(6) *Consensual validation is a practical necessity.* Finally, the principle helps groups to achieve effectiveness, direction, and clear-cut commitment. A primary aim, then, is to overcome frailties arising from the relativism encouraged by such a philosophy as progressivism which expresses, in turn, a transitional, moderative orientation. The stress is not only upon the continuous modifiability of this process but also upon its usefulness in the construction of worldwide cultural designs.

Our discussion of consensual validation closes with three questions. In searching for truths which may be sufficiently validated now or in the future, should we follow the perennialist in accepting supreme metaphysical or divine authority? Or should we agree with the essentialist's belief in the objectivity of established material or spiritual laws? Or can we accept the progressivist's belief that it is possible to function effectively through primary reliance upon his means-centered, reflective principles of truth-seeking? If, as we contend, our reply to such questions is more negative than positive (granting, of course, that each of these alternative philosophies, as well as others, contribute important ingredients to the inclusive principle), then we must consider another approach. In terms of far-reaching programs and objectives, the principle of consensual validation symbolizes the manifold attempt of mankind as a whole to rediscover and to reconstruct itself. In an age of crisis such as our own—an age which, left unreconstructed, suffers from disintegrating pressures and fearful catastrophes—this principle becomes imperative.

THE "GROUP MIND" AS END AND MEANS

Our concluding theme, the "group mind," enables the several themes previously discussed to bear again upon our present focal interest: the problem of knowledge. Knowledge is peculiarly the subject matter of what, in the history of philosophy and psychology, we have come to call "mind." Here, however, we are especially concerned with how the group thinks and utilizes its thinking to further the attainment of cultural goals that at once stimulate its actions and shape its institutional patterns.

Just as we saw earlier that societies are not organisms in any literal sense, so the "group mind" is not an entity that either exists in and of itself or possesses characteristics qualitatively different from those of individual minds. Even so, another meaning of "group mind" does reveal fruitful significance for the broad epistemological concerns we are now discussing. In every instance, the term is marked by quotes not only to distinguish it from more traditional meanings but to imply that it operates, thus far, only suggestively.

THE "GROUP MIND" AS END

"Group mind" as end is based on one assumption: a number of individuals or groups have joined and do join constantly for a purpose, more or less clearly expressed in the form of goals, that they endeavor to realize together. Obviously, therefore, "group mind" is a normative as well as descriptive term, and it is already partly implied in consensual validation. Although the latter, too, operates far from perfectly, it is evident that groups do consider evidence, carry on communication, and affect agreements; they do act on their decisions; and sometimes they do improve the range and reliability of their collective judgments. Here, then, is the "group mind" already functioning. Moreover, insofar as it functions as a fusion of its members, it helps to illustrate the reality of organism in history.

Thus far, however, we have scarcely examined the pertinence of other ontological features (namely, group conflicts, group allegiances, and group conditions) for the structure and operation of a "group mind." The point has been made, for example, that an important (though by no means the only) determinant of group conflicts and allegiances in our own culture is the dominant technological, socioeconomic structure. The impact of this structure upon a typical "group mind" has been potent indeed. Today, it affects the thought and actions of labor groups, owning groups, racial groups, nationality groups, and others in ways that reinforce stubborn ethnocentrisms, deepen tensions, and sometimes lead to local or even international violence. These are realities to be recognized and considered in any delineation of the "group mind" itself. Without considering them, we can hardly interpret either the role of ideology as a device that aims to transmit a particular cultural order or the role of utopia as a device that aims to transform that order.

Yet, though the influences of such potent conditioners do not produce a "group mind" qualitatively different from the individual mind, nevertheless, the degree of distinction between them is provocative. As discussed at an earlier point, if individual minds, too, can be subtly, sometimes deeply, affected by cultural conditioners, at least some of them can isolate themselves in order to reflect as objectively as possible upon the unrational forces at work within and upon them. But groups arc often less successful in achieving this kind of detachment. Negro and Jewish groups have repeatedly tried and failed; such economic groups as trade unions depend for their existence upon participation in, not merely dispassionate analysis of, economic struggle; and nations have certainly made meager headway in learning to subordinate their immediate interests to global objectives.

Testimony and agreement by the group about the goals it seeks are affected, in short, not only by logical or scientific considerations but also by the conditioners of cultural order. The group may be conscious that it defends or rejects a given cultural pattern; yet it may be confused or deceived about its own motivations or rationalizations.

Even so, the chief inference to be drawn is not that the group must invariably submit to such influences; it is, rather, that as men begin to realize the potent influence wielded by the "group mind," they can become equipped to diagnose the chief conflicts of our age and to build radical, more inclusive consensual validations. It is equally important to repeat, however, that the latter can function effectively only to the degree that the several steps of necessary procedure are employed—that is, when proper use is made of gathering maximum evidence about the goals we seek, when this evidence is communicated clearly, and when maximum agreement is reached on the pertinence of the evidence as well as the action that should be taken.

If, for example, sufficient consensus is reached among our black citizens that perpetuation of power in the hands of forces dedicated to the restriction of freedom deprives them of adequate standards of food, security, and education, then it follows that powerful programs and cutting-edge goals constructed in behalf of the forces of expansion of freedom can alone suffice. What in recent years has come to be known as "black revolution" in America is one consequence of this kind of consensus. But the question of widening such a "group mind" to embrace other citizens, white as well as black, has thus far been much more difficult to answer.

THE "GROUP MIND" AS MEANS

Thus we come to realize that, if ends are crucial determinants of the "group mind," then means are the strategies by which groups attain their end. Means, therefore, are also affected powerfully by conditioners affecting the choice of goals. Here the paramount problem is one of reaching the widest possible agreement about means—of developing strategies of action to be taken by those who agree upon their goals.

This problem is complicated by uncertainty as to when action in behalf of cultural reconstruction should occur. That is, reaching agreements which, when or if reached, still leaves uncertain the moment of commitment, the moment of action. To take action prematurely is dangerous: it could, and frequently does, generate still more hostility or stronger counterstrategies (one term for these is "backlash"). Yet to reach commitments for action too late could be just as dangerous; utopian "group minds" can be destroyed, as sometimes they have in the past, by ideological "group minds" whose own ends and means have crystallized sooner.

No formula guarantees avoidance of these twin dangers. Nonetheless, the guiderule that concerted effort to attain a fresh consensus about ends will assist in reaching commitment and action about means remains valid. Indeed, we shall make constant use of this ends–means dependency in considering a reconstructed theory and practice for education. Here, it is helpful only to emphasize that the means advocated are completely *democratic* means, in school and out. The aim is always to build a "group mind" that validates the maximum consensus of a majority whose opinions are continuously strengthened and, if necessary, revised by minority criticisms and by dissenting individuals. The principle is that normatively the "group mind" as end and means is the consensus of a culture that knows—in the most inclusive sense possible—both what it wants and how to satisfy what it wants.

KNOWLEDGE AND TRUTH DISTINGUISHED

The concept of the "group mind" provides still another instance of the indebtedness of reconstructionism to progressivism. Broadly speaking, progressivism, we recall in Part 2, distinguishes knowledge and truth: knowledge may be regarded as the reservoir of tried and tested experiences that people have already had; truth is the particular consequence that emerges in the solution of a present problem through the application of intelligence. Reconstructionism, in its still broader framework, makes a roughly parallel distinction: "knowledge" is the term used to designate the body of agreed-upon experiences utilized by past and present cultures; it is equivalent to "group mind" in its more ideological meaning and is an invaluable resource in building any new (that is, utopian) content. But just as the earlier reliability of a body of knowledge tends to decrease when it lags behind changes in an emerging culture, so "truths" recurrently established through the process of consensual validation can be distinguished, relatively speaking, from knowledge.

Truths thus become, we might say, the utopian content of the "group mind." They are active agreements both about dominant cultural goals and about means for achieving them. Such consensual validations are neither merely verbal nor static; they involve actions and, hence, include the utopian content of the "group mind" in rebuilding institutions, practices, habits, and attitudes. Their ultimate meanings are tested in the cultural demonstration, made possible with the aid of experimentation, that they produce the cultural designs that they were originally intended to produce. In short, the kind of truths most sought are achievements of the "group mind" as conceived in two ways: first, as *means* for active progress toward workable, acceptable utopian goals; and second, as *end* in possession of such goals.

THE IMPORTANCE OF THE PERSON

This and the preceding chapter emphasize cultural aspects of reality and knowledge, with special attention given to group experience. These aspects are not only often minimized by other philosophies of education but are among those most central to a reconstructed philosophy of education.

Although the importance of the person has also been frequently emphasized, we wish to make it very clear that the individual is never to be subordinated or disregarded by virtue of the importance of the group. Not only is he as fundamental as he is to other philosophies; in decisive respects, he is considered to be still more so. That is to say, his happiness and fulfillment are of paramount concern; but they are attainable, we contend, through coming to grips with the severe realities of our group-centered, increasingly technologized culture as well as by creating a theory and program of knowledge able to cope with these realities.

To avoid any possible misunderstanding, let it be reemphasized that the reciprocal relationship of personal and group goal-seeking is a basic motivation for seeking knowledge. Let us note, likewise, not only the indispensability of individual intelligence as interpreted by progressivists, but also the personal dimensions of prehended and/or unrational experience. Nor let us dismiss the point that, if consensual validation is to function properly, individual expression in the form of deviation and dissent is indispensable to due process.

What has not hitherto been stressed is a corollary of these observations: some of the most revolutionary contributions to knowledge have been (and, hopefully, always will be) made by individuals whose creative talents function best when the fewest possible restrictions are imposed upon them. This generalization holds equally, of course, for the artist and seminal thinker who, beginning as a "minority of one," may eventually succeed in influencing and even persuading large majorities.

We must not fail to recognize, either, the very rich contributions of both traditional philosophies and modern movements to the reconstructionist orientation. Certainly, personalism as developed by influential idealists is one. Even more contemporaneous are insights contributed by existentialists, neo-Freudians, and Zen Buddhists. All of these, with due qualifications, deserve to become amalgamated into the personality-culture syndrome that we have sought to portray and respect.

Our chief conclusion, then, is that any philosophy of culture viable for our age must permit ample elbowroom for the individual, for the innovator, and for the deviant. Furthermore, it must allow for the pursuit of truth by unorthodox, even unpopular means—that is to say, by means that are not only departures from those growing out of restorative, transmissive, and/or moderative cultural orientations, but, above all, that encompass the transformative orientation as well.

CHAPTER 17

Beliefs about value

REALITY, KNOWLEDGE, AND VALUE

IN THE PRECEDING two chapters, which deal with beliefs about reality and knowledge, we have avoided explicit discussion of values only at some cost. For values are closely related to both of these divisions of philosophy.

The "social construction of reality" (to recall Berger's and Luckmann's apt title) is inextricable from the struggle of races, religions, classes, or nations to achieve whatever they may regard in wide degrees of explicitness as the good life and to avoid equally disparate beliefs about the bad life. The place of values in this struggle is inherent.

Even more so is the interdependence of knowledge and values. Our frequent references to the operation of such factors as interest and purpose in all phases of the goal-seeking process are indications of this interdependence. In the context of culturology, it can be asserted that ontology and axiology, and to a still greater extent epistemology and axiology, can be separated from each other only for purposes of dissecting the whole.

Our approach to values, stated negatively, is opposition to any theory that considers values to be absolute in any way and that tries to fence off the area of values as separate and unique entities. Stated positively, values are want-satisfactions rooted in the proclivities of individuals and groups to seek and achieve goals. Furthermore, because values are considered according to the criteria of evidence, communication, agreement, and action, they too can be encompassed by the process of consensual validation.

Like any product of this process, they are thus never to be considered completely final or forever fixed. On the contrary, although strong commitment to values of the largest possible consensus in the widest range of cultures is called for, and although such commitment is necessary if needed utopian goals are to be achieved, we must encourage the keenest criticism and public discussion of every value. Contingencies are unavoidable in due process, for any attained agreement may itself prove erroneous. A correlative aim of this chapter, therefore, is to examine further and to broaden the several principles of knowledge and reality already stated or implied.

In order to proceed further, two operational distinctions are called for: one, between beliefs about reality and beliefs about values; the other, between beliefs about truth and beliefs about values.

The first distinction occurs between the description of a typical group reality and its desirability. To say that groups engage in conflict, for example, or that they are often ethnocentric, or that they are conditioned by far-reaching, powerful environmental forces is not to say that these social realities are to be condoned. On the contrary, the group may be condemned for them as wrong.

But the moment we speak of "wrongness," we introduce normative criteria of values which are not derived merely from descriptions of behavior. As with other philosophies of education, therefore, ontology alone is not enough; axiology is likewise required. Yet, to a greater extent than usual, the reconstructionist insists that an effective axiology must be based on recognition of the stubborn human realities that affect values themselves. These realities include hateful and violent, as well as loyal and cooperative, relationships within or between groups as well as individuals.

The second distinction follows in some situations between the methods and products of value determination and those of truth-seeking. In our discussion of truth-seeking, we emphasized a technique for attaining the most thorough, open, and active agreements possible—that is, consensual validations—in any given cultural situation. This type of agreement was also found to be indispensable to the pure natural scientist. After all, possible tests of a hypothesis have been made through examination of evidence, inference, verification, and other reputable canons of experimental investigation. Evidence must be offered publicly and communicated publicly before the hypothesis is accepted as scientific truth.

Implied here is the criterion of intersubjectivity, earlier mentioned. If, for example, you utter the word "two" in my hearing, you assume that I understand that you mean the number "two"; I assume that you have uttered the word "two"; and both of us assume the other's agreement that "two" represents the same numerical quantity. When scientists are dealing with such abstractions, or even with such physical objects and forces as stones and electricity, they may reach virtual universality. Here, moreover, the role of philosophic analysis in reducing the hazards of verbal agreement about concepts that are, in fact, disputable is one of its chief contributions. Precision of meaning has often been made more difficult thereby, but also more trustworthy.

When we enter the areas of psychological and sociological experience, the aseptic role of analysis may become even more useful. Although the physicist or the geologist often operates upon the assumption of consensus about basic data, the externality of his subject matter makes it possible for him, accepting and building on this assumption, to test another's results without reference to his own feelings, group relations, or other conditioners. The situation of the scientist working in the sphere of human experience is different. Although he may try to emulate the objectivity and methods of the physical scientist (as the mechanistic type of psychologist does, for example), and although he may achieve important experimental results thereby, the probability is that his investigations will, sooner or later, become narrow or sterile and his results dubious in direct proportion to the degree of that emulation.

The recent tendency in nonrealist schools of psychology and sociology, especially, has been to recognize that the qualitative and cultural aspects of human phenomena are legitimate objects of scientific investigation, and to accept the inseparability of the investigator from the human phenomena being investigated. (But even modern philosophies of physical science, it may be noted, have been influenced by a theory of inseparability—especially through quantum physics as interpreted by Werner Heisenberg.) These schools depend upon consensual validation, whether defined as such or not, even more than do physical scientists. The truths upon which investigators agree, although partly the result of utilizing conventional canons of scientific method, are also partly the result of communicating about the nature of experiences which are inseparable from the communicators. Earlier these experiences were characterized by such terms as unrational and prehensive. It may now be asserted that any science that can no longer accept psychologies of, say, connectionist behaviorism (or, of course, those of objective idealism or neo-Thomist absolutism) must not only utilize the process of consensual validation, but must regard its products as important instances of truth.

Yet if values are to be determined chiefly by the same process, what distinction remains at all between values and truths? Although operationally important, this distinction in cultural experience is one of degree only. Let us resort once more to the metaphor of the spectrum: at one extreme is research of the physical scientist, who is least dependent upon testimony and agreement as criteria of consensual validation; he is interested as a scientist in the kind of truths that can be established with minimum recourse to that process. At the other extreme is the concern of the axiologist who is most dependent upon testimony and agreement; he is interested in goal-seeking experiences involving, say, unrationality and existential immediacy as well as those involving experimental processes. Somewhere between the physical scientist and the axiologist are the psychologists and other scientists of man who, while they too depend upon consensual validation in reaching workable judgments of truth, range in interest from problems most resembling those dealt with by physics (animal reflexes, for example) to problems most resembling those in ethics (notably, the purposive behavior of individuals and groups).

It is the relevance of this interest in purposive behavior to which we next devote ourselves.

THE CONTENT OF VALUES

Because a primary need of our time is the construction of a philosophy of substantive ends as well as of viable means, we are under obligation to determine the nature and content of values as precisely as possible. In accordance with the belief, moreover, that values are part and parcel of the experience of real men living in real cultures, one expects them to be attached to, indeed to be identical with, certain specifiable goals. Through widening knowledge in such fields of psychological and social science as anthropology, through the arts and philosophy, above all, through growing skill in consensual validation as a process in politics and other areas of group life, many individuals and groups throughout the world are attaining increasing agreement upon what they do and do not want.

Let us try, therefore, to encapsulate and explicate as values the kinds of goals hitherto discussed or intimated:

(1) Most people do not want to be hungry; they cherish the value of *sufficient nourishment.*
(2) Most people do not want to be cold or ragged; they cherish the value of *adequate dress.*
(3) Most people do not want uncontrolled exposure, either to the elements or to people; they cherish the value of *shelter and privacy.*
(4) Most people do not want celibacy; they cherish the value of *erotic expression and celebration.*
(5) Most people do not want illness; they cherish the value of *physiological and mental health.*
(6) Most people do not want chronic economic insecurity; they cherish the value of *steady work, steady income.*
(7) Most people do not want loneliness; they cherish the value of *companionship, mutual devotion, belongingness.*
(8) Most people do not want indifference; they cherish the value of *recognition, appreciation, status.*
(9) Most people do not want constant monotony, routine, or drudgery; they cherish the value of *novelty, curiosity, variation, recreation, adventure, growth, creativity.*
(10) Most people do not want ignorance; they cherish the value of *literacy, skill, information.*
(11) Most people do not want to be continually dominated; they cherish the value of *participation, sharing.*
(12) Most people do not want bewilderment; they cherish the value of *fairly immediate meaning, significance, order, direction.*

ISSUES ARISING FROM DELINEATION OF VALUES

This list is obviously minimal; even so, it raises several issues requiring further consideration.

Values are inseparable from the cultural and psychological reality of goal-seeking already discussed. Economic conditions giving rise to group conflict and allegiance, for example, are related to such direct wants as food, shelter, security, and participation. A problem of pivotal concern is not merely that of determining exactly what our values are and what they should be; it is also that of eliminating cultural contradictions and frustrations that prevent them from being realized to the maximum.

In accordance, moreover, with "field" theory in social psychology, the values listed above not only overlap but suggest still others. Companionship, for one, is correlated sociopsychologically with appreciation, participation, and not infrequently with sexual union; together, they come close to Thomas' "response" or to Freud's "love." Mental health, as a value, overlaps all these and still others; indeed, according to the underlying premise of psychosomatic medicine, the wants of body and mind act profoundly upon each other. Moreover, just as the value of love is the common denominator of some of these values, so the value of religion may be considered the common denominator of these and others, particularly the last in our list above. Fromm's neo-Freudian connotation of *The Art of Loving* is by no means incompatible with such values as belongingness and direction that are conspicuous in several world religions. Nor are existential religious values as expressed by Buber, Harper, Marcel, and others. Finally, an example of the integrated character of values is suggested by those involving action—adventure, sharing, and the progressivist's favorite value, growth. Their familiarity, moreover, points in turn (as Veblen, Marcuse, and others have emphasized) to a deep-rooted desire to work at occupations that test man's mettle and produce results to be appreciated by others at the same time that they hold deep personal significance for him.

Nor is our cluster of values to be regarded as at all sufficient. Others, both more specific and more common, could be substituted for, or added to, those selected. Certainly, quite a different order could also be defended so that perhaps the only sequence is that of proceeding roughly from the less to the more complex. No hierarchical order is implied; the point to be emphasized is that each want-satisfaction is important both in itself and in its interweaving with others.

Still further, some of the values we have listed may seem to be incompatible. The want of security, for example, may appear to be inharmonious with the want of adventure. The want of privacy may seem to be at odds with the want of companionship and recognition, just as the want of novelty may seem opposed to that of order. We know from history, moreover, that men have at times chosen, or endured, domination or oppression as the price to be paid for security.

One easy explanation for such apparent contradictions is, of course, the sheer complexity and recalcitrance of human behavior. Another explanation is that no individual can satisfy all wants simultaneously: although wants are interfused, often they can be satisfied only in succession or alternation; therefore choice among conflicting values is imperative in every normal life. In language common to ethics, it is often necessary to select the most *desirable* values among many one may *desire*. As progressivist axiology has demonstrated, the need here for intelligent consideration of alternatives is almost continuous.

We have been speaking psychologically, but the apparent incompatibility of values is also due to the fact that the well-springs of man's behavior are as often to be found in the denials, inconsistencies, and struggles within a particular culture as within the individual himself. Certain values thus may be suppressed by cultural taboos or negations. Previously, some pains have been taken to note that our major orientations in educational philosophy are shot through with moral, economic, religious, and other conflicts.

But it is both unnecessary and vitiating to force human nature into a single mold. Uniformity is forlorn and colorless as an ideal. The supreme task of our age is to build a world civilization wide and flexible enough to provide for the expression and satisfaction of rich diversity among human wants. It is not the variety of values that is primarily to blame for the contradictions and ambivalences among them. Nor is it merely that there are always competing values. Far more crucially, it is the frustrations, alienations, and negations blocking the creation of flexible, workable designs—designs that could enable mankind to live *for* itself and thus for its maximum values, rather than so commonly *against* itself.

SOCIAL-SELF-REALIZATION: THE SUPREME VALUE

Instead of compelling us to select among them, our search, then, is for a pattern of values sufficiently inclusive to embrace their multiplicities. Such a pattern has been anticipated in discussing the cultural reality of history. There it was suggested that the forces of contraction or expansion are an index to the absence or presence of freedom. If freedom is so considered, however, the term must be understood to have connotations radically different from those familiar to more traditional philosophies and ideologies. This surely does not mean "freedom *from*"—negative value implying that the best life is one in which the individual is as little as possible responsible to, or controlled by, organized society. Rather, it should be understood to mean "freedom *for*"—freedom for the positive achievement of individual and social values; freedom to attain the widest possible range of goals; freedom to hope that the majority of people throughout the world are able to satisfy their maximum wants.

What, then, is an all-inclusive symbol of values that can serve as a measuring stick by which to estimate both the limitations of post-midcentury culture and as a normative criterion for the emerging one? It must be a symbol that excludes none of the goals that most men seek, yet one that encompasses such values as nourishment, adequate dress, shelter, erotic expression, health, work, devotion, appreciation, creativeness, literacy, participation, and direction.

One answer might still be freedom, especially if it is defined as ". . . the positive ideal of providing concrete opportunities for human development."[1] Or, if this value is too encumbered with traditional connotations, we might prefer the popular terms like "self-realization" or "self-actualization." But we must invariably remember that the self-discovering, self-expressing, self-fulfilling individual is not an isolated self; he is integral with others—a "group mind as end and means." In the last analysis, indeed, the realizing, actualizing organic culture, which is made up of individuals but yet is far greater than the sum of its parts, is the ultimate value. Let us therefore adopt the slightly cumbersome but more accurate term, *social–self-realization*, for the all-embracing value that we must seek. Let us, also, emphasize strongly that social–self-realization symbolizes a polaristic human experience—that is, at once *both* social-centered *and* self-centered. The norm it connotes is the maximum satisfaction of the wants of individuals and groups, not of either individuals *or* groups. Its locus is the culture—a normative, utopian, international culture.

In the present context, both knowledge and art are included within the meaning of this supreme value. Knowledge is included because each of our specific values comes to be known not only through apprehension and rational thought but, what is equally important, through unrational and prehensive processes that also embrace existential qualities. Art is included because it deals with unique, organic, Zenlike syncretisms achievable by individuals and groups—the unities symbolized in poetry, painting, music, sculpture, the dance, the architecture of buildings and cities, or merely in the homely products of everyday craftsmanship.

From whatever angle it is viewed, social–self-realization is, then, the all-embracing value. It is a dynamic fusion of economic, political, educational, and personal goals, as well as of scientific, esthetic, and religious goals—all to be sought, interwoven, and achieved.

[1] Edel, *Ethical Judgment*, p. 324.

But let us return now to an earlier assertion that the principal values encompassed by social–self-realization are increasingly demonstrable and are being accepted by ever-growing numbers of individuals and groups. To what extent can this assertion be defended?

Evidence supplied by science can be utilized in support. With the aid of biology and psychology, we learn that such important wants as nourishment, shelter, bodily covering, erotic expression, and physical and mental health are common to all peoples. With the aid of anthropology and history, it can be contended that the need for security, for companionship, and for the satisfaction of curiosity exists in many groups, on all levels of culture. Studies in social and industrial psychology offer substantial evidence for such complex wants as recognition, information, belongingness, and participation. Theorists and creators in the fine and applied arts strengthen the claim of authentic human needs for novelty, order, appreciation, and creativity.

Evidence from the sciences and arts is supplemented, moreover, by evidence of the widespread (though by no means universal) operation of the process of consensual validation—in itself an expression of social–self-realization in action. Through the machinery of popular government, through activities of multiple organizations such as consumer cooperatives, through the arts of communication as expressed in education, politics, religion, and other institutions—all help to demonstrate that great masses of people wish to achieve such values as sharing, recognition, and significance.

Yet, at the same time that social–self-realization may prove a demonstrable value, important qualifications mitigate against its operation. Certainly it fails to function with anything like maximum effectiveness. Popular government, to take an example in only one sphere, is, at best, a clumsy instrument of social–self-realization. The lack of articulated, defensible values and objectives, due in no minor sense to the shortcomings of conventional educational systems, is one obstacle. Another is the fact that certain individuals and groups refuse to testify fairly or to agree honestly about their values because of motives arising from self-interest.

Again, if Edel is correct, the kind of encompassing purpose symbolized by our term, social–self-realization, can be less easily demonstrated positively than can its negative corollaries—that is, what are *not* desirable as constituent norms of the good life:

> . . . the kinds of criteria for evaluation that have emerged [show that] . . . the negative ones have a sharper outline at the present stage of knowledge than the positive ones. By comparison . . . we do have a comprehensive view of evil—whether it be described biologically as death and illness, psychologically as neurosis and the inability to function, socially as wars, depression, mass hysteria, or historically as the decline of a civilization or the thwarting of a people's aspirations. . . . The definition of physical health is just getting to the point where it can be cast positively; that of mental health is still cast in terms of removing conflicts and anxieties. . . . The cultural criteria of disharmony are more manifest than those of positive well-being and creativeness. The historical thread of growing control over nature stands out more clearly than the human ends which such control can increasingly support. A . . . contemporary ethic is therefore weighted heavily with the effort to overcome known and scientifically describable evils. This effort implies some outline of the necessary conditions of the good, and should lead increasingly to the clarification of the positive good.[2]

Still another hindrance to demonstration of this value, albeit a welcome one, is questioning by critics such as analytic philosophers or empirical students of human nature who might dispute any ventured meaning of social–self-realization. And surely, they would be right if they contended that the full meaning of social–self-realization can never be exhausted. Not only do evidence, communication, and agreement, even in the most exact sciences, change from period to period, human–nature–living–in–culture constantly changes, too. We must, therefore, strongly reemphasize that social–self-realization is to be thought of as a "practical" universal value, not one in any sense complete or immutable. The effort to build an axiology based solidly on the inductive and tested findings of the human sciences has only begun. The evidence remains both limited and debatable. It will continue to be so in the foreseeable future.

Nevertheless, the reconstructionist is still not prepared to agree with the inference that some might draw from these limitations—namely, that no commitment to any supreme and universal value is ever legitimate. He is not persuaded merely by more growth, more change, more method, more process, more indeci-

[2] *Ibid.*, p. 307.

siveness, more analysis of language, more existential or affective immediacy. On the contrary, he desires more specificity, more testimony, more agreement about the minimum values already accepted by sufficient numbers of people on earth so that at least a nucleus of common values can be said to prevail. In the face of man's aggressive, even destructive drives; in the face of such cultural realities as social and political conflict; in the face of threatening confrontation between forces dedicated to its expansion; in the face of fashionable skepticism or flippant indifference among philosophers toward the choice of fundamental purposes appropriate to a revolutionary period; but also in the face of increasing, empirical support for the value of social–self-realization, we should be prepared to take sides now. The moment of choice, or commitment, is at hand.

This commitment is, of course, of crucial significance for the whole level of belief now under examination. The demand for commitment is certain to raise cries of alarm from moderative-minded philosophers of education as well as from either the transmissive-minded or the restorative-minded. Their own commitments, after all, have been achieved in terms of different theoretical formulations and with different cultural and often ideological objectives. The reconstructionist gladly concedes that social–self-realization or some symbolic equivalent is still an operational and debatable concept of value still seeking to clarify and unify axiological experience; hence, that it is still being built out of the experiences of individuals and groups living in ever-evolving cultures. He recognizes the importance to his case of demonstrating that a close correlation is demanded between the psychological *fact* of man's goal-seeking and the ethical *norm* that the goals we desire in the existential depths of our personal and cultural wants are profoundly worth seeking and, therefore, profoundly desirable as well. He is accordingly aware that, although both the process and product of consensual validation are intrinsic to his concern for both truth and value, the descriptive and normative judgments that eventuate may or may not always prove compatible, either with each other or with the overarching value. He is not insensitive to the acute differences of experience between groups and cultures of the past, present, and future. Finally, he appreciates that those who refuse to accept any one of the assumptions underlying the value of social–self-realization can hardly be persuaded by logical argument alone, nor should they be coerced into doing so.

Granting all this, we return to the imperative of commitment. Let those, says the reconstructionist, who are prepared to accept social–self-realization and its radical cultural correlate of a future-centered, world-wide democracy join forces with me, and let me join with them. Let those who are not prepared remain as critics and dissenters until the time comes when they have agreed with us, or, conceivably, we with them. Meanwhile, let us endeavor to widen the ranges of agreement already won. Let us learn how, through strategy and power, we can guarantee that the constellation of the forces dedicated to the expansion of freedom, including many of our critics, will realize ourselves together —will realize ourselves on a new, planetary level of man as a unified species.

The task of such a widening draws us into the arena of political philosophy.

SOCIAL–SELF-REALIZATION IN POLITICS

Thus far, relatively little has been said philosophically about such terms as democracy, because it has first been necessary to consider some of the principles of reality, truth, and value underlying political beliefs. From our viewpoint, democracy is adjudged normatively, of course, rather than merely descriptively. Nevertheless, after acknowledging all its defects, the representative system of government has, we believe, stupendous potentials to become the mature democracy that our revolutionary culture now demands of it.

Democracy, in short, is to politics what social–self-realization is to axiology. Both, broadly, mean self-government. But to the definition of democracy is added public, cooperative control and utilization of material and nonmaterial resources. This generalization deserves further attention.

THE MEANING OF MAJORITY RULE

Commitment to the descriptive-normative pattern of values thus far considered produces, in turn, a reasonable expectation that individuals and groups can unite in agreement upon what they want and how to obtain what they want. This is by no means to claim either that such agreement has been reached frequently or that validation, when and if consensually attained, invariably embraces vast proportions of citizens.

Thus restated, one principle, above all others, distinguishes democracy from other political orders: the principle of majority rule. The belief upon which majority rule depends is that the best long-run decisions affecting common welfare (that is, decisions working toward what we choose to call social–self-realization) are reached when the widest possible consensus of citizens is sought—when as many as possible testify, hear, see, or otherwise share, and then agree and act upon that consensus. No good reason prevails why a normative goal cannot sometimes even approximate unanimity—a goal not at all impossible among groups of various sizes and situations.

Thus, in democratic theory, it is being increasingly recognized that the more accurately and fully citizens are provided with dependable evidence, the more likely they are to make desirable majority decisions. Yet no one could maintain that possession of such evidence is the sole qualification for such decision-making; rather, it is assumed that people can also know in other ways what goals they cherish most. In the language of preceding discussion, a citizen should be able to recognize, for example, the prehensive unity of hunger and the intrinsic value of adequate nourishment whether or not he is familiar with the chemical composition of his digestive juices. It is precisely upon such simple recognitions as these that he then may join with others to help in establishing public policies and practices aimed at assuaging his and others' hunger.

The principle of majority rule thus further qualifies an earlier contention that, whereas the individual may be moral because he is reflective, society is frequently immoral because it is often so unreflective. However groups may act immorally, however majorities may err in judgment, however the body politic reaches agreements that may prove undesirable, the guiding principle still holds: if we accept democracy, we must also accept the belief that no more reliable political judgments can be effected than those reached by the method of consensual validation by the widest possible majority.

This kind of judgment is certainly not to be attained by counting noses; it is certainly not a mere quantitative one. Therefore, let us stress very strongly that voting as such is never *the* means to consensual validation: without the process of testimony, communication, and action, a majority decision is not a genuine consensus at all. Indeed, it justifies the belief held by Quakers and others that the voting technique is unsatisfactory as a way to assure the best possible agreements. As we interpret the principle, a majority decision is a judgment of optimal inclusiveness about something shared qualitatively—about values held in common on the basis of both unrational and rational or other manifestations of human experience. Since these values can best be epitomized by such a comprehensive, syncretic norm as social–self-realization, the test of majority rule is, therefore, the degree to which its policies approximate social-self-realization in its fullest meaning.

Of course, even casual inspection of political practices shows that the majority often fails appallingly to exercise its rule according to its own normative tests. We must reiterate how frequently dominant ideologists succeed in confusing public issues, thus forestalling public consciousness of, or agreement upon, fundamental interests of the majority. Millions of citizens, believing as they do in free enterprise and other shibboleths, frequently exercise one of their most precious democratic rights (majority rule itself), not in behalf of establishing policies that would assure utmost social-self-realization to themselves and their children, but in behalf of policies that distort or deny that magnificent goal. Nor is ideology alone responsible for destructive or outmoded judgments by the majority: feeble and incompetent education (illiteracy in large parts of the world is only the most glaring instance), superstition, religious and political dogmatism, advertising and other mass communication, nationalism, and nativism—these and other conditions, all interwoven with ideologies, deserve their heavy burden of blame.

The crucial political mandate of our time is, then, to reach far more substantial and radical consensuses—substantial and radical in the sense that, through their operating principles, the goals *of* the great majority may be sanctioned and achieved *by* the great majority. It is the mandate of making sure that majority rule is exercised by due process so that the values upon which most men can agree are publicly recognized and consented to. It is the mandate, finally, of integrating these values into the democratic structure and practice of a truly intercultural and international order.

THE MEANING OF MINORITY RIGHTS

The function of the minority in a democracy is sometimes stated in preventive terms—namely, to prevent tyranny by the majority. John Stuart Mill put it more succinctly when he said that there must always be a place for minorities so long as it remains unproved that the majority is infallible. Thus, in our present context, the prime political function of the minority is to criticize, through communication of additional or corrective evidence, whatever consensual validations may be reached by any majority. The more that data can be gathered as evidence, the more thoroughly that hypotheses are tested, the more fully that the content and form of existentially or otherwise directly perceived goals are enunciated rationally as well as experienced, the more dependable the attained agreements will be. Conversely, attainment of such agreements decreases in likelihood when facts known to the minority are suppressed, or when opportunities for any critic to communicate are in any respect limited. Each successive consensual validation, moreover, is endorsed by a majority which, although it usually excludes some citizens who are still unconvinced and who thus become a new critical minority, often includes some members of the former minority which led the way toward the new consensus.

In order that the function of criticism may be performed, the necessity of freedom of speech, press, assembly, and religion becomes even more indispensable than in other philosophies of education which frequently qualify their endorsement of these traditional rights in terms of their own culturological, if often implicit, assumptions. This is not to imply freedom to agree with judgments already reached, nor is this to imply freedom for "liberals" but not for "communists" or "fascists." This *is* to mean the privilege of advocating beliefs sometimes abruptly different from, and inimical to, those of a given majority—the right to challenge our most ancient and revered moral, political, religious, economic, educational practices, institutions, attitudes, or customs.

But minority rights do not, as a general principle, include the right to implement dissenting views through violence or through other practices that are overtly conflictive with policies already authorized politically and legally by the majority. True, any member of a minority willing to face the disapproval of those governed by conventional attitudes may fly in the face of sanctioned conduct as much as he pleases, so long as his course is not one clearly denied by law. (For example, he may dress himself in an "eccentric" fashion but he may not, thus far at least, walk naked in the street.) True, also, when legal lines between communicated advocacy and overt action have not been crystallized, any member of the critical minority is fully justified in deciding that the only way to measure the effectiveness of some controversial proposal is to try it; by doing so, he may also deliberately bring the legality of the proposal to a test in the courts. Finally, this minority critic may choose to question the constitutionality of a law which, he is convinced, perverts the normative standards of democracy. (Test cases, such as nonviolent protests that challenge discriminatory laws against minorities, have become heroic examples of the great importance of this process.) But where the distinction between advocacy and action has been established (by, say, the United States Supreme Court) and an action has been firmly declared contrary to law, the minority's right is limited strictly to advocacy until such time as the majority may authorize amendment or other constitutional correction.

It becomes only too apparent that, on these terms, reconstructionists themselves join a critical minority. They point out, for example, that our civil rights of freedom of the press and speech, including academic freedom, are often sharply circumscribed by agencies in control of public opinion. Therefore, a chief function of any such minority is to expose the ideological illusions that continue to deceive the majority, and to testify as publicly and as frequently as possible against those inherited beliefs and arrangements that deny social–self-realization to the vast majority. Meanwhile, reconstructionists continue to advocate thoroughgoing cultural changes—for example, public ownership of natural resources. But they cannot, and should not, act directly and concertedly to effect such changes insofar as these infringe upon majority-authorized institutions and practices.

But the critical minority's privileges and obligations are not confined merely to communicating its own normative alternatives. It should join whenever possible in organized, nonviolent attempts to test cases which bluntly distort constitutional rights. (Segregated schooling and the subverted Vietnam war have both been tragic cases of recent history.) In these efforts the critical minority occasionally succeeds in winning support of the majority for particular tests, so that some of its purposes may be demonstrated even while its role as both opponent and counterproponent continues. Women's political rights, old-age security, and integrated schoolings are examples of such partial successes.

Here one may discern, further, a direct connection with our emerging theory of value. It will be recalled that, although reconstructionists welcome examination of their own proposals, they are equally prepared to commit themselves to the keystone value of social–self-realization. They are prepared, in part, because of the imperiled juncture at which humanity stands. They are prepared, in further part, because the degree of consensus already gained through the behavioral sciences, through the arts, and through democracy-oriented movements makes it entirely possible that social–self-realization (both in its axiological meanings and its institutional imperatives) could now become the planetary goal of increasingly powerful majorities.

This commitment can be effected, still further, in the belief that the normative target of social–self-realization is more than just potentially *demonstrable*—although it is that, to be sure. In a crucial sense, it is already in the process of being *demonstrated* by and to the majority. It is being demonstrated also in the sense that individuals and groups, in larger proportions than of earlier historical periods, are becoming keenly aware of, and motivated by, goal-seeking interests. And this is true even though specific individuals or groups may not sufficiently recognize or articulate the meaning of such interests.

Let us carry a previous example further. The average man who is hungry may not explicitly declare that the value of balanced, sufficient nourishment is the normative correlate of hunger. But is it not probable, even virtually certain, that he could agree to that statement if he were given patient opportunity to consider it? Similarly, the average man who finds himself entangled in a chronic state of bewilderment may not analyze the problem and then communicate the belief that much of his frustration might be resolved by a conscious value of order and direction for himself and his culture. Yet, is there very plausible reason to suppose that, if he does require such a value, he would inevitably deny that he does? On the contrary: cumulative evidence demonstrates that he could very well agree.

Paradoxically, reconstructionists are, in certain respects, closer to perennialists at this point than at any other. Both philosophies believe that their obligation is to draw the "actual" from the "potential"—that is, to convince men consciously, clearly, actually, of the very values that they now hold (due to ignorance, concealment, or other factors) only unconsciously, vaguely, potentially. But, as considered in Part 4, the difference from perennialism is that the means by which the reconstructionist hopes to build consensus about these values and their cultural corollaries are openly cooperative, empirical, and naturalistic. Moreover, the values to which he is committed have themselves been crystallized, not as an a priori faith, nor as metaphysically posited forms, but as the product of living history, as the product of public and scientific testimony critically examined and tested, and as the product of agreements based upon such cultural realities and constituent principles of knowledge and value as hitherto outlined.

If, then, the reconstructionist willingly concedes that he is a minority spokesman for values of the kind already cherished by the majority (whether consciously so or not), he is equally prepared to concede that another minority thus far usually dominates the majority. This is the minority that now largely controls the instruments of power and that often "persuades" the majority that their interests are best served by perpetuating these controls. Indeed, one arduous task of the critical minority is that of proving how frequently the majority of citizens exercise their franchise of the secret ballot, not at all in behalf of their own interests, but rather in behalf of continued scarcity, insecurity, alienation, and war as these are covertly, if not openly, preferred by the dominant minority.

In this context, one may declare that the supreme political struggle of the dwindling decades still remaining in this millennium is not, after all, between the majority and a minority; like some others of history, it is more accurately depicted as a struggle between at least two organized minorities. Granting, of course, that still other minorities (racial, for one) may be involved, hence that all such generalizations as this deserve qualification, let us nevertheless venture to assert that the one minority aims to widen social–self-realization for and with the majority—for and with the forces of expansion. Such an undertaking, if successful, could create a world culture actually controlled by the majority—surely a unique achievement in history. The opposing minority aims to narrow the sphere of social–self-realization by perpetuating and strengthening the forces of contraction; therefore, it supports institutions, beliefs, and practices which, however much its ideology may protest otherwise, can only lead to increasing negation of human values, and thus to less and less control by the great majority.

Which of the two minorities may prove victorious remains, to be sure, a frightening conundrum of the future. But which of the two *ought* to be successful is not at all a conundrum—not at all, that is, if one accepts the guiding value of social–self-realization expressed through commensurate institutional designs and powerful strategies of action.

THE MEANING OF PUBLIC POLICY

We have said that the right of the majority to exercise its prerogative of formal rule (which is not necessarily, of course, actual rule) assumes that consensual validation is both an epistemological and axiological criterion of democracy. In other words, *the majority, in last analysis, is in a better position than any minority to decide what is true and what is good about the goal-seeking interests of its own culture.*

But just what *is* the majority qualified to decide? It is hardly in a position to decide all questions of truth or value. We have seen that a truth about the physical world accepted by, say, a physicist is (despite his own dependence upon intersubjective communication and agreement) also measured by exacting, objective tests. Nor is the majority equipped to formulate policies or legislation in the precise language of law, or to operate the intricate machinery of government. What the widest possible majority can, and should, determine is the central purposes of every policy. ("Policy" is defined here normatively as any consensually validated formulation of values—that is, want-satisfactions—generalized in political or other cultural purposes of a given period and given culture, and embracing the widest possible group for which the policy is intended.) A dramatic, magnificent example is the Universal Declaration of Human Rights of the United Nations—the most inclusive formulation of values that has ever been expressed by an international body. It is the cornerstone of both international and domestic policies which should eventually emerge from the Declaration.

Although values and policies are no more sharply divided in practice than are, let us say, advocacy and action, they do illustrate how one leads to the other. Assuming social–self-realization as the empirical universal value, the overall policy of democracy everywhere on earth must first guarantee adequate nourishment, clothing, and shelter, as well as literacy, companionship, participation, and every other constituent of that dominant value. A number of more specific policies constituent to this overall policy are thus required—some of them already endorsed, at least formally, by majorities in a number of countries, including America. Examples are protection against the insecurities of old age through retirement insurance; protection against ignorance through compulsory education; protection against domination of the industrial worker by the employer through labor organizations.

But world policies consistent with the overarching criterion of social–self-realization are by no means transfused into commensurate legislation. Today, most old people simply do not approximate genuine security. The great majority of people of every age are not assured of decent medical care. Vast millions of children receive little or no schooling. Moreover, although economic organizations protective of the consumer have increased in size and influence, the social orders in which they function are still largely dominated by monopolistic, corporate groups. The latter constitute a powerful minority which thwarts any effort to shift the center of economic power to the majority.

The role of the critical minority in formulating policies is, then, burdensome indeed. Nevertheless, policies are the heart of democracy. In reconstructionist terms, they are guiding principles, not of *private* "self-evidence" arising from subjective whim or arbitrary authority, but of *public* self-evidence. By the latter, we mean that the majority has agreed only after exhaustive, as well as scrupulous, communication of all practical judgments relevant to these policies.

THE MEANING OF POPULAR GOVERNMENT

Political implementation of policy is the process of guaranteeing that the values which the majority are *intended* to realize are *actually* realized through legislation and social practice. This is the apex of popular government assumed normatively by its legislative, executive, and judicial divisions. All three divisions consist, in whole or in part, of representatives chosen by the majority to carry out its interests.

The chief function of the legislative branch is to formulate, in specific terms, the policies desired by the majority. The chief function of the executive is to operate the machinery by which policies are carried out. This is the responsibility of governors to the governed: the majority is *the final judge* of whether legislatures and executives—the governors—are, in fact, serving its goal-seeking interests. If they are not, they should be replaced promptly by others who promise to do so. Here, again, the minority functions chiefly as critic of the effectiveness of legislatures and executives; thereby it assists the majority to arrive at consensual validations according to criteria previously established.

The role of the judiciary is, first, to interpret the meaning of any policy in the light of governing principles (embodied, for example, in a constitution); second, to examine the fidelity with which other divisions of government implement that policy; and, third, to determine whether actions of a private individual or group violate legal formulations of a given policy. The judiciary (whether the Supreme Court in general or other courts in particular) is less directly responsible to the governed than are the other two branches of government. Therefore it is less likely to be swayed by any temporary feeling or impulsive judgments of the majority. Nonetheless, in last analysis, the judiciary is equally responsible to the people it serves; hence, if its decisions do not usually reflect and advance majority policy, it too should be replaced.

EXPERTS IN DEMOCRACY

The fact that the majority authorizes a judiciary is one acknowledgement of the indispensable role that experts play in a democracy. The majority, although the final judge of policy, recognizes that every policy must be formulated, interpreted, and implemented as accurately and efficiently as possible. These are proper functions of the expert. Therefore, a thoroughly trained judiciary and a competently educated legislature and executive branch are imperative.

Especially in our unbelievably intricate technological culture, governments require services of physical and social scientists, engineers, statisticians, architects, plus innumerable others who associate closely with the judicial, legislative, and executive branches. Such experts are needed as technical planners—or, as ideologists might prefer to say, "bureaucrats." Their business is to translate general agreements into productive effects.

In addition to interpreting and implementing, the expert also demonstrates to the legislature and the executive branch (perhaps even more so than to the majority itself) both frequent mistakes already made and future changes that ought to be made. In this double function, he often plays the role of dissenter and creator. Yet it is never simply his place to decide for the majority; rather, he helps participants to decide for themselves by pointing out their goal-seeking interests as precisely and authoritatively as he can.

The expert, indeed the democratic leader in general, differs accordingly from the demagogue whose own business, after all, is to persuade the majority to follow his judgments whether they reflect genuine majority interests or not. In short, the democratic rather than demagogic expert is one who seeks to help majorities to distinguish spurious from viable values, to build the actual from the potential, to reach conscious acceptance of social–self-realization as democracy's highest normative criterion, to agree upon compatible policies, and finally to elect governments obligated to carry out the consensual policies of that majority.

Thus it becomes essential to disagree with the statement, however persuasively made, that one task of the democratic expert (indeed, a primary function of popular government) is to effect compromises between conflicting interests. Certainly, compromise on occasion is the only feasible way to resolve a particular dispute: each side yields some points and maintains others so that both sides may get back to work. Equally true is the fact that two groups, even though both sides agree upon a particular policy, may and often do compromise their differences over details of an act of legislation about which they have been painfully at odds.

Yet the decisive principle remains steadfast. Consensual validation (and here, after all, is the heart of the matter) is never to be construed as a mere patchwork of conflicting ends and conflicting means. Rather, consensual validation encourages a community of values aided by expert examination of evidence, nonverbal as well as verbal communication, and expert guidance in effecting agreement that eventuates in concerted, productive action.

NORMATIVE DESIGNS FOR A RECONSTRUCTED CULTURE

By "designs" is meant the flexible structures and practices of institutions—political, economic, scientific, educational, religious—that should serve as guides in building the future culture. Therefore, they are policies which are supported by values and, in turn, are ready for detailed implementation. Certain misconceptions may first be dispelled about designs before illustrative models are suggested below.

From earlier discussion of values, policies, and legislation, it is clear that no more exact correlation prevails between the value of social–self-realization and, say, a particular economic design than prevails between a general policy such as the promotion of health and a specific law providing "medicaid." Similarly, a value like participation is far more comprehensive than any design intended to maximize shared control over economic institutions.

Nor is it reasonable to assume that cultural designs are necessarily as permanent as the values that designs are intended to serve. Through the process of consensual validation, it is possible to attain majority agreement on certain values that rest on a long history. Yet the institutions established in their behalf vary greatly in structure and effectiveness from period to period. This does not mean that values are universal while institutions are merely particular; both are derived from, and react upon, cultures that change in time and space. But this does mean that the difficulty of both is intensified by the often greater permanence of values as compared with their translation into workable, empirical designs and institutions.

Implicit, too, in the need for flexibility of cultural designs is the precaution that they should never be regarded as ends divorced from means. The social psychology of goal-seeking, emphasizing both *goals* and *seeking*, is not only useful today; it should prove equally useful tomorrow when, and if, recreated designs are tested on a wider, even planetary, scale. The evolutionary ontology, always presupposed, should in itself dispel any notion that designs can ever become fixed or static. Or that they can ever lack provision for the *modus operandi* by which to realize constantly fructifying human ends.

Yet, after noting all such qualifications, the term, designs, still demands an emphasis different from that of other philosophies of education. This term implies deliberate, systematic, organized construction of plans for future cultural objectives. It implies not merely a process of planning alone but also a product —a concrete, harmonious, worldwide, and democratic plan. It implies that, despite the impossibility of proving in advance that any plan is sure to be tried fairly or to work successfully, we are still obliged to struggle for the widest possible approval of projections for the future. It implies that we possess frequently neglected reservoirs of both theoretical and factual knowledge about the kind of global culture that we could, and should, attain, whether physical, biological, psychological, anthropological, *or* philosophical.

The term, designs, likewise implies creativity. It implies that imaginative regard for beauty should play a central role in planning the future. It implies commitment—taking militant sides with the kind of order that assures maximum freedom for the peoples of every land. It implies acknowledgment that ours is a deliberately utopian approach to the crises of our time. And, finally, it implies that only the fullest possible social–self-realization for the largest possible number of individuals and groups becomes sufficient gauge of either the structure or the methodology of any axiologically, esthetically defensible design.

PRELIMINARY SKETCH OF DESIGNS

Although consideration of specific designs will be included in our subsequent discussion of education, it should be reiterated, meanwhile, that they are never to be regarded as so completely established as to preclude controversy. To be sure, they are presented as cultural policies that can, and should, be obtained upon the broad basis of values cherished by the majority.

Yet it must be reiterated that a chief intention is specificity rather than nebulosity about cultural goals. Therefore the outline that follows is sketched in as fairly concrete terms as can be expected from merely an outline. Appreciating again the need for relentless criticism and modification, they are minimum goals to which, we believe, the majority should now become committed as normative designs—designs supported both by emerging patterns of cross-cultural values and by magnetic, however still immature, contributions from the natural and social sciences, from the arts and religions, and from contemporary philosophy. The prime educational and political task is to present that evidence, to communicate its meanings in the multiple ways of both unrational and rational experience, and to test it as widely and persistently as the forces of expansion properly demand.

(1) We seek an *economy* to:
  (a) satisfy maximum wants of the consumer;
  (b) assure full employment for all citizens, in accordance with their abilities and interests, and under working conditions determined through their own organizations;
  (c) guarantee income for all families sufficient to meet expertly determined standards of adequate nourishment, shelter, dress, medical care, education, recreation;
  (d) utilize all natural resources and all large-scale enterprises in the interest of the majority of the people, with these resources and enterprises under majority control.

(2) We seek a *political system* responsible for:
  (a) placing major technological and agricultural enterprises by authority of the majority;
  (b) preventing pollution, despoliation, or other destructive forms of technological production;
  (c) integrating and publicly controlling transportation and communication systems, utilities, health, and all other public services;
  (d) maintaining a dynamic balance of centralized, federal direction with decentralized, local or regional administration and participation;
  (e) providing legislative, executive, and judicial representation of the chief occupations, interests, and purposes of all groups represented.

(3) We seek a *scientific order* committed to:
  (a) subsidizing pure and applied scientific research as a chief requirement of the people;
  (b) making use of industrial, medical, and all other scientific discoveries in the interests of the economy of abundance and the political system;
  (c) assuring complete experimental freedom to the scientist without military, political, or industrial supervision;
  (d) utilizing large numbers of men and women, trained

in the behavioral sciences, for democratic leadership and governmental service.

(4) We seek an *esthetic pattern* that will:
   (a) regard cultural transformation as an earthwide creative achievement of multiple dimensions;
   (b) express organic, functional direction in the planning and renewal of homes, cities, geographical regions, recreation centers;
   (c) encourage idiosyncratic as well as syncretic artistic talent, and reward creative achievement, while encouraging an equally complete freedom of expression, disagreement, or deviation as permitted the scientist;
   (d) offer publicly supported, uncensored access to works of fine and applied arts (music, drama, motion pictures, painting, sculpture, architecture, and others) by all citizens as a public privilege.

(5) We seek an *educational system* in which:
   (a) abundant support by federal taxation is supplemented by local and state taxation—each level governed by the principle of proportional capacity to pay;
   (b) facilities are free and universal, from nursery school through university and adult levels;
   (c) curriculums, teaching, guidance, and administration are geared to transformative purposes of the economy of abundance, political system, scientific order, and esthetic pattern;
   (d) mass communication and other instruments of public enlightenment are brought into direct cooperation with education and under similar controls.

(6) We seek a *humane order* which:
   (a) regards erotic expression an as affirmative value of great power, variety, and delight;
   (b) protects and encourages while transforming the values of intra- and interfamily life in accordance with plural cultural patterns, varying moral conduct or sibling-parent relationships, and birth control commensurate with democratically established population control;
   (c) provides complete security and meaningful experience to aged citizens and to the helpless or retarded of all ages;
   (d) guarantees full participation in every phase of cultural life by members of all minority groups.

(7) We seek a *world order* dedicated to:
   (a) application, internationally, of all principles specified in the preceding six objectives;
   (b) agreement, by due process, among the great and small nations that national sovereignty must now be subordinated to enforceable international authority;
   (c) maintenance of an internationally supported police force sufficiently powerful to prevent military aggression by any one nation;
   (d) inclusion of the exploited peoples of colonial territories within the widening convergence of peoples of all races and nationalities;
   (e) technological, esthetic, educational, medical, and other assistance to underdeveloped regions, with provisions for democratic controls and safeguards against discrimination or paternalism;
   (f) maximum educational, esthetic, scientific, social, and economic intercourse between nations, including free flow of immigration and emigration.

This bare outline lacks, of course, the magnetism and emotion that it must acquire in order to attract enthusiastic support for the crucial role it is intended to play. Quite differently stated, the outline may lack that quality of the "religious" as it was considered among our cluster of guiding values. Where, indeed, may we detect in our designs "immediate meaning, significance, order, and direction"—a value recognized as a want-satisfaction that is quite as fundamental as shelter or creative work?

Let us turn, therefore, to consideration of how such qualities may help to enfuse our cultural designs.

THE ROLE OF MYTH IN CULTURAL TRANSFORMATION

The term "myth" is hazardous. It is commonly identified either with superstitions and doctrinaire dogmas of the past or with fanatical, sectarian faiths and uncritical tradition-worship. In recent decades, myths have been perverted in fascist propaganda —the myth of the Italian nation and the myth of an Aryan elite are examples. Accordingly, we should rightly expect a good deal of skepticism toward the concept from philosophies that pride themselves on their rational, scientific approaches.

Still, it would be overhasty to conclude that the myth has always been, or need always be, a device intended merely to distort reality, conceal truth, or pervert values. As we regard them, on the contrary, *the great myths of civilization attempt to harmonize and to ennoble, by the use of esthetic, religious, scientific, and other symbols, the most universal and most profound meanings that men are able to perceive, however dimly, in a given epoch.* All great philosophies are thus, in some respects, myths: Platonism may be interpreted as an intellectual-poetic portrait of Athenian culture: Thomism, as a similar portrait of medieval culture. Even Deweyism, despite loud protests we may expect to hear from advocates, is the rather too dispassionate myth of the scientific-technological culture through which we have been speeding. Certainly, too, orthodox Marxism has become a myth for hundreds of millions of citizens whose symbol is the hammer and sickle. The point, then, is that myths may be "good" as well as "bad," depending upon the values they symbolize. And there are "true" as well as "false" myths, their truth or falsity depending upon the extent to which they serve either to disclose or to disguise the common character, the "folklife," of their periods of greatest influence.

Moreover, both ideologies and utopias may possess mythical characteristics. Ordinarily, we consider them to be more prosaic and detailed than myths. The conventional American ideology, for instance, is a somewhat bloodless portrayal of political and economic life, together with its cumbersome body of supporting beliefs and rituals. Yet the picture of our political and economic democracy as painted by Jefferson, for example, merges into a utopian myth of the American dream of freedom, opportunity, and success for every enterprising individual.

But myth is also significant, of course, in the great religions of the world—including Christianity. That this great force in Western civilization has its strong elements of myth would be denied today by no one except, perhaps, the strict fundamentalist. The story of the founding of Christianity is one of the most powerful, symbolic poems of all time. Such doctrines as belief in eternal salvation are vibrant with a profound sense of human destiny. Yet, they prove so defiant of literal translation that only a Michelangelo could portray the Christian myth so that all may understand.

That Christianity has frequently functioned as ideology is also a historic fact. It was so used in the Middle Ages; it serves as ideology today when the Church collaborates with the forces of contraction; or when American ministers and captains of industry join hands to celebrate business competition as a fine example of

Christian virtue; or when Southern segregationists cite Biblical quotations to bolster racist prejudice.

Granting that the ideological use of religion explains, in part, why the concept of myth is so often (and understandably) frowned upon by intellectuals, it should be pointed out, however, that Christianity has its own utopian aspects. The value of social-self-realization, for example, is anticipated by the ancient ideals of the dignity of personality and the brotherhood of man. In recent years, particularly, the struggle of Protestant leaders such as Martin Luther King and of certain Catholic priests and nuns (even in defiance of hierarchical mandates) has, at times, proved heroic—a point we have also tried to appreciate in our cultural appraisal of contemporary perennialism.

Mythical and visionary qualities in Christianity, paralleled in other religions such as Buddhism and Islam, are well interpreted by Cassirer. For him, the essence of mythical experience is the emotion aroused by symbols that acquire a ubiquitous power of their own. But the sophisticated religions of civilized peoples differ from primitive ones: the more enlightened adherents recognize that symbols of ritual and ceremony are actually *symbols*; hence they manifest no objective reality and magical powers. In more technical philosophic language, they are not "reified" or "hypostalized." The remarkable fact about the language of religion, indeed, is that it can shift back and forth from the level of pure myth to the sophisticated or philosophic plane ". . . with perfect freedom, and exhibit all the wealth and concrete exemplification of its creative power."[3]

In religion, myth plays a role that is also esthetic and thus suggests affinity between art and religion. The distinction, says Cassirer, is that the artist is more careful to distinguish between symbol and reality than is the theologian. The dramatist, for example, never claims that the characters he creates are actual persons or that they have special powers, whereas many religionists continue to do so.

In any case, whether myths are expressed through the use of religious or artistic symbols, no reconstructionist-oriented person would deny their often unscientific, often fanatic, character. What he would contend is that this character is not at all inevitable to the needed creative role of myth in modern culture. He wishes, in short, to imbue his designs with the spirit of com-

[3] Cassirer, *Language and Myth*, p. 81, and *Essay on Man*, Chaps. 7, 9. See also Mumford, *The Conduct of Life*, pp. 112–118.

mitment, zest, and emotion that progressivism, unfortunately, tends to subordinate and that perennialism, even more unfortunately, seeks in the restoration of beliefs that become eternal objects of awe and even absolute submission.

The myth yet to be created by and for the emerging age is, in contrast, a culturally therapeutic one. First, it lessens the tensions and bewilderments from which too many of us suffer. Second, it supplies the quality of affective involvement without which commitment to great cultural purposes and designs cannot hope to inspire, or even to occur at all. In more prosaic terms, the mythical mood should become enfused with practical designs for the future, based on voluminous scientific evidence and experimental research. The form and order of myth are symbolized in Cassirer's sense of esthetic-religious experience: they serve to harmonize personal and institutional polarities into marvelously dynamic, organic, cultural goals. The motivation and direction of myth may be linked, further, to the cross-cultural interests of individuals and groups who find unrational and prehended as well as rational and apprehended meanings in their creation of innovative designs.

Finally, the idea of myth, in the pervasive sense we have intended, encompasses various subtle qualities connoted by all five of the modern philosophic movements hitherto touched upon. It would probably be fruitless to argue that even philosophic analysis in some of its curious formulations (for example, certain quixotic writings by Wittgenstein) acquire mythical overtones; so, too, do neo-Marxism and certainly neo-Freudianism. But the two most obvious connections are discerned, of course, in existentialism and Zen Buddhism, each of which stresses noncognitive experience in its own diverse ways—both of which, likewise, point toward creative, holistic meanings for the life and culture of our age.

In different ways, then, the contribution of myth to beliefs about value is also Montague's concern for philosophy as "vision." Or, to quote the greatest of all utopian prophets of the coming scientific age: "By far the greatest obstacle to the progress of science and the undertaking of new tasks . . . is found in this, that men despair and think things impossible."[4] These words of Francis Bacon might well become the clarion call of a reconstructed culturology of education four centuries later.

[4] Bacon, as quoted in Hertzler, *The History of Utopian Thought*, p. 267. See also Farrington, *Francis Bacon, Philosopher of Industrial Science.*

SECTION 2

Educational beliefs of reconstructionism

CHAPTER 18

Learning as social–self-realization

AS EDUCATIONAL THEORY, reconstructionism emerges from, but continues to rest firmly upon, philosophic beliefs about reality, knowledge, and value. Still deeper, its roots reach into the historic soil of culture and thought that produced these beliefs. A basis has been laid in the preceding Section 1; its more precise relevance for education will now be developed in Section 2.

In this chapter, our theme is learning as transformation through social–self-realization. By way of broad background, let us first sample a few influences, both ancient and modern, upon the school as cultural vanguard.

UTOPIANISM IN THE HISTORY OF EDUCATION

The importance assigned to education by the great utopian thinkers is confirmed by the fact that virtually all of those mentioned in Chapter 14 gave it attention. Thus, both Plato and Aristotle, although their approaches are often quite different not only from each other but from the theory with which we are presently concerned, developed the outlines of a system of education which, if adopted, could have profoundly altered Greek practices. Several of their proposals could assuage needs of our own age as well: for example, they both insisted that schooling, at least for a few, should extend well into adult life. Their emphasis upon "gymnastics" and "music," although variant from those of today, is also in accord with certain recent educational theories.

Renaissance utopians, too, offered specific educational plans that still deserve careful consideration. Universal education, work experience, and development of the habit of reading in leisure time were urged by More. Bacon's design, embodied in his *New Atlantis*, centers upon the development of experimental method and the increase of scientific knowledge; but, unlike More, Bacon was more concerned with education of the superior few than the ordinary man. Campanella was prophetic in proposing a system of nursery schools for young children three years of age and over, and in believing, further, that schooling should not only emphasize learning by doing but employ pictures as effective tools of learning. Harrington advocated compulsory free schools and adult education on political issues; he also foresaw that effective education is the "plastic art" of government.

Only murmurings of the utopian mood were to be heard among professional educators of nineteenth-century America. There were, however, scattered anticipations in the writings of such educators as Horace Mann and Francis Parker. Mann's lifelong service to democratic education was too devoted to permit him to overlook the evils of an economic system that could produce such extremes of poverty and exploitation as he saw all around him. But he was also dedicated to the democratic values by which he believed education should be guided—values which were even more glowing beacons along Parker's course. Always a bitter opponent of lock-step education, Parker stressed the value of self-realization particularly. His views on the needs for world order and a thorough redistribution of wealth were almost clairvoyant of educational tasks.

Of educational theories among the Utopian Socialists, Owen's have had perhaps widest influence in America. He favored universal, compulsory schooling from which no one would be excluded because of social-class status. In the strong belief that human nature is shaped by the culture, he recommended that all education, from infancy onward, be designed to provide opportunities for experience in cooperation and creative work. He is credited with having founded the first "Infant Schools," as he and others termed them. Emphasis was placed upon singing, dancing, play, and moral instruction. Owen also founded schools in connection with his utopian communities in other countries. Thus, with his help, but under the administrative direction of his son, Robert Dale Owen, the famous community of New Harmony, Indiana, was founded. It included what has been acclaimed as the first kindergarten and nursery school in the United States.

Nor should we overlook the educational views of the American utopian, Bellamy. A brief section of *Looking Backward* considers the future of higher education. Bellamy's proposed schooling, which would be free to all citizens up to the age of twenty-one, would have as its primary aim the dissolution of class distinctions that have been sharpened in our own culture by the financial inability of great numbers of young people to afford schooling beyond the age of compulsory attendance.

Marx and Engels never devoted systematic attention to educational theory, yet their influence upon it has been powerful. They were among the first to examine the ideological role of such institutions as church and school. They emphasized the power of the school to reinforce an existing system of economic and political relations. Thus they write: "And your education! Is not that also social, and determined by the social conditions under which you educate, by the intervention, direct or indirect, of society by means of schools, and the like?" The aim of Marx and Engels, then, was to ". . . alter the character of that intervention, and to rescue education from the influence of the ruling-class."[1]

Twentieth-century English utopians have also given close, though intermittent, attention to education. For example, an almost completely forgotten novel by Wells, *Joan and Peter, the Story of an Education*, is both a scathing critique of English schools (to no small extent applicable to American schools also) and a broad outline of the schooling needed in an interdependent world. He writes: "I ask: what is this education of yours up to? What is the design of the whole? What is this preparation of yours for?" In sketching his answer, Wells implied the need for a "clear and guiding idea of a national purpose . . .," for "the limitlessness of the community . . .," and for the "World Republic" as "the proper teaching of all real education. . . . This idea of a world-wide commonwealth, this ideal of an everlasting world-peace in which we are to live and move and have our being, has to be built up in every school, in every mind, in every lesson."[2]

Numerous other prophetic Englishmen such as Shaw could be included, but we must turn instead to a few comments on such comparatively recent, American utopians as Veblen and Mumford. Veblen's most important contribution to education was his exposé of the control of the higher learning by business interests. Utilizing criteria of cultural reality, truth, and value, he demon-

[1] Marx, as quoted in Lee (ed.), *The Essentials of Marx*, p. 49.

[2] Wells, *Joan and Peter, the Story of an Education*, pp. 275, 554, 563, 565–566.

strated how the ideology of our "pecuniary culture" works upon the attitudes and practices of university instructors and administrators alike. No wonder, then, that there is ". . . a work of reconstruction to be taken care of in the realm of learning, no less than in the working scheme of economic and civil institutions." And ". . . if it is to be done without undue confusion and blundering it is due to be set afoot before the final emergency is at hand."[3]

Far in advance of his time but often advocated since, Veblen would have decentralization, democratic participation by the faculty in policy-making, and complete intellectual freedom to pursue scholarly and scientific problems without distraction by academic pageantry and the "conspicuous waste" of huge athletic stadiums and contests. Some of these recommendations were made in Veblen's famous early work, *The Theory of the Leisure Class*, in which he argued that typical college sports, fraternity activities, and other pursuits carried on in "the reputable seminaries of learning" are, in fact, holdovers from a "barbarian" (as opposed to a "civilized") culture.

Central to Mumford's position is the assumption that civilization now stands at the edge of an abyss. We must therefore choose between either the catastrophe that will accompany continued domination by the minority now holding economic-political control or the "dynamic equilibrium" of a "biotechnic" world order, which could be established if those controls were transferred to, and integrated by, the majority. The schools, moreover, could aid in helping to achieve this goal—one being to replace the mechanistic, atomistic bases of traditional education by a philosophy of "organism":

> This reorientation is a fundamental one. It means a shift from the belief in a science of dead things, analyzed, isolated, dissected, reduced to a tissue of simple abstractions, to a belief in a science of living things. In this new science, a qualitative understanding of pattern, form, configuration, history, is as important as statistical analysis; and in terms of the method that accordingly develops, no situation is fully resolved and no problem fully explored until it is seized in all its ultimate social relationship to human values and human purposes.[4]

[3] Veblen, *The Higher Learning in America*, p. 53.

[4] Mumford, *Values for Survival*, p. 147.

Although Mumford himself has never wavered in his conviction that "cultural renewal" (a favorite term of his) becomes the most urgent of all mandates, latter-day American educational philosophers have rarely reflected his own challenge in the decades since 1946 when this statement was written. It is true that a number of distinguished theorists have been future-minded—some, like the idealist, Alexander Meiklejohn, even taking a valiant utopian stance in *Education between Two Worlds*. Others of strong progressivist sympathy such as Harold Rugg, George S. Counts, and I. B. Berkson have also contributed influentially to the transformative orientation.

Yet it can scarcely be maintained that any of these able theorists express forthrightly the reconstructionist mood to the extent of several recent writers who (though not educational philosophers) have succeeded in reaching remarkably wide audiences. We refer to Paul Goodman, John Holt, Edgar Friedenberg, Jonathan Kozol, Peter Schrag, and other interpreters of the educational scene who, in several idioms of dissent and radical commitment, help to motivate us in the directions that we now wish to elucidate.

SOCIAL–SELF-REALIZATION AS CULTURAL MEANS AND END

Return, then, to the direct problem of this chapter as it has emerged, at least partly, from the utopian propensities of educational history. Perhaps one way to bridge the gap between where we have been and where we might wish to go is to recognize that, while all three philosophies of education thus far interpreted have recognized what may be termed, in psychological terms, "learning as goal-seeking," they do not agree upon the meaning of that concept.

Progressivists, we remember, call attention to the function of intelligence as continuous interaction of means and ends—the ends being "ends-in-view" which influence the original choice of means, but which are themselves modified in the process. Essentialists also recognize that goal-seeking is a legitimate aspect of learning: if idealists, they consider education as spiritual unfolding or as personal identification with an objective universe imbued with Divine purposes; if realists, they may think of goal-seeking largely as adjustment to the physical, economic, civic, and familial situations of modern life; if neither idealists nor realists, they may (along with philosophic analysts) still regard themselves as sophisticated proponents for educational transmission as culturally approbative goals. Perennialists, our third group, view goal-seeking as eternal striving by man to reach the end inherent in his nature—a striving primarily through empiriological clarification, or through revelation, or preferably through some combination of these means.

The reconstructionist interpretation of goal-seeking is indebted to all three of these philosophers of education. Nevertheless, the concept is sufficiently distinctive to warrant its own characterization. Psychological, sociological, axiological, and other aspects of goal-seeking discussed previously are not to be reiterated in detail, but are reformulated here as educational principles and practices considered in successive or overlapping dimensions. To these, we now turn.

Recall, to begin with, two complementary alternatives. On the one hand, reconstructionists stress the present stage of world history as a revolutionary one, so that restorative, transmissive, or moderative patterns of belief will no longer do. On the other hand, they insist that our revolutionary age demands unprecedented, transformative goals which a less precarious and more stable period would not have to demand.

Built upon the premises that all philosophies are, directly or indirectly, interpretations of culture, this philosophy of education thus obliges us to devote close attention to determining what purposes are needed if the vacillations and confusions so chronic to our civilization are to be dispelled. In education, it becomes necessary to agree as far as humanly possible not only on how we want to act but on where we want to go. Such an aim is surely not educational in any conventional, academic sense; it is, first of all, the aim of mankind. At the same time, it is the supreme justification of formal education as an institution of culture.

In broadest perspective, educational aims are therefore both national and international. They are national insofar as they focus attention upon the designs for a planned democracy of a country such as America; in these designs, every prime institution is organized and systematized in the interests and under the control of the majority of the people. (We have outlined their features in the preceding chapter.) Our purposes are international insofar as educational purposes assume that American civilization cannot survive, much less reorganize itself, unless its own transformations are geared throughout to those of other countries. On our technologically interdependent planet, isolation is now completely impractical even were it morally defensible.

The need for internationalism in education is, then, far from satisfied by innocuous generalizations about being a "good neighbor" or about cooperating with the United Nations. Only international commitment to a global order, in which authority is supported by police power superior to that of any single constituent member, can guarantee that in moments of crisis some nation will not repudiate its professions of peace. To expose the conflict between demands of national sovereignty and the need for responsible world sovereignty, and hence to commit ourselves unequivocally to world government and world citizenship, is not only one of our highest educational obligations—it is foremost among all such obligations.

In a critical sense, these two master purposes contain the one potential of energy far greater than that of all the radioactive elements on earth. They alone, if we decide to release the power within them, are capable of channeling the resources of science, economics, politics, religion, and art into the remaking of both our nation and our world. They alone, magnetized with cultural myth as we have delineated this value, can dissipate the confusions and frustrations that now so seriously weaken and stultify the educational enterprise. They alone are able to rejuvenate public education by validating a consensus of goals and strategies in which the common wants of mankind can be expressed and fulfilled. They alone, in short, are the means and end of social–self-realization regarded within the framework of democratic world culture.

MOTIVATIONS FOR LEARNING THROUGH SOCIAL–SELF-REALIZATION

Constructed upon the foundations thus far laid, the core of our theory of learning proves at once to be normative and descriptive. The criterion by which to judge whether any proposed experience should be included in an educational program is, therefore, whether that experience contributes to social–self-realization as we have sought to define this supreme value. It follows that requirements of such sciences of man as psychology and anthropology, insofar as their service to education is concerned, cannot be satisfied by the traditional canons of "objectivity" upon which some philosophers, especially realist essentialists and their allies, have insisted.

We can and should, to be sure, utilize precise and objective methods of experimentation in determining how individuals behave. Indeed, it is largely through these methodologies that the human sciences have begun to demonstrate that all human learning is at bottom a striving for expression, for fulfillment, for reciprocal functioning of the emotional, biological, and mental capacities of complex human organisms living interdependently with similar organisms. Also, it is largely because of the use of objective techniques that studies in educational psychology have strongly emphasized the importance of considering needs, desires, and drives in organizing an effective curriculum. Although research is far from complete, these studies bolster our case by providing evidence for the expectation that the reconstructionist kind of learning, while utopian, is also entirely workable.

But full understanding of the bearings upon education of social–self-realization also demands recognition of the fact not only that human beings are motivated by interwoven wants, but further that they *should* be so motivated. In other words, integrated satisfaction of these wants is a supreme good. It is the standard, moreover, by which, in the last analysis, we decide upon the worthiness of social institutions (including that of education itself).

Social–self-realization, far from being an abstract or dogmatic criterion of learning, thus becomes effective only in the degree to which its criteria are understood and applied. Let us next illustrate their usefulness with awareness of reconstructionist axiology and epistemology as background.

CONSTITUENT VALUES OF LEARNING

Social–self-realization connotes a cluster of specifiable values. Therefore, if we are to understand learning as goal-seeking, we must first try to answer the question: For *what* goals shall we learn?"

Consideration of such a "simple" value as sufficient nourishment suggests that learning can be motivated by study of the chemistry of food, the availability of food, and the customs related to it. Adequate dress, too, can generate interest in learning because of personal concern with comfortable and attractive clothing. The value of erotic expression encompasses both romantic and physical love as well as problems related to marriage and the family.

Although conventional schooling has by no means made sufficient use of such values, their power to stimulate the desire to learn has long been recognized. The fact that already they are more or less successfully employed in such fields as home economics easily explains the frequency of interest in these fields by comparison with typical academic subjects. As we proceed, however, from the less to the more complex and subtle values, opportunities for motivating the learner often decrease. Thus, such values as belongingness, appreciation, and participation, although they articulate wants just as important to social–self-realization as do physiological wants, enter only incidentally or haphazardly into the programs of many schools.

Consider the value of participation. From his earliest years, every child should feel that he is helping to create his school—that he has a share and a responsibility in that creation. He should learn to regard himself as a constructive critic who not only dares to question the rules and programs of a given classroom but who also is expected to offer suggestions for improvement—suggestions that will be criticized and weighed, in turn, by his fellow students and his teachers.

Participation is thus linked with such values as belongingness and appreciation: with belongingness, because the child (or adult, for that matter) may feel himself so much *within* the organic wholeness of his group that he is completely a part of it; with appreciation, because he may feel that others respect him for each effort and contribution, however modest it may be.

As a value, participation also extends beyond the school proper into educational activities of the community. Children should continually share in the experiences of a social environment which they enrich by that sharing and which, in turn, enriches them. Opportunities to do so, moreover, are boundless for the imaginative and adventuresome teacher in, say, ghetto life, political struggle, or neighborhood rehabilitation projects.

Remaining components of the supreme value of social–self-realization are equally applicable to learning. Thus, creativity, when it is related to a value such as steady work, opens an equally wide vista. Work experience—certainly all kinds of vocational training—should be geared not only to abilities and talents but also to the values of curiosity and adventure. Moreover, it should mean participation in purposeful, socially useful, community enterprises. But it should never be regarded merely as a means of acquiring skills or as a source of pocket money; rather, it should be considered as an end which lies close to the core of social–self-realization.

The main point is that the adequacy of any program of learning is to be measured by the extent to which it embodies *all* the constituent values of social–self-realization, not merely some of them. Otherwise, any school may excuse itself by showing that it is already guided by one or more of these values: literacy, skill, and information are among the most obvious, as well as physiological and mental health, steady income, and a few others. Moreover, schools founded on progressivist beliefs have made educational headway through utilizing the motivations provided by such values as growing and variation.

What even the best schools have not sufficiently accomplished is to make sure that (1) no constituent of social–self-realization is neglected; (2) each value receives consideration on the elementary, secondary, college, and adult levels; (3) choice among values, in terms of those most desirable in a given situation, is effected only after intelligent consideration of alternatives; and (4) continuous interplay among all constituent values is nevertheless cultivated, with a view to optimal satisfaction of them all. Social–self-realization, let us remember, is a normative fusion of the totality of want-satisfactions. Hence it is attained in the degree that no single value is forgotten or denied.

BASES OF LEARNING

Before this normative goal can be approached, we need to grasp more fully the relationships to learning of certain psychological and epistemological bases of social–self-realization. Let us be selective.

The phrase "continuous interplay" above is one basis; it implies that the experience of prehension (as we earlier chose to redefine this concept) both precedes and succeeds the conscious analyses and syntheses (the apprehensions) of experience. That the functional psychology of progressivism, supported often by aspects of Gestalt psychology, agrees at least implicitly with the concept of prehension is indicated by its beliefs in immediate experience, transaction, and "the whole child." Prehension underscores these familiar beliefs with richer sense of organic pattern. It is attuned to the Zennist spirit. It echoes certain qualities of existentialism. And it suggests, too, that the body responds to stimuli as *body* rather than as mere brain and nervous system. Every experience that is genuinely educative, moreover, contributes to the satisfaction of wants; each such satisfaction not only possesses its own unity but fuses with satisfaction of other wants in a still wider field. Only insofar as such widening patterns of want-satisfaction are built into the experience of human beings does fruitful learning occur.

The concept is, perhaps, still more helpful in bringing self-realization (regarded primarily in individual terms) together with social–self-realization (which may be redefined here as the entire culture fulfilling itself through interrelative and transformable institutions). Learning thus becomes social, utopian, and, above all, esthetic. All partners in an educational enterprise, not just students of art, enter into the cooperative creation of social designs—of "cultural gestalten."

The need to encourage the richest possible play of imagination and affect, both imperative to this kind of learning, cannot be overstressed. It is one of our least appreciated educational needs today. We have too widely assumed that learning is almost entirely cognitive—a mere apprehending of facts, parts, structures. Or, at best, it becomes a manipulation of these data by means of problem-solving which is more usually associated with "scientific" rather than with "esthetic" experience.

Another master principle upon which social–self-realization depends has been considered in Chapter 16 as the unrational. Because human wants cannot be understood as motivations until they have been traced ultimately to the unconscious or preconscious, the neglect of the Freudian and neo-Freudian schools by conventional schools of educational psychology is nothing less than scandalous. Much more careful attention should be paid to motivations springing from the value of love—love regarded frankly in its erotic sense as well as in broader senses. The potency of the craving for love should be recognized and taken into account in every program of education—and not only in the relationship of male and female but in those of teacher with student. Surely, it should provide the indispensable background for study of, and experience in, family life.

The significance for learning of the ego as mediator between id and superego also needs further consideration. In operational terms, the task of intelligence (centered in the ego) is to learn how to direct one's urges (centered in the id) so as to comply with or modify the social compulsions of conscience (centered in the superego). In terms of our concern with future cultural purposes, learning is facilitated by the attempt to answer such questions as these: What changes are desirable in the superego—or in the language of some authorities, in the creation of an "ideal superego"? What changes are needed so that the unrational goals of individuals may be more richly attained? What changes are needed in relationships of the sexes, and therefore in those of family life, in order to provide greater unity both in these relationships and among the larger unities of community, state, and world?

The unrational is equally important in its negative effects

on learning. Take only the process of rationalization, with its effect of thwarting or distorting actions or concealing motives. Countless young adults have rationalized themselves into "wanting" professional training beyond their interests or capacities because their families think that they should desire such training. Such an expectation on the part of one or both parents often has a neurotic basis. (An illustration: the ambition of a frustrated mother for the professional success of a son who, in her unconscious, becomes the image of the mate she had dreamed of.) The failures of children, moreover, to work constructively in school are often traceable to the unrational. Learning for such children is deleterious in that it often produces hatred rather than love of learning.

Even though psychotherapy is considered in some teacher-training and school programs, educational programs as a whole have only begun to confront such difficult personal problems in the behavior of individuals. Still more neglected, however, is the unrational in its cultural aspects. Whereas compulsions of the social environment (symbolized by the superego) are essential to Freudian theory, the typical psychoanalytic method aims to effect adjustment of the individual *to* the social environment rather than to inquire whether deep-seated disturbances of the social environment may not themselves be primarily responsible for troubles of the individual. Much the same criticism may be extended to some of the newer movements, such as existentialist psychotherapy.

To correct the culture rather than merely the personality is obviously beyond the powers of the physician of the mind. Hence, although his work is and will continue to be indispensable, it is also limited in efficacy. The greater task remains and, in a comprehensive sense, education's responsibility is to assume that task—to become, as Fromm and other influential neo-Freudians might well assert, physician to our maladjusted culture.

Here the twin concepts of ideology and utopia also become useful to learning as social–self-realization. Ideology, we recall, is seen as one social form of rationalization—that is, when a culture fashions a picture of itself that not only conceals actual conditions but may even justify or glorify institutions and practices that prove, in fact, to be outdated and harmful. Utopia becomes another concealment when utopians portray a kind of heaven into which people can escape by justifying their failures to confront the ongoing culture. In terms of learning, both ideology and utopia are constructs capable of penetrating through cultural patterns often transmitted by the schools. They can help students and teachers to understand whether, and in what degree, these patterns are accurate or deceptive images of cultural reality. Here the influence of neo-Marxian theory can prove unusually helpful.

CONSENSUAL VALIDATION AS EXPERIENCE IN LEARNING

Learning through social–self-realization requires, in addition to the philosophic concepts applied above to education, the correlative concept of consensual validation. Its fruitful operation, however, can be attained only through continuing experience—we learn about it best as we engage in it and, simultaneously, improve upon its workability. Education offers abundant responsibility to utilize its constituent phases by means of learning on every level from children to adults.

LEARNING THROUGH EVIDENCE

Knowledge as to the precise content, form, and relationships of learning comes from boundless sources: from science, history, art, religion, education itself, and, above all, from the experience of which each individual and group is directly aware.

It is this last source—direct experience—that is the point at which learners can begin to concern themselves with evidence. But they are prepared to learn the facts in a given situation that are pertinent to what they are learning only when their goal-seeking interests have motivated them sufficiently. Such learning is at first often characterized by uncertainty, doubt, a sense of confusion, and painful conflict among want-satisfactions. As emphasized by progressivists, the goal-seeking effort of an individual or group, being blocked, seeks to eliminate the blockage. Hunger quickens the perceptions of the primitive man seeking food. People lacking adequate shelter are induced to examine the political or economic reasons for shortage.

It is therefore sound for the teacher to encourage learnings rooted in problems. But he should go further—first, to appreciate that often the problems most worth considering are those created by interruption in satisfying specifiable wants; and second, to keep in mind that often such problems are eventually integral with cultural and intercultural purposes. Once he is so equipped, the teacher can more justifiably and quickly eliminate problems that are artificial or outdated, and he can encourage solutions appropriate to the age and environment of his students.

As friendly and astute critics have sometimes noted, however, progressivists may at times overemphasize problematic learning. Direct awareness of participation, creativity, and various other values can also be abundantly provided in a functional classroom. Interest is the key to learning—interest rooted in as many of the constituent values of social–self-realization as possible.

Moreover, if teachers sensitized to the principles of learning as goal-seeking appreciate that such learning embraces noncognitive motivations, they may appreciate, too, that these motivations are intrinsic to their possessors. This does not, of course, mean that if we cannot communicate or agree about our goals we do not possess them; it does mean that unrational, affective aspects are too often ignored or bypassed in the learning process because of the unconventionality or elusiveness of those aspects. Yet, just for this reason, they become all the more significant. Thus erotic powers, to take a familiar example, cannot be ignored by responsible educators, nor is there any reason for them to be ignored once a naturalistic ethic replaces customary fears that some of our desires are too nasty or too private to be honestly recognized. On the contrary, always remembering levels of maturation, such powers should properly occupy a large place in learning. Recognition of the unrational in its numerous manifestations contributes vitally to the denial or attainment of want-satisfactions; its suppression often does irreparable damage.

These comments may be highlighted by the recent developments of existentialism. Indeed, in its own terms, *direct* evidence in the way of subjective, untested, but often vivid, awareness, is precisely what existentialists insist upon. Surely they thus contribute a necessary dimension to the total outlook we are striving toward. So, too, is the directness of human perception so beautifully celebrated in delicate Zen rituals such as the tea ceremony.

But direct experience is not to be construed merely as personal. With neo-Freudians, such as Sullivan, we must insist, too, upon *interpersonal* experiences. With neo-Marxists, we must equally insist upon *intragroup* and, even more so, *intergroup* experiences that afford learners (again of varying maturation) innumerable occasions of struggles and conflicts within neighborhood, community, or national and international experiences. All were earlier described as the cultural reality of group concepts, allegiances, and conditioners.

What, now, is the main point to be emphasized? Simply this: fundamental to learning is the kind of evidence about our wants that springs from our own experience—individual and collective alike. Education that neglects or fails to provide generous opportunity for such experience and that does not recognize the importance of the libido, say, as a potent motivation to learn, cannot hope to succeed in the practice of consensual validation. Nor can education that neglects direct social involvement.

But let us turn next to what we shall term *indirect* experience in the search for social–self-realization. We have seen that such sciences as psychology, sociology, and anthropology give impressive support to the hypothesis that man is a goal-seeking, goal-achieving animal. Although experimental verification of this hypothesis is far from complete, a far greater mass of evidence is available than schools could easily use.

Take, as a simple instance again, the want of nourishment. The primary motivation in seeking food is, from infancy onward, direct experience of hunger. Beginning with this inescapable fact, we may study physiology in order to enrich our knowledge of what hunger means in terms of bodily processes and structures and of what nutrients are essential to the human organism. Thus we find (granting variations, of course) that persons of known weights, heights, and physical habits require specified numbers of calories and amounts of vitamins, proteins, carbohydrates, and other substances if they are to attain and maintain good physical health. Although taste and dietary habits range widely in different parts of the world, *standards* of adequate nourishment apply to Eskimos, Hottentots, Mongolians, or Americans. And these standards hold even if an Eskimo lives almost exclusively on blubber, or an American on "cokes" and drugstore sandwiches.

Evidence as to the nature of our more complex psychological wants—for creative work, let us say—is much more difficult to obtain. Nevertheless, anthropological research is laden with cross-cultural proof of artifacts that are both instrumental and esthetic—eating utensils, clothing, weapons, shelters, and hundreds of others. Industrial psychology, too, is producing evidence of high, positive correlations between monotony of work and low productivity, as well as between opportunities for originality and high productivity.

History is an equally abundant source of evidence for the study of wants and their satisfaction. Education as enculturation, for example, reveals man seeking to satisfy not only the wants of literacy, skill, and information but, likewise, all others of the spectrum which these wants assist in satisfying. Actually, the struggle for education throughout the ages could itself be interpreted as the struggle for social–self-realization. The story is often one of failure; yet the evidence of evolving cultures, when read in the light of man's effort to satisfy the want of education, sparkles with a relevance never equaled in history courses confined mainly to chronological events.

The ideal in learning is, of course, to provide continuous interplay between *both* experiences—direct and indirect. The indispensable understanding of one's goal-seeking interests is steadily deepened with the help of the arts, sciences, or history. The vast authoritative evidence available in these fields is deepened, too, as it becomes related to our efforts to confront the realities depicted in Chapter 15 or to achieve the personal-collective goals described in Chapter 17. Yet, such direct evidence proves meaningful only as we are able to read our own direct experience into it and to act in terms of that integration.

LEARNING THROUGH COMMUNICATION

The second aspect of learning through consensual validation—communication—is inseparable from the first. Hence, it should not be thought of as following the first aspect in sequence; rather, it operates simultaneously with the gathering of evidence. Both kinds of evidence, direct and indirect, are subject matter for communication. Thus I, for one, am able to express my own goal-seeking interests far better as I learn from others about theirs (and by "others" is meant scientists, artists, and historians as well as personal or group associates). Similarly, others may learn to express their interests more accurately as they listen to me. What does this capacity mean for educational method?

It means, to begin with, that the traditional classroom is completely transformed. Communication, instead of being limited to imparting indirect evidence from textbooks, pictures, or lectures, also includes reciprocal expression among students and teachers. The effort to articulate interests would be encouraged and respected. Likewise, the effort to interpret all evidence provided by science, art, or history would replace passive recitations. The more back-and-forth the communication, the more spontaneous it becomes and the more easily do more precise meanings emerge.

Here the "dialogic" philosophy of Buber appears to be peculiarly apt, especially as he has expressed his "I-thou" principle in educational terms. No longer is the teacher a mere conveyor of information or the student a mere recipient. Both learn from each other, both teach each other, and both thereby flower as personalities. Communication, moreover, takes place in various ways. Speech is of such importance that the teacher will often turn his classroom into a forum and exert every effort to draw out less assured students until they have attained confidence that they, too, have contributions to make. Writing is of equal importance, especially when it is communicated to the learning group as a whole; but themes that only the teacher reads, or that provide exercise in grammar through eclectic topics, should be taboo. Hence writing should be utilized much more generously in relation to cooperative problems or interests that govern total learning situations.

Nor should we forget the importance of communication through arts such as painting, music, drama, architecture, and the dance. Every school should provide wide ranges of creative expression. Here an underlying aim is to enable each person to express himself to himself and to others as authentically as he can in terms of his own unique talents. But learning through art is also frequently practiced in situations of common interest to all participants. The school orchestra with its variety of instruments, the interpretive group dance, the class-designed mural, the theatrical stage—all afford abundant opportunities for individualized communication in the socialized school.

But analytic philosophers and semanticists have also made us aware of the innumerable symbolic snares that prevent us from reaching one another even when we suppose that we have done so. Ludwig Wittgenstein, whose insights have led to so many contemporary puzzles about language; Alfred Korzybski, whose *Science and Sanity* established an entire "cult" of semantic studies; and Marshall McLuhan, the popularized exponent of revolutionary changes in the application of "new media" such as television—these are only three very different pioneers who, both directly and indirectly, point to the pitfalls as well as opportunities awaiting education. As Korzybski has emphasized, words function on levels of abstraction high above those of direct experience and sense perception—levels where words can synchronize only crudely or partially with such experience.

Here is another reason why schools should provide more opportunities for practice with other ways of dialogue than language—above all, with the arts. But we need also to remember that the artist, too, succeeds in communicating only to a degree: the composer of a symphony or the painter of a landscape may presume very well what he wishes to communicate, yet his work may convey an utterly different meaning to the listener or spectator.

Other mountainous obstacles to communication are ideological in nature—obstacles toward which, too often, philosophers of language appear remarkably oblivious. Patterns of beliefs, habits, attitudes, customs, and practices which become reflected as a given culture's word picture of itself are never completely accurate even in the youthful period of that culture; they usually become decreasingly accurate as time goes on. Yet we have seen how extremely powerful agencies of public opinion may skillfully reinforce ideologies—indeed, as changes accelerate in underlying cultural conditions (of politics, for one), these changes in turn stimulate ever more skillful, even frantic, efforts to convince us that no fundamental alterations of institutional arrangements need occur at all. Distortion of the evidence about group conflicts, allegiances, and conditioners can become a "fine art," practiced on a mass scale by radio and television commentators, by newspapers and motion pictures, and by public education.

As a means of learning, then, communication requires constant self-criticism by students and teachers as well as generous practice. At least an elementary knowledge of semantics should be part of the equipment of every teacher, and no student should be ignorant of the simple rules by which his use of words can be improved. Equally important is propaganda analysis—that is, detection of the common tricks by which we are so frequently prevented from understanding some aspect of cultural reality. Let it be remembered, however, that propaganda analysis is limited in usefulness without awareness of the ideological influences that often lies behind propaganda. Thus "Madison Avenue" advertising should be judged critically in terms of economic motives—for example, the pressure to purchase more and more electric appliances. Students should inquire to what extent people are actually led to healthful want-satisfactions and to what extent the ingenuity of mass conditioning generates artificial wants among insatiable consumers.

The concept of utopia can be equally helpful as a safeguard against pitfalls of communication. It provides normative standards by which the propaganda of ideology can be evaluated, and it helps to reduce cynical distrust of all evidence made available through communication. We must, however, remember that utopians may resort to propaganda which requires equally alert analyses.

But classroom learning needs to be supplemented by direct observation of the methods of communication that operate in the community. For this reason, critical study and use of such public opinion agencies as newspapers, radio, and television should be emphasized. More than this, the reconstructed community school should utilize all the technologically revolutionary instruments of communication; closed circuit television, for example, may well occupy at least as prominent a place as textbooks. Improved devices for measuring the effects—negative and positive—of these resources afford one important opportunity in the science of education. They include the whole gamut of programed instruction which students as well as teachers or other educators can learn to appraise for deleterious as well as constructive effects upon social–self-realization.

It becomes vital, too, for students to discover the cruciality of effective public communication by attending court trials, meetings of public commissions, political rallies, and debates of legislative bodies. Appreciation of the value of unrestricted freedom of speech and of the press thus can be deepened. For when students are alerted to the necessity of exposing special interests to the bright light of public scrutiny, they more readily learn how, in turn, these interests may be grossly ignored or distorted. Thus they may also learn not only how indispensable is one person's or group's testimony in the form of direct evidence, but how all such testimony must be checked scrupulously against the indirect evidence of experts in particular situations (jury trials are, again, first-rate examples) where the principle of consensual validation is in operation.

Learning through practice in public communication also helps young citizens to detect and avoid countless hindrances to dependable judgments. The sophistry of lawyers in court trials, the loaded testimony by lobbyists, the demagoguery of politicians —all provide fertile opportunity for the student to develop greater sensitivity toward virtually every process of public communication. But through such experience he can also develop appreciation of the fact that, despite all dangers inherent in these processes, democracy cannot succeed without them. For this reason, *continuous practice in classroom communication*—above all, dialogue—*is necessary for wider dialogue in the community.*

LEARNING THROUGH AGREEMENT AND ACTION

Whereas the processes of learning from evidence and learning through communication function interactively, learning through agreement follows both of these. That is to say, agreement (accompanied by implementation) is the step that is properly taken only when a group has learned as much as possible, by both direct and indirect experience, as to the nature of the goal-seeking interest that governs their effort.

Ideally, the aim of agreement is group unanimity. Sometimes this is possible, particularly if the quality and quantity of evidence are adequate and if processes of communication have been thorough. Yet, just as unanimity is not always feasible in political or economic life, and just as minority dissent must always be respected, so, too, are such limitations expectable in classroom experience. While a minority of student participants may propose some goal to which they wish to win the majority, they may fail either because the majority is not convinced or because freely given and communicated testimony persuades them that they themselves were wrong. Indeed, in classroom situations governed by the spirit and purpose of consensual validation, teachers themselves may belong to the minority—a position which they should gladly accept and for which, it is hoped, they will be respected.

But perhaps the richest reward accruing from minority-majority experiences is that of learning that agreements reached by the majority are proper conditions of policy and action. Commitment to goal-seeking is, at some point, imperative. Therefore classrooms should provide abundant opportunities to arrive at agreements and to translate them into *action* by the group. In such action, the dissenting minority (although it may, of course, continue to criticize at appropriate times and at other times may wish to withdraw from a proposed action) learns to recognize its obligation to respect majority decision.

If, for example, the majority of a high-school class in agriculture decides to grow a garden and to preserve the produce, those who have argued against the proposal should be encouraged to cooperate in carrying it out. In education as in politics, minority dissent does not ordinarily mean minority refusal to cooperate in policies decided upon by the majority.

It should be realized, of course, that action upon agreement is not always practicable. A social-studies group may devote several months to examining a local problem of low-cost housing and may then reach agreement upon a desirable policy. Obviously they cannot carry out the policy, because they cannot build the houses themselves. But what they can do is to discuss their ideas with civic authorities, perhaps persuade their parents to act, or resolve to take later action when they themselves become voting citizens. The community school, to be discussed further, affords exactly the kind of transformed learning environment in which such steps can and should occur.

GROUP DYNAMICS AND ANTHROPOTHERAPY

> *The re-educative process has to fulfill a task which is essentially equivalent to a change in culture. . . .* Only by anchoring his own conduct in something as large, substantial, and

> superindividual as the culture of a group can the individual stabilize his new beliefs sufficiently to keep them immune from the day-by-day fluctuations of moods and influences to which he, as an individual, is subject . . . re-education means the establishment of a new super-ego. . . .[5]

These provocative sentences from Lewin, the pioneer Gestalt social psychologist, anticipate both a need for large-scale cultural vision and the pivoted importance of consensual validation. The frontier area in applied social science called group dynamics, which probably owes more to Lewin than to any other thinker or experimenter, is indeed a promising one for the development, refinement, and testing of several guiding ideas congenial to reconstructionism.

Underlying "sensitivity training" and other contributions of group dynamics is a belief that the human group is as natural a phenomenon as the human individual—a "field of forces" that may be subjected to controlled investigation in the same intensive way that the individual is subjected to investigation by narrower psychologies. Enough evidence has already accumulated to show that genuine change does take place in the character of a group as it deals with its own unrational conflicts, its relationships to other groups, its failure to communicate caused by linguistic or emotional factors, its distortions of evidence, or its confusions as to goals as well as methods of action.

In the field of education, group dynamics, offers a number of simple, workable techniques by which group-mindedness may be improved. Here we shall provide a few brief examples that have benefited by decades of practice.

Role-playing, for example, is a device to clarify an imaginary or actual situation by spontaneous dramatization. Various members play the roles of real or typical persons involved. For example, a social-studies group is about to visit a local congressman, home from Washington, to determine why he voted against a bill to provide integrated housing on a national scale. In preparation for the visit, one student plays the role of the congressman, other students play a black labor leader, businessman, member of the League of Women Voters, and so on. After the scene has taken place, the players and the audience (remaining members of the group) join in analyzing what has occurred and try to anticipate

[5] Lewin, *Resolving Social Conflicts*, pp. 59, 65.

reactions to their forthcoming visit, thus improving their plans for the interview.

The "sociodrama" (or "psychodrama," as role-playing is sometimes called when concerned primarily with the problems of an individual) has abundant potentialities for learning. Not only may it clarify real situations; the acting group becomes more aware of itself and its members. Because it dramatizes situations at the same time that it verbalizes them, it also provides a perfectly legitimate quality of fun and imagination.

Another device is group self-evaluation, a process in which examination is made of the group's procedures and gains. The adequacy of evidence and communication, for example, depends upon the extent to which every member assumes a fair share of responsibility, takes part in the discussion, and may express dissent from the views of his fellows. Determining whether he functions as effectively as he might thus requires that other members help him to become aware of his part, just as he helps them. If this process of evaluation is well carried out, it includes awareness not merely of verbal behavior but also of unrationally motivated or other nonverbal behavior—for example, behavior arising from hostilities or insecurities of group members.

The process of group self-evaluation may be improved still further by use of the "observer." As a rule, he is a member of the group who becomes temporarily a nonmember—that is, he does not participate in the process at a given session but watches the group as critically as possible. As he observes he notes these points: Is the group moving ahead? Does it know where it wants to go? Are certain members resisting, thereby preventing cohesiveness (social prehension, we might say) from developing? Does the leader dominate too strongly? Does he hold the group "on the beam"?

The role of the leader (in the school, he may be either teacher or student) is of crucial importance in group dynamics. As the Lewinian social psychologist, Ronald Lippitt, has demonstrated, the aim is to avoid two extremes: on the one hand, autocratic leadership under which free participation, criticism, and group planning are impossible because the leader attempts to impose his own biases; on the other hand, laissez-faire leadership under which the group is allowed such complete freedom as to deny either direction or cohesiveness.

Democracy in leadership, although the most difficult to achieve, is a kind of Golden Mean. The democratic leader keeps the group moving forward, encourages the reticent, creates an atmosphere of constructive planning, sharing, and "groupness," offers suggestions, and tries always to insure that no one of the main aspects of group learning (evidence, communication, agreement, and action) is given such disproportionate attention as to throw the process and product of consensual validation off balance.

An extension of such examples in the theory and practice of group dynamics is also suggested by the concept of "anthropotherapy." The relevance of this concept for reconstructionism, however, is that it applies anthropological methodology more directly than does group dynamics—participant observation, for example. Furthermore, it connotes not only an extension of psychotherapy to cultural experience but reflects something of complementary neo-Freudian and neo-Marxian ideas.

The emphasis in anthropotherapy is thus upon change in the group experience of a subculture—change that requires its members to confront its own tensions and struggles by fairly prolonged efforts of patient, mutual involvement. Some of the same guiding techniques of group dynamics are, of course, applicable. So, informally, are those of consensual validation. Anthropotherapy in practice is social–self-realization at work in the life of a goal-seeking subculture.

THE PRACTICABILITY OF CONSENSUAL VALIDATION

So far, we have been discussing consensual validation as a general principle of learning without considering its educational practicability. Obviously the present philosophy and organization of many schools preclude its immediate practicability. Learning and teaching, particularly, reflect essentialist and/or perennialist beliefs much more often than other kinds.

Even in schools depending more or less completely upon progressivist and/or reconstructionist beliefs, group agreement is neither possible nor desirable in every learning situation. A group may find itself too divided to reach satisfactory consensus; the evidence may be too contradictory, feelings too hostile, or communication too blurred. Yet incomplete effort may have educative value, too: it helps students to appreciate the importance on occasion of suspending judgment, or of further factual investigation, or of seeking emotional harmony before reaching decisions. Both teachers and students should recognize, moreover, that group dynamics and anthropotherapy are still in the process of development and exploration, with much experimentation still to be done. Certainly leaders in group dynamics need to pay more thorough consideration to its philosophic assumptions: its relationships to cultural reality, its ambiguous values, its tendency at times to stress descriptive psychological process at the expense of normative cultural product, and the preference among some proponents for individual self-expression through, say, sensitivity training as against the values inherent in cohesive group-expression.

It is important to recall that any program of learning through consensual validation must provide for its component processes. Learning from evidence, for example, should occupy a substantial proportion of school time. Here is the proper place for subject matters studied *temporarily* in isolation from the total design. Both indirect and direct evidence of the types we have discussed are indispensable. Furthermore, since communication through the language arts as well as the graphic and musical arts requires sustained attention, generous periods should be allowed for practice and drill. During these periods, as during the study of evidence, the role of agreement may remain subordinated.

It should also be reemphasized that the reliability of agreement as a test of truth and value differs widely among various fields of learning. As was explained earlier, not even the physicist can avoid making use of the assumption of intersubjective consensus; but because of the relative objectivity of his subject matter and controls, this assumption may be less important to him than to the axiologist, to whom the factors of, say, unrational or existential awarenesses of goal-seeking interests are especially fundamental. Recall here that the range of importance of consensual validation can be likened to a kind of spectrum: the process is least crucial to scientific truth-seeking, most important to ethical or esthetic value-seeking. But so essential is it to both facts and values, certainly in education, as to obliterate the hard-and-fast line that often separates epistemology from axiology.

Finally, no claim should be made that this process is equally workable in all types of learning. Individual students must be encouraged to explore areas and problems by themselves whenever they will benefit by such independence. Also, learning in some fields (mathematics, for example) may not lend itself easily to this process. At the same time, as we shall find in the next chapter, opportunities to bring these subject matters into larger curriculum designs are much more abundant than hitherto assumed.

Indeed, when any school or program of schooling is dedicated to clarification and implementation of the governing purposes inherent in global reconstruction, all distinctions between the "steps" of consensual validation became artificial. The study of evidence is then never carried on exclusively for its own sake, whether in history, chemistry, or any other subject matter area. Likewise, practice in the skills of communication, verbal or non-verbal, is never wholly devoid of reference to the goal-seeking functions in which these skills are instrumental. In this perspective, public education itself becomes a kind of "group mind," a means of thinking and feeling its way toward achievement of those unified ends that are desirable to its members and that bind the curriculum into a unified whole.

But since the processes of seeking and communicating evidence are already more or less utilized (however often aimlessly) by education, special stress needs to be placed here upon the processes of reaching agreement and taking action. All levels of learning should provide continuous practice in group dynamics, in developing respect for and taking actions upon agreements reached, and in appreciating the need for strong cultural commitments.

Thus, in the context of the whole curriculum, utilization of evidence and of communication should always be correlated with efforts in which agreement and action are effected. To illustrate, obtaining evidence about nuclear physics properly invites communication of moral, political, and economic problems generated by atomic energy. Eventually such evidence extends toward the most viable agreements attainable as to what should be done about these problems. In a word, the principle of consensual validation becomes the symbolic instrument for achieving an "integrated curriculum" integrated *for* something—for powerful and encompassing commitments to goals which, far from being merely provincial, are worldwide. Normatively, this principle is nothing less than the process and product of the widest possible circle of mankind achieving social–self-realization.

EDUCATION FOR DEFENSIBLE PARTIALITY

Implicit, at least, in the foregoing discussion of learning as social–self-realization is a conviction that reconstructionist education takes sides. It encourages students, teachers, and lay members of the community to acquire knowledge about desperately pressing problems of our age of crisis, to make up their minds about the most promising solutions, and then to act concertedly to achieve those solutions. Emphasis on commitment to agreed-upon goals for the future thus raises, once more, the venerable problem of bias and indoctrination.

Is it not true, the critic may ask, that if a teacher believes in the purposes of national and international reconstruction, accepts the dominant value of social–self-realization, and implies in his teaching that mankind requires a democracy planned by and for the largest possible majority, he repudiates the ideal of scholarly objectivity, of fairness to "all sides of all questions"?

Stated in this fashion, the issue is sharp enough; it gains still sharper focus in the setting of our cultural crisis. For then we perceive that the question is whether public education should become the instrument of certain cultural forces and aims or whether it should remain as far as possible neutral and impartial. Will the "democratic way of life" be served by emulating in any way the educational systems of totalitarian countries which deliberately utilize these systems to instill unswerving loyalty to their own policies? Yet, if public education in the democracies does not do so, can it succeed in educating (and thus creating) a generation of citizens who deeply believe in their own future?

Hopefully, preceding expositions of philosophical and educational principles have prepared us to confront such questions. First, the reconstructionist strongly opposes the methods of totalitarian regimes, whatever their form. Second, he therefore opposes any kind of indoctrination. Third, he completely supports academic freedom by insisting upon impartial, thorough study of all kinds of evidence and alternatives. Fourth, vigorous utilization of the philosophic beliefs of reconstructionism is compatible with the transformative cultural orientation, both conceptually and behaviorally.

In short, partiality is also entirely defensible. The ultimate test is whether learning is woven into the woof and warp of individual and group behavior—whether patterns of belief are not only professed but also consistently, fully practiced in the life of the learner.

What, then, *is* education for "defensible partiality"?

Indoctrination redefined. To begin with, let us consider what defensible partiality is not. Opposition to indoctrination can be inferred from a definition of that term: a method of learning by communication that proceeds mainly in one direction—from "communicator" to "communicatee"—and that has the purpose of causing the latter to accept some doctrine or systematic body of beliefs about man and his universe that is held by the former.

Moreover, such doctrine is believed by its proponents to be so supremely true, or good, or both, as to eliminate the need for critical, scrupulous, thoroughgoing comparison with other doctrines.

This definition, if accepted, already points to the conclusion that most ways of learning that have been, and still are, practiced in the name of education are largely or wholly indoctrination. For many centuries, all of the great religions have deliberately taught that their respective doctrines are alone true and good, their chief indoctrinators being priests or monks vested with authority to communicate their tenets to receptive minds. Today, education in the form of indoctrination exists wherever a society is dominated by similarly unquestioned authority. Fascist Spain and Soviet Russia, however unlike they may be otherwise, both impose upon the people a belief in the supremacy of their respective systems. Within democracies, too, indoctrination of various kinds flourishes in the readily observed imposition of moral codes, religious creeds, social folklore, and especially of attitudes and programs identified with the traditional ideology.

Indoctrination may occur, also, within the kind of education ostensibly most opposed to it. Those who profess sincere devotion to honesty in learning often fail to recognize powerful influences of cultural reality and unrational motivations that work upon and mold both their own and their students' beliefs; such influences bring about all sorts of rationalizations and twisted interpretations of evidence. Moreover, some teachers of teachers who hold the experimental-liberal point of view have been known to provide little, if any, opportunity to consider in depth any alternative points of view.

Reconstructionist learning compared to alternative theories. That the educative process should not and cannot ignore sociopsychological forces is evident from the deliberate stress we have placed upon them. Rather, the aim is to bring them under scrutiny and control, using them continuously both in criticizing and shaping the guiding ends and means of the transforming culture. But scrutiny and control are possible only when such inner and outer influences as the unrational or ideological have been analyzed and appraised in a public process of shared experience which the teacher and students, too, share as members of the culture.

Indoctrination, it is true, may be approached more closely at some stages of education than at others. In their earlier years, children are conditioned in certain rules of conduct in order to become "socialized" in family and community. In high school and college, too, wherever consensual validation as a principle of learning is divided into its constituent aspects, impartation of evidence (the laws of society, for example) or training in communication (the rules of writing, for example) may prove both necessary and proper.

But this by no means suggests that the need for or desirability of indoctrination is, after all, conceded. Education as a whole is the proper frame of reference, not any one aspect of learning taken by or for itself. A school permeated with the reconstructionist philosophy will never limit itself to the mere inculcation of laws, rules, or training in skills. Nor are facts considered merely as facts. Whenever and wherever people learn, they need to appreciate both through precept and practice that every bit of learning they acquire must eventually be judged and accepted or rejected according to whether or not in harmony with their cooperatively, but critically, defined values and correlative cultural designs. This crucial attitude can and should begin to develop *not later than the nursery school.*

Take a single illustration. Children need to be informed at a very early age about traffic regulations—the meaning of red and green lights, for example—and it is important that they learn to obey them. At the same time, the effective teacher makes it clear that traffic regulations are devised by the community, that they may conceivably be improved upon, and that as the children grow older they should take part in the public process of examining legal regulations with a view to such improvement.

Propaganda: its role. Opposition to indoctrination is not, however, identical with opposition to propaganda, here defined as a "short-cut" device for shaping attitudes and consequent conduct.

Propaganda attempts, through the use of colorful symbolization rich in suggestion (advertising displays, various kinds of music, and rhetoric, for example), to persuade individuals or groups that a certain belief, practice, or product is either desirable or undesirable. Many of the meticulous arguments and much of the specific evidence that could be mustered in support of the propagandist's position are deliberately omitted from his techniques because the aim is to affect acceptance or rejection as directly as possible—not to persuade by slow, rational deliberation or the weighing of evidence.

Under certain conditions, propaganda is indispensable to other types of teaching than indoctrination. Indeed, whatever their philosophy, few instructors of any field can avoid the need of taking short cuts by omitting some of the evidence or some of the possible ways of communicating necessary to a learning situation. Moreover, propaganda often impresses a fact, rule, or value upon students much more effectively than would a neutrally analytical approach. There is no reason why learning for worthwhile ends should not be warmed with the persuasive qualities that commercial advertisers often exploit for unworthwhile ends.

Reconstructionism, more forthrightly than other philosophies (with the possible exception of perennialism), holds that if education is to become a great cultural force that shapes attitudes and inspires action, then it should reemphasize that affect accompanies cognition—hence, that learning is properly enfused with the colorful, dramatic qualities of normal human experience. The point may be underscored by recalling another helpful concept—cultural myth—for now it may be perceived to include, inevitably and properly, certain symbols of propaganda.

Let it be clearly understood that this heresy in no way concedes that propaganda and education are synonymous. Education in its totality, as we have said, encompasses the fullest possible consideration of evidence, the most thorough effort at clear communication, and the most scrupulous respect for disagreements as well as agreements. Accordingly, the legitimate role of propaganda in education should always remain subordinate to the complete process and product of learning for social–self-realization. This role is justified only in the degree that both students and teachers become aware of its limitations.

Here the teacher's duty includes two chief responsibilities: (1) to label propaganda for what it is, meanwhile giving students practice in the detection of its techniques; and (2) to develop, even in the very young student, a clear realization that he often learns facts, rules, attitudes, and beliefs by "short cuts" which, although necessary at certain times, should nevertheless be questioned for their accuracy or desirability at other times. Only thus can propaganda be transformed into education proper. For example, a rule of health that is learned by the child through propaganda (from, say, a Red Cross poster on the wall of a classroom) may be genuinely relearned and incorporated into the habits of adults through education in the causes of disease.

Indoctrination and propaganda compared. It appears, then, that the use of propaganda deserves more sympathetic understanding than does indoctrination. Opposition to indoctrination is fundamental, for the indoctrinator assumes not only that ultimate truths and values are in his possession but, further, that no due process —neither cumbersome, tedious exposure to the fullest possible comparative examination, nor the attainment of consensual validation—is essential. Hence, by its very nature, indoctrination contrasts sharply with a philosophy that teaches men to build concerted convictions only through public inspection and communication of pertinent evidence and only after exhaustive consideration of opposing or alternative convictions.

To be sure, propaganda is quite as indefensible as indoctrination when utilized to support presumably unchallengeable or authoritarian doctrines. Nevertheless, the use of certain forms of propaganda *as defined* is entirely consistent with learning through consensual validation. If propaganda, in other words, is employed as a subsidiary technique strictly governed by the principles of that theory of learning, why should not its fruits be frequently incorporated as legitimate aspects of the total process? Thus, if a school song celebrates the United Nations, its words as such not only may lack either logic and facts, but may seem to mold attitudes by direct suggestion and affect alone. Yet these attitudes may, upon careful study and dialogue, prove to be entirely consistent with evidence, communication, agreement, and concerted action.

At least one common type of propaganda, familiarly called "card-stacking" (weighting of evidence, or otherwise distorting it), is under no circumstances therefore acceptable. (Indeed, another reason for opposition to indoctrination is that it, too, may utilize card-stacking by disregarding or underplaying antithetical views.) But propaganda that resorts to "name-calling" or use of "glittering generalities" sometimes turns out to be legitimate when its claims are subjected to consensual validation.

Toward a purposeful education. A richer meaning of defensible partiality should now have developed from consideration of indoctrination as distinguished from propaganda: *What we learn is defensible insofar as the ends we support and the means we utilize stand up against exposure to open, unrestricted criticism and comparison. What we learn is partial insofar as these ends and means still remain definite and positive to their advocates after the defense occurs.*

In short, the commitments of public education, like those of the culture itself, are worth fighting for only if they are hammered out of the deepest, widest personal and group experiences. In the effort to achieve such commitments, a particular individual or group may find that, for the time at least, no satisfactory conclusion or commitment can occur because evidence and the results of experimentation simply do not warrant it. Thus the progressivist's moderative stance against undue haste may be well taken. Yet, the reconstructionist's emphasis is again different from his. Although a partiality that is defensible by no means always proves possible, the norm is *attainability* of such partiality—not unattainability.

Partiality, then, increases in defensibility only as it is tested by the kind of impartiality provided through many-sided evidence (unrational as well as rational), unrestricted communication by group learning, and complete respect for criticism and minority dissent. In this sense, it proves paradoxical: the more impartial we can become, the stronger and more defensible are the partialities that can emerge.

It follows that the teacher of reconstructionist inclination, being an important member of cooperative learning, is subject to the same guiding principles of practice as is any other group member. His classroom (whether enclosed by walls or embraced by a community) affords continuous opportunity for unrestricted, impartial study just because he and his students cannot otherwise reach effective agreements that are themselves partial.

By seeking constantly to articulate and delineate the complex influences that affect his own outlook; by sifting out his prejudices (opinions and attitudes hastily, illogically, or merely emotionally shaped) from his convictions (opinions and attitudes carefully, logically, consciously shaped) ; by warning his students repeatedly that even his clearest convictions are, like theirs, frequently touched with prejudice; by providing opportunities for guest speakers and consultants to be heard and resources to be collected for the purpose of weighing views alternative to his own —by these and other means, he encourages his students to develop sensitive awareness toward his own point of view. Furthermore, as this kind of teacher encourages them to take issue with him whenever they have reason to do so (to present counter-evidence and alternative proposals, for example, or to challenge the clarity of his language), he avoids the posture of superimposition that still remains the rule rather than the exception in education.

Insofar as he accomplishes these things, he becomes much more than a teacher. He becomes, in the senses defined earlier, a democratic leader as well.

CHAPTER 19

Curriculum designs for a transformative culture

CURRICULUM DESIGNS are to be erected upon the foundations of reconstructionist beliefs about learning, and this, in turn, about reality, knowledge, and value. The designs now to be considered, however, are conjectural: they are meant to suggest possible alternatives. While no single, fixed, or universal curriculum could or should be proposed, nevertheless experimental patterns of practice must have early and widespread adoption if public education is to meet its urgent obligations. The overall plan to be presented is, like the concept of social–self-realization, a normative one; it provides a goal toward which to move and a standard by which to measure alternative curriculums.

GENERAL EDUCATION: THE CENTER

WHY GENERAL EDUCATION?

Although curriculums on all levels, from elementary to adult, are of inestimable importance, the crucial focus of the proposed program embraces a span of four years: the last two years of the conventional senior high-school course and the two years of junior college. Here our special principles of learning bear directly upon the organization and content of all studies. Earlier schooling is brought to fruition and tested, while subsequent programs of the universities and of adult education retroact to the benefit of the general program. Success of the latter depends largely, therefore, upon the effectiveness of both the earlier and later levels, and its own effectiveness strongly influences them. We shall return to these levels later.

Although our proposed design could be adjusted to, say, the three-year senior high school, the ceiling age for average students, which has risen steadily for generations, may well be placed at about twenty years. During the period from seventeen through twenty, typical young men and women are confronting the responsibilities of citizenship, approaching marriage and family, and planning their own careers. This is not to insist that all average young people continue through the entire program; wide latitude certainly must be provided for those with special talents or interests. On the whole, nevertheless, a good case can be made for the 17–20 proposal—above all, if we assume, as we do, that the symptoms of maturity and seriousness of this age group are increasing with the growth of youth movements in many parts of the world.

General education, therefore, is envisaged on a worldwide scale. Let us grant that the capacity of nations to provide compulsory education of any kind, much less education up to the age of twenty, varies widely. Let us grant, too, that countries cannot construct good systems of public education at the same rate everywhere on earth. Nevertheless, this utopian objective (in a nonpejorative sense, of course) is not at all impracticable if a world order eventually sanctioned by the majority of people is not impracticable. Here it should thus be borne in mind that reconstructionists regard curriculum innovation just as they do any other kind, whether political, economic, moral, social, or hence cultural. Education *is not* the cause of such innovation; it *is* an indispensable partner.

A design covering the entire four-year program should help to illustrate some of the applications possible from underlying theory. We begin by considering practices followed more or less universally throughout the four-year period, and then outline a conjectural program for each of the four years in turn. The influence of numerous curriculum plans upon this program will be apparent to experts, but its departures from those most commonly considered will be equally apparent.

THE WHEEL CURRICULUM

The core curriculum, adapted from progressivism, can be approached through the metaphor of a wheel. The core proper, the hub, provides the central theme of the year. The spokes are the related studies—discussion groups, field experiences, content and skill studies, and vocational training; they support the hub as it, in turn, supports them. The rim is the synthesizing and unifying whole. We can even imagine four wheels—one for each year—all rolling forward together. They are connected by the common purpose of cultural transformation as both ends and means.

This design is not quite so mechanical, however, as a wheel suggests. In accordance with principles discussed earlier, the program is both organic and esthetic. Parts of the curriculum, both within a single year and between years, flow together and strengthen one another. General education is *designed*, to be sure, but by no means as geometrically as the limited image of wheel: flexibility is encouraged so that the unique, the dramatic, and the untried may have scope. Each four-year curriculum is, consequently, different from preceding ones. Each inherits problems and solutions of programs that have gone before but then moves on to fresh synthesis.

The metaphor of a wheel is, nevertheless, useful. The hub is rather large; it occupies approximately one-fourth of the total daily schedule, the spokes and rim the other three-fourths. In certain respects, moreover, the hub is identical for all four wheels in that the central theme of general education remains the same from beginning to end. The circumference of each wheel (that is, the scope of the year's program) is also comparable to the other three.

Bearing in mind that *no single arrangement is, by any means, the only one possible* (on the contrary, many alternative designs deserve consideration), the academic year on all levels—elementary, secondary, and higher—is conterminous with the calendar year. Traditional summer vacations are replaced by a summer recess of one month, a winter recess of the same duration, and a fall and spring recess of one week each. Even during these periods of recess, however, the schools remain in operation in the sense that they continue to provide expert assistance in a wide range of recreational and other activities related to the whole plan.

The formal schedule calls for average daily sessions seven and a half hours long, five days a week. The day is divided into four large blocks of time, each one and a half hours long, with another hour and a half allowed for relaxation and recreation. But here, too, responsibility of the school is not limited to this daily period; its recreational and adult program extends into the late afternoon and evenings, and into Saturdays and Sundays. Obviously, a staff large enough to accommodate this extensive schedule is essential.

During the first two years, half the day (that is, two of the four main periods) is devoted to the central area of the particular year; the other half is given to specialized, vocational or skill training that is less immediate to, although still integrated with, the overall program. Let us try this schedule:

8:30–10:00 A.M.:	discussion-group study of central area
	15-minute rest period
10:15–11:45 A.M.:	skill, content, vocational, or field study
	1-hour lunch period
12:45– 2:15 P.M.:	general assembly study of central area
	15-minute rest period
2:30– 4:00 P.M.:	skill, content, vocational, or field study

In the third and fourth years, the same schedule of four periods a day is followed, but an average of one whole day a week in Year Three is left open for intensive work in special fields of interest and, in Year Four, two whole days are left open for such work. The assumption is that occupational, preprofessional preparation or more extensive community involvement should be given increasing periods of time in the upper years.

The total number of students in each of the four years should not, ideally, exceed about 150. In large schools of metropolitan areas, it would not be impossible to have several parallel groups organized; each would be relatively autonomous, working in the same building or in clusters of buildings somewhat similar to decentralized "houses" already functioning in a few secondary schools.

The hub-spoke figure suggests the rationale of the schedule. The hub is the first of two afternoon periods. Here, in a general assembly, all students engaged in the study of a major theme or area learn together through various procedures and activities—television, motion pictures, panel discussions and debates, role-playing, demonstrations, lecture-and-question periods, and so on. Perhaps, still oftener than these, exchange of evidence and communication occurs among students and teachers, leading eventually to attempts at consensus. We shall see further how this period is utilized.

Practice in truth-seeking and value-seeking gained in the general assembly is based chiefly on work accomplished earlier in the day. The first period in the morning is also devoted to the major area under consideration, but in this period the students are divided into many small groups; in a sense, therefore, these morning groups, too, are part of the hub. Here students pursue various issues arising from the central area of the year, with primary concern for their more individualized choices and interests. Considerable time is spent in the study of evidence, but within these groups communication and agreement are also continually practiced. Techniques of group dynamics are freely utilized.

Teachers devote their time to moving among groups, sharing in the general assemblies, helping to clarify meanings, and frequently participating in field experiences. Some of them are specialists in general education; as they have no exclusive subject-matter field of their own, they serve as integrators and guides. Others are specialists in the various areas being studied. Several teachers, both specialists and general educators, continue with an entering class through four years, then begin with a new group. But responsibility also rests with students themselves, both for choosing their own leaders and for sharing in topics as well as methods of learning. (Students' decisions should be in harmony with policies established by planning councils to be considered in the following chapter.)

The second morning period provides for content study or practice in skills, which is integrated with the program of work in the periods before and after. For example, a first-period discussion group may decide to recommend that written reports of its findings be presented before the general assembly; therefore the second period is used for practice in composition that will be helpful in preparing such reports.

The final period of the day serves a function similar to that of the second period. If the problem of a certain block of time (three weeks, say) is city planning, certain students relate their vocational work in mechanical drawing to that problem. This period may or may not continue where the second one left off. In any case, its relationship to other periods need not always be direct.

Thus a considerable amount of election is available as to the second and fourth periods of the daily schedule. Students who want vocational training may devote both periods to it for a year or more. Every student is entitled to certain standards in writing, speaking, reading, and other skills. Ample leeway is provided, moreover, for independent study and creativity by students with special talents and curiosities. We therefore repeat that despite the centrality of group processes, individuality should be encouraged. Properly understood and utilized, the process of consensual validation itself affords such encouragement because it invites minority attitudes and interests. A student fascinated by painting, for example, should have open hours to express himself, even though his work may or may not find a place in the design of the whole.

Spoke and hub studies are equally integral as extracurricular activities—so much so that the prefix "extra" is misleading. Frequently, the last period of the day extends well beyond 4 P.M. for students who are building stage equipment, rehearsing a musical program, practicing a debate, or participating in neighborhood programs. In the area of physical education, little time is devoted to competitive interscholastic sports; emphasis is, rather, on intramural games, the dance as both a recreation and art form, and other shared activities.

If the physical, intellectual, or other needs of all students are not met through this fusion of the curricular and the extracurricular, additional periods can be provided each week by the simple procedure of substitution. Even in Years One and Two of the four-year program, it is not imperative that the assembly meet daily nor that discussion groups meet every morning. As a matter of fact, *the schedule should be cooperatively revised about once a month,* the frequency of revision depending upon the season of the year and the nature of the main theme of the year's program. In this way, although the basic structure prevails throughout the entire four years, time is found for additional sports, vocational activities, and field experiences that may occupy the better part of a week or possibly weeks.

Here, then, is the overall design of the four-year curriculum. It is not a rigid schedule of brief periods having little, if any, interconnection. It is a "curricular gestalt"—an organic pattern of flexibility and interrelated parts. The common denominator, the "carriage," of the entire program is governed by one encompassing question: *Where do we as a people want to go*? This question pervades, directly or indirectly, every specific issue; every period of history, science, or literature; every hour of practice in skills or vocations; every act of involvement in problems, tasks, and opportunities of the widening community.

To understand the transformative curriculum thoroughly, we need to scan major areas of knowledge and experience that it embraces. In terms of content, these include economics and politics, the natural sciences, the arts, the whole field of organized education itself, and the complex area of human relations. Let us sketch the content of each of the four years, noting how each year focuses upon one or more of these areas. Somewhat more extended attention will be given to the first year than to the other three, as it suggests the general procedure followed throughout.

YEAR ONE OF GENERAL EDUCATION

The first year has two chief objectives: (1) to provide motivation and orientation, and (2) to focus upon the sphere of economic-political reconstruction. Neither objective can, of course, be attained in a single year; these objectives, like those of the three remaining years, are constantly given further consideration as the student moves forward.

Nevertheless, the necessity of first-year concern with political-economic objectives should be made clear. However excellent his earlier schooling has been, the young person approaching adulthood may still need to perceive *why* it is important that general education be devoted to the tasks of goal-seeking. It is equally important for him to perceive that the crucial realities of such tasks center in economic-political experience; hence, that these realities must be discerned, analyzed, and refashioned early in his program if other areas are to receive proper consideration.

MOTIVATION AND ORIENTATION

Movement toward the first area can begin through cooperative examination of contemporary culture and of the empirical relations of individuals (in this case, students) to their culture. John's own interests—his uncertainties, tensions, instabilities, and confusions as well as his certainties and stabilities—are related to those of himself, his family, and to Centerville, where he lives.

In order to discover and motivate such interests, the school must foster a spirit of mutual respect and honesty of expression. Teachers share their own uncertainties and confusions, and the class seeks to enlist the interest of parents in its problems. Students estimate, preliminarily, how much security or insecurity or how much agreement or disagreement may be detected in the problems, practices, and plans of their own community. Meanwhile, the teacher, governed though he may be by his utopian values and therefore critical of many existing practices and future plans, does not impose his convictions upon any one. He lets the picture speak for itself.

John's understanding increases as Centerville is seen to depend upon other Centervilles and upon the state, region, nation, and world. *The aim is to widen perspective* both geographically and historically; to see how the prosperity or poverty of Centerville depends upon the state of the economy of the entire nation and indeed the world, and how this dependence emerges directly from the historic forces of contraction and expansion of freedom. A need to study the past is essential in order to foster concern for both present and future. History thus becomes an indispensable resource throughout the four years.

From consideration of the best evidence obtainable both through firsthand observation and authority, students begin to feel the impact of the crisis-culture on themselves and their community. They recognize the achievements of capitalism, of liberal democracy, of the arts, and human relations, and they assess them as dispassionately as possible. But they weigh these achievements against such stubborn realities as insecurity and war—in short, they begin to discover group conflicts, group allegiances, and group conditioners, and therefore begin to sense the power of the unrational that underlies those realities.

As more and more motivation is generated, students consider the question of what *would be* better by comparison with what now *is*. Technically speaking, ontological investigation soon gives rise to axiological study. With John, his family, and his community still in the forefront of attention, this introductory period engages in a crude, preliminary search for common values.

The temptation to jump quickly from the graphic level on which study has thus far proceeded to a nebulous level of generalization is to be strictly avoided. But once some of the insecurities that students discover in their own environment are detected, it should not be difficult to move toward the specific meaning of such values as security. Both in the immediate economic sense of adequate income and in its more complex psychological senses of the need of children for parental security or of adults for a sense of belongingness and recognition, this value, no less than others, is endemic.

Discussions of this sort should also awaken John's awareness of palpable inconsistencies in the value patterns of modern culture. The conflicts noted in Chapter 2 should be articulated in terms meaningful to the personal experience of students; for example, the belief that "honesty is the best policy" is very often associated in the same person with the belief that, in a competitive society, sharp dealing is necessary to economic success. Because the normative search for values is largely inductive, any imposition by the teacher of his own value system is unnecessary and undesirable. The value of social–self-realization (or some verbal equivalent), although it may emerge as a generalized ideal from our methods of learning, is not understood in exactly the same way by any two groups. It is a value too rich, too complex, too dynamic to be subjected to formal definition.

Here students should become aware of one question important to the entire curriculum: Is it, or is it not, reasonable to expect people of sharply different environments to reach any kind of agreements about their values and thus to provide a common guide toward the worldwide reconstruction of culture? Or, to put the issue in another way: If they could have access to dependable evidence and could communicate freely, would a majority of the people in such widely separated and different regions as our deep South, the far West, New England, China, India, Finland, and Liberia be likely to agree upon any kind of working definition of such a single goal as security? Would they be able to agree, also, that security means not only adequate food, shelter, and clothing—although these are basic—but group protectiveness and other satisfactions as well? And so with the other goals we named earlier: Can it be expected that these, too, could be agreed upon by a majority (two-thirds, shall we say?) of people of all races, nationalities, and classes?

These questions are not merely of intriguing interest. To the extent that they may or may not be reached, the answers determine the educational practicability of achieving national and international goals for our emerging age and therefore of the means essential to winning those goals. The teacher may believe, on the basis of increasing, though by no means conclusive, evidence that such a consensus *can* be won as his kind of learning-teaching reaches more and more people. But the extent to which students agree with him may vary, of course, according to their own socioeconomic position (upper-class and upper-status students are less likely to agree than others), upon the thoroughness of their study, upon their own experience with people belonging to different races, classes, religions, or other groups in their community. Given, however, widespread and conscientious participation, plus general meetings that pool the partial consensuses of small groups, does it not seem reasonable to anticipate varying ranges of agreements among people, in general, and students, in particular?

THE ECONOMIC-POLITICAL AREA

The length of time to be allowed for the economic-political area depends, obviously, upon the share earlier consumed in motivation and orientation. At least a third of the year may have been occupied, leaving approximately eight months for the second main task. The actual division of time is thus determined by the rapidity with which initial motivation is established. It is well not to wait too long, however, before plunging directly into the economic-political field, for this in itself should provide further motivation.

How shall we study the first area? A number of principles are guides to selection and organization of issues. Like those to be outlined in the succeeding areas, these principles do not exhaust but rather suggest their scope and character.

Although the long-range aim is to reach beyond the local community to encompass regional, national, and world transformation, the point of departure and point of return is, again, the immediate situation of John, his family, and Centerville. This motivation is aided because study of economic-political issues began in the introductory period of Year One. But in the second part of the year study becomes more intensive and systematic. It includes a critical survey of the community—the average income, kinds of employment, patterns of savings and expenditures, labor and employer organizations, taxes, structure and operation of local government, leading political groups, public services, and other pertinent factors.

But investigation of the community quickly reaches far beyond Centerville. The degree to which absentee ownership prevails is one factor of great importance. Local wage scales or strength of unions to which local workers belong may be typical ways in which Centerville's economy is linked to a complex, worldwide network.

This reaching-out process also extends into time. Far more than at the outset of the year, history helps to determine how Centerville reached its present stage of economic development; how the earlier, relative self-sufficiency of such communities has been supplanted by dependence upon a tightly interwoven technological system; how political institutions have tended toward more and more interdependence. History is also indispensable to the anticipation of future trends: with its help, students observe, for example, the trend away from small, free business enterprise toward corporate enterprise. They note the shift of population from the countryside to urban industrial districts. They observe how technology continues to increase productivity but, along with it, pollution and spoilage of nature. They find that the new, frightful weapons of twentieth-century technology could lead to mass destruction even more readily than to mass reconstruction.

Such study becomes an application of the ontological principle of "history as future." Time as duration, as we noted earlier, extends from the past through the present and into the future. Although study of trends by no means assures prediction of the inevitable, it does stimulate awareness of the course that history is running—a course that we may be able to redirect according to the ends we agree upon, thus actually creating our future. Here, the notion of *self-fulfilling prophecy* (in our terms, man experiencing social–self-realization because he has become convinced that this goal is entirely practicable) may be exemplified in dramatic ways. Japan's success in controlling population by careful planning is but one example.

Meanwhile, as already suggested, economic and political strands of culture are often treated interdependently since a chief, though by no means the sole, purpose of political arrangements is to provide effective operation of sanctioned industrial, agricultural, commercial, and other economic practices. Sharp critique of these practices is integrated with consideration of leading proposals for change: the one emphasis stimulates the other. Dispassionate consideration of all political parties among which the people of America and other countries are asked to choose (sponsorship ranges from the extreme right to the extreme left) is imperative. Equally imperative are the interpretation and comparison of economic programs as such, apart from directly political considerations. Students should study the free-enterprise school, the consumer-cooperative movement, the meaning of planned economy, and other basic theories and programs—not only the capitalist, but the socialist, communist, and mixtures of both as they function in various countries.

Finally, and by no means of least importance, are the major proposals for establishing a viable world order. The United Nations organization, World Federalists, and other plans should be analyzed and appraised. Involved in these proposals are such crucial issues as the abrogration of national sovereignty and the need for a program of policing aimed at the maintenance of world authority as democratically established.

Consideration of methods of learning in the economic-political area brings us back to the plan as a whole. Since the range of this area is clearly too broad to be encompassed equally well by all students, one important task of the curriculum is to locate points of concentration in accordance with particular interests. Such concentration is encouraged through work in small groups of the first daily period. Here, students practice together such techniques as role-playing and utilize resource persons from the faculty or community. Always, the aim is to delineate not only the economic-political problems of the group's individual members but its character as an emerging "group mind" in the sense noted earlier.

As an illustration, let us imagine five or six students who, because their families are "co-op" members, may find themselves intrigued by the consumer cooperative movement; several others may be interested in the Farmers' Union; still others by proposals of UNESCO for regional planning in various countries. Therefore, those with common interests join together for joint exploration of a specific program. Each group collects and analyzes pamphlets and other documentary material, reaches into the history of sponsoring organizations, interviews officers, attends local meetings, participates in exemplary community projects, and critically evaluates its own findings, conclusions, and disagreements. Eventually, all groups present their findings, agreements, and disagreements for critical reactions by the general assembly in the third period of the day.

This assembly thus serves as a sounding board for integration and comparison. Each of the small groups communicates with other groups; these, in turn, raise questions, frequently requesting particular groups to look still further into programs that have been investigated. At regular intervals throughout the approximate eight months devoted to the economic-political area, the general assembly attempts to reach formulations about institutional goals that square most satisfactorily with its axiological goals. A rough design is therefore in process of development from month to month; earlier versions are altered as later elements are added. As the year draws toward conclusion, the whole design is reexamined, reevaluated, and remodeled.

Meanwhile, students are at work in the second and fourth periods on more specialized skills and contents related, whenever possible, to the year's study. We have suggested that intensive practice in writing and speaking is geared to the work of discussion groups and general assemblies. Other methods and materials capable of integration include foreign languages, mathematics, commercial studies, and history. For example, although study of Spanish, Russian, French, or any foreign language is not compulsory, students who desire to do so may elect one or more of these in order to become acquainted with the problems and institutions of other countries through direct contact with their literature and, where possible, their people. The knowledge gained through language studies, moreover, can often be related to group and assembly study of world reconstruction—a central objective always. Mathematics and commercial training afford practice in a wide range of economic processes such as tax and interest computation. As is sometimes done in progressive education, a whole unit in arithmetic can be planned around a consumer cooperative or even around running a school store on cooperative principles. Intensive study of American or European history develops, as far as practicable, in direct relationship to the need for pertinent background. If this is done a student whose interest in history is especially strong may satisfy that interest systematically, meanwhile being motivated also by his desire to contribute to the entire class.

In addition, students who engage in vocational training are made more conscious of the relationship of their specialization to the wider economic and political pattern. One of the chief weaknesses of vocational education—its narrowness—is thus avoided. A young man who wishes to be an automobile mechanic could devote as much as a half day through a full year to this training, utilizing the second and fourth periods. But because he also shares the first-period groups and general assembly, he can hardly help but sense the relationships of his chosen occupation to the wider pattern. He comes to see that the chances of his achieving self-realization through that occupation depend upon the strength of the whole technology, upon labor organization, and upon the kind of government in power. In turn, he contributes to the learning of others through the special skills and know-how that he acquires.

These typical methods of learning are not, let us remember, confined to classroom or shop. Study groups utilize the community whenever possible by bringing resource materials (plants, soils, products) and people (black or other minority leaders, businessmen, politicians) into the school as consultants. They also go directly and purposefully into the community—into stores, farms, union halls, granges, produce markets, newspaper offices, legislatures, and courts. Of still greater value is their utilization of midwinter recesses (and often midsummer recesses as well) for trips to more distant regions, at home or abroad, or for working under educative supervision in factories, offices, or shops. Work experience is integral to any organic program.

Finally, learning in the economic-political area is geared to study of the remaining areas. This is accomplished not only by fostering constant awareness that scientific developments, let us say, exert profound bearings upon economic organization; more dramatically, representative delegations of students from Years Two, Three, and Four often join with students of Year One for mutual consultation in a particular discussion group or a general assembly. Reciprocally, first-year students join with those of succeeding years. Likewise, teachers of art or science may work with teachers of social studies or human relations at many specific points. The principle is one of learning not only *horizontally* across the first-year class but *vertically* through all four classes. Awareness and anticipation of the total design thereby develop from the beginning.

In this kind of interlearning, closed circuit television affords a marvelous opportunity for "instant communication" between several groups. If, for example, Year One students happen to be interviewing a Mexican-American activist on issues of exploitation, it is entirely feasible, technically, for students of the human relations area in Year Three to join by two-way television dialogue.

YEAR TWO OF GENERAL EDUCATION

As in the first year, two leading objectives govern the second: (1) to focus upon challenging problems, methods, needs, and goals of the area of science in relation to the guiding theme of general education; and (2) to do likewise with the area of art. About half the year could be devoted to each, but the precise division of time depends upon the program developed cooperatively by all personnel of the school, upon resources of the particular community, upon the character of the student body, and upon other variables.

THE AREA OF SCIENCE

The year opens with a period of recapitulation and anticipation. The entire class reports on summer projects, helps to plan the program, suggests improvements in teaching methods or in materials based on their experience in Year One. Above all, it considers connections between the preceding economic-political area and the science area. A typical question for early discussion is: To what extent does science affect the industrial order, both as it has been and as it ought to be? Considering this question enables students to review earlier problems and conclusions with a view to what lies ahead.

In the light of how science has functioned historically, such questions as these are then examined: How has science affected the life of Centerville? How does it differ from art or religion? What are some present-day characteristics of science? What distinctions emerge between natural science and social science?

Such study provides opportunity to deepen the student's understanding of values which began to develop early in Year One, and which requires further impetus early in Year Two. To the degree that the reconstructionist axiology can be sustained through the course of reexamining, communicating, and agreeing upon answers to these questions, students will recognize that scientific method is indispensable but not sufficient to the understanding of values. They see that understanding of a value like love, although it can be enormously aided by objective analysis of human urges, depends finally upon other functions as well, such as existential awareness and mutual recognition of the intrinsic qualities of this experience. The task of translating theoretical principles into terms familiar to young men and women eighteen years of age is by no means easy, but it is a highly important one.

The meaning of science begins to clarify as the relationships of science to axiology become clearer. Science is seen to be primarily a methodology rather than a body of knowledge. Analysis of language, with special emphasis upon the experimental method, proves applicable to a vast range of problems embracing both the nonhuman and human spheres of nature.

Further questions arise about the role of science in culture. The civic responsibilities of scientists; the place of experimenters who have little or no interest in making "useful" discoveries (the old question of "pure" versus "applied" science); the need for strong organization of scientific workers; the problem of freedom to experiment in the face of governmental security restrictions and, especially, the task of widening scientific method in thinking about and acting upon problems of cultural transformation—these are but samples.

Assuming that fair agreement may be reached in hub sessions of the general assembly upon the proposition that, in the emerging culture, science should be regarded as a great instrument of public welfare, in what precise ways shall science be financed and encouraged? Students need to consider, for example, how effective scientific investigation under government subsidy has resulted in military buildup while restricting other fields. Is it, indeed, practicable that strong public financing can assure intellectual freedom under clear control of majority policies?

Another important question is this: What knowledge does science already possess about improving health, shelter, and the satisfaction of other material and nonmaterial wants—knowledge that is basically important to social–self-realization but that has been far from adequately utilized? That science knows a great deal is unusually relevant to the second-period and fourth-period groups as they concentrate, according to their several interests, in chemistry, physiology, social psychology, biology, anthropology, or any one of a half-dozen other areas of natural and social science available in the curriculum.

For young students of physics, one of the most exciting areas of exploration is atomic energy. Universal interest in this fearful discovery can provide strong motivation for learning the principles of nuclear physics. At the same time, this interest helps students to exercise their imaginations as to the potentialities of atomic energy for such peacetime uses as industrial power.

As this picture of scientific resources is gradually put together in the general assembly, a correlative question arises: Why is society often so slow to make use of the discoveries of science in furthering its own welfare? History again helps to find an answer by showing the great influence of superstition and religious bigotry. Economic-politics, also with the aid of history, helps by showing how pecuniary interests often take precedence over public interests, how organized medicine has blocked national health services, and how some thousands of patents gather dust on the shelves of corporations because their release would lower the price or reduce the sale of this or that commodity.

All methods of learning in the area of economics-politics may be applicable here. For many students, one "course" in science is sufficient in general education. This may best be taken during the first half of Year Two, during which laboratory and demonstrations lend themselves to correlation with the overall theme. To choose one example: students analyze samples of typical patent medicines or radio-advertised foods to test the reliability of commercial claims, and from such analysis turn to proposals (perhaps in cooperation with Year One students) for strengthening controls over pure food and drug laws. Or students interested in social psychology study the effects of fatigue or monotony upon workers, and from this turn to proposals for improving industrial efficiency and the well-being of labor.

Opportunities for further study of science are, of course, available. The general science course is followed by more intensive work in physics, say, running into the fourth year. A good ideal of applied science is found in vocational training. Mathematics is offered in the second year, with sequences in Years Three and Four. But for the typical student, who has no intention to specialize in physics, courses in the "new math" or conventional algebra and geometry are not required. Sufficient acquaintance with their rudiments is provided in general science, economics, vocational training, and other fields. No student finishes the curriculum ignorant of their principles and their utility.

It is not only science and mathematics, however, upon which students may concentrate. The history of science invites similar concentration for interested students. Through foreign languages, students are enabled to learn at first hand of the scientific progress of other nations. Visits to industrial laboratories and university research centers, participation in community health projects during the winter recess, cross reference to the work of students in Years One, Three, and Four—all these offer endless opportunity in the science area. The second half of Year Two, to which we now turn, provides still further opportunity for relationships.

THE ART AREA

The intensive study of art, it will be noted, comes about halfway through the curriculum and is the most unifying of all areas. It reaches back into what has already been studied; it reaches forward into what is still to come, and it helps to fuse all areas into an esthetic design both for the school itself and for the culture of which it can be microcosmic.

We may anticipate, moreover, that the meaning of art, like the meaning of economics and science, begins to emerge only as each student discovers how art touches his own life. For John, awakening to the beauty existing all around him—in bridges, dishes, gardens, and buildings, as well as in music, painting, plays, and books—can in itself be an extraordinary learning experience. He may come to recognize that he has previously acquired a highly artificial conception of art—a conception associated with stuffy museums and memorized poetry. A gradual appreciation that the artist is anyone who works imaginatively and creatively, whether he be a carpenter, composer, or teacher, may be enhanced by intensive work in fields such as psychology, anthropology, and philosophy.

Art also permeates earlier study areas. Economic influences operate in the development of media such as the motion picture. Relationships of art to politics raise the provocative issue of whether the artist can legitimately play a propagandistic role. Science and art are found to be collaborators not only in architecture, photography, and engineering but in everything that invites the manipulation and reshaping of environment.

Students discern, then, that the dividing line between science and art is by no means hard and fast. Science is usually more precise, more quantitative. Ordinarily, the scientist tries to exclude from his calculations the "personal equation" of wishes or biases. Methods of the scientist, therefore, are more exacting, more dependent upon controls, laws, established findings, than are those of the artist. Art is more pliable, more qualitative, more affective, more often deliberately flavored with the personal equation. The most significant difference, perhaps, is the importance of unrational, existential, or Zennist factors in art as manifested in the expression of direct feeling either by the artist or by spectators who share vicariously in his works.

Assuming that an abundance of illustration has been made available, the esthetic meaning of "cultural myth" should begin to appear to the learner at this point. Consensuses that may develop about the functions and future of science, economics, politics, education, and human relations, all integrated by art, emerge as a unity of man's longings and expectations—as the myth of humanity in its authentic mood of utopian renewal and creativity.

Questions roughly parallel to those raised with regard to the social function of science are raised again here. Typical issues to be considered are the relations of "pure" and "applied" art. Home and city planning, as exemplified by the magnificent creations of Wright and the utopian projections of Mumford, illustrates what is meant by art for human welfare. Thereby, interconnections are strengthened between art and science as well as between art and economics. Again, descriptive and normative values complement each other, as exemplified in the glaring contrast between the urban explosion of the ugly "inner city" today and the "garden cities" of tomorrow—a contrast in which profits for the few become more "valuable" than social–self-realization for the many.

The role of fine arts in the future culture also receives investigation. Thus, the problem of whether radio and television should be transformed into publicly owned and controlled channels for wider appreciation of the fine arts requires further consideration of a difficult problem anticipated in Year One: If it is granted that today the majority of people prefer popular tunes and "soap operas," are these their deepest preferences? Or are these, rather, examples of what most people are conditioned to choose because they have been denied access to sufficient expression, sufficient opportunities for communication, sufficient agreement about their esthetic wants?

If, after the evidence has been examined, consensus favors the second of these answers, what must be done in order to assure that symphony orchestras and theaters are more numerous and available? How can books be produced much more cheaply and abundantly than at current inflationary prices? How can we discover, encourage, and support the artistic talent among countless people who have strong creative drives but who find no encouragement to develop them?

As for methods of learning, many students elect an additional course in art during the study of this area. More systematic work in painting, for example, may be integrated with the theme of the period. A mural of farming people, an original play dealing with an economic or political issue, thus tying in the first-year study—these are but two of a thousand imagination-stirring possibilities. Students with unusual creative talents and ambitions continue still further, either through intensive art courses in Years Three and Four, or through vocational work, or both. It should be stressed, again, that originality must be respected and encouraged, whether or not the young artist is able to synchronize his work with any group.

Nor is cooperation with the community and use of its resources by any means forgotten. Students may devote their long recesses to art in other sections of the country. Acting in summer stock; workshops in painting, sculpture, and writing; study trips to foreign art centers of, say, Florence or Kyoto—these are instances. Work experience during regular sessions provides further opportunities to learn directly through dress design, participation in civic orchestras, photography, landscape gardening, dance festivals, or stage and lighting design.

YEAR THREE OF GENERAL EDUCATION

The third year, with its twofold theme of education and human relations, is guided by objectives similar to those of the second. The overarching question to which an answer is sought may be: "Where do we as a people want to go in the organization and practice of education and, also, in the organization and practice of our relations to one another as human beings?"

The year opens with a period of review and preview similar to that which opened Year Two. One of the first outcomes to be sought is appreciation of the manner in which the two areas to be studied in Year Three are related to the areas of economics-politics and science-art. Another is appreciation of the interconnections between education and human relations. Allocation of time to the two areas to be studied is decided by cooperative planning and then modified in the course of the year. Perhaps this division will prove to be somewhat similar to that of the first year—about one-third to the first area (education) and two-thirds to the second area (human relations).

It should be remembered that as a rule one full day a week is set aside for specialized study, vocational training, or community involvement, thus reducing the amount of time directly devoted to the area by roughly 20 percent. But let us reemphasize that any isolation of this kind of intensive study from the total program is artificial. The assumption is that, as students move into their final two years, they are readier to focus their work in a field like language or agriculture without losing sight of the *interdependence* of particular parts and general plan.

THE EDUCATION AREA

Since we are attempting here only to suggest the approaches that seem fruitful for each area, let us briefly exemplify the way in which education becomes another important area as a theme for study.

An early problem is that of reaching fruitful definitions. In clarifying the deeper meaning of "education," such a concept as enculturation is translated with abundant illustration into terms familiar to the student (for example, education for creative work), who gradually learns that education is a personal and social want—a discovery to be reinforced by anthropological and psychological resources, among others.

It is also discovered that the role of formal education has shifted from time to time as the service of education to the culture has shifted. Although conventional schools have acted as a bulwark of the economic, religious, and political status quo, and although even today they serve as apologists for ideologies more often than not, their main responsibility for the future may be viewed quite differently. This responsibility, in keeping with the aim of the curriculum, is the definition and transformation of cultural and intercultural goals. Yet it is also entirely possible, in keeping with the principle of defensible partiality, that some groups or classes will reach very different consensuses as to the role of education in the culture.

A novel learning experience is thus provided for students to develop critical assessments of school programs, including their own. Equipped with normative instruments, they proceed to analyze subject matters, testing methods, field experiences, administration, vocational curriculums, finances, adult programs, guidance, teacher training, extracurricular activities, and virtually every other aspect of education viewed in its encompassing roles. Such study also includes the schools of other nations, thus becoming a comparative appraisal especially intriguing to students of foreign languages and cultures.

As learners familiarize themselves according to their group interests with the weaknesses and strengths of present educational practices, they also begin to develop an agenda of problems connected with future education. One of the most urgent items on this agenda is a budget commensurate with the desperate need for worldwide literacy, worldwide vocational training, and worldwide adult education. Such a program, obviously, requires not only greatly increased federal revenues but also revenues collected by world authority through international taxation.

THE AREA OF HUMAN RELATIONS

On a more sophisticated level than in Year One, the first objective of Year Three is to reach deeper *cognitive* understanding of and *noncognitive* identification with the values that govern the range of human relations. Once more, therefore, it is necessary for John to ask whether people of different parts of the world possess wants in common with the people of Centerville, and, if so, whether it is likely that they could attain majority agreement about them if free exchange of evidence and free communication were made possible. If social–self-realization is regarded, meanwhile, as the nearest approximation to a universal value, it bears upon several groupings of human relations; let us call them loosely, in ever widening circles, the interpersonal, intragroup and intergroup, and finally international and intercultural. Cross reference to the areas of economics-politics, art-science, and education produces helpful, illustrative material. For values permeate them all.

Interpersonal relations. Preoccupation with large-scale purposes for the future calls for a word of caution. In the effort to attain these great purposes, we cannot afford to lose sight of the importance of more intimate relationships among individuals, as exemplified in sexual conduct and family living. In urging that the student himself be considered the fulcrum of effective learning, we have already expressed this necessity. Values, it has been noted, are want-satisfactions rooted in the individual and in his relationships with other individuals. Nevertheless, dynamic continuity must be maintained between immediate values of everyday experience and comprehensive values of the new culture; neither can be meaningful without the other.

Family relationships are of two kinds—those existing within the family and those among families. The nature of a genuinely democratic family, where children and parents together share in planning, rule-making, and the work of the home, is always a normative theme of interest. The necessity for good education in homemaking becomes evident here; in fact, a general "course" in home economics for both young men and women is offered during this period of the year. So, too, is an elective in family living.

A central issue is whether such values as belongingness and recognition tend to become narrow and selfish unless families join together in neighborhood enterprises. The pseudo-anarchy of a city apartment house should be critically appraised at this point and suggestions offered for the development of, say, apartment cooperatives where families actually plan their food purchases or recreation programs in friendly association. The community school also becomes an important medium for such cohesiveness.

The topic of relations between the sexes is closely connected with that of family relations. The need for understanding the physiology and psychology of sex affords an opportunity for linking this area with the science area. Especially important is the need to consider unrational factors in love and, therefore, the psychoanalytic findings of Freud and his successors. It is assumed further that priggish attitudes toward the discussion of sex have been fairly well eliminated from the kind of general education we are picturing—a school in which learning is designed for and by young adults. Therefore, such problems of "the sexual revolution" as birth control, divorce, autoerotism and heteroerotism, and premarital and extramarital relations deserve mature scientific and moral consideration.

Such disciplines as history, anthropology, and literature also bear upon the study of sex relations all through this period. With their help, students become aware of the evolution of the family and compare strengths and weaknesses of the various forms of family organization as these might fit into their own future cultural designs. This stimulating study may deepen the student's belief that full sexual expression and affinity are among the foremost tests of happiness.

Relations between the sexes also raise complex questions regarding the status of women in the future social order. That women have often been denied fulfillment of their wants because of circumscribed spheres of opportunity is a historic fact. That careers limited to motherhood and homemaking sometimes provide such fulfillment, but often (and now, increasingly) produce widespread frustration, is also a fact. At this point, proposals for rebuilding curriculums to give women preparation in as wide a range of occupations and professions as men are urgent. So also are proposals to establish worldwide, publicly financed systems of nursery schools in order that little children may be cared for properly as their mothers choose to engage increasingly in wider events of the community.

Intragroup and intergroup relations. One problem of this sphere, again anticipated in study of the family, is the stratification of culture due to differences in age. Many long-range effects of rising longevity could be examined—for example, the tendency toward political and moral conservatism, the state's assumption of obligations to guarantee security to aged citizens, the need to provide continuous avenues of social–self-realization for older people in place of blind alleys of frustrating uselessness, and the encouragement of cooperation as well as communication between young and old in common enterprises. Here geriatrics, the relatively young science of aging, should receive attention.

The descriptive and normative are equally important in the study of races. Intensive courses in anthropology are available for election in the second and fourth periods during Year Three. In these, scientific evidence regarding racial stocks, racial intelligence, racial anatomy, and so on is brought to bear upon such axiological questions as: Shall races be assimilated or segregated in the world of tomorrow? Intensive study of Negro history and culture is aided by literature, drama, music, and other arts—a development that has achieved remarkable recognition due, in no minor part, to black militant action in various institutions of higher learning. As a matter of fact, enrichment of study in the whole area of human relations by correlation with studies in the art area is highly desirable. So, also, is utmost sociological realism regarding racial conflicts, conditioners, and allegiances.

What has just been mentioned about the study of races applies to nationalities. One additional emphasis, however, is upon the important place of nationalities (and races, too, obviously) within the framework of world order. The unrational obstinacy of national patriotism, so often an ideological bulwark against international amity, requires careful scrutiny within a view to determining how the cultural characteristics of various countries may be recognized and appreciated while being joined into a working federation of cultures. Here again, anthropology, foreign languages, history, and geography are among the most important resources.

Still another intergroup problem lies in class relationships. Earlier, we noted one of the aspects of interclass relationships—the leisure-class ideology with its complex rituals of ostentatious display, the emulation of those rituals by candidates for admission to the leisure class, and other phenomena contributing to social conflicts and ethnocentrisms. But of even greater importance is the problem of how far workers and employers, as groups, can achieve practical working agreements. That they do so on occasion is clear; that they do not do so on many other occasions is equally clear. The behavior of both classes is often thoroughly unrational, and their relationships often move in vicious circles. But if evidence and communication are forthright, students may find that the crisis-character of our time presses the defenders of the older configuration to employ hostile, undemocratic, and devious practices more frequently than do proponents of the newer configuration.

International and intercultural relations. The roots of these relations are, of course, interwoven with such intergroup relations as race and nationality. We shall only add that acquaintance with the world's great religions through comparative study of their common features, as well as their differences, is one of the first objectives of the human-relations area. The arts, history, anthropology, and other content studies are utilized once more. Examination is made of anti-Semitism as one of the most virulent forms of present day religious prejudice. Comparative courses in the religions of the Orient and the Occident are available to those most interested. Theological issues are largely excluded, but other issues (whether there should be "released time" for religious instruction is one) are raised by the general assembly as well as in cross-area investigations along with, say, the educational area.

The controversial place of religion in a transformative culture demands, further, that students reexamine the want that religious experience satisfies. If they find themselves in agreement as to the desirability of social–self-realization, they perceive that ". . . most men do not want bewilderment; they cherish the value of fairly immediate meaning, significance, order, direction . . .", and that religion, simple or sophisticated, provides just this direction. They perceive also that religious values are imbued with the cultural myth. They begin to appreciate the role of the existential as well as the visionary and utopian in great religions. Thus, they may gradually come to recognize how the preferred world order itself becomes an object of religious faith in the reconstructionist sense, albeit an object likewise grounded in such realities as technology and economic power.

The human relations area offers endless opportunities in learning. The use of the community is one important resource: study of the family, races, religions, nationalities, and economic classes all requires direct association with such groups. The school itself provides continuous experience in mixing of races among students, faculty, and parents. Equally, the more abundant that "vertical" associations are among various age and status levels, the better the educative experience is likely to be. It goes without saying that all classes are coeducational.

Guidance and counseling, provided from Year One onward, serve a more specialized function during this third year. Specialists offer courses in mental health to be taken during the study of personal and family relations. With their help, each student explores his own personality, ambitions, and talents, with a view to making decisions concerning his life occupation. Counselors approach their work with a sense of their responsibility to normative designs of the culture. In this way, they avoid directing students into narrow, "available," economic opportunities. As they encourage the attitude of "man-for-himself" instead of "man-against-himself," they help to correct the personal maladjustments and feelings of futility that often accompany social insecurities and economic frustrations.

Above all, we must reemphasize that human relations, as a major area of the curriculum, affords boundless resources for learning beyond classroom walls. This means that a very substantial part of the entire time—in this case, let us suggest more than half of the total year—should be devoted to *community experience* that flows all the way outward from Centerville to Africa and Asia and back again. Flexible schedules are so taken for granted that joint groups of Year One, Year Two, and Year Three students might spend two to four months in, say, Chile or Finland working on a cooperative housing project.

YEAR FOUR OF GENERAL EDUCATION

In the fourth year, students devote approximately 60 percent of their time to direct study of the guiding theme of the four-year curriculum and the remainder to concentrated study and training. The general assembly and discussion groups meet on an average of three days weekly. The specific theme of the year is again twofold: first, techniques and strategies for attaining agreed-upon goals; and second, reconsideration of all major areas of study, looking toward final synthesis. Let us assume that the two occupy one-third and two-thirds of the year, respectively.

TECHNIQUES AND STRATEGIES FOR ATTAINING GOALS

In accordance with our general theory, emphasis throughout is on goals—axiological goals of both a personal and cultural character—but the strategies by which they are to be attained are given intermittent attention from the outset. Major political and economic programs in Year One, for example, embrace both ends *and* means. Likewise, the chief goals considered in the three preceding years possess their own dynamic qualities; they are ends, but also means to other ends. As a matter of fact, the component values of social-self-realization are in the process of continuous—in one sense, endless—development. Nevertheless, this period of Year Four aims at more exacting analysis of and agreement about strategies than was accomplished during any of the previous study.

If reconstructionists are right, however, one of the most important motivations for formulating realistic *means* is concern with and commitment to strongly attractive, plausible *ends*. We assume, then, that the more fully students achieve defensible partialities toward the cultural designs they desire, the stronger will be an eagerness to develop programs through which their designs can be achieved.

Opportunities to fulfill that obligation have been provided continually from Year One. Work experience, particularly, is broadly interpreted to mean community activity—political, esthetic, interpersonal, intercultural, vocational. Direct experience of this kind sensitizes students as no amount of exhortation can to the imperative need to translate theory into practice.

Some time is also devoted to reconsidering relevant techniques and strategies that have been observed in preceding areas. Students find a great variety of "how's" already in operation throughout America and elsewhere. But since this variety lacks substantial or definitive purpose, they often seem in conflict. A typical problem thus arises of how to evaluate and select viable means.

Here the venerable ethical issue may well be reconsidered as to whether ends ever justify the means used in attaining them. Students learn that this issue requires semantic clarification. The term "justifies" is, in itself, ambiguous. In many situations its meaning is clearly a moral one: the end of racial equality, for example, justifies democratically organized attempts to abolish racial segregation as well as less overt discriminatory practices elsewhere. At the same time, as noted in previous pages, the major political principles of political democracy deny the right to violate policies legally authorized by the majority—except, of course, in the case of policies that clearly negate democratic values themselves.

Moreover, students become aware of the soundness of the progressivist belief that, since means help to shape the kind of ends that finally emerge, action and practice must prove to be in accord with the values inherent in the ends desired. To take the Negro again for purposes of illustration: If we believe in full equality for the black race as a cultural goal of tomorrow, must we not support such equality strictly in our relationships with him today? Means that would manipulate the Negro, even "for his own good," must be rejected.

At the same time, one of the most important outcomes of this period is the recognition that techniques and strategies must be aggressive and powerful if they are to be effective at all. Vacillating procedures are fatal in a time of grim conflict between polarizing forces. Organizational efforts limited to polite conversations or the passing of meek resolutions are inappropriate, indeed immoral, because they are irresponsible and evasive. A conception of education as a purely intellectual process devoid of feeling, commitment, or action becomes, in this context, equally immoral.

The emphasis here is on what we have termed the "group mind as end and means." Not only is the merely individualized approach to problems likely to be recognized by students as inadequate in an age of increasing collectivization; so, too, is the common progressivist approach—an approach that utilizes pluralistic, trial-and-error methods of group action. Although these methods retain much that can be productive, our greatest strategic priority is the alignment of all constructive forces of increasingly worldwide dimensions. Such solidarity is made feasible by the growing, if still implicit, commitment of mankind to the constituent values of social–self-realization—a solidarity sustained also by the history-long struggle for expansion of freedom against the forces of contraction.

The requirement of aggressiveness must not overlook the difficulty of translating general principles into precise programs of time and place. Especially grave is the danger of counteraction and backlash by reactionary groups before the forces of transformation are sufficiently organized to withstand assaults. In the fourth year, consequently, attention is given not only to what students can do immediately but what they should do in years that are to follow graduation. Both short- and long-range proposals invariably govern the responsibility of individual students and local situations—to John and to Centerville. Affiliation with black or other minority organizations concerned with effective democratic action, for example, must not be delayed because this would be "premature." Nor is it enough to imply that vigorous next steps *ought* to be taken; in this program, students and teachers *take* them.

THE CLIMAX OF YEAR FOUR: CONCLUDING NORMATIVE SYNTHESIS

The entire program of general education is characterized by dynamic wholeness. We have seen how each area draws upon all other areas for enrichment. Hence, even during study of the first systematic area (economics-politics), representative students on occasion join forces with those studying the final systematic area (human relations) and, similarly, with all others. The flow of educational traffic also continues back and forth between special fields and the central theme of the curriculum.

In the first major part of Year Four outlined above, this traffic between levels has already been continuous. Every area is reviewed for indications of workable means. Students are called upon for assistance to earlier areas where the need for strategy dovetails with consideration of the goals of, say, science or art. Thus, as the movement has been in the direction of integration from the outset, the aim of the concluding period is to achieve a *vision of the future* in which all areas coalesce with integrated *strategy for the future.* Both the end and the means are designed to make that vision a reality.

To illustrate, let us consider again the area of economics-politics. Since the period (three years earlier) in which this area was originally considered, we may safely assume that two important events have occurred. First, the culture has itself undergone inevitable degrees of change; fresh problems and proposals have therefore arisen. Second, the student's perceptiveness has sharpened; his knowledge of both domestic and foreign affairs has deepened and widened. Hence, although specifications of the original economic design have been modified from time to time during the study of each successive area, it is necessary now to reconsider it as a whole, to tighten connections between it and other designs, to eliminate superfluities or weaknesses, and to supply missing elements. Suppose that, in the first-year period, students have been unable for lack of time to consider proposals to reorganize Congress so that the people are represented occupationally as well as geographically. Here they carefully examine these proposals and make possible changes or additions.

This process of revision lends itself again to subdivided study within first-period groups. In the general assembly, however, the chief aim is now to attain as much agreement as may be warranted by the operating principles of consensual validation—that is, agreement based upon all of these principles in the cooperative quest for unified, complex, cultural design of economics–politics–art–science–education–human–relations–ends–means.

The same procedures are followed with regard to other axiological aspects of the curriculum. Earlier uncertainties about the fullest possible meaning of social–self-realization are reexamined, one of the most troublesome of these being the nature of religious values. Utilizing earlier exposure to religious experience in the human-relations area, students now seek to view this elusive goal-seeking interest in the perspective of all major areas. Free play of the esthetic imagination, including its unrational or existential qualities, is especially necessary. If motivation has been successfully established, parts of the design blend together like colors of the spectrum, from the intimately simple so exquisitely expressed in a Zen drawing, to the virile power of a Moore sculpture. Students come to appreciate more poignantly that life can be meaningful, exciting, and purposeful for anyone who feels himself part of both the age-old quest for earth-wide satisfaction of supreme human goals and man's "ultimate concern" as one frail segment of the boundless universe.

But there is need also for unexplored territory. Omissions are sure to be numerous. Therefore students must not only appreciate the vastness of the reality they have already scanned, but also that they have pointed the way for programs to be followed by their successors and for still more concentrated work in higher education.

Equally desirable are review and reformulation of minority disagreements that have been accumulating throughout the four years. Some may have become modified or been relinquished in the course of time; others may have been absorbed into majority agreements that thus approach unanimity. Nevertheless, when the final period is reached, certain disagreements are sure to remain. These are now carefully restated. And they, too, are left for later consideration by succeeding classes.

The year's work does not close, however, with emphasis upon omissions or differences. The minority is expected to understand and respect, while differing from, agreements reached by the majority, whereas the majority acknowledges the right of minorities to disagree. The range of concluding synthesis can never be predicted by any four-year program, nor should it be. Nevertheless, participants may hope for and seek to obtain whatever synthesis is warranted by the total design.

Although methods of learning previously outlined are continued in the fourth year, it is important to indicate how the extra periods now allowed for specialized work are organized. In the belief that greater blocks of time for uninterrupted study are educationally sound, during this year either an individual or a group working cooperatively may spend the larger share of whole days, weeks, or even months on one major project. Students concentrating on literature may develop an interest in the utopian novel and explore in depth the ideas of utopian writers—for example, Bellamy and Wells. A student of American history may raise the same question about utopian movements of earlier centuries.

Such concentrated work can still serve the theme of a particular area and its relations to the whole, but in no forced or artificial way. Accordingly, the many students who are learning a trade or specializing in a science or an art become conscious of the bearing of their study chiefly through their regular participation in the thrice-weekly assemblies, in discussion groups, and in community activities.

One word about techniques of evaluation. Throughout the program, modern instruments of measuring achievement and progress are utilized, students themselves sharing in the selection, administration, and evaluation of these examinations as helpful aids to learning. Like progressivists, however, teachers holding reconstructionist beliefs look upon "objective examinations" of contents and skills as decidedly inadequate. Accordingly, instruments that measure growth toward greater participation and other qualitative values fundamental to this kind of education are utilized much more frequently than quantitative ones. Near the end of the last year, comprehensive evaluations are prepared and evaluated together by students and teachers. The proposed evaluations have the unique aim, moreover, of genuinely *comprehending*, in the sense both of synthesizing and of judging accomplishment.

ELEMENTARY, HIGHER, AND ADULT EDUCATION

The fulcrum of our transformative design is general education. For this reason, its curriculum (preferably, but not necessarily, for ages seventeen to twenty) has been discussed at length. Not that other levels of education are unimportant. On the contrary, their success contributes to and depends upon the success of the designs just sketched. Chapters could be written about each of these levels without proceeding too far into the countless problems and proposals each would raise. We must be content, however, with presenting only the barest outline, remembering that philosophic and educational principles of reconstructionism apply equally to each level.

THE ELEMENTARY LEVEL

Although once more we must insist upon the conjectural character of all educational designs here considered, a reasonable division of time for the entire reconstructionist program below the university level could be described as the "4–6–5–4 plan." The first "4" stands for the early childhood period; the "6" and "5" stand for the lower and upper elementary schools, respectively, and the second "4" for the secondary school.

In other words, the *early school* spans ages two through five; the *lower elementary school*, ages six through eleven; the *upper elementary school*, twelve through sixteen; and the *secondary school* of general education is attended by young men and women of seventeen through twenty years of age.

A universal system of early schools. All children from two through five years of age are eligible to attend schools supported and controlled publicly in exactly the same way as all other schools. When both parents have assumed some out-of-the-home responsibility (as we should expect the vast majority to do), attendance of children after the second year of age is encouraged for two or more hours daily, depending on parental schedules and availability of home supervision.

When the mother remains throughout the day with her children in the belief that she is thus realizing herself more fully, attendance is optional until the age of about three and a half years; from that age until he is six, the average child must attend for a minimum of three hours daily. The assumption here is that a combination of home and school experience for average small children is desirable. Although the mother's care is needed, it should be supplemented by expert guidance in habit formation, for example, during these crucially formative years. Here mother and teachers should work often as partners, some of them serving as "paraprofessionals" or teachers' aides.

Children not yet born, and in their first months of life, likewise "go to school." Pre- and postnatal care is provided for all mothers in publicly supported centers—a program requiring well-trained, visiting teacher-nurses. Another function of these centers is to provide complete information and guidance regarding birth control and all other aspects of sexual and marital adjustment.

The lower elementary school. At this level, practices are strongly progressivist (as they are, indeed, in the early school). Learning through living situations, acquaintance with the expanding environment, participating in enriching experiences where play and work seem to become one—these are typical. The aim is to provide every opportunity for the kind of education that builds positive, self-reliant, growing personalities.

The distinctiveness of the lower elementary school, then, is less than that of the secondary school; yet it is already anticipatory of transformative attitudes and practices. Learning as social–self-realization serves from the nursery school onward as the conscious, normative measure of the school's effectiveness; hence all the dimensions of that supreme value, as earlier interpreted, come into full operation here. For example, every child deserves adequate nourishment and cleanliness; and, if the home does not assure them, the school does. But such values as creative work and novelty, though more difficult to realize, are equally important.

Group experience is abundant also. Although the individual child's interests are encouraged, so, too, are the common interests of other children. Projects that develop a sense of democratic *inter*-dependence are emphasized. Learning through consensual validation also begins in the earliest grades. The four steps in that process (learning through evidence, communication, agreement, and action) are practiced whenever a group of children discusses phenomena of nature such as flowers or rivers, the reasons for fire engines, the fact that schools and parks belong to the people, or countless other impressions and understandings.

Social responsibility, moreover, is developed from the earliest years upward. Here the remarkable achievement in Israel known as the "kibbutzim" is emulated, with children sharing in the planning and care of their own school-communities. Discipline, in this context, becomes cooperative, not superimposed—a value that extends to learning of skills or contents equally with extracurricular events. In this spirit, the kibbutzim are more in harmony with reconstructionist theory than, say, Summerhill, although A. S. Neill and his "child-centered" disciples are also to be admired immensely for their nonauthoritarian pioneering.

But let us remember also that such cooperative learning is by no means confined to a horizontal group—that is, to children of the same age. Group learning extends upward and downward from the child's age level, so that children of different ages join in student councils, community surveys, and interage learning groups. Each level contributes to the learning of others according to ability and maturation. Thus, if a playhouse is to be built, the larger children help with carpentry and the smaller ones concentrate on interior decoration. The "ungraded school" of interage groupings is taken for granted, but extended.

The upper elementary school. Although the dividing line between the lower and upper elementary schools is justified mainly by the fact of beginning puberty in the older group (this justification is, of course, far from clear-cut), most of the general characteristics of the lower school are also found on the upper level. More reasonably, perhaps, is the suggestion that the upper elementary school, five years in length, becomes a "suspension bridge" between the kinds of learning emphasized during the first ten years of public education (four years of early childhood and six years of the lower elementary school) and kinds already depicted in the last four (general education). All areas of the secondary program are, accordingly, given simple introductory consideration: problems of economics, politics, art, science, education, human relations, and others. Consensual validation, defensible partiality, and all other guiding principles of this educational philosophy are applied with gradually increasing refinement and awareness by all participants, including parents.

The utopian mood, as we have defined it, is also a characteristic of the upper and lower elementary schools: most crucially, they are schools permeated with values and goals of the future culture. The expression of these values and goals, to be sure, may seem more often indirect and implicit than direct and explicit. The needs, interests, and adjustments of children evolving in the "specious present" are by no means neglected. Yet, because teachers and administrators need to possess the clarity of vision, increasing numbers of parents and children should also come to possess it. Here, then, is the key principle. The multiple plans of study through which the principle is carried out may well prove of less long-range importance than that they are attempted and continuously tested.

For similar reasons, the burgeoning of educational "hardware" (teaching machines, computers, and audiovisual gadgetry, for example) is to be regarded strictly as subordinate to the facilitation of learning and fulfillment in the comprehensive meanings that have permeated this conception of education. Accordingly, the "new educational technology" becomes, potentially, both frightening and promising: it can either "automatize" the learning process and thereby the learner as well, or it can provide fruitful opportunities to decrease waste motion, to accelerate skills, and to release substantial time for creative experience among both students and teachers.

THE HIGHER LEARNING: COLLEGE AND UNIVERSITY

Every discerning reader will have appreciated that the questions and objectives examined in any one of the great areas of education call for vastly more knowledge than we now possess. To cite only barest examples of the need for research:

(1) psychological research in human wants and their satisfaction;
(2) economic research in needed forms of cooperative industrial enterprise;
(3) political research in regional, international, and interplanetary government;

(4) scientific research in atomic energy for industrial power;
(5) esthetic research in television as an art medium;
(6) educational research in consensual validation as a principle of learning;
(7) human-relations research in causes and cures of racial conflict; and
(8) philosophic research in the contributions of existentialism, philosophic analysis, neo-Marxism, and other relatively recent developments of the emerging revolutionary world view.

The universities are already engaged in comparable investigations. To an extraordinary extent, however, such projects now receive only a fraction of the attention they deserve. Like study on the lower levels, the higher learning has, for the most part, woefully lacked direction; too much of its research has been aimless, sterile, ideologically weighted, or circumscribed by the demands of government and private industry. The proposed philosophy aims to correct these weaknesses.

The researches just listed as examples are governed by the values of a humane world order, and therefore are undertaken with this great purpose in mind. But the college and the university must also provide opportunity to engage in scientific investigations and scholarly studies, and to exercise esthetic creativity along lines that promise no rewards whatever in terms of practical values or applications. Such disinterested learning may provide, of course, a high order of self-realization for those who engage in it. For this reason alone, every possible opportunity should be opened for talented scholars to explore independently and with minimum supervision.

But the term, "disinterested," itself challenges further research. What are the drives behind this sort of scholarly activity? When may objectivity, as advocated by analytic philosophers, for example, conceal ideological or unrational factors at work? What are the social responsibilities, if any, of the most cloistered scholar or deviant artist to the reconstructed order? What are the responsibilities of the college to the community? These are all provocative questions in higher education.

Another challenge arises when professional schools, influenced by the transformative orientation, find that older notions of training are becoming obsolete. Once this orientation is acknowledged by schools of medicine, say, problems of health on a national and worldwide scale become central, and every physician is finally acquainted with sociological, axiological, and other aspects of his profession about which hitherto he has often been kept ignorant. Law is no longer so circumscribed by its service to business; much more study is devoted to problems of international authority, to the philosophic and historic bases of law approached comparatively, and to the relationships of law to other fields. Architecture and engineering, in their concern with town and country planning, prefabricated housing, and countless other socioeconomic aspects of their fields, become far more future-centered than thus far.

As for the profession of teaching itself, the types of training hitherto common in teachers' colleges are largely discarded. Primary concern is with the interrelationships of the philosophic, cultural, and psychological aspects of education, which are treated always in the context of man's history. Careful attention is given to fields now too much ignored in teacher-training—the transformative role of the arts, for one; or the teaching of religion on a nonsectarian plane, for another. In addition, thousands of teachers are trained for service in fields where formerly there were but a few; these include specialists in general education who assume main responsibility for new curriculums, specialists in creative work experience, specialists in infant care, specialists in intergroup education (for example, in race relations), specialists in comparative and international education. Exchange of teachers among regions and countries, and continuous participation in the life of their communities during and after their training, are universal practices. A minimum of one semester's involvement in a foreign culture should be required.

A word should be added concerning the remarkable florescence of "free universities" that have sprung up in various cities and adjacent academic communities, chiefly under student impetus. Although they are relatively quite unstructured and impoverished, the thrust behind them is impressive. They repudiate much of what they consider to be fruitless subject matters and outmoded teaching procedures or standards. Instead, they aim to provide penetrating examinations and evaluations of the frontier problems confronting mankind. In these respects, they are warmly welcomed as congenial to the transformative orientation.

ADULT EDUCATION

The adult-education phase of the reconstructed program has been reserved to close this discussion, but it is not to be construed merely as an addendum. On the contrary, adult education is as important as any other level. In some respects, it is more so, for the hope of implementing theory by widening practice depends upon reaching adult citizens, especially parents who, in turn, will support both theory and practice on other levels than their own.

Although virtually all the methods and types of content already proposed may be utilized in adult education, learning is bound to be affected by the degree to which adult students have or have not been educated in schools operated upon reconstructionist principles. If they have not, the first need is for simple, careful orientation in the bases of this philosophy. Consensual validation, for instance, is of great importance as the chief process and product of adult learning—above all, in political conduct. It has probably been more successfully anticipated by experimentation on this level than on any other. So, too, have sensitivity training, group dynamics, and anthropotherapy.

The fact has been well tested that the average person not only continues to learn throughout his life; he can be stimulated to learn directly about any kind of experience if integral to his goal-seeking interests. Therefore it is perfectly plausible that adult education, if properly organized and interpreted, could attract literally hundreds of millions of students throughout the world. This is the ideal at which reconstructionists aim; indeed, they are convinced that the cultural order they propose cannot otherwise be attained. Moreover, as the bulk of the world's population consists of working and farming people, "workers' education" becomes equivalent to a large proportion of adult education as well.

Another important function embraces the problems and goals arising from sex morality, marriage, homemaking, and child care. Parents may also attend classes and participate with students in discussion groups, assemblies, and community learning. By becoming familiar with the school, they are better equipped also to share officially in the control of the school, as the next chapter will outline more precisely.

Active parent-education programs operate throughout the entire year. Neighborhood centers, with many kinds of vocational and recreational opportunities, are part of the typical program. Late-afternoon, evening, and weekend events provide opportunity for association with different races, religions, nationalities, and economic groups.

We conclude by reiterating our enthusiasm for the community school considered, curriculum-wise, as both a centripetal and centrifugal force for cultural transformation. It is *centripetal* because it draws the people of the community constantly toward its dynamic core. It is *centrifugal* because its membership of children and teachers radiates outward into the life of nearby and still further extended communities. All education, from early childhood to adulthood, is integral to this continuous inward-outward flow.

CHAPTER 20

The control of education: a reconstructed view

BEFORE ANY CURRICULUM such as the one that we have been designing can be put into operation on a broad scale, a number of problems involving both means and end, but especially means, must be solved—practical problems such as school administration, the role of teacher organizations, and community action, all centering around the concepts of control and power. These concepts are not, of course, to be considered only in relationship to education—their significance embraces the cultural realities of our age. The task of achieving social control of education in behalf of a reorganized culture is integral with the task both of estimating obstacles against cultural change and of developing powerful strategies to bring it about. Education is neither a panacea nor a sufficient cause of cultural reconstruction. It is a necessary, integral phase of the total configuration of cultural order, process, and goals.

Let us turn with this proviso to six large, interrelated topics as they bear upon the central theme of control: (1) ideology-utopia; (2) principles of educational authority; (3) federal aid and control; (4) the role of the profession for educational and cultural power; (5) organized religion and educational control; and (6) national responsibility to integration.

IDEOLOGY-UTOPIA: SIGNIFICANCE FOR THE ISSUE OF CONTROL

EDUCATIONAL CONTROL: APPROACH THROUGH IDEOLOGY

One of the first necessities, if education is to become a great cultural force, is that we "take our blinders off—that we confront the realities of our culture and our education. Granting the likelihood of overstatement in so brief a compass, the case for ideology may be reviewed first.

Previously, ideology has been considered as a symbolic expression of the complex of attitudes, beliefs, ideas, purposes, and customs that reflects, more or less systematically and accurately, the program and practices of the whole or important parts of any culture. The accuracy of this cultural rationalization varies in different historic periods. As a rule, an ideology is most "photographically" accurate during the period of maturity of a culture, less accurate in its youthful and aging periods.

Abundant evidence supports the contention that some of the most determinative cultural arrangements of Western civilization are now in their aging period. Our time is marked increasingly by tensions, stresses, and disparities between the inherited ideology and other transformations actually occurring. To take one crucial example: individual competition, private initiative, and national sovereignty are typical clichés of the early liberal or laissez-faire culture. They are clichés which, in fact, lag behind the increasingly noncompetitive, collectivized, international processes now fast emerging. Yet they are typical of an ideology that continues to exercise colossal influence over thinking and attitudes. Nowhere is this influence stronger than in education, including schools of the United States.

Though too few teachers, moreover, are free to challenge curriculums or educational practices shaped according to ideological precepts, very little research evidence is available to prove that they have wished to be much freer than they are. The fact is that, granting some exceptions to be noted shortly, the profession is itself so saturated with the beliefs, habits, and customs of the established culture that it is indeed feebly prepared to consider alternatives.

Many teachers are also imbued, by and large, with the attitudes of Veblen's "leisure class." Perhaps in part because of the traditional dignity attached to the status of the European "Herr Professor," of whom they are academic descendants, they prefer to think of themselves as members of middle- or upper-status groups. Their habits of conspicuous consumption encourage them, too, even though members of almost no profession can afford them less. Little wonder that often they become devoted allies of the ideology they reflect and portray. Little wonder, either, that teachers so frequently identify academic freedom (which they profess wholeheartedly) with what typical school boards prescribe as suitable for classroom consumption—with whatever the chamber of commerce, patriotic organizations, or the churches of Centerville regard as safe and proper learning.

For the most part, although again with important qualifications, the profession has also been trained and organized ideologically. Most teachers' colleges, like other institutions of higher education, maintain faculties that tend toward leisure-class attitudes, and most are markedly affected, if not actually regulated, by the same kind of pressure groups and conservatively oriented boards of trustees that control many lower schools.

The history of teachers' professional organizations is quite similar. Although classroom teachers hold many offices in the largest American body, the National Education Association (NEA), the establishment of policies and programs has been guided chiefly by superintendents of schools and other administrators who, in turn, reflect much the same patterns of control that operate in local communities.

This is not to deny that the NEA, and even more the American Federation of Teachers (AFT), have in recent years begun to manifest a more critical, even militant, posture. Indeed, both organizations have indicated a potential capacity to adopt policies and programs increasingly harmonious with what we have regarded precisely as a utopian, or at least anti-ideologist, orientation. But the historic effect of this overall situation is clear. The public schools have never been, and they are not now, impartial purveyors of "truth" and "virtue." Rather, they have been, and they are now, one of the most important institutional devices for strengthening group allegiances and group conditioners that serve the first constellation of forces.

That the children of America tend, in turn, to acquire much the same ideological outlook already possessed by the typical teacher is hardly surprising. Nor that parents, most of whom have been through similar schools, contribute generously to the saturation process—as do churches, the communication media, and all other attitude-forming agencies.

What, then, is the significance of this oversimplified profile?

It is unnecessary to contend that the dominant ideology is itself the sufficient cause of those patterns of control which, to a large extent, continue to prevail over schools at all levels in America. What is contended is that ideology provides an important opportunity to verbalize, justify, and thus to reinforce those patterns.

To state the point differently, the dominant Establishment that is determined to direct education in behalf of its own interests utilizes innumerable resources to prove its own determination —aids that become interwoven with its whole strategy, and that are aimed at maintaining control over the entire educational structure, its content, and its personnel with a view to gaining and holding maximum power over institutional patterns of the culture as a whole. In this sense, educational control is reciprocal with cultural control; each tends to strengthen the other.

EDUCATIONAL CONTROL: APPROACH THROUGH UTOPIA

The concept polaristic to ideology, as we have learned, is utopia. This has been defined as any word picture of attitudes, practices, institutions, ideas, and (to some extent) overt habits that supports a conception of culture admittedly different from the prevailing culture. We have learned also that utopia is best considered in a spectrumlike relationship to ideology, but that at moments of conflict and crisis the extremes of the spectrum become sharper. As people are drawn either toward defense of the existing order or toward support of quite a different order, they tend to become more unqualifiedly ideological or more utopian, as the case may be.

Education is far too immersed in culture to be aloof to this dynamic. Hence, although both ideological and utopian attitudes are likely to be reflected and often confused in the beliefs of countless teachers, students, or administrators, and although the ideological tends to remain the stronger, we should expect certain distinctions between these attitudes to become clearer in our present period than they were, perhaps, in the nineteenth century. To say that education is influenced by both kinds of attitudes is to soften the tones of the rather grim picture just sketched of its ideological character. Scattered all through the history of public schools in America and in other countries are hundreds of exceptions to the generalization that teachers are not, in fact, free.

These exceptions are of utmost importance. They do not disprove the assertion that schools tend to act as the servants of forces that impede the development of utopian beliefs and institutions. But they do indicate that public education also possesses a priceless quality of resilience.

One of the strongest utopian potentials in American education lies, for instance, in the democratic heritage itself. The noble belief in the decency and worth of common people has one of its epochal expressions in the establishment of free public education. To be sure, such education was regarded from the beginning, both by many businessmen and by some labor leaders, as a bulwark of the emerging industrial order. But for millions, it was also a new potent symbol of the forces of expansion. It meant that these millions at last could hope to acquire the same learnings and dexterities which, for too many centuries, had been the exclusive privilege of entrenched minorities—of the forces of contraction.

In the century or more that has passed since the establishment of our public school system, a good deal of this spirit and purpose has survived. It is seen, for example, in the inspiration given by American education to peoples of other lands who have hungered for similar opportunities. It is seen in the stubborn insistence of the American Federation of Labor—from its founding in the 1880s to the present—that public education shall not only provide services useful to the workingman but also that he shall have a strong voice in its direction. It is seen in those too rare courses in history and literature that treat the past as a decisive struggle for social–self-realization on the part of the widest possible majority, a struggle in which education itself has played a part. Hence, despite abundant distortions by ideologists who interpret tradition in their own terms, the belief that public schools should be controlled by, and in the interests of, the great majority is rooted deep in our culture.

Utopian propensities lie also in the chronic fact that teachers and students are restless. Dissatisfaction with the typical, ideology-weighted curriculum is widespread. Inadequate salaries, insecurity, overloaded schedules, restraints on their personal lives that many teachers are compelled to endure, outworn school plants and equipment in thousands of communities, discrimination suffered by black teachers and children—complaints such as these are no longer occasional; they are heard on every side.

The cross-national phenomenon of "student power" (touched upon earlier) that burst into the 1960s after decades of relative complacency has undoubtedly affected not only students themselves but the entire educational structure. This restlessness, to be sure, remains largely without clear direction. Although increasing numbers of teachers have supported aggressive organizations, many others are still as uncertain about what they should do as they are confused about philosophies of education.

As is true of confusions among individuals and groups in the culture at large, this condition has its dangerous aspects. It invites race-hating, labor-baiting, or totalitarian-minded groups to move in and capitalize upon the fears and frustrations that are at least as deeply felt among teachers as among other citizens. In a time of prolonged international strain, of uncertainty and pressure, such groups are unusually active in exploiting and intimidating a profession always hypersensitive to criticism. Much the same dangers of intimidation react upon student actions, especially so because the latter have themselves sometimes led to violence, just as have actions of frustrated and angry black movements of protest against ideological distortions and economic exploitation.

At the same time, widespread restlessness in education generates hope. It stimulates both teacher and student to become aware that they, too, are involved in far-reaching disturbances often rooted in unrational experience. It crystallizes the meaning of ideology-utopia toward more consistent, purposeful educational thought and action. It helps to clear the air of bewilderment—to expose the cultural significance of both ideological and utopian methods and contents. Thus, it enables the teacher, administrator, and student to choose more decisively between major alternative cultural alignments.

Nor should we overlook the significance of modern types of education—notably the progressivist. Critical and reflective learning is now advocated (and even beginning to be practiced) in various countries of the world. In the area of school administration, critics have so persistently called attention to inconsistencies between democratic ideals and autocratic authority that some school systems and universities have shifted to more participative policies. Innovative ventures, such as community schools, cooperative urban college projects, even "free universities," have aroused enthusiasm and support.

Moreover, the frequently heard contention that education must perform an ideological role because, throughout history, it has been a bulwark of cultural transmission is open to question on various grounds. To begin with, as anthropologists have demonstrated, cultures are never completely static; neither are their formal or their informal educational agencies. Enculturation, accordingly, can prove to be functionally both transmissive and innovative at varying places and times. The rising industrial order of earlier American history, for instance, was sufficiently dynamic so that the controlling minority could well afford to encourage schools with the expectation that they would support its interests. True, this minority gradually became more cautious, more resistant to change; so, too, did the schools. Yet even during the preceding century or more, the conception of education as a mere agent of the prevailing ideology has by no means been entirely accepted. Had it been, we could produce no record of intellectual or moral dissent in the field of education, but there is such a record. Had it been, we could not show, as we *have* shown, that the American culture continues to embody beliefs in education for the welfare of the people as a whole, not merely for the benefit of a minority—beliefs implying also that even thoroughgoing change may be justified when measured by that welfare. Similar values prevail in other cultures, too: in postwar Japan, Israel, Yugoslavia, Norway, India, and New Zealand—to mention only a few.

The argument of any transmissive theory of education may, in any case, exemplify the genetic fallacy. To insist that what *has been* must *always be* is a denial of the evidence of mutations in biology, of postorganic evolution, of abrupt turns in history, of the creation of new institutional forms, of new ideas, inventions, arts, and moral codes. History, including the history of education, does not necessarily repeat itself. For man *does* sometimes make himself.

The heart of the present view, in short, is that we need first to appraise the influence of ideology upon education throughout history—indeed, effective counteraction demands it—and then to advocate and achieve far-reaching departures from such influence. The alternative is nothing short of educational defeatism in the name of historical scholarship.

Such far-reaching departures add further support to the utopian potential because, we contend, these are more likely to prove *partially defensible* (according to the criterion earlier defined) than are characteristics typical of current ideologies. This contention follows from arguments of preceding chapters—the argument, for example, that social–self-realization can be increasingly demonstrated by consensual validation to be an empirical universal embracing our goal-seeking interests; or the argument that the national-international purposes commensurate with this value become more plausible as we learn about their character.

If then these are, or could become, reasonable convictions for the majority of men, are they not reasonable for the educational profession as well? For, with all its severe limitations, our profession is not only the largest single occupational group of formally educated people in America but probably in numerous other countries. Teachers do have more access to evidence regarding the historic and contemporary world than average citizens. They do communicate perhaps more frequently and more effectively than many others. Above all, because of the very nature of their profession, they do often concern themselves with the welfare of those whom they serve. Hence, when it is said that teachers belong to a profession of service, the statement is not merely trite; it is accurate. The irony is not that the intentions of large proportions of teachers are unworthy; rather it is that unfortunately, but quite innocently, they have misconstrued the nature of that service.

The argument here, then, is that the values of most school people are or at least could become sound. Once they (and we) are committed to these values as ends, they (and we) can anticipate recognition of the means to achieve them. From the point of view of teacher-training, the imperative task is to articulate the half-expressed. It is to make actual those potential goals that now influence the profession only vaguely, eclectically, intermittently, and myopically.

One further crucial factor that increases the utopian potential is the situation of the world at large—particularly, the solidifying of dynamic group amalgamations for or against the widening of economic, political, scientific, esthetic, and other freedoms. The great importance of this situation is that *the influence of education depends primarily upon the strength and sanction it receives from cultural forces with which it is interfused.* Thus far, but only thus far, are the advocates of education as cultural transmission correct. Where they are incorrect is in supposing that such forces are inevitably ideological. This is a generalization distorted to the point of fallacy: it ignores not only the utopian polarity present even in fairly stable and mature historic cultures but also, as Toynbee and other philosophers of history have shown, the militant utopianism that often emerges in unstable, aging cultures. Countless manifestations of this polarity are becoming more and more distinct. A new articulateness, a new sense of collective strength, a newly wrathful but righteous indignation, a new hope for the achievement of worldwide democracy for mankind—all these are mingled together.

In this vast, rumbling, clumsy, infinitely powerful mass of hundreds of millions of human beings lies the great reservoir of strength for tomorrow's education. Here, indeed, is the fountainhead of all other utopian potentials presently emerging. The immediate task before the profession is to draw upon this strength and thus to strengthen control of the schools by and for the goal-seeking interests of the overwhelming majority of mankind.

RECONSTRUCTED PRINCIPLES OF EDUCATIONAL CONTROL

On the basis thus far built, a more systematic design for the needed pattern of educational control may now be applied to public schools from the elementary grades through adult levels, always assuming that, in principle, they usually apply also to colleges and universities. Some aspects of this pattern are, or course, already being advocated and tested. But our proposals are again conjectural; they are working, experimental projections, not exclusive solutions.

POLICY-FORMULATING AND PLAN-MAKING BY CONSENSUAL VALIDATION

If consensual validation is an essential axiological, as well as epistemological, corollary of democratic government, then it should also operate in the control of education. In other words, every policy and plan for such control should be determined through the public process of gathering, communicating, agreeing about, and acting on whatever evidence is relevant to attaining the goals of all those concerned. Hence, in place of the kind of line-staff pattern in which authority filters down from the top, future schools should function in precisely the opposite way. Policies and plans should spring chiefly from the rank-and-file of students, teachers, parents, and citizens. The carrying out of policy should rest with the administrative and academic staff, which is, at all times, responsible to that rank-and-file.

Representative school boards. The principle of majority control has theoretically been recognized in some school systems (American and elsewhere) through provision for policy-formulating school boards (or boards of trustees) that are presumably representative of the majority. Actually, these boards have violated that principle much more often than they have protected it.

In the first place, most of their members have been recruited from a narrow segment of the population—the economically and socially dominant segment. In the second place, they have provided inadequate opportunity for the staff of the school or members of the community to indicate what services they expect education to perform. Teachers have been consulted too seldom; the student's voice has rarely been heard; except for the interests of alert patriotic or businessmen's pressure groups, the interests of the ordinary citizen are often ignored. In the third place, the ordinary citizen has not cared much one way or another: too often, he has been as indifferent to the policy-making of local school boards as to that of Congress. If he has allowed control of education to slip from his grasp, he must assume a large part of the blame.

The primary need, accordingly, is for every school board to become genuinely representative of the community. This is only to say that it should include men and women from and responsible to *all* groups of citizens. Teachers, parents, and alumni should also seek election according to their group purposes as well their common and earnest concern for good education. The aim is to guarantee that every possible interest is recognized, not just segments of the whole.

These obvious, yet often violated, proposals are not confined to local or state boards. A far more urgent need is for creation of federal boards organized on the principle of proportional representation according to economic and other interests.

Because the primary function of all boards is to formulate policies that serve values (that is, want-satisfactions) through education, they must be elected directly by the people whenever possible—certainly on the local, state, and regional levels. On the national and international levels, the question of effective representation is unresolved. The central principle of democratic representation is, however, in no way altered, and the task before us is to "spell out" such representation as we move toward it.

In any case, the powers of every board of education, regardless of level, *end* with policy formulation. All planning and translating of policy are left in the expert hands of those professionally involved in the educative process. For example, boards do not concern themselves with specific contents or methods of teaching; they have already established a policy of academic freedom according to principles expressed in such a theory as defensible partiality. Likewise, they do not interfere in the selection of faculty members and administrative personnel.

Widening participation within the school. Within the school itself, the process of sharing in the making of plans is continuous. A *council of citizens*, spokesmen for all shades of opinion (these include teachers, students, and delegates from representative community groups), meets regularly (at least once a month) to discuss with administrative and teaching staffs the more specific plans required by the board's general policies. For example, if the board has adopted our proposals for the secondary school, a host of issues arises as to its applicability to a particular community—issues of concern to parents, labor groups, chambers of commerce, black or other minorities, and surely to teachers and students.

Formally, the council of citizens has an advisory function;

actually, its influence increases with its concern. The processes of consensual validation continue to operate. Majority recommendations, although unofficial, are carefully considered by the all-school council to be described below.

In addition to the council of citizens, at least six other types of school councils are imperative. First is the *student council,* elected by the entire student body, including the elementary and adult divisions. (The question of the age at which children qualify for membership should be determined by the participating bodies.) The student council has several functions: to call general meetings of students; to make decisions within the boundaries of school-wide policy regarding all affairs, such as dances and athletic events; to set up and help enforce rules of conduct and discipline; to select and instruct representatives who meet with the advisory council of citizens, with the school board in public hearings, and with the all-school council (to be defined below). It elects its own teacher advisers, all of whom are without voting power.

Second is the *teachers' council,* to which all members of the academic staff belong but which, like the other councils, has an executive committee for interim work. Its responsibilities, too, are several: to bargain collectively with managerial officers regarding salaries, tenure, and other practicalities of professional status in the school system; to set up and regulate its own practices (again within the boundaries of school policy) in such matters as academic freedom and political participation; to select and instruct representatives to the several councils in which students are similarly represented; to carry on planning of the curriculum; and to be actively represented in state, regional, national and international bodies of teachers' organizations based upon comparable principles. Because, moreover, teachers are the primary professional section, they should hold proportionately larger memberships than any of the others.

Third is the *council of administrators*—principals, the superintendent, deans, registrars, and supervisors—whose responsibilities are roughly parallel to those of the teachers' council.

Fourth is the *council of service employees*—building superintendents, engineers, janitors, clerks, and gardeners. Its chief functions are two: to bargain collectively in the same manner as teachers, and to participate in the meetings of the council of citizens, the school board, and the all-school council.

Fifth is the *council of parents.* It consists of those whose children are in school; therefore it becomes involved mainly with the kind of day-to-day problems best solved when fathers, mothers, teachers, and children meet together. The council of parents also shares in many aspects of the adult-education program. It is actively represented on both the citizens' council and the all-school council, and it joins in public meetings of the school board.

The all-school council. The sixth and most important council consists of elected delegates from the councils of students, teachers, administrators, service workers, and parents. Its key responsibility is to crystallize plans and rules affecting the entire system rather than those which mainly concern one or another of the groups represented on the several subsidiary councils. One of its principal responsibilities is to determine, democratically, the respective powers of each of these councils. Also, it develops the operating program of the entire school within the boundaries of general policy established by the school board. In another direction, it mediates between recommendations of the advisory citizens' council and other councils, such as the students'.

To illustrate, let us suppose that the school board formulates a policy expressing Centerville's interest in the educational value of total integration among minority and majority groups—a policy integral to the goal-centered curriculum. The citizens' council then devotes a series of meetings to studying the policy in terms of Centerville's resources. After deliberation, it proposes alternative plans for utilizing these resources. Each of the several group councils, meanwhile, has studied the general policy, as well as whatever recommendations are made by the citizens' council. The all-school council then integrates the suggestions of the citizens' council with those of other groups and submits amendments, if any, for further consideration by the school board and by the several councils. Finally, it formulates a program agreeable to the majority and then authorizes the administrative and academic staff to put it into operation.

Educational planning: difficulties and advantages. Proposals for any general policy or any specific program may emanate from any member of the six councils. It is then submitted to the school board, citizens' council, all-school council, or all three, for further consideration. Before agreements are arrived at, as many as possible of the persons concerned are drawn into the presentation and communication of evidence and other steps of the group process.

It is to be expected that knotty difficulties arise in putting such educational planning to work. Less streamlined "efficiency" may result at times than business-minded executives would like.

But public education is not a business; it is an institution in the service of democracy. In any case, it seems likely that, through the practical operation of consensual validation, fewer errors will be made and more constructive results will emerge in the long run than could possibly be expected from benevolent commandments of the few.

The question is sure to be raised as to whether students and nonacademic personnel such as clerks and parents should be given joint responsibility with teachers and administrators. Certainly, the exact age of students and the number of such representatives on bodies set up for special purposes cannot be determined in advance of experimentation with viable arrangements. The most vital problems of education, however, are only in part professional. They are, in essence, those of the school-centered community. They stem from the wants, conflicts, and allegiances of ordinary men living together in culture. In fact, determination of the line of demarcation between professional and community responsibilities in a given situation is itself an empirical problem best solved in the all-school council. Hence, most educational decisions should be met by the same process of consensual validation as that which operates, or should operate, in the body politic.

On the whole, therefore, the reconstructionist viewpoint is evident. It is a confidence in the capacity of truly representative bodies to reach tenable decisions if afforded unrestricted right to express their criticisms and recommendations in the course of decision-making. This includes a fair, empirically determined representation of students, just as it does of teachers, administrators, or parents.

The six councils we have described are not, of course, the only ones possible. They have been chosen to dramatize the means of attaining a common norm—the planning of education by the largest possible number of lay and professional people. This planning is characterized by cooperative attack upon such problems of operation as those we have illustrated. And it is geared throughout to the philosophy of curriculum discussed in Chapter 19.

DISCIPLINE: A PERSPECTIVE

Innovative models of educational control also invite reconsideration of the problem of school discipline.

But what is the function of discipline? And what end should it serve? With the upsurge of student power, new and often complex issues have arisen concerning the treatment of recalcitrant students who, in turn, have protested what they consider to be the arrogant postures of administrative authority. Yet, long before militant student movements, everyday classroom teachers were expressing severe concern over the "right" way to maintain discipline. Some, of course, have insisted that the only solution is the age-old practice of "cracking down" (corporal punishment still remains rampant in some cultures, nor is it by any means rare within the United States). Others, notably progressivists, have preferred self-discipline as it develops from the student's interest in what he is doing, and from a correlative willingness to regulate his work according to what he intends to accomplish.

Reconstructionists recognize the psychological superiority of self-discipline over old-fashioned, military classroom rule. But they insist that progressivism often fails to follow through, one result being that the kind of discipline practiced in progressive schools varies widely. Some, of the child-centered type, try to encourage the student to discipline himself with minimum classroom regulation. Others, more social-centered, emphasize cooperative effort, with rules of discipline set by the learning group. Still, even this latter type leaves much to be desired. Not only does it alternate pendulum-fashion with the former, but the group effort it encourages may be piecemeal or its purposes frequently nebulous.

The needed concept of discipline rests upon several reconstructionist beliefs without which it cannot be understood. Let us recall two or three. One is belief in the increasingly collective character of our age—the belief that group allegiances and other cultural realities are so potent as to condition the status of every citizen. Another is the belief that actions capable of solving urgent cultural problems must often become socialized action. This means that for the individual to behave intelligently, experimentally, *as* an individual is rarely enough; what is required, in addition, is a revitalized "group mind" functioning as both end and means. Still another is belief in the necessity for cooperative means of seeking truth and values—that is, means of seeking goals at once psychological, cultural, and sufficiently specifiable so that education, as an agent of cultural renewal, can dedicate itself to them all.

In this perspective, discipline becomes the agreed-upon acceptance of orderly procedures through which members of a given group unite in systematic efforts to articulate and to attain their goals. It is not *super*imposed but it is, in a sense, *imposed*—imposed by the majority upon itself and upon any minority as well. The minority, although free to advocate, criticize, and persuade if possible, is expected to accept whatever rules of action are established by the group as necessary to group solidarity and accomplishment.

These beliefs, then, determine the connotations of discipline in reconstructionist classrooms and communities. Because students and teachers learn together, they also establish together whatever common responsibilities will best enhance such learning. For example, punctuality, order, and quiet may be necessary in the afternoon assemblies so that small groups can hear one another report on their respective investigations during morning periods. Summer work camps or field involvements often require step-by-step operations to be carried out cooperatively. Extracurricular activities and the operations of student councils—in fact, all educational activities, including those of teachers and parents—are similarly disciplined. These guidelines, however, must allow ample scope for the deviant student, who at times is to be encouraged to study and create independently of any group activity.

In some situations, discipline could, therefore, prove very strict. Yet "strictness" is a loaded term: it no more means superimposed authority than does the term "punishment" any longer deserve traditional connotations of retribution. At best, punishment suggests group-determined penalties for noncooperation with, or violation of, group-imposed regulations. Similarly, "reward" suggests group-determined appreciation of members who carry out the cooperative aims of classroom, team, or club.

Thus the whole creaking apparatus of competitive rewards and punishments—the pleasure-pain antithesis, operant conditioning, grade-seeking, and so on—is thrown on the rubbish heap. In its place is established the group morale (often, to be sure, a *stern* morale) that becomes possible only when significant work is to be accomplished. It is goal-directed work recognized by participants to be relevant to their own program and objectives, yet work which therefore provides distinctive opportunities for unique self-expression.

But what of our youngest educational initiates? Do they not require a different type of discipline? Must not they be told what the rules are, and be punished or rewarded according to their obedience to those rules? The answer to this question has likewise been anticipated. Degrees of inculcation are surely legitimate, especially in the lowest grades. Certain rules (against stealing or reckless driving, for example) are those upon which a given cultural group has already agreed. Therefore, even very little children need to understand them in order to be accepted into that group. Social scientists, we may recall, refer to this process as "socialization"—a process which they frequently reduce to behavioral conditioning and adjusting to given cultural routines.

From a reconstructionist viewpoint, this position is oversimplified and unduly constricting. Granting that such conditioning and adjusting perform a legitimate cultural role, they fail to underplay, if not to grasp, the total process of learning as social–self-realization. In short, the principle that guides effective teaching is the same in the case of discipline as in all other educational experience: to minimize mere obedience to rules from the nursery school onward and to maximize cooperatively established regulations.

The transformative school aims to provide just this kind of discipline and to provide it for every student, whatever his individual differences. A child whose intelligence is below average, or who is physically handicapped, needs to feel that he is competent to do his own best share, that he is respected for that contribution, and that, accordingly, he fills an important place. Equally, a young adult who possesses extraordinary intelligence or special talents should feel his own responsibilities to and appreciation by others at least as fully as those of average or lower than average ability.

EDUCATIONAL LEADERSHIP FOR THE NEW ORDER

Our sketch of reconstructed principles and practices of educational control has only meagerly referred to conventional leadership—notably, to principals and superintendents. This has been deliberate, for the importance assigned to their positions has been misplaced. Certainly the power, often immense and arbitrary, wielded by these officials should be repudiated.

Another and more positive reason for meager discussion of educational leadership is that understanding its role in the new order depends upon clarifying our conception of control itself. Let us note first, then, that administrators do hold a legitimate share of power both through their own council and through elected delegates to the all-school council. Moreover, their voices are heard both in the citizens' council, which they advise, and in public sessions of the school board. In professional responsibilities of chief concern to them, their own council exercises authority within the limits of school policy. When a question directly involves their particular sphere of duties (the election of a new registrar would be an instance), their representation on subcommittees of the all-school council is heavier than that of other groups. The superintendent and those associated with him also sit on subcommittees in advisory capacities.

But the crucial point is that administrators make no final decisions as to school- or system-wide policies and rules. They are, first of all, what their titles assert—officials whose duty it is to *administer*—to implement policies authorized by the respective councils. Yet, since it is obvious that every administrator must constantly make certain decisions, how shall jurisdiction be determined? Let us look back to the design for educational control with its four different levels of authority: *first*, the level upon which values themselves—the want-satisfactions of the majority—are determined (here authority derives from consensual validation and synthesizes in social–self-realization); *second*, the level of policy formulation, upon which authority is most directly vested in the democratically representative school board; *third*, the level of educational planning, involving rule-making and system-wide practices, upon which authority is vested chiefly in the several councils (especially, in the all-school council); *fourth*, the level of specific operation via values→policies→plans. It is strictly on this fourth level that administrators administer.

For example, it is their responsibility to budget all monies in the system, subject to approval by the councils. Again, they are presumably qualified to synchronize parts of the school program into a working whole. Yet many of their decisions are also of lesser scope. In work-experience programs, say, it is their business to negotiate for the involvement of students in economic enterprises of the community.

Before, however, we can sufficiently crystallize the role of the educational leader as administrator, he should be compared with the leader in political democracy. Here we find the primary roles to be two: first, implementing policy and program; second, suggesting plans, directions, and goals.

The first of these responsibilities is noted above in the delineation of administrative functions. Not only does the leader implement policy at the level of school operation; in addition, although he has no final authority of his own (at most, he has one vote in the all-school council), he is heard in school board meetings, in the council of citizens, and in all other groups that could benefit by his ability and professional training in enunciating school policy or refining school practice.

This kind of service is integral also with the leader's second major function. No less than of democracy at large, a never-ceasing need prevails in education to point out errors and failures in any program—above all, to suggest improvements, experimental ventures, short-range and long-range objectives. If the leader is to perform this function well, his single, most important area of professional preparation is educational philosophy. Moreover, preparation in this area should result in clear commitment to defensible, future-centered goals for both community and school.

FEDERAL AID AND FEDERAL AUTHORITY

THE NEED FOR FEDERAL AID

The issue of federal aid to the schools has become much less controversial than it once was in America. Consensual validation has, indeed, already been reached to a far greater degree than many experts on this issue might have predicted.

The fact that localities and states vary tremendously in their ability to finance education has been the most successful argument in behalf of federal aid. Not only does the quality of schooling vary; the economic and civic competence of citizens from region to region also varies. Southern states have been the chief losers: teachers' salary levels, the quality of equipment, and availability of schooling in the South are often well below the average of the country. But in both North and South, a double standard of schooling has usually prevailed for white and black children; blacks often receive far less schooling than do whites. At the same time, some Southern states earmark a larger proportion of their total income for education for both races than do far more prosperous states of the North.

But the issue of federal aid becomes more controversial when the question is raised as to the proportion of national or international budgets that should be set aside for public education. In the United States, the educational budget derived from federal sources remains not only proportionally small; it fluctuates erratically with other demands, such as burgeoning military programs and space adventures. The consequence is that states and communities still suffer from nearly impossible financial burdens. Yet American needs prove but a small segment of the total problem. Vast areas of the world have systems much weaker than ours: the high percentage of illiteracy in a single huge nation such as India dangerously weakens the entire prospects of world government and world economy.

True, establishment of the United Nations Educational, Scientific, and Cultural Organization (UNESCO) is an unprecedented achievement. But UNESCO remains by no stretch of the imagination a sufficient agency of international education. Its membership does not even include all the major nations. With regard to even a specific problem such as financial support for the world's schools, UNESCO is almost helpless, and its paltry annual budget must be spent chiefly upon small projects. The result is that it can do little to raise teachers' salaries or to help finance the school plants, books, and programs of countries such as the African.

If there were plenty of time in which to experiment with UNESCO, we could be "realistic"—that is, we could be satisfied to let its program develop slowly. But are those who advocate such a course actually as realistic as they suppose? On the contrary, would it not be far more realistic to insist that we have no time to lose, that a great program of education reaching into every corner of the earth is a desperate necessity *now*?

THE NEED FOR FEDERAL AUTHORITY

Administrative experts who advocate federal support for education may disagree as to the amounts essential or obtainable from a reluctant Congress or from the UN, but they still commonly agree on another point—namely, that federal aid can and should be divorced from federal control. Their argument stems from the venerable belief in a degree of local, educational autonomy and in states' right—and, on the international plane, in national sovereignty. They are fearful that, should the federal government (or the UN) exercise authority over education, there would be dictatorship over policies and practices and, finally, over subject matters.

That reconstructionists are, thus far, part of the critical minority is illustrated by this issue. They point out, for example, how absurd it is to suppose that either local or state authority over American education necessarily assures academic integrity or independence. School boards in America are sometimes tyrannical in establishing policies, in choosing personnel, in dictating the conduct of teachers, in selecting textbooks, in choosing courses of study and methods of teaching. But it would be equally absurd to assume that local authorities are actually as autonomous as they profess: we have also seen how often the thinking of school boards (and therefore of many superintendents) reflects ideologies that influence not only America but a large part of the world as well. The local pressure groups to which these boards yield usually have national affiliations (witness the American Legion). To claim that ideological influence over local schools is not part of a much wider network of power is to ignore cultural realities.

In the light of a democratic political philosophy, moreover, federal authority, as such, is neither good nor bad; it becomes good or bad according to whether it does, or does not, support the majority consensus in behalf of their universal wants. This statement implies a nationalism that is both legitimate and desirable—a nationalism created by people out of their own need for unity. Far from being chauvinistic or jingoistic, it can embody the dynamic loyalties, the mythlike qualities, the boldness that have always been characteristic of periods of great cultural health. This kind of nationalism is indispensable both as product and process. And education is one generating force.

In agreeing to federal aid, American educators acknowledge that final responsibility for schooling can no longer rest so exclusively where it has rested in the past—with localities or states. But frequently they fail to perceive the implications of this acknowledgment. In other words, whereas educators are willing that Congress, as representative of the people, should provide funds, they are not always willing to have representatives of the people control them. This implies a distrust in government that Congressmen who hold genuinely democratic convictions should resent. The national government should exercise the same authority over the spending of school funds as it does in other areas; otherwise, there would always be the danger of federal money being squandered by dominant minorities in states or localities. The spending of federal funds already provided for education in specific fields (through, for example, the Smith-Hughes law providing for agricultural, industrial, and home-economics education) is controlled by definite requirements which, although sometimes annoying, certainly have not given rise to wholesale corruption or rigidity of educational practice. To insist upon a working synthesis between federal aid and control with regard to general education is equally tenable.

More graphically, a Federal Education Authority (FEA) should be established, headed by a national board of representative citizens and including a newly authorized Secretary of Education. Just as in the democratic operation of school boards, as we have described them for lower levels, FEA policies should be established through the practice of consensual validation. That is, they stem from the "grass-roots" participation of the majority in gathering evidence as to what is commonly wanted by American schools (a measurable level of literacy, for example), in communicating this evidence through diverse channels (adult forums sponsored by public schools, for example), and in agreeing as widely as possible about the common denominators of policies that would aim to satisfy the widest range of educational wants. The incorporation of study of the education area into the curriculum of goal-centered, secondary schools (as noted in Chapter 19) illustrates the reciprocity of this kind of practice.

Once established, the FEA would be administered by the general principles of decentralized procedure discussed above. Grass-roots participation of students, teachers, parents, and citizens in controlling their community's schools or in establishing their own programs of learning and rules of discipline, for example, parallels citizens' active participation in carrying out mandates of the FEA in cities, states, and regions. The function of leadership, all the way from that of the new Secretary of Education down, is likewise a parallel one: what is needed is leadership that can discover and provide for satisfaction of educational requirements on a national scale.

But if emphasis upon American problems gives the impression that establishment of international authority for education is of minor importance, such is by no means our intention. Just as financial aid to the schools of all countries is a strict corollary of economic abundance, peace, and universal social–self-realization, so this aid should be accompanied by sufficient authority to guarantee that it will be used in their behalf. Thus, the case for an FEA can be made equally well for an International Education Authority (IEA). The policies and programs, the philosophy of leadership, the grass-roots techniques of participation in such an authority all are important, however complex are the translation of principles into daily practice. Here in the IEA, then, is another normative measuring stick by which to appraise UNESCO, both in its present frail structure and as it might become if and when the majority of people learn to exercise sufficient power in control of the UN and all its agencies.

ORGANIZED RELIGION AND EDUCATIONAL CONTROL

Returning to the American scene, further questions of explosive potentiality call for answers. Two of these emerge from the religious question. First, shall parochial schools receive support, along with public schools, from federal funds appropriated for general education? Second, if federal authority over public education is to be provided, shall this authority guarantee a place for religious instruction in the schools?

The first question has proved highly controversial. A five-to-four decision by the United States Supreme Court permits (although it does not compel) the use of state funds to pay for transportation of parochial-school pupils as well as those attending public school. Another decision, also a close one, forbids the use of public-school buildings for sectarian religious instruction. Still another permits schools to make provision for "released time" from regular schedules so that children may receive religious instruction under the auspices of their respective faiths, but off school property. These decisions point to the fact that the issue of religion in education is serious indeed, and one upon which the Supreme Court itself is by no means of one mind.

Moreover, bills that have been introduced into Congress to

provide federal aid for education would permit some funds to go to parochial schools. The arguments for and against such an arrangement are extremely involved; the most familiar one is that citizens of a given faith pay taxes as do all others; they are, therefore, entitled to a return in school services. Opponents reply that no one is compelled to send his children to parochial schools, that public schools are available, and that if parents do not care to make use of them they must expect to pay additional charges exactly as do parents who prefer to place their children in private schools.

The second question—that of permitting religious instruction in public schools under federal authority—has been precipitated by the Supreme Court's decision of 1963 which forbids sectarian prayers and scripture-reading in the public schools. This decision has been respected by many schools but flaunted by others. What many educators have apparently failed to appreciate, however, is the Court's intent: this is to deny indoctrination but not to deny any study of religious experience that is carried on according to fair-minded, comparative, critical learning and teaching.

Reconstructionists, of course, would applaud this decision. But they disapprove of the decision to authorize "released time" from public-school hours for religious instruction. A conspicuous effect, they are likely to contend, is to separate children of various faiths from one another and to emphasize group differences at the very time when our culture-in-crisis needs to concern itself with strengthening intergroup solidarities. Equally, they are dubious of strenuous efforts to obtain federal funds for parochial-school courses by means of "shared time" with "secular" subjects (such as physics) deemed distinct from those that are "religious" in content—a bifurcation having the devious purpose of further splitting the curriculum at the very time when a holistic conception of education and culture is just making headway.

Thus far, it may be safely assumed that the progressivist would endorse these reconstructionist views; more correctly stated, he has long anticipated them. Nevertheless, on the issue of religious education, too, variations appear—variations perhaps better highlighted by an early statement of Dewey than by others since. Writing in 1908, Dewey's point is simple: organized religion, as we have known it, is authoritarian. It claims a monopoly on absolute truths and values which presumably entitles it to impose its dogmas upon everyone it can reach. Such imposition is plainly antithetical to the proper function of public education, which is committed to no such dogmas: learning is open and experimental, not exclusive and ordained. Indeed, to bring teaching of religion into the schools, even in an objective fashion, is held to be hazardous; religionists would insist on directing the teaching or insist that particular religious dogmas be regarded as they regard them. Thus by introducing religion into the schools, we would be running the risk of forming "habits of mind" in severe conflict with the habits of mind that are harmonious with democracy and science. We would be wiser to do nothing than to do the wrong things, at least until education is much further developed.

The premise of Dewey's argument is that a fundamental distinction prevails between philosophic underpinnings of traditional religion and of public education. He would also be the first to agree that empirically this distinction is still by no means as great as it should be. The practices of public education, too, are constrained by dogmatic beliefs: certain teachers allow their religious beliefs to color secular studies; one may still easily discover theistic prayers, the use of religious music, and even sectarian exercises in many schools, while other types of authoritarianism—especially political and economic authoritarianism—are rampant. Nevertheless, the philosophic bases of traditional religion and democratic education remain incompatible, and it is for this reason, even when the incompatibility is concealed, that we cannot afford to encourage any movement, such as that for federal aid to parochial schools, that weaken barriers between them.

We should be grateful to Dewey and other progressivists for bringing the basic issue into sharp focus. From the reconstructionist perspective, however, it is desirable to restate and supplement their position at six points.

(1) The reconstructionist's opposition to authoritarian assumptions underlying much traditional religion may best be indicated in terms of his own opposition to indoctrination. Truths or values can never be built soundly by imposing any one doctrine as the only absolutely true and good one, all alternative doctrines, therefore, being regarded as false and bad. For this reason free public education should be extremely vigilant toward any religious institution that would substitute indoctrination for the kind of learning discussed in Chapter 18.

(2) It becomes essential to oppose any program of public education in which scrupulous consideration is not provided to doctrines other than the one that happens to be preferred by, say, a particular political regime at a given

time. For example, although strongly committed to certain beliefs, the reconstructionist insists upon the most thorough consideration of all beliefs at odds with his own; indeed, such consideration is indispensable to the whole process and product of truth-seeking or value-seeking through consensual validation. Hence, to advocate complete exclusion of the study of religious doctrines from the public schools is to advocate, in turn, a form of indoctrination: it is a convenient way of inisisting that another doctrine (that of the progressivists, in this case) is so clearly compatible with the requirements of good education that we need not, or should not, expose it to the unrestricted challenge of alternatives.

(3) If public schools are to give fair consideration to the traditional, contemporary, and future significance of religion, teachers need to be reeducated in this task. To date, they have been almost wholly unequipped and, in fairness to Dewey, we should observe that he was surely thinking of this lack of equipment when he made his own skeptical comments. But whereas he and most of his followers have offered little in the way of systematic or detailed proposals for overcoming the deficiency, we would urge no further delay in the study of religion within teacher-training programs. This training should acquaint teachers with the history of religion, together with its psychology and philosophy. It should provide direct contact with leaders and members of all major faiths. It should help teachers in training to deal with religious beliefs fairly and circumspectively, with the aim of understanding the contributions, negative or positive, of great religious institutions to past, present, and future cultures.

(4) Religion should be treated as a controversial issue and examined by the same canons of defensible partiality as any other issue. Any professionally qualified teacher is, of course, entitled to a position in the public schools regardless of the faith he professes, be it Humanism or Catholicism, and he is entitled to express his belief when religion is under group discussion. This does not, we repeat, mean indoctrination of any faith, religious or political. It does not mean that very young children should be indiscriminately exposed to religious beliefs or religious arguments. It does mean that, at least in the secondary school and college, every teacher must be willing, so

long as he accepts employment under its democratic policies, to submit evidence for his beliefs to public discussion, to other teachers of other faiths, and to students in terms of the same fundamental group processes of learning that function throughout the curriculum.

(5) It has been held in the preceding discussion that religion as a phenomenon of human experience can be subjected to intelligent consideration. This assumption has underlain a vast literature in such fields as the psychology, history, and philosophy of religion. It is evident, also, in the great organized religions of today—for example, in the Judaic, which is grounded in a profound philosophy of existence and life that has been interpreted by scholars of great competence.

True, the ultimate tenets of some, perhaps most, religions are considered to lie beyond the scope of rational analysis; they are, presumably, matters of revelation and faith. Even so, this contention does not prevent respectful examination and comparison, as far as possible, through the kind of educational process we have advocated for *all* human experience. Whether, after this process has taken place, any student concludes that some alternative set of beliefs is more satisfactory to him than one earlier accepted, or whether he reconfirms his earlier beliefs, he is fully entitled to his preference and is respected for it in exactly the same way as are other students whose conclusions prove at sharp variance from his.

(6) A far-reaching solution of the problem of educational authority in its relationships to organized religion is to provide worldwide schooling so rich in the values that sectarian religions have tried to supply (especially, the value of fairly immediate meaning and direction) that it becomes its own best protection against renewed encroachments upon secular education by organized religion. Progressivists and others approach a similar proposal when they talk of "a common faith," "character education," and "moral and spiritual values," and when they offer recommendations (psychologically dubious, if not inconsistent with the entire organismic or functional way of learning) that we may properly teach "about" religion, yet we must not teach religion itself. But their lack of regard for the unrational or existential qualities of personal and group experience; their reluctance to devote

thorough, searching consideration to the great religions in order to determine which values can be incorporated into the designs of a reconstructed culture; and their overconcern for methodology at the expense of substantive commitment—these and other difficulties invite us to look further.

In a word, we need to crystallize the promise embodied in what was earlier termed the revolutionary myth of a mature and free humanity. This is the answer to those who would restore perennial authority over education, however expressed in sophisticated symbols. By contrast, the myth of which we speak provides a religious dynamic that only a transformative-oriented education can help, we believe, to release. Given such education, we can expect the eventual assimilation of most, if not all, parochial schools by the school-centered community—a community no longer divided by walls of sectarian ethnocentrism but harmonized esthetically, organically, through maximum commitment to majority-defined values in their institutional projections.

NATIONAL RESPONSIBILITY TO INTEGRATION

Granting the cruciality of religion and public education, one may well contend that a second political issue looms even more urgently: the rights of minority citizens to achieve full, unqualified participation in all educational privileges. This issue has flickered intermittently since the Civil War, but it burst into flames only when the United States Supreme Court ruled, in 1954, that black children should enjoy the same standards of education as do white children—a right that cannot be fulfilled in segregated schools.

Nevertheless, bitter and hateful resistance has continued. Despite the belief of many white Southerners that "separate but equal" facilities are preferable for both races, a preponderant evidence (chiefly derived from the behavioral sciences) has painstakingly reinforced the Court's unanimous decision not only that such strictures are an ideological fiction but that, even if they are not, separate but equal arrangements affront basic values of American citizenship.

Yet it was not until a full 15 years later—1969—that the court decided, again unanimously, that "all deliberate speed" toward educational integration had become largely a shibboleth and a stumbling block. Almost at one stroke, it ordered several Southern communities to cease their subterfuges of procrastination. These communities complied more or less formally, but not without occasions of violent backlash by white groups and not without displays of sanctimonius breast-beating by white-supremacist politicians of Mississippi. Georgia, and other deep-South states.

What is to eventuate from the original decision is impossible to predict. Compromising and maneuvering that extend all the way up and down the political ladder are almost certain to continue for years, just as they will in the church-state controversy. In either case, the qualities of social–self-realization, as we have tried to express them, are likely to be mutilated by the forces of contraction at least as frequently as they are likely to be healed by the forces of expansion.

What is not in the least uncertain is the reconstructionist position toward integrated schools. This position supports the Supreme Court decision without equivocation. Integration, in other words, is a partiality that can be defended because it rejects human divisiveness just as vehemently as it accepts human cooperativeness. Granting that "bussing" of students or other clumsy expedients to promote integration are stopgaps at best; granting that Northern states are almost as guilty (perhaps, still more guilty, because more hypocritical) than Southern states; granting, too, that black movements of self-segregation such as nativism and nationalism are entirely explicable as desperate strategies forced upon their proponents by white racism and white power—nevertheless the guiding norm remains impregnable. Of course, integration cannot be achieved effectively as long as segregation and discrimination in housing, employment, marriage, or other institutional obsolescences remain largely intact. The fact is that integration *can* be achieved only when, and if, ghettos are totally abolished—when and if, too, citizens of all racial stocks are privileged to intermingle equally in residence, occupation, family life, and certainly education.

In short, patchwork solutions, however boastful of momentary accomplishment, will not do. To say this is, of course, to advocate exactly what reconstructionist-minded educators (whatever their preferred labels) invariably mean to advocate: a thoroughly rebuilt, democratically national and international order under unequivocal control by the overwhelming majority of people everywhere. This goal is entirely achievable through the aggressive but democratic processes that millions are only now learning to practice. On one condition, however: that the noble mandate of the Supreme Court in behalf of full educational integration attains mature and satisfying fruition.

ORGANIZING THE PROFESSION FOR DEMOCRATIC POWER

The interdependence of the policies or proposals that we have outlined above requires a strongly, powerfully organized profession. We shall not be able to establish effective federal aid and federal authority, for example, so long as teachers and administrators are weak and confused. It is our purpose to consider, finally, the hows and whats of this imperative.

Alliance between the educational profession and all the forces of expansion has been anticipated by so many implications in preceding chapters that only the most crucial of these need be reviewed. One basic contention that can hardly be reiterated too often is that we are rushing toward a decisive juncture of two mutually hostile constellations. The forces of expansion are those of ordinary citizens everywhere in the world. Although they are still much too inarticulate and disorganized and often remain under the highly articulate, ideologically dominant, tightly organized forces of contraction, nevertheless they are surging forward as never before. Moreover, in vast areas where hitherto they have been meekest—in Asia, South America, Africa—they are finally beginning to discover their own limitless strength.

Another important belief is that teachers can and should choose between these constellations. Indeed, how can they avoid choosing, if only by default, between antithetical patterns of value and hence around antithetical normative orientations? For the first constellation of forces hopes to achieve the translation of social-self-realization into terms of individual and social practice, while the second opposes such translation. Therefore the choice confronting teachers can be reduced to these fundamental questions: Do we or do we not wish to join with those who, in vast numbers and with solidarity, now struggle to transform the principle of majority rule into a worldwide, however generally enunciated, consensus epitomized by social-self-realization? And if we do, shall we or shall we not ally ourselves with those who constitute the great majority—the common peoples of all races and all nations?

Both questions are of such magnitude that we do not pretend to offer a practical, step-by-step program of action in behalf of the substantial proportions of teachers drawn toward the former of these alternatives. More so, perhaps, than any other events occurring at such swift tempo in the field of education, it is therefore important to avoid agendas or strategies for the profession that could easily prove outdated almost as soon as they are formulated. A more cautious approach is to limit ourselves here strictly to long-range guidelines only, always bearing in mind that each one is governed throughout by transformative premises. Let us state these guidelines as succinctly as possible.

(1) The profession of education should be so strongly organized that it is able to establish and maintain its own standards of competence and operation without intimidation or other interference.

(2) In accordance with the criteria of control hitherto outlined, teachers are the primary, but by no means exclusive, determinants of these standards. Communication of the profession with all representative sections of the community (local, state, national, and international) should be open and continuous in order to encourage criticisms, proposals, or modifications. But within general policies as represented by elected school boards or boards of trustees and implemented by all-school councils, standards of competence determined by consensual validation remain the prerogative of the teaching profession.

(3) It follows that organizations clearly and militantly representative of the forces of expansion are those with which the teaching profession should be continuously communicative and cooperative: black organizations, student movements seeking wider participation in educational affairs, international organizations (UNESCO, certainly), some sections of the labor movement, consumer cooperatives, organizations to conserve natural resources, family planning movements, and many others.

(4) A major criterion by which to determine the legitimacy of teacher organizations is the right of collective bargaining between teachers and, say, school boards according to working principles already well established by precedent in other employee-employer relationships. The right to strike also should be just as fully protected for teachers as for any other salary- or wage-workers of a democracy.

(5) The principles of due process should be exercised to assure protection of any teacher against arbitrary or unilateral discrimination, assignment, dismissal, or any other procedure related to his professional status.

(6) Due process also includes fully organized protection of the privilege of any teacher to practice academic free-

dom according to the principles of consensual validation and defensible partiality—both of these already inherent in the Bill of Rights.

(7) Any member of the organized profession may, also according to these principles, belong to and participate freely in any constitutionally recognized political party (radical or conservative) or any other constitutionally recognized group of the community (religious, civic, or otherwise).

(8) The teaching profession in America should be united nationally as one organization, according to the above guidelines, and under its own exclusive control. This includes all teachers in the higher learning (notably, the American Association of University Professors) as well as all other levels (notably, the National Education Association and American Federation of Teachers). Under the controlling policies of the overall organization, numerous subdivisions of specialization are entirely legitimate.

(9) The national American organization should become affiliated and vigorous on a worldwide scale with comparable organizations of foreign countries wherever their guiding principles meet such similar criteria as collective bargaining, the right to strike, due process, and all other democratic principles.

(10) All teachers' organizations, without exception, should endorse and endeavor to implement to maximum effectiveness the United Nations Charter of Human Rights.

SECTION 3

A culturological evaluation of reconstructionism

CHAPTER 21

In search of convergence

THROUGHOUT the present venture, a great deal of stress has been placed upon divergences. Particularly is this fact manifested in our interpretation of the four major philosophies of education that we have learned to call (in sequence of study but not of chronology) the progressivist, essentialist, perennialist, and reconstructionist. These, in turn, have been viewed from four respective culturological perspectives: the moderative, transmissive, restorative, and transformative.

In the case of the progressivist-moderative position, we have been compelled to conclude that this very cogent, influential approach to education and culture expresses a "later liberal" age of transition—an age between the "early liberalism" of preceding modern centuries and the democratically empowered world order to which mankind must now become committed if it is to survive and flourish at all.

In the case of the essentialist-transmissive position, we have contended that this is the frequently powerful ally of institutional and ideological forces at the same time that it is often both sophisticated and disunified as theory and practice—an orientation in education and culture that tends either subtly or overtly to perpetuate the still dominant, if often invisible, patterns of post-Renaissance civilization.

And in the case of the perennialist-restorative position, our culturological evaluation tends to the judgment—granting all the brilliance, devotion, and plasticity of this position—that it still emerges as a pro-aristocratic, absolutist-guided doctrine and program far more appropriate to much earlier ages of Western culture than it is to our own revolutionary one.

These generalizations do not begin to do justice, obviously, either to numerous qualifications and refinements that have permeated preceding chapters, or to an almost infinite range of others that have not. Nevertheless, "looking backward" at them, we feel compelled also to look forward. That is, we need to consider whether or not some of the severe divergences that have been noted are also capable of further, imperative convergences. We need to consider, too, whether the several movements of contemporary academic philosophy to which we have paid occasional attention (in Chapter 4 and beyond) do not deserve further, if still insufficient, consideration in terms both of their genuine differences and their common contributions.

But equally important is the necessity to emphasize again that opportunities to consider both differences and similarities are by no means motivated by an exercise in intellectual synthesis. Rather, they are motivated by the same concern that pervades this entire work—a quest for planetary unity among men that multiple crises of conflict, disintegration, and, quite conceivably, total destruction now thrust upon us.

If, then, one is willing to regard philosophies of education in this sense rather than as erudite theories that prove fascinating for their own sake, it becomes obligatory, likewise, to regard the fourth of our culturologies of education—the reconstructionist-transformative—with comparably critical appraisal. If, in other words, it has been profitable to develop the same parallel, three-step sequence (philosophic bases, educational formulations, and culturological evaluations) with which each alternative position was developed, then surely it becomes only fair to provide comparable opportunity to reconstructionism. This we have tried to do thus far in the preceding two sections of Part 5.

But now the third or final step creates a predicament. If the reconstructionist position is equally to be judged not merely as divergent from other major ones but as fairly entitled to a legitimate place in the search for convergence, how are we to achieve any kind of parallel, critical appraisal of its own role? Our predicament stems, of course, from the fact that reconstructionism has been frankly recognized as the first preference of this work; hence, it is treated on the premises of and also within a framework which has appeared to us as more defensibly partial than are the great alternative positions which we are obliged to view more externally, as it were, than would be true of our own position. Yet we are also aware, sometimes painfully so, that reconstructionism is vulnerable, too, and that if it is to join forces in behalf of convergence, it must prove just as eager to invite examination of its own weaknesses as it is to expose weaknesses in others. For convergence is possible only in the degree that open, unmitigated consideration of *both* weaknesses and strengths is guaranteed.

There are several ways through which it might be helpful to meet our obligation, but they may be dealt with under but two main headings. The first is, in a sense, merely instrumental to the second, the governing theme of this chapter: (1) some critical reactions; and (2) a reconstructionist approach to convergence.

SOME CRITICAL REACTIONS

The predicament of which we have spoken, although it can be overcome to our satisfaction only partially, now demands at least the conscious attempt to acknowledge representative instances of the many critical reactions to which reconstructionist beliefs have been subjected. Let us first consider, as forthrightly as we can, some of these reactions from our three alternative viewpoints in educational philosophy, and then include other likely reactions that might be expected from critics representing our several contemporary philosophic movements.

To begin with, it is a nice question as to whether progressivists have not often proved more severe in their response to reconstructionist ideas than they have to those of either essentialists or perennialists. We do not pretend to guess all the reasons for this conjecture. But from a culturological perspective (and this continues to govern our appraisal), one may inquire whether progressivists may be less comfortable about, or perhaps more defensive against, heretical deviations within their own naturalist, experimental orientation than in the case of positions which they are fairly sure of opposing anyway. We can hardly resist, indeed, a crude comparison with the political "left": over a century or more, communist and socialist intellectuals have probably expended at least as much energy in castigating each other as they have in attacking their common enemy, capitalism. Nor is this phenomenon too difficult to understand: they agree more or less explicitly that capitalism is iniquitous, but they frequently find much less agreement on the strategies of political action by which this iniquity should be dispelled. Similarly, progressivists and reconstructionists would both, as a rule, like to supplant a considerable portion of traditional educational systems, but they tend to differ in important ways about the processes by which that supplementation should occur both within and outside the school.

Yet to proceed even thus far with this sort of comparison is faulty. In one sense, progressivists and reconstructionists vary not only in their means but in their ends. Whereas, for example, reconstructionists fully endorse a future world community under completely democratic control (economically and otherwise), progressivists seem oftener to direct their talents and alliances to the most effective ways of bringing about gradual improvements in the educational and cultural condition. Whether carefully or carelessly, their critics depict reconstructionism not only as the fortunate advocate of the scientific method (or, in political terms, due process) but, equally, as the unfortunate advocate of magnetic purposes, militant programs of action, or strong substantive commitments. And it is precisely with all of these choices that the progressivist frequently takes issue.

Closely related to this type of criticism is the familiar one that, since all human experience is relative to time and place, we cannot and should not view human values as possessing any kind of universality that could justify our acceptance beyond much more than their plurality, tentativeness, and plasticity. When reconstructionists reach further than this toward an alleged amalgamation of values, they are no longer supported by the evidence of the sciences of man, and so they are simply encouraging a nonscientific, nonreflective approach to life that is, in actuality, contrary to the progressivist's fundamental posture—a posture which induces him, still further, to look pejoratively, if not indignantly, upon such favorite reconstructionist ideas as "utopia" or "myth."

We must be content with but one other fairly familiar criticism among progressivist educators—namely, that youngsters cannot be expected to engage confidently in consensual validation as a viable and crucial process of learning. The implication has been that teachers will almost inevitably load the dice in favor of their own preferred agreements and the kinds of actions that they want students to take. At the same time, and of perhaps equal dubiety, the heavy stress that is placed upon group decision-making may easily subject the individual learner, deliberately or not, to intimidation by his peers. Hence, the growth of selfhood and the encouragement of personal uniqueness may be seriously impaired.

Because the essentialist-oriented critic, especially if he is an idealist, may agree with some progressivists on the point just made, let us reiterate once more that philosophers of education must not, under any circumstances, become shackled to self-isolated domains of thought. This qualification is peculiarly apropos among essentialists because they themselves, as we have also repeatedly emphasized, reveal even less of a united front than do either progressivists or perennialists. On the contrary, it is possible to discover occasional essentialists (Ulich first occurs to us) who, in expressing affinity with certain of the reconstructionist's ideas, join vigorously with him in their transcending vision of man's future.

In general, however, the transmissive orientation is at least as skeptical, sometimes even more bitterly skeptical, of these ideas than it is of progressivist ones—above all, of the principal thesis that education already plays (but should much more effectively play) the role of powerful change agent in the human adventure. Thus the reconstructionist, advocating as he does the transformative and organizing powers latent in the enculturative process, is still more likely to be questioned from *both* philosophic and cultural perspectives.

From the former, the reconstructionist is sharply questioned because reality, truth, and value are regarded by essentialists as characteristics of which man is much less the maker than he is the accepter. In turn, consensual validation, to consider but one concept, is anathema, not so much because of progressivist objections of the sort mentioned above, but because of the contrary presupposition of, say, realist epistemologists (whether classical or modern) that the foundations of knowledge are anchored in far more solid, preestablished principles than are the fluctuating criteria that reconstructionists advance.

And from the latter perspective—the cultural—the reconstructionist may be challenged by essentialists because, not infrequently, he is regarded as a threat to social, moral, economic, and political stability. Indeed, it is hardly surprising that some essentialists (and some progressivists, too) appear uncomfortable about reconstructionist advocacy of both goals and tasks that they consider subversive. After all, is it not true that such advocacy extends to an economic system that would supersede long established practices of free enterprise by a far more completely socialized order, with natural resources and corporately controlled technologies under radically democratic public authority? Is it not true, also, that national sovereignty, with its long history in this and other countries, would be supplanted by international and world sovereignty? And so with other great features of our heritage—including the educational system: Does not our fourth educational philosophy urge that much of what has been so significantly achieved over a century of American progress now be rebuilt in favor of innovative and largely impractical proposals that do not guarantee even partial success?

We have resorted to rhetorical questions because, if not always entirely representative, they do, nevertheless, typify the kinds of attitudes and reactions to which reconstructionists have been frequently subjected not merely by such hatchetmen of modernized education as Rafferty, but by occasional pseudoessentialist philosophers who seem to delight in labeling reconstructionism as a "collectivist utopia," as "antirationalism," as "panacea," as a species of "economic determinism," and even as a "bad joke."

Perennialists have rarely resorted to comparable reactions. Still, they very frequently depart from reconstructionism for reasons not entirely unlike those of some essentialists: it simply does not provide the solid, philosophic groundwork of "first-order questions" that any philosophy (including, surely, that of education) must satisfy if it is to deserve painstaking attention and wholehearted loyalty. The ultimate source of this satisfaction—self-evident first principles—is virtually missing from the thinking of reconstructionists. Unfortunately, it seems unlikely that they can be persuaded to resolve the issue—certainly not on the level of philosophic discourse.

What, then, might perennialists say critically about other levels? Of many possibilities, consider but two quite different concepts—myth and evolution. The reconstructionist is right, they say, in holding that myth is a rich concept. But the trouble is that he fails to appreciate the core of reality from which the mythical spirit must radiate—in the case of ecclesiastic perennialism, of course, the absolute, revelatory faith of Christian doctrine that precedes and succeeds the rational processes afforded by philosophic sophistication.

The other concept arises over how we are to interpret the direction of human development. In accordance with the Darwinian theory of natural selection, the reconstructionist (equally, the progressivist) finds no ontologically ingrained purpose either in nature as a whole or in man as a creature of nature. But just here is the tragic weakness; granting within limits the scientific evidence of evolution, says the perennialist, we must also continue to realize (as we have realized ever since Aristotle) that the direction of reality is certainly not due simply to the capriciousness of mutational change. Rather, the goals of man are inherent in his hylomorphic, hence metaphysical, character. The reconstructionist, assuming the sincerity of his own finite goals, continues to deprive us of the invincible assurance that only perennialism guarantees.

Thus far, this selective review of critiques has confined itself primarily to examples gleaned from peers in educational philosophy. When, however, we turn to contemporary philosophers outside of education, it becomes necessary for the most part only to imagine their reactions. With few exceptions, these scholars reveal feeble interest, at best, in any serious educational thought—reconstructionist or otherwise. Nevertheless, if we return to our five selected positions among academic thinkers, it is not improper to suppose that in some cases they, too, might offer emphatic opinions indeed.

A number of these opinions could properly emanate from analytic philosophers, a few of whom do manifest a genuine interest in education. It has already been noted, for example, how frequently spokesmen distinguish between descriptive and normative judgments and, therefore, how they have challenged the logical defensibility of proceeding from such objective evidence as might be available concerning the nature of human desires to the inference that these desires are entitled to any warrant of desirability. The reconstructionist's attempt to resolve this dilemma by the several phases incorporated in the principle of consensual validation would not, we are sure, receive notice from most analytic philosophers if only because they rarely take into consideration the social character of truth- and value-seeking, much less what we have termed the culturology of knowledge that underlies this principle. At the same time, the analyst's insistence on meticulous meanings exposes reconstructionist ideas to insufficiencies of language—insufficiencies that may well be reduced in time with the aid of analytic philosophy itself.

Only one other hypothetical but important example may be selected from this influential philosophy. To what extent is our major concept of culturology itself open to question? Does it not become, rather, another case of the "culturalistic fallacy"—that is, a special case of the "fallacy of reductionism"—a simplistic attempt to reduce all effects, educational or otherwise, to the single cause of culture? To be sure, reconstructionists, as we observed earlier, do not follow the definition of culturology (by White, most influentially) that tries to relegate culture to an autonomous, self-sufficient reality. Rather, with Kluckhohn and others, we recall that culture is approached strictly as an operational construct. More than this, culture is interpreted in terms of interactional relationships that function dynamically between human individuals and the institutional patterns that encompass them. Nevertheless, the question that analysts could properly continue to raise is whether culturology—that is, anthropological philosophy—is anywhere nearly precise enough (linguistically, logically, or both) if it is to help us interpret and apply educational theories with as much fruitful significance as reconstructionists contend.

Turning next to existentialists, the single familiar question that might be anticipated is, of course, whether reconstructionists veer too far away from the fulcrum of human life: the existing self. The stress upon culture as the reality of paramount concern must, therefore, be suspect. Indeed, it is just the opposite stress that should become paramount. For it is not the human being but modern cultural institutions (scientific, religious, technological, educational, and others) that have often been responsible for subverting and devitalizing man.

For related reasons, most existentialists might protest the reconstructionist's frequent emphasis upon collective order and organized power. Yet it should not be forgotten that Buber, Sartre, and others are not averse to the social dimensions of existence as long as these are constantly and centrally interfused with personal dimensions—an interfusion which the reconstructionist must never overlook even amidst despair and absurdity.

To some extent, Zen Buddhists would join with existentialists in this admonition. The Zennist, however, would be likely to carry his doubts still further. Reconstructionism, no less than other philosophies under predominantly Western influence, suffers from an overdose of *vijnana* (that is, discordance and pluralism) and from an underdose of *prajna* (that is, the intuitive grasp upon a nonverbalized unification with the cosmos). Moreover, again like too many Western, scientifically oriented philosophers, the reconstructionist appears to be stunted in his capacity to appreciate the entrancing simplicity that everywhere permeates the minute objects and events of nature.

What may be said of an imagined neo-Freudian's critique? Those numerous psychotherapists influenced by existentialism would doubtless echo his own reactions closely; hence little is to be gained by reiterating them except, perhaps, to underscore the centrality of personal dignity and freedom. More distinctive, we suspect, is the neo-Freudian stress upon the theory of interpersonal relations—a theory which, because it varies from the reconstructionist's still heavier stress upon intergroup, social, and class relationships, might invite a vigorous demur. Equally so, neo-Freudians could, and should, raise the question whether reconstructionists, influenced here perhaps too heavily by progressivists, tend to exaggerate overoptimistically the extent to which intelligence (or, in Freudian and neo-Freudian terms, the ego) is capable of successfully regulating and directing the forces that play upon it amidst the unrational pressures of both id and superego.

If the question that we have just raised is apropos from the viewpoint of neo-Freudians, then perhaps, even more so, is it apropos from that of neo-Marxists. For, from both viewpoints, the reconstructionist may be criticized for overemphasizing the reflective capacity of "moral man" to regulate his own problems. At any rate, because of the neo-Marxist's never-ceasing attention to the social, economic, and political forces of contraction, he would surely insist that reconstructionists must avoid, at all costs, any temptation whatever to be diverted from the most tough-minded diagnoses and prognoses of which man is capable. They must, for example, confront those grim conditions of alienation that produce, in turn, man's own estrangement. Only if and when they do so can we expect reconstructionists to fulfill their obligations as culturologists of education.

A RECONSTRUCTIONIST APPROACH TO CONVERGENCE

No concept of the entire history of philosophy appears to us more appropriate to this concluding discussion than that of dialectic. Although its several specific meanings may seem unduly complex, a fairly common one need not: *dialectic is the process of intellectual movement which generates opposing ideas that in turn become transformed, by virtue of this very process, from earlier stages of such opposition to later stages of reconciliation.* So abstract a statement is, of course, question-begging in the sense that virtually every term invites elaboration. The term, "transformed," to select one, does not mean a literal replacement of previous ideas by entirely different ones. Nor does it mean a mere blending, compromising, or submerging of ideas. Rather, continuous (although uneven) development occurs in which each idea retains aspects of its originality at the same time that it becomes redefined because of the effect that contrary ideas exert upon it.

The bearing of dialectic on our present concern should be evident. Despite serious divergences that we have tried to specify, not only between the major orientations interpreted in preceding Parts, but now even between reconstructionism and real or hypothetical critics, we are not content to leave philosophies of education in this state of affairs. True, conflicts and oppositions have been, and continue to be, genuine—at times, explosively so. Nor do we wish to suggest that these should now be liquidated or forgotten. Our own insistence upon the importance of dissent, as exemplified by the role of the minority in political experience, surely demonstrates our objections to all kinds of monolithic, unilateral solutions to *any* great problem of man or nature, much less of education.

But neither does the dialectical process imply approval of disagreement, criticism, or disputation simply for its own sake—certainly not in our own stage of cultural history. Indeed, viewed culturologically, the concept of dialectic as an *intellectual* movement requires correction. It is this, yes; but far more pertinently it is best understood and applied, in the operational sense, as a dynamic process of *cultural* emergence, evolution, revolution, and renewal. Philosophy in its epistemological, axiological, and ontological functions is thus regarded as indispensable to the clarification, unification, and direction of this dynamic process.

Notwithstanding our friends, the analytic philosophers, we propose, therefore, to turn to the most central and decisive of all dialectical questions that could be raised, we believe, of either "educational" or "academic" philosophers. This question has haunted much of our deliberation but we wish to highlight it for a final time: *Is a future-centered world civilization desirable and, if so, attainable?* The reconstructionist reply is, of course, affirmative. But the question reaches further: To what extent can an affirmative reply prove warranted among *other* educational-cultural orientations?

Consider, to begin with, one or two of the essentialist-oriented philosophers discussed previously. Despite their more characteristic posture which is, we think, either aloof or hostile toward the "ideal superego" of world civilization, let us recognize a few essentialists who react otherwise. One of these, again, is Ulich: his loyal participation in the Council for the Study of Mankind itself testifies to his enduring concern. Still more explicit, perhaps, are Phenix's beliefs, as exemplified by this statement:

> For education, the inculcation of a world outlook is a clear imperative. A prime objective of the study of modern history should be to make vivid the story of the emergence of

> one world and the spread of the hunger and hope for freedom to people everywhere.[1]

Or consider the academic idealist, Hocking, and his aptly titled *The Coming World Civilization.* Influenced especially by Toynbee, he rejects nationalism and statehood in favor of a Christian-tempered but cosmopolitan outlook that challenges both parochialism and ethnocentricism. One may question, to be sure, how far Hocking is representative of essentialists, or even whether some of his presuppositions do not seriously mitigate against the adequacy of his own case. But it is also well to keep in mind that, throughout our discussion of the essentialist-transmissive orientation, we have repeatedly noted that it emerges as the least unified and most eclectic among our principal contenders. The point then is that, partly because of such characteristics, or partly perhaps in spite of them, it is not surprising that a few essentialists also seek far-reaching views of man and culture to which reconstructionists sympathetically respond.

Still more stimulating, we think, is the concern of some perennialists toward the future. Both Adler and Hutchins are among those who have at times expressed this concern. Nor should we be surprised that Maritain is still more audacious:

> Every authentic revolution presupposes that one day men have begun to turn away from the present and, in a sense, to despair of it . . . to be interested in the present primarily for the future . . . these are the first rudiments of a revolutionary attitude in the widest and most legitimate sense of the word.[2]

It should be remembered, too, that perennialists and reconstructionists here share a common interest—an interest in the purposefulness and goal-directiveness of life. That they differ widely in the philosophic presuppositions of this interest is not to be overlooked, but that some perennialists envisage planetary order as a converging norm is not to be overlooked either. Here, for example, is the sphere of agreement within which the Jesuit paleontologist, Teilhard de Chardin, and the humanist authority on evolution, Julian Huxley, have discovered unusual congenial-

[1] Phenix, *Education and the Common Good,* p. 231. See also his *Philosophy of Education,* pp. 217f.

[2] Maritain, *True Humanism,* p. 259.

ity. Indeed, one may well contend that the single most fertile idea in Teilhard de Chardin's writings has been convergence itself—a concept which, he contends, galvanizes the dialectic of diversity and unity in the cosmic thrust of evolution.

As for progressivism, surely Dewey has pointed in many intimations toward an "end-in-view" of a more viable human order than man has ever achieved. Nor should we forget that it was he, after all, who invited the term reconstructionism through his classic and still influential *Reconstruction in Philosophy.* In our own judgment, nevertheless, it is others who have built stronger bridges between Dewey's formulations and those toward which reconstructionists have been striving—especially Counts in *Education and American Civilization,* where he has written eloquently of "education for a world community," and, more recently, Berkson in his *Ethics, Politics, and Education,* which pays cautious attention to "the evolution of a world community." In both of these provocative works, however, this theme is treated with relative brevity, whereas, among most younger and still less reconstructionist-inclined progressivists, it has received either trivial attention or simply none at all.

When one turns to contemporary movements in philosophy, one is struck at once by further resources that contribute to a radically democratic world order. Among the most influential, surely, is Jaspers's existentialist-tempered *The Future of Mankind.* The neo-Freudian and neo-Marxist, Fromm, has also faced the issue in several stirring works. And there are others. Yet, for the most part, evidence of convergence among these movements may be exemplified less by commitment to the future of mankind than by quite unprecedented adventures in dialogue between varying protagonists. Whether this phenomenon may best be explained culturologically is in itself a question which, so far we know, has not yet been probed. But let us at least note, meanwhile, instances of philosophic communication that trespass across several boundaries: *Marxism and Psychoanalysis,* by Reuben Osborn; *Marxism and Existentialism,* by Walter Odajnik; *Psychotherapy East and West,* by Alan W. Watts; *Psychoanalysis and Religion,* by Erich Fromm; *Marxism and the Linguistic Analysis,* by Maurice Cornforth; *Zen Buddhism and Psychoanalysis,* by D. T. Suzuki and others; and *The Christian Marxist Dialogue* (Oestreicher, ed.).

Of even more importance are the direct or indirect, negative or positive, influences that contemporary positions may exert upon our dominant philosophies of education. A variety of such influences have been noted in the course of our culturological interpretations; here we must only recall the dialogue instituted between ecclesiastic perennialists and Zen Buddhists; Maritain's resilient but also acute judgments of both existentialist and Freudian metapsychology; Bruner's neoessentialist respect for the genius of Freud; the delightful rapprochement that has been advanced by Ames in his comparative study of Zen and pragmatism; and the strong threads of connection running between some analytic philosophers and pragmatists, between some other analysts and critical realists, or even between some analysts and Kantian idealists (as may be observed in the transmissive-weighted predilections of Peters).

Such instances are cited here (and noted further in *Suggested Readings*) partly to underscore a contention germane to preceding culturological appraisals of our principal educational theories. This contention is that in the decades following earlier and more conventional formulations of these theories, subsequent contemporary philosophic movements have either exerted considerable influence upon them, or, if not that, may well exert influence in the decades immediately before us.

Still more emphatically, we wish to observe again that much the same interplay (although by no means in parallel respects) occurs between contemporary philosophies and reconstructionist theory. Especially, two of the selected movements—neo-Freudianism and neo-Marxism—have consistently exerted more potent influence upon reconstructionism than on any of our alternative educational orientations. But the remaining movements (existentialism, analytic philosophy, and Zen Buddhism) have also, we believe, contributed freshly and significantly to its more recent explorations of practical intent and theoretical cogency. The extent to which such contributions may be attributed chiefly to their academic versions or to culturological influences (especially via the author's involvement in anthropological field studies) cannot be easily determined. What can be determined with some confidence is that both existentialism and Zen Buddhism have sensitized our reconstructionist orientation to the dialectical tension between (a) personality as an existing, affective self, and (b) culture as a powerful configuration of institutional forces. In the course of developing this dialectic, the analytic philosopher should be able also to contribute immensely by virtue of his sophistication in the refinements of meaning as well as his insights into the nature of ordinary language.

Nevertheless, we must be cautious lest our network of examples above, instead of aiding us to move toward the world perspective that is now so compelling, simply overwhelm us. When philosophy is viewed as we have tried repeatedly to view it—that is, as the supreme articulation of beliefs and practices indigenous to every culture—then the sheer magnitude of the challenge to our own period of cultural revolutions tempts us to settle instead for skepticism at best, or for chaos at worst.

Even so, the dialectic of convergence can, if we wish to treat it patiently, contribute fruitfully (speaking now in classical terms) to the "negation" of such "negations" as these. The disparateness of contemporary philosophy need not, in other words, become *necessarily* embroiled in endless disputation: granting all their very real confusions and frailties, we have also tried to indicate that these movements (not to mention others not even considered—phenomenology, for one) can, and should, help us to illuminate the quandaries that man-in-culture now confronts. At the same time, their contributions depend, we believe, upon a much wider framework than most leading protagonists are as yet prepared to take seriously. We refer again, of course, to the paramount crisis of our age and to the necessity of facing this crisis, not in the role of erudite scholars merely, but as inescapable participants in a time of extraordinary jeopardy. As existentialists such as Tillich have been warning us, this is indeed a time of "ultimate concern."

In the widest sense, here is the crucial motivation of the reconstructionist's approach to convergence. The conviction underlying this approach is that only a revolutionary vision of life crystallized in the future *of* mankind can hope to prevent much longer the likelihood of death *for* mankind. For it is this vision which, above all, is capable of generating the necessary power stored *within* mankind. A comparable conviction governs, not only the dialectic that is possible among our several contemporary academic philosophies, but also, and still more crucially for us, among our chief orientations toward education itself. To these orientations, then, we rightly return as a kind of climax.

The issue may now be restated: Amidst the acute divergences that prevail in education, may we likewise discover intimations of their own convergences?

The most apparent one, we suppose, is the dual partnerships frequently observed between essentialism-perennialism, as one, and progressivism-reconstructionism, as the other. These suggest at least a partial coalescence—one that could itself be elaborated a great deal further. We must refrain, however—except to reemphasize that both pairs also disclose marked differences not only between them but also within each partnership. What, then, may be said of our major philosophies of education if finally considered together? Can these disclose further common ground—even, perhaps, further hopes of synthesis?

To some extent, of course, they can. All four positions agree in certain important respects. For one thing, they continue to agree, at least ironically, that deep-seated disagreements—philosophically, educationally, and culturally—prevail among them, and hence that these would require much more communication than has ever been achieved thus far. In this respect, they would probably also welcome the methodology of dialectic, even though they might still be expected to differ, either about its best definition or about its capacity to achieve successful resolution between opposing theories.

For another thing, our respective advocates hold certain presuppositions that might seem obvious to many citizens of highly developed nations, yet would not necessarily seem obvious at all anywhere else. Imagine here an advocate of one of our orientations chatting with three colleagues of differing ones:

> But look. First of all, we do agree that people should become literate and skilled, don't we? We are all opposed to illiteracy and incompetence. That's something. You can still find plenty of individuals who would like to keep the masses of people illiterate, ignorant, and superstitious.
>
> Again, we agree that philosophy is a highly important discipline, not only in education but in culture. If we wouldn't all define philosophy similarly at every point, we could at least say that it is the effort to become as rational as possible about our beliefs—an effort that requires us to examine our assumptions, to attain maximum clarity about reality, knowledge, and value.
>
> And we're all opposed to tyranny. We repudiate fascism, as the most vicious form of modern tyranny. But, also, we do not want any kind of society in which leaders act arbitrarily and selfishly, without regard for the welfare of the people. Thus we'd say that the Soviet dictatorship has been acting ruthlessly. We also say that communism as Marxian theory, and communism in Russia, are by no means necessarily identical.

Then, too, we all respect the democratic heritage, don't we? We grant that certain inculcation of facts and rules is necessary in education just as it is in society. We know that you can't have schools or societies without some kind of order and discipline. We recognize the need for leadership and the fact that people are unequal in talents and abilities. We would like to see a lot more money spent on education. We resent pressure groups that try to scare teachers half to death and to confuse citizens about education.

Finally, isn't the most important agreement of all among us that history is passing through a period of grave crisis? Could we then go a step further and say that each of us, as well as the leading advocates of our preferred philosophies, reacts in various ways to the crisis through which we're passing? Essentialists, perennialists, progressivists, reconstructionists—all deeply sense the tensions endemic to our culture. All of us have been teaching and writing in terms of this situation, even when we don't always deal with it directly.[3]

The last paragraph of this comment brings us back to what we have termed "the most central and decisive of all dialectical questions"—that of world civilization. There is little doubt that behind much of the motivation for Vatican II or for the ecumenical tone that it has fostered lies the concern that this question generates. There is little doubt, either, that the contagion of unrest among millions of students and teachers around the world is likewise deeply, if not always rationally or consciously, influenced by the same question. Thus, while it remains true that a multitude of disturbing variations and even harsh conflicts in belief and action cut across our major orientations in education (just as they do across contemporary movements in philosophy, and just as they do, likewise, across politics, economics, art, and all other important phases of personality and culture), nevertheless it still remains true that so do a multitude of common concerns and common unities cut across these variations and conflicts.

In professing this judgment, we do not wish—let us reemphasize the point—to denigrate multiplicity in favor of commonalities. Moreover, exactly as any nation if it is to be creative

[3] Adapted from Brameld, *Toward a Reconstructed Philosophy of Education*, pp. 369ff.

must encourage diversity of racial, ethnic, and other groupings, so equally must any viable educational institution maintain academic freedom in the primary sense of what has been called *dissentual* thinking and action.

Yet, in last analysis, surely it is not the dissentual that offers sufficient justification for educational theory or practice. Rather, is it not also the implications of *consensual* validation, as we have considered it both descriptively and normatively, and on every level of human relationships from family and classroom to religions and nations? Reconsidered now as a primary dialectical principle in education, consensual validation stretches all the way from, say, interpersonal therapy and intergroup anthropotherapy to those international, planetary policies and controls requisite to a democratically empowered world government. In this encompassing sense, indeed, consensual validation enables philosophers of education themselves to explore their own capacities for such validation.

Furthermore, the same concept invites us to recrystallize another relevant concept of learning: defensible partiality. Viewed comprehensively enough, this provides every opportunity to weigh the case in behalf of essentialism or perennialism, for example, just as it does the case for progressivism or reconstructionism. In practicing defensible partiality, it is never to be expected that *any* educational theory is to be ridiculed or obliterated. On the contrary, we have tried to point out that at least as much may be learned from objections leveled against the reconstructionist orientation as from objections that it may level against others. At the same time, dialectically speaking, no alternative orientation ever remains quite what it was before an encounter took place. Nor do the polarizations that sometimes congeal between educational theories necessarily lead to permanent dichotomies. The same process of contradictions and reconciliations can and does occur, of course, in opportunities for dialogue among formal contemporary philosophers.

One further avenue in the direction of convergence in educational theory has been anticipated. This is by way of what is familiarly termed the "self-fulfilling prophecy." Negatively, the concept means a process by which one's image of oneself (for example, that of a student whose value judgments have become alienating and disillusioning because of forces that seem beyond his control) is reinforced and manifested in his future behavior by virtue of the very image he has chosen to expect of himself. Positively, however, the self-fulfilling prophecy may permit a radically different image—an image of oneself as, say, the active and responsible member of an intercultural and international community of all races and religions; as a full participant in educational planning and policy-making; and as the citizen of an industrial order under cooperatively shared authority. Here, again, one's capacity to fulfill one's prophecy becomes magnetized by the self-image that one etches. We may encapsulate this interest in another way: if powerful means are indispensable to the achievement of powerful ends, so are powerful ends also indispensable to powerful means.

Worth reiterating, too, is the fact that the transformative orientation is not interested in the kind of self-fulfilling prophecy that would try to embrace all other major educational philosophies within its own. This would result, at best, in a dubious compendium entirely devoid of the kind of dialectical direction that we are trying to apprehend. Nor does reconstructionism wish to refute, even if it could, such important critical reactions as we have tried frankly to summarize above. Some of these reactions, to be sure, seem to us much more trenchant than others; nevertheless, all of them, regarded dialectically, warrant consideration with the prospect always in mind that both their intended meanings and our own can benefit by vastly greater refinement and revitalization than could be claimed thus far. Self-fulfilling prophecy, in short, is itself in one sense a dialectical process: it occurs by discord and dispute but likewise by harmony and concordance.

For these reasons, if for no others, let no one suppose that any kind of prophecy somehow becomes underwritten by allegedly inviolable laws of reality and history. For the reconstructionist, it is true that to be prophetic is also to be committed intensively and extensively to partial and defensible goals. But this is not to contend that any prophecy, whatever else it may demonstate, must sooner or later reach inevitable achievement. Indeed, as has been often pointed out, the only inevitability we can count upon at all is that of choice. None of us, that is to say, can avoid choice if only because the decision not to choose at all between, for example, the prophecy of an alienated, corrupted future and that of a community of mankind proves to become itself a precipitous choice—a choice of futility, retreat, complacency, or an amalgam of all three.

Reconstructionists also choose. But in the choice of commitment to the future of world civilization, they seek dialectically to strengthen this commitment, not by exclusions, but by whatever inclusions may be tenable and fruitful—terms that again easily become question-begging, to be sure, yet need not become so at all when perceived once more in culturological perspective.

Consider, therefore, our continuum of educational orientations now in clearly temporal terms. What does it mean to speak of the restorative←→transmissive←→moderative←→transformative orientations no longer as philosophies of education as such, but rather as anthropological philosophies of education and therefore as symbols of the history of man? Does it not mean that all four play a potent role in the great cultures of history? When we appreciate, for example, the interpretations of a Plato, Aquinas, or Maritain, not exclusively as thinkers but as compatriots of their time, can we possibly ignore the importance that restorative beliefs continue to manifest upon our own time as well? Similarly, can we bypass the tremendous significance of a Locke, Hegel, Spencer, or others whose beliefs must be transmitted to and respected by each generation if only because these remain continuous with our own heritage? Finally, can we afford to minimize the vast impact that the moderative orientation of a Mill, James, or Dewey exerts not only upon the personal and social behavior of our own country and our own schools but upon that of many other countries?

Granting that answers to such questions seem all too obvious, they no longer remain so when regarded in both culturological and dialectical terms. Nor do they seem at all obvious when these concepts, in turn, interfuse still further with a third—the concept of self-fulfilling prophecy for which we have been pleading. For it is this prophecy and this choice of the future "city of man" that enable, above all, each circumscribed and partial pattern of belief and experience to become transformed—transformed into the planetary philosophy of education and culture that mankind now requires.

Here, in terms of whatever overarching symbol he might prefer, let the philosopher, Burtt, speak for the rest of us:

> . . . the greater philosophy has no wish to destroy its rivals and sit in solitary splendor on the speculative throne but rather knows that its role is best filled when, because of its presence, other philosophies are moved to develop to the utmost whatever constructive possibilities they harbor.

Thus, this "greater philosophy," of whatever name, is certainly not "greater" in any sense of superior wisdom or sophistication.

It possesses neither. But it is, we contend, of utmost relevance and utmost urgency. Again, in his own idiom, Burtt speaks for innumerable others:

> . . . while the basic source of insecurity for primitive man lay in his relation to the forces of physical nature, the basic insecurity of civilized man lies in his relations to his fellows —in his and their aggressive urges and hostile acts . . . civilized man is still struggling to achieve the discipline needed in the setting of the increasingly intimate interaction of people throughout the whole planet. He has won his victory over the environing world, but not yet over himself. All his other hopes and aspirations now wait on the removal of this insecurity, for unless it is removed he will not survive as a civilized man. . . . [4]

[4] Burtt, *In Search of Philosophic Understanding*, pp. 332, 302.

APPENDIX

SUGGESTED READINGS

CHAPTER 1

Stimulating anthologies of "the great debate" in education help to fill in our sketch. Examples are *Contemporary American Education* (Dropkin, Full, and Schwarcz, eds.); *Patterns of Power: Social Foundations of Education* (Linton and Nelson, eds.); *School, Society, and the Professional Educator* (Blackington and Patterson, eds.); and *School and Society* (Gross, Wronski, and Hanson, eds.). On alienation, including sexuality, consult this superb collection of readings: *Man Alone* (Josephsons, ed.).

CHAPTER 2

The characterization of culturology (although the author has not previously utilized the term) and of its bearings upon educational theory and practice is developed at length in Theodore Brameld's *Cultural Foundations of Education* and, more briefly, in *The Use of Explosive Ideas in Education: Culture, Class, and Evolution*, Part II. Extensive applications of the culturology of education to field studies are described in his *The Remaking of a Culture—Life and Education in Puerto Rico*; and in *Japan: Culture, Education, and Change in Two Communities*. Compare also "Learning through Involvement: Puerto Rico as a Laboratory in Educational Anthropology" (Brameld, ed.).

If readers are not yet exposed formally to the field of anthropology, we recommend such widely known overviews as Clyde Kluckhohn's *Mirror for Man*; Alfred L. Kroeber's *Anthropology* (or selections); *The Golden Age of Anthropology* (Mead and Bunzel, eds.); E. Adamson Hoebel's *Anthropology: The Study of Man*, 3rd ed.; and *They Studied Man* by Abram Kardiner and Edward Preble. The emerging "subdiscipline" of educational anthropology is perhaps best introduced by *Education and Culture* (Spindler, ed.); see also *Cultural Crisis and Education* by Francis A. Ianni and Edward Story. The anthropological philosophy of education is exemplified in *Modern Movements in Educational Philosophy*, chap. 3 (Morris, ed.).

Periodicals of direct importance include *Current Anthropology, American Anthropologist,* and *Ethnology.*

The range of resources for the concept of culture-crisis is too diverse to be representative. We may only mention such long-established scholars as Alfred Toynbee and Lewis Mumford (see References), or Pitirim Sorokin, who has entitled two of his books *The Crisis of Our Age* and *Social Philosophies of an Age of Crisis.*

Gunnar Myrdal's *An American Dilemma* is considered a classic. Jules Henry has written forcefully of *Culture against Man.* The term "man for himself" is, of course, the title of Erich Fromm's perhaps most influential book, while "man against himself" is the title of a book by another famous psychoanalyst, Karl Menninger. Other relevant works that throw light upon our crisis-culture will be noted as we proceed, especially in Part 5.

CHAPTER 3

Introductions to general philosophy, which are abundant, are recommended to anyone who has not become acquainted with the field. Comprehensive books of readings also contain helpful orientations to the meaning of philosophy as academic discipline: *Perspectives in Philosophy* (Beck, ed.); *Introductory Readings in Philosophy* (Singer and Ammerman, eds.); and *Philosophic Problems* (Mandelbaum, Gramlich, Anderson, and Schneewind, eds.). For a widely read, if controversial, history of this field, consult Bertrand Russell's *A History of Western Philosophy.* See also *A Hundred Years of Philosophy* by John Passmore.

In the philosophy of education, a compilation of definitions and explications is found in *What Is Philosophy of Education?* (Lucas, ed.). An unsatisfactory attempt to organize "topics and selected sources" is *Philosophy of Education* (Harry S. Broudy, Michael J. Parsons, Ivan A. Shook, and Ronald D. Szoke, eds.).

Collections of readings and commentaries in the philosophy of education also afford stimulating interpretations of the term:

The Philosophical Foundations of Education (Cahn, ed.); *Philosophy for the Study of Education* (Jarrett, ed.); *Philosophies of Education* (Phenix, ed.); *Selected Readings in the Philosophy of Education*, 3rd ed. (Park, ed.); *Philosophic Problems and Education* (Pai and Myers, eds.); Thomas O. Buford's *Toward a Philosophy of Education; Philosophy of Education* (Burns and Brauner, eds.); *Eclectic Philosophy of Education* (Brubacher, ed.); Kingsley Price's *Education and Philosophical Thought*; *Selected Educational Heresies* (O'Neill, ed.); and *Education for What?* (Monson).

Of numerous textbooks, three of wide usage also contain formulations of what the philosophy of education means: John S. Brubacher's *Modern Philosophies of Education*, 4th ed.; J. Donald Butler's *Four Philosophies and Their Practice in Education and Religion*, 3rd ed.; and Van Cleve Morris' *Philosophy and the American School.* All provide extensive sources in the field. For a fresh organization of major themes, see *Theories of Education* by John P. Wynne.

A number of influential periodicals in general philosophy can acquaint readers with current developments: *Journal of Philosophy, Ethics, Philosophical Review*, and others. In educational philosophy, the most widely read are *Educational Theory* and *Studies in Philosophy and Education.* But several other periodicals often deal with germane questions; these include *Harvard Educational Review, Kappan, School and Society, Educational Forum, Teachers College Record*, and *Educational Studies.* The annual yearbooks of the Philosophy of Education Society are also useful.

CHAPTER 4

Each of the five contemporary movements in "academic" philosophy selected for discussion is represented by an extensive literature, some of which may be found compiled in general works of philosophy such as those mentioned in Chapter 3.

For effective portraits of existentialism, see *Philosophies of Existence* by J. Wahl; E. A. Burtt, *In Search of Philosophic Understanding*, chap. 4; and Abraham Kaplan, *The New World of Philosophy*, lecture 3; also *Existential Psychology* (May, ed.). A fresh interpretation is Lionel Rubinoff's *The Pornography of Culture.* In educational philosophy, these are useful: *Existentialism and Education* by George F. Kneller; Van Cleve Morris, *Existentialism in Education*; and *Existential Encounters for Teachers* (Greene, ed.).

For neo-Freudianism, the single best interpretations for our interest are *Neo-Freudian Social Philosophy* by Martin Birnbach, and *Freud and the Post-Freudians* by J. A. C. Brown. These books also contain bibliographies of all the writers noted. Henry Murray is represented in a collection of pertinent readings: *Personality in Nature, Society, and Culture*, revised ed. (Kluckhohn and Murray, eds.). Kaplan, in *The New World of Philosophy*, offers a refreshing interpretation of the Freudian impact on philosophies (lecture 4). Relevant also is *Psychoanalysis and Contemporary American Culture* (Ruitenbeek, ed.).

For neo-Marxism, consult Erich Fromm's *Marx's Concept of Man*, and *Socialist Humanism* (Fromm, ed.), an "international symposium." As a fair sample of how philosophers in the socialist-communist orbit outside of Russia are modifying orthodox Marxism, we suggest *Marx in the Mid-twentieth Century* by Gajo Petrović and *A Philosophy of Man* by Adam Schaff. Herbert Marcuse's philosophy is developed in several works of importance, but see his brief *Essay on Liberation*. An excellent interpretation is *The Marxian Revolutionary Idea*, by Robert C. Tucker. See also, *Marx and the Western World* (Lobkowicz, ed.).

Analytic philosophy is well characterized again by both Burtt's *In Search of Philosophic Understanding* (chap. 3), and Kaplan's *The New World of Philosophy* (lecture 2). Ludwig Wittgenstein's most famous work is *Tractatus Logico-Philosophicus*, but we also suggest that intrigued readers dip into *Ludwig Wittgenstein: The Man and His Philosophy* (Fann, ed.). Anthologies include *Analytical Philosophy* (Butler, ed.) and *Readings in Philosophical Analysis* (Feigl and Sellars, eds.). Evolution of the field is portrayed in *The Age of Analysis* (White, ed.). Relevant to later chapters is also *Moral Principles in Political Philosophy* by Felix E. Oppenheim.

Finally, Zen Buddhism is, of course, best represented by D. T. Suzuki in such books as *Studies in Zen* and *Zen and Japanese Culture*. Alan Watts' *The Spirit of Zen* is also of great value. It contains a bibliography of Suzuki's major books. Huston Smith's *Religions of Man* (chap. 3) places Zen in relationship to Buddhism as a more inclusive doctrine. Here, again, Kaplan's *The New World of Philosophy* (lecture 9) is recommended for its lively treatment.

CHAPTER 5

The most thorough interpretation of pragmatism is *Meaning and Action: A Critical History of Pragmatism* by H. S. Thayer. Samples of classical works in pragmatism (broadly inclusive) are

Pragmatism by William James; *Chance, Love, and Logic* by Charles Peirce; *The Quest for Certainty* by John Dewey; *Mind, Self, and Society* by George H. Mead; *Paths of Life* by Charles Morris; *Mind and the World Order* by C. I. Lewis; *Humanistic Pragmatism* by F. S. C. Schiller; *The Structure of Science* by Ernest Nagel; *The Human Enterprise* by Max Otto; *Knowing and the Known* by Arthur F. Bentley (with Dewey); *The Logic of Modern Physics* by P. W. Bridgman. *Philosophers of Process* (Browning, ed.) contains selections and bibliographies of several pragmatists as well as of others. A fresh approach to axiology in this context is Rollo Handy's *Value Theory and the Behavioral Sciences.*

For a cross section of influential interpretations of Dewey, consult *The Philosophy of John Dewey* (Schilpp, ed.). See also, George Geiger's *John Dewey in Perspective.*

CHAPTER 6

Appropriate to this chapter as well as to subsequent chapters dealing briefly with historical backgrounds, the following works are fruitful: Edward D. Myers' *Education in the Perspective of History*; Henry J. Perkinson's *The Imperfect Panacea: American Faith in Education*; Edward J. Powers' *Evolution of Educational Doctrine*; and John S. Brubacher's *A History of the Problems of Education.* Merle Curti's *The Social Ideas of American Educators* embraces (as do others noted above) several major figures—not merely progressivists. A series of classics in educational history (edited by Lawrence A. Cremin) is published by the Teachers College Press, Columbia University. See also the influential *Education in the Forming of American Society* by B. Bailyn.

The emergence of American educational thought, leading to progressivism, is expertly treated by J. J. Chambliss in *The Origins of American Philosophy of Education.* Collections of sources are *Social History of American Education, Vol. II: 1860 to the Present* (Vassar, ed.); and *The American Legacy of Learning* (Best and Sidwell, eds.). A widely read but defective historical work on the development of progressivism is Lawrence A. Cremin's *The Transformation of the School.* For further background, consult Patricia A. Graham's *Progressivist Education: From Arcady to Academe* and Sol Cohen's *Progressives and Urban School Reform.* See also, Cremin's *The Genius of American Education.*

Dewey's own development is treated authoritatively in *The Dewey School* by K. C. Mayhew and A. C. Edwards; *Foundations of John Dewey's Educational Theory* by Melvin C. Baker; and *John Dewey as Educator* by Arthur G. Wirth. Both of the latter include important, but incomplete, bibliographies of Dewey's educational writings.

A cross section of Dewey's work in philosophy of education is in *John Dewey on Education* (Archambault, ed). Of his several books in the field, *The Child and the Curriculum* and *The School and Society*, both written at the opening of the twentieth century, are still often read; but the most monumental work is, of course, *Democracy and Education.*

Two highly influential interpreters of Dewey's educational thought, Boyd Bode and William H. Kilpatrick, speak in their original ways in (respectively) *Modern Educational Theories* and *Philosophy of Education.* Both are authors of several additional works of interest as, among others, are John L. Childs, *Education and Morals*; Harold Rugg, *Imagination*; V. T. Thayer, *Formative Ideas in American Education*; and Ernest E. Bayles, *Pragmatism in Education.*

Two younger progressivist-oriented writers with fresh perceptions are Donald Arnstine in *Philosophy of Education* and Philip G. Smith in *Philosophy of Education.* Both provide many useful sources, but are more constricted in themes (acutely different ones, at that) than one anticipates from their identical main titles. The problem-solving method in education is effectively developed in *Reflective Thinking* by H. Gordon Hullfish and Philip G. Smith.

CHAPTER 7

A pioneering work in progressivism viewed more or less culturologically is *The Educational Frontier* (Kilpatrick, ed.) in which Dewey, Childs, and others react to American life caught in the throes of the Great Depression. Dewey also anticipates the culturological viewpoint, especially in *Freedom and Culture,* as does George S. Counts in several works.

This interpretation of liberalism is especially influenced also by three English scholars: Harold J. Laski, *The Rise of Liberalism*; L. T. Hobhouse, *Liberalism*; and R. H. Tawney, *Religion and the Rise of Capitalism.*

Bode's critique of progressivism is discussed in his inadequately appreciated *Progressive Education at the Crossroads*; see also his *Democracy as a Way of Life.* Dewey's most widely read critique is *Experience and Education.* Kilpatrick's best work, in our opinion, is the neglected *Selfhood and Civilization.* Dewey's closest approach to Marxian ideas is in his *Liberalism and Social Action.* Kenneth D. Benne's "self-other" version of progressivism is perhaps best portrayed in his *Education as Tragedy*, which also scans reconstructionist horizons.

The disregard of neo-Marxian thought among critical interpreters of Dewey is remarkably exemplified in *Dewey on Education: Appraisals* (Archambault, ed.), but comparable disregard could be said also of neo-Freudianism, Zen Buddhism, and even existentialism. (The only definitive contemporary position represented here is that of analytic philosophy.) For a resilient interpretation of progressivism and other positions, chiefly from the analytic viewpoint, we especially recommend Bertram Bandman's *The Place of Reason in Education.* Rapprochement may still prove fruitful, however, between progressivism and other contemporary movements as illustrated by the awkward but valiant discourse of Leroy F. Troutner: "The Confrontation between Experimentalism and Existentialism: From Dewey through Heidegger and Beyond."

CHAPTER 8

Anthologies of modern philosophy representing such great figures as those mentioned in this chapter are noted in Chapter 3. The single most enlightening interpretation of the historical-cultural development of modern Western ideas, so far as we know, still remains *The Making of the Modern Mind* by John H. Randall, Jr.

See Brameld, *The Use of Explosive Ideas in Education*, Part IV, for a treatment of the concept of evolution, with bearings not only upon realist essentialism but upon other educational philosophies. Personalism is developed by E. S. Brightman in *A Philosophy of Religion*, and by Peter A. Bertocci in *Religion as Creative Insecurity*. Probably T. H. Green's most famous treatise is *Prolegomena to Ethics*, and Josiah Royce's may well be *The Philosophy of Loyalty*.

Exposure to some of the thought expressed by influential figures mentioned near the conclusion of this chapter is highly desirable: Oswald Spengler, *The Decline of the West*; Leslie White, *The Science of Culture*; Reinhold Niebuhr, *The Nature and Destiny of Man*; and Michael Polanyi, *The Tacit Dimension*. Sorokin is mentioned in Chapter 3, above. Compare a contemporary idealist interpretation, *The Alienation of Reason* by Lessek Kolakowski.

Our treatment of realist psychologies has benefited from Edna Heidbreder's *Seven Psychologies*.

CHAPTER 9

For histories of education that also provide backgrounds of essentialist thought, consult above, Chapter 6. Interesting commentaries with excerpts from several classical writers as well as from others are in Paul Nash's *Models of Man.* Critical portraits by contemporary writers of fifteen great educators are drawn competently in *The Educated Man* (Nash, Kazamias, and Perkinson, eds.). Another rich source is Robert Ulich's *History of Educational Thought.*

At least one writing from each of the pioneers of American essentialism as an organized movement deserves recording: *Education and Emergent Man* by William C. Bagley; *Introduction to the Philosophy of Education* by Michael Demiashkevich; *The Democratic Philosophy of Education* by H. H. Horne; *A Sociological Philosophy of Education* by Ross L. Finney; *Education and the New Realism* by Frederick S. Breed; and *Conflicting Theories of Education* by Isaac L. Kandel.

Robert Ulich's most creative work may well be *The Human Career*; see also his *Philosophy of Education.* Philip Phenix is ably represented by his *Philosophy of Education* and *Realms of Meaning.*

For Edward L. Thorndike, consult *Writings from a Connectionist's Psychology*; and for B. F. Skinner, *The Technology of Teaching.* Harry Broudy's *Building a Philosophy of Education* remains a widely studied interpretation from the classical realist viewpoint. Brief but helpful treatments are also Oliver Martin's *Realism in Education,* and J. Donald Butler's *Idealism in Education.*

For the neoessentialists mentioned, see References; also Jerome S. Bruner's *The Process of Education* and *On Knowing.*

The idea of "excellence" has been stressed since the heyday of progressivism. In addition to Broudy and Bruner, considerable attention has been paid to the theme in more superficial idiom by John W. Gardner in *Excellence* and *Self-Renewal.* James B. Conant has repeatedly sounded the same theme in *The Education of American Teachers* and other works.

It has been noted that Whitehead and Russell are hardly representative of essentialist theory as we view it culturologically, although both may be termed realists and provide stimulating contributions to education. Readers interested in their ideas and as well as their writings should consult Joe Park's *Bertrand Russell on Education* and Harold B. Dunkel's *Whitehead on Education.*

CHAPTER 10

For culturologically-toned interpretations, see Ernst Cassirer, *An Essay on Man,* and the interpretation of Cassirer in Brameld's *Cultural Foundations of Education* (appendix).

Our historical judgments are influenced by writers on liberalism (see Chapter 7, above) and by numerous others. See, for example, Merle Curti, *The Growth of American Thought*, and Max Weber, *The Protestant Ethic and the Rise of Capitalism.* The influence of Dewey in *The Quest for Certainty, Experience and Nature,* and other works is emphatic in our discussion of cultural lag in essentialism.

In addition to *Philosophy and Education* (Scheffler, ed.) on analytic interpretations of education, compare *The Concept of Education* (Peters, ed.); *Philosophical Analysis and Education* (Archambault, ed.); and Jonas F. Soltis, *An Introduction to the Analysis of Educational Concepts.* See also William K. Frankena's essay on "Public Education and the Good Life," in Scheffler, *op. cit.*

For an example of ameliorating influences, the importance of "sociological realism" is illustrated by the classic but until recently almost forgotten *Education and Sociology* by Emile Durkheim, a pioneer in culturology. Feigl's breadth of concern radiates from his essay in the *Fifty-Fourth Yearbook*, Part I, "Modern Philosophies and Education," National Society for the Study of Education.

CHAPTER 11

Histories of philosophy could be of great value here, but even more so would be the emulation of a favorite theme among perennialists —direct acquaintance with the "great books." For this purpose, we urge at least initial exposure to Plato's *The Dialogues; Works of Aristotle; Selections from Medieval Philosophy* (McKeon, ed.); and *Basic Writings of St. Thomas Aquinas* (Pegis, ed.).

Modern perennialist thought includes Etienne Gilson's *The Unity of Philosophical Experience*; Gabriel Marcel's *The Existential Background of Human Dignity*; and, among Jacques Maritain's many works, *The Twilight of Civilization* and *The Person and the Common Good.*

Our interpretation of *philosophia perennis* is especially indebted to Brother Benignus for his *Nature, Knowledge, and God.*

T. S. Eliot's most relevant work is *The Idea of a Christian Society*; Hillaire Belloc's may be *Essays of a Catholic Layman in England.*

CHAPTER 12

Histories of education are important here for background (see above, Chapters 6 and 9). Several others are available.

Robert Hutchins' first book on education, *The Higher Learning in America,* has been followed by several others (see References). The earlier humanists include Louis J. Mercier, *The Chal-*

lenge of Humanism, and Norman Foerster, *The Future of the Liberal College.* Interpretation of Aquinas as an educational philosopher is ably presented by John W. Donohue's essay in *The Educated Man,* chap. 5, and also in his *St. Thomas Aquinas and Education.* Maritain's most widely read treatise in this field is *Education at the Crossroads,* but a good collection is in *The Education of Man: The Educational Philosophy of Jacques Maritain* (Gallaghers, ed.). For a sympathetic interpretation of Maria Montessori, see E. M. Standing, *The Montessori Method.* Compare also Joseph McGlade, *Progressive Educators and the Catholic Church,* and *Catholic Education in America* (McCluskey, ed.). Joseph Schwab's views are expressed in *College Curriculum and Student Protest.*

Other useful sources will be found in the footnotes of this chapter.

CHAPTER 13

K. R. Popper's *The Open Society and Its Enemies* remains an influential work on the issues raised in a culturological interpretation of Plato and Aristotle. Compare John Wild's *Plato's Theory of Man* and Ronald Levinson's *In Defense* of Plato for challenging views. One of the most comprehensive and sensitive interpretations is also the much admired *Paideia,* by W. Jaeger. For references to Thomism, note sources indicated in previous chapter, but for further perspective consult George H. Sabine's *A History of Political Theory.*

Will Herberg's *Four Existential Theologians* is a collection of sources supporting our contention that convergence between hitherto polarized movements may be increased.

CHAPTER 14

William P. Montague's lecture will be found developed in his *Great Visions of Philosophy.* One of the best historic treatments of utopianism is Joyce O. Hertzler's *The History of Utopian Thought.*

A good collection of writings by Marx, Engels, and Lenin is *Reader in Marxist Philosophy* (Selsam and Martel, eds.). As representative of modern English utopians, see *A Modern Utopia,* by H. G. Wells. The most widely read work ever written by an American utopian is Edward Bellamy's *Looking Backward.* Thorstein Veblen's several classics are most famously represented by *The Theory of the Leisure Class.* Bourne is now almost forgotten, but his *Untimely Papers* should be revived. Lewis Mumford is represented by several works in the References, but we wish to recommend here, as among his later works, *The Transformations of Man* and *The Myth of the Machine.*

CHAPTER 15

Most of the anthropologists mentioned are listed in the References or found in works noted above (Chapter 2). We add only A. L. Kroeber's *An Anthropologist Looks at History* for its further bearing upon this chapter.

The prodigious literature upon which this chapter rests is illustrated by a classic in social science: George Simmel's *Conflict and the Web of Group-affiliations.* A voluminous collection of relevant materials is available in *The Planning of Change,* 2d ed. (Bennis, Benne, and Chin, eds.). The author's *Japan: Culture, Education and Change in Two Communities* includes his study of conflict between an outcaste minority and the majority; an earlier research work is *Minority Problems in the Public Schools*—a study of school systems in seven urban settings.

For two relevantly influential books by a social scientist, see *White Collar* by C. Wright Mills, and also his *Power, Politics, and People.* Comprehensive collections undergirding this and the next two chapters are *Philosophy of the Social Sciences: A Reader* (Natanson, ed.), and *Readings in the Philosophy of the Social Sciences* (Brodbeck, ed.). Also recommended is the respected *Social Theory and Social Structure* by Robert K. Merton. One of the most dramatic of many books on black–white conflict is *The Autobiography of Malcolm X.* See also the authoritative *The Nature of Prejudice,* by Gordon W. Allport. Works on student power proliferate rapidly, but two pioneering research studies in the 1960s may endure longer than most others: Kenneth Keniston's *The Uncommitted* and *Young Radicals.* A work having numerous implications in this and connected chapters is *The Coming Crisis in Western Sociology* by Alvin W. Goulder. Highly germane, too, is Gunnar Myrdal's *The Challenge of World Poverty.*

On the problems of "history as reality," Robert Heilbroner's *The Future as History* is timely. The concept of the "specious present" is developed further in Brameld's *The Climactic Decades: Mandate to Education,* chap. 2. Support for the reconstructionist philosophy of history is also exemplified by Herbert Muller's *The Uses of the Past.* Contributing much to Part 5 are also John McHale's *The Future of the Future*; Alvin Toffler's *Future Shock*; Earl Hubbard's *The Search is On*; and Donald N. Michael's *The Unprepared Society.*

Recommended as stimulating interpretations of the "reality"

of man viewed zoologically-anthropologically, see *The Naked Ape* and *The Human Zoo* by Desmond Morris; *The Territorial Imperative* by Robert Ardrey; *On Aggression* by Konrad Lorenz; and *Culture: Man's Adaptive Direction* (Montagu, ed.).

CHAPTER 16

Abraham Edel's contributions to culturology are fruitful in his *Ethical Judgment,* and again in his "The Contributions of Philosophical Anthropology to Educational Development." Older resources are Bronislaw Malinowski's *Freedom and Civilization*; W. I. Thomas' *Social Organization and Social Personality*; Robert S. Lynd's *Knowledge for What?*; Kurt Lewin's *A Dynamic Theory of Personality*; and Gordon W. Allport's *Personality.* Abraham Maslow's *Toward a Psychology of Being* contains a rich bibliography.

The concept of "prehension" is adapted loosely from A. N. Whitehead's *Science and the Modern World,* but influenced also by John Dewey's *Art as Experience*; Henri Bergson's *Creative Evolution*; and others. For the "unrational," Freud's extensive writings are, of course, most basic; *An Outline of Psychoanalysis* is an introduction. Of many interpretations in depth, it is difficult to surpass Philip Rieff's *Freud: the Mind of the Moralist.* See also Anna Freud, *The Psychoanalytic Treatment of Children.* A refreshing critique of the field of psychiatry by a political scientist congenial to culturological attitudes is Arnold A. Rogow's *The Psychiatrists.* Always appropriate to problems of this chapter is Erik Erikson's *Childhood and Society.*

The concepts of "ideology" and "utopia" are challengingly developed in Karl Mannheim's *Ideology and Utopia,* but other of his works, such as *Man and Society in an Age of Reconstruction,* are of great importance, too. The "culturology of knowledge," however, has benefited by several stimulating interpretations that have followed Mannheim, such as *The Role of Value in Karl Mannheim's Sociology of Knowledge* by F. Warren Rempel; *Philosophy, Science, and the Sociology of Knowledge* by Irving Louis Horowitz; and *The Social Construction of Reality* by Peter L. Berger and Thomas Luckmann. All of these works are reinforced by bibliographies.

The concept of consensual validation is applied further in Brameld's *The Climactic Decades: Mandate to Education,* chap. 6, but its implications are supported by many authorities. For one example, compare the philosophic analyst, John Wilson, in *Modern Movements in Educational Philosophy* (Morris, ed.), chap. 4. The contention that the jury system exemplifies important features of consensual validation is provocatively supported by elaborate research in *The Jury System* by Harry Kalven, Jr., and Hans Zeisel. See also, "Toward a Social Model of Consensus" by Thomas Scheff, *American Sociological Review*, February 1967.

CHAPTER 17

Werner Heisenberg's *Physics and Philosophy* helps to strengthen our case for the relationships of knowledge and value. More directly, see *The Encapsulated Man*, by Joseph R. Royce, and Ernest Becker's *The Structure of Evil*, both of which contain abundant sources and offer strong support for the theme of this chapter. Even more so does Floyd W. Matson's *The Broken Image* which is also a penetrating critique, heavily documented, of alternative orientations. For a pertinent axiological interpretation, see Richard L. Means, *The Ethical Imperative: The Crisis in American Values*. "Social-self-realization" is developed further in Brameld's *Education for the Emerging Age, Education as Power*, and elsewhere.

The meaning of freedom is strengthened and refined by the philosopher of education, Paul Nash, in his *Authority and Freedom in Education*, and this entire chapter presupposes the thought of several other philosophers (Perry, for one) whom we have previously cited, as well as anthropologists mentioned in Chapter 2, such as Dorothy Lee, *Freedom and Culture*. See also *Education and Human Values* by John Martin Rich and Margaret Mead's *Culture and Commitment*.

The philosophy of democracy is developed in *Man and the State* (Ebenstein, ed.), and by the contemporary philosopher, Charles Frankel, in *The Democratic Prospect*, but perhaps no more powerful single document on this theme exceeds Alexis de Toqueville's classic, *Democracy in America*. The problem of minority rights has become even more acute in the period of dissent that has followed the midcentury period; one recommended series of essays is *The New Left* (Long, ed.). Others of impact include *The Radical Liberal* by Arnold S. Kaufman; *The Politics of History* by Howard Zinn; *The Agony of the American Left* by Christopher Lash; *Anti-Politics in America* by John H. Bunzel; and *The Age of Aquarius* by William Braden. Michael Harrington's *Accidental Century* confronts some of our "normative designs." See also, Stuart Chase, *The Most Probable World*, and Kenneth Boulding, *The Meaning of the 20th Century*. The literature now appearing that bears upon and extends well beyond these designs is accelerating; for constantly enriching resources, contact the World Future Society (P. O. Box 19285, 20th St. Station, Washington, D.C. 20036). Earlier works that remain timely indeed are exemplary: Emery Reves' *The Anatomy of Peace* and Lewis Mumford's *Technics and Civilization.*

On the question of democratic policy-making, a work that has strongly influenced this one is *The Improvement of Practical Intelligence* by R. Bruce Raup and others.

CHAPTER 18

Utopian educators are often discussed in historical works on utopias (see Chapter 14, above). We should, however, note the influential writings of Paul Goodman (his *The New Reformation* is perhaps a fair sample) and other astute critics of American education with whom reconstructionists could be extremely sympathetic. An excellent anthology is provided in *Radical School Reform* (Ronald and Beatrice Gross, eds.).

The theories of social–self-realization and consensual validation in learning lean heavily upon such resources as are mentioned in Chapters 16 and, especially, 17 above, as well as upon the neo-Freudian, existentialist, and Zen positions, all of them listed in the References. Marshall McLuhan's *Understanding Media* deserves note, and the wealth of books on various types of automated learning require attention, as exemplified by *The New Media in Education* (Rossi and Riddle, eds.).

Although the literature varies immensely in quality, group dynamics is probably examined most expertly in *T Group Theory and Laboratory Method* (Bradford, Gibb, and Benne, eds.). Ronald Lippitt's pioneering work is illustrated in his *Dynamics of Planned Change.* Anthropotherapy is formulated as a "prolegomenon" in Brameld, *The Climactic Decades: Mandate to Education,* chap. 8.

CHAPTER 19

Resources for the hypothetical curriculum design rest primarily on those provided by most preceding chapters of Part 5. A great deal of curriculum literature is constantly appearing, however, some of which could be helpful but much of which is based on alternative assumptions. Let us mention only examples of useful sources: *Curriculum Planning for Modern Schools* by Galen Saylor and William A. Alexander; *Prospects for the Future of American Education* by William B. Ragan and George Henderson; *Inventing Education for the Future* by Werner Z. Hirsch and others; and *The Changing School Curriculum* by John I. Goodlad, Renata Von Stoephasius, and M. Frances Klein. The proposed model for general education is briefly restated in Brameld, "A Cross-cutting Approach to the Curriculum: The Moving Wheel," *Kappan,* March 1970. An unusually relevant interpretation of the often superficial field of guidance and counseling is James Allen Peterson's *Counseling and Values.*

One major area to be included in the proposed curriculum is education as an institution. Looking toward a more international and comparative outlook, one of the most widely read books is *Other Schools and Ours*, 3rd ed. by E. J. King. See also *Essays on World Education* (Bereday, ed.); Philip H. Coombs, *The World Educational Crisis*; and Morris Mitchell, *World Education.*

Art education has been a relatively neglected curriculum area which needs radical correction. We are able to suggest only *The Open Eye of Learning: The Role of Art in General Education* (Bassett, ed.); acquaintance with *The Journal of Aesthetic Education*; and familiarity with the work of Herbert Read (for example, *Education Through Art*), probably the foremost interpreter of art as a transformative power in education.

The classic *Summerhill,* by A. S. Neill, should also be read in connection with the education area. The kibbutzim as an educational adventure is interpreted in *Children of the Dream* by Bruno Bettelheim. See also *Education for Sexuality* (Burtt and Brower, eds.).

CHAPTER 20

Most of our case here, too, rests upon the preceding sources of Part 5.

One widely read treatise dealing challengingly with control and teacher organization is Myron Lieberman's *The Future of Public Education.* As is true of curriculum experts, much of the literature on administration is of relatively minor help to this study. We do, however, wish to suggest the following as forward-looking: *A Values Approach to Educational Administration* by Raymond C. Ostrander and Don C. Dethy.

On the issue of religion and education, one of the best historical studies is still *The American Tradition in Religion and Education* by Freeman Butts. See also Brubacher's *Modern Philosophies of Education,* chap. 9, and *The Role of the School in American Society* by V. T. Thayer and Martin Levit, chap. 19. The point raised by Dewey is found in *Intelligence in the Modern World: John Dewey's Philosophy* (Ratner, ed.), p. 706. Further discussion of the reconstructionist approach to religion and education is provided in Brameld's *The Climactic Decades,* chaps. 10–12.

CHAPTER 21

Of many direct influences upon this chapter, let us choose only three further ones: *Education and the Idea of Mankind* (Ulich, ed.) ; Erich Fromm *The Revolution of Hope*; and Eleanor Kuykendall, *Philosophy in an Age of Crisis.*

Readers who may be interested in pursuing criticisms of reconstructionism are invited to investigate three articles in *Educational Theory* by Brameld which annotate and respond to many: "The Philosophy of Reconstructionism," August 1951; "Causation, Goals, and Methodology," July 1952; and "Reconstructionist Theory: Some Recent Critiques Considered in Perspective," October 1966. See also, Frederick Lilge and Brameld's rejoinder in *Harvard Educational Review*, Fall 1952, and Spring 1953; George F. Kneller and Brameld, in *Educational Forum*, January 1958; Elizabeth R. Eames and Brameld, in *Studies in Philosophy and Education*, Winter 1966–67; Burnett, Palmer, and Brameld, in *ibid.*, Spring 1967, and Fall 1967. See also James E. McClellan, *Toward an Effective Critique of American Education*, chap. 3.

Concerning the "culturalistic fallacy," see David Bidney, *Theoretical Anthropology*, for a congenial interpretation.

The concept of dialectic is most famously developed in Hegel (see *Selections*), but is utilized creatively and subtly in our period by numerous thinkers such as Herbert Marcuse in *One-Dimensional Man* and *Eros and Civilization.*

The early interest of Mortimer J. Adler in convergence is exemplified by his *How To Think about War and Peace*, and by Robert M. Hutchins in numerous conferences at his Center for the Study of Democratic Institutions. See also Teilhard de Chardin's *The Future of Man*, and Julian Huxley's introduction to Teilhard's *Phenomenon of Man.*

The development of "reconstructionism" as a term is reviewed in I. B. Berkson's *Ethics, Politics, and Education.*

The associations of analytic philosophers with pragmatism are exemplified by Alan Pasch, in "Dewey and the Analytic Philosophers," and with other modern philosophic positions, including realism, in Herbert Feigl's *The "Mental" and the "Physical."* See also, Abraham Kaplan's *The Conduct of Inquiry* for a pragmatism-analysis rapprochement.

An idealist-essentialist quest for synthesis is Arthur W. Monk's *A Synoptic Philosophy of Education.*

We close our brief guide to reading with the hope that it will be utilized as constantly as it is selectively. With the mood and purpose which this final chapter tries to create, we especially urge attention to Warren W. Wagar's *The City of Man*, together with some of the excellent sources from which both it and this work are derived.

REFERENCES

These references include only works previously noted. Additional bibliographical opportunities are indicated at several points in the Suggested Readings.

ADLER, MORTIMER, J., *Art and Prudence*, Longmans, 1937.

———, *The Conditions of Philosophy*, Dell, 1965.

———, *How To Think about War and Peace*, Simon and Shuster, 1944.

———, *Problems for Thomists*, Sheed and Ward, 1940.

———, and Milton Mayer, *The Revolution in Education*, University of Chicago Press, 1958.

ALLPORT, GORDON, *The Nature of Prejudice*, Doubleday, 1958.

———, *Personality*, Holt, Rinehart and Winston, 1937.

AMES, VAN METER, *Zen and American Thought*, University of Hawaii Press, 1962.

ARCHAMBAULT, R. D. (ed.), *John Dewey on Education*, Modern Library, 1964.

———, *Philosophical Analysis and Education* (ed.), Humanities, 1965.

ARDREY, ROBERT, *The Territorial Imperative*, Atheneum, 1966.

ARISTOTLE, *Works*, Ross, W. D., and S. A. Smith (eds.), Oxford, various dates.

AQUINAS, see Thomas Aquinas.

ARNSTINE, DONALD, *Philosophy of Education*, Harper & Row, 1967.

———, "Review Article—The Cartography of Education: R. S. Peters' Ethics and Education," *Educational Theory*, Spring 1968.

AUGUSTINE, ST. AURELIUS, *Treatise on the City of God*, Macmillan, 1922.

BAGLEY, WILLIAM C., *Education and Emergent Man*, Nelson, 1934.

BAILYN, BERNARD, *Education in the Forming of American Society*, University of North Carolina Press, 1960.

BAKER, MELVIN C., *Foundations of John Dewey's Educational Theory*, Atherton, 1965.

BANDMAN, BERTRAM, *The Place of Reason in Education*, Ohio State University Press, 1967.

BARNETT, H. G., *Innovation: The Basis of Cultural Change*, McGraw-Hill, 1953.

BARNETT, GEORGE (ed.), *Philosophy*

and Educational Development, Houghton Mifflin, 1966.

BASSETT, RICHARD (ed.), *The Open Eye of Learning: The Role of Art in General Education*, MIT Press, 1969.

BAYLES, ERNEST E., *Pragmatism in Education*, Harper & Row, 1966.

BECK, ROBERT N. (ed.), *Perspectives in Philosophy*, Holt, Rinehart and Winston, 1961.

BECKER, ERNEST, *The Structure of Evil*, Braziller, 1968.

BELLAMY, EDWARD, *Looking Backward*, Modern Library, 1942.

BELLOC, HILLAIRE, *Essays of a Catholic Layman in England*, Sheed and Ward, 1931.

BENEDICT, RUTH, *Patterns of Culture*, Houghton Mifflin, 1934.

BENNE, KENNETH D., *Education as Tragedy*, University of Kentucky Press, 1967.

BENNIS, WARREN G., Kenneth D. Benne, and Robert Chin, (eds.), *The Planning of Change*, Holt, Rinehart and Winston, 1969.

BENIGNUS, BROTHER, *Nature, Knowledge and God*, Bruce, 1947.

BENTLEY, ARTHUR F., and John Dewey, *Knowing and the Known*, Beacon, 1949.

BEREDAY, GEORGE (ed.), *Essays on World Education*, Oxford, 1969.

BERGER, PETER L., and Thomas Luckmann, *The Social Construction of Reality*, Doubleday, 1967.

BERGSON, HENRI, *Creative Evolution*, Holt, 1913.

BERTOCCI, PETER A., *Religion as Creative Insecurity*, Association Press, 1958.

BEST, JOHN HARDIN, and Robert T. Sidwell (eds.), *The American Legacy of Learning*, Lippincott, 1967.

BETTELHEIM, BRUNO, *Children of the Dream*, Macmillan, 1969.

BIDNEY, DAVID, *Theoretical Anthropology*, Columbia University Press, 1953.

BIRNBACK, MARTIN, *Neo-Freudian Social Philosophy*, Stanford University Press, 1961.

BLACKINGTON, FRANK H., and Robert S. Patterson (eds.), *School, Society, and the Professional Educator*, Holt, Rinehart and Winston, 1968.

BOAS, FRANZ, "Anthropology," *Encyclopaedia of the Social Sciences.*

BODE, BOYD, *Democracy as a Way of Life*, Macmillan, 1939.

———, *Modern Educational Theories*, Macmillan, 1927.

———, *Progressive Education at the Crossroads*, Newson, 1938.

BOULDING, KENNETH, *The Meaning of the 20th Century*, Harper & Row, 1964.

BOURNE, RANDOLPH, *Untimely Papers*, Viking, 1919.

BOYD, MALCOLM (ed.), *The Underground Church*, Penguin, 1968.

BRADEN, WILLIAM, *The Age of Aquarius*, Quadrangle, 1970.

BRADFORD, LELAND, Jack Gibb, and Kenneth D. Benne (eds.), *T Group Theory and Laboratory Method*, Wiley, 1964.

BRAMELD, THEODORE, "Causation, Goals, and Methodology," *Educational Theory*, July 1952.

———, *The Climactic Decades: Mandate to Education*, Praeger, 1970.

———, "A Cross-cutting Approach to the Curriculum: The Moving Wheel," *Kappan*, March 1970.

———, *Cultural Foundations of Education*, Harper & Row, 1957.

———, *Education for the Emerging Age*, Harper & Row, 1965.

———, *Education as Power*, Holt, Rinehart and Winston, 1965.

———, *Japan: Culture, Education, and Change in Two Communities*, Holt, Rinehart and Winston, 1968.

———, (ed.), "Learning through Involvement: Puerto Rico as a Laboratory in Educational Anthropology, *Journal of Education*, December 1967.

———, *Minority Problems in the*

Public Schools, Harper & Row, 1946.

———, "The Philosophy of Reconstructionism, "*Educational Theory*, August 1951.

———, "Reconstructionist Theory: Some Recent Critiques Considered in Perspective," *Educational Theory*, October 1966.

———, *The Remaking of a Culture—Life and Education in Puerto Rico*, Harper, & Row, 1959.

———, *Toward a Reconstructed Philosphy of Education*, Holt, Rinehart and Winston, 1956.

———, *The Use of Explosive Ideas in Education*, University of Pittsburgh Press, 1965.

BREED, FREDERICK S., *Education and the New Realism*, Macmillan, 1939.

BRIDGMAN, P. W., *The Logic of Modern Physics*, Macmillan, 1927.

BRIGHTMAN, EDGAR S., *A Philosophy of Religion*, Prentice-Hall, 1940.

BRODBECK, MAY (ed.), *Readings in the Philosophy of the Social Sciences*, Macmillan, 1968.

BROUDY, HARRY S., *Building a Philosophy of Education*, 2d ed., Prentice-Hall, 1954.

———, Michael J. Parsons, Ivan A. Shook, and Ronald D. Szoke (eds.), *Philosophy of Education*, University of Illinois Press, 1969.

BROWN, J. A. C., *Freud and the Post-Freudians*, Penguin, 1964.

BROWNING, DOUGLAS (ed.), *Philosophers of Process*, Random House, 1965.

BRUBACHER, JOHN S. (ed.), *Eclectic Philosophy of Education*, Prentice-Hall, 1962.

———, *A History of the Problems of Education*, McGraw-Hill, 1947.

———, *Modern Philosophies of Education*, 4th ed., McGraw-Hill, 1969.

BRUNER, JEROME S., *On Knowing*, Harvard University Press, 1962.

———, *The Process of Education*, Harvard University Press, 1960.

BUBER, MARTIN, *Between Man and Man*, Macmillan, 1965.

———, *I and Thou*, Scribner, 1958.

BUFORD, THOMAS O., *Toward a Philosophy of Education*, Holt, Rinehart and Winston, 1969.

BUNZEL, JOHN N., *Anti-Politics in America*, Vintage, 1970.

BURNS, HOBERT W., and Charles J. Brauner (eds.), *Philosophy of Education*, Ronald, 1962.

BURTT, EDWIN A., *In Search of Philosophic Understanding*, New American Library, 1965.

BURTT, J. J., and L. Brower, *Education for Sexuality*, Saunders, 1970.

BUTLER, J. DONALD, *Four Philosophies and Their Practice in Education and Religion*, 3rd ed., Harper & Row, 1968.

———, *Idealism in Education*, Harper & Row, 1966.

BUTLER, R. J. (ed.), *Analytical Philosophy*, Barnes & Noble, 1962.

BUTTS, FREEMAN, *The American Tradition in Religion and Education*, Beacon, 1950.

CAHN, STEVEN M. (ed.), *The Philosophical Foundations of Education*, Harper & Row, 1970.

CASSIRER, ERNST, *An Essay on Man*, Yale University Press, 1944.

———, *Language and Myth*, Harper & Row, 1946.

CHAMBERS, GURNEY, "Educational Essentialism Thirty Years After," *School and Society*, January 1969.

CHAMBLISS, J. J., *The Origins of American Philosophy of Education*, Martinus Nijhoff (Hague), 1968.

CHASE, STUART, *The Most Probable World*, Harper & Row, 1968.

CHILDS, JOHN L., *Education and Morals*, Appleton, 1950.

COHEN, MORRIS R., and Ernest Nagel, *An Introduction to Logic and Scientific Method*, Harcourt, 1934.

COHEN, SOL, *Progressives and Urban School Reform*, Teachers College Press, 1964.

CONANT, JAMES B., *The American High School Today*, McGraw-Hill, 1959.

———, *The Education of American Teachers*, McGraw-Hill, 1963.

COOMBS, PHILIP H., *The World Educational Crisis*, Oxford, 1968.

CORNFORTH, MAURICE, *Marxism and the Linguistic Philosophy*, International Publishers, 1965.

COUNTS, GEORGE, S., *Education and American Civilization*, Teachers College Press, 1952.

CREMIN, LAWRENCE A., *The Genius of American Education*, Vintage, 1965.

———, *The Transformation of the School*, Knopf, 1961.

CUNNINGHAM, WILLIAM F., *General Education and the Liberal College*, Herder, 1953.

———, *The Pivotal Problems of Education*, Macmillan, 1940.

CURTI, MERLE, *The Growth of American Thought*, Harper & Row, 1943.

———, *The Social Ideas of American Educators*, Pageant Books, 1959.

DARWIN, CHARLES, *The Origin of Species*, Modern Library 1936.

DEMIASHKEVICH, MICHAEL, *Introduction to the Philosophy of Education*, American Book, 1935.

DEWEY, JOHN, *Art as Experience*, Putnam, 1958.

———, *The Child and the Curriculum*, University of Chicago Press, 1956.

———, *Democracy and Education*, Macmillan, 1916.

———, *Education Today*, Putnam, 1940.

———, *Essays in Experimental Logic*, University of Chicago Press, 1916.

———, *Experience and Nature*, Open Court, 1925.

———, *Experience and Education*, Macmillan, 1938.

———, *Freedom and Culture*, Putnam, 1939.

———, *Human Nature and Conduct*, Modern Library, 1930.

———, *Intelligence in the Modern World: John Dewey's Philosophy*. See Ratner, Joseph (ed.).

———, *John Dewey on Education*. See Archambault, R. D. (ed.).

———, *Knowing and the Known*. See Bentley, A. F.

———, *Liberalism and Social Action*, Putnam, 1935.

———, *The Philosophy of John Dewey*. See Schilpp, Paul A. (ed.).

———, *The Quest for Certainty*, Minton, Balch & Co., 1929.

———, *Reconstruction in Philosophy*, Holt, 1920.

———, *The School and Society*, University of Chicago Press, 1956.

DONOHUE, JOHN W., *St. Thomas Aquinas and Education*, Random, 1968.

DROPKIN, STAN, Harold Full, and Ernest Schwarcz (eds.), *Contemporary American Education*, Macmillan, 1965.

DUNKEL, HAROLD B., *Whitehead on Education*. Ohio State University Press, 1965.

DURKHEIM, EMILE, *Education and Society, Free Press*, 1956.

EAGLETON, TERENCE, *The New Left Church*, Helicon Press, 1966.

EBENSTEIN, WILLIAM, *Man and the State*, Holt, Rinehart and Winston, 1947.

EDEL, ABRAHAM, "The Contributions of Philosophical Anthropology to Educational Development," in G. Barnett (ed.), *Philosophy and Educational Development*.

———, *Ethical Judgment*, Free Press, 1955.

ELIOT, T. S., *The Idea of a Christian Society*, Harcourt, 1940.

———, *Notes towards the Definition of Culture*, Harcourt, 1949.

ENNIS, ROBERT, B. O. Smith, and others, *Language and Concepts in Education*, Rand McNally, 1961.

ERIKSON, ERIK, *Childhood and Society*, Norton, 1950.

ESSENTIALIST COMMITTEE, "Summary of Theses" (mimeographed pamphlet, N. D.).

FANN, K. T. (ed.), *Ludwig Wittgenstein: The Man and His Philosophy*, Dell, 1967.

FARRINGTON, BENJAMIN, *Francis Bacon, Philosopher of Industrial Science*, Abelard-Schuman, 1949.

FEIGL, HERBERT, *The "Mental" and the "Physical,"* University of Minnesota Press, 1967.

———, and Wilfrid Sellars (eds.), *Readings in Philosophical Analysis*, Appleton, 1949.

FINNEY, ROSS L., *A Sociological Philosophy of Education*, Macmillan, 1928.

FISCH, MAX H. (ed.), *Classic American Philosophers*, Appleton, 1951.

FOERSTER, NORMAN, *The Future of the Liberal College*, Appleton, 1938.

FORD, G. W., and Lawrence Pugno (eds.), *The Structure of Knowledge and the Curriculum*, Rand McNally, 1964.

FOX, JUNE T., "Epistemology, Psychology and Their Relevance for Education in Bruner and Dewey," *Educational Theory*, Winter 1969.

FRANK, LAWRENCE K., *Society as the Patient*, Rutgers University Press, 1948.

FRANKEL, CHARLES, *The Democratic Prospect*, Harper & Row, 1962.

FRANKENA, WILLIAM K., "Public Education and the Good Life," in I. Scheffler (ed.), *Philosophy and Education*, 2d ed.

FRASER, DOROTHY M., *Current Curriculum Studies in Academic Subjects*, National Education Association, 1962.

FREUD, ANNA, *The Psychoanalytic Treatment of Children*, Schocken, 1964.

FREUD, SIGMUND, *Civilization and Its Discontents*, Norton, 1962.

———, *An Outline of Psychoanalysis*, Norton, 1949.

———, and Osker Pfister, *Psychoanalysis and Faith*, Basic Books, 1963.

FROMM, ERICH, *The Art of Loving*, Harper & Row, 1956.

———, *Man for Himself*, Holt, Rinehart and Winston, 1947.

———, *Marx's Concept of Man*, Ungar, 1961.

———, *Psychoanalysis and Religion*, Yale University Press, 1961.

———, *The Revolution of Hope*, Harper & Row, 1968.

———, *Socialist Humanism* (ed.), Anchor, 1966.

GALLAGHER, Donald and Idella (eds.), *The Education of Man: The Educational Philosophy of Jacques Maritain*, Doubleday, 1962.

GEIGER, GEORGE, *John Dewey in Perspective*, McGraw-Hill, 1958.

GILSON, ETIENNE, *The Unity of Philosophical Experience*, Scribner, 1937.

GARDNER, JOHN W., *Excellence*, Harper & Row, 1961.

———, *Self-Renewal*, Harper & Row, 1964.

GEORGE, HENRY, *Progress and Poverty*, Modern Library, 1938.

GOODLAD, JOHN I., and others, *The Changing School Curriculum*, Fund for the Advancement of Education, 1966.

GOODMAN, PAUL, *The New Reformation*, Random, 1970.

GOULDER, ALVIN W., *The Coming Crisis in Western Sociology*, Basic Books, 1970.

GRAHAM, DON AELRED, *Conversations: Christian and Buddhist*, Harcourt, 1968.

———, *Zen Catholicism*, Harcourt, 1963.

GRAHAM, PATRICIA A., *Progressive Education: From Arcady to Academe*, Teachers College Press, 1967.

DE GRAZIER, ALFRED, and David A. Sohn (eds.), *Revolution in Teaching*, Bantam, 1964.

GREEN, T. H., *Prolegomena to Ethics*, Clarendon Press, 1929.

GREENE, MAXINE, (ed.), *Existential Encounters for Teachers*, Random, 1967.

GROSS, CARL H., Stanley P. Wronski, and John W. Hanson (eds.), *School and Society*, Heath, 1962.

GROSS, RONALD and Beatrice (eds.), *Radical School Reform*, Simon and Schuster, 1970.

HANDY, ROLLO, *Value Theory and the Behavioral Sciences*, Thomas Publishing, 1969.

HARRINGTON, MICHAEL, *Accidental Century*, Macmillan, 1965.

HEGEL, G. W. F., *Selections*, Scribner, 1929.

HEIDBREDER, EDNA, *Seven Psychologies*, Appleton, 1933.

HEILBRONER, ROBERT, *The Future as History*, Harper & Row, 1960.

HEISENBERG, WERNER, *Physics and Philosophy*, Harper & Row, 1958.

HENRY, JULES, *Culture against Man*, Knopf, 1965.

HERBERG, WILL, (ed.), *Four Existential Theologians*, Doubleday, 1958.

HERTZLER, JOYCE O. (ed.), *The History of Utopian Thought*, Macmillan, 1923.

HIRSCH, WERNER Z., and others, *Inventing Education for the Future*, Chandler, 1967.

HOBHOUSE, L. T., *Liberalism*, Williams and Norgate, 1911.

HOCKING, WILLIAM E., *The Coming World Civilization*, Harper & Row, 1956.

———, *Science and the Idea of God*, University of North Carolina Press, 1944.

———, *Types of Philosophy*, Scribner, 1939.

HOEBEL, E. ADAMSON, *Anthropology: The Study of Man*, 3rd ed., McGraw-Hill, 1966.

HORNE, HERMAN H., *The Democratic Philosophy of Education*, Macmillan, 1932.

HOROWITZ, IRVING L., *Philosophy, Science, and the Sociology of Knowledge*, Thomas Publishing, 1961.

HUBBARD, EARL, *The Search is On*, Pace Publications, 1969.

HULLFISH, H. GORDON, and Philip G. Smith, *Reflective Thinking: The Method of Education*, Dodd, Mead, 1961.

HUTCHINS, ROBERT M., "The Administrator," *Journal of Higher Education*, November 1946.

———, *The Atom Bomb and Education*, National Peace Council (London), 1947.

———, *The Conflict in Education in a Democratic Society*, Harper & Row, 1953.

———, *The Higher Learning in America*, Yale University Press, 1936.

———, *The Learning Society*, Praeger, 1968.

———, *No Friendly Voice*, University of Chicago Press, 1936.

———, *St. Thomas and the World State*, Marquette University Press, 1949.

———, *The University of Utopia*, University of Chicago Press, 1954.

IANNI, FRANCIS A., and Edward Storey, *Cultural Crisis and Issues in Education*, Little, Brown, 1970.

JAEGER, W., *Paideia: The Ideals of Greek Culture*, Oxford, 1939.

JAMES, WILLIAM, *Pragmatism*, Longmans, Green, 1907.

———, *The Principles of Psychology*, Holt, 1890.

———, *Talks to Teachers on Psychology*, Holt, 1900.

JARRETT, JAMES L. (ed.), *Philosophy for the Study of Education*, Houghton Mifflin, 1969.

JASPERS, KARL, *The Future of Mankind*, University of Chicago Press, 1961.

JOSEPHSON, ERIC and Mary (eds.), *Man Alone*, Dell, 1962.

KALVEN, HARRY, JR., and Hans Zeisel, *The Jury System*, Little, Brown, 1966.

KAPLAN, ABRAHAM, *The New World of Philosophy*, Vintage, 1961.

———, *The Conduct of Inquiry*, Chandler, 1964.

KANDEL, ISAAC L., *Conflicting Theories of Education*, Macmillan, 1939.

KAPLEAU, PHILIP, *Three Pillars of Zen*, Harper & Row, 1966.

KARDINER, ABRAM, and Edward Preble, *They Studied Man*, Mentor, 1963.

KAUFMAN, ARNOLD S., *The Radical Liberal*, Clarion, 1970.

KENISTON, KENNETH, *The Uncommitted*, Dell, 1965.

———, *Young Radicals*, Harcourt, 1968

KILPATRICK, WILLIAM H. (ed.), *The Educational Frontier*, Appleton, 1933.

———, *Philosophy of Education*, Macmillan, 1951.

———, *Selfhood and Civilization*, Macmillan, 1941.

KIMBALL, SOLON, and James E. McClellan, *Education and the New America*, Random, 1962.

KING, E. J., *Other Schools and Ours*, 3rd ed., Holt, Rinehart and Winston, 1967.

KLUCKHOHN, CLYDE, and Henry Murray (eds.), *Personality in Nature, Society, and Culture*, rev. ed., Knopf, 1953.

———. *Mirror for Man*, McGraw-Hill, 1949.

KNELLER, GEORGE F., *Existentialism and Education*, Philosophical Library, 1958.

KOERNER, JAMES D. (ed.), *The Case for Basic Education*, Little, Brown, 1959.

KOHN, HANS, *The Twentieth Century: A Midway of the Western World*, Macmillan, 1949.

KOLAKOWSKI, LESSEK, *The Alienation of Reason*, Anchor, 1969.

KORZYBSKI, ALFRED, *Science and Sanity*, Science Press, 1933.

KROEBER, ALFRED L., *Anthropology*, Harcourt, 1948.

———, and Clyde Kluckhohn, *A Critical Review of Concepts and Definitions*, Peabody Museum, 1952.

———, *An Anthropologist Looks at History*, University of California Press, 1963.

KUYKENDALL, ELEANOR, *Philosophy in the Age of Crisis*, Harper & Row, 1970.

LASH, CHRISTOPHER, *The Agony of the American Left*, Vintage, 1968.

LASKI, HAROLD J., *The Rise of Liberalism*, Harper & Row, 1936.

LEE, ALEXANDER (ed.), *The Essentials of Marx*, Vanguard, 1926.

LEE, DOROTHY, *Freedom and Culture*, Prentice-Hall, 1959.

LEVINSON, RONALD, *In Defense of Plato*, Harvard University Press, 1953.

LIEBERMAN, MYRON, *The Future of Public Education*, University of Chicago Press, 1960.

LINTON, THOMAS E., and Jack L. Nelson (eds.), *Patterns of Power: Social Foundations of Education*, Pitman, 1968.

LEWIN, KURT, *A Dynamic Theory of Personality*, McGraw-Hill, 1935.

LEWIS, C. I., *Mind and the World Order*, Dover, 1924.

LIPPITT, RONALD, *Dynamics of Planned Change*, Harcourt, 1958.

LOBKOVICZ, NICHOLAS (ed.), *Marx and the Western World*, University of Notre Dame Press, 1967.

LONG, PRISCILLA (ed.), *The New Left*, Porter Sargent, 1969.

LORENZ, KONRAD, *On Aggression*, Harcourt, 1963.

LUCAS, C. J. (ed.), *What Is Philosophy of Education?*, Macmillan, 1969.

LYND, ROBERT S., *Knowledge for What?*, Princeton University Press, 1939.

MCCLELLAN, JAMES E., *Toward an Effective Critique of American Education*, Lippincott, 1968.

MCCLUSKEY, NEIL G. (ed.), *Catholic Education in America*, Teachers College Press, 1964.

MCGLADE, JOSEPH, *Progressive Educators and the Catholic Church*, Newman Press, 1953.

MCHALE, JOHN, *The Future of the Future*, Braziller, 1969.

MCKEON, RICHARD P. (ed.), *Selections from Medieval Philosophy*, Scribner, 1929.

MCLUHAN, MARSHALL, *Understanding Media*, New American Library, 1964.

MALCOLM X, *Autobiography of Malcolm X*, Grove, 1965.

MALINOWSKI, BRONISLAW, *Freedom and Civilization*, Roy, 1944.

MANDELBAUM, DAVID G. (ed.), *Selected Writings in Language, Culture, and Personality* [of Edward Sapir], University of California Press, 1949.

MANDELBAUM, MAURICE, Francis W. Gramlich, Alan Ross Anderson, and Jerome S. Schneewind (eds.), *Philosophic Problems*, Macmillan, 1967.

MANNHEIM, KARL, *Ideology and Utopia*, Harcourt, 1936.

———, *Man and Society in an Age of Reconstruction*, Harcourt, 1940.

MARCEL, GABRIEL, *Creative Fidelity*, Farrar, Straus, 1964.

———, *The Existentialist Background of Human Dignity*, Harvard University Press, 1963.

MARCUSE, HERBERT, *Eros and Civilization, Vintage*, 1955.

———, *An Essay on Liberation*, Beacon, 1969.

———, *One-dimensional Man*, Beacon, 1964.

MARITAIN, JACQUES, *Art and Scholasticism*, Scribner, 1933.

———, *Christianity and Democracy*, Scribner, 1945.

———, *Education at the Crossroads*, Yale University Press, 1943.

———, *Existence and the Existent*, Pantheon, 1948.

———, *On the Grace and Humanity of Jesus*, Herder, 1969.

———, *On the Use of Philosophy*, Princeton University Press, 1961.

———, *The Peasant of the Garonne*, Holt, Rinehart and Winston, 1968.

———, *The Person and the Common Good*, University of Notre Dame Press, 1966.

———, *Ransoming the Time*, Scribner, 1941.

———, *Scholasticism and Politics*, Macmillan, 1940.

———, *True Humanism*, Bles, 1939.

———, *The Twilight of Civilization*, Sheed and Ward, 1943.

MARTIN, OLIVER, *Realism in Education*, Harper & Row, 1969.

MARX, KARL, *Economic and Philosophical Manuscripts*, McGraw-Hill, 1964.

———, *The Essentials of Marx*. See A. LEE (ed.).

MASLOW, ABRAHAM, *Toward a Psychology of Being*, Van Nostrand, 1962.

MATSON, FLOYD W., *The Broken Image*, Anchor, 1966.

MAY, ROLLO, Ernest Angel, and Henri F. Ellenberger (eds.), *Existence*, Basic Books, 1958.

———, *Existential Psychology* (ed.), Random, 1961.

MAYHEW, K. C., and A. C. Edwards, *The Dewey School*, Appleton, 1936.

MEAD, GEORGE H., *Mind, Self, and Society*, University of Chicago Press, 1934.

———, "The Philosophies of Royce, James, and Dewey in their American Settings," *International Journal of Ethics*, January 1930.

MEAD, MARGARET, *Culture and Commitment*, Natural History Press, 1970.

———, and Ruth Bunzel, *The Golden Age of Anthropology*, Braziller, 1960.

MEANS, RICHARD L., *The Ethical Imperative: The Crisis in American Values*, Anchor, 1970.

MEIKLEJOHN, ALEXANDER, *Education between Two Worlds*, Harper & Row, 1942.

MENNINGER, KARL, *Man Against Himself*, Harcourt, 1938.

MERCIER, LOUIS J., *The Challenges of Humanism*, Oxford, 1933.

MERTON, ROBERT K., *Social Theory and Social Structure*, Free Press, 1957.

MICHAEL, DONALD N., *The Unprepared Society*, Basic Books, 1968.

MILLS, C. WRIGHT, *Power, Politics, and People*, Ballantine, 1963.

———, *White Collar*, Oxford, 1951.

MITCHELL, MORRIS, *World Education*, Pageant, 1967.

MONK, ARTHUR W., *A Synoptic Philosophy of Education*, Abingdon, 1965.

MONSON, C. H., JR., (ed.), *Education for What?*, Houghton Mifflin, 1970.

MONTAGU, ASHLEY (ed.), *Culture: Man's Adaptive Direction*, Oxford University Press, 1968.

MONTAGUE, WILLIAM P., *Great Visions of Philosophy*, Open Court, 1950.

MORRIS, CHARLES, *Paths of Life*, Harper & Row, 1942.

MORRIS, DESMOND, *The Naked Ape*, Dell, 1967.

———, *The Human Zoo*, McGraw-Hill, 1969.

MORRIS, VAN CLEVE, *Existentialism in Education*, Harper & Row, 1966.

———, *Modern Movements in Educational Philosophy* (ed.), Houghton Mifflin, 1969.

———, *Philosophy and the American School*, Houghton Mifflin 1961.

MULLER, HERBERT, *The Uses of the Past*, Oxford, 1952.

MUMFORD, LEWIS, *The Condition of Man*, Harcourt, 1944.

———, *The Conduct of Life*, Harcourt, 1951.

———, *The Culture of Cities*, Harcourt, 1938.

———, *The Myth of the Machine*, Harcourt, 1966.

———, *The Story of Utopias*, Liveright, 1933.

———, *Technics and Civilization*, Harcourt, 1934.

———, *The Transformations of Man*, Collier, 1956.

———, *Values for Survival*, Harcourt, 1946.

MURRAY, HENRY A. (ed.), *Myth and Myth-Making*, Braziller, 1960.

MYRDAL, GUNNAR, *An American Dilemma*, Harper & Row, 1944.

———, *The Challenge of World Poverty*, Pantheon, 1970.

MYERS, EDWARD D., *Education in the Perspective of History*, Harper & Row, 1960.

NAGEL, ERNEST, *The Structure of Science*, Harcourt, 1961.

NASH, PAUL, *Authority and Freedom in Education*, Wiley, 1966.

———, Andreas M. Kazamias, and Henry J. Perkinson (eds.), *The Educated Man*, Wiley, 1965.

———, *Models of Man*, Wiley, 1968.

NATANSON, RONALD (ed.), *Philosophy of the Social Sciences: A Reader*, Random, 1963.

NATIONAL SOCIETY FOR THE STUDY OF EDUCATION, *Forty-First Yearbook*, Part I, "Philosophies of Education," Public School Publishing Co., 1926.

———, *Fifty-Fourth Yearbook*, Part I, "Modern Philosophies and Education," University of Chicago Press, 1955.

NEILL, A. S., *Summerhill*, Hart, 1960.

NELSON, BENJAMIN (ed.), *Freud and the 20th Century*, World Book Company, 1957.

NELSON, WILLIAM (ed.), *Twentieth Century Interpretations of Utopia*, Prentice-Hall, 1968.

NEWMAN, JOHN HENRY, *The Idea of a University*, Longmans, 1947.

NIEBUHR, REINHOLD, *Moral Man and Immoral Society*, Scribner, 1932.

———, *The Nature and Destiny of Man, Scribner*, 1955.

NORTHROP, F. S. C. (ed.), *Ideological Differences and World Order*, Yale University Press, 1949.

———, *The Meeting of East and West*, Macmillan, 1947.

O'CONNOR, D. J., *An Introduction to the Philosophy of Education*, Philosophical Library, 1957.

ODAJNIK, WALTER, *Marxism and Existentialism*, Anchor, 1965.

OESTREICHER, PAUL (ed.), *The Christian-Marxist Dialogue*, Macmillan, 1969.

O'NEILL, WILLIAM F., *Selected Educational Heresies*, Scott, Foresman, 1969.

OPPENHEIM, FELIX E., *Moral Principles in Political Philosophy*, Random, 1968.

OSBORN, REUBEN, *Marxism and Psychoanalysis*, Dell, 1965.

OSTRANDER, RAYMOND C., and Don C. Dethy, *A Values Approach to Educational Administration*, American Book, 1968.

OTTO, MAX C., *The Human Enterprise*, Appleton, 1940.

———, *Science and the Moral Life*, New American Library, 1949.

PAI, YOUNG, and JOSEPH T. MYERS (eds.), *Philosophic Problems and Education*, Lippincott, 1967.

PARK, JOE, *Bertrand Russell on Education*, Ohio State University Press, 1963.

———, (ed.), *Selected Readings in the Philosophy of Education*, 3rd ed., Macmillan, 1963.

PASCH, ALAN, "Dewey and the Analytic Philosophers," *Journal of Philosophy*, October 8, 1959.

PASSMORE, JOHN, *A Hundred Years of Philosophy*, Pelican, 1970.

PEGIS, ANTON C. (ed.), *The Basic Writings of St. Thomas Aquinas*. See Thomas Aquinas.

PEIRCE, CHARLES, *Chance, Love, and Logic*, Harcourt, Brace, 1923.

PERKINSON, HENRY J., *The Imperfect Panacea: American Faith in Education 1865–1965*, Random, 1968.

PERRY, RALPH BARTON, *Realms of Value*, Harvard University Press, 1954.

PETERS, R. S. (ed.), *The Concept of Education*, Humanities, 1967.

———, *Ethics and Education*, Scott, Foresman, 1967.

PETERSON, JAMES ALLEN, *Counseling and Values*, International Textbook, 1970.

PETROVIĆ, GAJO, *Marx in the Mid-twentieth Century*, Doubleday, 1967.

PLATO, *The Dialogues* (Jowett edition), Random, 1937.

———, *The Republic*, Scribner, 1928.

PHENIX, P. H., *Education and the Common Good*, Harper & Row, 1961.

———, *Philosophies of Education* (ed.), Wiley, 1961.

———, *Philosophy of Education*, Holt, Rinehart and Winston, 1958.

———, *Realms of Meaning*, McGraw-Hill, 1958.

POLANYI, MICHAEL, *The Tacit Dimension, Doubleday*, 1966.

POPPER, K. R., *The Open Society and Its Enemies*, Routledge, 1945.

POWERS, EDWARD J., *Evolution of Educational Doctrine*, Appleton, 1970.

PRICE, KINGSLEY, *Education and Philosophical Thought*, Allyn and Bacon, 1962.

RAGAN, WILLIAM B., and George Henderson, *Prospects for the Future of American Education*, Harper & Row, 1970.

RANDALL, JOHN H. JR., *The Making of the Modern Mind*, rev. ed., Houghton Mifflin, 1940.

RATNER, JOSEPH (ed.), *Intelligence in the Modern World: John Dewey's Philosophy*, Modern Library, 1939.

RAUP, R. BRUCE, and others, *The Improvement of Practical Intelligence*, Harper & Row, 1950.

READ, HERBERT, *Education Through Art*, Pantheon, 1945.

REMPEL, F. WARREN, *The Role of Value in Karl Mannheim's Sociology of Knowledge*, Mouton (Hague), 1965.

REVES, EMERY, *The Anatomy of Peace*, Harper & Row, 1945.

RICH, JOHN MARTIN, *Education and Human Values*, Addison-Wesley, 1968.

RIEFF, PHILIP, *Freud: The Mind of the Moralist*, Doubleday, 1961.

ROGOW, ARNOLD A., *The Psychiatrists*, Putnam, 1970.

ROSS, W. D., and J. A. SMITH (eds.), *Works of Aristotle*. See Aristotle.

ROSSI, PETER H., and Bruce J. Riddle (eds.), *The New Media in Education*, Aldine, 1966.

ROSZAK, THEODORE, *The Making of a Counter Culture*, Anchor, 1969.

ROUSSEAU, JEAN-JACQUES, *The Social Contract*, Putnam, 1906.

ROYCE, JOSEPH R., *The Encapsulated Man*, Van Nostrand, 1964.

ROYCE, JOSIAH, *Philosophy of Loyalty*, AMS Press, 1908.

RUBINOFF, LIONEL, *The Pornography of Power*, Quadrangle, 1968.

RUGG, HAROLD, *Imagination*, Harper & Row, 1963.

———, *Foundations for American Education*, World Book Company, 1947.

RUITENBEEK, HENDRIK M. (ed.), *Psychoanalysis and Contemporary American Culture*, Dell, 1964.

RUSSELL, BERTRAND, *A History of Western Philosophy*, Simon and Schuster, 1945.

SABINE, GEORGE H., *A History of Political Theory*, Holt, Rinehart and Winston, 1937.

SAPIR, EDWARD. See D. G. MANDELBAUM (ed.).

SAYLOR, GALEN, and William A. Alexander, *Curriculum Planning For Modern Schools*, Holt, Rinehart and Winston, 1966.

SCHAFF, ADAM, *A Philosophy of Man*, Dell, 1963.

SCHEFF, THOMAS, "Toward a Social Model of Consensus," *American Sociological Review*, February 1967.

SCHEFFLER, ISRAEL, *The Conditions of Knowledge*, Scott, Foresman, 1965.

———, *The Language of Education*, Thomas, 1960.

——— (ed.), *Philosophy and Education*, 2d. ed., Allyn and Bacon, 1966.

SCHILLER, F. S. C., *Humanistic Pragmatism*, Free Press, 1966.

SCHILPP, PAUL A. (ed.), *The Philosophy of John Dewey*, Northwestern University Press, 1939.

SELSAM, HOWARD, and Harry Martel (eds.), *Reader in Marxist Philosophy*, International Publishers, 1963.

SIMMEL, GEORGE, *Conflict and the Web of Group-affiliation*, Free Press, 1955.

SINGER, MARCUS, and Robert R. Ammerman (eds.), *Introductory Readings in Philosophy*, Scribner, 1962.

SKINNER, B. F., *The Technology of Teaching*, Appleton, 1968.

———, *Walden Two*, Macmillan, 1948.

SLOCHOWER, HARRY, *No Voice Is Wholly Lost*, Farrar, Straus, 1945.

SMITH, HUSTON, *The Religions of Man*, Mentor, 1958.

SMITH, PHILIP G., *Philosophy of Education*, Harper & Row, 1965.

SOLTIS, JONAS F., *An Introduction to the Analysis of Educational Concepts*, Addison-Wesley, 1968.

SPENGLER, OSWALD, *The Decline of the West*, Knopf, 1932.

SPINDLER, GEORGE S. (ed.), *Education and Culture*, Holt, Rinehart and Winston, 1962.

SOROKIN, PITIRIM, *The Crisis of Our Age*, Dutton, 1941.

———, *Social Philosophies of an Age of Crisis*, Beacon, 1951.

SPIER, LESLIE A., Irving Hallowell, and Stanley Newman (eds.), *Language, Culture, and Personality*, Banta, 1941.

STANDING, E. M., *The Montessori Method*, Academy Library Guild, 1962.

SUMNER, WILLIAM GRAHAM, *Folkways*, Ginn, 1906.

SUZUKI, DAISETSU T., *Studies in Zen*, Dell, 1955.

———, *Zen Buddhism and Japanese Culture*, Pantheon, 1958.

———, ERICH FROMM, and Richard DeMartino, *Zen Buddhism and Psychoanalysis*, Grove, 1960.

TAWNEY, R. H., *Religion and the Rise of Capitalism*, Harcourt, 1926.

TAYLOR, HAROLD, "Education as Experiment," *Antioch Review*, Summer, 1949.

———, *Students without Teachers*, McGraw-Hill, 1969.

TEILHARD DE CHARDIN, P., *The Future of Man*, Harper & Row, 1964.

———, *The Phenomenon of Man*, Harper & Row, 1959.

THAYER, H. S., *Meaning and Action: A Critical History of Pragmatism*, Bobbs-Merrill, 1968.

THAYER, V. T., *Formative Ideas in American Education*, Dodd, Mead, 1965.

———, and Martin Levit, *The Role of the School in American Society*, Dodd, Mead, 1966.

THOMAS AQUINAS, *Basic Writings*, A. C. PEGIS (ed.)., Random, 1945.

THOMAS, W. I., *Social Organization and Social Personality*, University of Chicago Press, 1966.

THOMPSON, LAURA, *Culture in Crisis*, Harper & Row, 1950.

———, *Toward a Science of Mankind*, McGraw-Hill, 1961.

THORNDIKE, EDWARD L., *Selected Writings from a Connectionist's Psychology*, Appleton, 1949.

TOFFLER, ALVIN, *Future Shock*, Random, 1970.

de TOQUEVILLE, ALEXIS, *Democracy in America*, Knopf, 1945.

TOYNBEE, ARNOLD J., *A Study of History*, Oxford, 1947.

TROUTNER, LEROY F., "The Confrontation between Experimentalism and Existentialism: From Dewey through Heidegger and Beyond," *Harvard Educational Review*, Winter, 1969.

TUCKER, ROBERT C., *The Marxian Revolutionary Idea*, Norton, 1969.

TYLOR, EDWARD B., *Primitive Culture*, 5th ed., Murray, 1929.

ULICH, ROBERT, *Crisis and Hope in American Education*, Beacon, 1951.

———, *Education and the Idea of Mankind* (ed.), Harcourt, 1964.

———, *Fundamentals of Democratic Education*, American Book, 1940.

———, *History of Educational Thought*, American Book, 1945.

———, *The Human Career*, Harper & Row, 1955.

———, *Philosophy of Education*, American Book, 1961.

VASSAR, RENA L. (ed.), *Social History of American Education, Vol. II: 1860 to the Present*, Rand McNally, 1965.

VEBLEN, THORSTEIN, *The Higher Learning in America*, Viking, 1918.

———, *The Theory of the Leisure Class*, Modern Library, 1934.

WAGAR, WARREN W., *The City of Man*, Penguin, 1963.

WAHL, J., *Philosophies of Existence*, Schocken, 1969.

WATTS, ALAN A., *Psychotherapy East and West*, New American Library, 1961.

———, *The Spirit of Zen*, Grove, 1958.

WEAVER, RICHARD, *Ideas Have Consequences*, University of Chicago Press, 1948.

WEBER, MAX, *The Protestant Ethic and the Rise of Capitalism*, Allen and Unwin, 1930.

WELLS, H. G., *Joan and Peter, the Story of an Education*, Macmillan, 1918.

———, *A Modern Utopia*, Chapman and Hall, 1905.

WILD, JOHN, *Plato's Theory of Man*, Harvard University Press, 1946.

WHITE, LESLIE, *The Science of Culture*, Farrar, Straus, 1949.

WHITE, MORTON G. (ed.), *The Age of Analysis*, Houghton Mifflin, 1955.

WHITEHEAD, ALFRED N., *The Aims of Education*, Mentor, 1929.

———, *Science and the Modern World*, Macmillan, 1925.

WIRTH, ARTHUR G., *John Dewey as Educator*, Wiley, 1966.

WITTGENSTEIN, LUDWIG, *Tractatus Logico-Philosophicus*, Routledge, 1960.

WYNNE, JOHN P., *Theories of Education*, Harper & Row, 1963.

ZINN, HOWARD, *The Politics of History*, Beacon, 1970.

NAME INDEX

I

J

K

L

M

N

O

P

SUBJECT INDEX

D

S

V

W

Z